Your students live in the real world. Here's a textbook that does, too.

Real Writing

WITH READINGS

Paragraphs and Essays for College, Work, and Everyday Life

Also available without readings

BY SUSAN ANKER

Like other workbooks written for the developmental writing course, *Real Writing* covers what you need in a format you and your students can use. But *Real Writing* works better.

Here's <u>why</u> *Real Writing* works . . .

Several nationwide surveys, a committed editorial board of experienced instructors, a thorough program of reviewing and class testing, and hundreds of conversations with instructors across the country over the past fifteen years all told us the same two things: If students are to succeed in developmental writing, they must see the relevance of the course to their own real lives and goals. And if a textbook is to be useful, it must help make this connection.

Real Writing works better because it is grounded in the reality of students' lives. It connects the content of the course to the real worlds of college, work, and everyday life, and it equips students with skills that will work in these worlds. It gives students a real reason to write and a realistic chance of success.

Real Writing is based on instructors' real lives as well. An Editorial Advisory Board consisting of experienced instructors from around the country helped us shape the book's approach, content, and features. And the extensive array of ancillaries is intended to simplify and enrich your busy professional life.

Here's how *Real Writing* works . . .

Teaches Practical Writing and Editing Skills.

Real Writing focuses on the practical skills that instructors told us form the corner-stone of writing competence in the real world. *Real Writing* avoids grammar jargon (which is not useful) and focuses on the skill of editing (which is). Plentiful options for collaboration and writing with a computer—increasingly important skills in the real world—are available for instructors who want to incorporate these into their course. If students can master practical writing and editing skills, they are well on their way to becoming successful writers in the real worlds of college, work, and everyday life.

The focus of *Real Writing* reflects the well-established consensus about what developmental writing students need to learn. But *Real Writing* goes beyond other books by showing students how these skills are usefully applied in the real world.

PARAGRAPHS

74   Part Two • Writing Different Kinds of Paragraphs   Guided Practice

Step 5. Revise Your Draft

After completing your draft, take a break. Then reread it, searching for examples that don't fit, additional details to make your examples more lively and specific, and ways to connect the examples so that they flow smoothly. This is your chance to improve your illustration paragraph before getting a grade. Do not just copy over your draft; make changes that will improve the paragraph

TEACHING TIP
You may want to model giving feedback for the students. Read a paragraph aloud and give feedback according to the guidelines.

> **Teamwork: Get Feedback**
>
> When you have completed the draft of your illustration paragraph, you may want to show it to someone else or read it aloud in a small group, asking for feedback and suggestions that will help you revise.
>
> **GUIDELINES FOR GIVING FEEDBACK**
> - Start with a positive comment.
> - Throughout, offer comments rather than "You should's."
> - Start with the paragraph as a whole and move to smaller points.
>   — Tell the writer what you think the main point is.
>   — Ask questions about the examples and the writer's meaning.
> - Tell the writer what works for you and what you think might be done better (and how).
> - Be as specific as you can. Don't just say "It's good" or "I liked it." Explain why.
> - If you get confused, tell the writer what's confusing.
> - Help the writer.

Here is the revised example paragraph, with notes to show what changes the writer made to revise the draft.

REVISED PARAGRAPH

COMPUTER
Advise students to copy their draft and save the original. Tell them to make changes only on the copy so that if they want to go back to an idea from the original, they will still have it. Also advise them to print out a hard copy of the original before revising.

    Although they don't consider it stealing, many people regularly

take things from their companies. The most common items to disap- ⌐—less wordy—⌐

pear are pens and pencils that employees almost unconsciously stuff

into their purses, knapsacks, or briefcases. Over time, they may accu- ⌐word changed

mulate quite a stash of them. Another big item is all kinds of paper: ⌐transition added

pads of lined paper, handy little notepads that can be used for shopping ⌐———added detail———⌐

Because editing skills are useful only if students can apply them, every editing chapter concludes with opportunities for students to edit their own writing.

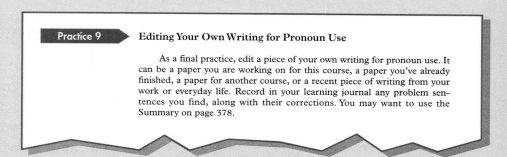

Practice 9 Editing Your Own Writing for Pronoun Use

As a final practice, edit a piece of your own writing for pronoun use. It can be a paper you are working on for this course, a paper you've already finished, a paper for another course, or a recent piece of writing from your work or everyday life. Record in your learning journal any problem sentences you find, along with their corrections. You may want to use the Summary on page 378.

Real Writing Is Easy to Use.

In addition to being an ideal classroom text, *Real Writing* is a book students can use on their own. Chapters have a predictable three-part organization that makes it easy for students to *understand* the importance of the lesson, *practice* the skills involved, and *apply* them to their own writing. Lessons are accompanied by plenty of models and exercises. The clear and open design highlights key information and places tips and options in the margins. Every chapter ends with a summary of core content, and every grammar chapter also includes a Quick Review Chart.

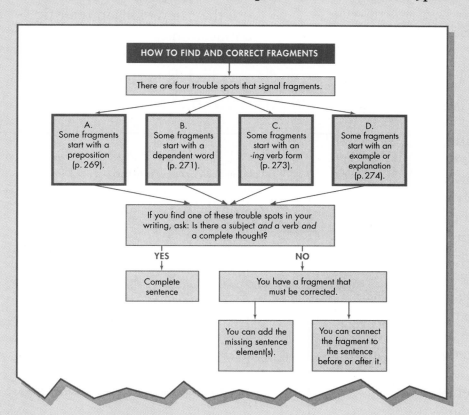

HOW TO FIND AND CORRECT FRAGMENTS

There are four trouble spots that signal fragments.

A. Some fragments start with a preposition (p. 269).

B. Some fragments start with a dependent word (p. 271).

C. Some fragments start with an -ing verb form (p. 273).

D. Some fragments start with an example or explanation (p. 274).

If you find one of these trouble spots in your writing, ask: Is there a subject *and* a verb *and* a complete thought?

YES → Complete sentence

NO → You have a fragment that must be corrected.

You can add the missing sentence element(s).

You can connect the fragment to the sentence before or after it.

"My students loved the summary charts. They liked the overviews that the charts provide."

— **Eddye S. Gallagher**
Tarrant County Junior College, Northeast Campus
Editorial Advisory Board Member and Class Tester

Real Writing Uses Real-World Assignments and Examples.

Real-World Writing Assignment: The Service Learning Course

You are taking a course in your major that has a service learning requirement. To fulfill this requirement, you volunteer for several hours per week at the Helping Hand Center, an organization run by the college that helps anyone in the community with any kind of problem. Fortunately, this semester a lot of people need help with exactly the kind of subject matter you're currently studying for your major. (Please choose a skill that you know well, that is part of your major, and that people visiting a neighborhood help center might want to learn.)

To earn academic credit for this work, you must write an essay-length report and submit it to your instructor. Choose one of these topics.

1. **PROCESS ANALYSIS:** To help other people that might need your expertise in the future, you decide to write out a complete set of instructions for the course-related skill you're best at teaching. Remember that your process analysis has to be clear enough for people to use on their own.

2. **PROCESS ANALYSIS:** One of the people you meet at the center is a man in his forties with interests and a background similar to your own. He wants to go to your college, but he has been out of school for a long time and has no idea how to apply for admission or sign up for a course. You help him either apply or sign up and then write an essay-style report that traces the process step by step.

3. **CLASSIFICATION:** An elderly woman, newly widowed, has no idea how to ~~ her ~~ ses, ~~ what ~~ She needs ~~ ~~ a

Throughout the book, all assignment topics, exercises, models, and examples are drawn from college, work, and everyday life. Each paragraph- and essay-writing chapter culminates in a Real-World Writing Assignment, in which students apply writing skills to a realistic situation, either in college, work, or everyday life. Students can see how the lessons of the book apply to real life, and they get a chance to use their new skills in realistic applications.

Real Writing Uses Checklists and Guided Practices to Make the Process Approach Work.

Like any up-to-date writing text, *Real Writing* presents writing as a process. But *Real Writing* also gives students the practical tools they need to make the process approach work. Each writing assignment is accompanied by a Checklist that gives a clear, easy-to-follow structure to the process for that type of writing. In addition, the two assignments most likely to be used first in the semester— Illustration and Narration— have extensive Guided Practices that walk students through each step of the assignment with explanations, examples, critical thinking questions, and opportunities to work on their own paragraphs.

Checklist: How to Write Comparison/Contrast

Check off items as you complete them.

1. **Narrow and explore your topics.**

____ Narrow your general topics to topics that have enough in common to be compared or contrasted, that you are interested in, and that can be compared or contrasted in a paragraph. Jot down some ideas about the two topics.

____ Decide why you are comparing or contrasting these two things. Is it to help readers choose between them? Or is it to give readers a better understanding of their relationship?

____ Decide whether you will compare or contrast your topics.

2. **Write a topic sentence.**

____ Review your ideas about the topics you are comparing or contrasting.

____ Write a topic sentence that includes your topics, the main point you want to make about them, and whether you are comparing or contrasting them.

3. **KEY STEP: Find points of comparison or contrast.** (See p. 158.)

____ Use a prewriting technique to find similarities and / or differences. Many people find that making a two-column list (one for each topic) is the easiest way to come up with parallel similarities or differences.

____ Select the points of comparison or contrast you will use, ch~~ ~~sing points that your readers w~~ ~~understand.

Real Writing Helps Students Overcome the Four Most Serious Errors.

In the Real World, Why Is It Important to Correct Fragments?

SITUATION: Karen has just graduated from the licensed practical nurse (LPN) program, and she's applying for a job at an excellent hospital. She sends her résumé along with a cover letter. She really wants a job at this hospital. Unfortunately, her cover letter hurts her chances. Here is a portion of her letter:

I graduated from the Nurse Practitioner program at Roxbury Community College. In May of this year. Even though I have just graduated, I have held responsible positions that will help me become part of your team quickly. Including Office Assistant at the Pediatrics Center, Assistant Manager at TLC Day Care, and Shift Manager at Pizza Hut. These positions have given me experience in office procedures, child care, and patient interaction. This experience will help me in the position on the nursing staff at Children's Hospital. Because it is directly relevant to the job.

RESPONSE: We gave Ann Colangelo, director of Critical Care Nursing at Children's Hospital in Boston, a cover letter containing Karen's paragraph. This is how Colangelo reacted to the letter:

I'm not a stickler for perfect grammar, and our business is health care, not writing. But I noticed the errors in the letter right away. The résumé looks decent, but those kinds of mistakes mark Karen as either sloppy or lacking in basic writing skills. I don't need nursing staff with either of those traits, and we have lots of applicants for every position.

People outside the English classroom notice major grammar errors

Bedford Books conducted an extensive nationwide survey to determine which grammar problems were the most serious and most damaging to students' writing success in the real world. Instructors cited four errors—fragments, run-ons, subject-verb agreement problems, and verb form problems—as the most troubling. We targeted these troublemakers with fuller coverage in Part Five, The Four Most Serious Errors, providing real-life examples, additional instruction, and more extensive exercises.

Real Writing Motivates with Profiles of Success.

An interview with and photograph of a former developmental student who has "made it" in the real world opens each paragraph-writing chapter (Part Two). The people profiled, many of whom are recipients of the Outstanding Alumni Award presented annually by the National Association for Developmental Education, were not good writers in college and did not believe that they would need writing in their lives after school. Their honest words of advice and encouragement help students see that success is possible and that writing skills are an important part of getting there.

Reggie Harris, Coordinator of Recruitment

PROFILE OF SUCCESS

Reggie Harris

WRITING THEN: "The importance of writing was never a big issue until I got to college. My reading instructor, Vashti Muse, showed me the importance of it. Before meeting her, I didn't think about writing. I was an athlete, not a writer, so I thought it wasn't important for me."

WRITING NOW: "My major responsibility is recruiting students for Hinds Community College, and I travel to visit prospective students. But back in the office, I have to write a lot. In addition to responding to writ-

Real Writing Contains Guides to Thinking Critically in Every Chapter.

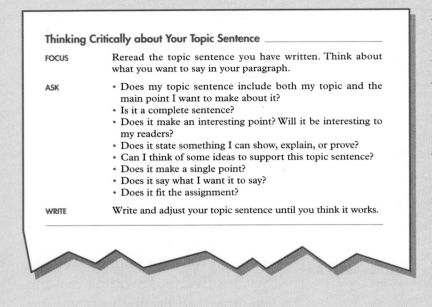

Thinking Critically about Your Topic Sentence _____

FOCUS   Reread the topic sentence you have written. Think about what you want to say in your paragraph.

ASK   • Does my topic sentence include both my topic and the main point I want to make about it?
             • Is it a complete sentence?
             • Does it make an interesting point? Will it be interesting to my readers?
             • Does it state something I can show, explain, or prove?
             • Can I think of some ideas to support this topic sentence?
             • Does it make a single point?
             • Does it say what I want it to say?
             • Does it fit the assignment?

WRITE   Write and adjust your topic sentence until you think it works.

Most developmental students need help with learning how to learn, with gaining awareness of and control over their own thinking rather than continuing to follow instructions blindly. The Thinking Critically guides for each crucial skill taught in *Real Writing* help students *focus* on the matter at hand—their own writing —*ask* themselves some key questions, and *write* or *edit* based on their answers. They help students *think* like writers.

Real Writing Connects Reading with Writing.

"Readings for Writers," at the end of the longer edition of *Real Writing*, is a collection of twenty-one high-interest selections in the areas of college, work, and everyday life, all of which have been reviewed and approved by developmental writing students.

The organization of the selections according to rhetorical method parallels the arrangement of the paragraph and essay chapters, which makes it easy for students to see the connection to their own writing and easy for you to integrate readings into the course.

Like the rest of the book, the reader promotes active learning. An introduction explains and demonstrates strategies for active, critical reading, while the unique apparatus includes Guiding Questions and quotations from student reviewers.

Mike Royko

Two Extremes Miss Target over Guns

Mike Royko (1932–1997) got his first job as a reporter by lying about previous journalist experience. From then on, he worked for virtually every Chicago newspaper in virtually every capacity. For more than twenty years, Royko reigned in his home town, holding the title of Chicago's most prominent journalist. In his daily column Royko often tackled controversial topics.

In "Two Extremes Miss Target over Guns," Royko, who was a gun owner himself and a member of the LaSalle Street Rod and Gun Club, criticizes both gun lovers and gun haters about their attitudes toward gun control. He examines the lack of communication that plagues the debate on gun control by comparing and contrasting the attitudes of opponents and supporters. The article originally appeared in the *Chicago Tribune* (1995).

GUIDING QUESTION
Based on Royko's title, what do you expect the essay to focus on?

> "I'm glad to see both sides of the gun control issue. I have read a lot about guns and gun control, but I never read anything like this."
> —Mark Herrmann, Student

When the subject is guns, we definitely have a failure to communicate.

Those who hate guns seem to believe that those who don't are a lot of lowbrow, beady-eyed, beer-guzzling neofascists who are constantly leaving pistols around the house so children can find them and shoot their siblings.[1]

Those who defend gun ownership seem to think that gun-control advocates[2] are a bunch of left-wing, government-loving, wine-sipping sissies who believe that the best way to handle a criminal is to kneel at his feet and blubber: "Don't hurt me. Take my money. I know you had a disadvantaged childhood, and I share your pain."

That's why I seldom write about the endless struggle between gun owners and gun haters, even though I think I understand them better than they understand each other.

For example, many gun lovers seem to believe that any gun-control law that imposes any restriction on gun ownership is a bad law.

If you carry that to its illogical[3] conclusion, we would have no gun laws and no restrictions. It would be legal for anyone — responsible citizen or nut — to buy a gun as easily as a bottle of root beer. And for anyone to carry it everywhere and anywhere, openly or concealed.

We might even have a situation that I once jokingly proposed[4] — and the Archie Bunker show shamelessly stole — in which all passengers on airplanes would be issued loaner pistols so they could blow away skyjackers.

We need gun laws. How restrictive they should be, I don't know. But

---

Real Writing Reflects the Classroom Experiences of Instructors and Students across the Country.

Real Writing was developed with the guidance of an editorial board of experienced instructors in a variety of institutions. The real-world insights of these people—who teach every day at large and small schools across the country—have shaped the project from beginning to end. In addition, every chapter has been thoroughly reviewed by numerous other instructors, and every section has been tested in developmental writing classrooms. Finally, because motivation and interest are so essential to student success, student reviewers helped us improve the chapters and choose the reader selections.

Susan Anker (B.A., M.Ed., Boston University) has a uniquely broad perspective on the challenges of teaching the developmental writing course. She taught English and developmental writing for several years before entering college publishing, where she has worked for seventeen years: as a sales representative and English/ESL editor at Macmillan Publishing Company; as developmental English/ESL editor, executive editor, and editor in chief at St. Martin's Press; and as editor in chief for humanities at Houghton Mifflin Company. In each of these positions, she worked with developmental writing instructors, maintaining her early interest in the area. Anker and her husband are the principals of Anker Publishing Company, which publishes professional development materials for higher education instructors and administrators. Her many years of experience talking and working with developmental writing instructors across the country and developing textbooks that meet the needs of these instructors and their students have culminated in *Real Writing*.

EDITORIAL ADVISORY BOARD

Real Writing was developed with the guidance of an editorial board of experienced instructors. The practical, real-world insights of these people—who teach every day at large and small schools across the country—have shaped the project from the very beginning. The board members have brainstormed with us; commented extensively on multiple drafts; class-tested chapters, features, and readings; contributed student and instructor material; helped with the design; and planned and written ancillaries. Their time and energy have improved every page.

Eddye S. Gallagher
Tarrant County Junior College
Hurst, Texas

Eddye Gallagher has taught writing for twenty-eight years at Tarrant County Junior College. The recipient of numerous local and regional teaching awards, she encourages confidence and enthusiasm in her students and works to eliminate the fear that developmental writers experience when faced with a writing situation. Over the years, she has offered her expertise and support to many teachers. This history of mentoring has culminated in *Teaching REAL WRITING: 1. Practical Suggestions*, an instructor's manual that helps both new and veteran instructors teach the developmental writing course. She has also written *The Computer Assistant* (McGraw-Hill, 1996), a spiral-bound book for computer-assisted composition classes. She is a former editorial board member and current consulting reader of *Teaching English in the Two-Year College*.

Beverly A. Butler
Shippensburg University of Pennsylvania
Shippensburg, Pennsylvania

Beverly Butler is professor of English and director of the Learning Assistance Center at Shippensburg University of Pennsylvania. In 1992, the Pennsylvania Association of Developmental Educators recognized her work in the university's tutoring center, where she and her staff foster among students an understanding of, confidence with, and appreciation of the writing process. As an instructor of writing and director of the tutoring center, she has developed critical strategies for building both the skill level and comfort level of developmental writers. She is the author of *At the Source: A Text for Basic Writers* (McGraw-Hill, 1993).

You live in the real world, too.

Here are practical resources to help in your complex challenges.

Real Writing's extensive ancillary package takes instructors' real lives into account. We know how busy you are and how little assistance you have. These are practical tools that simplify class preparation, promote student success, and enrich instructors' professional lives.

FOR INSTRUCTORS

Instructor's Annotated Edition for REAL WRITING

Teaching REAL WRITING: *1. Practical Suggestions*

Teaching REAL WRITING: *2. Additional Resources*

Teaching REAL WRITING: *3. Background Readings*

Teaching REAL WRITING: *4. Classroom Posters*

FOR STUDENTS

Notebook Dividers to Accompany REAL WRITING

SOFTWARE

Electronic Supplements for REAL WRITING: *1. Interactive Writing Software*

Electronic Supplements for REAL WRITING: *2. Interactive Grammar Tests and Exercises*

Electronic Supplements for REAL WRITING: *3. Additional Resources on Disk*

Instructor's Annotated Edition for REAL WRITING gives practical page-by-page advice on teaching with *Real Writing*.

by Susan Anker

The *Instructor's Annotated Edition for REAL WRITING*, which you are holding in your hands, is a unique classroom resource. In addition to answers to all exercises in the student text, marginal annotations offer practical suggestions for using each page of the text in the classroom. To make these tips even more convenient, each one is labeled according to content:

- *Teaching Tip*—ideas about presenting the material and ensuring comprehension in class
- *Discussion*—discussion prompts and ideas for conveying difficult or complex concepts through discussion
- *Teamwork*—suggestions for facilitating peer editing and collaborative work
- *Computer*—suggestions for instructors whose students use computers
- *ESL*—suggestions for instructors with nonnative speakers in the class
- *Resources*—cross-references to relevant material in the ancillaries
- *Reading Selections*—cross-references to relevant selections in *Readings for Writers*, in the longer version of *Real Writing*

Many of these tips were contributed by members of the Editorial Advisory Board, a team of experienced instructors who have collaborated with the author on *Real Writing*. Each such tip includes the board member's initials at the end.

> **TEACHING TIP**
> Emphasize that support points must be factual; an opinion alone will not convince readers. If students use an opinion, they should immediately support it with a fact. (EG)

Teaching REAL WRITING: 1. Practical Suggestions helps you plan and teach the course.

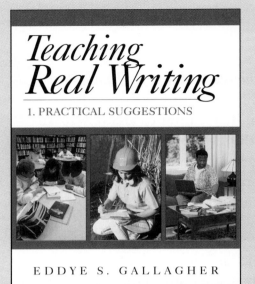

Teaching Real Writing
1. PRACTICAL SUGGESTIONS

EDDYE S. GALLAGHER

by Eddye S. Gallagher
Tarrant County Junior College

This useful volume contains practical advice on teaching the course with *Real Writing*, from what to do on day one of class to integrating the real world into the writing course to preparing students for assessment. Particular emphasis is placed on the needs of new instructors and on the need of all instructors to grow. *Practical Suggestions* also features a special section on critical thinking written by Chet Meyers, professor of humanities at Metropolitan State University and author of *Teaching Students to Think Critically*, along with suggestions and activities for promoting this skill.

Contents

Teaching Real Writing: 2. *Additional Resources* provides useful classroom resources.

EDDYE S. GALLAGHER
SUSAN ANKER

by Susan Anker and
Eddye S. Gallagher (Tarrant County Junior College)

This handy collection of materials for classroom use supplements the materials in *Real Writing* with additional self-assessment tools, writing guides, planning forms, diagnostic grammar tests, grammar review tests, and editing exercises. In addition, reproducible versions of writing guides, checklists, and quick review charts in the student text are included here so that instructors can distribute copies for students to complete and hand in. (*Additional Resources* is also available in electronic form.)

Contents

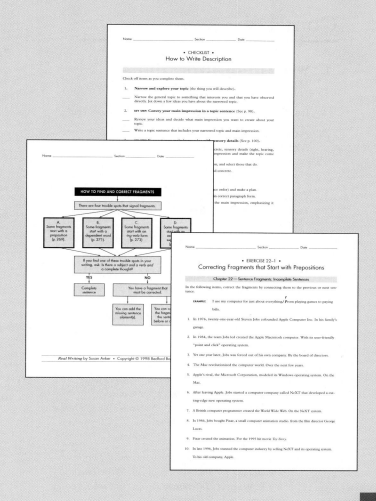

Teaching REAL WRITING 3. *Background Readings*
broadens your professional perspective.

by Susan Naomi Bernstein
Shippensburg University of Pennsylvania

This anthology includes twenty-five professional articles on topics of interest to developmental writing instructors, by both well-known writers such as Mina Shaughnessy, Mike Rose, and Rei Noguchi and newer voices of instructors currently teaching across the country. The selections are made more useful by analytical introductions, informative headnotes, and commentaries pointing out practical applications to the classroom.

Contents

Teaching REAL WRITING: 4. Classroom Posters reinforces key messages.

by Susan Anker

These four colorful, attractive posters—which can be displayed in your classroom, office, or writing center—visually reinforce the messages that success is attainable and that good writing is an important part of getting there.

1. **Profiles of Success**
2. **Using a Writing Process**
3. **Defeating the Four Most Serious Errors**
4. **Your Real Purpose and Audience**

Notebook Dividers to Accompany REAL WRITING helps students organize their course materials.

by Lois Hassan
Henry Ford Community College

Many developmental writing instructors find that their students have difficulty with being effective *students*, organizing and managing course materials and responsibilities. Our own research confirmed that this is a widespread problem and revealed that many instructors make these skills an implicit part of the curriculum, in part by helping their students set up class notebooks. The eight notebook dividers offered with *Real Writing* simplify this task. Each one is preprinted with a tab corresponding to a conventional section in a class notebook and useful tips on organizing and keeping on top of that material.

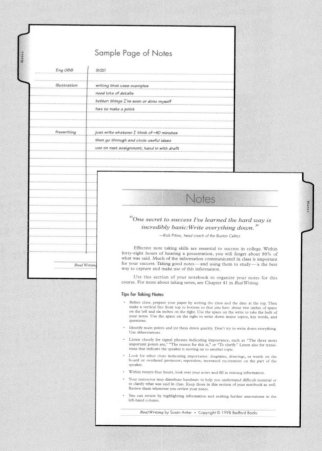

Electronic Supplements for REAL WRITING: *1. Interactive Writing Software* **transfers the pedagogy and approach of the book to a practical writing tool for the computer lab.**

These interactive writing guides use the Guided Practice format in the student text to walk students through the process of writing each type of paragraph and essay in the book. For each step of the clearly defined process, students are given explanations, examples, critical thinking questions, and opportunities to work on their own paragraphs. The network-compatible version also facilitates collaboration. (Available for both Windows and Macintosh.)

Electronic Supplements for REAL WRITING: *2. Interactive Grammar Tests and Exercises* **provides diagnostic tools and further opportunities for editing practice.**

The interactive diagnostic tests and editing exercises on this disk can be used for either study or assessment. The network-compatible version allows you to diagnose the needs of the class as a whole and simplifies record keeping. (Available for both Windows and Macintosh.)

Electronic Supplements for REAL WRITING: *3. Additional Resources on Disk* **allows instructors to customize instructional materials and store them in a convenient format.**

The materials in *Additional Resources* are reproduced here in word processing files that can be edited and printed as needed. (Available for both Windows and Macintosh.)

REAL WRITING
with Readings

*Paragraphs and Essays
for College, Work, and
Everyday Life*

Advisory Board

REAL WRITING

with Readings

Paragraphs
and Essays for
College, Work,
and Everyday Life

Susan Anker

Bedford Books ♨ Boston

For Bedford Books

President and Publisher: Charles H. Christensen
General Manager and Associate Publisher: Joan E. Feinberg
Managing Editor: Elizabeth M. Schaaf
Developmental Editors: Denise B. Wydra, Sarah E. Cornog
Editorial Assistants: Michelle M. Clark, Adrian Harris
Production Editor: Karen S. Baart
Production Assistants: Melissa Cook, Arthur Johnson
Copyeditors: Barbara G. Flanagan, Rosemary Winfield
Text Design: Claire Seng-Niemoeller
Cover Design: Night and Day Designs
Cover Photographs (from left to right): Copyright Charles Gupton, Stock, Boston.
Copyright Mark Burnett, Stock, Boston. Martin Paul, Ltd.
Composition: Ruttle, Shaw & Wetherill, Inc.
Printing and Binding: RR Donnelley & Sons Company

Library of Congress Catalog Card Number: 97–74954

Manufactured in the United States of America.

2   1   0   9   8   7
f   e   d   c   b   a

For information, write: Bedford Books, 75 Arlington Street, Boston, MA 02116
(617–426–7440)

ISBN: 0–312–13344–8   (Instructor's Annotated Edition)
       0–312–13342–1   (Student Edition)

Acknowledgments

Raphael Allen, "A Need for Affirmative Action." Originally appeared in the *Spectator*, March 1, 1996. Reprinted by permission of the author.

Maya Angelou, "Our Boys." From *Wouldn't Take Nothing for My Journey Now*, by Maya Angelou. Copyright © 1993 by Maya Angelou. Reprinted by permission of Random House, Inc.

Isaac Asimov, "What Is Intelligence, Anyway?" Reprinted by permission of the Estate of Isaac Asimov c/o Ralph M. Vicinanza, Ltd.

Russell Baker, "The Plot against People." From the *New York Times*. Copyright © 1968 by the New York Times Co. Reprinted by permission.

William J. Bennett, "Leave Marriage Alone." From *Newsweek*, June 3, 1996. Copyright © 1993 by Newsweek, Inc. Reprinted by permission.

Janice Castro, "Spanglish Spoken Here." From *Time*, July 11, 1988. Copyright © 1988 by Time Inc. Reprinted by permission of Time Inc.

Terry Crawford, "Affirmative Action Causes Imbalance." Originally appeared in *The Cavalier Daily*, June 29, 1995. Reprinted by permission of the author.

Stephanie Ericsson, "The Ways We Lie." Copyright © 1992 by Stephanie Ericsson. Originally published in *Utne Reader*. Permission granted by Rhoda Weyr Agency, NY.

Clif Garboden, "Windchill" (excerpt). Originally appeared in *The Boston Globe Magazine*, January 19, 1992. Reprinted by permission of the author.

Joey Green, "Beauty and the Beef." Copyright © 1987 by Joey Green. Reprinted by permission.

Rose Del Castillo Guilbault, "Americanization Is Tough on 'Macho'." From *The San Francisco Chronicle* (World Magazine). Copyright © 1989. Reprinted by permission of the author.

Roger Hoffmann, "The Dare." From the *New York Times*. Copyright © 1986 by the New York Times Co. Reprinted by permission.

Maxine Hong Kingston, excerpt from *The Woman Warrior* by Maxine Hong Kingston. Copyright © 1975, 1976 by Maxine Hong Kingston. Reprinted by permission of Alfred A. Knopf, Inc.

Preface for Instructors

In *Real Writing with Readings: Paragraphs and Essays for College, Work, and Everyday Life,* I worked with a talented collaborative team of Bedford editors and academic advisers, and together we set out to do two things. First, we decided to put writing in a real-world context, to make clear the vital importance of writing to students' lives, to present it as something students need not only to pass the course but also to succeed in every arena of their lives — now and in the future. We set out to demonstrate, in other words, that writing is fundamentally connected to students' past experiences and future goals — and thus is real. Second, we wanted to give students and instructors a solid collection of concrete, class-tested tools for mastering the crucial writing skills students need in college, work, and everyday life.

We did not try to re-create the wheel. A look at the contents of the many other writing workbooks reveals similar coverage, a sound framework that has evolved over time and reflects a consensus about what students need to know. *Real Writing* builds on that foundation. The basic scope and content of *Real Writing* parallel those in other workbooks. The topics and sequence will therefore look familiar, as will the workbook format providing lots of examples, practices, and opportunities for writing.

What seems to be missing in the available workbooks, however, is a compelling link to students' lives, something that will draw them into the book and help them connect to writing. While most workbooks have examples of student writing and maybe some student-oriented topics, they seem otherwise divorced from their audience and even oblivious to the realities of students' lives. More than ever, students aren't only students: They are also workers, parents, people with myriad responsibilities for whom "student" is just one of many demanding roles. If what they learn is not directly related to the rest of what they do, it is easily lost among other pressing concerns. When their textbooks fail to make the connection, it is not surprising that writing remains for students something that is done only in college, or even only in the writing class.

Everything we've done in *Real Writing* works toward making this connection, toward giving students a real reason to write and a realistic chance of success. We started with a clear understanding of where and who your students are — and where and who they want to be. To make *Real Writing* a better writing text, we have responded on every page and in a variety of ways to the question lurking in so many students' minds: "Why should I learn this? It's not important to my life." We know that writing is important. Success in the modern world — whether in college, at work, or in private life — is virtually impossible without good writing skills. To be practical, we have focused on the skills that will truly make a significant difference in students' writing and students' lives. And to be effective, we have refined the tools and techniques used to get those lessons across.

Personal experience, insightful collaborators, thorough reviewing, and nationwide surveys have bolstered our confidence that we know what's needed and what will work. For more than fifteen years I have held editorial and editorial management positions in college textbook publishing. In each position I've had the opportunity to talk at length with developmental writing instructors and students, to see what goes on in their classrooms, to hear about the challenges they face. This has given me a unique perspective; it also has helped me see what a tremendous advantage it would be to involve some of these instructors in the development of the book and to bring their real-world experiences into the mix. Consequently, an Editorial Advisory Board was established early in the life of the project.

Six talented and experienced instructors from across the country—Eddye Gallagher, Beverly Butler, Steven Garcia, Jack O'Keefe, Betty Owen, and John Silva— were enlisted to help shape the book, test ideas, and try them out on their students. Over the course of developing the book, these people became close and constant collaborators; their input, contributions, and reactions—along with those of their students—have infused this book with the hard-earned lessons of many classrooms. Once we were confident of being on the right track, we took the book to other classrooms. Every section of *Real Writing* has been class-tested thoroughly, and, once again, the perspective we gained from this real-world experience led to significant improvements. In addition, we have conducted several extensive surveys, asking teachers across the country to tell us more about their students and their needs. Working as a team and forging connections of our own, we have worked to shape a text that makes connections among instructors, students, writing, and the real world.

Organization

Real Writing with Readings: Paragraphs and Essays for College, Work, and Everyday Life uses an organization that is both straightforward and flexible. The book is divided into four sections: "Paragraphs," "Essays," "Editing," and "Readings for Writers." A briefer version of the book without the last section is also available. Within each section, two or more parts group the chapters into manageable chunks. "Paragraphs" contains Part One, "How to Write a Paragraph," which goes over the general writing process for paragraphs, and Part Two, "Writing Different Kinds of Paragraphs," which covers each of the different paragraphs that students are typically asked to write: illustration, narration, description, and so on. The next section, "Essays," mirrors this organization, with Part Three, "How to Write an Essay," and Part Four, "Writing Different Kinds of Essays." The third section, "Editing," is divided into four parts: Part Five, "The Four Most Serious Errors"; Part Six, "Other Grammar Concerns"; Part Seven, "Word Use"; and Part Eight, "Punctuation and Capitalization." The final section, "Readings for Writers," has ten chapters: an introduction on active reading and nine other chapters, each of which contains readings using one of the rhetorical methods students have studied in the text.

Features

Real Writing not only presents the information students need but also shows students how and why writing is relevant to them—connecting them to writing, to the content of the book, and to the course. Here are some of the ways *Real Writing* forges this connection.

Teaches practical skills.   *Real Writing* covers the writing forms and strategies that are the cornerstone of practical writing competence in the real world: assessing purpose and audience, developing topic sentences, organizing material, using methods of paragraph development, writing informational and argumentative essays, creating summaries, and so on. *Real Writing* focuses on the practical skill of editing rather than the abstract system of grammar. Throughout the book are options for working collaboratively and using computers—increasingly important skills in the real world. *Real Writing* also includes useful appendices that cover skills needed in real life: setting goals, giving oral presentations, and writing résumés.

Is easy to use. The format makes complex information easy to find, so students can use *Real Writing* on their own. Chapters have a predictable three-part organization that makes it easy for students to *understand* the importance of the lesson, *practice* the skills involved, and *apply* them to their own writing. Plenty of models, exercises, and readings accompany the lessons. The clear and open design highlights key information and offers tips and options in the margins. Every chapter ends with a summary of core content, and every grammar chapter also includes a "Quick Review Chart" in the summary. To acquaint students with these elements, an illustrated introduction at the beginning of the book walks them through the book and its features.

Connects the content to students' own goals for college, work, and everyday life. All three aspects of a student's world—college, work, and everyday life—are reflected in the examples, readings, exercises, and assignments. Every paragraph- and essay-writing chapter (Parts Two and Four) presents information on how the type of writing under discussion is used not only in college but also at work and in everyday life. "Real-World Assignments"—the culminating assignments in these chapters—require students to apply what they've learned to realistic situations, from either college, work, or everyday life. Exercise and writing topics have been chosen to reflect the diversity of the developmental writing population in terms of age, background, goals, and learning styles. "In the Real World" sections in Part Five, "The Four Most Serious Errors," present situations and examples in which grammar lapses had significant consequences. "What Will You Use?" prompts at the ends of many chapters ask students to connect what they have studied and how they will apply it.

Supports a process approach to writing and editing with practical tools that work. There are six chapters on how to write a paragraph (Part One) and three chapters on how to write an essay (Part Three). In the paragraph- and essay-writing chapters in Parts Two and Four, students work primarily on their own paragraph assignments rather than drilling with unconnected exercises. Each writing assignment is accompanied by a "Checklist" that gives a clear, easy-to-follow structure for the type of writing under discussion. In addition, the two forms of writing that are often introduced first in the semester—illustration and narration—have extensive "Guided Practices" that walk students through each step of the process with explanations, examples, critical thinking guides, and practices. Editing chapters have plentiful exercises, many in connected discourse. And because editing and grammar lessons are useful only if students can apply them to their own writing, editing chapters end with assignments to help students find and correct problems in their work.

Focuses on a limited number of essential skills—so mastery becomes a realistic goal. The four most serious grammar errors—those mistakes that are truly detrimental to a writer's credibility—are given special emphasis and attention in Part Five, "The Four Most Serious Errors." Essential grammar terminology is limited to twelve key terms. Chapter 32, "ESL Concerns," gives students whose native language is not English the practical advice and handy references they need to increase English-language competency. The emphasis throughout is on improving writing, not on learning theory or jargon.

Shows students an image of themselves as successful, competent writers and people. "Profiles of Success" in the paragraph-writing chapters (Part Two) consist of pictures and interviews with former developmental students who now use writing in their successful careers. Each profile gives specific examples of the kinds of writing the person's job demands and contains honest words of advice and encouragement to help students see that success is possible and that writing skills are an important part of getting there. Quotations and pictures of basic writing students open many chapters; others begin with quotations from successful people who hold jobs that students might aspire to. "You Know This" tips remind students that they already have many of the skills and experiences they need to be strong writers. Examples of student writing are shown throughout, including two student-written selections in "Readings for Writers."

Helps students become active and critical learners. "Thinking Critically" guides in every chapter improve students' metacognitive skills by asking them to *focus* on the task at hand, *ask* some key questions, and *write* or *edit* based on their answers. "Learning Journal" prompts at the end of many chapters ask students to evaluate both the usefulness of the content and their own success as learners.

Features a reader that connects reading with writing. "Readings for Writers," at the end of the longer edition of *Real Writing,* is a collection of twenty-one high-interest selections in the areas of college, work, and everyday life, all of which have been reviewed and approved by developmental writing students. Student voices are also heard in two student-written essays at the end of the argument chapter. The organization of the selections according to rhetorical method parallels the arrangement of the paragraph and essay chapters, making it easy for students to see the connection to their own writing and easy for you to integrate the readings into the course. Like the rest of the book, the reader promotes active learning. An introduction explains and models strategies for active, critical reading, and the unique apparatus includes not only headnotes, comprehension and critical thinking questions, and writing prompts, but also guiding questions (which give students a purpose for reading) and quotations from student reviewers.

Ancillaries

Just as students' lives are busier than ever, so too are the lives of instructors. Our Editorial Advisory Board, along with reviewers, helped us construct an extensive ancillary package that takes the real world of instructors into account and provides practical tools that simplify class preparation, promote student success, and enrich professional development. (To read more information on any of these ancillaries and to see sample pages, please turn to the special section at the beginning of the Instructor's Annotated Edition.)

ANCILLARIES FOR INSTRUCTORS

- *The Instructor's Annotated Edition for REAL WRITING* gives practical page-by-page advice right where you need it: in the book. Not only does it contain answers to all exercises, but it offers unique marginal annotations containing helpful teaching tips on a variety of topics.

- *Teaching REAL WRITING: 1. Practical Suggestions* is a thorough instructor's manual that helps all instructors teach the course and contains special advice for new instructors. It includes a special section on teaching critical thinking in the developmental classroom.

- *Teaching REAL WRITING: 2. Additional Resources* supplements the materials in the workbook itself with additional exercises, checklists, writing guides, transparencies, assignments, and other materials for classroom use. (It is also available on computer disk.)
- *Teaching REAL WRITING: 3. Background Readings* offers twenty-five professional articles on topics of interest to developmental writing instructors, accompanied by useful suggestions for practical applications to the classroom.
- *Teaching REAL WRITING: 4. Classroom Posters* reinforces key messages about the importance of writing and the attainability of success with four attractive, colorful posters.

ANCILLARY FOR STUDENTS

- *Notebook Dividers to Accompany REAL WRITING* helps students organize their course materials.

SOFTWARE

- *Electronic Supplements for REAL WRITING: 1. Interactive Writing Software* contains interactive writing guides that transfer the pedagogy and approach of the book to a practical writing tool for the computer lab.
- *Electronic Supplements for REAL WRITING: 2. Interactive Grammar Tests and Exercises* provides diagnostic tools and further opportunities for editing practice.
- *Electronic Supplements for REAL WRITING: 3. Additional Resources on Disk* allows instructors to customize the instructional materials in *Additional Resources* and store them in a convenient format.

Acknowledgments

Many voices shaped *Real Writing*. I fear I will forget some people whose insights helped inform this book over the years of its development, but what follows is my best attempt to thank those who contributed to *Real Writing*.

Editorial Advisory Board

The thanks must start with the Editorial Advisory Board. When I agreed to write this book, I had no idea how intense and prolonged that commitment would be. I would guess that the members of the Advisory Board similarly underestimated the amount of work their participation would involve. Each of the board members carefully scrutinized seemingly endless drafts and revisions. During the course of the book's development, I felt sure that board members would at some point cry "uncle" and retreat from the project. But no one dropped out; and they all remained active, involved, and insightful throughout every stage. *Real Writing* blends their voices with mine and those at Bedford Books. Thanks to each of you; I admire your tenacity along with your insights into teaching and learning and your good humor.

Eddye S. Gallagher, Tarrant County Junior College, Northeast Campus (TX). Eddye was the first of the board members to be involved with *Real Writing*, and her straightforward, pragmatic, plentiful suggestions infuse each chapter. Her years of classroom experience enabled her to give us an accurate reading of what would ring true for developmental writing students. Throughout the writing of the book, Eddye candidly pointed out things that didn't work and helped to replace them with things that do.

Beverly A. Butler, Shippensburg University of Pennsylvania. In a quiet but persistent voice, Beverly reminded us that the book had to help students think like writers, that we must distill and model our thought processes for students. The Thinking Critically guides had their genesis in Beverly's promptings.

Steven A. Garcia, Riverside Community College (CA). In addition to reviewing and testing the manuscript, Steve was generous with his teaching tips and frequently urged us to use visual images and provide for a variety of learning styles. His many good suggestions reminded us always to link new knowledge to concrete things that students are already familiar with.

Jack O'Keefe, Richard J. Daley College, City Colleges of Chicago (IL). Jack is a masterful collector of reading selections that are well written and of great interest to students. He gave us many of his surefire classroom successes as we put together the readings in the book. He also is an astute judge of good writing assignments, and we relied on him to painstakingly scrutinize our writing chapters (in addition to all other parts).

Betty Owen, Broward Community College (FL). Betty has a true appreciation for her students and how they see things. She kept us thinking about how the book should look and feel to students and how it could be relevant to them.

John Silva, LaGuardia Community College, City College of New York. John was an active voice in all aspects of the book's development and was especially helpful in two areas: making sure that we challenged and stretched students rather than spoon-fed them and keeping us sensitive to the concerns of nonnative speakers.

Students and Their Instructors

Many students and former students have contributed immensely to this book. The seven former students featured in the Profiles of Success are inspiring, and I have been honored to get to know them. I thank them for their patience as I called and wrote again and again for more information for the profiles. It is no surprise to me that they are successful: They are patient, gracious, and grateful, in addition to their other talents. I sincerely thank Rocío Avila, Rosalind Baker, Valeria Edwards, Reggie Harris, Gary Knoblock, Jeffrey Lee, Jill Lee, and Ignacio Murillo.

Other students and former students also contributed many elements to *Real Writing*. Some supplied model paragraphs and essays, among them Karen Branch, Carol Benson, Marcella Cross, Danny Fitzgerald, Mark Herrmann, Tiffany Johnson, Jackie LeFrançois, Jason Sifford, Janet Wade, and Kevin Willey.

Some offered observations about writing that we used as quotes: Pedro Babiak, Mayerlin Fana, Fritz Gourdet, Ken Hargreaves, Jimmy Lester, Minh Nguyen, Ingrid Panosh, Robyne Petty, Matt Pierce, Emily Quinn, Kathleen Reid, John Rich, Naomi Roman, Ray Stone, and Rosanna Valdez.

Other students served as reviewers and class testers, offering written comments: Ricky Alyassi, Susan Andreas, Michael Avila, Deborah Baker, Cesar Barajas, Maria Barcenas, Rochelle Basaldua, Juan Belmontis, Michelle Brown, Farrah Burgos, Monica Cacho, Julieta Carretero, Maricela Chavez, Derrick Clarke, Jennifer Desmangles, Chris Devine, Desserine Drake, Ignacio Duran, Sherry Durgan, Matt Edsall, Christel Esparza, Mario Flores, Jason Foices, Nicole Foley, David Frey, Ricardo Galvez, John Geeter, Lorenzo Gilbert, Chris Gilliam, Genoveva Guillén, Lucrecia Guillén, Ramzey Haddad, Brad Hammond, Kimberly Harviley, Lori Hassan, Guadalupe Hernandez, Yvonne Herrera, Mark Herrmann, Barbara Hildreth, Ginger Hollingsworth, Karen Hoover, Kawana Horton, Kimberly Hurdle, Jammie Jackson, Shelontay Jackson, Donnette James, Teresa Janociak, Joanna Jarzabek, Tiffanie Johnson, Fatemah S. Kalleh, Kim Klein, Brent Knaak, Maria Kubacka,

Kelly-Gene Lawson, Naun Leanos, Jr., Sinar Lomeli, Lilia Lopez, Mario Lopez, Elizabeth Luna, Anna Laura Madrazo, Melinda Manzo, Zerlma Martinez, Elizabeth Mena, John W. Mills, Jessica Miranda, Nancy Mota, Alina Munoz, Jimmy Munoz, Geania Navarro, Victoria Ojeda, Li Pan, Pablo Pérez, Terri Petty, Gwen Quefenne, Cecilia Ramos, Michele Ramsey, Janda Reed, Beverly Rehfeldt, Hector Reyes, Joy Richardson, Shelly Rivet, Sandra Scott, Braulio Segoviano, John Sidaros, Maria Soto, Rachel Soto, Laura Sterck, Connie Temple, Elizabeth Terriquez, Noe Jesse Trejo, Brent Turner, Darché Turner, Rachel Uziel, Vivian Vaccarino, Marie Vazquez, Elizabeth Velasco, Barbara Walker, Erica Walsh, Roosevelt White, Marilyn Whitton, Andre Williams, Nathan Wissick, Pieter Wycoff, Gloria Zapata, and Jehad Zatar.

Jim Rice and Pat Toney at Quinsigamond Community College, Worcester, MA, allowed me to be a part of Pat's English 110 class. Pat and her students patiently talked with me about books, practice exercises, writing, grammar, jobs, courses, expectations, problems, and myriad other things: life in the real world. Among these students were Letitia Anaya, Joseph Chedid, Raul Figueroa, Ken Hargreaves, Jimmy Lester, Theresa Peltier, Emily Quinn, Yesenia Reyes, Naomi Roman, Ray Stone, and Tan Vuu.

Many of the former developmental students profiled in the book are recipients of the Outstanding Alumni Award presented annually by the National Association for Developmental Education (NADE). I spoke with their mentors and former teachers, the people who submitted their names to NADE. Many of the profiled former students believe that these teacher/mentors were directly and single-handedly responsible for helping them to rechart their lives. Without question, these people have made a profound difference in the lives of their students: Sally Brown, Puente Project (Rocío Avila, Ignacio Murillo); Mary Kay Healey, Puente Project; Maxine Elmont, Massachusetts Bay Community College (Rosalind Baker); Laura Geyer, Forsyth Technical and Community College (Valeria Edwards); Elnetta Jones, Shippensburg University of Pennsylvania (Jeffrey Lee); Karen Miller, University of Toledo Community and Technical College (Jill Lee); and Vashti Muse, Hinds Community College (Reggie Harris).

I was helped by various people involved in NADE, including Vickie Kelly, Louisiana College, and Ada Belton, Keystone Junior College, who helped me track down the NADE award winners.

Reviewers and Class Testers

In addition to the Editorial Advisory Board, a group of unusually thoughtful reviewers and class testers helped us to develop and fine-tune the book. We are particularly indebted to Pat Malinowski of Finger Lakes Community College (NY) who was with us every step of the way, thoughtfully evaluating each chapter and graciously supplying student writing. My thanks also to Alan Ainsworth, Houston Community College—Central; Ann Aronson, Metropolitan State University; Karen Ball, Vincennes University; Sandra Bavra, North Carolina Central University; Susan Bernstein, Shippensburg University of Pennsylvania; Judy Boles, Chattanooga State Technical Community College; Gene Booth, Albuquerque Technical Vocational Institute; Vivian Brown, Laredo Junior College; Joanne Buck, Guilford Technical Community College; Deborah Callen, Harold Washington College; Sandra Carey, Lexington Community College; John Cegielski, Anoka Ramsey Community College; Wendy Chen, Minneapolis Community College; Carolyn Chism, Montgomery College; Jeffrey Cofer, Atlantic Community College; Judith Coleman, University of Massachusetts at Boston; Jean Crockett, Cleveland State Community College; Francine DeFrance, Cerritos College; Stephanie Doijka, Lakewood Community College; Eileen Eliot, Broward Community College—Central; Clara

Fendley, Scottsdale Community College; Ann George, Penn State University; John Gregg, San Diego Mesa College; Elizabeth Griffey, Florida Community College at Jacksonville; Connie Gulick, Albuquerque Technical Vocational Institute; Patricia Hare, Brevard Community College; Crystal Harris, Sinclair Community College; Judy Harris, Rochester Community College; Lois Hassan, Henry Ford Community College; Julie Hendrickson, University of Maine at Augusta; Harriet Hornblower, University of Massachusetts at Lowell; Christine Howell, West Virginia University; Lauri Humberson, St. Philip's College; Ronald Illingworth, University of Alaska—Fairbanks; Deborah James, University of North Carolina at Asheville; Patricia Jenkins, Cleveland State Community College; Susan Jones, University of Tennessee at Chattanooga; Scott Kassner, Minneapolis Community College; Steve Kaufman, Minneapolis Community College; Gilda Kelsey, University of Delaware; Cindy Krause, Wilbur Wright College; Jo Libertini, East Tennessee State University; Debra Lilli, Community College of Rhode Island; Patricia Malinowski, Finger Lakes Community College; Linda Matthews, South Suburban College; Tim McLaughlin, Bunker Hill Community College; Kim McSherry, Houston Community College—Central; Chet Meyers, Metropolitan State University; Caryl Ann Minor, Edinboro University of Pennsylvania; Mercy Moore, Broward Community College—Central; Bridget Murphy, North Hennepin Community College; Sarita Mutscher, Blinn College; Victoria Nelson, West Virginia University; Heather Newburg, Lake Superior State University; Marsha Olivers, Anoka Ramsey Community College; Bonnie Orr, Wenatchee Valley College; Myra Peavyhouse, Roane State Community College; Gary Phillips, Grossmont College; Hazel Phillips, Collin County Community College; Jim Rice, Quinsigamond Community College; Carolyn Russell, Rio Hondo College; Lois Ryan, Manchester Community College; Andrea Sanders, Walters State Community College; Bill Schlientz, Philander Smith College; William Shute, San Antonio College; Rosemary Smith, Prince George's Community College; Billie Unger, Shepherd College; Dorothy Voyles, Parkland Community College; Steve Whiting, Sinclair Community College; Joann Wilcox, Aims Community College; Lisa Windham, College of the Mainland; Jay Wootten, Kent State University—Salem; Rose Yesu, Massasoit Community College; and Teena Zindel-McWilliams, Richland Community College.

Colleagues

Some of my own earliest authors taught me about good teaching, good authorly ways, and strong author-editor relationships. Thanks forever to those early authors: Ann Raimes, Trudy Smoke, Karen Greenberg, and Dick Nordquist, among others.

Contributors

Various people contributed ideas and material to *Real Writing*. First, I thank the Editorial Advisory Board—once again—for many good suggestions for the teaching annotations. I am grateful to Beth Mezaros for her many insightful comments and suggestions; to Mitchell Evich for exercises; and to Deborah Repplier for her work on "Readings for Writers."

Rita Losee kindly allowed me to use much of her material in goal setting after I participated in and was much impressed by a workshop she gave. The guide to writing a résumé was written by Jill Lee at the University of Toledo Community and Technical College. Jill is also one of the profiles of success (Chapter 10).

Eddye S. Gallagher, Editorial Advisory Board member and a steady supplier of pragmatic advice and ideas, wrote *Practical Suggestions,* the instructor's manual, and contributed exercises and tests to *Additional Resources.* From the moment I met

Eddye, I knew she would be integrally involved in *Real Writing,* and indeed she has been. Chet Meyers of Metropolitan State University (MN) supplied critical thinking material in *Practical Suggestions,* and Pamela Ozaroff wrote exercises for *Additional Resources.* Lois Hassan of Henry Ford Community College (MI) wrote the notebook dividers that will help students get and stay organized.

Susan Naomi Bernstein, Shippensburg University of Pennsylvania, wrote *Background Readings,* sifting through stacks of journals and books to find reading selections that would be useful and informative for instructors. She then surrounded these fine selections with apparatus to help instructors apply the material.

Bedford Books

I held editorial and editorial management positions at several different publishing houses before hooking up with Bedford Books to create *Real Writing.* Bedford is different: Each person there insists upon excellence, nudges toward improvement, and pushes to do it again (and again, and again), to try all ideas before selecting the best, and to work until everyone is ready to drop. All the editors are active teachers, learners, and collaborators. They know how to get the best from people and are at once—and to a one—exceptionally demanding, unswervingly gracious, and eternally patient.

Karen Baart, production editor, took an uncommonly messy manuscript and somehow miraculously produced a book, overseeing the complex process of book production. Melissa Cook skillfully assisted her, as did Arthur Johnson in the later stages. Barbara Flanagan's eagle eye and unflagging expertise in all things grammatical rooted out errors, infelicities, and downright embarrassments. Sarah Cornog, associate editor, ably handled many of the details of the project early on, added insightful comments, and ultimately took full responsibility for the reader section of the book. This section benefited from Rosemary Winfield's judicious copyediting. Michelle Clark, editorial assistant, shaped the numerous drafts of *Background Readings* and efficiently managed the constantly shifting landscape of ancillaries and the endless rounds of reviews—always cheerfully, always well. During her tenure as editorial assistant, Adrian Harris also provided early able assistance with the selection of readings, early reviews, and organization of the first meeting of the Editorial Advisory Board.

Karen Henry, executive editor, contributed steady and sound advice that helped turn a collection of good but unintegrated features into a book with a message. Charles Cavaliere, marketing manager, energetically and enthusiastically helped us take the book into the world, and the talented folk in the Promotion Department—Donna Dennison, Susan Pace, Terry Govan, Stephanie Westnedge, and Zoe Langosy—worked to get that message into visual and verbal print form. Elizabeth Schaaf, managing editor, supervised endless rounds of design and production decisions to bring *Real Writing* out in a timely fashion. Claire Seng-Niemoeller brought admirable amounts of talent and patience to the design of this book, combining the many elements into an aesthetically pleasing, coherent whole.

I've known Chuck Christensen, president and publisher of Bedford Books, and Joan Feinberg, general manager and associate publisher, for many years. One of the first things I did upon becoming a rookie English editor was to visit Chuck and Joan at the newly established Bedford Books office, hoping that some of their editorial brilliance and magic would rub off. We struck up a lasting collegiality, with mutual respect and friendship that has grown over the years. Joan always assured me that the people at Bedford had no magic formula for publishing good books; they just knew the right questions to ask and keep asking until they were satisfied that each book had a sound reason for being. Other publishers strive to publish good books; Chuck and Joan do something far beyond that: they insist on it. They are in a league by themselves.

I've left for next-to-last the thanks to Denise Wydra, senior editor, because I'm not sure that I have the words to adequately communicate my profound gratitude for her contribution (partly because she's made me write so many words, again and again, that I am literally in short supply). Denise saw what was there and made it much better; she saw what wasn't there, and together we explored the world of possible ideas. I have worked with many talented editors; Denise is, quite simply, the best. She has been my collaborator and coauthor for nearly three years, and I have grown to depend on her advice and appraisal. Thank you, Denise.

Finally, I thank my husband, Jim Anker. Ever patient, ever strategic, ever encouraging, he helped me to stay the course. I learn from him every day of my life.

Introduction for Students

How to Use This Book

TEACHING TIP
Going through this introduction, the practice, and the questionnaire works well as an activity on the first day of class. It acquaints students with the book and its features, gives both them and you a profile of them as writers, and focuses their attention on what they actually want from the course. For other ideas about what to do on the first day or week of class, see *Practical Suggestions*.

Why Use *Real Writing*?

The easy answer is that it's been assigned by your instructor. But that just means you need to buy the book; it's your decision whether or not to actually use it to help you improve your writing. Probably you're juggling lots of time-consuming commitments (like college, a job, family responsibilities, and commuting), and each commitment grabs a chunk of your time. You need to make wise decisions about how to spend your time in the most useful ways.

The real answer to why you should use this book is that it will benefit you personally. As the title suggests, *Real Writing: Paragraphs and Essays for College, Work, and Everyday Life* isn't just academic. Its purpose is to improve your writing so that you can succeed not only in this course, but in other courses, on the job, and in your everyday life. Writing is a skill that you'll need to get through college, but it is also a skill that most jobs require. College graduates earn about 75 percent more than high school graduates; community college graduates earn 60 percent more than high school graduates and 320 percent more than high school dropouts. People in industry cite good communication skills as the most important ability they look for in job candidates. Mastering basic writing skills may be the most important thing you do in college.

How will *Real Writing* help? Mainly by being practical: It focuses on the most important writing and editing skills you need to succeed and gives you simple explanations, reality-based assignments, concrete steps for completing tasks, and tips for moving ahead if you get stuck. *Real Writing* isn't removed from your life; it starts where you are and helps you get to where you want to go.

How to Find Information in *Real Writing*

Your instructor will assign chapters, practice exercises, writing assignments, and so on. First, find the time to do the assigned work—carefully and thoroughly. Then as you write, check back in the book for anything you're not sure about (such as the steps for writing a particular kind of paragraph, or how to edit your writing to see if you've made a grammar mistake, or whether to use *they're* or *their*). How do you get to that information quickly, without thumbing through the whole book? There are several ways, and you may find some more useful than others, depending on what you are looking for.

TEACHING TIP
Walk students through each of these "access routes" to make sure they understand how they can find information in the book.

Brief table of contents.   Inside the front cover of the book is a brief table of contents. Here you can scan all the chapter titles and see at a glance where the various writing and editing topics are in the book. You'll also see that the book moves from writing paragraphs (Parts One and Two) to writing essays (Parts Three and Four) to editing (Parts Five through Eight). If you're looking for a whole chapter or a general section of the book, the brief table of contents is a good place to turn.

Table of contents.   At the front of the book is the longer, more detailed table of contents. When you are trying to find something specific within a chapter, this may be more useful than the brief table of contents. For example, you might recall that there is something about keeping a journal in one of the first few chapters but not remember whether it's in Chapter 1 or Chapter 2. A quick look at the table of contents will help you see that Keeping a Journal is a section in Chapter 2 and will give you the exact page number to turn to.

Index.   At the end of the book is a complete index, organized alphabetically, that lists what's in the book and what page it's on. Using the index will almost always direct you to the right place. For example, to find how to write a topic sentence, you would look up *topic sentence*. There you'd find the page number not only for the section that covers this skill in general but for other sections that cover topic sentences in specific types of writing. In creating the index, we tried to think of the many ways you might look something up and included a variety of terms so that you won't have to look in several places.

List of useful charts and quick references.   Facing the inside of the back cover is a list of charts and quick reference tools (such as writing checklists, a list of irregular verbs, and so on). If you find yourself turning repeatedly to a page in the book after you're done with the chapter it's in, that page is probably listed here. If it's not, you can add it so that you'll know where to find it next time.

Headings at the tops of pages.   Along with the page number at the top of each page is a useful reminder of exactly where you are in the book. The first line next to the page number gives the name of the section of the book you're in—Paragraphs, Essays, Editing, or Readings. On each left-hand page under the name of the section are the number and name of the part you're in. On the right-hand page are the number and name of the chapter you're in. The following sample shows that you are in Part One, on paragraphing, and within that in Chapter 5, on drafting.

Finding Information in *Real Writing*

Using each of the aids mentioned in the preceding section, find these items in the book:

- The definition of *fragment*
- A chart showing how to find and correct fragments
- The difference in meaning between *they're* and *their*
- A checklist that will help you write an argument paragraph
- The definition of the term *classification*
- A list of irregular verbs

How to Use *Real Writing* When You Write

Real Writing is full of elements that are intended to help you make your way through your writing assignments and become a better writer. Here are descriptions of a few of them with samples from the book.

Marginal notes. Throughout the book you will see notes in the margins, the space to the left of where most of the type appears. These notes provide tips on how to do something, reminders of information that you may have forgotten, references to other pages in the book where you can review material, ideas for journal writing, and quotations from other students. Most of these notes aren't crucial—you don't have to read or under-stand them to benefit from the chapter—but they're always useful and informative.

Thinking critically guides. Each chapter has short guides that help you focus and collect your thoughts as you begin a task. These guides make completion of the task easier and give you useful practice in thinking before acting—it's practice you'll use both in and out of college.

Thinking Critically about Your Topic Sentence _____

FOCUS   Reread the topic sentence you have written. Think about what you want to say in your paragraph.

ASK   • Does my topic sentence include both my topic and the main point I want to make about it?
         • Is it a complete sentence?
         • Does it make an interesting point? Will it be interesting to my readers?
         • Does it state something I can show, explain, or prove?
         • Can I think of some ideas to support this topic sentence?
         • Does it make a single point?
         • Does it say what I want it to say?
         • Does it fit the assignment?

WRITE   Write and adjust your topic sentence until you think it works.

Checklists. Because the writing process consists of a num-ber of small steps that are some-times easy to overlook, we've included a checklist for each assignment that will help you keep track of what you've done and point out what you should do next.

Checklist: How to Write Comparison/ Contrast	Check off items as you complete them.
	1. Narrow and explore your topics.
	_____ Narrow your general topics to topics that have enough in common to be compared or contrasted, that you are interested in, and that can be compared or contrasted in a paragraph. Jot down some ideas about the two topics.
	_____ Decide why you are comparing or contrasting these two things. Is it to help readers choose between them? Or is it to give readers a better understanding of their relationship?
	_____ Decide whether you will compare or contrast your topics.
	2. Write a topic sentence.
	_____ Review your ideas about the topics you are comparing or contrasting.
	_____ Write a topic sentence that includes your topics, the main point you want to make about them, and whether you are comparing or contrasting them.
	3. KEY STEP: Find points of comparison or contrast. (See p. 158.)
	_____ Us~~e a~~ prewriting technique to find simil~~arities~~ and / or differ~~ences~~

Guided practices.   The first two paragraph assignments, illustration and narration, are the two that instructors are most likely to assign first in

Guided Practice: How to Write Narration	Step 1. Narrow and Explore Your General Topic
	After you have chosen a general topic to write about, find your own story within that general topic. Write down one or two ideas for possible stories and ask yourself if there _is_ a story to tell, if you are interested in the story, and if you can tell it in a paragraph.
TIP: For a review of the Three-Question Test for Good Topics, see Chapter 2.	Sometimes people choose experiences that are too big to tell in a paragraph. For instance, one student first chose as his story "life as a Buddhist." There may be a fascinating story there, but it's too big to tell thoroughly in one paragraph. The student had to narrow the general topic to something more focused: "an important Buddhist ceremony." You need to be able to communicate the important events in your story in one paragraph.

GENERAL TOPIC:	_A situation I learned from_
POSSIBLE STORIES:	_When I fell before my wedding, when I hurt Naomi's feelings, when my grandfather died_
NARROWED TOPIC / STORY:	_When I fell before my wedding_
IDEAS:	_A horrible experience, one I learned from, behavior the day before, the fall, how it changed things_

Thinking Critically to Narrow and Explore a Narration Topic _____

FOCUS	Think about the general topic and your experiences with it.
ASK	• What experiences in my life are connected to this topic?
	• Which would make a good story?
	• Which seem interesting to me?
	• Which one should I focus on?
	• When I think of this experience, what are the first things ~~come to my mind?~~

the course. For these assignments, we've provided Guided Practices, an additional layer of support to help you work effectively through the writing process. Each Guided Practice follows the steps of the assignment, accompanied by explanations, examples, critical thinking questions, and opportunities to work on other writing.

Hand-edited sentences.   In the editing section of the book, the examples of grammar mistakes actually *show* handwritten corrections. You can see at a glance both what the problem was and how it was corrected.

> *When the*
> ~~The~~ interviewer stands, the candidate should shake hands firmly.
> ^

Perspective pictures.   Sometimes we need to change our perspective on things in order to see and understand problems — and to correct them. At the end of each of the editing chapters on the four most serious errors is an activity involving an image that you can see in two ways: the way you first perceived it and the way you saw it after a closer look. This exercise is similar to the kind of focusing you need to do when you read your own writing looking for errors. If you find that you often can't see the errors in your own writing, try doing one of these activities.

FOCUS — AND REFOCUS

Focus on this picture and write what you see.

Boxes.   Throughout the book, boxes contain useful lists and key concepts that you will need as you write. The boxes make important information easy to locate quickly.

Present-Tense Forms for Two Irregular Verbs			
BE		**HAVE**	
I am	we are	I have	we have
you are	you are	you have	you have
he, she, it is	they are	he, she, it has	they have
the editor is	the editors are		
Denise is	Denise and Sarah are		

Summaries.   Each chapter ends with a summary that defines key concepts and gives page numbers for places in the chapter where full explanations appear. The summaries are a good way to review the material in a chapter or to check a basic definition.

Summary: Fragments

- A **sentence** is a group of words that has a subject and a verb and expresses a complete thought. (See p. 267.)
- A **sentence fragment** seems to be a complete sentence but is only a piece of one. It lacks a subject, a verb, or a complete thought. (See p. 267.)
- There are four **fragment trouble spots** that often signal sentence fragments:
  - A word group that begins with a preposition: *about, in, of* (see p. 269)
  - A word group that begins with a dependent word: *because, until, when* (see p. 271)
  - A word group that begins with an *-ing* verb form: *eating, driving* (see p. 273)
  - A word group that begins with an example or explanation: *like my apartment, such as flowers* (see p. 274)
- To correct fragments, you can add the missing sentence elements or connect the fragment to the sentence before or after it. (See p. 269.)

Quick review charts.   Each chapter on grammar topics in the editing section ends with a quick review chart that provides a visual summary of the chapter content. These charts are a good way to see at a glance how the topics in the chapter are related; in many cases, you can use the charts to troubleshoot for problems in your writing.

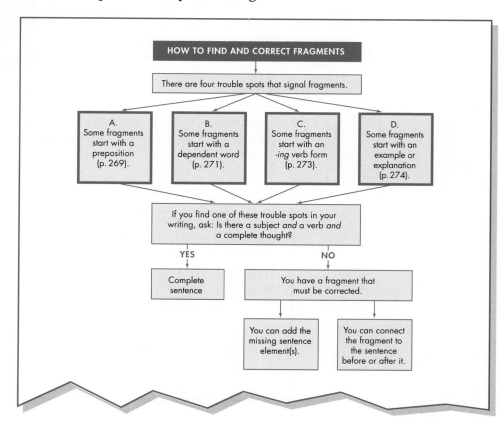

Other Helpful Information

Besides the information contained in the chapters of the book, *Real Writing* has several items that will be useful to you in college, work, and everyday life.

Three useful appendices.   Following the chapters in the text are three appendices containing useful information, tips, and strategies for three activities you may do in this course or beyond: giving oral presentations, writing a résumé, and setting goals. We guarantee that these appendices will come in handy in the near future. (See p. 569.)

Grammar reference.   After the appendices is a grammar reference, a quick review of key grammar points that you are likely to need as you write. (See p. 586.)

Chart of correction symbols.   Printed on the inside of the back cover is a chart showing symbols that many instructors use to indicate writing or grammar problems in drafts of student work. When you have received a paper back from your instructor, use this chart to understand what his or her symbols mean.

What Kind of Writer Are You?

You may not think that you're a writer at all, but everyone has some experience with writing. As you begin the course, it is helpful for you to identify for yourself what kind of writer you are and what your experience has been. This will give you a clear idea of your starting point. Take a few minutes to fill out the writing questionnaire on page xxiii.

What Kind of Writer Do You Want to Be?

Whether you elected to take this course or you've been placed into it, you should determine what you want to get out of it. "A grade" isn't sufficient; one way or the other, you'll receive a grade, but you should identify what skills or abilities you want to learn or improve.

Take an opportunity to list three specific things you want to learn from this course. Be as specific as possible. For example, "learn to write better" is pretty general; what do you mean by "better"? In the past, what sort of problems have you had in writing? Do you get points taken off for misspellings? for fragments or run-ons? Has the teacher commented, "Ideas not sufficiently developed"? Do you have trouble deciding what to say or expressing the main idea in a topic sentence? How do you do on essay exams? Think of three specific things you want to improve during this course and write them down on a piece of paper to turn in to your instructor. Also record them on the following page, so at the end of the term you can judge whether you've achieved them.

RESOURCES
A reproducible version of this questionnaire, which you can distribute and have students hand in, is found in *Additional Resources*.

TEACHING TIP
You can start off by listing students' answers to question 1 on the board. If students worked in pairs or small groups, you can have those same groups work together on question 1.

DISCUSSION
After they answer question 2, ask students what real writing is and list some answers on the board. Lead them to understand that all writing they do is real writing and that what they learn in the course will help them with other kinds of writing outside the course.

TEACHING TIP
Collect responses and make a list. Distribute the list to the class and discuss the different goals people have. Tell them that you'll review the goals together at the end of the course.

1. _____

_____

2. _____

_____

3. _____

_____

Writing Questionnaire

This questionnaire will help you become more aware of your own experience as a writer. Take some time to fill it out now, to determine where you are before you start the course.

1. List everything that you have written in the past three days. Include any kind of writing: reminder notes, homework, shopping lists, forms—anything that caused you to put words on paper or on screen. You may want to compare your list with some of your classmates' lists or talk about this in a small group before you make your list. The comparison or discussion may remind you of things you've written.

2. Pick any two of the things from question 1 to focus on—circle them in the list. For each one, do you consider this *real writing*? Why, or why not? What is *real writing*?

3. Why did you write each one? Who eventually read each one?

4. For each one, did you have any problem getting your message across? Could people figure out what you meant? (If you wrote a note to yourself, did it make sense later?)

5. In general, what do you find the hardest thing about writing? What is the easiest part?

Contents

ESSAYS

Part Three
How to Write an Essay   177

Part Four
Writing Different Kinds of Essays   211

REAL WRITING
with Readings

*Paragraphs and Essays
for College, Work, and
Everyday Life*

PARAGRAPHS

Part One

How to Write a Paragraph

1

Overview

Prewriting, Drafting, Revising, and Editing

RESOURCES
Additional Resources contains a reproducible form that students can use to plan their paragraphs. It details the steps of the writing process and provides spaces for the topic sentence, support sentences, and concluding sentence. (EG)

Understand What a Paragraph Is

A **paragraph** is a group of sentences that work together to make a point. A good paragraph has three necessary parts — the topic sentence, the body, and the concluding sentence — which serve specific purposes.

PARAGRAPH PART	PURPOSE OF THE PARAGRAPH PART
1. The **topic sentence**	states the **main point.** The topic sentence is often the first sentence of the paragraph.
2. The **body**	supports (shows, explains, or proves) the main point. It is made up of about three to five **support sentences,** which contain facts and details supporting the main point.
3. The **concluding sentence**	reminds readers of the main point and often makes an observation.

Paragraphs have a standard format or arrangement. When writers follow the format, they give readers important clues about how to understand what they see on the page.

On page 4 is a sample paragraph, in standard format, with the topic sentence, body, and concluding sentence labeled.

RESOURCES
See "Oral Connections to Literacy: The Narrative," by Aku Duku Anokye, and "Arguing from First Hand Evidence," by Caryl Klein Sills, in *Background Readings.*

> The mind's power to affect the body through conditioning became crystal clear to me when I was six or seven years old. My Uncle Dick, a confirmed cheese hater, was eating Sunday dinner with us. For dessert there was a cheesecake camouflaged with ripe strawberries. It was so good that he ate two pieces. About an hour later my mother expressed her surprise at Uncle Dick's delight in the dessert, since she knew how much he hated cheese. At the sound of the word *cheese*, Uncle Dick turned pale, began to gag, and ran for the bathroom. Even as a child it was obvious to me that the problem was not the cheese itself, but some mental conditioning about cheese that produced such a violent reaction.
>
> —Joan Borysenko, "Mind/Body Programming"

Topic sentence
• first sentence
• starts with indent

Body
• made up of support sentences
• follows topic sentence

Concluding sentence
• last sentence

Understand the Writing Process for Paragraphs

The Writing Process for Paragraphs

STAGES	STEPS IN EACH STAGE
1. **Prewrite**	*Why am I writing? What do I want to say? Who will read this?* • Find and explore your topic (Chapter 2) • Write a topic sentence (Chapter 3) • Support your point (Chapter 4)
2. **Draft** (Chapter 5)	*How can I show my reader what I mean?* • Arrange ideas in a plan • Write a draft using complete sentences • Write a concluding sentence and a title
3. **Revise** (Chapter 6)	*How can I make this clearer or more convincing to my reader?* • Add, delete, or change sentences to make your paragraph stronger
4. **Edit**	*Are there errors that my reader will notice? Are there errors that confuse my meaning?* • Find and correct errors in grammar (Chapters 21–32), word use and spelling (Chapters 33–35), and punctuation (Chapters 36–39)

> **Tips on Paragraph Form**
>
> • Indent the first line to signal a new paragraph. If you are using a word processor, press the tab key once to indent.
> • Use margins of one inch on both left and right sides of the page. If you are using a word processor, the margins are probably preset at one inch.
> • All sentences express a complete thought and end with either a period (.), a question mark (?), or an exclamation point (!).

A paragraph does not happen all at once. Writers go through several steps, each step bringing them closer to a finished paragraph. All of these steps, taken together, are called the **writing process for paragraphs.**

The writing process is not so different from other processes you use every day, like taking a shower or tying a shoelace: They seem complicated at first, but once you are familiar with the stages and steps, you hardly notice that you are doing them.

Practice 1 ▶ Analyzing a Process

Choose a process that you have used recently, one that requires some careful thought and decision making. You can choose one of the processes in this list or some other process that you are familiar with.

buying a car (or a computer, a stereo system, a TV)
buying clothing for a special event
throwing a party
buying a gift for someone you want to impress
finding day care
studying for a test
looking for a job

On a separate piece of paper, list all the steps involved in this process, from the very beginning to the very end. What does your list tell you about this process? Were you surprised at the number of steps?

Understand the Role of Purpose and Audience

In the outline of the writing process on page 4, each stage began with questions about the audience and purpose of the paragraph. Why?

Everything you write has a **purpose,** a point or a reason—otherwise you wouldn't write it. In college, your purpose for writing is usually to show something, explain something, or create a convincing argument.

students, identify the original audience, and ask what they would change if it were for a different audience, which you specify. Groups should revise with the new audience in mind.

TIP: There will be more Thinking Critically guides throughout the book to lead you through the writing process. When you see one, stop and answer the questions.

Everything you write also has an **audience**, someone who reads it, thinks about it, and responds to it. For most college writing, your primary audience is your instructor. Outside of school you have different audiences.

Why are purpose and audience important? As you work through the writing process, you will be making many decisions: What would be an interesting topic? What details should I include? What order should they go in? Keeping your purpose and audience in mind will help you make these decisions.

Thinking Critically about Purpose and Audience

	PURPOSE	AUDIENCE
FOCUS	Remember that you are writing for a reason.	Remember that someone will read what you write.
ASK	• What is my assignment? What topic will I be writing about? • What point do I want to make about my topic? • What do I want my audience to think about my topic? • What do I need to tell my audience so that they will get my point?	• Who is my audience? • What does my audience already know about my topic? • What does my audience want or need to know about my topic? • Does my audience have a particular attitude or opinion about my topic? Do I need to address that specifically?
WRITE	Always write with your purpose and your audience in mind.	

Summary: Paragraph Overview

- A **paragraph** is a group of sentences that together make a point. (See p. 3.)
- A paragraph has a **topic sentence, support sentences,** and a **concluding sentence.** (See p. 3.)
- There is a standard **paragraph form.** (See p. 5.)
- To write a paragraph, follow a **process: prewrite, draft, revise, edit.** (See p. 4.)
- The process of writing is like other processes you use. Focus on mastering the smaller steps of writing a paragraph. If you do each step well, you will write a good paragraph. (See p. 5.)
- Everything you write is for a particular reason (**purpose**) and for a particular reader (**audience**). (See pp. 5–6.)

TEAMWORK
Have students share examples of a difficult process they learned with help from someone else. Give an example from your own life. (BO)

What Will You Use?

What is a current goal you have? What are the steps in the process you might use to reach that goal? Does thinking about it as a process help?

Write about whether the idea of a *process* will or won't help you plan for and reach goals.

2

Finding and Exploring Your Topic

Choosing Something to Write About

EVER THOUGHT THIS?
"I have nothing to say. How can I write a whole paragraph?"
—Ray Stone, Student

If you have nothing to say, you probably have not found anything that you are interested in saying. You need to dig around for something that interests you. Then you will have something to say. Take the first step in the writing process: Finding and exploring a good topic.

TEACHING TIP
This chapter includes the first part of a writing assignment that continues through Chapter 6. It asks students to respond to the prompt *Where do you want to be in five years?* You can have students work on this assignment as they work through this chapter or begin it when the assignment appears, on page 16.

Understand What a Topic Is

A **topic** is who or what you are writing about. A good topic is one that interests you, that you know something about, and that is specific. Any topic for a paragraph should be able to pass the following three-question test.

Three-Question Test for Good Topics

Does it interest me?	If you don't care about a topic, you will find it hard to say something about it. You will get bored, and so will your audience. Try to find a topic that you care about.
Do I know something about it?	You are most likely to have something interesting to say if you already know something about the topic. Unless the assignment specifically asks you to do research, write about something you know.
Is it specific?	If a topic is too general, you may end up writing a series of broad, bland statements that don't say much at all. Focus on a single idea that you can cover in a paragraph.

When you are given a topic to write about (whether by an instructor or by a supervisor), the topic may at first seem uninteresting, unfamiliar, and very general. It is up to you to find a *good* topic based on the general one. There are two steps involved:

1. **Narrowing:** focusing on the smaller parts of a general topic until you find one that is interesting, familiar, and specific
2. **Exploring:** investigating what you already know about the narrowed topic, to find out what you want to write about

Practice Finding and Exploring a Topic

A. Find a Good Topic by Narrowing

Break the general topic into smaller, more manageable parts. Then you can choose which of these narrower parts would make a good topic for you.

There are many ways to narrow a topic. You can try dividing a general category into smaller subcategories (*pollution: air pollution, water pollution, noise pollution*). Or you can think of specific examples (*crime: my car got stolen last year; the church was vandalized in March*). Or you can limit yourself to what has happened in the last week or the last twenty-four hours (*community issues: the traffic light that still isn't working*).

After you have narrowed the topic to write about, be sure to test it by using the Three-Question Test for Good Topics. You may need to narrow and test several times before you find something that will work for a paragraph.

Jackie's assignment is "Write a paragraph about something you find stressful." First she jots down some examples of things that she finds stressful:

taking tests	*arguments*
dealing with the kids	*when my car breaks down*
dealing with my mother	*making sure everyone's ready*
paying bills	* in the morning*
writing	*starting a new class*
interviewing	*starting a new job*
speaking in front of a group	

Then she looks over her list and picks one idea to write about: *speaking in front of a group*. Finally, she tests it to see if it is a good topic for her to write about.

1. Does it interest me?   *Yes, because when I have to speak in front of a group I'm terrified. It's an intense experience for me.*

2. Do I know something about it?   *Yes! Too much!*

3. Is it specific?

Yes, but it's really more like when a teacher assigns an oral presentation; that's the only kind of public speaking I do.

After using this test, Jackie narrows her topic a little more: *oral presentations*. This is a good topic for her to write a paragraph about.

Practice 1 ▶ **Narrowing a General Topic**

Choose one of the general topics listed here, circle it, and jot down five narrower ideas that might make good topics. Then choose one of the narrower ideas that you think would make a good topic for a paragraph and circle it.

a living hero	an essential survival skill	an issue on this campus
moods	minimum-wage jobs	community service

1. *Answers will vary.* _____

2. _____

3. _____

4. _____

5. _____

TEACHING TIP
If time is a concern, limit the number of prewriting techniques students try to three.

B. Explore Your Topic with Prewriting Techniques

Use **prewriting techniques** to come up with ideas at any time during your writing: to find a topic, to get ideas for what you want to say about it, and to support your ideas. Ask yourself: What interests me about this topic? What do I know? What do I want to say? Then use prewriting techniques to find the answers. This section presents five different prewriting techniques. No one uses all five; writers choose the ones that work for them. Before you know which ones work best for you, though, you have to try them all out.

When prewriting, don't judge your ideas yet. Later you can decide whether they're good or not. At this point, your goal is to get as many ideas as possible, so don't say "Oh, that's stupid" or "That won't work" or "Yeah, right." Just get your brain working by writing down all the possibilities.

Kevin was given the assignment "Write a paragraph about yourself." He narrowed that to *myself as a student*. The examples of prewriting techniques are on Kevin's narrowed topic.

Listing / Brainstorming

List all of the ideas about your topic that you can think of. Write as fast as you can for five minutes without stopping.

> **LISTING EXAMPLE**
> *Topic:* Myself as a student
> nervous
> disorganized
> not very successful
> sometimes don't understand
>   assignment
> trouble with writing
> no time to do homework
> brilliant!
> stupid!
> bored
> frustrated
> more motivated than I used to be
> desperate to pass

Practice 2   Listing

Use listing to come up with ideas about your narrowed topic at the end of Practice 1 (p. 10). Try to answer the questions What interests me about the narrowed topic? What do I know? What do I want to say?

COMPUTER
Freewriting and questioning lend themselves particularly well to doing on computer.

Questioning: Asking a Reporter's Questions

Ask questions to start getting ideas. These questions give you different angles on ideas:

Who?
What?
Where?
When?
Why?
How?

> **QUESTIONING EXAMPLE**
> *Topic:* Myself as a student
> *Who?* Kevin, 24, male, like school
> *What?* commuter, part-time, 2 courses, no major
> *Where?* Carriston County CC, 5 miles from home, 15 miles from work
> *When?* early morning classes, study when I can — usually late at night or during lunch
> *Why?* to get a better job and make more money, to get an apartment, like learning new things and better skills, but have trouble studying, not a good writer
> *How?* finding the time, getting better at organizing my life, have to do things in bits as I find time, maybe get one of those organizers or a calendar, wish I could get a computer.

| Practice 3 | > | Questioning |

Use questioning to come up with ideas about your narrowed topic at the end of Practice 1 (p. 10).

WHO? *Answers will vary.* _____

_____

WHAT? _____

_____

WHERE? _____

_____

WHEN? _____

_____

WHY? _____

_____

HOW? _____

_____

Discussing

Many people find it helpful to discuss ideas with someone before they write. As they talk, they get more ideas, and they get immediate feedback from the other person.

Team up with another person. If you both have writing assignments, first explore one person's topic, then the other's. The person whose topic is being explored is the *interviewee*; the other person is the *interviewer*. The interviewer should ask questions about anything that seems confusing or unclear and should let the interviewee know what sounds interesting. The interviewee should give thoughtful answers and keep an open mind. It is a good idea to take notes when you are the interviewee.

DISCUSSING EXAMPLE
Kevin: I want to write about myself as a student. All I can come up with is that I'm not a very good student.
Jorge: Give me an example.
K: Well, like I'm really disorganized. I never have enough time to do my homework, so it's usually only half done.
J: Is it the same with all your classes?
K: No, this is the worst. In my other courses, it's clear what I need to do to pass the course and use the stuff I learn at my job. But here, I have trouble fitting it all together.
J: I know what you mean—I feel like that sometimes, too.
K: You do? But you always seem to know what's going on.
J: Yeah, but I <u>feel</u> lost. Maybe lots of us do. Maybe that would be a good topic to write on. . . .

| Practice 4 ▶ | ### Discussing |

Use discussion with a partner to come up with ideas about your narrowed topic at the end of Practice 1 (p. 10). The interviewer can try asking these questions: What interests you about the narrowed topic? What do you know about it? What do you want to say?

Freewriting

Freewriting is like having a conversation with yourself, on paper. To freewrite, just start writing everything you can think of that comes into your brain about your topic. Write nonstop for at least five minutes. Don't go back and cross anything out, and don't worry about using correct grammar, spelling, and so on; just write.

FREEWRITING EXAMPLE
Topic: Myself as a student

This is a dumb assignment. How can I describe myself as a student when I'm not one? I go to school but I'm not really a student I just take courses so I can get a job. Don't know why I'm in this course. In high school they said I was a good writer. I think they made a mistake. Now I have to pass this before I can take anything else. I thought I was a good student. Now maybe I'm not. I work hard and my grades are okay. It doesn't come easy but I want to pass. Maybe I'm just not good at writing. I never knew why my high school teacher said my writing was good, and now I don't know why it's not good. It's confusing.

| Practice 5 ▶ | ### Freewriting |

Use freewriting to explore your narrowed topic at the end of Practice 1 (p. 10). To get yourself started, ask yourself these questions: What interests me about this topic? What do I know about it? What do I want to say?

Clustering/Mapping

Clustering, also called mapping, is like listing except that you arrange your ideas in a more visual way. Start with your narrowed topic in the center. Then use the three questions to write three things about that narrowed topic, circle those things, and draw lines connecting them to the narrowed topic. Then add three things about each of the three things, and so on. You might want to start by writing down these three questions as your first three things about the topic: What interests me? What do I know? What do I want to say?

| Practice 6 ▶ | ### Clustering |

On a separate piece of paper, use clustering to explore your narrowed topic at the end of Practice 1 (p. 10).

CLUSTERING EXAMPLE

C. Keep a Journal

Another good way to get ideas is to keep a journal. If you set aside a few minutes on a regular schedule to write in the journal, it will be a great source of ideas when you need them. Another benefit is that you will get used to writing regularly, so writing will not seem like such a chore.

To get the most from your journal writing, you should commit yourself to keeping a journal all semester and write in it for at least ten minutes (or ten lines) at least three times a week. The writing in your journal doesn't need to be long or formal. Your journal is for you.

There are many ways to use a journal:

- To record and explore your personal thoughts and feelings
- To comment on things that happen, either things that happen to you, or political events, or things going on in the neighborhood, at work, in college, and so on
- To explore ideas to see what you know and think about them
- To explore things you don't understand (as you write, you may figure them out)

ESL
Some ESL students may feel uncomfortable with journal writing. Emphasize that journal entries will not be graded, are confidential, do not have to be too personal, and don't have to be written in polished prose.

TEACHING TIP
It helps to give students journal assignments each week or so. Here are some suggestions:
• Something that was discussed in a class and your thoughts on it
• At least one positive thing that happens every day and why it is positive
• Something you read in the newspaper or heard on the news (not only the facts, but what you think about them—your observations)
• A goal of yours and what specific things you plan to do to achieve it
• Two things you're interested in and why

TEACHING TIP
Explain to students that journal entries do not have to be too personal: They are for recording ideas rather than for emptying emotions. (BO)

List three other ways you might use a journal (there are no wrong answers).

1. _Answers will vary._

2. _____

3. _____

Marcella started a journal entry with a statement of how she's been feeling and explores some reasons. This entry helped her analyze her unexplained tiredness, so she's learned something (even though it won't keep her from disliking shorter days).

JOURNAL ENTRY

11/2/97—I've been feeling tired all week. I can't figure out why. I've been getting the same amount of sleep, and I'm not sick. As I was driving home around 7:00, I thought I was going to have to stop for coffee I was so sleepy. A car coming toward me turned on its headlights which gave me kind of a start and woke me up. I wonder if I'm more tired because it's starting to get dark earlier. I hate the end of those long summer days when you feel full of energy because it's still daytime. I think that's probably it. I'm adjusting to the earlier darkness (and I hate that summer's ended).

This book contains two kinds of journal assignments. The kind of journal just described can be called an **idea journal:** a place to record and explore your personal ideas. Many chapters have idea journal assignments on the first page or somewhere in the margins. These ask you to think about and comment on your personal experience with a topic or idea. They can be very useful in helping you finish the assignments—and besides, they are interesting possibilities for future writing.

Another way to use journals is to keep a **learning journal,** a written record of what you have learned. This helps you see where you have improved—and where you still have questions. Many chapters include assignments for such a learning journal.

| Practice 7 | Writing in a Journal |

For the next week, write in a journal for ten minutes (or at least ten lines) each day at the same time of day. Put the date and time at the start of each entry. For each of the entries, write on the topic "Something I noticed about myself today."

At the end of the week, reread the entries and write a sentence or two about an observation you can make about yourself based on what you noticed all week. Don't worry; these entries will not be graded.

TEACHING TIP
It is important to get students to use these Thinking Critically guides rather than skipping over them. If students are already working on a paper, read each question aloud, giving a minute or so between questions for students to jot down responses. You may want students to turn in these responses along with their drafts.

Thinking Critically about Your Topic

FOCUS	Reread the general topic you have chosen or been assigned.
ASK	• How can I divide this topic? What are the smaller parts? • Which of these would be a good narrowed topic for a paragraph? • Does this topic pass the Three-Question Test for Good Topics? • What do I already know about this topic? • What do I want to write about? • What will other people want to read about?
WRITE	Narrow to find a good topic for your paragraph and then use prewriting techniques to explore your ideas about the topic.

Write to Find and Explore Your Own Topic

TEACHING TIP
For this first writing assignment, the single topic for the whole class allows you to compare students' writing abilities in an "apples to apples" context. If the suggested topic doesn't appeal to you, use another. This one was selected because it has the secondary objective of getting students to think about longer-range plans and goals.

Paragraph Assignment, Step One

GENERAL TOPIC: Where do you want to be in five years?

AUDIENCE: Your instructor and your class

PURPOSE: To present yourself to the class in a way that will give your audience a sense of your goals

This is the beginning of a writing assignment that will continue through the rest of the chapters in Part One. It will give you a chance to practice the steps of the writing process while writing about something that is interesting and useful to you. In each chapter, you will complete one step in the writing process, until you have a complete, revised draft by the end of Chapter 6. Keep any notes or drafts you write as you work on this assignment; you will need them later.

RESOURCES
See "A Basic Writer's Portfolio," by Sharon Hileman and Beverly Six, in *Background Readings,* for a discussion of student writing portfolios.

Narrow and Explore Your Topic.

With your audience and purpose in mind, narrow and explore the general topic for this assignment: *Where do you want to be in five years?*

1. Narrow by jotting down five goals or hopes you have for yourself. Or focus on a specific part of your life (personal, academic, professional, and so on). Choose one idea to write about.
2. Apply the Three-Question Test for Good Topics (p. 8) to the idea you have chosen. Choose a new topic if you need to.
3. Use a prewriting technique to explore your topic.

(For more help, use the Thinking Critically guide on this page.)

Topic Assignment

1. Choose one of these broad, general topics, or find one of your own (make sure it doesn't require any outside research).

work	family	school
public transportation	vacations	children

2. Write down the topic and give it to a partner or someone in your group. Someone should give you his or her topic.

3. Take the broad topic someone else has written and narrow it.

4. Spend five minutes using a prewriting technique to come up with at least three *interesting* ideas that you could write about.

5. Read both your narrowed topic and your interesting ideas aloud to the group.

Summary: Topic

- A **good topic** interests you, is something you know about or can find out about, and is specific enough to write about in a paragraph. (See p. 8.)
- **Narrow a general topic** to find a good topic to write about. (See p. 9.)
- **Explore your narrowed topic** to get ideas: what interests you about the topic, what you know about it, what you want to say. (See p. 10.)
- There are five popular **prewriting techniques: listing, questioning, discussing, freewriting,** and **clustering.** Use prewriting techniques to get ideas anytime during the writing process. (See pp. 11–14.)
- Keeping a **journal** also is a good way to build up a supply of ideas. (See p. 14.)

What Will You Use?

How might you use prewriting techniques to investigate possible career choices? explore possible academic goals or plans? find possible solutions to problems?

EVER THOUGHT THIS?
"I have enough ideas, but I don't know what to do with them."
—*Fritz Gourdet, Student*

You have come up with some interesting ideas about a topic. Now what? You need to think about what all these ideas add up to. What is the main point you want to make? You are ready for the next step in the process: making your point in a topic sentence.

TEACHING TIP
Emphasize that the topic sentence should include an opinion, not simply state a fact. Many students can't see the difference between "I have two brothers" and "My two brothers have totally opposite personalities," so you may need to discuss the difference. (EG)

TEACHING TIP
Tell the students that a topic sentence is like a contract with readers in which the writer promises to convey specific information on the topic using 50 to 150 words. Realizing how few words they have to fulfill their promise helps students narrow their scope. (BO)

3

Writing Your Topic Sentence

Making Your Point

Understand What a Topic Sentence Is

The **main point** of your paragraph is the main idea you want to get across about your topic. A good main point is one that interests you; one that you can show, explain, or prove; and one that is limited to one idea.

The **topic sentence** states your main point and prepares your readers for what is to come. It is often the first sentence in a paragraph. A good topic sentence makes one point clearly and prepares readers for the rest of the paragraph.

TOPIC: Skills employers value

MAIN POINT: Communication skills are more important than technical skills to employers

A recent survey reported that employers consider communication skills more critical to success than technical skills. Employees can learn technical skills on the job and practice them every day. But they need to bring well-developed communication skills to the job. They need to be able to make themselves understood to colleagues, both in speech and in writing. They need to be able to work cooperatively as part of a team. Employers can't take time to teach communication skills, but without them an employee will have a hard time.

— Topic sentence

— Body (Support sentences)

When developing a topic sentence for your paragraph, make sure it has these four features:

FOUR FEATURES OF A GOOD TOPIC SENTENCE

1. It states one main point clearly.
2. It interests you.
3. It is something you can show, explain, or prove.
4. It prepares readers for the rest of the paragraph.

Practice Finding a Main Point and Writing a Topic Sentence

YOU KNOW THIS
What was the point of a movie you saw recently? Think of an argument you had recently. What was it about? What was your point?

ESL
Some cultures (particularly Asian ones) avoid making direct points in writing. You may need to explain that in English, the rhetorical convention is that the writer make a clear, direct point. Ask students if writing conventions in their countries approach the main point differently.

IDEA JOURNAL: How do you react to speaking in public? Think of a time you were embarrassed in public.

A. Find a Main Point

Any writing you did to explore your topic will help you find a main point. Look over your ideas to find the strongest message there. Try circling or underlining key ideas and repeated phrases.

In Chapter 2 you saw examples by a student named Jackie, who has been told to write a paragraph about something she finds stressful. Here is her progress so far:

GENERAL TOPIC: Something that you find stressful

JACKIE'S NARROWED TOPIC: Oral presentations

JACKIE'S FREEWRITING ON THE TOPIC

I can't stand giving them. I avoid doing them until the last minute, why do people assign them, anyway? everyone hates them. When I'm up there I feel like an idiot and my face is all red. Sometimes I get short of breath. I sound stupid. I just want to sit down. It's the most stressful thing I can think of.

Now Jackie needs to find the main point. Jackie's ideas added up to a more general point: her nervousness about making oral presentations. Although she didn't write the word *nervousness,* the ideas she circled added up to it. Don't worry if the main point you find doesn't cover all the ideas you wrote down as you explored your topic. You are looking for the *strongest* message.

JACKIE'S MAIN POINT: I get nervous when I have to give an oral presentation.

Practice 1 Finding a Main Point

Find a main point in each of the following prewriting examples.

TEAMWORK
This works well as a small-group activity.

1. **NARROWED TOPIC:** Parking at school

   FREEWRITING ON THE TOPIC

       I really hate the parking lots here. They're always filled by the time I get here. I circle and circle, then get a spot that's far as possible from my first class and I get blamed for being late. Maybe I should take earlier classes and I'd get a spot but that doesn't solve the problem. It just means other students would be doing the circling Why can't there be more parking? The school has more land. They could pave over by the Admin. building. There should be enough parking, we pay enough.

   MAIN POINT: *Possible answer: The school should provide enough parking for all students.*

DISCUSSION
You may want to discuss this topic in class since many students have strong but unexpressed feelings about these tests. (Also see "The First Day of Class: Passing the Test" by Ira Shor, in *Background Readings*.)

2. **NARROWED TOPIC:** Placement test for this course

   LISTING ON THE TOPIC

Not enough time	Didn't like or understand the topic
I was nervous	
I got good grades in high school	Not fair
Couldn't understand the questions	Not a good way to show what you know
Person didn't explain the directions clearly	

   MAIN POINT: *Possible answer: My score on the placement test doesn't reflect what I really know.*

3. **NARROWED TOPIC:** Write your narrowed topic from Practice 1 in Chapter 2 (p. 10) here.

   Answers will vary.

   Reread your prewriting ideas from Chapter 2 to find a main point.

   MAIN POINT: *Answers will vary.*

B. Write a Topic Sentence

You are now ready to combine your narrowed topic and your main point into a topic sentence. Try using this basic formula:

Narrowed topic	+	Main point	=	Topic sentence

JACKIE'S TOPIC SENTENCE

narrowed topic   main point

Oral presentations make me very nervous.

The formula (topic + main point = topic sentence) isn't an exact translation: You may want to change some words to make sure your topic sentence is clear and strong.

JACKIE'S REVISED TOPIC SENTENCE: The thought of giving an oral presentation turns me into a nervous wreck.

Thinking Critically about Your Topic Sentence

FOCUS   Reread the topic sentence you have written. Think about what you want to say in your paragraph.

ASK
- Does my topic sentence include both my topic and the main point I want to make about it?
- Is it a complete sentence?
- Does it make an interesting point? Will it be interesting to my readers?
- Does it state something I can show, explain, or prove?
- Can I think of some ideas to support this topic sentence?
- Does it make a single point?
- Does it say what I want it to say?
- Does it fit the assignment?

WRITE   Write and adjust your topic sentence until you think it works.

| Practice 2 | ⟩ | **Identifying Topics and Main Points** |

In each of the following topic sentences, underline the topic and double-underline the main point about the topic.

EXAMPLE: Aging airplanes have increased the likelihood of plane crashes.

1. The level of nicotine in cigarettes is kept high by the tobacco industry.

2. The oldest child in a family is often the most independent and ambitious child.

3. Gadgets designed for left-handed people are sometimes just jokes.

4. The city's new mayor enjoys practical jokes.

5. Dinnertime telephone sales calls are not for the weakhearted.

6. The magazine *Consumer Reports* can help you decide which brands or models are the best value.

7. Of all the fast-food burgers, Burger King's Whopper is the best buy.

8. At 5 o'clock every afternoon, Route 128 becomes a death trap.

9. Some song lyrics have serious messages for people of all ages.

| Practice 3 | Choosing Topic Sentences |

TEAMWORK
This works well as a small-group activity; students can discuss which sentence is better and why.

In each of the following pairs of sentences, circle the letter of the better topic sentence, considering what you have learned about what a good topic sentence is. In the space below each pair, give one reason that the sentence you *did not* circle is weak.

a. Most people take vacations because they need them.
b. Most people take vacations.

We know that most people take vacations. There isn't a main

point to discuss.

1. a. Students spend time studying.
   b. Good students make time to study.

   Answers should indicate that weak topic sentences state

   facts rather than make points — there's nothing to discuss.

2. a. Paying taxes takes money.
   b. Taxes take a big chunk of your weekly paycheck.

   _____

   _____

3. a. History repeats itself.
   b. History is in the past.

   _____

   _____

4. a.   Many things are addicting.

    (b.)   Many people are addicted to the Internet.

_____

_____

5. a.   December 22 has the least daylight of any day of the year.

    (b.)   Lack of daylight causes depression in some people.

_____

_____

| Practice 4 | Writing Topic Sentences |

TEACHING TIP
Instead of these topics, you could have students use topics and ideas from the journal writing they've done in response to the idea journal prompts in this chapter.

Narrow each of the following topics into something you could write about in a paragraph. Then choose a main point that interests you; that you can show, explain, or prove; and that is specific. Finally, write a topic sentence that combines the topic and the main point.

1. Cigarette smoking

   NARROWED TOPIC: *Answers will vary.* _____

   TOPIC SENTENCE: _____

   _____

2. Credit cards

   NARROWED TOPIC: _____

   TOPIC SENTENCE: _____

   _____

3. Minimum wage

   NARROWED TOPIC: _____

   TOPIC SENTENCE: _____

   _____

4. Your narrowed topic and main point from number 3 in Practice 1 (p. 20)

NARROWED TOPIC: _____

TOPIC SENTENCE: _____

_____

C. Topic Sentences versus Titles

Because a topic sentence and a title both express the main point of a paragraph, you might wonder what the difference is. A topic sentence is a sentence. A title is a group of words but not a sentence. Make sure your topic sentence is a sentence and not a title.

TITLES	The Agonies of the Oral Presentation
	Public Speaking Nervousness
TOPIC SENTENCE	The thought of giving an oral presentation turns me into a nervous wreck.

Practice 5   **Telling Topic Sentences from Titles**

Each of the following pairs contains one topic sentence and one title. (For the purpose of this practice, sentences have no end punctuation and important words in titles are not capitalized.) Circle the topic sentence in each pair.

    a. Communication problems between men and women
    (b.) Men and women often experience communication problems

1. a. The disastrous Flight 409
    (b.) The crash of Flight 409 was disastrous

2. (a.) California residents experience a constant threat of earthquake
    b. The constant threat of earthquake in California

3. a. Early differences between men and women
    (b.) Differences between men and women appear early in life

4. a. The difficulties of working and going to school
    (b.) Many students find it difficult to work and go to school

5. (a.) Central Bank has unfair lending practices
    b. Unfair lending practices at Central Bank

Write Your Own Topic Sentence

Paragraph Assignment, Step Two

Write a Topic Sentence.

In Step One (p. 16), you found and explored a topic for your paragraph on the general topic *Where do you want to be in five years?* Now write a topic sentence for your paragraph.

1. Look back over your points and decide on a main point.
2. Put your main point in a topic sentence. Remember that you want to give your professor and classmates a clear idea of your goals.

(For more help, use the Thinking Critically guide on p. 21.)

Topic Sentence Assignment

Choose one of the journal entries that you wrote in response to an idea journal suggestion in this chapter and that you might like to write more about. Using what you've learned in this chapter, find a main point and develop a good topic sentence for a paragraph based on your journal entry.

Summary: Topic Sentence

- The **main point** of your paragraph is the main idea you want to get across about your topic. A good main point interests you; is something you can show, explain, or prove; and is limited to one idea. (See p. 18.)
- **To find a main point,** review your ideas about your narrowed topic and look for the strongest message. (See p. 19.)
- A **topic sentence** presents the topic and the main point of a paragraph. A good topic sentence makes one point clearly; prepares readers for the rest of the paragraph; and is a complete sentence. (See p. 18.)
- **To write a topic sentence,** start with the basic formula (narrowed topic + main point = topic sentence). Then adjust the sentence until you are satisfied with it. (See p. 20.)

What Will You Use?

Consider an assignment you have in another class or at work. How can you use what you have learned in this chapter to do the assignment? How can making a clear point help you in everyday life? in college? in your job?

EVER THOUGHT THIS?
"I've spent all this time writing my main point. Isn't that enough?"
—Minh Nguyen, Student

Your main point is right there in your topic sentence, but saying something doesn't make it true. To help your readers understand your main point, you need to take the next step in the process: supporting your main point.

IDEA JOURNAL
Write about a time that you were overcharged for something. How did you handle it?

DISCUSSION
Ask the class this question: "Assume the bill in question is from a restaurant. What support points could the writer use?" Some possible answers could be pointing to the price, showing a math error, showing something on the bill that the writer didn't eat, and so on.

4

Supporting Your Point

Finding Details, Examples, and Facts

Understand What Support Is

Support points are details or facts that show, explain, or prove your main point. Support points usually follow the topic sentence and make up the largest part (the body) of the paragraph.

Without support, you *state* the main point, but you don't *make* the main point. Consider these unsupported statements:

1. The amount shown on my bill is incorrect.
2. I deserve a raise in salary.
3. I am innocent of the crime.

The statements may be true, but without good support, they are not convincing.

Writers sometimes confuse repetition with support. The same point repeated several times is not support. It is just repetition.

REPETITION, NOT SUPPORT   The amount shown on my bill is incorrect. You overcharged me. It didn't cost that much. The total is wrong.

As you develop support for your main point, make sure that it has these three features.

THREE FEATURES OF GOOD SUPPORT

1. **It relates to your main point.** The purpose of support is to show, explain, or prove your main point, so the support you use must be directly related to that main point.

YOU KNOW THIS
When have you had to give support for your position?

2. **It considers your readers.** What information will convince your readers? If your support points aren't aimed at the people who will read your writing, they are unlikely to help you get your main point across.

3. **It is detailed and specific.** Give readers enough detail, particularly through examples, to see what you mean.

Practice Finding and Selecting Support

TIP: For a review of prewriting techniques (listing, questioning, discussing, freewriting, clustering) see Chapter 2.

A. Find Support

Use the prewriting technique that works best for you for three to five minutes to come up with as many ideas as you can to support your topic sentence. If you find yourself staring at your topic sentence with no ideas at all, try these three tips to get going.

EVER THOUGHT THIS?
I sometimes get papers back with the comment "You need to support/develop your ideas." (If you get this comment, this section will help you.)

THREE QUICK TIPS FOR FINDING SUPPORT

1. **Circle a word** in your topic sentence and write about it for a minute or two. Reread the topic sentence and make sure you're on the right track. Keep writing about the word.

2. Reread your topic sentence and **write down the first thing you think of.** Then write the next thing you think of. Keep going.

3. **Reread your prewriting** from earlier in the process and add to it. After a couple of minutes, stop and review what you've just written. Keep going.

TEACHING TIP
Emphasize that support points must be factual; an opinion alone will not convince readers. If students use an opinion, they should immediately support it with a fact. (EG)

In Chapters 2 and 3 you saw examples by Jackie, who has been told to write a paragraph on something she finds stressful. Here is a reminder of her topic sentence and an example showing the ideas that Jackie came up with at this stage by using the technique of listing.

JACKIE'S TOPIC SENTENCE: The thought of giving an oral presentation turns me into a nervous wreck.

IDEA JOURNAL
Write about a time that you had to speak in front of a group.

JACKIE'S LISTING ON HER TOPIC:

worry for weeks	*sweaty*
put it off	*sound dumb*
dumb topic, nothing to say	*boring everyone*
feel angry at professor	*want to sit down*
skip class	*shaky hands*
watch TV, make calls, eat junk	*slump*
lose assignment	*my face is hot and red*
buy new notebook	*I look terrible*
can't sleep before	*forget what I wanted to say*
don't do a good job	*wasn't good anyway*
shaky voice	

TIP: Remember that in prewriting, the goal is to get as many ideas on paper as possible. Write whatever you think of—don't judge the ideas yet.

Thinking Critically about Your Support

FOCUS	Think about the main point you make in your topic sentence.
ASK	• What can I say that will show, explain, or prove what I mean? • What do my readers need to know or understand in order to be convinced? • What examples come to mind? • What have I experienced myself? • What points could I make to convince my readers? • What details could I use to strengthen the support?
WRITE	Use a prewriting technique for three to five minutes to find as many support points as you can.

<blockquote>Practice 1</blockquote>

Finding Supporting Ideas

Choose one of the following suggested topic sentences or one of your own and use one prewriting technique (listing, questioning, discussing, freewriting, clustering) for a few minutes. You will need a good supply of ideas from which to choose support for your main point.

SUGGESTED TOPIC SENTENCES

1. This year's new TV programs are worse than ever.
2. Today there is no such thing as a "typical" college student.
3. Last year was full of surprises.
4. Learning isn't just for students.
5. Practical intelligence can't be measured by grades.

B. Drop Unrelated Ideas

Reread your topic sentence to remind yourself of your main point. Then review your prewriting carefully and cross out (drop) ideas that are not directly related to your main point. Also consider your readers—cross out anything that would confuse them. If new ideas occur to you, jot them down. Here is what Jackie did at this point.

JACKIE'S TOPIC SENTENCE: The thought of giving an oral presentation turns me into a nervous wreck.

JACKIE'S LIST, WITH UNRELATED IDEAS DROPPED

worry for weeks   *sweaty*
put it off   *sound dumb, feel like an idiot*
~~dumb topic, nothing to say~~   *boring everyone*

TIP: If you have explored your topic using a computer, it is better *not* to drop ideas by deleting them. You might find out later that you need something you have deleted. Either make a copy of the list and keep the original file as a backup copy, or move ideas that you want to drop to another part of the document (like the very end).

~~*feel angry at professor*~~
~~*skip class*~~
watch TV, make calls, eat junk
~~*lose assignment*~~
~~*buy new notebook*~~
can't sleep before
don't do a good job
shaky voice

want to sit down
shaky hands
slump
my face is hot and red
~~*I look terrible*~~
forget what I wanted to say
~~*wasn't good anyway*~~
exhausted after
can't wait to leave class
can't listen to anyone else

| Practice 2 | Dropping Unrelated Ideas |

TEAMWORK
You may want to have students discuss their answers to this practice, either in small groups or as a class.

In each of the following groups of possible support points, cross out the unrelated ideas. Be ready to explain your choices.   *Answers may vary.*

1. **TOPIC SENTENCE:** Business letters must be clear and focused.

   POSSIBLE SUPPORT POINTS
   can't have things readers won't understand
   readers' time is important
   writing should be direct, not fancy
   business writing not the place for self-expression
   ~~creative writing courses are good for self-expression~~
   should tell readers what to do in response
   avoid jargon
   should give readers answers to any questions
   ~~use friendly words to put readers at ease~~

2. **TOPIC SENTENCE:** The original *Star Trek* television program showed a peaceful, integrated society that appealed to people in the 1960s.

   POSSIBLE SUPPORT POINTS
   no prejudice among humans on ship

   bridge crew included
       a black (Uhura)
       a Russian (Chekov)
       a Japanese (Sulu)

   ~~Uhura a strong female figure — first time black woman in such a position of authority~~

   first officer (Spock) a different species

~~sometimes Spock is victim of racial slurs~~

meet many different species on their travels

little prejudice toward other species

Star Trek an escape from real racism

in real life, U.S. full of racial unrest in 1960s

> **Practice 3** ▸ **Dropping Unrelated Ideas**
>
> Reread your topic sentence and prewriting from Practice 1 (p. 28). Cross out any ideas in your prewriting that are unrelated to your main point or are not aimed at your readers.

C. Select Best Support Points and Add Supporting Details

Review your remaining ideas and select the best points to use in your paragraph. Consider which ones will be clearest and most convincing to your readers. For most paragraphs, you need about three to five support points.

See if you can group the ideas in any way. For example, Jackie discovers that she can group her ideas into three categories: things that happen before, during, and after the oral presentation.

TEACHING TIP
Tell students to ask themselves the kinds of questions their readers will ask: Such as? In what way? For example? If their support points answer those questions, readers should understand their main point. (EG)

JACKIE'S TOPIC SENTENCE: The thought of giving an oral presentation turns me into a nervous wreck.

JACKIE'S SUPPORT POINTS

1. *Avoid preparing for it*

2. *Exhausted afterward*

3. *Fall apart while giving it*

When you have selected your major support points, ask yourself: "Do I have the details or specific examples I need to help my readers understand what I mean?" Try to make each support point stronger by adding supporting details.

COMPUTER
Have students type in possible support and then use cutting and pasting to group it. They can easily move the points around to try new groupings.

JACKIE'S SUPPORT POINTS	JACKIE'S DETAILS
1. *Avoid preparing for it*	—*worry about doing it*
	—*do anything to avoid: watch TV, call friends, eat junk food*
2. *Exhausted afterward*	—*completely drained of energy*
	—*can barely make it through rest of class*

3. *Fall apart while giving it*   — *sweaty, shaking hands*

                                           — *red, hot face*

                                           — *feel boring*

Practice 4 ▶ Selecting the Best Support Points

TEAMWORK
This works well as a small-group activity.

Find the three points you would choose to support the following topic sentence and write them in the spaces provided. Be ready to explain your choices.

TOPIC SENTENCE: Most Americans are not good listeners.

POSSIBLE SUPPORT POINTS

people talk more than they listen

competitive streak—everyone wants to say the most

even when quiet, thinking about what to say next, not listening

good listening is hard work

preparing a good "comeback"

good listening is active, not passive

if you can't talk most of the time, talk faster

talk louder

good listening = processing what the other person is saying

Answers may vary.

SUPPORT POINT 1: *competitive streak—everyone wants to say the most*

SUPPORT POINT 2: *good listening is hard work*

SUPPORT POINT 3: *even when quiet, not listening*

Practice 5 ▶ Selecting the Best Support Points and Adding Supporting Details

TEAMWORK
Have students work in pairs to read their topic sentences aloud and share possible support points. Together, they can select the three best points. Suggest that they use the Thinking Critically guide on page 28.

Reread the prewriting you did for Practice 1 and worked with for Practice 3 (pp. 28 and 30). Now select the three strongest support points. In the spaces provided, write your topic sentence and the three support points.

Then, for each support point, add supporting details—something that will give readers a clearer picture of what you mean.

Answers will vary.

TOPIC SENTENCE:

SUPPORT POINTS	DETAILS
1. _____	_____
	_____
	_____
2. _____	_____
	_____
	_____
3. _____	_____
	_____
	_____

Write Your Own Support Points

Paragraph Assignment, Step Three

Support Your Point.

In Step Two (p. 25), you wrote a topic sentence for your paragraph on the general topic *Where do you want to be in five years?* Now support your point with details and examples.

1. Prewrite for three to five minutes on your topic sentence. Try to think of examples that will show your professor and classmates exactly what you mean.

2. Choose the best ideas from your prewriting to use in your paragraph. Add more details if you can.

(For more help, use the Thinking Critically guide on p. 28.)

TEACHING TIP
This second assignment is provided in case you do not wish to use the cumulative Paragraph Assignment, which continues from Chapter 2 through Chapter 6.

Support Point Assignment

Choose one of the journal entries you wrote in response to an idea journal suggestion in this chapter and find a main idea that you might like to write a paragraph about. Using what you've learned in this chapter, develop four support points for the main idea. Make sure you have at least one supporting detail for each support point.

Summary: Support Points

- **Support points** are examples or facts that show, explain, or prove your main point. They usually follow the topic sentence and make up the body of the paragraph. (See p. 26.)
- Good support points are directly related to your main point, are aimed at your readers, and are detailed and specific. (See pp. 26–27.)
- To **find support,** prewrite to come up with ideas. (See p. 27.)
- **Supporting details** can make the support points clearer and more convincing to your readers. (See p. 30.)

What Will You Use?

How could knowing how to support your main point help you in college or at work?

5

EVER THOUGHT THIS?
"I can't believe I'm finally getting out of the pre-writing stage. If drafting takes as long as pre-writing, I'll never finish."

—*Rosanna Valdez, Student*

Good news! When you get to the stage of drafting, you have done most of the legwork you need to write a good paragraph. You are more than ready to take the next step in the process: writing a draft.

YOU KNOW THIS
What is a dress rehearsal? Have you ever rearranged the furniture in a room? Have you ever rehearsed in your head what you're going to say to someone?

TIP: For more on standard paragraph form, see Chapter 1.

COMPUTER
Have students draft on the computer, saving the draft on disk and printing it out. Explain how using the computer will make changing their draft much easier.

Drafting

Arranging Your Ideas and Writing a Paragraph

Understand What a Draft Is

A **draft** is the first whole version of all your ideas put together in a paragraph. You have been gathering ideas for your draft: narrowing and exploring a general topic, finding your main point, writing a topic sentence, and supporting your main point. You have your ideas; now you need to arrange them and put them in paragraph form. Do the best job you can in drafting your paragraph, but remember that you will have more chances to make changes. Think of your first draft as a dress rehearsal for your final paper.

FIVE FEATURES OF A GOOD DRAFT

1. It has a topic sentence.
2. It has support points and supporting details or examples that are arranged in a logical order.
3. It has a concluding sentence.
4. It may have a title.
5. It follows standard paragraph form and uses complete sentences.

Practice Writing a Draft

A. Arrange Your Ideas in a Logical Order

Order means the sequence in which you present your ideas: what comes first, what comes next, and so on. If you don't put your points in a logical order, they will not be easy for your readers to follow.

As you arrange your ideas, consider using space order, time order, or order of importance.

TIP: Space order is some-times called *spatial order*.

Space Order

Use space order to arrange ideas so that your readers can see your topic as you do. Space order usually works best when you are writing about a physical object or place. You can move from

TEACHING TIP
To introduce the organizational patterns, read a list of ten words (such as *your room, a musical group, a music concert, a mall, a picnic, a restaurant, a subway ride, a classroom, a car*). Have students write down which type of organization would work best for each word. Have them share their answers so that they will see that there is more than one way to approach a draft. (BO)

- Top to bottom / bottom to top
- Near to far / far to near
- Left to right / right to left
- Back to front / front to back

EXAMPLE USING SPACE ORDER

The new elementary school does not look like a welcoming place. There is no landscaping, so it looks barren and cold. The gray foundation is not softened by bushes, plants, or trees at its base. The yellow brick walls rise straight up from the ground like a huge box. There are no interesting jogs or details to break the lines of the walls. There are few windows, and they are flush with the harsh exterior lines. The huge roof is completely flat too, with the exception of a square steel structure that looks like a guard tower, sticking rudely out of the roof. In fact, the new building looks more like a prison than a school.

What type of space order does the example use? ___*bottom to top*___

| Practice 1 | Using Space Order to Arrange Ideas |

TEAMWORK
Practice 1 works well as a paired or small-group activity.

Arrange the supporting details for each of the following topic sentences according to a space order. Indicate which point comes first, which second, and so on, by writing the number on the blank at the left. Then indicate the type of space order you used (top to bottom, near to far, and so on). In some cases, more than one order is possible. Choose an order that makes sense to you. Example:

IDEA JOURNAL
What is the most spectacular place you have ever seen? What did you notice about it? How did you react to it?

TOPIC SENTENCE: The inside of the ancient cathedral was spectacular.

___*4*___ a finely carved mahogany lectern raised on a pedestal

___*2*___ 300 rows of polished mahogany pews

___*6*___ an altar topped by a 40-foot crucifix and gold turrets

___*1*___ entryway with two huge, brilliantly painted and lifelike statues

___*5*___ gleaming white marble stairs leading up to the altar

___*3*___ stained-glass windows rising 50 feet

TYPE OF SPACE ORDER: ___*near to far*___

COMPUTER
If you are working in a network environment, input the practice in advance and have students move the ideas around to get them into spatial order. Do the same for Practices 2 and 3.

1. **TOPIC SENTENCE:** Dona looked very professional for her interview.

   Answers may vary.

   _2_ hair held back with gold clip

   _1_ small gold hoop earrings

   _6_ black, low-heeled shoes

   _4_ black A-line skirt brushing the top of her knees

   _3_ white silk blouse with only top button undone at throat

   _5_ black nylons

   TYPE OF SPACE ORDER: _top to bottom_

2. **TOPIC SENTENCE:** The view in front of us looked like a postcard.

   _2_ wide, calm river just beyond the green field

   _5_ misty peaks of mountains in the far distance

   _1_ nearby, cows grazing in a green field

   _3_ a couple of picturesque cabins on the other side of the river

   _4_ steep, rocky slopes of the mountainside

   TYPE OF SPACE ORDER: _near to far_

3. **TOPIC SENTENCE:** My new desktop computer was an intimidating sight.

   _2_ an off-white box containing the actual computer sitting on top of the keyboard's frame

   _1_ a keyboard with lots of unfamiliar buttons right in front of me

   _5_ a mysterious "glare guard" on the front of the monitor

   _3_ several scary-looking lights and switches on the box containing the computer

   _4_ the heavy monitor sitting on top of the computer

   TYPE OF SPACE ORDER: _bottom to top_

TIP: Time order is sometimes called *chronological order*.

Time Order

Use time order to arrange points according to when they happened. Time order works best when you are writing about events. You can go from

- first to last/last to first
- most recent to least recent/least recent to most recent

EXAMPLE USING TIME ORDER

Because I'm not a morning person, I have to follow the same routine every morning or I'll just go back to bed. First I allow myself three "snooze" cycles on the alarm. That gives me an extra fifteen minutes to sleep. Then I count to three and haul myself out of bed. I have to do this quickly, or I may just sink back onto the welcoming mattress. I run the shower so the water will be warm when I step in. While waiting for it to warm up, I wash my face and brush my teeth with cold water. It's a shock, but it jolts me awake. After showering and dressing, I'm ready for the two cups of coffee that are necessary to get me moving out of the house.

What kind of time order does the author use? ___*first to last*___

| Practice 2 | Using Time Order to Arrange Ideas |

TEAMWORK
Practice 2 works well in pairs.

Arrange the supporting details for each of the following topic sentences according to a time order. Indicate the sequence of ideas by writing a number on the blanks at the left. In some cases, more than one order is possible. Choose an order that makes sense to you. Example:

TOPIC SENTENCE: Using a computer, rearranging paragraphs is simple.

_2_ click on the edit menu to open it

_6_ open the edit menu again and pull down to the paste command and click

_3_ pull down to the cut command and click

_4_ the paragraph disappears

_5_ click in the place where you want to move the paragraph

_1_ drag the mouse across the paragraph to highlight it

_7_ the paragraph appears in the new location

1. **TOPIC SENTENCE:** It was one of those days when everything went wrong.

    _5_ boss was waiting for me   *Answers may vary.*

    _2_ no hot water for a shower

    _7_ got sick at lunch and had to go home

    _3_ burned my toast

    _4_ missed the regular bus to work

    _1_ alarm didn't go off

    _6_ forgot to save work on computer and lost it

2. **TOPIC SENTENCE:** Selena Quintanilla's story is both inspiring and tragic.

    _6_ murdered right before her album was to be released in English

    _3_ sang in English with her father's band

    _4_ started singing Tejano music in Spanish (*Tejano* literally means "Texan")

    _5_ became very popular and successful

    _8_ only twenty-four when she died

    _7_ her English album sold 175,000 copies in a single day

    _1_ born in southern Texas

    _2_ started singing at a very young age

3. **TOPIC SENTENCE:** On the advice of an attorney, I am withholding rent until the heat in my apartment is returned to normal.

    _4_ I called the Board of Health

    _5_ representative was sent to my apartment

    _6_ representative agreed that the temperature exceeded "comfortable" range

    _7_ my attorney sent you a letter warning you to fix the problem

IDEA JOURNAL
How do you usually deal with people who aren't treating you fairly?

_3_ for six weeks, I left messages for you describing the problem with my heat

_1_ in February, the temperature in my apartment was ninety-three

_2_ even with all the windows open, I was sweltering

_8_ now I have no heat

Order of Importance

Use order of importance to arrange points according to their importance, interest, or surprise value. Usually, save the most important for last.

EXAMPLE USING ORDER OF IMPORTANCE

People who keep guns in their houses risk endangering both themselves and others. Many accidental injuries occur when a weapon is improperly stored or handled. For example, someone cleaning a closet where a loaded gun is stored may handle the gun in such a way that it goes off and injures him or her. There have also been many reports of "crimes of passion" with guns. A couple with a violent history has a fight, and in a fit of rage one gets the gun and shoots the other, wounding or killing the person. Most common and most tragic are incidents in which children find loaded guns and play with them, accidentally killing themselves or their playmates.

What is the writer's most important point? _that children sometimes find loaded guns and accidentally kill themselves or their playmates_

| Practice 3 ▶ | Using Order of Importance to Arrange Ideas |

TEAMWORK
Practice 3 works particularly well in small groups because students have to discuss why they think one idea is more important than another. Point out that each person has his or her own sense of importance and that it's easier to make decisions about order of importance in their own writing than in an exercise. (EG)

Arrange the supporting details for each of the following topic sentences according to order of importance, starting with least important. Indicate the sequence of ideas by writing the number in the blank at the left. In some cases, more than one order is possible. Choose an order that makes sense to you. Example:

TOPIC SENTENCE: It is important to read the fine print in advertisements.

_1_ gives more information about the product

_3_ explains any misleading parts of the ad that might trick you

_4_ includes any warnings about the product

_2_ often gives the address in case you want to order

1. **TOPIC SENTENCE:** Smoking should be banned at all restaurants.

Answers may vary.

____2____ nonsmoking sections aren't enough, since the smoke always floats into them

____1____ smell of cigarette smoke is unpleasant

____3____ inhaling secondhand smoke is nearly as unhealthy as smoking yourself

2. **TOPIC SENTENCE:** Restaurants have no right to ban smoking.

____4____ smoking is legal, and discrimination is illegal

____3____ most restaurants already have a nonsmoking section

____1____ smoking at the end of a meal is an important part of overall dining pleasure

____2____ smokers pay as much to eat as nonsmokers, so why should non-smokers get preferred treatment?

3. **TOPIC SENTENCE:** All students should learn to work with computers.

____3____ more and more jobs require basic computer skills

____1____ computers are fun and have good games

____2____ writing on computers is faster than writing on paper

B. Make a Plan

TIP: It is easy to try out possible orders if you are writing on a computer. Just use the cut and paste functions to experiment with rearranging points. Doing this will give you a good sense of how your final paragraph will look. And it's easy to try out a different order if you do not like what you see.

When you have decided how to order your ideas, make a written plan for your paragraph, starting with your topic sentence. A good, visual way to plan your draft is to arrange your ideas in an outline. The outline provides a map of your ideas that you can follow as you write. An outline does not have to be formal; it is for your own use.

Jackie chose to order her paragraph by time and to arrange her details from first to last. Here is her informal outline.

JACKIE'S OUTLINE

Topic sentence: The thought of giving an oral presentation turns me into a nervous wreck.

1. *Avoid preparing*

   —*worry every time I think about it; don't do anything about it*

   —*do other things instead: watch TV, call friends, eat junk food*

2. *Fall apart while giving it*

   —*hands shake, start sweating, red face*

   —*feel boring*

3. *Collapse afterward*

   —*exhausted, no energy*

   —*can barely make it through the rest of the class*

Thinking Critically While Making a Plan

FOCUS	Reread your topic sentence and support points.
ASK	• What would be the best organization for my support points? space order? time order? order of importance? • Does this organization help me get my main point across? • Will my readers be able to follow my paragraph easily? • What point should come first? what next? what after that? what last? • Do I want to add any additional details?
WRITE	Write a plan (an outline) that shows how you want to arrange your points.

C. Write a Draft Using Complete Sentences

You are now ready to write a draft of your paragraph. You have done most of the work—now you just have to put everything in paragraph form. Work with your outline in front of you. Be sure to include your topic sentence (usually at the very beginning) and express each point in a complete sentence. As you write, you may want to add things or change the order. That's fine—an outline is only a plan. As you draft, write the best paragraph you can, but remember that you will have another chance to revise it.

JACKIE'S DRAFT PARAGRAPH

> The thought of giving an oral presentation turns me into a nervous wreck. When I get the assignment, it makes me feel so worried that I avoid working on it. I do other things instead, like watching TV, calling friends, and eating junk food. When I give the report, I completely fall apart. My hands shake, I start to sweat, and my face turns all red. And I'm sure that everyone thinks I'm boring. When I'm finally done, I'm so exhausted that I collapse in my seat. I feel I can hardly make it through the rest of class.

— Topic sentence

— Support point 1

— Support point 2

— Support point 3

D. Write a Concluding Sentence

A **concluding sentence** refers back to the main point in the topic sentence and makes an observation based on what you have written in the paragraph. The concluding sentence is not just a repeat of the topic sentence.

POSSIBLE CONCLUDING SENTENCES FOR JACKIE'S PARAGRAPH

~~I don't like giving oral presentations.~~

~~Giving oral presentations is nerve-racking.~~

From start to finish, oral presentations are stressful.

Oral presentations are number one on my personal stress scale.

Jackie eliminates the first two concluding sentences because they repeat the topic sentence rather than make an observation based on the whole paragraph. She decides that either of the remaining sentences would make a good concluding sentence.

Practice 4 ▶ Choosing a Concluding Sentence

Each of the following paragraphs has several possible concluding sentences. Circle the letter of the one you prefer, and be prepared to say why you chose it.

1. A recent survey reported that employers considered communication skills more critical to success than technical skills. Most important to those surveyed was a person's ability to get ideas across to others, both in speech and in writing. Ideas are good only if they are understood by others. The ability to work cooperatively in groups was also cited as highly important. With work teams used more frequently, employees need to be able to function as part of a team effort. Employers also want people who can understand problems and come up with solutions that can be shared with others.

 (a.) Employers surveyed felt employees could learn technical skills on the job but needed to come to the job with good communication skills.

b.   Employers who were surveyed valued communication skills more than technical skills.

c.   Communication skills and technical skills are not equal.

2. Have you ever noticed that people often obey minor rules while they ignore major ones? For example, most people cringe at the thought of ripping off the "Do not remove under penalty of law" tag from a new pillow. This rule is meant for the seller so that the buyer knows what the pillow is made of. Once someone owns the pillow, it is okay to remove the tag, but people hesitate to do so. Another minor rule that people obey is the waiting-line procedure in a bank. Ropes often mark off where a line should form, and a sign says "enter here." Customers then zigzag through the rope lines. Even when there is no one in line, many people follow the rope trail rather than walking right up to a teller. The same people who tremble at the thought of removing a tag or ignoring the rope lines may think nothing of exceeding the speed limit, even at the risk of a possible accident.

a.   This doesn't make sense to me.

b.   What is it about those minor rules that makes people follow them?

c.   Apparently "under penalty of law" is a greater deterrent than "endangering your life."

3. Student fees should not be increased without explanation. These fees are a mystery to most students. Are these fees for campus improvements? Do they support student activities and, if so, which ones? What exactly do we get for these mysterious fees? We are taught in classes to think critically, to look for answers, and to challenge accepted wisdom. We are encouraged to be responsible citizens. As responsible citizens and consumers, we should not blindly accept increases until we know what they are for.

a.   We should let the administration know that we have learned our lessons well.

b.   Student fees should be abolished.

c.   Only fees that go directly to education should be approved.

Practice 5 ▶ **Writing Concluding Sentences**

Read the following paragraphs and write a concluding sentence for each one.

1. In many ways, life in the United States has improved in the last fifty years. Personal computers, VCRs, microwave ovens, CD players, and cable TV are but a few of the modern conveniences that weren't around fifty years ago. Air travel, once limited to the country's wealthy, is now experienced by much of the population regularly. Since 1970, air travel has tripled as people have greater freedom to see other parts of the country and the world. More adults are college graduates. In the last twenty-five years, the number of college graduates has increased from 11 percent to 22 percent of the total pop-

ulation. The economy, which is often criticized, has created more than 18 million jobs since 1985.

POSSIBLE CONCLUDING SENTENCE: *Answers will vary but should include "life"*

and "improved."

2. There are certain memory devices, called *mnemonics,* that almost everyone uses. One of them is the alphabet song. If you want to remember what letter comes after *j,* you will probably sing the alphabet song in your head. Another is the "Thirty days hath September" rhyme that people use when they want to know how many days are in a certain month. Another mnemonic device is the rhyme "In 1492, Columbus sailed the ocean blue."

POSSIBLE CONCLUDING SENTENCE: *Answers will vary but should refer to the*

memory devices and how commonly they are used.

E. Title Your Paragraph

TIP: Paragraphs are not always titled, so ask your instructor whether you should write a title.

TIP: For more on capitalizing titles, see Chapter 40.

The title is the first thing readers see, so it should give them a good idea of what your paragraph is about. Decide on a title by rereading your draft, especially your topic sentence. A paragraph title should be fairly short and should focus on the main point.

JACKIE'S POSSIBLE TITLES
Stressful Speaking
Oral Presentations: Hard on the Nerves
A Nerve-Racking Experience
A Stressful Experience from Start to Finish

Practice 6 ▶ **Writing Titles**

Write possible titles for the paragraphs in Practice 5 (p. 43).

1. *Answers will vary.* _____

2. _____

Write Your Own Draft Paragraph

Paragraph Assignment, Step Four

Write a Draft.

In Step Three (p. 32), you found support for your paragraph on the general topic *Where do you want to be in five years?* Now make a plan for your paragraph and write a draft.

1. Choose an order (space, time, or importance). If you will tell a story in your paragraph, you should probably use time order. If you are describing a number of goals or accomplishments, you might want to start with the least important and end with the most important.

2. Arrange your support points and supporting details in a plan.

3. Write a complete draft with a concluding sentence and a title.

(For more help, use the Thinking Critically guide on p. 41.)

Summary: Drafting

- A **draft** is the whole version of your ideas put together in paragraph form. Think of your first draft as a dress rehearsal for your final paper. (See p. 34.)

- A **logical order** helps readers follow your ideas. (See p. 34.)

- Three common orders for paragraphs are **space order, time order,** and **order of importance.** (See p. 34.)

- An **outline** is a useful way to plan your draft. (See p. 40.)

- A draft should be in **paragraph form,** with complete sentences. (See p. 41.)

- A **concluding sentence** refers back to the main point and adds a further observation. (See p. 42.)

- The **title** should be short and should indicate what the paragraph is about. (See p. 44.)

What Will You Use?

How can understanding the process of drafting help you in your everyday life or at work? in classes other than this one?

6

Revising

Improving Your Paragraph

EVER THOUGHT THIS?
"When I finish my draft, I'm done with the assignment. I don't want to think about it anymore."
— Emily Quinn, Student

Don't think about your draft anymore—for the moment. Give yourself some time away from it, at least a few hours, preferably a day. Forget about it for a while. But come back to it again. Taking a break will result in a better piece of writing and a better grade or result. Take the next step in the process: revising your draft.

TIP: The editing section of the book begins on page 253.

TEACHING TIP
Stress that revision is not just copying over neatly; it is a reworking of ideas based on analyzing the draft.

Understand What Revision Is

Revising and editing are two different ways to improve a paper. **Revising** is changing the ideas in your writing to make it clearer, stronger, and more convincing. When revising, you might add, cut, or change whole sentences. **Editing** is finding and correcting problems with grammar, style, usage, and punctuation. While editing, you usually add, cut, or change words and phrases.

Most writers find it difficult to revise and edit well if they try to do both at once. It is more efficient to solve bigger, idea-level problems (by revising) and then move on to smaller, word-level ones (by editing).

REVISION GOALS
- Search for ideas that do not fit into the paragraph.
- Search for ideas that are not as specific or complete as they can be.
- Search for ways to connect ideas so that they flow smoothly from one to the next.

Revision is critical to good writing. You have already invested time and energy in writing your draft; don't waste those efforts by avoiding the final important steps that will bring you to a successful finish.

Practice Revising for Unity, Detail, and Coherence

A. Revise for Unity

Unity in writing means that all the points you make are related to your main point; they are *unified* in support of your main point. As you draft a paragraph, you may detour from your main point without even being aware of it, as the writer of the following paragraph did with the underlined sentences. The diagram after the paragraph shows what happens when readers read the paragraph.

> Car mechanics don't always have the answers to car problems. Today while I was driving, my car started weaving and wobbling, and the steering seemed loose. I pulled into a gas station and asked the mechanic to take a look at it. He seemed to know what he was doing, as he walked around the car, looking at various parts, nodding his head, and saying, "Um hm." The mechanic told me his cousin has a Tracker just like mine and loves it. I really like mine, too. It's like a sports car. The mechanic finished his inspection of the car and told me there was absolutely nothing wrong. I got back in and continued driving. After about half a mile, one tire spun right off the car and rolled off the road, leaving my car lying on its side. I learned later that two of the lug nuts attaching the tire to the wheel had come loose and that the mechanic should have checked them first. Next time I won't be so quick to accept a mechanic's answer.

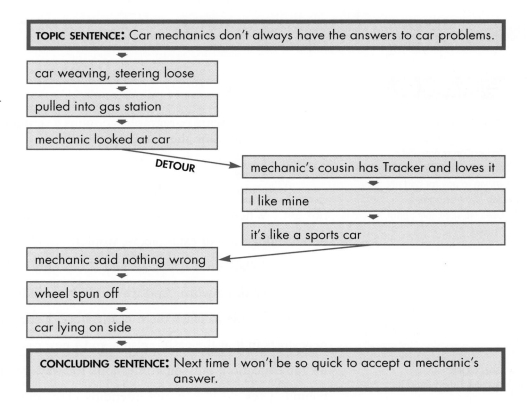

Detours in your paragraph lead your readers away from your main point and weaken it because the readers' focus is broken. As you revise, check to make sure that your paragraph has unity.

Five Revision Tips

1. **Give yourself a break.** A few hours or a day away from your draft will give you the fresh eyes you need for revising.
2. **Read aloud.** Sometimes hearing what you have written will help you find things that aren't quite right.
3. **Imagine you are someone else reading your draft.** In particular, imagine you are the person who actually *will* read this piece of writing.
4. **Get help from a friend, classmate, or colleague.** Ask someone to read what you have written and to make suggestions for improvement. This person will not "judge" your writing but will make friendly, constructive suggestions about your work. Offer to do the same in return.
5. **Get help from a "pro."** If there is a writing center at your college, it may have tutors available to read and comment on your draft—with no grade involved. You have paid for this service as part of your tuition; don't hesitate to use it.

> **Practice 1**   Revising for Unity

Each of the following paragraphs contains a sentence that detours from the main point. Underline the detour. Example:

Circles are answers for Practice 4 (page 55).

"(Education) is one of the few things people are willing to (pay for) and not get." When we (buy) something expensive, we make sure we take it home and use it. For example, we wouldn't think of (spending) a couple of hundred dollars on a new coat and shoes only to hide them away in a closet never to be worn. And we certainly wouldn't (pay for) those items and then decide to leave them at the store. I once left a bag with three new shirts in it at the cash register, and I never got it back. People (pay) a lot for (education,) but sometimes look for ways to leave the "purchase" behind. They do this by not attending class, not paying attention, not studying, or not completing assignments. At the end of the term, they have a grade but didn't get what they (paid for: education) and knowledge. They have wasted their money, just as if they had (bought) an expensive sound system and had never taken it out of the box.

TIP: One of the advantages to writing on a computer is that revising is much easier than it is on paper. You don't have to retype everything; you can just make the changes you want. You can even try out different versions and then decide later which one you like best.

1.   One way to manage time is to keep a (written)(calendar) or schedule. It should have an hour-by-hour breakdown of the day and evening, with space for you to (write) next to the time. As appointments or responsibilities come up, (write) them in on the right day and time. Before the end of the day, consult your (calendar) to see what's in store for the next day. Using a (calendar) saves your memory, because once you write down the appointment or activity, you don't have to think about it anymore. Calendars come in all sizes, colors, and shapes. Once you are in the habit of using a (calendar,) you will see that it frees your mind because you are not always trying to think about what you're supposed to do, where you're supposed to be, or what you might have forgotten.

Circles are answers for Practice 4 (page 55).

2.   As you use a calendar to manage your (time,) think about (how long) certain activities will take. A common mistake is to (underestimate) the (time) needed to do something, even something simple. For example, when you are (planning) the (time) needed to get cash from the cash machine, remember that there may be a line of people. Last week in the line I met a woman I went to high school with. When you are (estimating) (time) for a more complex activity, such as reading a chapter in a textbook, (block out) more (time) than you think you will need. If you finish in less (time) than you have (allotted,) so much the better. (Allow) for interruptions. It is better to (allow) too much (time) than too little.

3.   Effective time management means (allowing)(time) for various ("life") (activities.) For example, it is important to (budget)(time) for (chores), like paying bills, buying food, picking up a child, or going to the doctor. It seems as if my dentist is always a half hour behind schedule. A daily (schedule) should also account for communication with other people, such as family members, friends, service people, and others you might need to contact. It is important to (allow) for relaxation (time). Do not (schedule) something for every minute; give yourself some "down" (time). Finally, (leave time) for unexpected things that are a huge (part of life), like last-minute phone calls, a car that won't start, or a bus that is late.

IDEA JOURNAL
Today, what are your must-do, want-to-do, and hope-to-do things? Keep track of these for a week.

B.   Revise for Detail and Support

Look carefully at the support points and supporting details you developed and imagine yourself as your reader: Do you have enough information to understand the main point? Are you convinced of the main point?

In the margin of your draft (or between the lines, if you have enough space), note ideas that seem weak or unclear. Add at least three additional support points or supporting details to your draft.

COMPUTER
Have students double-space their drafts so that they are easier to read and so that the printed copy has room for comments and suggestions (their own and those of the peer reader).

JACKIE'S DRAFT, WITH HER NOTES

The thought of giving an oral presentation turns me into a nervous wreck. When I get the assignment, it makes me feel so worried that I avoid working on it. I do other things instead, like watching TV, calling friends, and eating junk food. *Or even cleaning!* When I give the report, I completely fall apart. *Voice? What about when I forget?* My hands shake, I start to sweat, and my face turns all red. And I'm sure that everyone thinks I'm boring. When I'm finally done, I'm so *Why? Tell more here.* exhausted that I collapse in my seat. I feel I can hardly make it through the rest of class. From start to finish, oral presentations are stressful.

JACKIE'S REVISED PARAGRAPH

Underlines are answers for Practice 2.

Additional details will vary.

The thought of giving an oral presentation turns me into a nervous wreck. When I get the assignment, it makes me feel so worried that I avoid working on it. I do other things instead, like watching TV, calling friends, eating junk food, and even cleaning. When I give the report, I completely fall apart. My hands shake, I start to sweat, my face turns all red, and my voice cracks. I forget for a minute what I wanted to say and feel like a complete idiot. And I'm sure that everyone thinks I'm boring. When I'm finally done, I'm so exhausted that I collapse in my seat. I am totally drained of energy. I feel I can hardly make it through the rest of class. All I want to do is go home and crawl into bed. From start to finish, oral presentations are stressful.

Revising for Support and Detail

Jackie added several details to make her point clearer. Underline the details she added.

Then add two or more supporting details, based either on your own experience of giving an oral presentation or on one that is similar to Jackie's other support. Insert your additional supporting details in Jackie's revised paragraph.

C. Revise for Coherence

Coherence means that the parts of something connect to form a whole. The parts need to be assembled in a particular order and need "glue" to connect them.

Coherence in writing helps readers see how one point leads to another— a paragraph that lacks coherence can sound like a string of unrelated statements. Individual ideas should be so well arranged and connected that they leave readers with a clear overall impression.

Here are two paragraphs, one that is not coherent and one that is. Read them and notice how much easier the second paragraph is to follow. Both paragraphs make the same points, but the underlined words in the second paragraph help "hold it together."

NOT COHERENT

It is not difficult to get organized—it takes discipline to stay organized. All you need to do is follow a few simple ideas. You must decide what your priorities are and do these things first. You should ask yourself every day what is the most important thing you have to accomplish. Make the time to do it. You need a personal system for keeping track of things. Making lists, keeping records, and using a schedule help with this. It's a good idea not to let things stack up. Get rid of possessions you don't need, put things away every time you use them, and don't take on more responsibilities than you can handle. It isn't a mystery; it's just good sense.

COHERENT

It is not difficult to get organized—even though it takes discipline to stay organized. All you need to do is follow a few simple ideas. You must decide what your priorities are and do these things first. For example, you should ask yourself every day what is the most important thing you have to accomplish. Then make the time to do it. To be organized, you also need a personal system for keeping track of things. Making lists, keeping records, and using a schedule help with this. Finally, people who are organized do not let things stack up. Get rid of possessions you don't need, put things away every time you use them, and don't take on more responsibilities than you can handle. Organization isn't difficult; it's just good sense.

Common Transitions

SPACE

above	below	near	to the right
across	beside	next to	to the side
at the bottom	beyond	opposite	under
at the top	farther/further	over	where
behind	inside	to the left	

TIME

after	eventually	meanwhile	soon
as	finally	next	then
at last	first	now	when
before	last	second	while
during	later	since	

IMPORTANCE

above all	in fact	more important	most
best	in particular	most important	worst
especially			

EXAMPLE

for example	for instance	for one thing	one reason

AND

additionally	and	as well as	in addition
also	another	furthermore	moreover

BUT

although	in contrast	nevertheless	still
but	instead	on the other hand	yet
however			

SO

as a result	finally	so	therefore
because			

Add Transitions.

Transitions are words or phrases that connect your ideas so that one point moves smoothly to the next. Use transitions when moving from one main support point to another. Also use them wherever you want to improve the flow of your writing.

Practice 3 ▶ **Adding Transitions**

TEAMWORK
This practice works well in small groups.

Read the following paragraphs and in the blanks add transitions that would smoothly connect the ideas. In each case, there is more than one right answer. Example:

Bishop Jacques Gaillot, a French priest, has found a new way to spread the word. In 1995, Gaillot was removed from his church by decree of the pope. _____*After*_____ the pope learned that Gaillot was promoting condom use to curb the spread of AIDS, Gaillot was exiled to a diocese in the Sahara Desert. _____*When*_____ he arrived at his new mission, he found that it no longer existed. Instead of giving up, Gaillot thought about how he could reach people. _____*Finally*_____, he came up with the idea of a virtual diocese that could run on the Internet. _____*Now*_____ his Web page, Partenia, is set up and is open to people all over the world. Gaillot is the first cyberspace priest, reaching potentially millions of people over the worldwide computer network.

Answers will vary.

1.   The advertisement for corned beef is deceptive. It is topped by the brand name, Hormel, printed in large, bright red letters. _____*Under*_____ the name, the words "Corned Beef" capture your attention with their huge and bold lettering. _____*Next*_____ is an eye-catching red triangle that assures "premium quality." _____*Beside*_____ the red triangle is a big picture of thick, color-

ful slices of corned beef. _At the bottom_ of the ad is a box surrounding the words "Made in the USA. It matters!" If you don't look closely, you will hardly notice the line of smaller letters sandwiched between the large bold "Corned Beef," the red triangle, and the picture of the beef. It says, "Product of Brazil." Is this dual claim of Brazilian/USA origin a simple mistake, or is the ad designed to make us think we are "buying American"?

2.   Selena Quintanilla's story is both inspiring and tragic. _When_ she was very young, Selena sang in English in her father's band. _As_ a teenager, she started singing Tejano music in Spanish. _Tejano_ literally means "Texan," but it has come to represent a culture of Mexican Americans. Selena's new Tejano music became very popular and successful, and she was ready to release an album in English. _However,_ she was murdered right before the album's release. _After_ it was released, her album sold 175,000 copies in a single day, becoming one of the best-selling albums in history. At twenty-four, Selena experienced almost simultaneous death and stardom.

3.   Smoking should be banned at all restaurants. The smell of cigarette smoke is downright unpleasant. It also makes my eyes water and sting, which is not a very pleasant experience while I am trying to eat. _In addition,_ it ruins the taste of the food I've just paid for. _Most important,_ inhaling secondhand smoke is nearly as unhealthy as smoking yourself. Smokers may claim that having separate smoking and nonsmoking sections is enough, but it isn't. Smoke from

the smoking section wafts steadily over to the nonsmoking one, damaging both my evening out and my good health.

Repeat Key Words.

Another way to give writing coherence is to focus readers on the main point by repeating key words—words that are closely related to your topic and main point. In the following paragraph the key words are underlined.

> The Scholastic Assessment Test (SAT) is at the center of controversy once again—some people claim that the time restrictions are unfair. A group representing the rights of specially challenged test takers claims that the SAT's time limits are unfair to people who, for physical or mental reasons, cannot complete the test items within the time allotted. For example, someone with multiple sclerosis may simply need more time on the SAT than someone without a physical challenge. Another group disagrees strongly, arguing that an important part of the test is the time restrictions. All students would do better if they had more time. This group demands that if time limits are eased for anyone, they be eased for everyone. Otherwise the results are unfair. This new controversy, like past ones, will undoubtedly be settled, and the SAT will remain powerful, fair or unfair.
>
> KEY WORDS: SAT, test; controversy; time restrictions, time limits, time; unfair, fair

Note that key words can be different words with the same meaning. For example, *test* and *SAT* are different words but refer to the same thing.

Practice 4 ▶ Repeating Key Words

Reread Practice 1 (p. 48). In each paragraph, circle key words that are repeated. In the spaces here, write the key word or words. The topic sentences are printed to remind you what paragraph the blanks are for. Example: *Answers may vary.*

"Education is one of the few things people are willing to pay for and not get."

KEY WORDS: *education; pay for, buy, spending, pay, bought*

1. One way to manage time is to keep a written calendar or schedule.

    KEY WORDS: *written, write; calendar*

    _____

2. As you use a calendar to manage your time, think about how long certain activities will take.

KEY WORDS: *time; how long, underestimate, planning,*
estimating, block out, allotted, allow

3. Effective time management means allowing time for various "life" activities.

KEY WORDS: *allowing, budget, schedule, allow, leave time;*
time; "life" activities, chores, part of life

RESOURCES
Practical Suggestions contains a discussion of peer
feedback. See also the
three articles in Chapter
7, "Collaborative Learn-
ing," in *Background
Readings.*

Teamwork: Getting Feedback

One of the best ways to work with other students is to get and give feedback on early drafts, before you have done the work of revision. Other people will be able to look at what you've written with a fresh perspective. They will see things that you cannot—both good qualities and parts that need to be strengthened or clarified.

You can get feedback either from a partner or in a small group. If you are working with a partner, exchange papers. Each partner should read the other one's paper and jot down a few comments. You may want to talk about the papers and the comments afterward. If you are working in a group, it's probably easiest to read your paper aloud and have group members take notes while you are reading. They can give you their comments when you are done reading.

Often it is useful for the writer to ask the person or people giving feedback a couple of questions to focus on as they read or listen: Is anything unclear? Is this boring? Do you understand what I mean?

Revise Your Own Paragraph

As you revise your own paragraphs, use this Thinking Critically guide to remind yourself of what to look for and think about.

Thinking Critically While Revising

TEACHING TIP
Make revision concrete
by challenging students to
find at least one place in
their drafts where detail
can be added and at
least one place where a
transition can be added.
(BO)

FOCUS   After a break, reread your draft with concentration and a fresh perspective.

ASK
- Have I completed the assignment?
- Will my readers understand what I've written? Will they be convinced?
- What is my main point? What did I want to say? Did I say it?

- Does everything in my paragraph relate to my main point?
- Do I have enough support? Can I add any details?
- Does my paragraph hold together? Is it clear how one idea connects to another? Do the sentences flow?

WRITE   Revise your draft, making any improvements you can.

REFOCUS   Reread your revised paragraph to make sure it is as good as you can make it.

Paragraph Assignment, Step Five

Revise Your Draft.

In Step Four (p. 44), you wrote a draft for your paragraph on the general topic *Where do you want to be in five years?* Now revise it.

1. Reread your draft with a fresh perspective, looking for ideas that don't fit, points that need more detailed information, and places that need to be smoothed with transitions. Keep your audience and your purpose in mind.

2. Revise your draft, making these improvements and any others you think of.

(For more help, use the Thinking Critically guide on p. 56.)

Congratulations! You now have a complete, revised paragraph, ready to be edited.

Revision Assignment

Take a paragraph-length paper you have written for this course or another college course and revise it, using what you have learned in this chapter. Use the Thinking Critically guide on page 56.

Editing—making changes in grammar, word use, punctuation, and capitalization—follows revising and is the final stage in the writing process. After you have revised your paragraph to make the ideas clear and strong, you need to edit it to be sure there are no errors or distractions that could prevent readers from understanding your message. When you are ready to edit your writing, turn to Chapter 21, the first chapter in the editing section.

Summary: Revising

- **Revision** is the process of reading your draft with fresh eyes. It is a search for ideas that don't fit, points that can be more specific, and ways to connect the points. (See p. 46.)

LEARNING JOURNAL
In your own words, what is revision? What do you look for when you revise?

- Revise for **unity**—all points should support your main point. (See p. 46.)

- Revise for **support**—you should have enough support points and details. (See p. 50.)

- Revise for **coherence**—all points should blend together to form a whole. (See p. 51.)
  - Use **transitions** to move smoothly from one point to the next. (See p. 53.)
  - **Repeat key words** to keep readers focused on the topic and the main point. (See p. 55.)

What Will You Use?

How can what you have learned about revising in this chapter help you in other areas of your life?

PARAGRAPHS

Part Two

Writing Different Kinds of Paragraphs

7

Illustration

Paragraphs That Show Examples

Rocío Avila, Teacher

Rocío Avila

WRITING THEN: "As a college student, I dreaded writing. Writing an essay was a torturous journey for me. Writing seemed to be a task only required in college."

WRITING NOW: "I do a lot of writing on the job. For example, I write letters to parents, administrators, and businesses where I have to give examples to explain what I mean, what I need, what I propose doing. I've realized that writing is essential for all aspects of my life."

(For more about Rocío Avila, see p. 74.)

Understand What Illustration Is

Illustration is writing that uses examples to show, explain, or prove a point. Giving examples is the basis of all good writing and speaking: You make a statement; then you give an example that shows (illustrates) what you mean.

GOOD ILLUSTRATION

- Makes a point
- Gives detailed and specific examples to show, explain, or prove the point
- Gives enough examples to get the point across

SAMPLE ILLUSTRATION PARAGRAPH

All of a sudden, it seems that everyone is online. Rosie O'Donnell tests out punch lines under dozens of names on America Online, and Madonna "reads bedtime stories" to promote her new

RESOURCES
For a discussion of how to use the profiles in Part Two, see *Practical Suggestions.*

READING SELECTIONS
For examples of and activities for illustration essays, see Chapter 42.

YOU KNOW THIS
If you have *any* communication with other people, you have experience illustrating your point. For example:
• You suggest to a friend, "Let's do something fun." He says, "*Like what?*"
• You tell a friend, "You've been acting weird." She asks, "*How?*"

DISCUSSION
Ask students to think of one other way that they have used illustration.

IDEA JOURNAL
Give some examples of things that annoy you.

single on the Underground Music Archive. ("You can interact with me," she begins, "but you can't touch me.") Rush Limbaugh and Billy Idol, NBC and *Scientific American* are online. There are downy-cheeked B-1 pilots and grizzled B-36 vets, gay square-dance clubs and bagpipe players. For all the high-minded, high-tech visions, a lot of the Net is soft-core porn on ThrobNet, discussions of Spam and *Star Trek* on Prodigy, sad-sack stories in "discussion rooms," and lounge-lizard come-ons on Teen Chat on AOL's People Connection. It's the Internet, and an estimated ten to twenty million people around the world use it.

—Phil Patton, "Life on the Net"

1. Annotate the paragraph to highlight its structure:
   • Double-underline the topic sentence.
   • Underline the examples that demonstrate the topic sentence.

2. What is the main point of the paragraph? *Many people now communicate over the Internet.*

3. The **topic sentence** of an illustration paragraph usually includes the topic and the point the writer wants to make about it.

The bus drivers in my city have no sense of courtesy.

Fill in the blanks with the topic and the point for the sample paragraph:

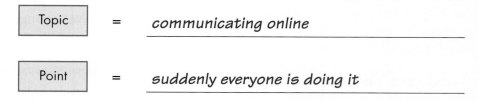

Topic = *communicating online*

Point = *suddenly everyone is doing it*

4. The **support** in an illustration paragraph is the example or examples the paragraph contains. List two examples from the paragraph.

Answers will vary.

COMPUTER
Ask students who use the Internet to list other uses. Develop a set of Internet options as the basis for a writing assignment.

The writer gives several examples of people who are online and how they use the Internet. These various examples give the readers a better chance of knowing who some of the people are. For example, maybe a reader doesn't know who Rosie O'Donnell is but knows Madonna or *Star Trek*. Using a variety of examples helps readers identify with the paragraph and its meaning.

Write an Illustration Paragraph

TIP: Look back at your idea journal entry (p. 62) for ideas.

The key to writing a good illustration paragraph is to use a variety of **specific, detailed examples** that will appeal to your readers and help them understand your main point.

Illustration Assignment

Choose one of the following topic sentences (or one of your own) and write a paragraph that gives specific, detailed examples showing, explaining, or proving your main point.

NOTE
Because this is the first paragraph-writing chapter, the topic sentence is provided. In all other chapters, students must narrow the topic and write their own topic sentences.

Topic Sentences

COLLEGE

- I hope to accomplish several goals by taking this course.
- My [name of a course you are taking] course is very hard.
- Before registering for a particular college course, students should consider several things.
- I chose [your college] because it offered several advantages.

WORK

- I am interested in a number of different careers.
- My job requires a number of skills.
- Although I don't consider myself a writer, I find that I have to write fairly often.
- A résumé should contain certain basic information.

EVERYDAY LIFE

- Stress is a part of my daily life.
- I have been lucky to have had some good role models.
- _____ is my hero.
- Like most people, I have certain pet peeves.

Guided Practice: How to Write Illustration (p. 64) walks you through each step of writing an illustration paragraph, giving guidance and examples. Checklist: How to Write Illustration (p. 72) puts the steps into a checklist. To write your illustration paragraph, use either the Guided Practice, the Checklist, or parts of both.

Guided Practice: How to Write Illustration

TIP: Because you have already been given a topic sentence, in this chapter you start with Step 3, supporting your main point.

TEACHING TIP
Tell students that the number of examples they need will vary. For some topics, one extended example is enough; other topics call for more examples presented in less detail. Emphasize that examples should be varied, not just the same one repeated in different words. (EG)

TIP: For a reminder about prewriting techniques, see Chapter 2.

Step 3. Support Your Main Point with Examples

Find and Choose Supporting Examples.

You already have a topic sentence. Now use a prewriting technique to come up with examples that will show, explain, or prove your main point. Your examples will help your readers understand your main point.

First, use a prewriting technique to find as many examples as you can. Then go over your prewriting and drop examples that will not help you get your point across to your readers. Choose the best examples to use in your paragraph; think about combining smaller points.

TOPIC SENTENCE: Although they don't consider it stealing, many people regularly take things from their companies.

PREWRITING LIST

pens and pencils

pads of paper

~~erasers~~

products they make

long-distance calls
personal calls

~~paper clips~~

file folders

| Practice 1 | ▶ | Finding Examples to Support a Point |

NOTE
The Guided Practice (p. 64) and the Checklist (p. 72) cover the same material. Students can use the Checklist if they do not need the more in-depth support provided in the Guided Practice, which offers
(continued)

Read the following topic sentences and jot down three examples you might use to support each one.

EXAMPLE: My boss is very cheap.

makes us reuse envelopes

has a lock on the phone

gives us only a certain amount of paper each week

explanations, models, heuristics, and step-by-step instructions.

Guided Practices are provided in Chapters 7 and 8; thereafter the Checklist is augmented by explanations of and practices for the key elements of the type of writing covered.

TEAMWORK
Practice 1 can be done in pairs or in small groups. Have groups share their examples.

1. This town (city) has several major problems.

Answers will vary.

_____

_____

_____

2. My boss is fair (unfair). [Choose one or the other.]

_____

_____

_____

3. I have many things to do this weekend.

_____

_____

_____

4. This school is "user-friendly" ("user-unfriendly"). [Choose one.]

_____

_____

_____

5. Taking even just one course in college is expensive.

_____

_____

_____

Add Supporting Details.

Your illustration paragraph will only be as good as the examples you provide, and your examples will only be as good as the details you use. Reread the examples you have chosen and look for additional details or examples you can use to make them stronger.

TOPIC SENTENCE: Although they don't consider it stealing, many people regularly take things from their companies.

TIP: Check the pre-writing you did for supporting examples (p. 64) to see if there are some good additional details there.

EXAMPLES AND DETAILS CHOSEN FOR PARAGRAPH

Supporting example: *pens and pencils*

> *Added detail:* *accumulate in bottom of purse or knapsack*

Supporting example: *personal long-distance calls*

> *Added detail:* *to family or friends, short but frequent*

Supporting example: *products they make*

> *Added detail:* *think they're entitled to; sometimes even give to friends*

Supporting example: *paper*

> *Added detail:* *pads of paper, notepads, file folders*

TEACHING TIP
Walk students through the Thinking Critically guide, explaining the importance of asking and answering the questions.

Thinking Critically to Support Your Main Point with Examples

FOCUS	Reread your topic sentence carefully.
ASK	• What is a good example of what I mean? • What are some examples I've experienced myself? What have I heard about from friends and relatives? • What kinds of examples will my readers relate to? • Which of these examples are directly related to my main point? • What details will help my readers see what I mean?
WRITE	List the supporting examples and additional details you will use.

Practice 2 Supporting Your Main Point with Examples and Details

Use the Thinking Critically guide on this page to help you find supporting examples and details for your illustration paragraph. Follow these steps:

1. Use a prewriting technique to find possible examples. List them on the lines labeled "Example."
2. Cross out unrelated ideas and anything that won't help you get your point across to your readers.
3. Circle the three or four strongest examples to use in your paragraph.

4. Try to add one detail to each example you have circled, to make it lively and clear to your readers. Write each detail on the line labeled "Detail" next to its example.

EXAMPLE: *Answers will vary.*   **DETAIL:** _____

_____   _____

EXAMPLE: _____   **DETAIL:** _____

_____   _____

EXAMPLE: _____   **DETAIL:** _____

_____   _____

EXAMPLE: _____   **DETAIL:** _____

_____   _____

EXAMPLE: _____   **DETAIL:** _____

_____   _____

EXAMPLE: _____   **DETAIL:** _____

_____   _____

Step 4. Write a Draft

Arrange Your Examples and Write a Draft.

Illustration paragraphs may use space order, time order, or order of importance. Reread your topic sentence and your supporting examples to decide how to arrange them so that they will have the most impact on your readers.

Once you have decided how to order your ideas, make a plan by putting them into an informal outline. Then use this outline as a guide to write your draft.

INFORMAL OUTLINE

Topic sentence: Although they don't consider it stealing, many people regularly take things from their companies.

1. *Pens and pencils*

   —accumulate in bottom of purse or knapsack

2. *Paper*

   —pads of paper, notepads, file folders

3. *Personal long-distance calls*

   —to family or friends, short but frequent

4. *Products they make*

   —think they're entitled to; sometimes even give to friends

TEACHING TIP
Remind students that
the draft is not the final
copy.

DRAFT PARAGRAPH

Although they don't consider it stealing, many people regularly take things from their companies. The items that most frequently disappear are pens and pencils that employees almost unconsciously stuff into their purses, knapsacks, or briefcases. Over time, employees may accumulate quite a stash of them. Paper is a big item, including pads of lined paper, notepads, and file folders. Few people consider long-distance personal phone calls at work actually stealing, but it is using company time and money to chat, even briefly, with friends and family. One of the more significant ways people "steal" from their companies is by taking home samples of the products the company makes: food, clothing, supplies, and so on. Employees seem to think they are entitled to these products and even give them to friends. In this way, they hurt the company by robbing it of a product it depends on for revenue.

Thinking Critically While Drafting Your Illustration Paragraph _____

FOCUS   Reread your topic sentence and the supporting examples and think about the best way to present your ideas.

ASK   • Which of the three orders (space, time, importance) would work best with these examples to make my point to my readers?
             • Now that I have an order, are there any "gaps" that I should fill in with other examples?

WRITE   Write an outline that shows the plan for your illustration paragraph. Then write a draft paragraph with complete sentences in paragraph form.

Practice 3 ▶ Making a Plan and Writing a Draft

Use the Thinking Critically guide on this page to make a plan for your illustration paragraph in the spaces on the next page. Then write a draft on a separate piece of paper.

TOPIC SENTENCE: _Answers will vary._ _____

_____

SUPPORTING EXAMPLE **1**: _____

    ADDED DETAIL(S): _____

_____

SUPPORTING EXAMPLE **2**: _____

    ADDED DETAIL(S): _____

_____

SUPPORTING EXAMPLE **3**: _____

    ADDED DETAIL(S): _____

_____

SUPPORTING EXAMPLE **4**: _____

    ADDED DETAIL(S): _____

_____

Write a Concluding Sentence.

    A concluding sentence ties your examples back to your main point. It makes a further observation about what the topic sentence and the supporting examples add up to.

    CONCLUDING SENTENCE FOR ILLUSTRATION PARAGRAPH: Taking things from work may not seem like stealing, but the results are the same: extra costs to the company, which may result in lower pay raises.

Thinking Critically to Write a Concluding Sentence

FOCUS   As you reread your paragraph, think about what observation you can make based on the examples you have given.

ASK   • What observation do these examples add up to?
            • How can I tie the observation back to my topic sentence?
            • What can I say that will end my paragraph on a strong note?

WRITE   Write your concluding sentence.

Practice 4

Writing Your Concluding Sentence

DISCUSSION
Read aloud a paragraph with a poor concluding sentence, and ask students to jot down ideas for a better one. Ask some students to read their sentences aloud. Ask the class why the original concluding sentence was weak.

TIP: For a review of revising strategies, see Chapter 6.

Read your draft paragraph and write two possible concluding sentences here. Then circle the best one and add it to your draft paragraph.

CONCLUDING SENTENCE 1: _____

_____

CONCLUDING SENTENCE 2: _____

_____

Step 5. Revise Your Draft

After completing your draft, take a break. Then reread it, searching for examples that don't fit, additional details to make your examples more lively and specific, and ways to connect the examples so that they flow smoothly. This is your chance to improve your illustration paragraph before getting a grade. Do not just copy over your draft; make changes that will improve the paragraph.

TEACHING TIP
You may want to model giving feedback for the students. Read a paragraph aloud and give feedback according to the guidelines.

Teamwork: Get Feedback

When you have completed the draft of your paragraph, you may want to show it to someone else or read it aloud in a small group, asking for feedback and suggestions that will help you revise.

GUIDELINES FOR GIVING FEEDBACK

- **Start with a positive comment.**

- **Throughout, offer comments and observations rather than "You should's."**

- **Start with the paragraph as a whole and move to smaller points.**
  —Tell the writer what you think the main point is.
  —Ask questions about the examples and the writer's meaning.

- **Tell the writer what works for you and what you think might be done better (and how).**

- **Be as specific as you can. Don't just say "It's good" or "I liked it." Explain why.**

- **If you get confused, tell the writer what's confusing.**

- **Help the writer.**

COMPUTER
If students compose on computers, they can exchange disks and write feedback in files on the disks.

COMPUTER
Advise students to
copy their draft and
save the original. Tell
them to make changes
only on the copy so
that if they want to go
back to an idea from
the original, they will
still have it. Also
advise them to print
out a hard copy of the
original before
revising.

Here is the revised example paragraph, with notes to show what changes
the writer made to revise the draft shown on page 68.

REVISED PARAGRAPH

Although they don't consider it stealing, many people regularly
take things from their companies. The most common items to disappear are pens and pencils that employees almost unconsciously stuff
into their purses, knapsacks, or briefcases. Over time, they may accumulate quite a stash of them. Another big item is all kinds of paper:
pads of lined paper, handy little notepads that can be used for shopping
lists and phone messages, and file folders to organize home records. Yet
another "innocent theft" is the long-distance personal phone call.
Those calls cost the company in two ways: they use company time for
personal business, and the company has to pay for the calls. Even
though companies may have special discounted telephone rates, no call
is free. Finally, one of the more significant ways people steal is by taking home samples of the products the company makes: food, clothing,
supplies, and so on. Employees seem to think they are entitled to these
products and even give them to friends. By doing so, they hurt the
company by robbing it of a product it depends on for revenue. These
examples may not seem like stealing, but the results are the same:
extra costs to the company, which may result in lower pay raises.

less wordy
word changed
transition added
added detail
added detail
transition
added more concrete detail
transition added
added concluding sentence
observation

Thinking Critically to Revise an Illustration Paragraph

FOCUS   After a break, reread your draft illustration paragraph with a
             fresh perspective. Think about what you want your readers to
             learn from the paragraph.

ASK   • What do I want to say? Have I said it?
             • Are there any examples or details that don't fit?

NOTE
This chapter does not take students through the process of editing their papers. That material is covered in "Editing," Chapters 21–40.

- Are there enough detailed examples to show my readers what I mean?
- Do the pieces fit together into a whole paragraph that flows smoothly? Do I need to add transitions or repeat key words?
- Will my readers get my point? Will they find my paragraph interesting?

WRITE   Revise by making improvements to your draft.

Practice 5 ▶ **Revising Your Draft**

Reread your draft and ask yourself the questions in the Thinking Critically guide on page 71. Revise your draft by making at least three changes. Be prepared to explain how those changes improve the draft.

Checklist: How to Write Illustration

NOTE
Because students are given topic sentences in this chapter, they should skip to Step 3. The complete Checklist is provided so that students can use it for other assignments.

TEACHING TIP
All paragraph chapters have Checklists, which are also reproduced in *Additional Resources.* You can photocopy and distribute them if you want students to hand Checklists in with their assignments.

Check off items as you complete them. Because you are given a topic sentence in this chapter, you can skip over the first two steps and start with number 3.

1. **Narrow and explore your topic.**

    ✓ Narrow the general topic to a specific idea that you are interested in and that you can show, explain, or prove in one paragraph. Jot down some ideas about the narrowed topic and why it's important.

2. **Make your point in a topic sentence.**

    ✓ Decide what is most important about your narrowed topic. What do you want to say to your readers? What point do you want to make?

    ✓ Write a topic sentence that contains both your narrowed topic and the point you want to make about it.

3. **Support your main point with examples.**

    ____ Use a prewriting technique to find supporting examples that will show, explain, or prove your main point.

    ____ Drop unrelated ideas. Select the best examples to use in your paragraph.

    ____ Add supporting details to make the examples specific.

4.   **Write a draft.**

_____ Arrange your examples in a logical order (space, time, or importance) and make a plan.

_____ Write a draft paragraph using complete sentences in paragraph form.

_____ Write a concluding sentence that relates back to your main point but does not just repeat it.

_____ Title your paragraph, if required.

5.   **Revise your draft.**

_____ Get feedback from others.

_____ Cut any details that do not support your main point.

_____ Make sure that you have enough examples to appeal to your audience and to get your point across.

_____ Make sure your paragraph flows. Add transitions and repeat key words as necessary.

_____ Do not just copy over your draft. Make some changes to improve it.

6.   **Edit your revised draft.**

_____ Find and correct any problems with grammar, spelling, word use, or punctuation.

_____ Produce a clean, final copy.

_____ Ask yourself: Is this the best I can do?

Use Illustration in Real-World Situations

RESOURCES
For an additional real-world assignment for this chapter, see _Additional Resources._

It is hard to explain anything without using examples, so you use illustration in almost every communication situation: in college, at work, and in everyday life.

COLLEGE	An exam question asks you to explain and give examples of a concept.
WORK	Your boss asks you to tell her what office furniture or equipment needs to be replaced and why.
EVERYDAY LIFE	You complain to your landlord that the building superintendent is not doing his job. The landlord asks for examples.

Real-World Assignment: Improving the College Experience

SITUATION: Your college has a new president who is interested in making changes that will improve students' college experience. As part of a campus-wide request for input, your class is asked to submit ideas about how the college experience could be improved.

ASSIGNMENT: Generate a list of three changes you think would improve your college experience. Come up with specific examples of how those changes would be improvements. Working with the list of changes and specific examples, write an illustration paragraph.

Summary: Illustration

- **Illustration** is writing that uses examples to show, explain, or prove a point. (See p. 61.)
- **Good illustration** makes a point, gives detailed and specific examples to explain, demonstrate, or prove the point, and gives enough examples to get the point across. (See p. 61.)
- The **topic sentence** in an illustration paragraph usually includes the topic and the main point. (See p. 62.)

What Will You Use?

List something from this chapter that you will use in the future.

PROFILE OF SUCCESS

Rocío Avila

Rocío Avila is a teacher of bilingual children, many of whom are struggling to learn a new language, English. To ensure that they learn the information they need to keep up with the class, Rocío gives lots of examples of key points. Through the examples, the children are better able to understand and relate to the information.

When Rocío was in college, she was mentored by counselors and teachers from the Puente Project, a group in California that advises Hispanic students, helping them adjust to the demands of college.

COLLEGES: El Camino College and University of California, Irvine

EMPLOYER: Santa Ana (California) Unified School District

POSITION: Bilingual teacher

MAJOR JOB RESPONSIBILITIES: Teach classes; create lesson plans; hold parent conferences; participate in workshops and conferences; organize field trips

TYPES OF WRITING REQUIRED: Lesson plans; letters to parents, administrators, and businesses; memos to other teachers; grant proposals

PROUDEST ACHIEVEMENT: In one year, I completed my teaching credentials, survived a diabetes diagnosis, moved into my own apartment, and completed my first year of teaching. None of my accomplishments could have been possible without the continuous support of my two best friends: my mom and my boyfriend.

BEST PIECE OF ADVICE I EVER RECEIVED: Your education is the most valuable thing you have that can never be taken away from you.

BEST PIECE OF ADVICE I CAN GIVE: Believe in yourself and all is possible.

Narration

Paragraphs That Tell Stories

Valeria Edwards, Assistant Principal

PROFILE OF SUCCESS

Valeria Edwards

WRITING THEN: "In high school I had no idea where I was going or that I would need writing skills. I was raised by my grandparents who themselves didn't have much formal education. When I took a writing test for college and realized the deficit in my writing skills, I was glad there was a program to help bridge the gap."

WRITING NOW: "As assistant principal, I am the editor of our weekly newsletter, and I coedit a student handbook that is distributed to all students in the school. I also write memos every day—to staff, parents, and other colleagues. In most of this writing, I am reporting on something that has happened or will happen. For example, the newsletter often recounts what happened at a school event."

(For more about Valeria Edwards, see p. 93.)

Understand What Narration Is

Narration is writing that tells a story of an event or an experience. People like stories, so narration is a good way to make a point.

GOOD NARRATION

- Reveals something of importance
- Includes all of the important events of the story
- Brings the story to life with detailed examples of what happened
- Presents events in a clear order (usually according to when they happened)

SAMPLE NARRATION PARAGRAPH

At age 14, a gawky and shy James Earl Jones was transformed. Transplanted from rural Mississippi, he felt out of place at Dickson High School in Brethren, Michigan. His stutter was so pronounced that he never spoke out in class. Under-

RESOURCES
For a discussion of how to use the profiles in Part Two, see *Practical Suggestions*.

DISCUSSION
Jones was the voice of Darth Vader in *Star Wars* and of the father lion in *The Lion King*. A very successful actor, he has starred in many movies and television programs. Tell students that when Jones was asked what he would say to anyone hoping to be successful in life, he answered, "Whatever you are interested in, just do it. Don't let anyone say you can't."

IDEA JOURNAL
Write about something that happened to you today.

READING SELECTIONS
For examples of and activities for narration essays, see Chapter 43.

YOU KNOW THIS
You often use narration. For example:
• You tell a friend what happened over the weekend.
• You give the plot of a movie you saw.
• You say, "You won't believe what happened." Then you tell the story.

standably, he often felt alone. Jones found refuge in writing poetry. (One day) in class, he wrote a poem and submitted it to his English ①
teacher. The teacher, surprised at how good it was, wondered whether Jones had copied it and challenged Jones, "The best way for you to ②
prove that you wrote this poem yourself is for you to recite it by heart to the class." Jones (then) walked to the front of the room, thinking it ③
would be better to be laughed at for stuttering than to be disgraced. He was scared, (but) he opened his mouth and began to speak. To the aston- ④
ishment of everyone in the class, the words flowed smoothly. The stutter disappeared. He had stumbled upon what speech therapists would one day discover: that the written page can be a stutterer's salvation. He went on to become a high school public-speaking champion and ⑤
won a scholarship to the University of Michigan. (Today,) 50 years ⑥
later, the voice of James Earl Jones is among the most familiar in the world.   *(Exact number of incidents will vary.)*

—Wallace Terry, "When His Sound Was Silenced"

1. Annotate the paragraph to highlight its structure:
   • Double-underline the topic sentence.
   • Underline events that tell the story.
   • Circle the transitions.

2. What is important about the story? *overcame stuttering*

   _____

3. The **topic sentence** of a narration paragraph usually includes the topic and a preview of what is important about it.

My first day at my new job was nearly a disaster.

Fill in the blanks with the topic and the preview for the sample paragraph.

RESOURCES
See "Oral Connections to Literacy: The Narrative," by Aku Duku Anokye, in *Background Readings*.

Topic	=	*James Earl Jones*

Preview	=	*overcame his stuttering when he was 14*

4. The **support** in a narration paragraph is a series of events. The events tell readers what happened. Write the first event in the sample paragraph here.

Jones wrote a poem.

5. What type of **order** does the sample paragraph use: space, time, or importance?

time order

Write a Narration Paragraph

TIP: Look back at your idea journal entry (p. 76) for possible stories.

The key to writing a good narration paragraph is to include the important events that make up the story in enough detail for your readers to understand what happened. The story should reveal something about the people involved in the story.

Narration Assignment

Choose one of the following general topics or one of your own.

COLLEGE
- Something that happened on the first day of classes
- A run-in with authority
- An experience where you felt a strong emotion: happiness, sadness, relief, fear, regret, nervousness
- A project, assignment, or activity that was fun

WORK
- A work experience that you'd rather forget
- A work achievement you are proud of
- A funny work story
- How you got your first job

EVERYDAY LIFE
- A childhood memory
- A day you'll never forget

TEACHING TIP
Suggest to students that they make journal entries on some of the topics that they don't write about for this assignment. (EG)

- A situation where you learned from a mistake
- An important event that didn't go as you expected
- An experience of winning

Guided Practice: How to Write Narration walks you through each step of writing a narration paragraph, giving guidance and examples. Checklist: How to Write Narration (p. 91) puts the steps into a checklist. To write your paragraph, use either one or parts of both.

Guided Practice: How to Write Narration

TIP: For a review of the Three-Question Test for Good Topics, see Chapter 2.

TEAMWORK
Give small groups of students a few very broad topics and have them narrow the topics to something that would be manageable in a paragraph. Example of some broad topics: being a student at [your college]; living in [your town, city, or state]; a major holiday.

Step 1. Narrow and Explore Your General Topic

After you have chosen a general topic to write about, find your own story within that general topic. Write down one or two ideas for possible stories and ask yourself if there *is* a story to tell, if you are interested in the story, and if you can tell it in a paragraph.

Sometimes people choose experiences that are too big to tell in a paragraph. For instance, one student first chose as his story "life as a Buddhist." There may be a fascinating story there, but it's too big to tell thoroughly in one paragraph. The student had to narrow the general topic to something more focused: "an important Buddhist ceremony." You need to be able to communicate the important events in your story in one paragraph.

GENERAL TOPIC	*A situation I learned from*
POSSIBLE STORIES	*When I fell before my wedding, when I hurt Naomi's feelings, when my grandfather died*
NARROWED TOPIC / STORY	*When I fell before my wedding*
IDEAS	*A horrible experience, one I learned from, behavior the day before, the fall, how it changed things*

Thinking Critically to Narrow and Explore a Narration Topic _____

FOCUS	Think about the general topic and your experiences with it.
ASK	• What experiences in my life are connected to this topic? • Which would make a good story? • Which seem interesting to me? • Which one should I focus on? • When I think of this experience, what are the first things that come to my mind? • What do I want my readers to get from the story?
WRITE	Write down your narrowed topic and ideas that you have.

| Practice 1 ▶ | Narrowing and Exploring Your General Topic |

Use the Thinking Critically guide on page 78 to find two different narrowed topics you might write about. Then circle the topic you will use and jot down some of the things that come to your mind as you think about it.

GENERAL TOPIC: *Answers will vary.* _____

NARROWED TOPICS *(circle the one you will use)*:

1. _____

2. _____

IDEAS ABOUT THE NARROWED TOPIC *(jot down at least five)*:

_____

_____

_____

_____

_____

_____

Step 2. Make Your Point in a Topic Sentence

Decide What Is Important about the Story.

The point of the story is simply what makes the story important to you and to your readers.

If you need to discover what about the story is important to you, reread the list you made in Practice 1. Is the point of the story there? Ask yourself what you would want a good friend to get out of this story. (Or what would you answer if your friend asked, "So what?") Consider why the story was interesting to you in the first place. Then write a statement of why you think the story is important.

| NARROWED TOPIC/STORY | *When I fell before my wedding* |
| WHAT'S IMPORTANT ABOUT THE EXPERIENCE | *I learned that getting married was more than the wedding. I focused on what was really happening. I was happy about the important things and forgot about the small things like flowers, weather, how I looked.* |

TIP: When you have the basic topic sentence, try changing it to make it sound stronger, clearer, or more interesting.

• An accident on the eve of my wedding helped me put things in perspective.

• I remembered the true meaning of marriage by ending up in a hospital the night before my wedding.

• An accident the night before my wedding reminded me of what was really important.

Write a Topic Sentence.

In the topic sentence, you introduce the topic and give the reader a preview of what will happen. Your topic sentence should give readers some idea of why the story is important. Try starting with this basic formula:

An accident the night before my wedding reminded me of what was important.

Thinking Critically to Make Your Point

FOCUS   Reread your narrowed topic and think about why you chose this experience to write about.

ASK   • How did this experience affect me? Why is it important to me? Why is it interesting?
               • What do I want to reveal by telling this story? What do I want readers to learn from it?
               • How can I get readers interested in the story without giving it away?

WRITE   Write a topic sentence that identifies your topic and gives a preview.

Practice 2 ▶ Making Your Point in a Topic Sentence

Using the Thinking Critically guide on this page, complete the sentence about what's important and then write a topic sentence.

WHAT'S IMPORTANT TO ME ABOUT THE EXPERIENCE IS *Answers will vary.* _____

_____

_____

TOPIC SENTENCE: _____

_____

Step 3. Support Your Main Point with Events That Tell the Story

In a narration paragraph, the events you include and the way you describe them create a story with a certain point of view. For example, two people who witness the same event may give very different accounts of it because they focused on different events or perceived those events differently. The stories the two people tell reflect different points of view. Read these two accounts of the same experience.

CHARLENE'S STORY

This morning I could have killed my husband. While I was running around yelling at the kids, trying to get them fed and off to school, he sat there reading the newspaper. When I finally sat down, he just kept on reading that newspaper, even though I needed to talk with him. After several attempts to get through to him, I finally barked out, "Daryl! I have a few things I need to say!" He looked up, smiled, got another cup of coffee, and said, "What?" But as I began talking, he resumed reading the paper. Does he live in another world?

DARYL'S STORY

This morning my family enjoyed some "quality time" together. The children were all in the kitchen eating and talking with each other. After they left for school, my wife and I were able to sit and share some quiet time at the table. We chatted about various things while drinking coffee and looking at the newspaper. It really started the day out right.

As you can see, the events are the same, but the stories aren't; they repeat two different points of view. Be careful to use events that will tell the story you want to tell.

Presenting Your Point of View (Teamwork)

Either in a small group or as a class, choose a television program you can all watch this week. Then choose a major character in the program that you will focus on. Each person will report on what happened in the program, but half the group should start with a positive idea of the character and half with a negative one.

EXAMPLE: Group 1: Phoebe is incredibly funny.

Group 2: Phoebe is incredibly stupid.

Write a one-paragraph account of what happened. Have each student share his or her account with the rest of the group. See how the stories differ depending on the point of view.

Find and Choose Events.

Once you know the story you want to tell and the message you want to get across, you need to find and choose the events you will use to tell that story to your readers.

Use a prewriting technique to come up with a list of the events in your story. Start by writing down every event that you can think of. Then go back over your prewriting and cross out anything that isn't central to the story you want to tell. Think about what you want your readers to know. Look for minor events that can be combined into larger ones. You should end up with about three to six events that will be useful in telling your story.

TOPIC SENTENCE: An accident the night before my wedding reminded me of what was really important.

PREWRITING LIST OF EVENTS

finding fault with everyone, really nervous
~~*stubbed my toe*~~
arguments with my mother and Jim
~~*couldn't get in touch with maid of honor*~~
~~*phone kept ringing*~~
~~*ate too much leftover Halloween candy*~~
~~*left my raincoat in my apartment*~~
~~*umbrella broke*~~
fell
couldn't sleep
got up
splashed water on my face
went to hospital — 35 stitches
talked with Jim, felt better

Add Details.

Look for examples and details that will make each event lively and specific. Remember that you want your readers to share your point of view and see the same message in the story that you do.

TOPIC SENTENCE: An accident the night before my wedding reminded me of what was really important.

EVENTS AND DETAILS CHOSEN FOR THE PARAGRAPH

Event:	*finding fault with everyone and everything*
Details:	*hemline on wedding dress looked crooked, rain predicted, fights with my mother and fiancé*
Event:	*fell*
Details:	*tripped over suitcase and hit corner of night table*
Event:	*couldn't sleep*
Details:	*got up to splash warm water on my face*

Event:	*went to hospital*
Details:	*35 stitches, doctor's reaction, thinking how terrible I'd look*
Event:	*talked with Jim and felt better*
Details:	*he was there when I woke up, said I looked beautiful, remembered what's important*

TIP: For complete information on using quotation marks, see Chapter 38.

Use Conversation.

As you remember the experience, you may recall something that someone said or a brief conversation that took place. If what was said was important to the story, put it in your paragraph. If you are reporting exactly what the speaker said, use quotation marks.

I said, "I'm going to be one ugly bride."

He said, "That would be impossible."

TEACHING TIP
Ask students why conversation can be effective. Quickly review the use of quotation marks (Chapter 38). Remind students of the difference between direct and indirect quotations.

Thinking Critically to Support Your Main Point _____

FOCUS	Reread your topic sentence and think about what happened.
ASK	• What happened first? What next?
	• Which events do I need to tell the story? Which get my message across? Which will my readers relate to?
	• Should any minor events be combined?
	• What details make these events come alive?
	• Do I want to report anything that was said?
WRITE	List the events and additional details you will use.

Practice 4

Supporting Your Main Point with Events and Details

Use the Thinking Critically guide on this page to help you find supporting details for your narration paragraph. Follow these steps:

1. Use a prewriting technique to find possible events. List them on the lines on the next page labeled "Event."
2. Cross out events that are not essential and combine smaller events.
3. Circle the three or four strongest events to use in your paragraph.
4. Add at least one detail or example to make the events you have chosen lively and specific. Write the details on the lines labeled "Details" next to each event.
5. Write down any pieces of conversation you might use.

EVENT: _____*Answers will vary.*_____   DETAILS: _____

_____   _____

EVENT: _____   DETAILS: _____

_____   _____

EVENT: _____   DETAILS: _____

_____   _____

EVENT: _____   DETAILS: _____

_____   _____

EVENT: _____   DETAILS: _____

_____   _____

CONVERSATION: _____

_____

TIP: For a review of time order or a review of outlining, see Chapter 5.

Step 4. Write a Draft

Arrange Your Events and Write a Draft.

When you tell a story, most often you arrange the events according to when they happened: in time order. Before you write a draft of your narration paragraph, arrange the events in a logical time sequence, usually working from what happened first to what happened last. Make a plan (usually an outline) for your paragraph, using the topic sentence as the first sentence. Then write the draft paragraph, using complete sentences and correct paragraph form. If you think of more details and examples related to your main point as you write, put them in.

INFORMAL OUTLINE

Topic sentence: An accident the night before my wedding reminded me of what was really important.

1.   *Finding fault, nervous and cranky*

     — hemline on wedding dress looked crooked, rain predicted, fights with my mother and fiancé

2. *Couldn't sleep*

    —got up to splash warm water on my face

3. *Fell*

    —tripped over suitcase and hit corner of night table

4. *Went to hospital*

    —35 stitches, doctor's reaction, thinking how terrible I'd look

5. *Talked with Jim*

    —he was there when I woke up, said I looked beautiful, remembered what was really important

DRAFT PARAGRAPH

An accident the night before my wedding reminded me of what was really important. All day I had been nervous and ready to find fault. Nothing was right: The hem on my wedding dress looked crooked, the weather report predicted rain, and one of the bouquets was the wrong color. I argued nonstop with my mother and my fiancé. That night I couldn't sleep, so I got up to splash some warm water on my face. I tripped and crashed headfirst into the corner of the night table. I felt blood, and I screamed for help. At the hospital, the doctor sewed my lip and cheek together with thirty-five stitches. I asked him how I would look for the wedding, and he shrugged his shoulders. I awoke on my wedding day to see my fiancé sitting in a chair beside the bed holding my hand. I said, "I'm going to be one ugly bride." He placed his hand on the side of my face and said, "That would be impossible."

Thinking Critically While Drafting Your Narration Paragraph

FOCUS   Reread your topic sentence and detailed events and think about how to tell your story.

ASK   • Does time order work best?
             • Should I go from what happened first and work up to what happened last?
             • Have I left out any important incidents?

WRITE   Write an outline that shows the plan for your narration paragraph. Then write a draft paragraph with complete sentences in correct paragraph form.

> Practice 5   **Arranging Events as They Happened**

The events following each topic sentence are out of order. Number the events according to time sequence, 1 for the earliest and so on. Example:

TOPIC SENTENCE: Sojourner Truth was a remarkable woman.

_1_ Born a slave in 1797

_3_ At forty-six, heard heavenly voices urging her to spread word of emancipation and women's rights

_2_ Freed and moved to New York City to be a maid

_6_ Died at age eighty-six

_5_ Educated many people

_4_ Traveled around the country giving speeches even though she never learned to read or write

1. **TOPIC SENTENCE:** Alan Page has followed his dreams and helps others to follow theirs.

   _3_ Played professionally for the Minnesota Vikings

   _2_ In college, played football for Notre Dame

   _6_ Became a Minnesota Supreme Court justice

   _1_ As a child idolized sports heroes and lawyers

   _4_ Realized many of his teammates couldn't read the playbook

   _5_ Went to law school

2. **TOPIC SENTENCE:** I'll never forget the most unlucky day of my life.

   _1_ First thing had an argument with someone I work with

   _6_ Glass everywhere; couldn't drive

   _5_ Got to parking lot and someone had shot the windshield

   _2_ My lunch taken from the refrigerator

_3_ Got back to my desk and had a message from my husband saying our apartment had been robbed

_7_ Burst into tears wondering if someone was after me

_4_ Decided to go home

3. **TOPIC SENTENCE:** I have work experience that qualifies me for the position of office manager.

_3_ In college worked in busy admissions office; managed two other students

_1_ Always worked in my mother's home office helping her with billing, accounting, correspondence

_5_ Now assistant office manager at Norton Company

_2_ In high school worked in doctor's office organizing patient files and setting up appointments

_4_ Also worked at night in college cafeteria processing food orders, doing inventory, tabulating day's sales

Practice 6 ▶ Making a Plan and Writing a Draft

Use the Thinking Critically guide on page 85 to make a plan for your narration paragraph in the following spaces, and then write a first draft on a separate sheet of paper.

RESOURCES
A blank diagram of a narration paragraph (big enough to write in) is in *Additional Resources.* You may want to copy it and give it to students to plan their paragraphs.

TOPIC SENTENCE: *Answers will vary.* _____

EVENT 1: _____

DETAILS: _____

EVENT 2: _____

DETAILS: _____

EVENT 3: _____

DETAILS: _____

EVENT 4: _____

DETAILS: _____

Write a Concluding Sentence.

A concluding sentence relates back to your main point and sums up what is important about the story.

> **CONCLUDING SENTENCE:** At that moment I remembered what was important: not a dress, the weather, or how I looked, but the beauty of our relationship.

Thinking Critically to Write a Concluding Sentence

FOCUS	As you reread your paragraph, think about what is important about the experience.
ASK	• What is the point of my story? • What message do I want to leave my readers with?
WRITE	Write your concluding sentence.

Practice 7 ▶ **Writing Your Concluding Sentence**

Use the Thinking Critically guide on this page to write two possible concluding sentences for your narration paragraph. Then circle the best one and add it to your draft paragraph.

CONCLUDING SENTENCE 1: *Answers will vary.*

_____

CONCLUDING SENTENCE 2: _____

_____

TIP: For a review of revising strategies, see Chapter 6.

Step 5. Revise Your Draft

You have your story on paper. Now reread it looking for ways to improve it: making the point clearer; getting rid of events that don't fit; adding other, more important events; adding detail; connecting the events with transitions. Do not just copy over your draft; make changes that will improve the story.

COMPUTER
Have students reread their drafts and highlight the time transitions. List the ones they used on the board.

Add Transitions.

Transitions connect your ideas so that they flow smoothly from one to the next. Because narration usually uses time order to arrange ideas, **time transitions** are the best connectors, indicating when one event occurred in relation to another.

COMMON TIME TRANSITIONS

after	eventually	meanwhile	soon
as	finally	next	then
at last	first	now	when
before	last	second	while
during	later	since	

The revised example paragraph has comments that show where the writer made changes to her draft, including adding transitions.

REVISED PARAGRAPH

An accident the night before my wedding reminded me of what was really important. All day I had been nervous and ready to find fault. Nothing was right: The hem on my wedding dress looked crooked, the weather report predicted rain, and one of the bouquets was the wrong color. I argued nonstop with my mother and my fiancé. That night I couldn't sleep, so I got up to splash some warm water on my face.

— added detail —
Returning to the bedroom in the dark, I tripped and crashed headfirst
— added detail —
into the corner of the night table. Blood gushed from my face, and I
— transition —
screamed for help. Later at the hospital, the doctor sewed my lip and
— added detail —
cheek together with thirty-five stitches, a visible seam in the middle of
— transition —   — added detail —
my face. When I asked him how I would look for the wedding, he tilted his head, grimaced, and shrugged his shoulders. I awoke on my wedding day to see my fiancé sitting in a chair beside the bed holding my hand. I
— added detail —
said, "I'm going to be one ugly bride." He placed his hand so gently on
— detail —   — detail —
the side of my face, kissed me, and whispered, "That would be impossible." At that moment I remembered what was important: not a dress, the weather, or how I looked, but the beauty of our relationship.

added concluding sentence

COMPUTER
If students compose on computers, they can exchange disks and write feedback on one another's disks.

Teamwork: Get Feedback

When you have completed the draft of your paragraph, you may want to show it to someone else or read it aloud in a small group, asking for feedback and suggestions that will help you revise.

GUIDELINES FOR GIVING FEEDBACK

- Start with a positive comment.

- Throughout, offer comments and observations rather than "You should's."

- Start with the paragraph as a whole and move to smaller points.
    — Tell the writer what you think the main idea is.
    — Review the events that make up the story.
    — Ask questions about the events that might help the writer give more detail.

- Tell the writer what works for you and what you think might be done better (and how).

- Be as specific as you can. Don't just say, "It's good" or "I liked it." Explain why.

- If you get confused or lost somewhere in the paragraph, tell the writer where.

- Help the writer.

Thinking Critically to Revise a Narration Paragraph

FOCUS   After a break, reread your draft narration paragraph with a fresh perspective. Think about what you want your readers to take away from the story.

ASK
- What is the point of my story? Why is it important to me? What do I want my readers to learn or understand?
- Are there any incidents or details I should cut because they are unimportant to the story?
- Have I included all the important incidents? Will my readers be able to follow the sequence of events?
- Have I included enough concrete, specific details?
- Do the pieces fit together and flow smoothly? Do I need to add transitions to show how one event leads to another?
- Is it a good story?

WRITE   Revise by making improvements to your draft.

| Practice 8 | Revising Your Draft |

Use the Thinking Critically guide on page 90 to revise your draft. Make at least three changes and be prepared to explain how they improve the draft.

Checklist: How to Write Narration

Check off items as you complete them.

1. **Narrow and explore your general topic** (the story you will tell).

_____ Narrow the general topic to a specific experience that you are interested in and can tell in a paragraph. Jot down some ideas about the story and why it's important.

2. **Make your point in a topic sentence.**

_____ Decide what is important about the experience. What do you want your story to reveal? How were you or others affected by what happened?

_____ Write a topic sentence that hints at what is important about your story.

3. **Support your main point with events that tell the story.**

_____ Use a prewriting technique to find the events that were part of the experience.

_____ Read the prewriting and choose the events that are most important to the reader's understanding of the story. Drop events that are not important to the story.

_____ Add details to make the events more lifelike. Consider adding conversation.

4. **Write a draft.**

_____ Arrange the events in chronological order and make a plan.

_____ Write a draft paragraph using complete sentences in paragraph form.

_____ Write a concluding sentence that reveals what is important about the story and relates back to your topic sentence.

_____ Title the paragraph, if required.

(continued)

RESOURCES
All paragraph chapters have Checklists. They are also in reproducible form in *Additional Resources*. Copy and distribute the form if you want students to check off the steps as they go and hand in the Checklist with their draft or revision.

TEACHING TIP
Caution students to proofread carefully for tense consistency. In writing narration, students have a tendency to shift tenses incorrectly. (EG)

5. **Revise your draft.**

_____ Get feedback from others.

_____ Cut any details that distract readers from the story.

_____ Add any other events that are important to the story.

_____ Make sure the sequence is logical. Add transitions (especially time transitions) to take readers from one event to another.

_____ Do not just copy over your draft. Make changes to improve it.

6. **Edit your revised draft.**

_____ Find and correct any problems with grammar, spelling, word use, or punctuation.

_____ Produce a clean, final copy.

_____ Ask yourself: Is this the best I can do?

Use Narration in Real-World Situations

Stories are a big part of our communication with others. They can be entertaining, but they also provide information and examples that show, explain, or prove a point. People like stories; when you are trying to make a point, you are more likely to get people's attention if you tell a story.

COLLEGE   In a reading or an English course, you are asked to recount, in your own words, the basic story of a piece of literature.

WORK   You are part of a team at work whose charge is to come up with the "company story," a story that can be presented to potential customers to show the company in a positive light.

EVERYDAY LIFE   Someone asks you how you and your mate first met.

TEAMWORK
This assignment works well as a collaborative, small-group activity.

Real-World Assignment: Your Job Interview Story

SITUATION: Many job interviews require you to tell "your story." Think of a job that you might interview for in the near future or one that you have already interviewed for. Then read the following excerpt from a magazine article.

Plan your interview story carefully. Most successful interviews follow a three-scene script. Cooperate with the script and you increase your chances of being hired. Fight it or ignore it and your interview may run aground.

Scene One: Lasting about three minutes, this scene consists of small talk and is really a compatibility contest. As you shake hands, make eye contact and smile. Show that you are courteous, friendly, and at ease with yourself and the situation. These "small" points are not trivial.

Scene Two: Lasting about 15 minutes to an hour or more, this scene is mainly you telling your story. You need to explain your skills, abilities, accomplishments, and ambitions. Emphasize your ability to add value to the employer. If you can claim credit for increasing sales, reducing costs, or improving quality, now is the time to do so. . . . As you conclude this scene, stress your ability and willingness to perform at a high level.

Scene Three: Lasting only a minute or two, this scene closes the interview and sets up the next steps.

— "How to Land a Job," *Psychology Today*

ASSIGNMENT: First generate a list of your strengths, including (1) skills, (2) abilities, (3) accomplishments, and (4) ambitions. Then write a statement claiming how you would add value to the company you are interested in, based on these qualities. Next identify an experience or event that demonstrates that you have these qualities and that you could tell in a paragraph. Finally, write your "story" in a paragraph, using what you know about narration. Be sure to include your statement of added value.

PROFILE OF SUCCESS

Valeria Edwards

Writing did not come easy to Valeria Edwards. She became a better writer through the developmental writing courses she took at Forsyth Technical Institute.

As assistant principal at the Bolton Elementary School in North Carolina, Valeria uses narration in her job every day, both in writing and in speech. In 1989, Valeria won the Outstanding Alumni Award given annually by the National Association for Developmental Education (NADE).

COLLEGES: Forsyth Technical Institute, Winston-Salem State University, North Carolina Agricultural and Technical State University

EMPLOYER: Winston-Salem/Forsyth County (North Carolina) Schools

POSITION: Assistant principal (K–5)

MAJOR JOB RESPONSIBILITIES: Edit and publish newsletter; advise volunteers; observe and evaluate faculty and staff; coordinate intersession programs

TYPES OF WRITING REQUIRED: Weekly newsletter to parents informing them of activities and events; write student handbook with rules, regulations, procedures; write memos to staff, parents, and colleagues

PROUDEST ACHIEVEMENT: Receiving the NADE Outstanding Alumni Award in 1989 and the first-ever Distinguished Alumni Award from Forsyth Technical Institute in 1996

BEST PIECE OF ADVICE I EVER RECEIVED: When I graduated from high school I had no plans to attend college, nor could I afford it. With the encouragement of friends, I enrolled, but things got tough fast. My adviser said to me, "Don't give up." I took her advice and not only finished community college but went on to get a bachelor's degree.

BEST PIECE OF ADVICE I CAN GIVE: Believe in yourself. Don't get bent out of shape, fall to pieces, or feel hurt when things don't go as you expect. We aren't perfect, but we can strive for excellence.

Summary: Narration

IDEA JOURNAL
Reread your journal entry on something that happened to you today (p. 76). Make another entry, either about the same experience or about another one. This time, use what you know about narration to tell the story.

- **Narration** is writing that tells a story. (See p. 75.)
- **Good narration** reveals something of importance, includes all the events of the story, brings the story to life with details, and presents events in a logical order (usually time order). (See p. 75.)
- The **topic sentence** introduces the story and gives the reader a preview of what's important about it. (See p. 76.)

What Will You Use?

Give some examples of how you will use narration in your own life.

9

Description

Paragraphs That Create Pictures in Words

Gary Knoblock, Police Officer

PROFILE OF SUCCESS

Gary Knoblock

WRITING THEN: "A teacher in high school had been pretty down on me. She told me that I wasn't going to amount to much. I didn't understand a lot of things, and I didn't know how to ask the questions I needed to ask. I had pretty poor grammar skills in the beginning, so I took some remedial courses. I had a poor opinion of the way I wrote."

WRITING NOW: "One part of my job is to take statements from suspects and witnesses. Based on the detailed questions I ask in the interviews, I write descriptions of people and places involved in crimes. The more detailed these descriptions are, the more likely we are to break the case."

(For more about Gary Knoblock, see p. 105.)

Understand What Description Is

Description is writing that creates a clear and vivid impression of the topic. Description translates your experience of a person, place, or thing into words, often by appealing to the physical senses: sight, hearing, smell, taste, touch.

GOOD DESCRIPTION

- Creates a single main impression about the topic. The main impression is the overall effect, feeling, or image you want to create about your topic.
- Uses concrete, specific details to support the main impression.
- Uses details that appeal to the five senses: sight, hearing, smell, taste, touch.

95

IDEA JOURNAL
Describe your dream job
or your dream home.

SAMPLE DESCRIPTION PARAGRAPH

   A green guava is sour and hard. You bite into it at its widest point, because it's easier to grasp with your teeth. You hear the skin, meat, and seeds crunching inside your head, while the inside of your mouth explodes in little spurts of sour. You grimace, your eyes water, and your cheeks disappear as your lips purse into a tight O. But you have another and another, enjoying the crunchy sounds, the acid taste, the gritty texture of the unripe center.

—Esmeralda Santiago, When I Was Puerto Rican

YOU KNOW THIS
You use description in
various ways every day.
For example:
• When you describe
  what someone looks
  like
• When you describe
  something you want to
  buy or sell
• When you describe
  where you want some-
  one to meet you

1. What is the main impression about the topic? <u>*sour, hard*</u>

2. Underline the <u>details</u> that support the main impression.

3. What senses do the details appeal to? <u>*taste, sound, sight*</u>

Write a Description Paragraph

RESOURCES
For a discussion of how
to use the profiles in Part
Two, see *Practical
Suggestions.*

   The keys to good description are **choosing a clear main impression** and **using vivid details** that create the image for your readers. Sensory details—details that are related to the five senses of sight, hearing, smell, taste, and touch—are necessary for effective description. Choose a topic that you have observed firsthand so you can come up with details about it.

   In this section, you will write your own description paragraph. Before you begin, you can analyze the structure of a description paragraph and practice the key steps to writing one.

Analyze a Description Paragraph

ESL
You may need to define
"looker" for ESL students.

   Amy was a looker; I privately thought that she was the most beautiful child on earth. She inherited our father's thick, wavy hair. Her eyes were big, and so were her lashes; her nose was delicate and fluted, her skin translucent. Her mouth curved quaintly; her lips fitted appealingly, as a cutter's bow dents and curls the water under way. Plus she was quiet. And little, and tidy, and calm, and more or less obedient. She had an endearing way—it attracted even me—of standing with her legs tight together, and peering up and around with wild, stifled hilarity and . . . curiosity, as if to see if—by chance—anybody has noticed small her and found her amusing.

—Annie Dillard, An American Childhood

READING SELECTIONS
For examples of and ac-
tivities for description essays, see Chapter 44.

DISCUSSION
Bring in a noisemaker of some sort. While students close their eyes, make the noise. Repeat. Ask students to open their eyes and write a description of the noise. Call on students to read what they wrote.

1. Annotate the paragraph to highlight its structure:

   • Double-underline the <u>topic sentence</u>.

   • Underline the <u>details</u> that help create an image.

   • Circle the (transitions.)

2. What is the main impression about Amy? <u>*Amy is beautiful.*</u>

   _____

3. The **topic sentence** of a description paragraph usually includes the topic and conveys the main impression.

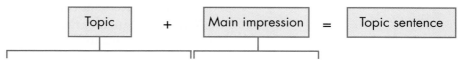

   My English professor's office is a complete mess.

   Fill in the blanks with the topic and the main impression for the sample paragraph:

Topic	=	*Amy*
Main impression	=	*beautiful*

COMPUTER
Have students select a classmate or a well-known place on campus and, using the computer, write descriptive terms about the person or place (without naming it). Have students move to another computer, read the other student's description, and try to guess who or what the subject is. If students can't guess, the original writer should add more description. (EG)

4. The **support** in a description paragraph is the details that contribute to the main impression. They are often details that appeal to the senses of sight, hearing, smell, taste, and touch. What sense or senses do the details in the sample paragraph appeal to?

   sight
   _____

   List one detail from the paragraph for the sense or senses you listed.

   Answers will vary.
   _____

5. Description usually uses **space order:** The description starts on one side and moves to another, or starts at the back and moves to the front, and so on. How does the sample paragraph move (where does it start and where does it end)?

   It starts at the top of Amy and moves to the bottom.
   _____

TIP: For more on space order and space transitions or on outlining, see Chapter 5.

RESOURCES
A reproducible form containing a diagram students can use to plan their definition essays is in *Additional Resources*, which also contains a complete Guided Practice for this chapter, with worked-out examples and exercises for each step.

Key Step:
Convey a Main Impression in a Topic Sentence

Find a Main Impression.

A main impression is the overall feeling, effect, or image created by a description. Every good description has a main impression—and all the details in the description help to create it.

Thinking Critically to Find a Main Impression

FOCUS   Think about your topic and what its most intense quality is.

ASK
- What do I think of first when I think of this topic? What are the first words that come to mind about it?
- What is the quality that best characterizes the topic for me?
- What do I want my readers to think about my topic?
- Can I write a paragraph about that quality?
- Can I think of sensory details that create that quality?

WRITE   Write your main impression next to your topic.

Practice 1 ▶   Finding a Main Impression

For the following items, jot down five impressions that appeal to you and circle the one you would use as a main impression. Use the Thinking Critically guide on this page. Example:

Topic: A fire in the fireplace

IMPRESSIONS: *(cozy,) warm, comforting, smells good, bright*

1. Topic: a movie theater lobby

   IMPRESSIONS: *Answers will vary.* _____

2. Topic: a fireworks display

   IMPRESSIONS: _____

3. Topic: a pizza place

   IMPRESSIONS: _____

4. Topic: an old person

   IMPRESSIONS: _____

TIP: For a review of the Three-Question Test for Good Topics, see Chapter 2.

5. Topic: the room you're in

IMPRESSIONS: _____

Write a Topic Sentence.

Your topic sentence should include your topic and the main impression you want to convey about it. Try starting with this basic formula:

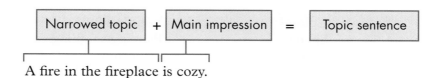

A fire in the fireplace is cozy.

Practice 2 ▶ Writing a Topic Sentence

TIP: When you have the basic topic sentence, revise it to make it sharper and more specific. Use a dictionary or a thesaurus to find words that are more specific and descriptive.
• A fire in the fireplace is cozy.
• A fire in the fireplace makes the atmosphere in the room cozy and safe.

Choose three of the items from Practice 1 to use in this practice. In the spaces, write the topic, the main impression you chose, and a topic sentence. Then revise the topic sentence to make the main impression sharper and more specific. Example:

TOPIC / MAIN IMPRESSION: *a fire in the fireplace / cozy* _____

TOPIC SENTENCE: *A fire in the fireplace is cozy.* _____

REVISED: *A fire in the fireplace fills the room with coziness.* _____

1. **TOPIC / MAIN IMPRESSION:** *Answers will vary.* _____ / _____

    TOPIC SENTENCE: _____

    REVISED: _____

2. **TOPIC / MAIN IMPRESSION:** _____ / _____

    TOPIC SENTENCE: _____

    REVISED: _____

3. **TOPIC / MAIN IMPRESSION:** _____ / _____

    TOPIC SENTENCE: _____

    REVISED: _____

TIP: For a review of prewriting techniques, see Chapter 2.

Key Step: Support Your Main Impression with Sensory Details

Good description uses specific details that appeal to one or more of the five senses: sight, hearing, smell, taste, and touch. Your description should *show* your readers what you mean, not just *tell* them. Sensory details can bring your description alive. Here are some things to consider as you develop some sensory details to support your main impression.

TEAMWORK
Put students in small groups and give each group an object to describe using the questions in the text.

SIGHT
Colors?
Shapes?
Sizes?
Patterns?
Shiny/dull?
Does it look like
  anything else?

SOUND
Loud/soft?
Piercing/soothing?
Continuous/
  off-and-on?
Pleasant/unpleasant?
  (how?)
Does it sound like
  anything else?

SMELL
Sweet/sour?
Sharp/mild?
Good? (like what?)
Bad? (rotten?)
New? (new what?
  leather? plastic?)
Old?
Does it smell like
  anything else?

TASTE
Good? (What does
  good taste like?)
Bad? (What does bad
  taste like?)
Bitter/sugary?
  metallic?
Burning? spicy?
Does it taste like
  anything else?

TOUCH
Hard/soft?
Liquid/solid?
Rough/smooth?
Hot/cold?
Dry/oily?
Textures?
Does it feel like
  anything else?

Thinking Critically to Support Your Main Impression with Sensory Details

DISCUSSION
Read the Thinking Critically questions aloud and discuss how to "supercharge" the main impression.

FOCUS   Reread your topic sentence and think about the last time you observed your narrowed topic.

ASK
- What does this thing look like? sound like? smell like? feel like? taste like?
- Which details are needed to get my main impression across to my readers?
- Which details will appeal to my readers?
- Should any minor details be combined?
- What can I do to "supercharge" these details? How can I make them stronger and more convincing?
- Will my readers get a good sense of what I mean from these details?

WRITE   List the concrete, specific details you will use.

| Practice 3 | ▶ | Finding Details to Support a Main Impression |

TEAMWORK
This practice works well in small groups. Assign it at the end of a class period and ask for responses during the next class.

Read the topic sentences and write five sensory details you might use as support for the main impression. Example:

Even at night, New York City echoes with noise.

a. *police and fire sirens*

b. *garbage trucks*

c. *jackhammers*

d. *laughter of people coming home from clubs*

e. *car horns*

Answers will vary.

COMPUTER
Have students write one sensory detail on their screen and then move to the next computer and write another, and so on until all items are complete.

1. My favorite meal smells as good as it tastes.

a. *Possible answers: sweetness of sweet potatoes*

b. *sage in stuffing*

c. *buttery roasting turkey*

d. *sharp, tangy roasting onions*

e. *cinnamon apple pie*

2. The new office building has a very contemporary look.

a. *Possible answers: lots of glass*

b. *concrete*

c. *steel*

d. *tall*

e. *lots of angles*

3. A classroom during an exam echoes with the "sounds of silence."

a. *Possible answers: people coughing*

b. *rustle of papers*

c. _____ *radiator hissing*

d. _____ *sound of pens scratching paper*

e. _____ *lights buzzing*

4. The dog standing in the middle of the road looked mean and threatening.

a. _____ *Possible answers: foaming at mouth*

b. _____ *teeth bared*

c. _____ *scarred body*

d. _____ *missing an ear*

e. _____ *other ear standing up*

5. The person sitting next to me is very obviously sick.

a. _____ *Possible answers: sneezing*

b. _____ *coughing*

c. _____ *face flushed with fever*

d. _____ *watery eyes*

e. _____ *blowing nose*

TIP: Look back at your idea journal entry (p. 96) for something you might want to describe.

Description Assignment

Choose one of the following general topics or one of your own to write about.

COLLEGE
- A classmate or a teacher
- The bookstore
- A classroom
- The main area of the student union

WORK
- A co-worker or a boss
- A particular area at work
- An office at work
- Your own work space

EVERYDAY LIFE
- A relative or friend
- A room in your home
- A season
- Your favorite piece of clothing

ESL
Have students describe a famous place in their countries or a favorite ethnic meal.

Checklist: How to Write Description

RESOURCES
All paragraph chapters have Checklists. They are also in reproducible form in *Additional Resources*. Copy and distribute the form if you want students to check off the steps as they go and hand in the Checklist with their draft or revision.

Check off items as you complete them.

1.   Narrow and explore your topic (the thing you will describe).

_____   Narrow the general topic to something that interests you and that you have observed directly. Jot down a few ideas you have about the narrowed topic.

_____   Consider your purpose for describing this topic. What main quality do you want your readers to learn about the topic?

2.   KEY STEP: Convey your main impression in a topic sentence. (See p. 98.)

_____   Review your ideas and decide what main impression you want to create about your topic.

_____   Write a topic sentence that includes your narrowed topic and main impression.

3.   KEY STEP: Support your main impression with sensory details. (See p. 100.)

_____   Use a prewriting technique to come up with concrete, sensory details (sight, hearing, smell, taste, touch) that will support your main impression and make the topic come alive for your readers.

_____   Drop details that don't support the main impression, and select those that do.

_____   Add information to make the details more vivid and concrete.

4.   Write a draft.

_____   Arrange the details in a logical order (probably space order) and make a plan.

_____   Write a draft paragraph using complete sentences in correct paragraph form.

_____   Write a concluding sentence that relates back to the main impression, emphasizing it one last time for your readers.

_____   Title the paragraph, if required.

5.   Revise your draft.

_____   Get feedback from others.

_____   Cut any details that do not support your main point or help show readers what you mean.

(continued)

_____ Add any sensory details that will make your paragraph stronger.

_____ Make sure the order of details is logical. Add transitions to make the paragraph easy to follow (especially space transitions).

_____ Do not just copy over your draft. Make changes to improve it.

6.   Edit your revised draft.

_____ Find and correct any problems with grammar, spelling, word use, or punctuation.

_____ Produce a clean, final copy.

_____ Ask yourself: Is this the best I can do?

Use Description in Real-World Situations

TEACHING TIP
As an additional assignment, have students create a profile of someone they know who is "together" (has steady job). They should model their profile on the Knoblock profile. Say you'll be sending some to the publisher for the next edition of the book (and please do!). Encourage students to get a picture as well.

RESOURCES
For an additional real-world assignment for this chapter, see *Additional Resources*.

TEACHING TIP
For a model interview for this assignment, see *Practical Suggestions*.

Description and the ability to probe for details are useful not only in school but also in other settings. Some descriptions rely less on sensory details and more on other concrete and specific kinds of details. For example, a good job description will include specific details about what the job is, what skills it requires, what responsibilities it includes, and what experience it requires. It may also give details about salary range and other benefits. Although it does not use sensory details, it does rely on other specific details.

In most areas of your life, you will have occasion to write description, using specific, concrete details.

COLLEGE
• On a nursing test, you describe symptoms observed in a patient.

WORK
• You write a memo to your boss describing how the office could be arranged for increased efficiency.

EVERYDAY LIFE
• You must describe something you lost to the lost-and-found clerk at a department store.

Real-World Assignment: An Information Interview

SITUATION: A good job search strategy is to arrange "information interviews" with people who have jobs you might be interested in. Even very busy people are often willing to give you half an hour for an information interview. In return, they expect you to come prepared with questions they can respond to. The interview will be useful to you only if you get detailed information that you can *use* to get a job or decide on a career path.

Both conducting an interview and writing a description require the same key skill: the ability to probe for specific details. You have written a description by discovering and developing specific details; now you can apply that critical skill to conducting an interview.

ASSIGNMENT: Interview a classmate, a friend, or someone you know to get information about the job that person has (or has had recently). You will write a brief description of the job based on your interview.

Before the interview, prepare a list of questions. What information do you want to get? Use both closed and open questions.

CLOSED QUESTIONS: Require one- or two-word answers only

EXAMPLE: How long have you worked here?

OPEN QUESTIONS: Require more detailed answers

EXAMPLE: Describe an average day on the job.

Prepare an interview guide with five to ten questions. Leave space for notes about the person's responses and for additional questions that occur to you during the interview.

After the interview, follow what you have learned about description to write a job description based on your interview.

PROFILE OF SUCCESS

Gary Knoblock

Gary Knoblock was not always a good writer. However, he took courses to improve his writing, and he now writes very well. As part of his job as a police officer, Gary Knoblock often has to interview witnesses and suspects and then write a brief description based on the information he has gathered.

COLLEGE: Tarrant County (Texas) Junior College

EMPLOYER: Fort Worth Police Department

POSITION: Gang Intelligence Officer

MAJOR JOB RESPONSIBILITIES: Taking statements and depositions from suspects and witnesses; developing intelligence of newly formed and established street gangs; providing intelligence to other police agencies; identifying emerging organized crime trends; maintaining a central information base

TYPES OF WRITING REQUIRED: Writing up interviews with suspects and witnesses; preparing search and arrest warrants that flow in a logical sequence and establish probable cause; writing detailed intelligence reports that demonstrate emerging trends in the Dallas–Fort Worth metroplex; preparing criminal cases for prosecution

PROUDEST ACHIEVEMENTS: Receiving the Medal of Valor; winning the Tarrant County Junior College's Distinguished Student Scholarship

BEST ADVICE I EVER RECEIVED: What you put into something is exactly what you get out of it; no more, no less.

BEST ADVICE I CAN GIVE: Go beyond your limits from time to time. People limit themselves by believing they can't do things.

Note: Gary has received another promotion in the Fort Worth Police Department, where he is now a member of the Special Weapons and Tactics (SWAT) unit.

Summary: Description

IDEA JOURNAL
Reread your entry on the dream job or dream home (p. 96). Write another entry on the same topic using what you have learned about good description to improve your writing.

- **Description** is writing that creates an image with words. (See p. 95.)
- **Good description** creates a single main impression; uses concrete, specific details; and uses details that appeal to the five senses—sight, hearing, smell, taste, and touch. (See p. 95.)
- The **topic sentence** in a description paragraph introduces the topic and conveys the main impression about it. (See p. 97.)

What Will You Use?

List some ways that you might use description in your life.

Process Analysis

Paragraphs That Explain How Things Happen

Jill Lee, Coordinator of Career Services

Jill Lee

WRITING THEN: "I didn't have confidence in myself or in my writing. I never thought I'd have a job where I'd have to write."

WRITING NOW: "I do a lot of writing, like guides to writing résumés or letters and memos. People like the guides to practical skills; they are short, 'how to' pieces that help students in their careers."

(For more about Jill Lee, see p. 118.)

Understand What Process Analysis Is

Process analysis either explains how to do something (so your readers can do it) or explains how something works (so your readers can understand it). Both types of process analysis explain by presenting the steps involved in the process.

GOOD PROCESS ANALYSIS

- Either helps readers perform the steps themselves or helps them understand how something works
- Presents the essential steps in the process
- Explains the steps in detail
- Presents the steps in a logical order (usually time order)

RESOURCES
For a discussion of how to use the profiles in Part Two, see *Practical Suggestions.*

TEACHING TIP
Read the paragraph aloud (or choose a student to read) and give students a couple of minutes to respond to the questions. Then discuss the answers as a group.

READING SELECTIONS
For examples of and activities for process analysis essays, see Chapter 45.

IDEA JOURNAL
Write about something you recently learned how to do—and how you do it.

SAMPLE PROCESS ANALYSIS PARAGRAPH

A microwave oven cooks food with a powerful device called a magnetron. First the magnetron sends out microwaves, magnetic waves ①   that in length are between infrared and short-wave radio wavelengths. When these microwaves connect with food, they make the tiny water ②   particles in food move around. As the unevenly shaped particles rub against each other, the rubbing action produces friction. That friction ③   then produces heat, just as when you rub your hands together quickly to ④   warm them. Cooking then takes place by heating up the water either on ⑤   the surface of foods or inside them. The microwave doesn't brown food; it steams it. Food is "zapped" by the tiny magnetron.

—Adapted from *How Things Work*

1. What is the process being analyzed? *how a microwave oven cooks*
    food

2. Does this paragraph tell how to do something or explain how somethings works? *explains how something works*

3. Underline and number the steps.   *Number of steps may vary.*

Write a Process Analysis Paragraph

The key to good process analysis is presenting the essential steps in detail and in a logical order.

In this section, you will write your own process analysis paragraph. Before you begin, you can analyze the structure of a process analysis paragraph and practice the key steps to writing one.

Analyze a Process Analysis Paragraph

To remember what you read, pay attention to what you are doing, and why. Before beginning, think about what you need and gather it to- ①   gether. Get your reading material, along with a pen, some paper, a highlighter, glasses if you wear them, and whatever you might want to drink or eat. Otherwise, you will keep finding excuses to stop reading and go get something you need. Once you have everything together,

remind yourself of why you are reading so that you will focus on what ②
is important. Are you reading for a class discussion? for a test? to give a
report? to summarize for someone else? What, specifically, do you need
to do with what you are reading? Next preview the material quickly, ③
looking at major headings, material in boxes, and pictures. Now you
are ready to read—actively. Don't just sit there: Pay attention; do
something. Highlight important points, make notes, ask yourself ques- ④
tions. When you have finished, go back and review what you have read, ⑤
looking at important points and making additional notes to yourself. If
there is a summary in the book, see if it matches what you got from
what you read. Finally, test yourself: Do you remember? If you don't ⑥
pay attention to what you read and how you read it, you may find that
you turn the last page without remembering anything.

1. Annotate the paragraph to highlight its structure:

    • Double-underline the topic sentence.

    • Underline each step in the process.

    • Circle the transitions.

2. Is this a paragraph that tells how to do something or a paragraph that
    explains how something works? *tells how to do something*

    What is the process being analyzed? (What should you be able to do
    after reading the paragraph?) *how to read effectively*

3. The **topic sentence** of a process analysis paragraph usually includes
    the process being analyzed and the point the writer wants to make
    about it.

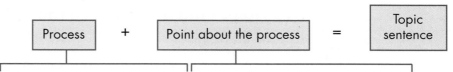

Applying for a driver's license is time-consuming and exhausting.

Fill in the blanks with the process and the point from the sample paragraph.

Process	=	_reading_

Point about process	=	_paying attention will help you remember_

4. The **support** in a process analysis paragraph is a series of steps. The steps tell readers how to do the process or how the process takes place. How many steps are in the sample paragraph?

   6 (Number may vary.)

TIP: If you have written a narration paragraph already, you will notice that narration and process analysis are alike in that they both depend on presenting incidents or steps in time order—the order in which they occur. The difference is that narration reports what happened while process analysis describes how to do something or how something works.

5. Process analysis paragraphs usually use **time order:** the first step in the process is described first, and so on. They use **time transitions** to guide readers from one step to the next:

   COMMON TIME TRANSITIONS

after	eventually	meanwhile	soon
as	finally	next	then
at last	first	now	when
before	last	second	while
during	later	since	

   List some of the transitions the writer used in the sample paragraph:
   Before, Otherwise, Once, Next, Now, When, Finally

6. Review the **steps** in the sample paragraph. Do you think the writer has left out anything essential? If so, what?

   Answers will vary.

7. What **details** does the writer use for the first step?

   examples—reading material, pen, paper, highlighter,

   glasses, food and drink

Key Step: Find and Choose the Essential Steps in the Process

To perform or understand a process, your readers must know all of the essential steps. Because you are describing a process that you are familiar with, you may not think about each individual step. For example, as you tie your shoe, you probably aren't aware of the steps involved; you just do them. As you describe a process, you need to think carefully about what the individual steps are so that you do not leave out any essential ones.

TIP: For a review of supporting a main idea with examples, see Chapter 4.

Thinking Critically to Find and Choose the Essential Steps

FOCUS	Reread your topic sentence and any prewriting you've done. Think about your readers and what you need to explain so they can either perform or understand the process.
ASK	• Exactly how is this process performed? What are the essential steps? • What steps do my readers need to know to perform or understand the process? • How much detail do I need to give about each step? What are good examples of the steps? • Have I left any essential steps out? • Will my readers understand the process based on the steps I've chosen?
WRITE	List the steps and the supporting details you'll use.

Practice 1 ▷ Supplying Missing Steps

In each of the following process analysis paragraphs, an essential step is missing. In real life, the writer would naturally do that essential step, but he or she left it out of the paragraph.

Either by yourself, with a partner, or in a small group, supply the missing step in each paragraph. Indicate with a caret sign (∧) where it should appear in the paragraph.

Placement of carets may vary.

1. Getting myself ready for work in the morning is a mad dash. First I shut off the alarm clock and drag myself out of bed. I turn on the shower and splash cold water on my face while waiting for the shower to get hot. Then I jump into the shower for a quick shampoo and lather up with soap. After rinsing myself off and shutting off the water, I grab for the towel and dry myself off.∧ Blow-drying my hair takes just two minutes. Then I go down to the kitchen for coffee that my roommate has already made. I gulp down one cup at the table and then walk around with a second one, gathering up what I need to take with me to work. After running a comb through my hair, I'm out the door. I run down to my bus stop and off to another fast-paced day. From beginning to end, the whole process takes only twenty minutes.

WHAT'S MISSING?   *getting dressed*

2. Anyone can make cake from a packaged cake mix. First get the package and read the directions. Then assemble the ingredients you will need to add. These usually include water, eggs, and sometimes oil. If the instructions say so, grease the cake pan or pans you will use to bake the cake. Next mix the ingredients together in a bowl, and stir or beat as directed. Then transfer the batter into the right-sized cake pans. Put the pans into the oven and set the timer for the baking time indicated. It's hard to go wrong.

WHAT'S MISSING? _*turning on the oven*_ _____

Practice 2 ▶ **Finding and Choosing the Essential Steps**

TEAMWORK
This practice works well as a small-group assignment. As an extension, have groups choose a similarly familiar process and list all the steps involved in it. Then have them choose one step to leave out. Groups can exchange papers and fill in the missing steps. You might also want the paragraphs to be read aloud so students can listen for the missing steps.

For each of the topic sentences, write the essential steps in the order you would perform them.

1. To operate the washing machine, follow the directions.

    _____

    _____

    _____

    _____

2. Writing a good paragraph isn't hard if you follow the right steps.

    _____

    _____

    _____

    _____

3. I think I could teach anyone how to _____ .

    _____

    _____

    _____

    _____

TIP: For a review of out-lining, see Chapter 5.

Key Step: Arrange the Steps in a Logical Order

When you are describing a process, most often you will arrange the steps according to time: what should be done first, second, next, and so on. When you are writing a process analysis paragraph, review the steps you have chosen to make sure that they are arranged in a logical time sequence.

Thinking Critically to Arrange the Steps in a Process

FOCUS	Reread your topic sentence and steps. Think about the best order for presenting the steps.
ASK	• What happens first? What next? What comes after that? • What time transitions can I use to emphasize when each step happens? • Now that I have an order, are there any gaps that need to be filled?
WRITE	Make an outline with your steps arranged in time order.

Practice 3 ▶ Arranging Steps in Time Order

TEAMWORK
This practice works well as a group activity.

COMPUTER
Have students type all three topic sentences and the first step for one of them. Then have them move to the next computer and add another step, continuing to move and add until the practice is completed. Read some finished answers aloud. Have the class listen for any missing steps and offer suggestions.

The steps following each topic sentence are out of order. Number the steps according to time sequence, 1 for the earliest and so on. There may be more than one correct order.

Answers may vary.

1. It is faster to use an automatic teller machine (ATM) to get cash than to wait for a human teller.

    _3_ Push the button next to "withdraw"

    _1_ Insert ATM card into machine

    _7_ Count the money to make sure the amount is correct

    _2_ Punch in personal identification number (PIN) or password

    _8_ Take your card and your receipt

    _6_ Collect the cash from the drawer

    _4_ Tell the machine what account to make the withdrawal from

    _5_ Enter the amount of cash you want

PARAGRAPHS

ESL
Ask students if they have had any experiences where the order of steps in a process is different in one place or culture than in another. Give an experience of your own as an example (if only something like traffic conventions that are different from one city to the next).

2. To choose the course(s) you will take next semester, just follow a few simple steps.

1 ____ Get the current course catalog

5 ____ Decide which courses match your schedule

3 ____ Decide what courses you need most

2 ____ Pick up a course schedule

4 ____ Find times of the courses you want

6 ____ Make a list of the courses

3. All pay phones work the same way.

3 ____ Insert the right amount of change

2 ____ Listen for a dial tone

1 ____ Pick up the receiver

4 ____ Listen for another dial tone

5 ____ Dial the number and wait

4. If you follow these few steps, you should have no trouble recording a welcome message on your phone machine.

4 ____ Press the "record message" button

1 ____ Read the directions in the manual

2 ____ Write out what you want to say

5 ____ Say your message into the machine speaker

3 ____ Make sure the tape is in the machine

COMPUTER
Have small groups of students list the steps in a process that you supply (a different one for each group). Ask each group to type the steps on the screen in paragraph form, but out of order. Groups should then move to another screen and unscramble the steps, moving them so that they are in the right order, still in paragraph form.

5. Everyone should know how to use a checkbook register to keep track of the money in a checking account.

4 ____ Write the new balance in the next space

1 ____ Record the number of the check, the date, and the payee

2 ____ Write the amount of the check in the right column

5 ____ Check against the bank statement to make sure there are no mistakes

3 ____ Subtract it from the balance in the account

TIP: Look back at your idea journal entry (p. 108) for ideas to write about.

ESL
Suggest that students write about a process that they used in their native country or culture but don't use where they live now.

COMPUTER
Have students write about how to do something on a computer (open programs, highlight, delete, underline, and so on). Read some of the finished paragraphs aloud to compare the steps.

DISCUSSION
Ask students for other examples of how they might use process analysis.

Process Analysis Assignment

Write a process analysis paragraph on one of the following general topics or one of your own. You can decide whether you want to teach your readers how to do something or simply explain how something works. Use the Checklist on this page to write your paragraph.

COLLEGE: HOW TO
- Study (for an exam and so on)
- Apply for something (financial aid, admission, and so on)
- Use a library (find a book, find a magazine article)
- Use a computer (use a spell checker, open up a word processing program, save what you have done, and so on)

WORK: HOW TO
- Do something you do regularly as part of your job
- Use a piece of equipment
- Prepare for a job interview
- Ask for a raise

EVERYDAY LIFE: HOW TO
- Make something (coffee, food, a decoration, a sign, and so on)
- Build something
- Apply for something (a credit card, a loan, an apartment, and so on)
- Improve your health (reduce stress, play a sport, and so on)

Checklist: How to Write Process Analysis

Check off items as you complete them.

1. **Narrow and explore your topic** (the process you will analyze).

   ____ Narrow the general topic to a specific process that you know about, are interested in, and can describe in a paragraph. Jot down a few ideas about the narrowed topic.

   ____ Consider your purpose for describing this process: Do you want to teach your readers how to do it themselves? Do you want to give your readers an idea of how it happens?

   (continued)

RESOURCES
A reproducible copy of this Checklist for a process analysis paragraph is in *Additional Resources.* Copy and distribute this version if you want students to hand in the completed Checklist with their paper.

2.   **Make your point in a topic sentence.**

_____   Decide what you want to say about the process you are analyzing.

_____   Write a topic sentence that includes the process you are analyzing and the point you want to make about it.

3.   KEY STEP: **Choose the essential steps in the process.** (See p. 110.)

_____   Use a prewriting technique to find all the steps you can think of.

_____   Drop any steps that are not important to the process. Choose steps that are necessary for the reader to perform the process or to understand how it works.

_____   Add details to make the steps more concrete, specific, and easy to follow.

4.   KEY STEP: **Arrange the steps in a logical order and write a draft.** (See p. 113.)

_____   Arrange the steps in time order and make a plan, using the topic sentence as the first sentence.

_____   Write a draft paragraph, using complete sentences and correct paragraph form.

_____   Write a concluding sentence that reminds the reader of your main point about the process.

_____   Title the paragraph, if required.

5.   **Revise your draft.**

_____   Get feedback from others.

_____   Cut unnecessary steps and detours.

_____   Add any other steps that readers need to understand the process, and add detail to any steps that aren't clear.

_____   Make sure the sequence is logical; add time transitions where connections are unclear.

_____   Do not just copy over your draft. Make changes to improve it.

6.   **Edit your revised draft.**

_____   Find and correct any problems with grammar, spelling, word use, or punctuation.

_____   Produce a clean, final copy.

_____   Ask yourself: Is this the best I can do?

Use Process Analysis in Real-World Situations

Any time you give someone directions about how to do something or explain how something works, you are using process analysis. Here are some ways you might use process analysis.

COLLEGE

- In an automotive engineering course, you write out the procedures for installing a new muffler.
- In a science course, you explain how photosynthesis works.

WORK

- You write instructions for how to operate something (the copier, the fax machine).
- You write a memo to a co-worker explaining how to do one of your job responsibilities while you are on vacation.

EVERYDAY LIFE

- You give a friend directions to where you live.
- You write a recipe for a friend.

Real-World Assignment: Write a Memorandum

TEAMWORK
This assignment works well as a collaborative, small-group activity.

Memorandums (memos), a common means of communicating in the workplace, often present and describe a process. In this assignment, you will write a memo to your co-workers, at the request of your boss.

SITUATION: Your boss has asked you to participate in the training of a group of new employees. You're pleased since this is an opportunity to make a good impression on your boss.

RESOURCES
For an additional real-world assignment for this chapter, see *Additional Resources.*

ASSIGNMENT: Using the steps of writing a process analysis, write a memo giving instructions on how to do a specific task in your job (you can choose anything you know something about). Your audience will be the new employees, but your boss will also receive a copy of your memo. Generate the essential steps in the process. Write a memo, using the following guidelines and the Checklist on page 115.

IDEA JOURNAL
Reread your journal entry on how to do something you recently learned (p. 108). Make another entry on the same process, using what you have learned about process analysis. Assume you are teaching someone else this same process.

FORMAT FOR A MEMO

Date: [*Put today's date here*]

To: New Employees

From: [*Put your name here*]

Subject: Instructions on how to [name the process you are analyzing]

In the opening sentence, tell what process you are describing and why. Then list the essential steps either in paragraph form or in a bulleted list. In the concluding sentence, tell the new employees how to contact you if they have any questions.

Summary: Process Analysis

RESOURCES
For a discussion of how to use the profile, see *Practical Suggestions*.

NOTE
The National Association for Developmental Education (NADE) honors one outstanding alumnus or alumna of developmental education each year. For more information, see *Practical Suggestions*.

- **Process analysis** is writing that explains how to do something or how something works. (See p. 107.)
- **Good process analysis** presents all of the essential steps in the process, explains the steps in detail, and presents the steps in a logical order (usually time order). (See p. 107.)
- The **topic sentence** in a process analysis paragraph includes the process being analyzed and a point about that process. (See p. 109.)

What Will You Use?

List some situations in your life where you will use process analysis.

PROFILE OF SUCCESS

Jill Lee

Jill Lee always thought she was a terrible student and a terrible writer. In fact, when she was first accepted to college, she thought the college had made a mistake and worried that someone would find out and make her leave. She didn't know that the college had an open admissions policy that allowed any student to enroll who completed the application form.

In time Jill overcame her self-doubts and low self-esteem, completing not only her associate's degree but also going on to get a bachelor's and a master's degree. In 1993, Jill was the recipient of the NADE (National Association for Developmental Education) Outstanding Alumni Award.

In her job as coordinator of Career Services at the University of Toledo, Jill works closely with students to help them find and secure jobs. Although she never expected to have a job that required so much writing, through practice she has become good at writing. The kind of writing she does most often is process analysis — in student guides, such as how to write a résumé; in memos to faculty and business leaders about how they can improve career training for students, and in job descriptions.

COLLEGE: University of Toledo/Community and Technical College

MAJORS: Legal secretarial, gerontology and psychology, guidance and counseling education

DEGREES RECEIVED: Associate of applied business, bachelor of science, master of education

EMPLOYER: University of Toledo/Community and Technical College

POSITION: Coordinator of Career Services

MAJOR JOB RESPONSIBILITIES: Direct Career Services operations; market university programs, services, and graduates to local and national employers; assist students with employment

TYPES OF WRITING REQUIRED: Student résumés; annual reports; letters of recommendation; memos to professors and staff; job trend descriptions; presentation outlines; notes on student skills and interests

PROUDEST ACHIEVEMENT: Working as a professional at the very same institution that initially helped me to overcome my inadequacies.

BEST ADVICE I EVER RECEIVED: A person told me: "It's time to take the obstacles and barriers that life brings and turn them into stepping-stones." At a time in my life when I was feeling defeated and without purpose, those words gave me the incentive to start school.

BEST ADVICE I CAN GIVE: Know that you're not alone and never be afraid to ask for help from others. This means raising your hand to ask questions, going to faculty, and tapping into all the resources available to you.

11

Classification

Paragraphs That Put Things into Groups

Ignacio Murillo, Civil Engineer

PROFILE OF SUCCESS

Ignacio Murillo

WRITING THEN: "A writing assignment in college was always a burden to me. As a result, I procrastinated. I never thought that writing was going to be an integral part of the career I had chosen."

WRITING NOW: "Although people don't usually think of engineers as having to do any writing, my work requires a lot. For example, when field investigations are completed, I have to write a report that summarizes and explains the results. To explain the results, I often group them into categories that make sense to the client."

(For more about Ignacio Murillo, see p. 131.)

Understand What Classification Is

Classification is writing that organizes, or sorts, things into categories.

GOOD CLASSIFICATION

- Makes sense of things by organizing them into categories
- Uses useful categories
- Uses a single organizing principle
- Gives examples of what fits into each category

Imagine the following situation, where the classification does not follow these principles.

You walk into your college bookstore looking for a math textbook and expect to find it in the math textbook area, classified according to the subject area. Instead, the books on the shelves aren't classified in any way you can make sense of.

119

RESOURCES
For a discussion of how to use the profiles in Part Two, see *Practical Suggestions.*

IDEA JOURNAL
Write about the kinds of students in this class or the kinds of friends you have.

When you ask the sales clerk how to find the book, he says, "What color is it? The right half of the store has them arranged by color: blue over there, green in the middle, and so on. The left half of the store has them arranged by author."

You may never find your book because (1) the categories of organization (color and author) are not useful and (2) there is not a single organizing principle. Instead there are two: by color and by author. Even if you know the color, you still won't know whether you will find it in the color section; it might be in the author section. The following diagram shows how you would expect textbooks to be classified.

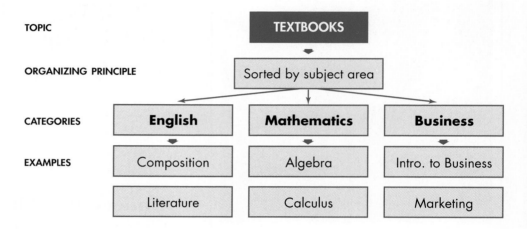

TOPIC — **TEXTBOOKS**

ORGANIZING PRINCIPLE — Sorted by subject area

CATEGORIES — **English**   **Mathematics**   **Business**

EXAMPLES — Composition / Literature   Algebra / Calculus   Intro. to Business / Marketing

READING SELECTIONS
For examples of and activities for classification essays, see Chapter 46.

The **organizing principle** is *how* you sort the group of things, not the categories themselves. Here is another example of classification.

SAMPLE CLASSIFICATION PARAGRAPH

Test questions generally fall into two categories: objective and subjective. Objective questions have a definite right and wrong answer. Multiple choice, matching, and fill in the blanks are objective questions. Although these can be tricky because of their wording, most students prefer objective questions, particularly multiple choice and matching. The answers are already there, and the student just has to choose the right ones. Subjective questions, such as short answer and essay, have no single correct answer: There is a range of possibilities. Students have to know the information requested by the questions and present it in their own words. For most people, the more concrete, objective questions are less intimidating than the subjective ones. You can make a lucky guess on an objective question, while the subjective question doesn't hold much hope for dumb luck.

YOU KNOW THIS
You have had experience classifying things. For example:
• You walk into a video store looking for a specific video. How are the videos arranged?
• You're packing to move and are surrounded by your possessions. How do you decide what to put in which box?
• You have just done a huge load of laundry. How do you sort it?

1. What is the topic (group of things) being classified? _test questions_

2. How many categories are there? What are they?

    2: objective, subjective

3. Underline the examples of things in each category.

Write a Classification Paragraph

TEACHING TIP
Read the paragraph aloud and give students a few minutes to respond to the questions. Then discuss the answers as a group.

The keys to good classification are **choosing useful categories** that all follow a single organizing principle and **giving examples** of things that fit into the categories.

In this section, you will write your own classification paragraph. Before you begin, you can analyze the structure of a classification paragraph and practice the key steps to writing one.

Analyze a Classification Paragraph

Attacking the stack of résumés that she had received in response to the job ad, the human resources manager sorted the applicants into three types. The first were the "No Ways." These were people who had no experience or none of the qualifications for the job. She could hand this stack off to her assistant, who would send brief but polite form letters telling the applicants they were not in the running. The second type was the "Definites," people who looked, at least on paper, like good candidates for the position. She would contact these people to set up interviews. The third type, with the most résumés in the stack, were the "Maybes." These applicants did not seem ideally qualified, but they would be worth considering if none of the "Definites" worked out.

RESOURCES
A reproducible form containing a diagram students can use to plan their classification essays is in *Additional Resources*, which also contains a complete Guided Practice for this chapter, with worked-out examples and exercises for each step.

1. Annotate the paragraph to highlight its structure:
    *   Double-underline the topic sentence.
    *   Underline the categories.
    *   Circle the transitions.
2. What is being sorted in this paragraph? _résumés_

3. The **topic sentence** of a classification paragraph usually includes the topic being classified and how it is being classified. Sometimes the categories themselves are named:

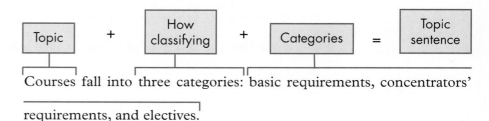

Courses fall into three categories: basic requirements, concentrators' requirements, and electives.

Fill in the blanks with the topic and the method of classifying for the sample paragraph.

Topic	=	*résumés*

How classified	=	*three types*

4. The **support** in a classification paragraph is a group of categories that all follow a single organizing principle. The categories help make sense of the topic for readers. What are the categories in the sample?

"No Ways," "Definites," "Maybes"

5. Classification paragraphs can use **time, space,** or **importance order.** Transitions move the reader from one category to another.

    COMMON CLASSIFICATION TRANSITIONS
    the first kind, the first type, the first group
    the second kind, the second type, the second group
    the third kind, the third type, the third group

List the transitions used in the sample paragraph. *The first, The second type, The third type*

6. Classification uses a single organizing principle to sort things. What organizing principle does the sample paragraph use?

Answers should have to do with strength of the applications.

7. What **examples** does the writer use for the first category?

people with no experience, people with no qualifications

| Practice 1 | Diagramming the Classification Paragraph |

TEACHING TIP
Some students may prefer a linear outline rather than this diagram. Give them the option of using a traditional outline format.

Fill in the following diagram for the sample paragraph on page 121.

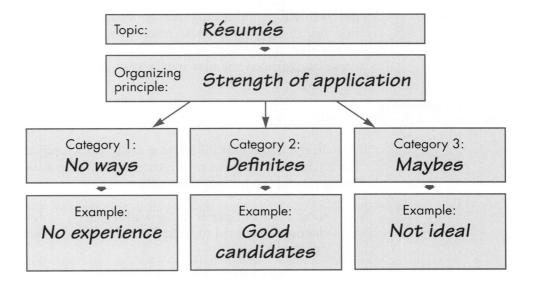

TIP: For a review of supporting a main idea with examples, see Chapter 4.

Key Step: Choose Useful Categories and Give Examples

The categories you choose for your classification paragraph will tell your readers how you are organizing your topic. First, you need to find useful categories. Second, you need to make sure all the categories follow a single organizing principle. Third, you need to supply examples for each category.

TEACHING TIP
Walk the students through this feature. Use a simple topic (stores in town or a local mall, clothing students are wearing, courses offered at the college) and demonstrate how you would classify it. Or break the class into small groups and give each group a topic. Have them work through the questions, writing responses. Then call on students from each group to tell what they did.

Thinking Critically to Find Categories and Examples

FOCUS	Think about your topic and how you might sort it.
ASK	• What is my purpose in sorting (classifying) the topic? What do I want to show my readers?
	• What categories would help me achieve that purpose?
	• What organizing principle do these categories follow?
	• What examples can I give of things that fit into the categories so that my readers will understand them? Will one example be enough, or do I need several to make the categories clear?
	• Have I overlooked any categories?
WRITE	Write a list of your categories with examples.

Find Useful Categories.

To classify or sort things in a logical way, you need to find the categories to put them into. For example, say you need to sort the stack of paper on your desk. Before making random piles, you decide what useful categories might be: things that can be thrown away; things you need to take action on; things you need to read; things that can be passed on to others; things that you've seen and that need to be filed; and so on. Deciding on these categories is the first step in classification.

Practice 2   Finding Useful Categories

In the items that follow, you are given a topic and a reason for sorting. For each item, list three useful categories (there are more than three correct categories for each item). Example:

TOPIC: Pieces of paper in my wallet   *Answers will vary.*
PURPOSE: To get rid of what I don't need   *Sample answers given.*
CATEGORIES:

a. *Things I need to keep in my wallet*

b. *Things I can throw away*

c. *Things I need to keep, but not in my wallet*

1. **TOPIC:** Animals in a pet shop
    PURPOSE: To decide what kind of pet to get
    CATEGORIES:

    a. *dogs*

    b. *birds*

    c. *fish*

2. **TOPIC:** College courses
    PURPOSE: To decide what I'll register for
    CATEGORIES:

    a. *English*

    b. *Accounting*

    c. *Math*

3. **TOPIC:** Stuff in my notebook
    PURPOSE: To organize my schoolwork
    CATEGORIES:

    a. _____ *homework* _____

    b. _____ *notes* _____

    c. _____ *doodles* _____

4. **TOPIC:** Wedding guests
    PURPOSE: To arrange seating at tables
    CATEGORIES:

    a. _____ *family members* _____

    b. _____ *neighbors* _____

    c. _____ *friends* _____

5. **TOPIC:** Clothing
    PURPOSE: To get rid of some clothes
    CATEGORIES:

    a. _____ *out of style* _____

    b. _____ *don't fit* _____

    c. _____ *good* _____

Make Sure Categories Follow the Same Organizing Principle.

Once you have useful categories, check to make sure that they follow the same organizing principle. Otherwise the classification may not be useful (like the bookstore with the two organizing principles).

Practice 3 ▶ **Eliminating the Misfit Category**

For each of the topics that follow, one of the categories does not fit the same organizing principle as the rest. Circle the letter of the category that does not fit, and write the organizing principle the rest follow in the space provided. See the example at the top of the next page.

DISCUSSION
You may need to discuss the idea of a single organizing principle. Remind students of the bookstore example (p. 119), and give another example in which two organizing principles used together prevent useful organization.

COMPUTER
Have students type in a topic (similar to the ones in Practice 3) and write one example of a category. Then have them move to the next computer and write another category that would fit that topic. Keep adding until each topic has five categories. Then have students return to their original computers and see if the categories all follow one organizing principle. Have students read the categories aloud and have the class decide whether they fit.

Answers may vary.

TOPIC: Shoes
CATEGORIES:
a.   Running
(b.) Leather
c.   Golf
d.   Bowling

ORGANIZING PRINCIPLE: By *activity*

1. **TOPIC:** Relatives
    CATEGORIES:
    a.   Aunts
    (b.) Uncles
    c.   Sisters
    d.   Mother

    ORGANIZING PRINCIPLE: By *female relatives*

2. **TOPIC:** Jobs
    CATEGORIES:
    a.   Weekly
    b.   Hourly
    c.   Monthly
    (d.) Summer

    ORGANIZING PRINCIPLE: By *pay period*

3. **TOPIC:** Animals
    CATEGORIES:
    a.   Dogs
    b.   Cats
    c.   Rabbits
    (d.) Whales

    ORGANIZING PRINCIPLE: By *pets; four legs*

4. **TOPIC:** Sports
    CATEGORIES:
    a.   Volleyball
    b.   Tennis
    (c.) Football
    d.   Badminton

    ORGANIZING PRINCIPLE: By *net sports*

TEAMWORK
Have small groups make up three more of these practice items and exchange with another group.

5. **TOPIC:** Consumer products
    CATEGORIES:

    (a.) Candy

    b.   Orange juice

    c.   Liquor

    d.   Milk

    ORGANIZING PRINCIPLE: By   *liquids, beverages*

Give Examples of Things That Fit in the Categories.

Your readers need specific examples of things that fit into each category. After you find useful categories, look for examples.

Practice 4 ▶ **Giving Examples**

TEAMWORK
This practice works well as a small-group activity.

In the spaces provided, give at least two examples of things that fit into the category. Example:

Answers will vary.

TOPIC: Pieces of paper in my wallet
PURPOSE: To get rid of what I don't need

a. Things I need to keep in my wallet

   EXAMPLES: *money, license, phone numbers*

b. Things I can throw away

   EXAMPLES: *ticket stubs, old receipts, old grocery lists*

c. Things I need to keep, but not in my wallet

   EXAMPLES: *bank receipts, addresses on slips of paper*

1. **TOPIC:** Animals in a pet shop
    PURPOSE: To decide what kind of pet to get

    a. dogs

       EXAMPLES: _____

    b. birds

       EXAMPLES: _____

c. fish

EXAMPLES: _____

2. **TOPIC:** College courses
PURPOSE: To decide what I'll register for

a. English

EXAMPLES: _____

b. Accounting

EXAMPLES: _____

c. Math

EXAMPLES: _____

3. **TOPIC:** Stuff in my notebook
PURPOSE: To organize my schoolwork

a. homework

EXAMPLES: _____

b. notes

EXAMPLES: _____

c. doodles

EXAMPLES: _____

TIP: Look back at your idea journal entry (p. 120) for ideas to write about.

Classification Assignment

Choose one of the following topics or one of your own to classify and write about in a paragraph. Use the Checklist on page 129 to write your paragraph.

COLLEGE

Types of . . .
- Teachers
- Courses offered
- Financial aid
- Students
- Degree/certificate programs

WORK

Types of . . .
- Bosses
- Things in a supply closet or room
- Workers/employees
- Work areas/spaces/offices
- Office technology

EVERYDAY LIFE

Types of . . .
- Monthly expenses
- Pets
- Drivers
- Friends
- Cars

Checklist: How to Write Classification

Check off items as you complete them.

1. **Narrow and explore your topic** (the thing or collection of things you will categorize).

____ Narrow the general topic to one that you are familiar with, can break into groups, and are interested in. Jot down a few ideas about the topic and possible categories.

____ Consider your purpose for classifying the topic: What do you want to show your readers?

2. **Make a point in a topic sentence.**

____ Review your ideas and decide how you want to sort your topic.

____ Write a topic sentence that includes your topic and how you are classifying (sorting) it. You may want to mention the categories in the topic sentence: *There are three types of lies: white lies, little lies, and big, bad lies.*

3. **KEY STEP: Choose useful categories and give examples.** (See p. 123.)

____ Use a prewriting technique to find possible categories into which you could sort your topic.

____ Drop categories that do not follow the organizing principle. Choose the most useful categories.

____ Find examples of things that fit into each category.

(continued)

4.   Write a draft.

_____   Decide on an order of presentation and make a plan, using the topic sentence as the first sentence.

_____   Write a draft paragraph, using complete sentences and correct paragraph form.

_____   Write a concluding sentence that reminds readers of your topic and makes an observation about the topic and the categories.

_____   Title the paragraph, if required.

5.   Revise your draft.

_____   Get feedback from others.

_____   Cut any categories that do not follow the one organizing principle you've chosen and any examples that do not fit their categories.

_____   Add transitions to let readers know you are moving from one category to another.

_____   Add any other necessary categories or examples.

_____   Do not just copy over your draft. Make changes to improve it.

6.   Edit your revised draft.

_____   Find and correct any problems with grammar, spelling, word use, or punctuation.

_____   Produce a clean, final copy.

_____   Ask yourself: Is this the best I can do?

Use Classification in Real-World Situations

You use classification any time you want to organize things. Here are some ways you might use classification.

COLLEGE   In a criminal justice course, you are asked to discuss the most common types of chronic offenders.

WORK   Your boss asks you to classify the kinds of products the company produces for a sales presentation.

EVERYDAY LIFE   You classify your typical monthly expenses to make a budget.

Real-World Assignment:
The Survey

A common way to gather information is to conduct a survey, either in person, by phone, by mail, or via the Internet. Surveys can be long and complicated, or they can consist of just one or two questions. In this assignment, your survey will consist of two questions, and you will organize the responses into categories.

SITUATION: The college has just set up an advisory board composed of representatives from the college and from local businesses. The chair of the board wants to know what kinds of jobs students have while they are in school. You have been asked to help gather the information.

ASSIGNMENT: Conduct a survey of five students on campus that asks these two questions: (1) Do you have a paying job? (2) If so, where, and what do you do? Classify the responses by the kinds of jobs students have (full-time, part-time, retail, manual, clerical—whatever categories make sense to you). Make sure that the categories follow a single organizing principle. For example, part-time and clerical are different: One is by the amount of time; the other is by the type of work. Using the survey responses, give examples for each category. Write a one-paragraph summary of the survey results, using the Checklist on page 129.

PROFILE OF SUCCESS

Ignacio Murillo

Ignacio Murillo, the first in his family to graduate from a four-year university, is a successful engineer who was president of an engineering society for two years in college and was elected Engineer of the Year during his senior year.

Ignacio once had trouble with writing, and he still doesn't think of himself as a good writer, although his written work on the job is consistently strong. He has to do a lot of writing, so he takes it seriously, works hard at it, and does it well.

COLLEGE: University of California, Irvine

MAJOR: Civil engineering

DEGREE RECEIVED: Bachelor of science

EMPLOYER: Montgomery Watson

POSITION: Associate civil engineer

MAJOR JOB RESPONSIBILITIES: Perform and organize environmental field investigation activities; review and interpret analytical results; assist project managers in completing reports and proposals

TYPES OF WRITING REQUIRED: Reports summarizing field investigations and results for clients and state and local agencies; proposal preparation; client and agency letters and memos; applications for city, state, and federal permits

PROUDEST ACHIEVEMENT: Completion of my college education after five arduous years

BEST ADVICE I EVER RECEIVED: Never sit in the back of the room. Instead, sit up front and make yourself known and heard. Apply this to both school and work.

BEST ADVICE I CAN GIVE: Don't be afraid of criticism; your first effort or draft is not your last one. There is always room for improvement.

Summary: Classification

RESOURCES
For a discussion of how to use the profile, see *Practical Suggestions*.

IDEA JOURNAL
Reread your journal entry on the kinds of students in this class or the kinds of friends you have (p. 120). Make another entry on the same topic, using what you have learned about classification.

RESOURCES
For an additional real-world assignment for this chapter, see *Additional Resources*.

- **Classification** is writing that organizes things into categories or groups. (See p. 119.)
- **Good classification** organizes things into useful categories, uses a single organizing principle, and gives examples of things that fit into each category. (See p. 119.)
- The **organizing principle** is *how* you sort the groups of things. (See p. 120.)
- The **topic sentence** in a classification paragraph includes the topic and how you are classifying it. You may also include the categories you will use. (See p. 122.)

What Will You Use?

List some situations in your life where you will use classification.

12

Definition

Paragraphs That Tell What Something Means

Rosalind Baker, Adult Education Specialist

Rosalind Baker

WRITING THEN: "I didn't think much about writing, period. It wasn't part of my life. Neither was the rest of school."

WRITING NOW: "I do many kinds of writing: reports, referrals, recommendations, plans for workshops. I have to *define* terms in writing for almost every workshop we offer. For example, one workshop is on household finance, rate of interest, etc. We give these to participants to keep for reference—and they use our handouts."

(For more about Rosalind Baker, see p. 143.)

Understand What Definition Is

Definition is writing that explains what a term means.

Having a clear understanding of what a term means can avoid confusion and mistakes. Some words have definite, concrete meanings, like *glass, book,* or *tree,* and you can depend on a dictionary definition for their meanings. Others depend more on a person's point of view, like *beautiful, good,* or *fun.* These words need to be carefully explained, or they could be misunderstood.

For example, if a friend says, "Don't take that class. It's terrible," you don't know exactly what she means by *terrible.* Until you do, you won't know whether you would think the course is terrible or not.

You ask your friend what she means by *terrible,* and she says, "It's offered only one night a week from four to seven, and you have to use computers. Plus, the class isn't on campus; it's downtown."

In fact, that time slot one night a week

RESOURCES
For a discussion of how to use the profiles in Part Two, see *Practical Suggestions*.

DISCUSSION
Using a food that your students eat regularly, say aloud, "This burger is great." Then quickly call on students, asking them to give a word that means *great burger* to them. List the words on the board. The different responses should illustrate the point of subjectivity.

IDEA JOURNAL
Write about what *relevant* means.

READING SELECTIONS
For examples of and activities for definition essays, see Chapter 47.

YOU KNOW THIS
When you talk with people, you often ask what they mean, or you have to tell them what you mean. For example:
• A friend tells you, "I think my relationship with Marty is getting serious." You ask, "What do you mean by *serious?*"
• You're about to register for a course when a friend says, "Don't take that class. It's terrible." You say, "What do you mean by *terrible?*"
• A young child hears you use the term *jet lag* and asks what it means.

fits your schedule perfectly, and you'd prefer to write with a computer. And you work downtown, so it's a much more convenient location for you than the campus. By asking your friend to define *terrible*, you discovered that it's not terrible for you at all: It's ideal. In this situation, it is important to clarify the meaning of *terrible* to each of you.

Definition helps you to convey what you mean and to avoid being misunderstood. It also helps you to understand what other people mean.

GOOD DEFINITION

• Tells readers what term is being defined
• Presents a clear and precise basic definition
• Uses examples to show what the writer means
• Uses words and examples that readers will understand

SAMPLE DEFINITION PARAGRAPH

Windchill, a concept defined in 1939 by meteorologist Paul Siple and tested in Antarctica during the winter of 1941, is a measure of discomfort, i.e., how cold you feel due to the combined effects of temperature and wind speed. Windchill applies only to the effects of wind and temperature on human skin. The windchill formula factors in our skin's talent for losing heat through conduction, radiation, evaporation, and convection, but obviously can't take into account individual metabolism, diet, blood circulation, etc. For practical applications (including weather reports), windchill numbers are converted to "effective" or "equivalent" temperatures. So on a blustery Boston day — temperature, 20 degrees; wind speed, 10 m.p.h. — we're told that the windchill factor is 3 degrees. What this means is that at 20 degrees in a 10 m.p.h. wind, human skin loses heat at the same rate it would at 3 degrees at 4 m.p.h. (standard wind speed generated by walking on a calm day). Windchill above minus 20 degrees is not considered to be dangerous; below minus 70 degrees is considered very dangerous.

— Clif Garboden, "Primer"

1. What term is being defined? _windchill_

2. What is the basic definition? _measure of discomfort — how cold you feel_

3. Underline the facts the writer gives in defining *windchill*.

Answers may vary.

Write a Definition Paragraph

The keys to good definition are presenting a clear, basic definition and explaining it with facts or examples your readers will understand.

In this section, you will write your own definition paragraph. Before you begin, you can analyze the structure of a definition paragraph and practice the key steps to writing one.

Analyze a Definition Paragraph

Assertiveness means standing up for your rights—politely but firmly. My friend Teresa is assertive. (Once) when we were in a restaurant and her hamburger was well done instead of rare, Teresa signaled the waiter and nicely asked if she could return the excellent but well-done burger for one that was a bit rarer. I braced myself for an argument, but the waiter just replaced the burger. (Another time) as we stood in line for movie tickets, a guy cut in front of Teresa. She tapped him on the shoulder, smiled, and said, "I see there was a gap that looked as if it were the end of the line, but it's really back there." (When) the guy stared at her and said, "I'll just stay here. You don't mind, right?" she answered, "Well, yes, I do mind." She (then) made sure the people in back of us were listening and said, "And you're not being fair to all these other people, either." The guy left. Assertiveness helps you get what you want and deserve without creating a scene.

1. Annotate the paragraph to highlight its structure:

    • Double-underline the topic sentence.

    • Underline the examples.

    • Circle the (transitions.)

2. What term is being defined? _____*assertiveness*_____

3. The **topic sentence** of a definition paragraph usually identifies the term being defined and provides a brief, basic definition.

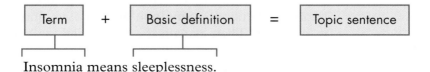

Insomnia means sleeplessness.

RESOURCES
A reproducible form containing a diagram students can use to plan their definition essays is in *Additional Resources,* which also contains a complete Guided Practice for this chapter, with worked-out examples and exercises for each step.

TEACHING TIP
Have several (five or so) dictionaries available to students for some of the practices and any in-class drafting or revising. Tell them that they should buy their own dictionary if they don't already own one and tell them they can find paperback versions in the reference section of the bookstore.

TEACHING TIP
This chapter is a good place to emphasize the benefits of vocabulary building and keeping a list of new words. Reinforce this practice by giving students a new word at the end of each class and challenging them to use the word during the next class.

Fill in the blanks with the term and the basic definition for the sample paragraph.

Term	=	*assertiveness*

Basic definition	=	*standing up for your rights*

4. The **support** in a definition paragraph usually consists of details and examples that explain the term so that readers can understand what you mean by it. The sample paragraph uses stories as examples. How do these help readers understand the definition?

make it easy to relate to, easy to imagine

TIP: For a review of writing topic sentences, see Chapter 3.

Key Step: Write a Topic Sentence That Presents a Clear, Basic Definition

The topic sentence in a definition paragraph should tell readers what term is being defined and present a clear, basic definition. When you are writing a definition paragraph, first develop that basic definition and then find a good way to present it to your readers.

Thinking Critically to Write a Definition Topic Sentence

FOCUS	Read the dictionary definition and any ideas you have written about the term.
ASK	• What do I mean by this term? What do I want to tell my readers about it? • What basic definition should I use in my topic sentence? • How can I present my definition in a topic sentence so my readers will know what I mean?
WRITE	Write a topic sentence that includes both the term and the basic definition, using one of the common patterns. (See p. 137.)

Choose a Basic Definition.

You need to understand the term before you can define it for others. Read the dictionary definition of your term and any ideas you wrote about its meaning. Then explain the term briefly in your own words. Do *not* just copy the definition from the dictionary.

Here is the basic definition of *assertiveness* that the writer of the sample paragraph started with.

Assertiveness: Standing up for your rights. Calmly defending your rights without getting angry.

Practice 1 ▷	**Choosing a Basic Definition**

For the following five items, look up the meaning(s) in the dictionary. Then write a basic definition that you might use in a paragraph. It does not need to be a complete sentence.   *Answers will vary. Sample answers given.*

1. Stress (noun): _a mentally or emotionally upsetting condition_

2. AIDS: _a severe disease affecting the immune system_

3. Vacation (noun): _time devoted to pleasure and relaxation_

4. Confidence: _trust or faith in a person or thing_

5. Conservation: _preservation from loss, damage, or neglect_

TEACHING TIP
These patterns can be difficult for students, so you may want to go over this carefully in class.

Choose a Pattern for the Topic Sentence.

There are several patterns for a good topic sentence in a definition paragraph. You do not have to follow one of these patterns, but they provide reliable formulas if you want to use them.

Term	+	*means/is*	+	basic definition	=	Topic sentence

This pattern is the simplest, presenting the term, the word *is* or *means*, and the basic definition. In some cases, the basic definition might be a synonym (a word with the same meaning that your readers are more likely to know), as in the definition of insomnia.

TERM	MEANS / IS	BASIC DEFINITION
Assertiveness	is	standing up for your rights.
Insomnia	means	sleeplessness.

The "class" is a larger group that the term belongs to; the "detail" is a unique characteristic that sets it apart from other things in the class. This pattern for a topic sentence gives readers a precise, basic definition of the term, as long as you are clear about what the class is and can give a brief but revealing detail.

TERM	CLASS	DETAIL
Insomnia	is a sleep disorder	that prevents people from sleeping.
A Rottweiler	is a dog	that can be very violent.

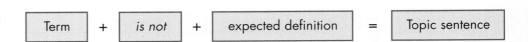

This pattern can be effective when you are defining a word differently than your readers may expect. In the following examples of the term *depression*, for example, many people do think that depression is just a bad mood. This topic sentence alerts readers that the term will be defined differently, as more than just a bad mood.

TERM	IS NOT	EXPECTED BASIC DEFINITION
Depression	is not	just a bad mood.
Wealth	is not	the amount of money someone has.

Because the topic sentence in this pattern does not give the definition of the term, make sure you do provide a basic definition somewhere else in the paragraph. You may want to state it clearly as part of the concluding sentence.

Practice 2   Writing Topic Sentences

For each of the following terms, write a topic sentence for a definition paragraph using the pattern indicated in brackets. First look up the meaning of the word in the dictionary and then write the topic sentence. If you completed Practice 1, you can use the basic definitions you wrote there for items 1–5 instead of looking them up in the dictionary.

EXAMPLE: Cirrhosis [term/class/detail]: *Cirrhosis is a liver disease often caused by alcohol abuse.*

Answers will vary. Sample answers given.

1. Stress [term + class + detail]: _Stress is an emotionally upsetting condition that can have physical effects._

2. AIDS [term + class + detail]: _AIDS is a disease of the immune system that leaves its victims in a weakened state._

3. Vacation [term + *means/is* + basic definition]: _Vacation means taking time off to relax._

4. Confidence [term + class + detail]: _Confidence is a feeling of trust or faith._

5. Conservation [term + *means/is* + basic definition]: _Conservation means preserving something from damage, loss, or neglect._

6. Marriage [term + *is not* + expected definition]: _Marriage is not a lifelong love affair._

7. Baseball [term + class + detail]: _Baseball is a sport that Americans love._

8. Happiness [term + *means/is* + basic definition]: _Happiness is joy and satisfaction._

9. Collaboration [term + *means/is* + basic definition]: _Collaboration is working together with others._

10. A good family [term + *is not* + expected definition]: _A good family is not always a father, a mother, and adorable children._

TIP: For a review of supporting a main idea with examples, see Chapter 4.

Key Step: Select Examples to Explain the Definition

When you have presented a basic definition in your topic sentence, you will then need to provide information to explain your definition. This information can be facts or examples or stories—whatever will be the most likely to explain the term to your readers.

Thinking Critically to Select Examples That Explain a Definition

FOCUS   Read your topic sentence, focusing on the basic definition.

ASK
- What do I know that can explain the term? Use a prewriting technique to come up with ideas.
- What examples would most appeal to my readers?
- Will a brief story reveal the term's meaning in real life?
- Are there facts or additional information that will fill in the basic definition?
- Which ideas will best help readers understand the term?

WRITE   Write a list of your examples.

Practice 3   **Selecting Examples to Explain the Definition**

List three examples or pieces of information that you could use to explain each of the following definitions.   *Answers will vary.*
Sample answers given.

EXAMPLE: Insomnia means sleeplessness.

a. *hard to fall asleep*

b. *wake up in the middle of the night*

c. *wake up feeling not rested in the morning*

1. Confidence is feeling that you can conquer any obstacle.

a. *you focus on chances of success*

b. *you know you have skills needed*

c. *you let others know you are optimistic*

2. A true vacation is not just time off from work.

a. *need to relax*

b. *need to have something fun & unusual to do*

c. *need enough time to unwind*

3. A family is a group you always belong to, no matter what.

a. *you can always count on family*

b. *distance, divorce, even death won't change it*

c. *sometimes might want to escape, but can't*

TIP: Look at your idea journal entry (p. 134) for ideas to write about.

Definition Assignment

Choose one of these terms (or one of your own choice) to define in a paragraph. Use the Checklist on this page to write your paragraph.

ESL
Suggest that students define a common term in their language that has no direct counterpart in English.

COLLEGE
- A useful course
- Learning
- Standardized tests
- Cheating
- Plagiarism

WORK
- A good job
- Sexual harassment
- A term used in your work that other people in the class may not know
- Benefits
- Self-starter

EVERYDAY LIFE
- Discrimination
- Success
- A good relationship
- Destructive behavior
- Self-esteem

Checklist: How to Write Definition

RESOURCES
A reproducible Checklist for a definition paragraph is in *Additional Resources.* You may want to copy and distribute it to students, having them check off the steps as they go and hand in the Checklist with their draft or revision.

Check off items as you complete them.

1. **Narrow and explore your topic** (the term you will define).

    ____ Use a dictionary to find the meaning(s) of the word you plan to define.

    ____ Make sure your topic is a term that you can define in a paragraph. Jot down a few ideas about its meaning. Consider both the dictionary meaning and other meanings.

    ____ Consider your purpose for defining this term: What do you want your readers to know about it?

2. **KEY STEP: Write a topic sentence that presents a clear, basic definition.** (See p. 136.)

    ____ Review your ideas and decide what basic definition you will give in your paragraph.

    ____ Write a topic sentence that includes the term and a basic definition. You can use one of these patterns:

    - Term + *means / is* + basic definition = topic sentence
    - Term + class + detail = topic sentence
    - Term + *is not* + expected definition = topic sentence

    Do *not* just copy the dictionary definition.

    (continued)

3.   KEY STEP: **Support your definition with examples.** (See p. 139.)

_____ Use a prewriting technique to find details and examples that explain the term.

_____ Drop examples that do not support the definition.

_____ Select the best examples to use in your paragraph. Add any details necessary to make your definition clearer.

4.   **Write a draft.**

_____ Arrange the examples and make a plan, using the topic sentence as the first sentence. Definition might use any of the orders of organization: space, time, or importance. Arrange your ideas so that readers will understand them.

_____ Write a draft paragraph using complete sentences and correct paragraph form.

_____ Write a concluding sentence that reminds readers of the term and its meaning and makes an observation about it based on the examples you've given.

_____ Title the paragraph, if required.

5.   **Revise your draft.**

_____ Get feedback from others.

_____ Cut anything that doesn't help communicate your definition.

_____ Add other examples or details that you think help explain the term.

_____ Make sure the sequence is logical; add transitions that move the readers smoothly from one example to the next.

_____ Do not just copy over your draft. Make changes to improve it.

6.   **Edit your revised draft.**

_____ Find and correct any problems with grammar, spelling, word use, or punctuation.

_____ Produce a clean, final copy.

_____ Ask yourself: Is this the best I can do?

Use Definition in Real-World Situations

TIP: To study for a test, see if you can explain a term aloud in your own words. Often trying to explain a term in your own words will show you things about it that you don't understand.

RESOURCES
For discussion of how to use the profile, see *Practical Suggestions.*

TEAMWORK
This assignment works well as a collaborative, small-group activity.

Many situations—in college, at work, or in your everyday life—require you to explain the meaning of a term. Here are some ways that you may find yourself using definition.

COLLEGE	On a math exam, you are asked to define *exponential notation.*
WORK	On an application that says, "Choose one word that describes you," you must define yourself in a word and give examples that support this definition. (This is also a very common interview question.)
EVERYDAY LIFE	In a relationship, you define for your partner what you mean by *commitment* or *communication.*

Real-World Assignment: Defining Important Skills

SITUATION: A recent survey of businesses asked what skills are most important to employers. The top five skills cited were

1. Motivation
2. Interpersonal skills
3. Initiative
4. Communication skills
5. Maturity

PROFILE OF SUCCESS
Rosalind Baker

Rosalind Baker defines herself at eighteen as "a mess." A homeless, unemployed single mother, she was living at the Pathways Family Shelter. She felt that she had hit bottom. Fortunately, she decided it was time to take charge of her life. She finished high school and left the shelter. She then enrolled at Massachusetts Bay Community College, where she met a mentor, Dr. Maxine Elmont. Rosalind graduated from Massachusetts Bay and went on to Suffolk University to get a bachelor's degree. She is now the adult education specialist at the same shelter that she called home for a while and is working toward a master's degree in public administration.

Rosalind writes often in her job, including defining terms that are part of educational programs or workshops for residents of the shelter.

COLLEGES: Massachusetts Bay Community College; Suffolk University, Boston

MAJOR: History, minor in public policy

DEGREES RECEIVED: Associate of arts, bachelor of science

EMPLOYER: South Middlesex Opportunity Council

POSITION: Adult education specialist/family advocate

MAJOR JOB RESPONSIBILITIES: Assessment of education and training needs of the adult residents of the house; provide workshops, tutoring sessions, and programs to meet the educational goals of residents; as programmer, provide guest speakers to give relevant and interesting talks to shelter residents

TYPES OF WRITING REQUIRED: Monthly reports, recommendations, referrals, case documentation, workshop handouts

PROUDEST ACHIEVEMENT: Finishing my bachelor's degree. I didn't think I could ever do it.

BEST PIECE OF ADVICE I EVER RECEIVED: Take charge of your life before someone else does.

BEST PIECE OF ADVICE I CAN GIVE: Don't be easily discouraged. Believe in yourself and question authority.

RESOURCES
For an additional real-world assignment for this chapter, see *Additional Resources*.

ASSIGNMENT: Use what you have learned about definition to define the five skills (terms). For each skill, give at least two examples of how the skill could be used on the job. Write a paragraph that defines and gives examples of any *one* of the terms, particularly as it applies to the workplace. (If you prefer, apply the skills in school situations or in situations in everyday life.) Use the Checklist on page 141.

Summary: Definition

IDEA JOURNAL
Reread your journal entry on the term *relevant* (p. 134). Make another entry using what you have learned about definition.

• **Definition** is writing that explains what a term means. (See p. 133.)

• **Good definition** tells readers what is being defined, presents a clear and precise basic definition, and uses examples readers will understand to explain the term or concept. (See p. 134.)

• The **topic sentence** in a definition paragraph usually includes the term being defined and a basic definition. (See p. 135.)

What Will You Use?

List some situations in your life where you will use definition.

Reggie Harris, Coordinator of Recruitment

13

Comparison and Contrast

Paragraphs That Show Similarities and Differences

PROFILE OF SUCCESS

Reggie Harris

WRITING THEN: "Writing was never a big issue until I got to college. My reading instructor, Vashti Muse, showed me the importance of writing. Before meeting her, I didn't think about it. I was an athlete, not a writer, so I thought it wasn't important for me."

WRITING NOW: "My major responsibility is recruiting students for Hinds Community College, and I travel to visit prospective students. But back in the office, I have to write a lot. In addition to responding in writing to requests for information, I have to write reports on yearly recruitment results. Part of that report is comparing the current year's enrollments with past years'. By comparing the results, we can see how successful we have been in our recruitment efforts."

(For more about Reggie Harris, see p. 157.)

Understand What Comparison and Contrast Are

Comparison is writing that shows the similarities among things; **contrast** shows the differences. Often people will use the word *compare* to mean either compare or contrast, but as you work through this chapter, the terms will be separated:

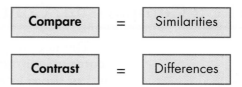

Comparing and contrasting are used both to explain things and to help you make decisions between two options.

145

GOOD COMPARISON / CONTRAST

- Uses topics that have enough in common to be compared/contrasted
- Serves a purpose—either to help readers make a decision or to help them understand the topics
- Presents several important, parallel points of comparison/contrast
- Arranges points in a logical organization

SAMPLE COMPARISON / CONTRAST PARAGRAPH

When they get lost while driving, women and men have very different ways to find the right route. As soon as a woman thinks she might be lost, she will pull into a store or gas station and ask for directions. If as she continues on, she's still not sure of the directions, she will stop again and ask someone else for help. Until they know they are on the right track, women will continue to ask directions. In contrast, men would rather turn around and go home than stop and ask for directions. First, a man doesn't readily admit he is lost. When it is clear that he is, he will pull over and consult a map. If he still finds himself lost, he will again pull out that map. Either the map will finally put the man on the right route, or—as a last resort—he will reluctantly stop and let his wife go in and ask for directions. Many battles of the sexes have raged over what to do when lost in the car.

1. Is this a comparison or a contrast paragraph? *contrast*

2. What is being compared or contrasted? *men and women drivers*

3. Underline the points of comparison and contrast.

Write a Comparison/Contrast Paragraph

The keys to good comparison/contrast are **presenting clear points of comparison/contrast with strong examples** to explain them and **arranging them either point-by-point or whole-to-whole.**

In this section, you will write your own comparison/contrast paragraph. Before you begin, you can analyze the structure of a comparison/contrast paragraph and practice the key steps to writing one.

Analyze a Comparison/Contrast Paragraph

READING SELECTIONS
For examples of and ac-
tivities for comparison/
contrast essays, see
Chapter 48.

TEACHING TIP
Tell students that some-
times an exam question
that says "Compare x
and y" may mean to give
both similarities and differences.

RESOURCES
A reproducible form con-
taining a diagram
students can use to plan
their comparison/contrast
essays is in *Additional
Resources*, which also
contains a complete
Guided Practice for this
chapter, with worked-out
examples and exercises
for each step.

As revealed in the fine print, the financial terms offered by the two credit cards are very different. One difference is the annual membership fees. Big Card has no fee at all; Mega Card charges $35 each year for the privilege of membership. Another difference is what they charge for cash advances. Getting an advance using Big Card costs $1 per withdrawal, while the same activity using Mega Card will cost $1.50. Also, Big Card is more gracious than Mega Card, offering a "grace" period of thirty days before imposing finance charges on unpaid balances. Mega's finance charge starts after twenty-five days. The biggest difference between the two cards is the finance charge rates. Big Card's finance charge is 15.5%; Mega Card's is a whopping 17.9%. That difference in percentage rates is even bigger when you recall that Mega has a shorter grace period, so the finance charges start adding up earlier. Over the course of a year, unpaid balances will cost a lot more on the Mega Card than they would on Big Card. The several differences in the financial terms point to Big Card as the better choice.

1. Annotate the paragraph to highlight its structure:

    • Double-underline the topic sentence.

    • Underline each point of comparison.

    • Circle the transitions.

TIP: This chapter will
describe comparison/
contrast papers as having
two topics instead of one.
Each thing being exam-
ined is considered a topic
(*men drivers, women
drivers* = two topics).

2. What are the two topics? *financial terms of two credit cards:*

    Big Card and Mega Card

    Are they being compared or contrasted? *contrasted*

    Is the purpose of the paragraph to help readers make a decision or to help them understand the topics better?

    make a decision — which credit card to get

3. The **topic sentence** of a comparison/contrast paragraph usually identifies the topics and tells the main point you want to make about them. It should also indicate whether the topics are being compared or contrasted, through words such as *alike, similar, same, compare, both, different, dissimilar, unlike,* or *opposite.*

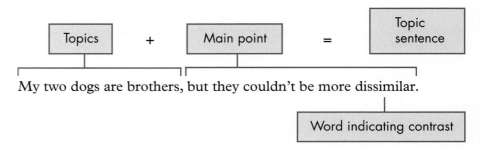

My two dogs are brothers, but they couldn't be more dissimilar.

Fill in the blanks with the topics, the main point, and the contrast word for the sample paragraph.

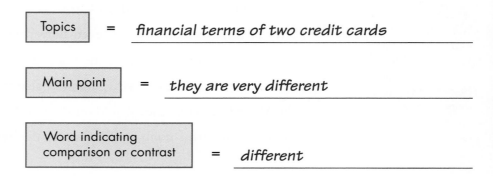

4. The **support** in a comparison/contrast paragraph is a series of important, parallel points of similarity or difference between the two topics. What is the first point of contrast in the sample paragraph?

membership fees: Big Card has none, and Mega Card charges

$35 per year

5. Comparison/contrast paragraphs usually use one of two standard organizations: **point-by-point** or **whole-to-whole**.

POINT-BY-POINT	WHOLE-TO-WHOLE
Topic sentence	Topic sentence
Point 1	Topic 1
Topic 1	Point 1
Topic 2	Point 2

Point 2	Point 3
Topic 1	Topic 2
Topic 2	Point 1
Point 3	Point 2
Topic 1	Point 3
Topic 2	Concluding sentence
Concluding sentence	

Transitions are used to move readers smoothly from one part of the comparison/contrast paragraph to the next.

COMMON COMPARISON TRANSITIONS	COMMON CONTRAST TRANSITIONS
One similarity	One difference
Another similarity	Another difference
Similarly	In contrast
Like	Unlike
Both	While

What kind of organization does the sample paragraph use? _____

point-by-point

TIP: For a review of supporting a main point with examples, see Chapter 4.

COMPUTER
Have students freewrite on the computer, responding to one word that you supply. Students should spend one minute typing in words that come to them. Then they move to another person's computer and review the words to see which could be compared/contrasted. They should underline those on the screen.

Key Step: Find Points of Comparison or Contrast

Once you have chosen two topics, decided on your purpose, and decided whether to compare or contrast them (or both), you need to find specific points of comparison or contrast. Keep your purpose in mind. If you want to help readers choose between two models of CD players, you should probably compare or contrast them in terms of price, features, and reliability — or whatever other points you think are important for making that decision. Many writers make a list with two columns, one for each topic, with parallel points of comparison or contrast lined up underneath.

TOPIC SENTENCE: As revealed in the fine print, the financial terms offered by the two credit cards are very different.

BIG CARD	MEGA CARD
no annual fee	*$35 annual fee*
$1 fee per advance	*$1.50 per advance*
30 days before interest charges	*25 days before interest charges*
15.5% finance charge	*17.9% finance charge*

Three Questions to Ask about Comparison / Contrast Topics

Before you begin looking for points of comparison/contrast, ask yourself these questions about your topics.

1. What is my purpose?

   Do you want to help your readers choose between the two things? For example, you might compare or contrast two cars, hoping to show your readers that one is better than the other. Or do you want to give your readers a clearer understanding of the two topics, without implying that one is better? For example, you might objectively compare or contrast two routes to get somewhere so that readers understand the options.

2. Do I want to compare these two topics, contrast them, or both?

   What will help you make your point? Do you need to show how these two things are similar, how they are different, or both? What do readers need to know to understand your point?

3. Do these topics have enough in common to make a comparison or contrast worthwhile?

   You may have heard the expression "That's comparing apples and oranges"—which means that the two things being compared/contrasted aren't alike enough to result in meaningful comparison.

   For example, comparing/contrasting a light in your room with a sneaker wouldn't help explain either of the items; they're so different to begin with that showing either similarities or differences makes no sense. Choose things that are similar enough to be compared or contrasted in a reasonable way.

Thinking Critically to Find Points of Comparison or Contrast _____

FOCUS	As you look for points of comparison or contrast, think about your purpose.
ASK	• Do I want to explain two things or help readers to make a choice between two things? • Do I want to show the similarities, the differences, or both? • What are some parallel points of the two topics? • Do these points reveal important characteristics of the two topics? • What else would help show how the topics are alike or different?
WRITE	Write a list of points of comparison or contrast.

| Practice 1 | **Finding Points of Contrast** |

Each of the following items lists some points of contrast. Fill in the blanks with more. Example:

CONTRAST: Hair lengths

Long hair	*Short hair*
takes a long time to dry	dries quickly
can wear a lot of ways	*only one way to wear it*
doesn't need to be cut often	needs to be cut every five weeks
gets tangled, needs brushing	*low maintenance*

1. **CONTRAST:** Snack foods

Potato chips	*Pretzels*
high fat	low fat
Answers will vary but	twists or sticks
should focus on differences.	

2. **CONTRAST:** Ethnic foods

Mexican	*Chinese*
beans as a starch	_____
_____	common condiment: soy sauce
_____	_____

3. **CONTRAST:** Buildings

The most modern in town	*An older building*
_____	_____
_____	_____
_____	_____

4. **CONTRAST:** Dancing and exercising

Dancing	*Exercising*
purpose: social, for fun	_____
_____	done at a gym
_____	_____

Practice 2	**Finding Points of Comparison**

Each of the following items lists some points of comparison. Fill in the blanks with more.

1. **COMPARE:** Sports

Basketball	*Soccer*
Team sport	Team sport
Answers will vary but	_____
should focus on similarities.	_____

2. **COMPARE:** Ethnic foods

Mexican	*Chinese*
Relatively inexpensive	_____
Can be mild or spicy	_____
_____	_____

3. **COMPARE:** Dancing and exercising

Dancing	*Exercising*
Done to music	Done to music
_____	_____
_____	_____
_____	_____

Key Step: Decide on an Organization and Arrange the Points

TIP: For a review of outlining, see Chapter 5.

There are two ways to organize a comparison/contrast paper: point-by-point or whole-to-whole. A point-by-point organization presents one point of the two topics with examples of each and then moves to the next point with examples and so on. A whole-to-whole organization presents all the points of the first topic and then all the points of the second topic. You have to decide which will best serve your purpose. Choose one of the two organizations and stick with it throughout the paragraph; otherwise you will confuse your readers.

To review, the two organizations look like this:

RESOURCES
Focus students on the two organizations. Tell them that they need to review their drafts carefully to make sure that they follow one of them consistently. Hand out diagram forms from *Additional Resources* and have students turn in completed copies with their drafts.

POINT-BY-POINT	WHOLE-TO-WHOLE
Topic sentence	Topic sentence
Point 1	Topic 1
Topic 1	Point 1
Topic 2	Point 2
Point 2	Point 3
Topic 1	Topic 2
Topic 2	Point 1
Point 3	Point 2
Topic 1	Point 3
Topic 2	Concluding sentence
Concluding sentence	

You must also decide on an order of presentation. Comparison/contrast can use any order of presentation—time, space, importance. Choose an order that suits what you have to say.

Thinking Critically to Arrange Your Points

FOCUS	Review your topic sentence and points of comparison or contrast, and think about how to arrange your ideas.
ASK	• Should I use a whole-to-whole or point-by-point organization? • Which organization would make the comparison or contrast easier for my readers to understand? Which seems more natural? • Within that organization, how should I arrange my points? by importance? by time? by space?
WRITE	Write an outline that shows the plan for your paragraph.

> **Practice 3**   Organizing a Comparison/Contrast Paragraph

The first outline is for a comparison paper using a whole-to-whole organization. Reorganize the ideas and create a new outline using a point-by-point organization. The first blank has been filled in for you.

The second outline is for a contrast paper using a point-by-point organization. Reorganize the ideas and create a new outline using a whole-to-whole organization. The first blank has been filled in for you.

COMPARISON PAPER USING WHOLE-TO-WHOLE ORGANIZATION

TOPIC SENTENCE: Training your boss to treat you right is like training a small child to behave.

1. Training small child
   - let him know what the rules in your house are
   - don't respond to tantrums
   - when he misbehaves, tell him firmly but calmly that what he's doing is not OK

2. Training your boss
   - let her know what you will tolerate
   - don't respond to bullying or yelling
   - when she misbehaves, tell her firmly but calmly that she is out of line

COMPARISON PAPER USING POINT-BY-POINT ORGANIZATION

TOPIC SENTENCE: Training your boss to treat you right is like training a small child to behave.
                                                    Answers will vary.

1. Let him or her know what is acceptable
   - *child - house rules*
   - *boss - what you will tolerate*

2. *Don't respond to bad behavior*
   - *child - tantrums*
   - *boss - bullying, yelling*

3. *Speak firmly but calmly*
   - *child - what he's doing not OK*
   - *boss - out of line*

CONTRAST PAPER USING WHOLE-TO-WHOLE ORGANIZATION

TOPIC SENTENCE: Boston and Detroit are completely different cities.

1. Boston
   - small: metro area has about 1 million people
   - old: dates back to the colonial period
   - quaint and sophisticated culture: ballet, symphony, museums

CONTRAST PAPER USING POINT-BY-POINT ORGANIZATION

TOPIC SENTENCE: Boston and Detroit are completely different cities.

1. Size
   - *Boston - small, 1 million people*
   - *Detroit - large, 4 million people*

2. *Age*
   - *Boston - old, colonial period*

2. Detroit
   • large: metro area has about
     4 million people
   • young: mostly a twentieth-
     century city
   • raw and urban culture:
     Motown music, gangs

• *Detroit - young, 20th century*

3. *Culture*

• *Boston - quaint, sophisticated*

• *Detroit - raw, urban*

TIP: Look back at your idea journal entry (p. 146) for ideas.

Comparison/Contrast Assignment

Choose one of the following general topics or one of your own to compare or contrast in a paragraph. Use the Checklist on this page to write your paragraph.

COLLEGE
• Two teachers/two courses
• Writing on a computer and writing by hand
• High school and college

WORK
• Two bosses/two jobs
• Management and workers (clothing, offices, and so on)
• Two offices

EVERYDAY LIFE
• How you dress now and how you dressed five years ago
• Two friends
• Two stores/two magazines/two modes of transportation

ESL
Give students the option of comparing/contrasting some aspect of their native culture with that in the United States.

Checklist: How to Write Comparison/ Contrast

Check off items as you complete them.

1.   Narrow and explore your topics.

_____ Narrow your general topics to topics that have enough in common to be compared or contrasted, that you are interested in, and that can be compared or contrasted in a paragraph. Jot down some ideas about the two topics.

_____ Decide why you are comparing or contrasting these two things. Is it to help readers choose between them? Or is it to give readers a better understanding of their relationship?

_____ Decide whether you will compare or contrast your topics.

(continued)

RESOURCES
A reproducible copy of this Checklist is in *Additional Resources.* You may want to copy and distribute it to students, having them check off the steps as they go and hand in the Checklist with their draft or revision.

2. **Write a topic sentence.**

_____ Review your ideas about topics you want to compare or contrast.

_____ Write a topic sentence that includes your topics, the main point you want to make about them, and whether you are comparing or contrasting them.

3. **KEY STEP: Find points of comparison or contrast.** (See p. 149.)

_____ Use a prewriting technique to find similarities and/or differences. Many people find that making a two-column list (one for each topic) is the easiest way to come up with parallel similarities or differences.

_____ Select the points of comparison or contrast you will use, choosing points that your readers will understand.

_____ Add examples or explanations of points, if necessary.

4. **KEY STEP: Decide on an organization and arrange the points in a draft.** (See p. 153.)

_____ Decide whether to use a point-by-point or a whole-to-whole organization.

_____ Arrange the points of comparison/contrast in the order you want to present them. Outline or diagram the paragraph.

_____ Turn the points of comparison/contrast into complete sentences and put them in paragraph form.

_____ Write a concluding sentence that reminds readers of what you are comparing or contrasting and makes an observation or decision based on the similarities or differences.

_____ Title the paragraph, if required.

5. **Revise your draft.**

_____ Get feedback from others.

_____ Make sure your points of comparison/contrast are parallel and important. Cut anything that does not help make your point.

_____ Add any other information that will help you show important similarities or differences.

_____ Add any transitions needed to move readers smoothly from one part of the comparison/contrast to the next.

_____ Do not just copy over your draft. Make changes to improve it.

(continued)

RESOURCES
For a discussion of
how to use the profile,
see *Practical Sugges-
tions.*

6.   Edit your revised draft.

_____ Find and correct any problems with grammar, spelling, word use, or punctuation.

_____ Produce a clean, final copy.

_____ Ask yourself: Is this the best I can do?

Use Comparison/Contrast in Real-World Situations

NOTE
The National Associa-
tion for Developmental
Education (NADE) hon-
ors one outstanding
alumnus or alumna of
developmental educa-
tion each year. For
more information, see
Practical Suggestions.

Many situations require you to understand similarities and differences. Here are some examples of how you may find yourself using comparison and contrast.

COLLEGE

• In an accounting course, you contrast the two most common inventory valuation methods.

• In a pharmacy course, you contrast the side effects of two drugs prescribed for the same illness.

PROFILE OF SUCCESS
Reggie Harris

Reggie Harris played football in college, and although he was successful on the football field, he lacked confidence in the classroom. By the time Reggie was in college, he was convinced that it would be difficult to succeed academically. His teacher and mentor, Vashti Muse, says that when Reggie first walked into her class, he kept his head and eyes down and wouldn't make eye contact. Her first goal was to get him to look her in the eye and to keep his head up. Working together, they achieved much greater goals.

Today Reggie travels to schools and businesses recruiting and speaking to prospective students for Hinds Community College. He also works with student athletes who feel, as he once did, uncertain about their academic skills. He and Vashti Muse are very close friends. In 1993, Reggie won the Outstanding Alumni Award given annually by the National Association for Developmental Education (NADE).

COLLEGES: Hinds Community College; Delta State College, Missouri

MAJOR: Business administration

EMPLOYER: Hinds Community College

POSITION: Coordinator of Recruitment

MAJOR JOB RESPONSIBILITIES: Recruit prospective students at high schools and businesses; coordinate campus visits and tours

TYPES OF WRITING REQUIRED: Weekly objective report to supervisor; year-end results report; written responses to information requests from institutions and individuals

PROUDEST ACHIEVEMENT: Being nominated by my former teacher, Vashti Muse, for the NADE (National Association of Developmental Education) Outstanding Alumni Award—and then winning it

BEST PIECE OF ADVICE I EVER RECEIVED: Both my wife, Angela, and my mother, Ada Harris, said the same thing: "Give 100 percent to everything you do and help someone else whenever you can."

BEST PIECE OF ADVICE I CAN GIVE: Work hard and don't give up. Hard work does pay off.

WORK

- You must contrast sales this year to sales for last year.
- For a sales conference, you compare the product your company makes with that of your closest competitor.

EVERYDAY LIFE

- At the supermarket, you contrast brands of the same food to decide which to buy.
- You contrast two banks' checking account rules before opening an account.

TEAMWORK
This assignment also works well as a small-group collaborative assignment.

Real-World Assignment:
Analyzing a *Consumer Reports* Rating Chart

SITUATION: You've decided to buy a portable CD player. You know you'll have many choices, so before buying, you check a recent *Consumer Reports* issue on CD players.

RESOURCES
For an additional real-world assignment for this chapter, see *Additional Resources*.

ASSIGNMENT: Read the rating chart on the next page about portable CD players and contrast two of the models. Identify three important points of contrast and look at what the chart says about each model for each point. After analyzing the points, choose which model you would buy. Write a paragraph contrasting the two models. You can end with a statement of which you chose and why. Use the Checklist on page 155.

Summary: Comparison/Contrast

IDEA JOURNAL
Reread your journal entry on the differences between men and women (p. 146). Make another entry on the same subject, using what you have learned about comparison/contrast.

- **Comparison** is writing that shows similarities; **contrast** shows differences. This form of writing can be used either to explain two things or to make a choice between them. (See p. 145.)
- **Good comparison/contrast** uses two topics that have enough in common to be compared and contrasted, presents several points of comparison or contrast, and arranges the information in either point-by-point or whole-to-whole organization. (See p. 146.)
- The **topic sentence** should include your topics and tell the main point you want to make through your comparison/contrast. You should also indicate whether you are comparing or contrasting. (See p. 148.)
- The **points of comparison/contrast** should be parallel. (See p. 150.)

What Will You Use?

List some situations in your life where you will use comparison/contrast.

Within type, listed in order of overall quality

Ratings legend: Excellent ● | Very good ◕ | Good ○ | Fair ◔ | Poor ●

Brand and model	Price	Overall score (0–100)	ERROR CORREC.	LOCATE SPEED	BUMP RESIST.	OVERALL CONVENIENCE	TAPING EASE	CALEN. DISPLAY	TRACK KEYPAD	FAVORITE TRACK	AUTO-EDIT	REMOTE VOLUME	REM. DISC KEYPAD
CAROUSEL CHANGERS													
Onkyo DX-C211	$270		●	◕	◔	○	◔	—	—	—	—	—	✓
Sony CDP-C445	230		○	◕	○	●	●	✓	✓	—	—	—	✓
Denon DCM-340	260		●	◕	◔	○	◔	—	✓	✓	✓	—	—
Technics SL-PD1000	260		◔	●	◔	◕	○	✓	✓	✓	✓	—	—
Philips CDC935	240		◕	◕	◕	◕	◕	✓	✓	—	✓	—	—
Kenwood DP-R6060	250		○	◕	●	◕	◕	✓	✓	✓	✓	✓	✓
Marantz CC-45	300*		◕	◕	●	○	◕	✓	—	—	✓	✓	—
Yamaha CDC-645	270		○	◕	○	◕	○	◕	—	—	—	✓	—
Teac PD-D900	155		○	○	○	◕	◔	✓	—	—	✓	—	✓
Fisher DAC-2403	265		○	○	◔	○	◔	—	—	—	✓	✓	✓
MAGAZINE CHANGERS													
JVC XL-M415TN	230		◔	○	○	○	●	✓	—	—	✓	—	✓
Optimus CD-7300 (Radio Shack)	250		○	○	○	◕	○	—	✓	—	✓	✓	✓
Pioneer PD-M703	240		○	◔	◔	◕	○	✓	✓	—	✓	✓	✓
SINGLE PLAY													
Technics SL-PG440	140		◕	◔	○	◕	●	✓	✓	—	✓	✓	—
Pioneer PD-203	150		◕	◔	○	◕	◕	✓	✓	—	✓	✓	—
JVC XL-V261TN	155		○	◕	◔	◕	◕	✓	✓	—	✓	—	—
Sony CDP-315	130		○	◔	◔	○	○	✓	✓	—	—	—	—
100 DISC CHANGERS													
Sony CDP-CX151	655		◕	◔	◕	◕	◕	✓	✓	✓	—	—	✓
JVC XL-MC100	700		◕	○	○	◕	◕	✓	✓	✓	—	—	—
Pioneer PD-F100	560		○	○	○	○	◕	—	—	—	—	—	✓
PORTABLES													
Panasonic SL-S180	130		◕	◔	◕	◕	◕	—	—	—	—	—	—
Sony D-131, **A BEST BUY**	95		◕	○	◕	◕	◕	—	—	—	—	—	—
Sony D-235CK	180		◕	○	◕	○	◕	—	—	—	—	—	—
Panasonic SL-S351C	180		○	◔	◕	◕	◕	—	—	—	—	✓	—

Notes on the table

Price is the estimated average, based on a national survey. An * indicates the price we paid. **Overall score** is based mostly on performance. To a lesser degree, it covers **features** and convenience. (Sound quality, excellent on all models, is not scored.) **Performance. Error correction** shows how well a player compensates for dirty or scratched discs. **Locate speed** is how quickly the player starts playing and goes from track to track and disc to disc. **Bump resistance** is how well the player handles heavy footsteps and other jarring or, for portables, being carried around. **Features. Overall convenience** includes both usefulness and ease of use of a player's controls and programming features. **Taping ease** measures how easy it is to perform all the functions you need to copy a disc onto tape. A **calendar display** shows a disc's tracks as a block of numbers, and highlights the track being played. A **keypad** on the console makes it easy to choose tracks; most remotes also have a track keypad. **Favorite-track** selection lets you choose the tracks you want to hear, and, by pushing a button, play them each time you play the disc. **Auto-edit** shows which selection of tracks will most nearly fill one side of a tape cassette. A remote with **volume** control is useful if your receiver's remote lacks a volume control. A remote with a **disc keypad** makes choosing discs from your armchair easier.

14

Argument

Paragraphs That Persuade

Jeffrey Lee, Regional Sales Manager

PROFILE OF SUCCESS

Jeffrey Lee

WRITING THEN: "I didn't think much about writing. I wanted to be successful, but it didn't occur to me that writing well would help me in that goal."

WRITING NOW: "I am challenged with a diversity of writing projects. Because my position is sales management, I often have to write persuasively, both to suggest sales and marketing strategies and to 'sell' my ideas to the eighty employees I oversee in my region."

(For more on Jeffrey Lee, see p. 175.)

Understand What Argument Is

Argument is writing that takes a position on an issue and defends it with evidence to persuade someone else of the position.

Knowing how to argue is critical. We use argument every day: to persuade someone to lend us something or to do something for us. We persuade someone to give us a job, or not to give us a traffic ticket, or to buy something we're selling, or to give us more time. And we argue when something important is at stake, like keeping a job, or protecting our health, or defending our community. We need to do more than just say what we want or believe; we need to give reasons or evidence.

Argument helps you persuade people to see things your way, or at least to understand your position. Most of us have experienced the feeling of being a helpless victim—just standing by while something that we don't want to happen, happens. Although knowing how to argue won't eliminate all such situations, it will help you to defend your position. While you may not always win, you can at least put up a good fight.

RESOURCES
For a discussion of how to use the profiles in Part Two, see *Practical Suggestions*.

IDEA JOURNAL
Convince a younger brother, sister, or friend to finish high school.

TEACHING TIP
One of the reasons that students should give in the activity at the bottom of this page is that the classes will make them more valuable employees. Many reasons are possible; the point is to show students that they don't have to be passive or angry; they can use argument.

This is a real situation, and the student used the following reasons to persuade her boss: She'd paid a lot of money that was nonrefundable; she was learning things that

(continued)

GOOD ARGUMENT

- Takes a strong and definite position on an issue
- Gives good evidence to defend and support the position
- Considers the opposing view
- Has energy from start to finish

SAMPLE ARGUMENT PARAGRAPH

Many doctors are convinced that Ritalin [a drug used to treat attention deficit/hyperactivity disorder, ADHD] is overprescribed. "I fear that ADHD is suffering from the 'disease of the month' syndrome," says Dr. Peter S. Jensen, chief of the Child and Adolescent Disorders Research Branch of NIMH [National Institute of Mental Health]. Teachers—even in preschool—are known to pull parents of active kids aside and suggest Ritalin. Overwhelmed with referrals, school psychoogists (averaging one for every 2,100 students) say they feel pressed to recommend pills first before they have time to begin an evaluation. Psychiatrists nationwide say that about half the children who show up in their offices as ADHD referrals are actually suffering from a variety of other ailments, such as learning disabilities, depression, or anxiety—disorders that look like ADHD, but do not need Ritalin. Some seem to be just regular kids. A St. Petersburg, Fla., pediatrician says parents of nomal children have actually asked him for Ritalin just to improve their

---

SITUATION: You are working while going to school, and you always have to find classes that fit into your schedule. This semester, you are taking two classes that you've paid for yourself, without any financial aid. Halfway through the term, your boss tells you that he wants to change your shift. The different shift conflicts with your classes, and it's too late to get a refund on your tuition. When he tells you about the shift change, you say, "But that's when my classes meet." He replies, "Sorry. We need you when we need you. I assume your job comes first."

At this point, you might keep quiet and just quit the classes. Or you might get angry but keep the anger to yourself, carrying on imaginary battles with your boss in your head. Or you might get angry and

quit your job. None of these responses gets you what you want, which is somehow to finish the classes *and* keep your job.

If you know how to argue, you can construct an argument that might persuade your boss not to change your shift—at least not immediately. You can think of good reasons for allowing you to finish the course and then present them to your boss, either orally or in writing.

ACTIVITY: Either in small groups, as a class, or individually, come up with reasons to give your boss for allowing you to finish your classes and not change your shift. Try to give some reasons that show how he and the company will benefit.

PARAGRAPHS

would improve her skills as an employee (writing skills to write her weekly report and reading skills to more quickly understand manuals she had to use). She also argued that she had just five weeks left in the courses and asked if the change could be postponed for that length of time. She was allowed to finish the courses.

grades. "When I won't give it to them they switch doctors," says Dr. Bruce Epstein. "They can find someone who will." Finding someone who will is distressingly easy.

—Lynn Nell Hancock, "Mother's Little Helper"

1. What is the issue? _Ritalin's rate of prescription_

2. What is the author's position? _it's prescribed too much_

3. Underline the evidence the author gives. What do you think the strongest evidence is? Why? _Answers will vary._

Write an Argument Paragraph

The keys to good argument are **taking a definite position on an issue** and **presenting convincing evidence.** It is important to choose an issue that you are interested in and feel strongly about; otherwise it will be difficult to persuade anyone else of your position.

In this section you will write your own argument paragraph. Before you begin, you can analyze the structure of an argument paragraph and practice the key steps to writing one.

Analyze an Argument Paragraph

READING SELECTIONS
For examples of and activities for argument essays, see Chapter 50.

Prisoners have more rights and privileges than law-abiding citizens. They are guaranteed certain facilities that not everyone else has. For example, a prisoner in Massachusetts recently sued a prison because he didn't have a toilet in his cell and had to use one down the hall. My grandmother, who lives in a nursing home, also has to go down the hall to use the bathroom, and we *pay* for her to be there. Prisoners have the right to three square meals a day. I eat macaroni and cheese from a box several times a week because it's cheap. Is that a square meal? Worst of all, my taxes pay for prisoners to get college degrees. Last year my state proudly reported that one hundred prisoners had received college degrees. I can't even afford that for myself; why should I help someone who's being "punished"? I realize that education is supposed to help rehabilitate prisoners, but why should someone who has broken the law get more help than I do? I wish the state took as good care of me as it does of its prisoners.

RESOURCES
A reproducible form containing a diagram students can use to plan their argument essays is in *Additional Resources,* which also contains a complete Guided Practice for this chapter, with worked-out examples and exercises for each step.

RESOURCES
See "Arguing from First-Hand Experience," by Caryl Klein Sills, in *Background Readings*.

ESL
Ask students how their native cultures deal with confronting authority.

YOU KNOW THIS
You have been in situations where you have a definite opinion and want to defend it.
• You persuade someone to lend you money or to let you borrow a car.
• You and a mate have different ideas about how to spend a sum of money (you want a washing machine; he or she wants a car stereo). You argue by giving reasons and trying to persuade your mate.
• The college announces a tuition increase, and you want to protest. You argue your case, giving reasons against the increase.

TEACHING TIP
Tell students that argument is not like bickering or fighting. It is a reasoned defense of a position.

1. Annotate the paragraph to highlight its structure:

• Double-underline the topic sentence.

• Underline each piece of evidence.

• Circle the transitions.

2. What is the issue in this paragraph? *prisoners' rights and privileges*

3. The **topic sentence** in an argument paragraph should include the issue (topic) and your position on that issue.

Smoking in restaurants should be banned completely.

Fill in the blanks with the issue and the position for the sample paragraph.

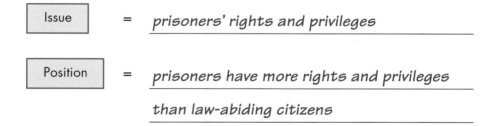

Issue = *prisoners' rights and privileges*

Position = *prisoners have more rights and privileges than law-abiding citizens*

4. The **support** in an argument paragraph is the evidence—facts, examples, and expert opinions. The support helps persuade readers that your position is a good one. What is the first piece of evidence in the sample paragraph?

prisoners are guaranteed facilities that other people don't have, like private toilets

5. Argument paragraphs usually use **order of importance,** starting with the least important and ending with the most important idea. Transitions are used to move from one piece of evidence to the next and to add emphasis.

TRANSITIONS FROM ONE POINT TO ANOTHER

also	in addition	consider that
another thing	another fact to consider	
for example	another reason	

TRANSITIONS TO ADD EMPHASIS

above all	the last point to consider	best of all
especially	in particular	worst of all
in fact	more important	
remember	most important	

What transition does the writer use to indicate his final, most important piece of evidence in the sample paragraph?

Worst of all

TIP: For a review of exploring a topic, see Chapter 2.

Key Step: Explore the Issue and Take a Position

Once you have an issue in mind, you need to find a position you are interested in writing about. Try turning the issue into a question (for example, Is Ritalin overprescribed?) and taking some time to build your energy around this question. Then write a strong statement about your position.

Thinking Critically to Explore an Issue and Take a Position

DISCUSSION
Introduce the idea of looking at the opposite point of view. Ask, "Why is it important to preserve prisoners' rights?" Give students a few minutes to talk in groups and then ask for responses.

TEACHING TIP
Focus students on these questions, especially putting the issue in question form. Aloud, state some issues (legalizing marijuana, assisted suicide, some campus issue) and call on students to express the issues in question form.

FOCUS	Think about the issue.
ASK	• How can I put the issue in question form?
	• Why is the issue important to me? How does this issue affect me and my family? What do I have at stake?
	• How would I answer the question? What is my position?
	• Why do some people take a different position?
	• Can I defend my position with energy and conviction?
	• Can I defend it in a paragraph?
	• How should I present my position to my readers?
WRITE	Write a topic sentence strongly stating your position.

Put the Issue into Question Form.

The first thing to do is to put the issue into question form. This helps you understand what the issue is, and it also gives you a way to frame your argument: as an answer to the question. Try starting the question with the word *should*.

Practice 1 Turning the Issue into a Question

For each of the following issues (topics), write a question. Example:

Answers will vary.
Sample answers given.

ISSUE: Prisoners' rights

QUESTION: *Should prisoners have the rights they do?*

1. ISSUE: Lab testing on animals

   QUESTION: *Should lab testing be conducted on animals?*

2. ISSUE: Married priests

   QUESTION: *Should priests be allowed to marry?*

3. ISSUE: Flat-rate income tax

   QUESTION: *Should we have a flat-rate income tax?*

4. ISSUE: Curfews for teenagers

   QUESTION: *Should cities impose curfews on teenagers?*

5. ISSUE: Affirmative action in hiring practices

   QUESTION: *Should affirmative action hiring practices be abandoned?*

Build Energy.

   A good argument has energy; when you read it you know that the writer is committed to his or her position. Get yourself energized or you aren't likely to persuade or convince anyone. You should feel like a lawyer about to go to court to present a case.

   When you are free to choose the issue to write about, you will probably choose something you personally care about. But even when you are assigned an issue, you still need to defend it powerfully by finding something in it that you care about.

   Take a full minute to either think about the issue, talk about it with a partner, or jot down ideas about it. Here are some prewriting techniques to get you started.

COMPUTER
Have students respond to the prompts on the computer.

• Imagine yourself arguing your position to someone you really dislike (who, naturally, holds the opposite position).

• Imagine that your whole grade rests on persuading your teacher of your position.

- Imagine how this issue could affect *you* or your family personally.
- Imagine that you are representing a large group of people who do very much care about the issue and whose lives will be forever changed by it. It's up to you to win their case.

TIP: When you have a basic topic sentence, try revising it to make it sound stronger, clearer, or more interesting.
- Day care facilities should be provided by companies at a low cost to employees.
- Companies should provide day care facilities at a low cost to employees.
- Employees are entitled to low-cost, company-sponsored day care.

Write a Topic Sentence.

Once you have a position that you feel strongly about, you are ready to answer the question you posed about the issue. The answer to that question is your topic sentence. Your topic sentence should answer the question you wrote and express your position on the issue strongly.

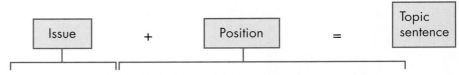

Day care facilities should be provided at a low cost to employees.

Most good topic sentences for argument paragraphs use words like these:

could	should	should not	would
must	must not	ought	ought not
needs	requires	must have	

Practice 2   ▶   ### Writing a Topic Sentence

Write a topic sentence for each item in Practice 1 by answering the questions you wrote there. Make sure your topic sentences are complete sentences. Example:

TEAMWORK
Practice 2 works well in pairs or small groups.

ISSUE: Prisoners' rights

QUESTION: Should prisoners have the rights they do?

ANSWER / POSSIBLE TOPIC SENTENCE: *Prisoners should not have more rights and privileges than law-abiding citizens.*

Answers will vary. Sample answers given.

1. ISSUE: Lab testing on animals

ANSWER / POSSIBLE TOPIC SENTENCE: *Animals should continue to be used for lab testing.*

2. ISSUE: Married priests

   ANSWER / POSSIBLE TOPIC SENTENCE: *Priests must be allowed to marry.*

3. ISSUE: Flat-rate income tax

   ANSWER / POSSIBLE TOPIC SENTENCE: *The United States should not adopt a flat-rate income tax.*

4. ISSUE: Curfews for teenagers

   ANSWER / POSSIBLE TOPIC SENTENCE: *Teenagers need a midnight curfew.*

5. ISSUE: Affirmative action in hiring practices

   ANSWER / POSSIBLE TOPIC SENTENCE: *Affirmative action in hiring practices should be maintained.*

TIP: For a review of supporting a point, see Chapter 4.

Key Step: Present Convincing Evidence to Support Your Position

A strong position must be supported with convincing evidence. Remember that you want to persuade readers that your position is a good one. Use strong evidence, consider your opposition, and end on a strong note.

TEACHING TIP
Go over the concept of evidence carefully. Students' arguments are often weak because of poor evidence or lack of evidence.

Thinking Critically to Present Convincing Evidence

FOCUS	Think about your position and the readers you must persuade.
ASK	• What facts, examples, and expert opinions can I use to defend my position?
	• Is all my evidence strictly related to the issue?
	• What is my strongest evidence? (Save it for last.)
	• What objections could my opponents raise to each point of evidence? How would I answer those objections?
	• What evidence will appeal strongly to my readers?
	• How can I make a final pitch for my position in the concluding sentence?
	• If I were to argue my case with this evidence, would I stand a chance of persuading an opponent?
WRITE	Write a list of the evidence you will use; arrange it to build in importance, saving the most persuasive piece for last.

TEACHING TIPS
Have students read a newspaper or a news-magazine and bring in examples of evidence (facts, examples, expert opinion). Bring in a mis-leading ad that uses poor evidence (such as one of the diet aid ads that promise instant weight loss). Critique the evidence with students. Have them bring in other examples.

Use Good Evidence.

Supporting your position with convincing evidence is the most important part of an effective argument. What is evidence? It isn't just your own beliefs stated with conviction. Good evidence consists of facts, specific examples, and expert opinions.

FACTS: Things that are real; their existence can be proved. Statistics—real numbers from actual studies—can be persuasive factual evidence to back up your position.

> **POSITION:** Students are a powerful consumer group.
> **FACT:** A report issued by the University of California indicates that three out of five college students have a major credit card.

EXAMPLES: Specific information or experiences that support your position.

> **POSITION:** Joe Camel cigarette ads specifically target young people.
> **EXAMPLE:** The ads use a character who is "cool" to young people, and the tobacco companies produce all kinds of Joe Camel merchandise that appeals to people under eighteen.

EXPERT OPINION: The opinion of someone who is considered an expert in the field. The person must be known for his or her expertise in the area of your topic. For example, the opinion of the head of the FBI about the benefits of eating a low-fat diet isn't good evidence. The FBI chief isn't an expert in the field of nutrition.

> **POSITION:** The drug Ritalin is overprescribed for attention deficit / hyperactivity disorder.
> **EXPERT OPINION:** Dr. Peter Jensen, a pediatric specialist, warns, "I fear that ADHD is suffering from the 'disease of the month' syndrome, and Ritalin is its 'cure.'"

It's tempting when writing an argument paragraph to cite as evidence something that "everyone" knows or believes or does. But be careful of the "everyone" evidence; everyone usually doesn't know or believe it. It is better to stick with facts (including statistics), specific experiences, and expert opinions.

Practice 3 ▶ Finding Evidence

For each of the following positions, give the type of evidence indicated. Example:

POSITION: Pesticides should not be sprayed from planes.

FACT: *Scientific studies prove that both plant life and people*

are harmed.   *Answers will vary.*

1. **POSITION:** The parking situation on this campus is impossible.

    EXAMPLE: _____

    _____

2. **POSITION:** People should be careful about "going overboard" when dieting.

    FACT: _____

    _____

3. **POSITION:** Smoking is harmful to smokers and nonsmokers alike.

    EXPERT OPINION: _____

    _____

4. **POSITION:** Rich people get special privileges.

    EXAMPLE: _____

    _____

5. **POSITION:** Adolescents and alcohol are a dangerous mix.

    FACT: _____

    _____

Review Your Evidence and Consider Your Opposition.

Your evidence may be convincing to you, but will it persuade your readers? Review your evidence using these five strategies:

1. Reread your evidence from your opponent's perspective, looking for ways to knock it down. Anticipate your opponent's objections and include evidence to answer it.
2. Ask someone else to "cross-examine" your evidence, looking for weak spots.
3. Stay away from generalities. Statements about what "everyone" else does or what "always" happens are easy to disprove.
4. Make sure that you have said enough. Take the time to present the evidence in full; your argument depends on the quality of your evidence.
5. Reread your evidence to make sure that it supports your position. If it is the least bit off track, you leave your opponent room to find a hole in your argument.

| Practice 4 ▶ | Reviewing the Evidence |

For each of the following topic sentences, one piece of evidence is weak: It does not support the position. Circle the letter of the weak evidence and in the space provided state why it is weak. Example:

Advertisements should not use skinny models.

a.   Skinny should not be promoted as ideal.

(b.) Everyone knows that most people are not that thin.

c.   A survey of young girls shows that they think they should be as thin as models.

d.   People can endanger their health trying to fit the skinny "ideal."

e.   Three friends of mine became anorexic trying to get skinny.

Not good evidence because ___*"Everyone knows" is not good*___

evidence; everyone obviously doesn't know that.

1. It is dangerous to keep a gun in the house.

a.   Guns can go off by accident.

b.   Reports indicate that most guns are kept loaded, in case of emergency.

c.   Within the past year, more than twenty children have died playing with guns.

d.   Just last week a story in the newspaper reported on a man who, in a fit of rage, took the gun out of the drawer and shot his wife.

(e.) People always panic when their house is broken into.

Not good evidence because ___*too general*___

2. Schoolchildren in the United States should go to school all year.

a.   A survey of teachers across the country showed that multiple shorter vacations interrupt learning less than entire summers off.

b.   Many children are bored and restless after three weeks of vacation and would be better off returning to school.

c.   Test scores improved when a school system in Colorado went to year-round school sessions.

(d.) All of my friends would like to end the long summer break.

Not good evidence because ___*wanting it doesn't mean it should*___

happen

3. Capital punishment should be abolished.

    (a.)   It is immoral.

    b.   Data show that it does not deter criminals.

    c.   There have been too many instances of mistaken convictions where people were later found to be innocent.

    d.   Just last year two people on death row were retried and found innocent.

Not good evidence because *a personal opinion, not a fact, example, or expert testimony*

4. People should not be required to retire at age sixty-five.

    a.   Many people are still youthful at sixty-five and perform perfectly well.

    b.   With an increased life expectancy, few retired people can support themselves on their pensions for twenty to twenty-five years.

    (c.)   Older people often can't perform as well as younger people.

    d.   Retirement should be based on performance, not on age.

Not good evidence because *doesn't support the topic sentence*

5. The "three strikes and you're out" law that forces judges to send people to jail after three convictions should be revised.

    a.   A week ago a man who stole a slice of pizza was sentenced to eight to ten years in prison because it was his third conviction.

    b.   It makes prison overcrowding even worse.

    (c.)   Judges can make mistakes.

    d.   It too often results in people getting major prison sentences for minor crimes.

Not good evidence because *doesn't support the topic sentence*

End on a Strong Note.

Argument is almost always organized by order of importance. Save your most persuasive evidence for the end, building up force and leaving a strong impression. Save the best for last.

Your concluding sentence is the last opportunity you have to win your case. Make it memorable and dramatic. Remind your readers of the issue, your position, and the rightness of your position.

Before writing your concluding sentence, build up your energy again. Then reread your topic sentence and draft paragraph. As soon as you finish reading, write the most forceful ending you can think of. Aim for power; you can tone it down later.

TIP: Look back at your idea journal entry (p. 161) for ideas to write about.

Argument Assignment

Choose one of the following issues or one of your own choice to write about in an argument paragraph. Try to choose one that you care about; if none of these appeals to you, look through the college paper, the local newspaper, or a newsmagazine or watch the evening news to find an issue that's important to you. Use the Checklist on page 173 to write your paragraph.

TEACHING TIP
If you know of a "hot issue" that students are likely to feel strongly about, suggest it as a topic.

COLLEGE

- School uniforms for public school children
- Sex education in schools / condom distribution
- AIDS children in public schools
- Persuade your teacher to raise your grade this semester
- A controversial issue on your campus

WORK

- On-site day care
- Flextime
- Mandatory drug testing
- A new company policy (or an existing one)
- Persuade your boss to give you a raise or to let you take some time off

EVERYDAY LIFE

- Smoking in restaurants (or elsewhere)
- Tobacco companies' responsibility for death by lung cancer
- Assisted suicide
- Rights of gays to marry
- A controversial issue in your community

**Checklist:
How to
Write
Argument**

Check off items as you complete them.

1.   KEY STEP: Explore the issue and take a position.
(See p. 164.)

_____   Turn the issue into a question. Jot down some ideas about the issue and what your position is.

_____   Build energy by taking a minute to think about how you are personally affected or involved. Take a position.

_____   Make sure the issue and your position are narrow enough to be covered in a single paragraph.

2.   Write a topic sentence that states your position.

_____   Write a topic sentence that answers your question. It should include the issue and your position on that issue.

3.   KEY STEP: Present convincing evidence to support your position. (See p. 167.)

_____   Consider what makes good persuasive evidence (facts, examples, expert opinions).

_____   Use a prewriting technique to come up with possible evidence.

_____   Drop unrelated evidence and evidence that will not be convincing to your readers.

_____   Consider the opposing position and anticipate objections. Find more support for your position.

_____   Select the best evidence to use in your paragraph. Find additional details or examples as needed to back up your position.

4.   Write a draft.

_____   Arrange the evidence in order of importance (probably least important to most important). Make a plan, using the topic sentence as the first sentence.

_____   Write a draft using complete sentences and correct paragraph form.

_____   Write a concluding sentence that reminds readers of the issue and reaffirms your position based on the evidence. Make your final pitch—with energy.

_____   Title your paragraph, if required.

(continued)

RESOURCES
A reproducible Checklist is in *Additional Resources*. You may want to copy and distribute it to students, having them check off the steps as they go and hand in the Checklist with their draft or revision.

5.   Revise your draft.

_____   Get feedback from others.

_____   Read it from the perspective of someone who strongly defends the opposite position.

_____   Cut any evidence that does not support your position.

_____   Add any other evidence that might help your case.

_____   Make sure the sequence of ideas is logical. Add needed transitions, especially transitions for emphasis.

_____   Do not just copy over your draft. Make changes to improve it.

6.   Edit your revised draft.

_____   Find and correct any problems with grammar, spelling, word use, or punctuation.

_____   Produce a clean, final copy.

_____   Ask yourself: Is this the best I can do?

Use Argument in Real-World Situations

Every day you defend your positions or persuade people. Knowing how to put together a good argument is one of the most useful skills you can develop. Here are some examples of how you may find yourself using argument.

COLLEGE

A common type of exam question presents a statement and asks you to agree or disagree with it, giving evidence to support your opinion.

- A question in a business exam might read: " 'A CEO's annual compensation should not be tied to company performance.' Agree or disagree and support your opinion."
- You might argue for or against make-up exams for students who don't do well the first time.

WORK

- You decide to defend your group at work against a policy that is unfair.
- You need to leave work an hour early one day a week for twelve weeks to take a course. You must persuade your boss to allow you to do so.

EVERYDAY LIFE

- You try to negotiate a better price on something you want to buy.
- As a representative of your tenant organization, you try to block a proposed rent increase.

Real-World Assignment: Debating an Issue

Often you will find yourself arguing with someone about an issue you feel strongly about, and it's hard to get your points out. Knowing how to construct an argument allows you to express your opinions convincingly.

SITUATION: What is an important issue on campus or in your community? As a class, list possibilities and vote on an issue to debate. Your professor will divide you into small groups according to your position on the issue; if you have not yet decided your position, your professor will assign you to a group.

ASSIGNMENT: Use what you have learned about argument to come up with convincing evidence for your position. When you have agreed upon the most convincing evidence, write a paragraph defending the group's position. Use the Checklist on page 173. The groups can then debate the issue.

PROFILE OF SUCCESS

Jeffrey Lee

As a regional sales manager, Jeffrey Lee uses persuasion almost constantly. Sales is persuasion, and a good salesperson must understand how to construct a good argument, particularly how to find evidence that will appeal to the customer and how to overcome the customer's objections.

Jeff was the winner of the NADE (National Association of Developmental Education) Outstanding Alumni Award in 1995. He now manages $15 million in revenue for PepsiCo, oversees eighty employees, and has a six-figure income. He cites as his keys to success the following: setting life goals; having a positive attitude; being committed to excellence; and developing the self, continuously.

COLLEGE: Shippensburg University, Pennsylvania

MAJOR: Psychology

EMPLOYER: PepsiCo

POSITION: Business development manager, regional sales manager

MAJOR JOB RESPONSIBILITIES: Develop and execute strategic plans for the Pittsburgh market, including pricing, marketing, personnel, financial targeting, and forecasting; give presentations; manage sales teams

TYPES OF WRITING REQUIRED: Memos, presentations, strategic plans (including my vision, top priorities, objectives, action plans with dates), quality training programs, financial forecasts; extensive writing both to senior management and to employees I supervise

PROUDEST ACHIEVEMENT: Achieving a major sale with a Fortune 100 company that my employer thought was impossible. I was rewarded with a bonus check of $55,000. My earnings exceeded $100,000 at the age of twenty-nine.

BEST PIECE OF ADVICE I EVER RECEIVED: To raise my personal standards from focusing on mediocrity and getting by to standards of excellence. Learn to ask questions to clearly understand what people are looking for in any situation; then exceed their expectations.

BEST PIECE OF ADVICE I CAN GIVE: Start with a dream of where you want to go in life and support it with a five-to-ten-year game plan. This game plan should include clear written goals, action steps, and concrete measurement targets.

TEAMWORK
These two assignments work well as collaborative, small-group activities.

Real-World Assignment:
Making a Sales Presentation

Whether you are in an official sales job, such as Jeffrey Lee's, or some other position, all work is sales in one way or another. You sell your boss on a new idea; you sell your colleagues on a plan; you convince someone's secretary to put your call through; you present a case for getting a new desk or piece of equipment.

SITUATION: You are part of a sales team that is near its goal of being the company's top-performing group. Your group is eager to win the all-expenses-paid vacation in Hawaii. Many other teams are competing for the prize, so you have to be very persuasive and present a great case for your product.

RESOURCES
For an additional real-world assignment for this chapter, see *Additional Resources*.

ASSIGNMENT: Use what you have learned about argument to write a paragraph persuading a customer that he or she should buy your product. Come up with evidence of value to your customer (how he or she will benefit from it). As evidence, you can use facts, studies, endorsements from users, expert opinions, and examples. (And you can make these up, so have some fun.) Use the Checklist on page 173 to write your argument paragraph.

You can use a product you actually have some experience with or one of the following. It should be something you're familiar with, such as

a pen	a pad of paper
a sweatshirt	a kind of coffee or soft drink
a cleaning product	a bag (book, purse, knapsack, and so on)
a textbook	a kind of food

Summary: Argument

IDEA JOURNAL
Reread your journal entry on convincing someone to finish high school (p. 161). Make another entry, using what you know about argument and evidence.

- **Argument** is writing that takes a position on an issue and defends it with convincing evidence to persuade other people. (See p. 160.)
- **Good argument** presents enough good evidence—facts, examples, and expert opinions—and enough detail about that evidence to convince readers. It anticipates and fends off opposing views. (See p. 161.)
- The **topic sentence** should state the issue and give your position on it. A good topic sentence for an argument is usually an answer to a question. (See p. 163.)
- Good argument is full of energy and conviction.

What Will You Use?

List some situations in your own life where you will use argument.

ESSAYS

Part Three

How to Write an Essay

15

Overview
Moving from Paragraphs to Essays

TEACHING TIP
Tell students that the quotes in Chapters 15–20 are from *real* people who hoped to give them the message that writing has an impact on their futures.

Understand What an Essay Is

An essay is a piece of writing with more than one paragraph; it is usually between three hundred and six hundred words long. The parts of an essay correspond to the parts of a paragraph: An essay's thesis statement is like a paragraph's topic sentence; an essay's support paragraphs are like a paragraph's support sentences; an essay's concluding paragraph is like a paragraph's concluding sentence.

Here is an example of an essay with the parts underlined and labeled.

Thesis statement
Introductory paragraph

Life is full of traps of various kinds: money traps, security traps, emotional traps. While we may like to think that we do not fall into those traps, most of us do at one time or another. The best thing we can do is to be aware of the traps, so that when we fall in, we might be able to climb out.

Topic sentence
Support paragraphs

One of the more common traps is the money trap. People continue to pour money into a car, for example, even when all reason tells them it isn't worth it. At first they think the small repair is worth the investment. But then as things continue to fail, they keep paying for the repairs. People often think, "I've spent

— Support

179

this much; I might as well spend a little more to make it right." Before they know it, they've spent much more than the car is worth and sell it for a loss.

— Supp•

Topic sentence

LEARNING JOURNAL
Without looking back or ahead in the book, jot down what you know about paragraph form and the process of writing paragraphs.

A more serious trap is the security trap. A common example of this is when people stay in jobs they hate. They are afraid to leave the security of a paycheck, benefits, regular employment. They are afraid they will never find anything better—or anything at all. So they wake up each morning dreading going to work. They wait for each day to pass, and they wait for each endless week to end. They wish their lives away, caught in the security trap.

—Supp•

Support paragraphs

Topic sentence

Emotional traps take the largest toll on people, and they are the hardest to break out of. Emotional traps involve relationships that are unhealthy or just don't work: a bad marriage; an abusive relationship; an inability to break away from someone close. The ties are strong and irrational, and they are therefore very difficult to break. Unfortunately, people who cannot escape emotional traps become weak emotionally and increasingly unable to break out. Eventually, the unhealthy relationship seems normal.

—Supp•

TEACHING TIP
Have students interview a second- or third-year student in their major to find out what kind of writing the person does for his or her classes.

Concluding paragraph

Few of us go through life free of traps. Although we may not be able to avoid all traps, we can try to recognize them for what they are and work to minimize our stays. We can learn from the traps we are certain to fall into; we just shouldn't live there forever.

—Adapted from Jeffrey Z. Rubin, "Psychological Traps"

IDEA JOURNAL
Write about a trap that you have been in—and how you got out.

A diagram showing the relationship is at the top of the next page. The diagram shows three support paragraphs, but there isn't a set rule about how many support paragraphs are required. Between two and five is usual for college papers.

RELATIONSHIP BETWEEN PARAGRAPHS AND ESSAYS

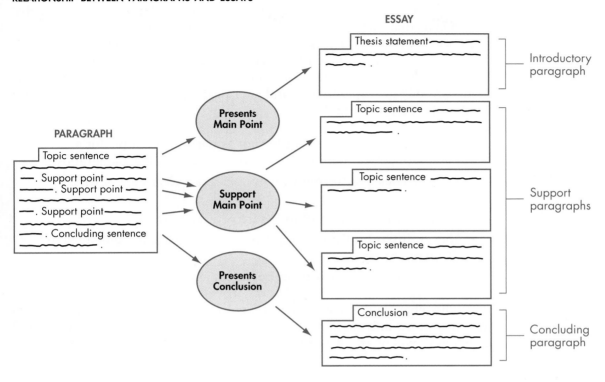

Understand the Writing Process for Essays

The basic process for writing an essay is the same as the process for writing a paragraph: prewrite, draft, revise, and edit.

WRITING PROCESS FOR ESSAYS

TIP: To review prewriting, see Chapters 2–4. To review drafting, see Chapter 5. To review revising, see Chapter 6. To review the writing process in general, see Chapter 1.

1. **PREWRITE** • Narrow and explore your topic.
   • Find a main point and write a thesis statement.
   • Find and select support points.

2. **DRAFT** • Arrange your ideas in an outline.
   • Write a draft using complete sentences and paragraphs.
   • Write an introduction, conclusion, and title.

3. **REVISE** • Improve the unity, support, and coherence of your essay.

4. **EDIT** • Find and correct errors in grammar, word use, punctuation, and mechanics.

You are familiar with the basic writing process by now, so this section of the book won't go over it again. (For a review, see Chapters 1–6.) Instead, this chapter and the next two will focus on the things that are *different* about writing an essay. A complete checklist of steps for writing essays begins on page 213.

The most important difference between writing an essay and writing a paragraph is that essays are longer and go into more depth than paragraphs. This means that there are more opportunities for the writer (and the reader) to get lost. (Think of the difference between driving across town and driving across the country.) If you've been writing paragraphs, you've already learned all the skills you need to write an essay—now you just need to use them carefully to keep both you and your readers on track. In particular, you need to do the following things.

- Choose an **essay-sized topic** (not as narrow as a topic for a paragraph, but still limited enough to cover in a few paragraphs).
- Use the **thesis statement** to give readers a clear idea of what is to come.
- Have a well-organized **plan** before you start drafting.
- Use an **introduction,** a **conclusion,** and a **title** to guide readers through the essay.
- Revise carefully for **unity, coherence,** and **support**.

This chapter will cover prewriting and drafting an essay. Chapter 16 will give more information on introductions, conclusions, and titles; and Chapter 17 will offer advice on revising essays.

Practice Prewriting and Drafting an Essay

A. Narrow Your General Essay Topic

As you already know, all topics for writing should pass this three-question test (for more information about the test, see p. 8):

THREE-QUESTION TEST FOR GOOD TOPICS

- Does it interest me?
- Do I know something about it?
- Is it specific?

TEACHING TIP
You might use a camera analogy to explain the wide angle/closeup action for narrowing a topic. (SG)

You will usually need to narrow the general topic your instructor assigns down to one that is a good topic for an essay.

ASSIGNED GENERAL TOPIC	NARROWED ESSAY TOPIC
A great vacation	→ A weekend camping trip
Public service opportunities	→ Volunteering at a homeless shelter
A personal goal	→ Paying off my debts

Essays are longer than paragraphs, so their topics can be a little broader. But be careful: Most of the extra length in an essay should come from handling ideas in more depth (giving more examples and details, explaining what you mean), not covering a larger area.

TIP: Before choosing a topic that you know will need research, ask your instructor whether it fits the assignment.

For essays, writers sometimes turn to sources outside their own experiences to find information: They may talk to friends and colleagues, do some extra reading, or even conduct research. You may come up with a topic that you are interested in but don't know much about. If you have the time and the resources to find out more, this may be a good topic for you.

Practice 1 ▶ **Narrowing an Essay Topic**

For each general topic given here, write down a possible narrowed topic. Then answer the lettered questions and revise the topic if necessary. Example:

GENERAL TOPIC: A problem in your community

POSSIBLE NARROWED TOPIC: *The lack of recycling facilities in my city*

a. If you were going to find out more about this topic, what is one thing you could investigate? *Whether there are any plans to build a recycling plant*

b. What is one source you could consult? *City hall*

c. Does it pass the Three-Question Test? *No — too broad*

d. If you answered no to question c, revise your possible topic here: *Why my city should try to recycle more glass*

1. GENERAL TOPIC: The worst experience you have had in school

   POSSIBLE NARROWED TOPIC: *Answers will vary.*

a. If you were going to find out more about this topic, what is one thing you could investigate? _____

b. What is one source you could consult? _____

c. Does it pass the Three-Question Test? _____

d. If you answered no to question c, revise your possible topic here:

   _____

2. **GENERAL TOPIC:** Physical exercise

    POSSIBLE NARROWED TOPIC: _____

    a. If you were going to find out more about this topic, what is one thing you could investigate? _____

    b. What is one source you could consult? _____

    c. Does it pass the Three-Question Test? _____

    d. If you answered no to question c, revise your possible topic here:

    _____

3. **GENERAL TOPIC:** Job interviews

    POSSIBLE NARROWED TOPIC: _____

    a. If you were going to find out more about this topic, what is one thing you could investigate? _____

    b. What is one source you could consult? _____

    c. Does it pass the Three-Question Test? _____

    d. If you answered no to question c, revise your possible topic here:

    _____

B. Write Your Thesis Statement

A **thesis statement** is a sentence that presents the main point of an essay, just as a topic sentence presents the main point of a paragraph. The thesis statement is the topic statement of the introductory paragraph, usually either the first or the last sentence of that paragraph.

A STRONG THESIS STATEMENT
- States a single main point that you can show, explain, or prove
- Prepares readers for the rest of the essay
- Is specific, not vague
- Is a forceful statement written in confident, firm language

To form your thesis statement, you can use the same technique you used to form a topic sentence:

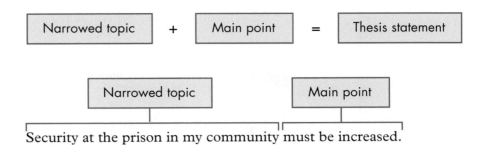

Security at the prison in my community must be increased.

Remember that an essay is longer than a paragraph. To guide your readers through this longer paper, you sometimes need to give them more information in the thesis statement than you would in a topic sentence. One way to do this is to make the thesis statement refer to each of the main support points you will cover in your paper. Adding these points also makes the thesis statement more specific and concrete—stronger overall.

VAGUE   Our campus cafeteria has many problems.

CONCRETE   Our cafeteria's problems include poorly cooked meals, a bad floor plan, and an unhelpful staff.

By including specific details, you not only make your thesis statement more interesting, you also give your readers a clearer idea of your point.

GENERAL   I saw an interesting movie.

SPECIFIC   The movie *Dead Man Walking* forces viewers to confront the death penalty.

A weak, boring thesis statement will result in a weak essay that leaves readers thinking, "So what?" Write a forceful, definite statement. Do *not* write a thesis statement that begins, "In this essay I will show. . . ." Don't say you *will* make a point; just make it.

WEAK   In this essay, I will show the importance of body language.

FORCEFUL   Body language reveals much about a person.

Practice 2 ▶ Writing Strong Thesis Statements

Rewrite the weak statements on the next page to make them more concrete, specific, and forceful. Example:

I have many things to do every day.

Raising three children, working long hours, and taking

college courses make every day a real challenge.

1. Let me tell you what happened today.

    Answers will vary.

    _____

2. Most people watch television.

    _____

    _____

3. Drunk driving is dangerous.

    _____

    _____

4. A lot has been written recently about natural wonder drugs.

    _____

    _____

5. Going to college is expensive.

    _____

    _____

6. I will prove that drug testing in the workplace is an invasion of privacy.

    _____

    _____

7. I don't believe that affirmative action in college admissions is right.

    _____

    _____

8. Children are a lot of work.

    _____

    _____

9. The words to [a song you know] are interesting.

_____

_____

10. My cousin has a good job.

_____

_____

C. Support Your Thesis

An essay usually has between two and five main points that support the thesis statement. Each main support point is presented in its own paragraph with its own topic sentence and supporting details.

To find and select support for your thesis, use a prewriting technique (listing, questioning, discussing, freewriting, or clustering) to come up with ideas. Then read over those ideas, first to drop any that are not related to your main point and then to group similar ideas.

Think of what you could use as major support for your thesis statement. Jot down three or four possible major support points and then move any additional supporting ideas and details under them. The major support points will become the topic sentences of the paragraphs in your essay. The ideas and details under them will support the topic sentences.

TIP: For a complete review of prewriting techniques, see Chapter 2. For a complete review of supporting your point, see Chapter 4.

D. Make a Plan and Draft Your Essay

Because an essay is longer than a paragraph and has more points, you need a more definite plan than you do to write a single paragraph. The plan will be your map, or blueprint, as you write. The most reliable way to arrange your ideas is to make an outline that includes your thesis statement, topic sentences (major support points), supporting details, and a possible main point for the concluding paragraph.

To write an outline, first consider how you will order your major support points. Think about your readers and what presentation of ideas will help them understand or agree with your main point. Here is a quick review of the common ways to order your ideas: time, space, and importance.

- **Time order:** arranged according to when things happened (first to last/last to first)
- **Space order:** arranged according to how things might be seen (top to bottom/bottom to top; near to far/far to near; side to side/left to right/right to left; back to front/front to back)
- **Order of importance:** arranged according to the importance of things, particularly how strongly they will affect readers (least important to most important/most important to least important)

TIP: For more complete information on the ways of ordering ideas, see Chapter 5.

TIP: Remember, a paragraph has a topic sentence that presents the main point and at least two or three support sentences.

RESOURCES
A reproducible blank outline for essays is in *Additional Resources*.

Start by filling in the main support points (the topic sentences for the support paragraphs) in the order you think is most effective. Then review the supporting ideas you wrote and select the ones that will best show, explain, or prove each topic sentence. Add other support that occurs to you. If you can, add a concluding statement that reminds readers of your main point and makes an observation based on your support points.

Sample Outline

Main point and support for introductory paragraph

THESIS STATEMENT: The prison in my community must step up its security.
—very loose
—beautiful country setting
—looks like a college campus
—but it's a prison, with convicted criminals
—people strolling on grounds

Main point and support for first support paragraph

TOPIC SENTENCE 1: Although it is a minimum-security prison, there are some dangerous inmates.
—many have served years in more secure prisons; now awaiting parole
—escape within months of their parole hearings
—panic and become desperate to get out

Main point and support for second support paragraph

TOPIC SENTENCE 2: The inmates who were convicted of less violent crimes may still be very violent characters.
—recent escapee in for burglary
—would have murdered ninety-year-old resident if he'd known she was still alive

Main point and support for third support paragraph

TOPIC SENTENCE 3: A home invasion last month brought the issue of prison security to the fore.
—escapee broke into home

Main point for concluding paragraph

CONCLUDING STATEMENT: Town residents must keep up the pressure to ensure adequate security at the prison.

COMPUTER
Suggest to students that when they write their draft they highlight (using boldface or underlining) their support points. This will keep them on track and will also help peer editors to focus. (JS)

When you are satisfied with your outline, you should be able to work from it to write a complete first draft. Use each main point in the outline as the topic sentence of a new paragraph; use each minor point as support for the corresponding paragraph. Draft a series of related paragraphs that each have a main point and adequate support. Don't let yourself get stalled at this point if you're having trouble with one word or sentence. Just keep writing. If you are writing by hand, use every other line to leave space for changes.

The introductory and concluding paragraphs can be especially challenging. You may want to leave them until the end. Advice and models for introductory and concluding paragraphs are found in Chapter 16.

When you have completed your draft, set it aside for a day or two (or at least a few hours) before revising it. Revising essays is covered in Chapter 17.

Practice 3 ▸ **Arranging Topic Sentences to Support a Thesis**

Each thesis statement is followed by topic sentences for support paragraphs for an essay. Number each set of topic sentences according to the order you think is best; in some cases, more than one answer may be considered correct. Be ready to discuss your choices.   *Answers may vary.*

TEAMWORK
Practice 3 works well in pairs or small groups.

1. **THESIS STATEMENT:** According to a recent survey, students returning to school after being out for a while are similar in terms of experience, motivation, and goals.

   __2__ They are highly motivated, much more than when they were younger.

   __3__ They are much more interested in learning than in just getting a grade.

   __1__ They have solid life experience that they bring to the classroom.

2. **THESIS STATEMENT:** My family's work history matches our country's changing industrial profile.

   __3__ Now, my sister and two cousins work in the high-tech fields of computers and engineering.

   __1__ Half a century ago, my immigrant grandfather worked in the coal mines and steel mills of Pennsylvania.

   __2__ My father was a middle manager who worked for a supermarket chain.

3. **THESIS STATEMENT:** It is possible to successfully balance work and school, but doing so takes careful planning.

   __2__ Keep all the things you need for class together in one place.

   __1__ Make sure the courses you take are scheduled at times that are possible for you.

   __3__ Have a regular place where you write down assignments and due dates.

Summary: Essay Overview

LEARNING JOURNAL
What is one thing you learned in this chapter?

- An **essay** is a piece of writing with several paragraphs that make a point together. (See p. 179.)
- The **parts of an essay** correspond to the parts of a paragraph. (See p. 179.)

PARAGRAPH		ESSAY
topic sentence	→	thesis statement
support sentences	→	support paragraphs
concluding sentence	→	concluding paragraph

DISCUSSION
Ask students how they would explain what an essay is to someone who has no idea. (SG)

- The **process** of writing an essay is the same as that for writing a paragraph: prewrite, draft, revise, and edit. (See p. 181.)
- The **topic** of an essay should be interesting; should be something you know about; and should be specific enough to show, explain, or prove in the essay. (See p. 182.)
- The **thesis statement** of an essay should include the narrowed topic and the main point you will make about it. It should be forceful and specific and should give readers a sense of what the essay will cover. (See p. 184.)
- **Support** the main point by using a prewriting technique. Select major support points (for topic sentences) and group similar ideas for paragraphs (supporting details). (See p. 187.)
- A **plan** for an essay should show the order of the topic sentences for paragraphs and also supporting details for the topic sentences. (See p. 187.)

TEAMWORK
Have students work in groups to come up with ideas about how each of them might use the essay process.

What Will You Use?

Will you have to write an essay or extended piece of writing in the next two months? Consider course work, exams, business correspondence, reports, and anything else you might have to write.

16

Introductions, Conclusions, and Titles

Writing the Special Elements in Essays

Understand Introductions, Conclusions, and Titles

Strong introductions, conclusions, and titles are crucial to the success of an essay. Essays are longer and more complex than paragraphs, and readers need these devices to stay focused and interested. The title hints at the main point of the essay; the introduction gets readers' interest and presents the main point; the conclusion reminds readers of the main point.

Practice Using Good Introductions, Conclusions, and Titles

A. Introductions

Think of your introductory paragraph as a marketing challenge. Ask yourself: How can I sell my essay to readers?

A GOOD INTRODUCTION

- Should catch readers' attention
- Should present the thesis statement of the essay
- Should give readers a clear idea of what the essay will cover

191

ESL
Remind nonnative speakers that it is a convention of English to present the main point in the first paragraph, stated explicitly.

The thesis statement is usually either the first or the last sentence in the introductory paragraph.

Here are some common kinds of introductions that meet this challenge. The thesis statement is underlined in each one. These are not the only ways to start essays, but they should give you some useful models.

A Quote

A good short quote definitely gets people's interest. It must lead naturally into your main point, however, and not be there just for effect. If you start with a quote, make sure that you tell the reader who the speaker is.

1.   "God help me. I'm alone. There's no hope." Those thoughts represented rock bottom for Marie Balter. Abandoned by her mother, abused by her adoptive parents, at times depressed and perhaps suicidal, the intelligent, willful Balter was confined for twenty years to a state mental hospital, where she was misdiagnosed as a schizophrenic and was nearly killed by massive doses of an experimental drug. <u>Rather than giving in, however, she decided to fight.</u>

—Bruce McCabe, " 'Mental Illness': Escape from Hell"

Example or Story

READING SELECTIONS
The full essays for the introductions by Staples, Hoffmann, and Del Castillo Guilbault are in the Readings section at the end of the book (if you are using the edition with readings).

People like stories, so opening an essay with a brief story or example often draws them in.

2.   It has been more than two years since my telephone rang with the news that my younger brother Blake—just twenty-two years old—had been murdered. The young man who killed him was only twenty-four. Wearing a ski mask, he emerged from a car, fired six times at close range with a massive .44 Magnum, then fled. The two had once been inseparable friends. A senseless rivalry—beginning, I think, with an argument over a girlfriend—escalated from posturing, to threats, to violence, to murder. <u>The way the two were living, death could have come to either of them from anywhere.</u> In fact, the assailant had already survived multiple gunshot wounds from an accident much like the one in which my brother lost his life.

—Brent Staples, "A Brother's Murder"

Surprising Fact or Idea

IDEA JOURNAL
Write about a time someone dared you to do something.

Surprises capture people's interest. The more unexpected and surprising something is, the more likely people are to take notice of it.

TEACHING TIP
In the inverted pyramid strategy, the introductory paragraph starts with a general statement and narrows to the thesis statement. (EG)

3.   The secret to diving under a moving freight train and rolling out the other side with all your parts attached lies in picking the right spot between the tracks to hit with your back. Ideally, you want soft dirt or pea gravel, clear of glass shards and railroad spikes that could cause you instinctively, and fatally, to sit up. Today, at thirty-eight, I couldn't be threatened or baited enough to attempt that dive. <u>But as a seventh grader struggling to make the cut in a tough Atlanta grammar school, all it took was a dare.</u>

—Roger Hoffmann, "The Dare"

Strong Opinion or Position

The stronger the opinion, the more likely it is that people will pay attention. No wimpy introductions! Make your point and shout it!

IDEA JOURNAL
Respond to Steele's statement.

4.   The problem is familiar: Black students are not faring well in college. The national dropout rate for African Americans is nearly 70 percent, while for whites it's 40 percent. Now there's a new idea, one that is offering some hope. Claude Steele, a professor of social psychology at Stanford University, calls it "stereotype vulnerability," which means that if you tell kids they're part of a group that can't succeed, they won't.

—Connie Leslie, "You Can't High-Jump
if the Bar Is Set Low"

IDEA JOURNAL
What does the word *macho* mean to you?

A Question

A question needs an answer, so if you start your introduction with a question, your readers will need to read on to get the answer.

ESL
Ask students what words from their native languages don't translate well into English.

5.   What is *macho?* That depends on which side of the border you come from. Although it's not unusual for words and expressions to lose their subtlety in translation, the negative connotations of macho in this country are troublesome to Hispanics.

—Rose Del Castillo Guilbault,
"Americanization Is Tough on Macho"

Thinking Critically to Write an Introduction

FOCUS   Reread your draft essay and your assignment.

ASK   • What do I know about my readers? What kind of introduction will work best with them?
        • What is my purpose in this essay? What point do I want to make? How can my introduction help me make that point?
        • How can I catch my readers' attention?
        • How should I present my thesis statement?
        • How can I give my readers a good sense of what the essay will cover?

WRITE   Write a strong introduction.

Practice 1   ## Marketing Your Main Point

IDEA JOURNAL
Write on one of the topics in Practice 1.

As you know from advertisements, you can make just about anything sound interesting. For each of the following topics, write an introductory statement using the method indicated. Some of these topics are purposely pretty dull to show you that you can make a punchy statement about almost anything if you put your mind to it.

TOPIC: Welfare to single teenage mothers
TECHNIQUE: Question

What would happen if the government stopped making welfare

payments to single teenage mothers tomorrow?

1.   **TOPIC:** Smoking cigarettes
     TECHNIQUE: Strong opinion

     Answers will vary.

2.   **TOPIC:** Food in the cafeteria
     TECHNIQUE: Example or story

3.   **TOPIC:** Credit cards
     TECHNIQUE: Surprising fact or idea

4.   **TOPIC:** Role of the elderly in society
     TECHNIQUE: Question

5.   **TOPIC:** Stress
     TECHNIQUE: Quote (you can make up a good one)

Practice 2   Identifying Strong Introductions

In a newspaper, a magazine, an advertising flier—anything written—find a strong introduction. Bring it to class and be prepared to explain why you chose it as an example of a strong introduction.

TEACHING TIP
If you use the inverted
pyramid for introductions,
explain the conclusions
as a regular pyramid.
The tip of the pyramid,
(the narrowest point) is
the first sentence of the
concluding paragraph,
moving to the most gen-
eral point: the main idea
that the writer wants
readers to remember.
(EG)

B. Conclusions

Conclusions too often just fade out because writers feel they're near
the end and think the task is over—but it isn't *quite* over. Remember, people
usually remember *best* the thing they see, hear, or read *last*. Use your conclusion to drive your main point home one final time. Make sure your conclusion has the same energy as the rest of the essay, if not more.

A GOOD CONCLUSION

- Should refer back to the main point
- Should sum up what has been covered in the essay
- Should perhaps make a further observation or point

In general, a good conclusion creates a sense of *completion*: It brings readers
back to where they started, but it also shows them how far they have come.
Think of a spiral:

SPIRAL VIEW OF AN ESSAY

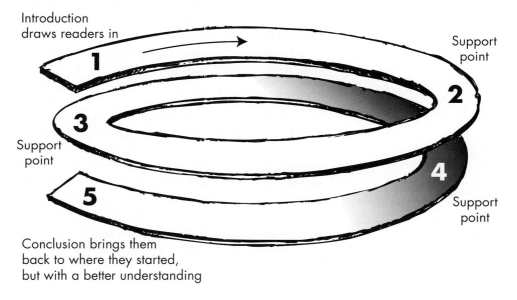

Introduction
draws readers in

Support
point

Support
point

Support
point

Conclusion brings them
back to where they started,
but with a better understanding

One of the best ways to end an essay is to refer directly to something in the
introduction. If you asked a question, reask it and answer it. If you started a
story, finish it. If you used a quote, use another one—maybe by the same
person or maybe by another person on the same topic.

1.   **INTRODUCTION**

"God help me. I'm alone. There's no hope." Those thoughts represented rock bottom for Marie Balter. Abandoned by her mother,
abused by her adoptive parents, at times depressed and perhaps suicidal, the intelligent, willful Balter was confined for twenty years to a
state mental hospital, where she was misdiagnosed as a schizophrenic
and was nearly killed by massive doses of an experimental drug. Rather
than giving in, however, she decided to fight.

IDEA JOURNAL
Do you know someone like Marie Balter, someone who refuses to give up?

CONCLUSION

"God has plans for all of us. We don't know what they are yet. He uses pain and suffering for growth." Marie Balter had plenty of both, and indeed she did grow. Despite physical and mental abuse, strong and dangerous drug treatments, and a diagnosis of hopelessness, she escaped her shadow world. Armed with her experience, her three college degrees, and her conviction, she teaches and lectures on overcoming life's obstacles. Marie has helped herself, and she is no longer alone.

— Bruce McCabe, " 'Mental Illness': Escape from Hell"

2.   **INTRODUCTION**

It has been more than two years since my telephone rang with the news that my younger brother Blake — just twenty-two years old — had been murdered. The young man who killed him was only twenty-four. Wearing a ski mask, he emerged from a car, fired six times at close range with a massive .44 Magnum, then fled. The two had once been inseparable friends. A senseless rivalry — beginning, I think, with an argument over a girlfriend — escalated from posturing, to threats, to violence, to murder. The way the two were living, death could have come to either of them from anywhere. In fact, the assailant had already survived multiple gunshot wounds from an accident much like the one in which my brother lost his life.

CONCLUSION

TEACHING TIP
Have students repeat Practice 2, this time for strong conclusions.

As I stood in my apartment in Chicago holding the receiver that evening in 1984, I felt as though part of my soul had been cut away. I questioned myself then, and I still do. Did I not reach back soon or earnestly enough for him? For weeks I awoke crying from a recurrent dream in which I chased him, urgently trying to get him to read a document I had, as though reading it would protect him from what had happened in waking life. His eyes shining like black diamonds, he smiled and danced just beyond my grasp. When I reached for him, I caught only the space where he had been.

— Brent Staples, "A Brother's Murder"

Thinking Critically to Write a Conclusion

FOCUS   Reread your draft essay and your introduction.

ASK
- What is my main point? What do I need to remind readers of?
- What is the most important thing for my readers to remember about what I have written?
- What is the strongest or most interesting part of my introduction? How can I refer back to that?
- Do I have any further observations to make?

WRITE   Write a good conclusion.

Practice 3 ▶	### Analyzing Conclusions

How is the conclusion to the essay on Marie Balter linked to the intro-duction (example 1 on p. 195)? How does it refer back to the introduction? How does it show readers how far they have come?

Answers will vary. _____

_____

_____

Practice 4 ▶	### Finding Good Introductions and Conclusions

In a newspaper or magazine or anything written, find an example of a piece of writing that has a strong introduction and conclusion. (You may want to use what you found for Practice 2.)

1. What method of introduction is used? _____

2. What does the conclusion do? (restate the main idea? sum up the sup-

    port? make a further observation?) _____

    _____

3. How are the introduction and the conclusion linked? _____

    _____

TIP: Do not put quotation marks around your title or underline it. Center it at the top of the page be-fore the first paragraph.

C. Titles

Even if your title is the *last* part of the essay you write, it is the *first* thing readers read. Use your title to get your readers' attention and to tell them what your paper is about. Use vivid, strong, specific words.

Remember, a title is different from a thesis statement or topic sentence.

A TITLE

• Is not part of the first paragraph
• Is not a complete sentence
• May hint at the main point, but usually does not state it outright

One way to find a good title is to consider the type of essay you are writing. If you are writing an argument, state your position in your title; if you are writing a process analysis, try using the term *steps* or *how to* in the title. This way, your readers will know immediately not only *what* you are writing about but how you will discuss it.

TEACHING TIP
Except for the first and fourth ones, the titles here are taken from the Readings section.

Illustration	My Husband the Dictator
Narration	A Brother's Murder
Description	The Monster
Process Analysis	How to Apply for Financial Aid
Classification	The Ways We Lie
Definition	What Is Intelligence, Anyway?
Comparison and Contrast	Two Extremes Miss Target over Guns
Cause and Effect	Why Marriages Fail
Argument	Affirmative Action Causes Imbalance

Thinking Critically to Write a Good Title

FOCUS	Reread your introduction to remind yourself of how you've marketed your main point.
ASK	• How can I let my readers know what the topic of my essay is? • How can I hint at my main point? • How can I let readers know what kind of essay this is? • Will my title get my readers interested? • Have I used vivid, specific language?
WRITE	Write two or three titles and pick the best one.

Practice 5   Writing Titles

TEAMWORK
Practice 5 works well as a group activity.

The following are possible alternate titles for introductory paragraphs 3, 4, and 5 on pages 192–93. After rereading the paragraphs, choose the best title by circling the letter. Be prepared to explain why you made that choice.

1. Introductory paragraph 3
   a. The Dangerous Dive
   b. Seventh Grade
   c. The Freight Train
   d. A Tough Grammar School

2. Introductory paragraph 4
   a. Black Students at Stanford University
   b. If You Don't Believe, You Won't Succeed
   c. Stereotypes at Stanford
   d. Stereotypes Affect Success

3. Introductory paragraph 5
   a. "Macho" Means Bad
   b. What Does "Macho" Really Mean?
   c. Translations Blur Meaning
   d. Macho, Macho Man

Practice 6 ▶ **Name That Essay**

Reread the paired paragraphs 1 and 2 on pages 195–96 and write alternate titles for the essays that they belong to.

Introduction/conclusion 1: _____*Answers will vary.*_____

Introduction/conclusion 2: _____

Summary: Introductions, Conclusions, and Titles

LEARNING JOURNAL
In your own words, explain what introductory and concluding paragraphs should do.

• Your **introduction** should get your readers' attention. Some ways to start an essay are with a quote, an example, a surprising fact or idea, a strong opinion, or a question. (See pp. 192–93.)

• Your **introductory paragraph** presents your main point and indicates what you will cover in your essay. (See p. 191.)

• Your **concluding paragraph** refers back to the main point, sums up what has been covered, and perhaps makes a further observation. (See p. 195.)

• To give readers a sense of completion, your concluding paragraph should be linked back to your introductory paragraph. (See p. 195.)

• Don't let your conclusion fade. Make it powerful. (See p. 195.)

• The title should catch readers' attention and indicate the main point of the essay. (See p. 197.)

What Will You Use?

How will you use what you've learned about introductions and conclusions in college, at work, or in your everyday life?

17

Revising
Improving Your Essay

"I am in the computer and technology field where, traditionally, people have not been required to write much. As you progress in your career though, you have to be able to present your ideas to management. If you can't express them clearly and concisely, you may never be heard. For me, the bottom line is if you can't write well, don't expect to make it in today's business world."

—Ingrid Panosh, Senior Information Consultant, West Information Publishing Group, Eagan, Minnesota

Understand What Revising an Essay Is

A. What Is Revision?

Revision is reseeing: reading your draft with fresh eyes to see what you can improve. Revising an essay is much like revising a paragraph. You follow the same steps and search for the same things: ideas that don't fit into the essay, words or ideas that could be more specific, and ways to connect ideas so that they flow smoothly. For a complete explanation of the basic revision process, see Chapter 6.

Five Revision Tips

1. Give yourself a break from your draft (a few hours or a day).
2. Read your draft aloud and listen to your words.
3. Imagine yourself as your reader.
4. Get feedback from a friend, classmate, or colleague. (See pp. 56, 205.)
5. Get help from a pro at the college writing center or lab.

See page 48 for more ideas about revision.

No one gets everything right in a draft, so do not skip the revising stage. Commit yourself to making at least five changes in any draft. Revising isn't optional: It is a critical part of any kind of writing you do, whether it is for college, for work, or for everyday life.

LEARNING JOURNAL Describe what you actually do when you revise a draft.

Thinking Critically to Revise an Essay

FOCUS	After a break, reread your draft with concentration and a fresh perspective.
ASK	• Have I completed the assignment? • Will readers understand what I've written? • What is my main point? What did I want to say? Did I say it? • Does everything in my essay relate to my main point in my thesis statement? Does everything in each paragraph relate to the topic sentence for that paragraph? • Do I have enough support? Can I add any details? • Does my essay hold together? Is it clear how one idea connects to another? Is it clear how one paragraph connects to another? • Does my introduction catch readers' attention and present the thesis? • Does my conclusion end on a strong note?
WRITE	Revise your draft, making any improvements you can think of.
REFOCUS	Reread your revised essay to make sure it is as good as you can make it.

B. Revising versus Editing

ESL
ESL students are often tempted to edit without revising because they focus on first-language interference errors. Stress that first they must look at the bigger picture.

Revising and editing are two different ways to improve a paper. **Revising** is changing the ideas in your writing to make it clearer, stronger, and more convincing. When revising, you might add, cut, or change whole sentences or even whole paragraphs. **Editing** is finding and correcting problems with grammar, style, usage, punctuation, and mechanics. While editing, you usually add, cut, or change words and phrases.

DISCUSSION
Ask students what "He can't see the forest for the trees" means. Then ask them how it might relate to revising and editing.

Most writers find it difficult to revise and edit at the same time. It is more efficient to solve bigger, idea-type problems first (by revising) and then move to smaller, mechanical ones (by editing). Of course, if you notice a spelling mistake and want to fix it while you are still revising, go ahead. Just don't fall into the trap of looking only at individual words when you should be looking at ideas.

The editing section of this book begins on page 253.

Practice Revising for Unity, Detail, and Coherence

Revising for unity, detail, and coherence is covered in detail in Chapter 6. This section reviews the information there. If you need practice, go back to the exercises in Chapter 6.

COMPUTER
Tell students to first use the copy function to move an idea to another paragraph. They can read it over in the two different places and decide where it fits better. Remind them to then use the cut function to remove it from one place.

COMPUTER
If you can send material to students' monitors, type in a short essay (you could use one from the reader). Have students read the essay on screen and for each paragraph add a sentence that doesn't support the main point. Then have them move to another computer and find the unrelated sentence. They should put the offending sentence in italics. Have them return to the original computer and see if the correct sentences are italicized.

C. Revise for Unity

Unity means that all the points you make are related to your main point. If your essay includes ideas that do not relate to the main point, it lacks unity.

Thinking Critically to Revise for Unity

FOCUS	Reread your draft essay.
ASK	• What is my main point? • What are my support points? • Does the topic sentence in each support paragraph show, explain, or prove my main point? Do they actually help me make my point? • Do the sentences in each of the support paragraphs relate to the point in the topic sentence for that paragraph? • Are there any ideas that seem to detour from the main point?
REVISE	Drop or move any ideas that take a detour from the point.

D. Revise for Detail and Support

However strong your main point is, you won't get it across to your readers unless you include support that clearly shows, explains, or proves your point.

The thesis statement has to be supported by topic sentences that are related to the main point. The topic sentences have to be supported by examples and details in the support paragraphs.

Revise for detail and support by rereading your essay and looking for places where you have not supplied enough examples or proof. Keep your readers in mind and think about what they know and need to know in order to see your point.

Thinking Critically about Detail and Support

FOCUS	Reread your thesis statement and the topic sentence for each body paragraph.
ASK	• Do I have enough support for my thesis? • From these topic sentences, will my readers be convinced of my thesis? • Should I add any other support points?
REVISE	Add or change any topic sentence in any support paragraph as necessary.

FOCUS   Reread each topic sentence and the supporting examples, facts, and details in that paragraph.

ASK
- Do I have enough support for this topic sentence?
- From these examples, facts, and details, will my readers be convinced of the point in my topic sentence?
- Should I add any other support in the paragraph?

REVISE   Add or change supporting examples, facts, and details as necessary.

COMPUTER
Encourage students to use the cut and paste function rather than retyping to avoid the risk of introducing new errors. (EG)

E. Revise for Coherence

Coherence means that the parts of the essay—the sentences and paragraphs—"stick together" and connect to form a whole essay. Coherence in writing helps readers see how one point connects to another so that they blend into a single essay.

Three devices help ensure coherence in essays:

- Transitional words
- Repeated key words
- Transitional sentences

Here is part of an essay showing what devices the writer used to achieve coherence. In the essay, the student writer compares and contrasts different pediatricians she has used.

Transitional words (double-underlined)

Repeated key word (circled)

Transitional sentence (underlined)

Fortunately, I have found a pediatrician who listens to my thoughts and concerns. No matter what is going on outside of the examining room during our visits, Dr. Johnson is courteous enough to ignore the distractions and finish examining my children before leaving the room.

He is also very understanding about my parental concerns. For example, my oldest daughter had trouble learning to walk. Dr. Johnson called in three other doctors to check her leg development, and he also asked me if I wanted to schedule X-rays of her legs if I was not satisfied with the specialists' opinions. Instead of my concern being dismissed as unwarranted, Dr. Johnson's findings reassured me that she would be all right.

—Denise Washington (student)

Common Transitional Words and Phrases

SPACE

above	below	near	to the right
across	beside	next to	to the side
at the bottom	beyond	opposite	under
at the top	farther/further	over	where
behind	inside	to the left	

TIME

after	eventually	meanwhile	soon
as	finally	next	then
at last	first	now	when
before	last	second	while
during	later	since	

IMPORTANCE

above all	in fact	more important	most
best	in particular	most important	worst
especially			

EXAMPLE

for example	for instance	for one thing	one reason

AND

additionally	and	as well as	in addition
also	another	furthermore	moreover

BUT

although	in contrast	nevertheless	still
but	instead	on the other hand	yet
however			

SO

as a result	finally	so	therefore
because			

TIP: For a review of how to use transitional words and repeated key words, see Chapter 6.

TEACHING TIP
Ask students to bring in a newspaper article with all transitions circled and highlighted. (SG)

Transitions help ideas flow smoothly. You practiced using transitional words and repeated key words or ideas when revising paragraphs for coherence. (See the box on p. 204 for a reminder of common transitions.) In essays, you can also connect paragraphs with transitional sentences (see the example essay on p. 203). A transitional sentence begins a paragraph and tells readers, "I'm done with that point and I'm moving on." If your final essay seems choppy, you may want to try adding a transitional sentence to the beginning of some paragraphs.

Thinking Critically to Create Coherence

FOCUS   Reread your essay.

ASK
- Are there any places where one idea just seems to stop abruptly?
- Are there any places where readers might wonder why I go on to the next point or how the point fits into the whole?
- Does every paragraph have a topic sentence?

WRITE   Try adding transitional words and sentences and repeating key words and ideas from earlier paragraphs.

TEAMWORK
Try modeling peer review. Bring in a short essay and have students answer the questions in small groups, with one person acting as recorder. You can join each group for a few minutes to make sure they understand the process. Then discuss the answers as a class.

Teamwork: Getting Feedback

If you can, show your draft to someone else and ask for that person's opinion. The first time someone else comments on what you have written, you may feel a little awkward or embarrassed, but you'll get over it. Don't explain your essay to the person; see if it stands on its own. Ask the person some of these questions:

- Do you know what the main point is?
- Can I do anything to make the introduction more interesting?
- Is there enough support for my main point? Do you know what I'm talking about?
- Are there too many details? If so, what should I leave out?
- Are there any places where you have to stop and reread something to understand it?
- What about the conclusion? Does it fade out? Could I make the point more forcefully?
- Where could the essay be better? What would you do if it were your essay?
- Do you have any other comments or suggestions?
- Do you see any errors in grammar, spelling, or punctuation?
- If you were getting a grade on this, would you turn it in as is?
- What else do you have to say about my essay?

TEAMWORK
Have students work in pairs to suggest other changes for the draft essay. Also ask them if they agree with the annotations that the student and teacher made.

F.   An Example of Revision

Here are a first draft and a revised draft of the same paper, "Secure the 'Campus.'" The first draft shows the comments of three different people: the writer (in green), a peer editor (in black), and the instructor (in black capital letters). The revised draft shows the changes the student writer made based on these comments.

FIRST DRAFT

TITLE?

good intro!

Add "eyes adjust to dark"

THESIS?

GIVE NAME OF PRISON

Add transition— connection unclear

common where?

POINT LACKS COHERENCE

Cut? Doesn't really support my topic sent.

What happened? Give us more details!

The young man quietly opened the door to the stately brick building and sprinted across the spacious grounds toward the street. As he sank into thick lawn, he heard the din of crickets and inhaled the scent of roses. He smiled and took a deep breath. Is this a college student taking an evening walk? No, it is a prisoner escaping from prison.

Although (it) is a minimum-security prison, many of the inmates are dangerous. Those who were convicted of very violent crimes have served long terms in other prisons and are now close to parole. Many prisoners attempt escape within months of their parole hearings. The police chief indicates that this is a common phenomenon, and experts think that the possibility of being denied parole causes some prisoners to panic and become desperate to get out before that could happen.

The inmates who were convicted of less violent crimes may still be very violent characters. For example, a recent escapee was in for burglary. When he broke into the house, he clubbed a ninety-year-old woman to near death and left her for dead. By his own admission, had he known she was still alive, he would have finished the job. This near-killer and others like him roam free in our minimum-security facility. Inmates also form work crews who perform jobs around the town and, in the process, get to "scope out" possible escape routes. They then use their knowledge to break out.

A home invasion last month brought the issue of prison security to the public's attention. In the middle of the night, a prisoner escaped and broke into a home right down the road. The incident and the publicity left little doubt that the prison's security is too casual.

Under pressure from the governor and the news media, the prison is taking steps to increase its security. One has to wonder, though, what will happen when the publicity dies down. Will the prison lapse back into its lax security? Town residents must keep up the pressure to ensure adequate security at the prison.

Like what?

Could be stronger here

REVISED DRAFT

Secure the "Campus"

The young man quietly opened the door to the stately brick dormitory and sprinted across the spacious grounds toward the street. As he sank into thick lawn, he heard the din of crickets and inhaled the scent of roses. Once his eyes adjusted to the darkness, he surveyed the area and saw no other humans. He smiled and took a deep breath. Is this a college student taking an evening walk? No, it is a prisoner escaping from prison—a prison that must increase its security.

Although the Middle County Correctional Facility is a minimum-security prison, many of the inmates are dangerous. Those who were convicted of very violent crimes have served long terms in other prisons and are now close to parole. Surprisingly, though, many prisoners attempt escape within months of their parole hearings. The police chief indicates that this is a national phenomenon, and experts think that the possibility of being denied parole causes some prisoners to panic and become desperate to get out before that could happen.

The inmates who were convicted of less violent crimes may still be very violent characters. For example, a recent escapee was in for burglary. It was a very violent burglary, however—when he broke into the house, he clubbed a ninety-year-old woman and left her for dead. By his own admission, had he known she was still alive, he would have finished the job. This near-killer and others like him roam freely in our minimum-security facility.

A home invasion last month brought the issue of prison security to the public's attention. In the middle of the night, a prisoner escaped and broke into a home right down the road, where a family was asleep on the second floor. Hearing the prisoner break in, the father, mother, and oldest daughter ran into the hall to see what the noise was. They were greeted by the prisoner, who was halfway up the stairs and was wielding a baseball bat and threatening their lives. He awakened the two younger children and announced his intent to take them as hostages. Somehow, the father convinced him not to do so. Instead, the terrorized family hovered in a bedroom while the escapee cleaned out their house of all small valuables and took off in their van. Within two hours, television and news media swarmed the town and continued close coverage for several days, at which point the prisoner was apprehended. The incident and the publicity left little doubt that the prison's security is too casual.

IDEA JOURNAL
Write about a recent crime and your reactions to it.

Under pressure from the governor and the news media, the prison is taking steps to increase its security. Expensive, high-tech, state-of-the-art security systems will be installed and monitored at all times. Guards will be retrained and held more accountable for security. An additional evening roll call will be implemented. One has to wonder, though, what will happen when the publicity dies down. Will the prison lapse back into its lax security? Town residents must keep up the pressure to ensure adequate security at the prison; their safety is at stake.

Practice 1 ▶ Revising an Essay

TEAMWORK
This practice works well in small groups. Have groups share revisions and point out to students that there is no one right way to revise—that they have options to consider.

Using the ideas in this chapter, revise the following essay for unity and coherence. Cross out any words or sentences that don't support the main point. Use arrows to show what should be moved. Write any new words or sentences in the margins or between lines.

Answers will vary.

Body language is often more revealing than words. By just looking at the way people are sitting or standing, you can tell a lot, even if they are not speaking. Certain positions tend to mean certain things, and it is helpful to understand these unspoken messages.

transition added

Different arm positions signal different attitudes toward the situa-

unrelated idea

tion or the speaker. ~~Some people have longer arms than others.~~ *For example,* Arms crossed tightly over a person's chest suggest that the person is not open to what is going on or being said. The position expresses disagreement, resistance, or anger. More neutral arm positions are resting at a person's side, or crossed loosely, or one resting lightly on the other.

transition

also   *attitudes (more specific)*

Leg positions reveal ~~things.~~ Tightly crossed legs indicate a closed or unreceptive attitude. People who sit with one leg wrapped tightly around another are tense about something. And if they also have their arms tightly crossed, you can be pretty sure that they aren't happy with what's going on, even if they say otherwise.

transitions

is also revealing and   *For example,*

Basic posture sends messages. The basic body slump can mean a few different things. Constant slumping with head hung down and back hunched can signal poor self-esteem. Or it might just mean someone is tired or bored. ~~Then there is~~ $s$tanding up straight/ A chin tilted *, on the other hand, signals alertness.* upward looks snobby. A head to the side indicates either questioning or sympathy. Leaning back in a chair is casual; leaning forward slightly is attentive. Leaning forward dramatically indicates aggression.

transition and support

Body language messages are at least as strong as speech messages. Take a look around a room and notice how people are sitting, standing, or walking. Or take a look at yourself. What does your own body language reveal? Understanding body language, both your own and others', helps you give and get the real message. So when you want to project a certain attitude, consider your body as well as your words.

Summary: Revising an Essay

LEARNING JOURNAL
How would you explain the terms *unity, support,* and *coherence* to someone who had never heard of them?

- **Revision** is reseeing: reading your draft with fresh eyes. It is a search for ideas that don't fit, points that could be more specific, and ways to connect the points. (See p. 200.)
- Revise for **unity**—all points should relate to and support your main point. (See p. 202.)
- Revise for **support**— topic sentences that relate to the thesis statement and details that relate to and support the topic sentences. (See p. 202.)
- Revise for **coherence**— points should blend together to form a whole. Use **transitional words and sentences** to move smoothly from one point to the next. **Repeat key word(s) and ideas** to keep your readers focused on the topic and main point. (See p. 203.)
- Ask a friend, a colleague, a classmate, or a member of your family to read your draft. (See p. 205.)
- Always revise a draft; commit yourself to making at least a few changes to any draft.

What Will You Use?

Which suggestions for revision in this chapter will you use on your next essay, and why?

ESSAYS

Part Four

Writing Different Kinds of Essays

18

Informative Essays
Essays That Explain

TEACHING TIP
In addition to traditional academic-style assignments, each type of informative essay also has an applied writing assignment. (See pp. 232–34.) Students are given real-world situations and must use their writing and critical thinking skills to write essays in response.

Checklist:
How to
Write an
Essay

In Part Two of this book, you practiced writing paragraphs that used different methods of developing your ideas: illustration, narration, description, process analysis, classification, definition, comparison and contrast, and argument. In this chapter, you will write essays that use some of those same methods. For more information about any of them, refer to Part Two where they are explained in more detail.

This chapter focuses on **informative writing,** writing that tells or explains something to readers. Many reports, applications, memos, instructions, technical manuals, and college essays are examples of informative writing. Writing that tries to prove a point, win an argument, or persuade readers is called argument; it will be covered in Chapter 19.

You can use this writing process Checklist for all the informative essays covered in this chapter.

Check off items as you complete them.

1. **Narrow and explore your topic.**

_____ Narrow the general topic to something that interests you and that you have direct experience with. Jot down a few ideas about the narrowed topic.

_____ Consider your purpose for writing about this topic. What point do you want to make? What do you want your readers to learn?

2. **Make your point in a thesis statement.**

_____ Review your ideas and decide what main point you want to make about your topic.

(continued)

ESSAYS

Part Four • Writing Different Kinds of Essays

copy of this Checklist is in *Additional Resources*. If you want students to complete the Checklist as they write their essays, you can make and distribute photocopies.

_____ Write a thesis statement that includes your main point and gives readers an idea of what the essay is about.

3. Choose details and examples to support your main point.

_____ Use a prewriting technique to come up with specific details and examples that will support your main point and make the topic come alive for your readers.

_____ Drop details that don't support the main point, and select those that do.

_____ Group the support into paragraphs, one for each major support point.

_____ Add information to make the details and examples more vivid and convincing.

4. Write a draft.

_____ Write a topic sentence for each main support paragraph.

_____ Arrange the topic sentences and supporting details and examples in a logical order and make a plan that arranges the paragraphs in the body of the essay.

_____ Write a draft using complete sentences in correct essay form.

_____ Write the introduction, conclusion, and title.

5. Revise your draft.

_____ Get feedback from others.

_____ Cut any details that do not support your main point or help show readers what you mean.

_____ Add any points, details, or examples that will make your essay stronger.

_____ Make sure the order of the paragraphs is logical. Add any transitions needed to make the essay easy to follow.

_____ Do not just copy over your draft. Make changes to improve it.

6. Edit your revised draft.

_____ Find and correct any problems with grammar, spelling, word use, or punctuation.

_____ Produce a clean, final copy.

_____ Ask yourself: Is this the best I can do?

Narration

TIP: For more on narration, see Chapter 8.

READING SELECTIONS
For examples of and activities for narration essays, see Chapter 43 in the Readings section.

er Janet Wade won the
say contest, the executive di-
ctor of the Illinois Community
llege Board recommended
at Janet be named Student
ureate of Illinois, an award
rmally reserved for seniors
four-year institutions who ex-
plify the spirit and value of
hievement.
About winning the contest
d the award, Janet said,
ttle did I know how writing
e essay would change my
. I thought I was developing
-confidence just going to
rper, but this award has
ven me so much more. The
essage I got from the award
that it's possible to be a re-
ning adult student and be
t as competitive as a regular
llege student. In spite of hav-
g family obligations and
erything, you can do this
."
Janet has now graduated
m Harper with a 4.0 aver-
e and is continuing her edu-
tion, working toward a B.A.
DePaul University in
icago.

Narration is the telling of a story about an event or experience. Good narration reveals something of importance, includes the important events of the story, brings the story to life with detailed examples of what happened, and usually presents events according to when they happened (time order). In college writing, narration is used often: for example, whenever students recount a historical event, summarize a work of fiction, or give background on the development of a medical technique or theory.

Read and Analyze a Narration Essay

Janet Wade, who was a student at William Rainey Harper College in Illinois, wrote the following essay, which won the Illinois Community College Trustees Association essay contest.

How Community College Has Changed My Life

Allow me to introduce myself, because you might not recognize me as a "coed" at first glance. I am a middle-aged mother of three who did not have the opportunity to attend college when I graduated high school twenty-something years ago. I have been attending Harper College on a part-time basis for five years now and am pursuing a liberal arts degree with a major in English. Community college has forever changed my life.

When I was a high school student, I received mostly B's and C's — all right, more C's than B's. As a college student, however, I maintain a 4.0 average and am a member of Phi Theta Kappa, the honor society for two-year colleges, as well as Harper's own honor society. With my self-esteem thus bolstered, I now have a goal of graduating Harper with a 4.0 average, and with hard work and a little luck, I am confident that I will do it. This level of confidence is something that could not have been acquired through the maturation process alone; I give ample credit to my community college experience.

While going to college, I have developed a true affection for the works of William Shakespeare and consequently was delighted to have

1

2

3

TEACHING TIP
You might check to see if there is any contest in your community, county, or state similar to the one Wade entered and work with students to enter.

brunch with some professors of English prior to accompanying them to a production of *Othello*. I have joyfully discovered my creative side in a creative writing course and a Women and Creativity class taken here at Harper. I never realized I could wear the hat of a poet, a fiction writer, a playwright, and a producer/director and love it!

Over the years I have met published poets, seen wonderful theater productions at rock-bottom prices, and found a fascination for American and British history that I would never have known existed within me, without the community college influence. I've listened to some wonderful guest lecturers, engaged in some lively debates, and seen fascinating videos and documentaries while a student here at Harper College.

Now I use what I have learned. The knowledge I gained from an environmental science class is being put to practical use—I now recycle with a vengeance—and I will be helping to plan the Earth Week activities at my children's school.

I look forward to completing my education here at Harper College, which will bring me even closer to earning my bachelor of arts degree. Community college has taught, and continues to teach, me many things, the most important of which is not any particular subject or theme, but that the love of learning can and should go on.

IDEA JOURNAL
What happened on your first day of college? during your first week?

1. In the first paragraph, double-underline the thesis statement.

2. In the body paragraphs, underline examples that support the thesis statement. Find at least five.

3. What kind of order does Wade use? Space? Time? Importance?

   Time

   Circle the transitions.

4. What lesson is revealed by Wade's narrative? (What is her main point?)
   Community college has vastly improved her life and is worth the effort.

Narration Essay Assignments

Using the Checklist on page 213 and the Thinking Critically guide on this page, write a narrative essay on one of the following topics.

1. Look back at your idea journal entry about starting college (p. 216). Write an essay about the best or worst thing that happened on your first day of college.
2. Write about an achievement of which you are proud.
3. Write an essay about a very embarrassing experience.
4. Tell about a time when you learned something significant about or from your mother, father, or grandparent.
5. Look back at the paragraph you wrote in Chapter 8 and write an essay using that paragraph as a starting point.

Thinking Critically about Your Narration Essay

FOCUS	Reread the assignment and think about what you want to say to your readers in your narrative essay.
ASK	• What experience or event do I want to write about? Why? • What is important about this story? What should it reveal to my readers? • Can I write a thesis statement that introduces the story and tells why it is important? • To convey my main point, what events do I need to tell about? What details, facts, and examples will bring the events to life for my readers? • Should I use a chronological order or some other order? • At the end of the essay, will my readers understand what they have been told and why?
WRITE	Write a clear, strong, and convincing narrative essay that gets your main point across to your readers.

Description

Description is writing that gives a vivid impression of the topic. It translates your experience of a person, place, or thing into words, often by appealing to the physical senses: sight, hearing, smell, taste, touch. Good description creates a strong main impression (overall effect, feeling, or image) about your subject and uses specific details to support the main impression. The details are often related to the five senses. In college writing, description is used often: for example, whenever students write news reports in a journalism class, present information about materials and conditions in a lab report, or identify their ideal customer in a marketing or advertising course.

Read and Analyze a Description Essay

Tiffany Johnson, a student at Broward Community College in Florida, wrote the following essay for a writing class.

IDEA JOURNAL
Write about someone you think is beautiful.

READING SELECTIONS
For examples of and activities for description essays, see Chapter 44 in the Readings section.

The Beautiful Person in My Life

My friend, who was so important to me growing up, had a beauty   1
that was both inward and outward. He was very tall and pencil-slim.
His hair was full and long, thick and wavy. It curled wildly around his
head. His face was as soft as a baby's cheeks, and his skin was the light-
est soft brown. His eyes were deep brown and welcoming.

When he greeted people, he seemed almost shy, smiling just a little   2
and tilting his head a bit to one side. He always wore simple clothing
such as a long, baggy, slightly wrinkled, dark-colored shirt and loose-
fitting jeans. He never wore brightly colored or tight-fitting clothes. He
never wore jewelry—not even a watch—and he never wore cologne. I
can't even remember his shoes, though I think they were just cheap
tennis shoes. If you didn't know him, you would never notice him. I
guess that's what he wanted.

To people who knew him, he was very special: He definitely stood   3
out from the crowd. He was talented at everything, from sports to
music. Some days he would sit on the front stoop hunched over his
guitar and would softly pick a tune he'd made up. He might sing along
quietly in his deep, melodious voice. Or he might bring out his har-
monica and make it cry. Other times, he'd play basketball, wordlessly
slicing by the guards, jumping high in the air, and cleanly dropping the
ball through the net. Everyone liked him.

DISCUSSION
Ask students which of the senses they think of when they hear the word *beautiful*. Discuss why we first think visually of beauty and explore nonvisual things that can be beautiful: music, song lyrics, a fabric, a personality.

Everyone relied on him because he was always there to lend a   4
helping hand. He helped everyone in the neighborhood through one
crisis or another, and he was respected by everyone. I learned from him
to care as much for others as for oneself. I learned from him that
beauty is inside and out.

1. Double-underline the <u>thesis statement</u>.

2. Underline some <u>sensory details</u> the author uses—find at least ten. What sense does she use most? _*sight*_____

3. How does the author order the details? _*space: top to bottom*_ *(hair → shoes)*_____

4. In your own words, what main impression does the author create? *Answers will vary.*_____

5. Without looking at the essay, describe the person. Has the author given you a memorable impression? _____

   _____

   _____

6. How does the author tie the conclusion back to the introduction? *uses "inside and out"—like "inward and outward"* *in introduction*_____

Description Essay Assignments

Using the Checklist on page 213 and the Thinking Critically guide on page 220, choose one of the following topics and write a description essay.

1. Look back at your idea journal entry (p. 218) and write an essay describing someone you think is beautiful. Consider what effect that beauty has on you.

2. Listen to a musical group that you like and describe the sounds of the music.

3. Where are you right now? What is your general impression of the room or space you're in? Write about how it looks, sounds, and smells.

4. Describe in detail the experience of eating a favorite food or meal. Don't do this from memory. Concentrate as you eat to get the details that you don't usually notice.

5. Describe the perfect car, house, or job.

6. Look back at the paragraph you wrote in Chapter 9 and write an essay using that paragraph as a starting point.

Thinking Critically about Your Description Essay

FOCUS	Reread the assignment and think about what you want to describe for your readers.
ASK	• What person, place, or thing do I want to write about? Why?
	• What main impression about it do I want to convey?
	• Can I write a thesis statement that introduces my subject and states the main impression?
	• To convey my main impression, what elements of my subject do I need to describe? What sensory details will my readers need to understand my subject?
	• Should I use space order or some other order?
	• At the end of the essay, will my readers understand what I have told them and why?
WRITE	Write a clear, strong, and convincing description essay that gets your main point across to your readers.

Process Analysis

TIP: For more on process analysis, see Chapter 10.

Process analysis is writing that explains how to do something or how something works by presenting the steps. Good process analysis tells the reader what process is being analyzed, presents the essential steps in the process, explains the steps in detail, and presents the steps in a logical order (usually chronological). In college writing, process analysis is used often: for example, whenever students write out the procedures for a lab experiment, explain how to make an electrical repair, or identify the steps in a government process.

Read and Analyze a Process Analysis Essay

READING SELECTIONS
For examples of and activities for process analysis essays, see Chapter 45 in the Readings section.

Karen Branch wrote the following paper as part of a writing class project to put together information for new students.

Number of steps identified in each paragraph will vary.

How to Apply for Financial Aid

IDEA JOURNAL
Have you ever avoided doing something because it seemed too complicated or overwhelming? What?

Why do so many students who qualify for financial aid fail to receive it? Many students simply don't know how to apply for it. The process of financial aid is time-consuming, but not difficult—and it's a process you should learn. If you think there's any chance you will be attending college in the fall, start the process by April 1.   1

(The first step) is to call the college admissions department and ask   2
3 to speak to the financial aid department. Ask if you can make an ap-

pointment to talk with a financial aid officer. Also ask for information on all available financial aid. The person will ask for your name and address and will mail you information. It should take only a few days to arrive, so if you haven't received the package in a week, call again.

When you receive the package, take a quick look at everything to see what's there. The package should include information from the college and information from the U.S. Department of Education. For example, you should receive a pamphlet on direct loans, a Free Application for Federal Student Aid, and a *Student Guide: Financial Aid from the U.S. Department of Education.* If you are missing any of these items, call the college again and request them.

Next review the forms and booklets for deadlines. Financial aid officers say the biggest reason students don't get loans or aid is that they miss deadlines. Don't lose out on real money because you've missed a deadline. Start a file labeled "Financial Aid" and staple a sheet of paper with deadlines to the inside front. Also mark important dates on your personal calendar.

After this previewing, you then need to decide what aid you are eligible for. Read the information you have received very carefully and determine what you should apply for. If you are confused, call the financial aid office again; it is the job of people there to help you, so don't hesitate to call.

Once you know what aid you will apply for, gather together all the forms you will need to complete. Fill in the application completely. Most people make mistakes on forms, so it is smart to make a couple of copies of the application forms and fill out the information on the copies first. Then proofread the information carefully, and when you're sure it's right, transfer it to the real application. If you have any questions, call the financial aid office again. You might want to have someone there review your draft application.

When you have completed the actual application, make sure that you have attached any additional information requested. For example, you will probably have to attach a financial statement or your high school transcripts. Reread the pamphlet and the application to make sure your package is complete. When everything is ready, make a copy for your file and mail the application materials.

2

(Then) you wait for a while. The financial aid office can tell you when you should expect a response. If you haven't heard anything within that time, call financial aid to see if you should follow up in any way. With any luck, you should be notified that you have received some money. This will make the whole thing worth it. Don't miss out on easy money just because you didn't understand the process!

1. Double-underline the thesis statement in the first paragraph.

2. In each paragraph, underline the steps. Beside each paragraph, write the number of steps in that paragraph in the left margin.

3. What kind of order has the writer used? Space? Time? Importance?

   Time
   _____ Circle all the (transitions.)

4. Double-underline the sentence in the concluding paragraph that ties the concluding paragraph to the introductory paragraph.

Process Analysis Essay Assignments

Using the Checklist on page 213 and the Thinking Critically guide on page 223, write a process analysis essay on one of the following topics.

1. Look back at your idea journal entry (p. 220) and describe the process of doing whatever it is you were avoiding. Let readers know whether you've mastered the process by now—or are still avoiding it.

2. What do you do particularly well? Write an essay that teaches someone (a younger friend or sibling, for example) how to do it.

3. Write about how to impress a date (or your boss or your teacher).

4. Write about how to make _____ [topic of your choice].

5. Write about how to plan a good vacation or trip.

6. Look back at the paragraph you wrote in Chapter 10 and write an essay using that as a starting point.

Thinking Critically about Your Process Analysis Essay

FOCUS   Reread the assignment and think about what process you want to explain to your readers.

ASK
- What process do I want to write about? Why?
- What do I want my readers to be able to do? Perform the process themselves? Understand how the process works?
- Can I write a thesis statement that contains the process and my purpose?
- What steps in the process do my readers need to know about? What details, facts, and examples will help my readers understand each step?
- Should I use a chronological order or some other order?
- At the end of the essay, will my readers understand what I have told them?

WRITE   Write a clear, strong, and complete process analysis essay.

Classification

TIP: For more on classification, see Chapter 11.

Classification is writing that sorts things by putting them into groups or categories. Good classification makes sense of things by organizing them, uses categories that follow a single organizing principle, and gives examples of what fits into the categories. In college writing, classification is used often: for example, whenever students categorize mental and physical disorders, organize the different expenses in a budget, or identify the parts of a computer system.

Read and Analyze a Classification Essay

READING SELECTIONS
For examples of and activities for classification essays, see Chapter 46 in the Readings section.

This essay was written by Danny Fitzgerald, a business student interested in Japan.

Blood Type and Personality

In Japan, the question "What's your blood type?" is as common as "What's your sign?" in the United States. Some Japanese researchers claim that people's personalities can be classified by their blood types. You may be skeptical about this method of classification, but don't judge its validity before you read the descriptions the researchers have put together. Do you see yourself?

IDEA JOURNAL
How could you divide the people in your class (or at work or in your family) into groups?

1

If you have blood type O, you are a leader. When you see something you want, you strive to achieve your goal. You are passionate, loyal, and self-confident, and you are often a trendsetter. Your enthusiasm for projects and goals spreads to others who happily follow your lead. When you want something, you may be ruthless about getting it or blind to how your actions affect others.

Another blood type, A, is a social, "people" person. You like people and work well with them. You are sensitive, patient, compassionate, and affectionate. You are a good peacekeeper because you want everyone to be happy. In a team situation, you resolve conflicts and keep things on a smooth course. Sometimes type As are stubborn and find it difficult to relax. They may also find it uncomfortable to do things alone.

People with type B blood are usually individualists who like to do things on their own. You may be creative and adaptable, and you usually say exactly what you mean. Although you can adapt to situations, you may not choose to do so because of your strong independent streak. You may prefer working on your own to being part of a team.

The final blood type is type AB. If you have AB blood, you are a natural entertainer. You draw people to you because of your charm and easygoing nature. ABs are usually calm and controlled, tactful and fair. On the downside, though, they may take too long to make decisions. And they may procrastinate, putting off tasks until the last minute.

Classifying people's personalities by blood type seems very unusual until you examine what researchers have found. Most people find the descriptions fairly accurate. When you think about it, classification by blood type isn't any more far-fetched than classification by horoscope sign. What will they think of next? Classification by hair color?

TEAMWORK
If most students know their blood type, form groups according to blood type and have students determine if they have the traits in the essay. They could then write a classification essay on their own blood type's characteristics.

1. Double-underline the thesis statement.

2. What introduction technique does the writer use to get attention?
   Surprising statement

TIP: To review introduction techniques, see Chapter 16.

3. According to what characteristic does this essay classify people?

   blood type

4. What categories does the writer present? *O, A, B, AB*

5. Underline the <u>topic sentences</u> of paragraphs 2–5.

Classification Essay Assignments

Using the Checklist on page 213 and the Thinking Critically guide on this page, write a classification essay on one of the following topics.

1. Look back at your idea journal entry (p. 223). Write a short essay classifying people in the class, people at work, or people in your family. Try to come up with categories no one has thought of before.
2. Write an essay on the kinds of writing you have done in the past two weeks, for college, for work, or for yourself.
3. Classify the kinds of foods that are usually in your refrigerator or kitchen.
4. If you get a college degree, what kinds of jobs will you be qualified for?
5. Look back at the paragraph you wrote in Chapter 11 and write an essay using that paragraph as a starting point.

Thinking Critically about Your Classification Essay

FOCUS	Reread the assignment and think about what you want to classify for your readers.
ASK	• What group or collection of things do I want to write about? Why? • What is my purpose? To make sense of my subject for my readers? To make some additional point about my subject? • To accomplish my purpose, how should I sort things? • Can I write a thesis statement that introduces the subject and states my main point? • What categories will help my readers understand my subject? Which items fit into each category? What details, facts, and examples will my readers need to understand how I have classified things? • Should I use order of importance or some other order? • At the end of the essay, will my readers understand what I have told them?
WRITE	Write a clear, strong, and logical classification essay that gets your main point across to your readers.

Comparison and Contrast

TIP: For more on comparison and contrast, see Chapter 13.

Comparison shows similarities among things; **contrast** shows differences. Good comparison and contrast uses subjects that have enough in common to be compared or contrasted, serves a purpose (to make a decision or to analyze the subjects), presents several points of comparison or contrast, and arranges the points in either point-by-point or whole-to-whole form. In college writing, comparison or contrast is used often: for example, whenever students evaluate various solutions to an environmental problem, analyze competing scientific theories, or set two political systems side by side.

Read and Analyze a Comparison/Contrast Essay

READING SELECTIONS
For examples of and activities for comparison/contrast essays, see Chapter 48 in the Readings section.

The following essay was written by Mark Herrmann, a student at Finger Lakes Community College in Canandaigua, a town in upstate New York.

My Street Then and Now

Ten years ago, I lived in Rochester, New York, on a street in the outskirts of the nineteenth ward. The neighborhood was considered trendy at the time, and I felt very lucky to find an affordable apartment there. It was a convenient location; a ten-minute drive got me to work or just about anywhere else I wanted to go. Last summer I drove down my old street six years after leaving it and only four years after moving out of the city. I was dismayed to see the changes that had occurred in such a short time.   1

When I lived on this street, most of the houses were well cared for with neatly mowed lawns and flowers planted in the front. In the summer, children played outside; they rode bikes on the sidewalks or ran back and forth through sprinklers. The adults sat on the porch talking or cooked on gas grills. I enjoyed walking my dogs around the block, and while it was wise to be cautious, I never feared for my safety.   2

Now, however, I found myself locking the car doors. The house I used to call home had been sold; it did not look the same. The grass and weeds were very high, and a window had been broken. Garbage bags were piled in front; some of them had broken open and their contents were spilling out everywhere. As I looked around, I found other houses in similar condition. There were no children playing outside or   3

IDEA JOURNAL
Write about a place you are familiar with and how it has changed over the years. Be as specific as you can.

any adults. The only sign of life was a man staggering down the street clutching a bottle. I knew that I would not feel safe living here now.

I wondered how this street could have changed so much. Then I 4 remembered reading about the rising crime rate in the city. Shootings and stabbings happened ten years ago, but they were not everyday occurrences as they seem to be today. Perhaps this crime is driving people to move to the safer suburbs. I was saddened to see how this "up and coming" neighborhood appears to be on the decline.

1. Double-underline the thesis statement.

2. Is this a comparison or a contrast essay? __*contrast*__

3. What organization (point-by-point or whole-to-whole) does the writer use? __*whole-to-whole*__

4. List at least four examples of things that have changed. __*Answers will vary.*__
   Possible examples: grass and weeds around house, window
   broken on house, garbage bags piled up, no children outside

5. Where does the writer move from past to present? (Circle) the transition word.

6. What does the writer cite as a possible reason for the changes?
   rising crime rate driving people out

Comparison/Contrast Essay Assignments

Using the Checklist on page 213 and the Thinking Critically guide on page 228, write a comparison or contrast essay on one of the following topics.

1. Look back at your idea journal entry (p. 226) and write an essay that contrasts the place then and the place now.

2. Think back to what you were like ten years ago: what you looked like; what you did for fun; what you wore; what TV shows, movies, or songs were popular; what was going on in the world. Write an essay comparing or contrasting then and now for one of these topics.

3. Contrast a good college course you've taken with a bad one.

ESL
ESL students can compare or contrast some elements of their native culture or country with life in the United States.

4. Compare your favorite book with your favorite movie. Look for similarities you were unaware of before.

5. Look back at the paragraph you wrote in Chapter 13 and write an essay using that paragraph as a starting point.

Thinking Critically about Your Comparison/Contrast Essay

FOCUS
Reread the assignment and think about what you want to compare or contrast for your readers.

ASK
- What two things do I want to compare or contrast? Why? Are they similar enough to be compared or contrasted?
- What do I want my readers to be able to do? Make a decision? Understand how my two subjects are alike or different? Is there some other point I want to make?
- To accomplish my purpose, what approach should I take? Comparing? Contrasting? Both?
- Can I write a thesis statement that introduces my subjects and states my main point?
- To convey my main point, what aspects of my subjects do I need to compare or contrast? What details, facts, and examples will help my readers understand each comparison or contrast?
- Should I use a whole-to-whole organization or a point-by-point organization?
- At the end of the essay, will my readers understand what I have told them?

WRITE
Write a clear, strong, and convincing comparison or contrast essay that gets your main point across to your readers.

Cause-Effect

READING SELECTIONS
For examples of and activities for cause-effect essays, see Chapter 49 in the Readings section.

A **cause** is what made an event happen. An **effect** is what happens as a result of the event. In college writing, cause and effect is used whenever students trace the development of a historical situation, identify the consequences of poor nutrition, or describe why a mechanical device fails.

TEACHING TIP
Explain to students the differences between *effect* (noun) and *affect* (verb). (SG)

CAUSE
You get your laundry out of the washing machine, and everything is pink. You want to know why. You determine that the **cause** of the laundry turning pink was washing your new red T-shirt with everything else.

EFFECT
You're about to put your clothes in the washing machine. The label on your new red T-shirt says, "Wash separately." You consider what the **effect** might be of washing the T-shirt with the rest of the clothes. You determine that a likely effect is that the red will run and turn your laundry pink.

Jim Rice of Quinsigamond Community College helps his students visualize the cause-effect relationship by suggesting that they think of three linked rings:

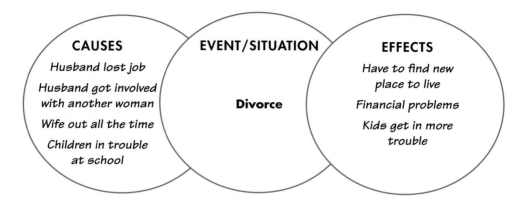

Practice 1   **Listing Causes and Effects**

Fill in the diagram with three possible causes and effects of the situation (finding a job).   *Answers will vary.*

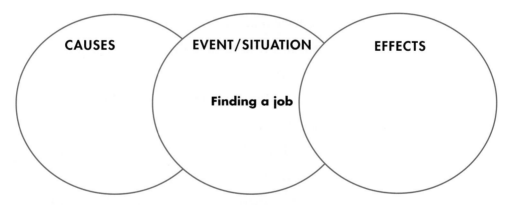

Read and Analyze a Cause-Effect Essay

Carol Benson wrote this cause-effect essay for her writing class. She said writing about these events helped her put things in order.

Learning from Loss

Two years ago, a good friend died from AIDS. Since that time,   1
Kevin's death has had many effects on me. Although most of them
have been painful, in the end I've grown from the experience.

The (first) effect I experienced was rage. How could this have happened, and why? The world seemed full of unfairness and cruelty. I spent hours crying, slamming my fist against walls and tables, cursing a world where criminals lived while Kevin died. I couldn't sleep or eat much. I lived on my rage alone.

(After) the effects of rage came those of sorrow and loss. I missed my friend. I kept picking up the phone to call him, only to realize while dialing that he was dead. Something would happen at work that I knew he'd appreciate, and I'd think, "Wait till Kevin hears this." During this time I sighed a lot and felt tired. For the first time I understood what people meant by the phrase "Part of me died."

(Months later,) I turned a corner and stopped sitting around feeling like a victim. I had to do something. I called the local AIDS hotline and asked about volunteer opportunities. Now I visit four AIDS patients often and just spend time with them. Sometimes we talk, or watch TV, or have dinner. Sometimes we just sit together, and they doze off. I also got involved in organizing an AIDS walk to raise money for research. The walk raised $5,000. About 700 people showed up, and together we marched through the streets, feeling part of a powerful group joined by the deaths of friends and family.

I (still) think of Kevin often, but not with rage or even so much with sorrow. In some ways I feel connected to him through my work with AIDS patients. I know that I can't control everything in life, but I can take control of my own life. The effects of Kevin's death have helped me to look beyond myself and to work for a better world.

TIP: To review introduction techniques, see Chapter 16.

1. What method does the writer use to get your attention in the introductory paragraph? _*strong statement*_

2. Double-underline the <u>thesis statement</u> in the first paragraph.

3. How many effects does the writer present? __*3*__ Underline the sentence that introduces each of the <u>main effects</u>.

4. In what order (space, time, importance) are the effects arranged?

   time _____ Circle the (transitions.)

5. List the examples the writer gives in the second paragraph to support

   the topic sentence of that paragraph. *Answers will vary. Possible*

   examples: world seemed unfair, spent hours crying and

   raging, couldn't eat or sleep

6. Double-underline the sentence in the last paragraph that <u>sums up</u> the main point of the essay.

Cause-Effect Essay Assignments

Using the Checklist on page 213 and the Thinking Critically guide on this page, write an essay on one of the following topics.

1. Look back at your idea journal entry (p. 229) about the event that either annoyed or pleased you. Write an essay on either the causes or the effects, or both, of that event.
2. Think of a difficult decision you made recently. What caused you to have to make that decision? What were the effects of that decision? Write a short essay on the causes, the effects, or both.
3. Write an essay explaining what caused you to enroll in college and what the effects have been so far.
4. Have you ever made a conscious decision to change a bad habit or improve your lifestyle? Write about the effects.

Thinking Critically about Your Cause-Effect Essay _____

FOCUS   Reread the assignment and think about what causes or effects you want to describe for your readers.

ASK
- What situation do I want to write about? Why?
- What is important about this situation? What main point do I want to make about it? To do this, what approach should I take? Exploring causes? Exploring effects? Both?
- Can I write a thesis statement that introduces the situation and states the main point?
- To make my main point, what important causes and/or effects do I need to present? Am I sure that my causes are *real* causes, not just things that happened afterward? Am I sure that my effects are *real* effects, not just things that happened before? What details, facts, and examples will my readers need to understand each cause and/or effect?

- Should I use a chronological order or some other order?
- At the end of the essay, will my readers understand what I have told them?

WRITE   Write a clear, strong, and convincing cause-effect essay that gets your main point across to your readers.

Use Essay Skills in Real-World Situations

Real-World Assignment: The Interview

You have an interview at a company you really want to work for. You are determined to get this job, so you go to the library and check out a book on interviewing for jobs. It has a chapter entitled "The Most Frequently Asked Questions," which you turn to.

You have no trouble answering many of the questions that ask about your employment history and about the company itself, such as "What jobs have you had in the past?" "What types of responsibilities have you had in other jobs?" and "What are you looking for in an employer?"

But then you come across a series of questions that require you to talk about *yourself*. You realize that you are less prepared for these, and you decide to write out an answer to help you get ready for the interview.

Write a complete essay in response to one of these standard interview questions. Remember that you want to present yourself as a strong candidate. To do this, you will need to present your strengths as an employee and to support your claims with concrete details and examples.

1. **DESCRIPTION:** How would you describe yourself as an employee? You might tell about your habits or about your strengths and weaknesses.

2. **DESCRIPTION:** How would you describe your ideal job? You might tell about the range of activities or responsibilities you'd like or the sort of environment you'd like to work in.

3. **NARRATION:** What is your greatest personal or professional strength? Narrate a story that shows this strength in action.

4. **NARRATION:** What accomplishment or achievement are you proud of? Narrate the story of this accomplishment or achievement; be sure to let the interviewer know what you think this story says about you.

Real-World Assignment: The Service Learning Course

You are taking a course in your major that has a service learning requirement. To fulfill this requirement, you volunteer for several hours per week at the Helping Hand Center, an organization that helps anyone in the community with any kind of problem. Fortunately, this semester a lot of people need help with exactly the kind of subject matter you're currently studying for your major. (Please choose a skill that you know well, that is part of your major, and that people visiting a neighborhood help center might want to learn.)

To earn academic credit for this work, you must write an essay-length report and submit it to your instructor. Choose one of these topics.

1. PROCESS ANALYSIS: To help other people that might need your expertise in the future, you decide to write out a complete set of instructions for the course-related skill you're best at teaching. Remember that your process analysis has to be clear enough for people to use on their own.

2. PROCESS ANALYSIS: One of the people you meet at the center is a man in his forties with interests and a background similar to your own. He wants to go to your college, but he has been out of school for a long time and has no idea how to apply for admission or sign up for a course. You help him either apply or sign up and then write an essay-style report that traces the process step by step.

3. CLASSIFICATION: An elderly woman, newly widowed, has no idea how to handle her expenses or even what bills to expect. She needs to create a monthly budget. Write an essay that classifies the types of monthly expenses she will probably have, along with examples of those expenses. You can use your own expenses as a model.

4. CLASSIFICATION: The Helping Hand Center wants to set up a course for the college's students that focuses on "academic survival skills," and you are asked for ideas about what kinds of things might be considered useful skills. Write an essay that presents the various academic skills you think the center should teach, with examples of specific activities that should be covered in a course.

Real-World Assignment:
The Restaurant Management Job

You have been hired as a management trainee at the Oxford House, a famous old restaurant. Your first assignment is to act as host: You greet the customers, escort them to their tables, and check in with the diners partway through their meals.

After your first week, the manager confides that the restaurant has been losing business in the past couple of years. The manager asks you to spend the next few weeks observing the customers and their behaviors and to write a report offering any suggestions for change that you can think of. You observe the following:

- Most of the customers are older; very few young people come in.

- All of the waiters are men. They dress in formal attire.

- The restaurant atmosphere is very dark, very formal, very quiet.

- There is no specially designated smoking area. The smell of smoke fills the entire restaurant.

- The menu is limited.
  - The entrees are either beef or pork.
  - Soups are always either chowders or cream of something.
  - The only salad is iceberg lettuce with tomatoes and cucumbers.
  - The vegetable is either plain green beans or carrots.
  - The wine list is short and expensive. The only beers are domestic (Miller and Budweiser, for example).

You realize that the restaurant has been losing business because it is failing to attract new, younger customers. If the Oxford House is to survive, it needs to appeal to people in their twenties and thirties. Write one of the following reports.

1. **COMPARISON / CONTRAST:** Write a report for your manager in which you contrast the dining preferences of younger and older customers. You can focus on the food, the atmosphere, or something else. Use examples from the Oxford House and make recommendations for specific changes.

2. **CAUSE-EFFECT:** Your manager thinks that some of your recommendations make sense but is confused by your suggestion for a designated smoking area. Write an essay-length report in which you discuss the effects that such a change might have on the atmosphere of the restaurant or the type of customers it attracts.

3. **COMPARISON / CONTRAST:** Assume your manager has followed your recommendations. Now you need to let potential customers know how the Oxford House has changed so they will try the restaurant. Write a short, upbeat essay contrasting the old and the new Oxford House, which you can reproduce as a flyer and use for advertising the restaurant.

4. **CAUSE-EFFECT:** After your recommended changes have been made and the Oxford House starts making money again, the owner of the restaurant starts to take an interest. She wants to know why things are suddenly looking up. Write a report to the owner in which you explain the causes of the Oxford House's new success.

What Will You Use?

List some ways you might use the types of informative writing covered in this chapter in your real life.

19

Argument Essays
Essays That Persuade

TIP: For more on argument, see Chapter 14.

DISCUSSION
Read the essay aloud and ask students to agree or disagree with the position. After reading, give students a couple of minutes to jot down some ideas and discuss.

IDEA JOURNAL
Who has the right to decide on medical treatment: the doctor or the patient?

Argument is writing that takes a position on an issue and defends it with evidence in order to persuade someone else of the position. Good argument takes a strong and definite position, presents convincing evidence to defend and support the position, considers the reader's position and the opposing view, and has energy from start to finish.

Read and Analyze an Argument Essay

The following essay was written by Jason C. Sifford at Tarrant County Junior College in response to the question "Who has the right to decide on medical treatment: the doctor or the patient?"

Life or Death: Who Decides?

Too many hospital beds are taken up by basically dead bodies. 1 Many patients who will never wake up again are kept alive because their families have the money. While these "dead" patients take up room in the hospitals, there are many who cannot be admitted but who could be saved with immediate care. Also, many people do not care about their spouse or family member when money is involved, be it medical bills or the anticipation of a large sum from the insurance company. Therefore, doctors should have the sole authority to recommend that a patient sustain treatment or be cut off from it.

Doctors are trained to make these decisions.

Families are too emotionally involved.

READING SELECTIONS
For examples of and activities for argument essays, see Chapter 50 in the Readings section.

Space is needed for those who can benefit.

✓ or ?

✓ or ?

TEACHING TIP
For complete coverage of argument, see Chapter 14.

Doctors go through strenuous training for at least eight years to learn how the body works and, for that matter, how the body does not work. After the conventional four years of college comes medical school. After medical school comes the internship, which can last up to three years. Obviously, becoming a doctor is no trivial task. These doctors become, after all their studies, the most elite and intelligent people on earth, at least in the areas of health and patient care.

Many families do care deeply about their loved ones and would do anything to keep them alive for as long as possible. "Alive" is the key word here. Many families, with unsupported hopes that some supernatural force or miracle will happen, keep their loved ones on life support long after the brain has expired. On the other hand, some people have family members who go into the hospital and ask that needed treatment be denied. Or the family members will not sign the needed waivers so that treatment may begin because they have taken out large insurance policies and wish to collect on them. Doctors have no personal ties to these people and are trained specifically for these situations. Furthermore, they can determine if a patient will recover or not and, therefore, should have the last word on the matter.

Many people cannot enter the hospital because of a lack of beds. A recent poll by the *American Medical Journal* estimates that 15 percent of all hospital beds are taken up by clinically dead patients. These numbers are staggering, considering that another 30 percent of the general population cannot receive treatment because of hospital overcrowding. In Freemont, Georgia, Jessica Freeman, twelve years old, died in her home from an infection after being treated in the emergency room for a ruptured appendix and then released because no beds were available.

With tragedies such as Jessica's happening every day, it is evident that something is wrong with our medical system. Giving doctors authority either to dismiss patients who are not treatable or to stop treatments for those who will not recover can only help save more lives.

1. Double-underline the thesis statement.

2. In your own words, what three supporting points does Sifford use to defend his position? Write these points in the margin next to their paragraphs. Which do you think is the most convincing?

3. What surprising statistics does the author cite? Underline them. Put a check (√) in the margin next to each one if you find it convincing, a question mark (?) if you don't.

Argument Essay Assignments

Using the Thinking Critically guide on this page and the Checklist on page 238, write an argument essay on one of the following topics. For some topics, you may need to do some background reading.

ESL
Some cultures (many Asian ones, for example) are not as direct in their arguments as U.S. culture is. Emphasize to students that their position must be clear, direct, and supported by evidence.

1. The same question that Sifford considered, using your journal entry (p. 235) as a starting point and not using any of Sifford's evidence

2. A counterargument to Sifford's essay, presenting evidence that the patient or the patient's family should have complete control over medical treatment

3. Legalization of marijuana or cocaine

4. Gay couples adopting children

5. A controversial current issue at college, at work, or in your community

TEACHING TIP
Suggest to students that they use some of the topics for journal entries. You may want to assign topics of local interest for assignments.

6. Pornography on the Internet

7. Prerequisites for college courses

8. Gun control

9. The law that requires students to stay in school until they are sixteen

10. An essay using as a starting point the paragraph you wrote in Chapter 14

Thinking Critically about Your Argument Essay

FOCUS   Before and as you write, think about your position on the issue and how you can persuade your readers.

ASK
- Why is the issue important to me? What do I have at stake?
- What is my position on the issue?
- What is my reader's position—the same as mine or different? If different, for what reasons?
- What points can I make to support my decision? What points can my opposition make? How can I counter them?
- How do I get energy into my argument?

WRITE   Write a strong, persuasive essay that states your position, supports it with evidence, and defends it against opposition.

Checklist: How to Write an Argument Essay

TEACHING TIP
You may want to review the section in Chapter 14 on how to narrow the topic by forming a question (p. 164).

Check off items as you complete them.

1.   **Explore the issue and take a position.**

_____   Turn the issue into a question.

> **Issue:** Smoking in restaurants

> **Question:** Should smoking be allowed in restaurants?

_____   Use a prewriting technique to find and explore your position, your readers' position, and the opposition's position.

_____   Build energy/get involved/take a stand. Take a minute to think about how this issue affects *you* or your family.

2.   **Write a thesis statement.**

_____   Write a thesis statement that answers your question. Make it strong and clear.

3.   **Find and select evidence that supports your position.**

_____   Use a prewriting technique to come up with support points and evidence (facts, examples, expert opinions) for each support point.

_____   Consider the opposing position; anticipate objections.

_____   Drop points and evidence that don't support your thesis well, and select those that do.

_____   Get someone to listen to and challenge your support points and evidence. Find new evidence if necessary.

4.   **Write a draft.**

_____   Write a topic sentence for each support point.

_____   Arrange support points and evidence in a logical order (usually from least important to most important) and make a plan.

_____   Write a draft using the complete sentences in correct essay form.

_____   Write an introduction that draws readers in. Write a strong conclusion that makes your final pitch with energy.

5.   **Revise your draft.**

_____   Get feedback from others.

RESOURCES
A reproducible Checklist for an argument essay is in *Additional Resources.* You may want to copy and distribute it to students, having them check off the steps as they go and hand in the plan with their draft or final paper.

(continued)

COMPUTER
Have students list evidence for their topic on the computer. Then have each student move to another student's computer and write down opposition to the evidence that the student has written. Students should then return to their own computers and answer the objections.

_____ Cut any details that do not help you persuade readers of your position.

_____ Add any other support points or evidence that might help your case.

_____ Make sure the order is logical and add importance transitions.

_____ Do not just copy over your draft. Make changes to improve it.

6.   Edit your revised draft.

_____ Find and correct any problems with grammar, spelling, word use, or punctuation.

_____ Produce a clean, final copy.

_____ Ask yourself: Is this the best I can do?

Use Argument Essay Skills in Real-World Situations

Real-World Assignment: The College Council

You are a student representative to the College Council, which reviews requests and issues that affect the college as a whole. The college president opens today's session by saying, "We have before us a very tricky question to consider that affects not only the student involved but others as well." The president then presents the case.

Professor Johnston teaches EN100A, the basic writing course in the English department. A passing grade is required of all students in the course before they can be accepted into a degree program. A student in Professor Johnston's course, Joe M., has made a request of Professor Johnston that she does not feel able to grant without advisement by the College Council.

Joe M. is a mechanic at a large automotive repair center. He has a wife and four young children, one of whom has a chronic illness that requires expensive medical treatments. Joe must make more money or he will have to apply for welfare. Joe recently applied for a supervisor position that includes a substantial pay raise, but the company requires its supervisors to have a degree in automotive engineering. Because Joe is a good employee, his boss will make an exception to the rule, _if_ Joe enrolls in a degree program.

Joe is failing EN100A, a prerequisite for enrolling in the automotive engineering degree program. Joe attends every class, does all the homework, and completes all the writing assignments—but his writing is so poor that he receives F's. He has finally approached Professor Johnston, hoping that she will give him a passing grade if she knows how important it is. Professor Johnston is caught between the needs of this student and her responsibility both to the college and to other students. She applies to the College Council for advice.

The president says, "I would like each of you to write your opinion about what should be done and send me your responses. But first, here are some of the issues I would like you to think about. I'm sure there are others; please raise them in your opinion."

- Joe has very serious reasons for wanting to enter the program.
- If he fails EN100A, he will not get a much-needed promotion.
- His writing is so bad that there is no question in Professor Johnston's mind that he should not pass the course.
- Other students in the basic writing course also have good reasons for needing a passing grade.
- The college made a passing grade in EN100A necessary for good reasons. For the college degree to mean anything, certain basic skills must be guaranteed.
- Nothing is secret on a college campus. Any exception to any rule has a way of getting around.
- As a supervisor at the automotive center, Joe has to write weekly production reports and performance reviews.

Write a complete essay on one of the following topics, based on the facts of the case.

1. Write an argument either for or against giving Joe a passing grade in EN100A.
2. From Joe's perspective, write an argument essay in support of "bending the rules."
3. From the perspective of a businessperson on the College Council, write an argument essay against "lowering the standards."

Argument Writing Tests

Many states and colleges require students to take a writing test. Often the test calls for an argument essay on an assigned topic, and students must argue pro (for) or con (against) as directed. Many people believe that a good writer should be able to argue either side of an issue regardless of his or her personal feelings. Choose one of the following topics, come up with evidence to support both sides of the issue, and write an essay defending each side.

1. People convicted of drunk driving should lose their licenses forever.
2. Recently a popular and well-respected high school teacher in Illinois was dismissed from his position because it came out that in high school he had been charged with possession of marijuana (two joints). The law in the state says that no one convicted of any drug crime may serve as a teacher in a public school, so the principal had no choice but to dismiss the teacher despite his superb record of fifteen years of teaching. Argue for and against the law.
3. First-degree murder should have a mandatory death penalty.
4. The government should make it more difficult for couples to divorce.
5. Students should be penalized for poor attendance.

20

The Essay Exam and the Summary

Important College Writing Tasks

Everyone gets nervous about taking exams. The trick is to turn that nervousness into positive energy by learning test-taking strategies. This chapter will give you some all-purpose study strategies for exams and then some special advice about writing essay exams and summaries.

Studying for Exams

If you don't study for an exam, panic and poor performance are the likely results. Here are five reliable tips to help you study for any exam.

Ask about the Test

The more you know, the better off you'll be. Start with the person who knows the most: your professor. It's reasonable to ask about the test, so don't be afraid. Just know what questions to ask.

ASK	NOT
• What part of the course or text will it cover? (a chapter? a unit?)	• What's on the test?
• Will the format be multiple choice? short answer? essay?	
• Will I be allowed to use notes? a textbook? reference books?	

ASK	**NOT**
• What percentage of my course grade is the exam?	• Is this test important?
• Do you have any recommendations about what to review? (the text, notes, lab reports, and so on)	• Do I need to read the book? Are your lectures important?
• Will I need any special materials? (calculator, dictionary, and so on)	
• Will I have the whole period to complete the exam?	• Is there a make-up test?

Write down your professor's answers to your questions. Don't rely on your memory; it's going to have enough to do to remember the material without having to recall what the professor said.

Study with Another Person or Other People

Although everyone is busy, the effort needed to form a study partnership or group is well worth it. If you're studying for a writing course exam, probably the most important thing you can do is exchange notes on what's likely to be on the test and how to approach it. When you study by yourself, you have only your own perception of what's important. Another person's ideas add to your ability to "scope out" the test.

For other courses, study group members can help each other learn and review the content of the course. Do some prep work before meeting as a group so that you make the most of your group study time. Here are some ways to prepare and study as a group or with a partner.

- Each person can have responsibility for a particular section of material, preparing a list of five to ten questions that might be asked about that section. The questions and possible responses can then be discussed in the group.
- Each person can copy his or her notes—including study questions—on a particular chapter, section, or topic and distribute them to group members. (Decide ahead of time who will copy which notes.)
- Each person can come with a list of "ten things I'm sure will be on the test."
- Each person can come with a list of "things I don't understand."

Predict What Will Be on the Exam

Whether you are studying with other people or by yourself, it's a good exercise to make a list of what you think will be covered on the exam. Look over your notes, assignments, and previous tests or quizzes. What has the instructor stressed the most? Try writing questions for that material, and then try answering your own questions.

If there are things you're confused about, ask your professor about them, or ask another person in the class—someone who knows the material. If you are studying in a group, try writing a mock exam and showing it to your professor to see if you are on the right track. Don't go into an exam knowing that you don't understand a major concept.

Use Study Aids

Discover what study aids you have available and use them.

- Reread your notes, looking especially for anything you've underlined, starred, or highlighted.
- If you are being tested on material from your textbook, review any chapter summaries or "key concepts" sections.
- Review any handouts your instructor may have given you.
- Consider other available ways to review material—audiotapes, videos, computer exercises, study guides, and so on.

Be Active

You are more likely to understand and remember material if you have reviewed it actively. If you're reviewing material in a book, take notes. This helps you remember information because you put it in your own words, you write the information, and you see it on the page of your notebook or in the margin of the book.

Say aloud concepts that you want to remember. Many people learn well by hearing something rather than just by seeing it.

If studying from notes, modify your notes somehow. For example, if you've written an outline, transform it into a map. *Do* something.

Double Your Chances of Passing Exams before You Even Begin

Some students who fail or get low grades on exams simply don't know or understand the material. But many others fail because they don't know how to take an exam. Here are five things you should do for every exam.

Be Prepared

If you've found out everything you could about the exam and studied for it, you've already done the most important preparation. But don't get to the exam and discover that you've left something essential at home. Do you need paper? pen? books? a notebook? a calculator? Make sure you have what you need.

Manage Your Nerves

Get plenty of rest the night before and allow extra time to get to class. Arrive early enough to settle in. Before class or while the exam is being distributed, breathe deeply and talk to yourself (silently, of course). Sit up straight, take a deep breath, remind yourself that you know the material. You're prepared; you're ready; you will pass. When your professor starts to talk, look up and listen.

Understand the Directions

TEACHING TIP
Tell students that for some people, listening is not enough; they need to jot down the directions or highlight them if they are on the page.

First, listen to the directions your professor gives. It's tempting to start flipping through the exam as soon as you get it rather than listening to your professor. Resist temptation. Your instructor may be giving you key advice or information that's not written elsewhere.

Then, slowly and carefully, read the directions for each part of the test. Most of us have had the experience of answering all of the questions in a section, only to find out later that the directions said to answer only two. If you don't understand any part of the directions, ask your professor for clarification.

Survey the Whole Exam before Starting

Surveying is a crucial step that will help you budget your time. Often the toughest questions (and the ones worth the most points) are at the end. You don't want to have answered all the two-point questions and leave the thirty-point ones unanswered. Ask yourself:

- How many parts are there? Be sure to look on both sides of the page.
- How many points is each part worth? This will help you decide how much time each part is worth.
- What questions can I do quickly and easily? Start with these. It will get you going on the test, give you points, and build your confidence.

Develop a Plan

TEACHING TIP
Tell students that surveying and developing a plan don't take much time away from the test taking; they shouldn't use more than three to five minutes.

First, budget your time. After surveying the whole test, write down how much time you will allow for each section. Make sure you leave enough time for sections with the highest point values. Also leave enough time for any essay questions. They usually take longer than you think.

As you budget, keep in mind how much time you *really* have for the exam: A "two-hour" exam may really be only one hour and fifty minutes. Remember also to subtract a few minutes at the beginning for settling in and a few at the end for checking your work.

Second, decide on an order. Decide where you should start, what you should do second, third, and so on. Start with the sections you can answer quickly and easily.

Third, make a schedule and stick to it. You can calculate what time you want to start each section: Part 1 at 9:40, Part 2 at 9:55, and so on.

As you take the exam, monitor your time. If you find you're really stuck on a question and you're going way over your time budget, move on to another question or section. If you've thought about the question and can't come up with an answer, just move on. If you have time at the end of the exam period, you can go back to it.

Answering the Essay Question

Essay questions are often worth the most points, so they deserve special strategies. Here are five steps you can use to attack the essay exam question.

Read the Question Carefully

Be sure to read the essay question carefully so you know *exactly* what to write. Look for three kinds of key words in the essay question: words that tell you *what subject* to write on, those that tell you *how* to write about it, those that tell you *how many* parts your answer should have. Circle those words.

(Discuss) the (three) major (stages in the consumer buying process.)

(Describe) (someone who has played an important role) in your life.

TEACHING TIP
Have students bring in exams with essay questions from other classes. Look for any other words that are used and discuss what they mean.

TEACHING TIP
Give some topics to students and ask them what they would focus on. Examples: Discuss the Million Man March. Explain the meaning of "sexual harassment." Discuss a major figure in the civil rights movement. (SG)

COMMON KEY WORDS IN ESSAY EXAM QUESTIONS

Key Word	*What It Means*
Analyze _____	Break into parts (classify) and discuss
Define _____	State the meaning and give examples
Describe the **stages** of _____	List and explain steps in a process
Discuss the **causes** of _____	List and explain the causes
Discuss the **concept** of _____	Define and give examples
Discuss the **differences** between _____	Contrast and give examples
Discuss the **effects / results** of _____	List and explain the effects
Discuss the **meaning** of _____	Define and give examples
Discuss the **similarities** between _____	Compare and give examples
Discuss the **stages / steps** of _____	Give a process analysis

Key Word	*What It Means*
Explain the **term** _____	Define and give examples
Follow the development of, the process of _____	Give the history; narrate the story; analyze the process
Identify _____	Define and give examples
Should _____	Argue for or against
Summarize _____	Give a brief overview or narrative
Trace _____	Narrate; explain the process

Practice 1	**Identifying and Decoding Key Words**

Answers may vary.

Read the following essay questions and circle the key words. In the space below each item, write what the question asks you to do. Example:

(Discuss the meaning) of (*psychotic.*)

Define the term psychotic and give examples of it.

1. (Discuss) the (effects of alcohol.)

    List and explain the effects of alcohol.

2. What are the main (differences) between (Christianity and Judaism?)

    Contrast Christianity and Judaism and give examples.

3. (Discuss) the (four) main (stages of collective bargaining.)

    Give a process analysis with four steps for the collective

    bargaining process.

4. (Identify and discuss) the (three) major (sources of stress in humans.)

    Define and give examples of three main sources of stress.

5. Give (examples) of (something in our local economy that is changing) very rapidly.

    Identify and describe several examples that illustrate one

    change in the local economy.

6. (Trace the development) of the (steam engine.)

    Give the history of the steam engine.

Write a Thesis Statement

Write a thesis statement that is simple and clear; it should say exactly what you will cover in your answer. (In some cases, you may get partial credit for correct information contained in the thesis statement, even if you did not get the chance to write about it in your essay.)

The best way to stay on track in an essay exam is to write a thesis statement that contains the key words in the essay question. Usually you do not need to include a word such as *discuss* or *explain*.

ESSAY QUESTION   Explore one important consequence of women's entering the workforce in large numbers in the 1940s.

THESIS   One important consequence of women's entering the workforce in large numbers in the 1940s was the recognition that women could do "men's work."

| Practice 2 | ▶ | **Writing Thesis Statements** |

TIP: For more on developing thesis statements, see Chapter 15.

Write thesis statements in response to the following sample essay exam questions. Even if you do not know much about the topic, you should be able to write a thesis statement that follows the guidelines in this section.

1. Describe someone who was important to you when you were in high school.

   Answers will vary.

   _____

   _____

2. Identify three ways to relieve stress; give examples.

   _____

   _____

3. Should smoking be banned from all public places?

   _____

   _____

4. Discuss the differences between your eating habits now and your eating habits five years ago.

   _____

   _____

5. Choose two people who made a difference in twentieth-century America and explore their contributions.

_____

_____

Make an Outline

If you haven't done this already, jot down some notes on how you want to answer the question. Write down any important names, dates, or facts that pop into your head. Make a short outline so that you have a basic map for your answer. Each main point in your outline should represent a separate support point and a separate paragraph.

Write Your Answer

Your answer to an essay question should be in essay form, with an introductory paragraph, support paragraphs, and a concluding paragraph. Don't forget to use separate paragraphs for separate support points.

Here is an essay written by Lorenzo Gilbert at Broward Community College in Florida for the final exam in his basic writing course. He wrote in response to this question: "Describe someone who has played an important role in your life."

In today's society with all of the violence and drugs in the black community, it really helps to see a black man rise above other people's expectations.

When my uncle Dr. Gerald Johnson was a little boy, he used to take care of sick or wounded animals. When he got a little older, he worked for an animal doctor in an animal clinic. He cleaned cages, walked dogs, bathed dogs, and assisted the doctor any way he could. Although he earned only seventy-five cents an hour, the knowledge he received from working under a doctor would make him rich later.

Johnson graduated from Miami Central and received a band scholarship to attend Tuskegee University in Alabama. Tuskegee was an all-black school, so he felt very much at home. After marching in the band for four years and taking a lot of pre-veterinarian courses, it was time for him to move on. Although Tuskegee had a veterinary school, Johnson decided to go to the University of Florida since it was closer to home. Unfortunately, going to UF made him feel out of place. The university was predominantly white, and the veterinary school had only two blacks including Johnson. After the second year the only black other than Johnson dropped out because of the pressure. Since Johnson was black, none of the white students would work, study, or help him.

Even though he did not receive the extra help the others got, he still graduated, making him the first black to graduate from the University of Florida's veterinary school.

Now he owns three animal clinics and employs two assistant doctors, four receptionists, seven technicians, and one groomer.

If you really want something and work hard for it you can have it. Johnson really wanted to be a veterinarian and he got it. That is why he plays an important role in my life. He helped me see that anything is possible.

Reread Your Answer and Revise

Ask yourself:

- Does my essay answer the question? Look back at the question and your notes on what it asks you to do. Have you done it?
- Is it in essay form? Are there separate paragraphs for each point?
- Is it free of major grammar and spelling errors?

TIP: To see the symbols that are commonly used to make corrections, see the inside back cover of this book.

You can revise your essay by neatly crossing out mistakes, adding extra words or sentences in the margin or on extra lines, and using the paragraph symbol (¶) to show where you want a new paragraph to start.

Practice 3 **Answering an Essay Question**

Choose one of the following possible topics and write an essay on it, using the five steps discussed in this chapter. If you are doing this independently, give yourself a forty-five-minute time limit.

1. In a well-developed essay, agree or disagree with one of the following statements.

   People should live together before they get married.

   Marriage is an outdated custom.

   People should be required to retire at age sixty-five.

   Most students cheat on exams.

   Admissions policies at colleges should be made stricter.

   English should be the only official language in the United States.

   Tobacco should be banned entirely.

   People would be better off if they never watched television.

   People in this state do not care about the environment.

   All people should have religious training.

   Schoolchildren have too many vacations.

2. Discuss a major problem on this campus.

3. Define "heroism."

4. Discuss the types of crime in this area.

5. Narrate an event that impressed you in high school.

6. Summarize the events that led to your taking this course.

Writing Summaries

A **summary** is a condensed version of a longer piece of writing. A summary presents the main idea and key support points, stripping down the information to its essential elements. A summary is always stated in your own words.

In college, you are often asked to summarize something you have done in a course: a chapter you read, an experiment, an event in history. To summarize something well, you have to understand it thoroughly so that you can explain its important parts in your own words. For that reason, teachers often ask summary questions on exams. In the workplace, you often have to summarize events, situations, or information for your boss, who needs to know what's going on but doesn't have the time to hear every small detail.

A GOOD SUMMARY

- Has a topic sentence that identifies what you are summarizing
- States the main point of the longer text being summarized
- Includes the key support points
- Includes any concluding observations or recommendations
- Is written in your own words

The following example is a summary of the student essay on page 220, "How to Apply for Financial Aid." First read that essay, and then read the summary.

main point

The essay "How to Apply for Financial Aid," by Karen Branch, describes how to go about applying for aid. The author says that many students who are eligible for financial aid don't get it because they don't know how to apply for it. The author then presents the steps a student should follow, starting with calling the college admissions department and talking to the financial aid officer, who can provide information, directions, and an application form. It is then up to the student to read the information, determine what aid he or she qualifies for, and accurately complete the various forms. It is important to send the forms in on time and to follow up with the financial aid office. The author urges students not to overlook this source of funding.

| Practice 4 | **Analyzing a Summary** |

1. Double-underline the <u>topic sentence</u> of the summary.

2. What is the <u>main point</u> of the longer essay as it appears on page 250? Underline it and write "main point" in the margin.

3. What is the final observation? <u>Underline</u> it.

Thinking Critically to Write a Summary

TEAMWORK
Bring in a short article from a newspaper or use an essay from the back of this book. Break students into small groups and have them work through the Thinking Critically guide to answer the questions about the article. Compare answers and ideas. Have them write a summary.

FOCUS   Read or reread the longer work carefully, focusing on the most important information in it.

ASK
- If I could say one thing to sum up the main point in one sentence, what would I say?
- What other key information supports or demonstrates the main point?
- What observations or conclusions are drawn?
- Are these my own words?

WRITE   Write a summary that includes the main points in your own words.

| Practice 5 | **Writing a Summary** |

Use any essay that you have written for this course and write a summary of it. When you pass it in, make sure to attach the longer piece you are summarizing.

Your professor may prefer that you summarize a paragraph you wrote, something you have read, or something he or she will give you to read. In any case, using the Thinking Critically guide on this page, write a concise summary of the longer piece in your own words.

Summary Assignments

1. Read the front page of today's newspaper and summarize one of the news items.

2. Summarize the cover story from a recent issue of a magazine.

3. Watch one of the television news magazines (such as *60 Minutes*) and summarize one of the stories. To do this assignment, take notes while you are watching and listening.

4. Summarize a movie you have seen recently.

5. Summarize the strategies for taking an exam that are presented in this chapter.

TEACHING TIP
As a journal assignment, have students read an article, summarize it in one paragraph, and react to it in a second paragraph. (EG)

EDITING

Part Five

The Four Most Serious Errors

21

Overview

The Basic Grammar Tools

TIP: Put a bookmark or a paper clip at the beginning of this chapter. You will need to come back to it often as you edit your writing.

RESOURCES
Additional Resources contains supplemental exercises for this chapter and a test that assesses students' attitudes toward grammar.

LEARNING JOURNAL
Write about something that you're an expert in — a sport, part of your job, caring for children, whatever. Write responses to these questions: Were you always good at this? How did you get to be an expert? If you had to help someone else learn this thing you are good at, what would you do?

The first two sections of this book ("Paragraphs" and "Essays") focus on how to plan, draft, and revise your writing — in other words, how to get, develop, and refine ideas. This section focuses on the last step in the writing process: editing. In editing, you make sure that your ideas are expressed correctly and well. You shift your focus from looking at the ideas themselves to looking at words or phrases. You find and correct problems with grammar, style, usage, punctuation, and mechanics. Because editing calls for a different kind of focusing and thinking, it is usually done last, after the ideas in a piece of writing are in good shape.

Focus on What Is Most Important

Grammar probably isn't new to you. You've probably studied it before but found that for some reason it didn't sink in or transfer to your writing. You now have a chance to do it differently, though. This book and this course will help you learn and use the grammar that you need by focusing on what is most important — editing concerns.

A. The Four Most Serious Errors

DISCUSSION
You might explain that the author surveyed teachers from all over the country to come up with the four most serious errors.

This book puts special emphasis on four grammar errors, the four that people most often notice. These four errors may make your meaning harder to understand, but even if they don't, they give a bad impression of you.

THE FOUR MOST SERIOUS ERRORS

- Fragments
- Run-ons
- Problems with subject-verb agreement
- Problems with verb form and tense

255

If you can edit your writing to correct the four most serious errors, your writing will be clearer, and your grades will improve. By focusing on these errors, this book will help you make a significant difference in your writing.

B.   A Dozen Sentence Terms

Writing teachers use words such as *subject* and *verb* to describe how the different parts of a sentence fit together. The terms are tools that allow people to talk about how English works. Right now, you don't need to master all grammar terms. But you do need to learn the few terms that will allow you to edit your writing for the four most serious errors.

This book tries to avoid terms that are not tools you need right now. This chapter presents twelve terms (an even dozen) that you need to know—and use—now. These terms are highlighted and definitions are printed in the margin so that if you need to remind yourself later what a term means, you can find and review it quickly. Other terms are introduced in this chapter; but focus on the dozen sentence terms that are highlighted. These are the tools you need to start editing your writing.

The Basic Sentence

1. Sentence: The basic unit of a written communi-cation. It must have a subject and a verb, and it must express a complete thought.

A **sentence** is the basic unit of written communication. A complete sentence in standard written English must have these elements:

- A subject: the person, place, or thing that the sentence is about
- A verb: tells what the subject does or links the subject to a word that describes it
- A complete thought: an idea that makes sense independent of other sentences around it

TIP: A sentence begins with a capital letter and ends with a period (.), a question mark (?), or an exclamation point (!).

Editing starts with a clear understanding of what *is* a sentence and what *is not* a sentence. You can make sure that a group of words is a sentence by checking to make sure it has a subject, a verb, and a complete thought.

Here are some examples of sentences, some long, some short, but all with subjects, verbs, and complete thoughts. In each of the examples, the subject is underlined once, and the verb is underlined twice. This system of indicating subject and verb will be used throughout the rest of the book.

I work.

After my morning class, I work at the dry cleaner.

I am working there until midnight every night this week.

At the end of the week, I collapse.

My schedule is exhausting.

C. Subjects

The **subject** of the sentence is the person, place, or thing that the sentence is about. To find the subject, ask: Who or what is the sentence about?

Maureen studies all week long.

> [Who is the sentence about? *Maureen.*]

The parking garage is full by the time I get there.

> [What is the sentence about? *Parking garage.*]

The subject of a sentence is either a noun or a pronoun. A **noun** can be the name of a specific person, place, or thing:

Jack is overweight.

A noun can also name a nonspecific person, place, or thing:

Computer technicians can make a good salary.

A **pronoun** stands in for a noun. People use pronouns to avoid repeating nouns.

The students finished the test. ~~The students~~ They passed in their exams.

Pam bought a new car. ~~The car~~ It is red with a convertible top.

Common Pronouns

PERSONAL PRONOUNS	POSSESSIVE PRONOUNS	INDEFINITE PRONOUNS	
I	my	all	many
me	mine	another	much
you	your	any	neither
she	yours	anybody	nobody
her	her	anything	none
he	hers	both	no one
him	his	each	nothing
it	its	either	one
we	our	everybody	several
us	ours	everyone	somebody
they	their	everything	someone
them	theirs	few	something

| Practice 1 | **Identifying the Subject** |

Underline the subject in the following sentences.

> **EXAMPLE:** <u>Ralph</u> was convicted of breaking and entering.

1. Normally, <u>he</u> would have been given a jail sentence.
2. But a new rehabilitation <u>program</u> kept Ralph out of prison.
3. Young <u>people</u> who are convicted of nonviolent crimes can take a special literature course.
4. The <u>convicts</u> read, discuss, and write about particular works of literature instead of serving time in jail.
5. <u>They</u> learn about society and themselves.
6. The success <u>rate</u> with the students has been very high.
7. <u>Students</u> feel better about themselves and are more confident.
8. Similar <u>programs</u> are being started all over the country.
9. The <u>courses</u> are held at local schools rather than in jails.
10. Many "<u>graduates</u>" enroll in college programs and stay out of trouble.

D. Verbs

5. Verb: Tells what the subject does or links the subject to a word that describes it.

Every sentence has a main **verb**, the word or words that tell what the subject does or that link the subject to another word that describes it. There are three kinds of verbs: action verbs, linking verbs, and helping verbs.

An **action verb** tells what action the subject performs. To find the main action verb in a sentence, ask: What action does the subject perform?

TIP: In the examples in this section of the book, verbs will be indicated with a double underline: Darla <u>diets</u>. Verb is sometimes abbreviated *vb.* or *V.*

> <u>Kevin</u> <u>snores</u> all night.
>
> > [What is the subject? *Kevin.* What action does the subject perform? *Snores.*]
>
> <u>Ian</u> <u>plays</u> in the band Groovasaurus.
>
> > [What is the subject? *Ian.* What action does the subject perform? *Plays.*]

| Practice 2 | **Identifying Action Verbs** |

In the following sentences, underline the subject and double-underline the action verb.

> **EXAMPLE:** A Michigan <u>company</u> <u>offers</u> an unusual college souvenir.

1. Oak Grove International <u>sells</u> customized coffins.

2. The <u>company</u> <u>paints</u> coffins in school colors.

3. <u>Oak Grove</u> also <u>creates</u> customized lids with footballs, basketballs, or beer cans.

4. Deep blue <u>coffins</u> <u>account</u> for half the company's sales.

5. A customized <u>coffin</u> <u>costs</u> between $2,000 and $3,000.

6. <u>Alumni</u> <u>love</u> the expensive souvenir.

7. Extra-expensive <u>coffins</u> <u>carry</u> the school insignia.

8. <u>Customers</u> even <u>buy</u> coffins as gifts.

9. The <u>owners</u> <u>started</u> a very profitable business in school coffins.

10. The <u>profits</u> <u>surprised</u> even the owners.

A **linking verb** connects (links) the subject to another word or words that describe the subject. Linking verbs show no action.

The <u>professor</u> <u>is</u> late.

> [The verb *is* links the subject *professor* to a word that describes the professor: *late*. The sentence essentially means "the professor = late."]

<u>I</u> <u>feel</u> great today.

My <u>jacket</u> <u>looks</u> very shabby.

<u>Prices</u> <u>seem</u> higher this year than last.

Some words can be either action verbs or linking verbs. It all depends on how the verb is being used in a particular sentence.

ACTION VERB   Pat <u>tasted</u> the meat.

LINKING VERB   The <u>meat</u> <u>tasted</u> terrible.

> [No action performed. It could read *The meat was terrible*.]

Common Linking Verbs

FORMS OF *BE*	FORMS OF *SEEM* AND *BECOME*	FORMS OF SENSE VERBS
am	seem, seems, seemed	look, looks, looked
are	become, becomes, became	appear, appears, appeared
is		smell, smells, smelled
was		taste, tastes, tasted
were		sound, sounds, sounded
		feel, feels, felt

| Practice 3 | **Identifying Linking Verbs** |

In the following sentences, underline the subject, double-underline the linking verb, and draw an arrow from the subject to the word that describes it.

EXAMPLE: M&M's became popular in the United States in the 1940s.

1. They taste good, and they "melt in your mouth, not in your hands."

2. The colored coatings look different but should taste the same.

3. However, the colors taste different to people.

4. The first M&M's were all purple.

5. Forrest Mars and Bruce Murries were the inventors of M&M's.

A **helping verb** joins with another verb. The helping verb is often a form of *be, have,* or *do.* Together, the helping verb and the other verb (called the main verb) are called a complete verb.

I was studying for the test.

> [The helping verb is *was*; the complete verb is *was studying.*]

Elena is feeling sick.

Daniel might lose his job.

Common Helping Verbs

FORMS OF *BE*	FORMS OF *HAVE*	FORMS OF *DO*	OTHER
am	have	do	can
are	has	does	could
been	had	did	may
being			might
is			must
was			should
were			will
			would

Practice 4 ▶ **Identifying Helping Verbs**

In the following sentences, underline the subject and double-underline the complete verb. (Remember, the complete verb is made up of the helping verb and another verb.)

EXAMPLE: More families are teaching their children at home.

1. Students can learn at their own rates.

2. Home schooling has increased to over one million children.

3. Some school officials have claimed that children won't learn basic skills.

4. Some parents, however, have responded that education at home is best.

5. To get into college, home-schooled students must compete with school-educated students.

E. Complete Thoughts

6. Complete thought: An idea that makes sense independent of other sentences around it.

A **complete thought** is an idea that makes sense by itself, without other sentences. An incomplete thought leaves readers wondering what's going on.

INCOMPLETE THOUGHT   because my alarm didn't go off

COMPLETE THOUGHT   I was late because my alarm didn't go off.

INCOMPLETE THOUGHT   the people who won the lottery

COMPLETE THOUGHT   The people who won the lottery were happy.

To identify a complete thought, ask: Do I get the basic idea, or do I have to ask a question to get it?

In the wallet.

[Do I get the basic idea, or do I have to ask a question to understand? *You would have to ask a question, so this is not a complete thought.*]

Practice 5 ▶ **Identifying Complete Thoughts**

Some of the items on the next page contain complete thoughts, and others do not. In the space to the left of each item, write either *C* for complete thought or *I* for incomplete thought. If you write *I*, add words to make a sentence.

EXAMPLE: _I_   A good friend of mine. *is coming for a visit*

Answers will vary.
Sample answers shown.

_I_   *I will wait*
___   1. Until the store closes at midnight.
          ^

_I_   *you should say what you think*
___   2. At the next meeting.
                    ^

_C_   3. My keys are missing.

_I_   *was for rent*
___   4. The apartment on the third floor.
                              ^

_C_   5. I rented it.

Building Up the Basic Sentence

Any basic sentence must have a subject, a verb, and a complete thought. Sometimes you want to give your readers more detail, so you add other words to make your idea clearer. You can give more information about the subject or the verb or both. Regardless of how much information you add, the subject and the verb remain the same.

BASIC SENTENCE	<u>Birds</u> <u>fly</u>.
MORE INFORMATION ABOUT THE SUBJECT	The two <u>birds</u> <u>fly</u>.
	The two mangy <u>birds</u> <u>fly</u>.
MORE INFORMATION ABOUT THE VERB	The two mangy <u>birds</u> <u>fly</u> awkwardly.
	The two mangy <u>birds</u> <u>fly</u> awkwardly around the room.

F. Adjectives

A word or group of words that modifies (gives more information about) the subject is an **adjective**. To build up the subject, add adjectives.

The old <u>man</u> laughed.

   [The adjective *old* gives more information about the subject *man.*]

Adjectives can also modify nouns and pronouns that are not subjects. You can add as many adjectives as you need.

The nervous new <u>teacher</u> walked into the ugly old classroom.

The skinny little <u>man</u> laughed.

G. Adverbs

8. **Adverb:** A word or group of words that modifies (gives more information about) a verb (or an adjective or another adverb). Often an adverb ends in *-ly*.

A word or group of words that modifies (gives more information about) a verb is an **adverb**. To build up a verb, add adverbs.

The skinny man <u>laughed</u> loudly.

Tom suddenly <u>left</u> the theater.

You can add as many adverbs as you need.

The poisonous gas <u>seeped</u> quickly and quietly into her office.

TIP: *Adverb* is sometimes abbreviated *adv.*

An adverb can also modify an adjective or another adverb.

The very old <u>man</u> laughed.

[The adverb *very* gives more information about the adjective *old.*]

The fire <u>spread</u> too quickly to save the building.

[The adverb *too* gives more information about the other adverb *quickly.*]

Practice 6

Building Up the Subject with Adjectives and the Verb with Adverbs

ESL
Remind students that in English adjectives do not change form when they modify a plural noun or pronoun. (JS)

In each of the following sentences, underline the subject and double-underline the verb. Then add an adjective that gives more information about the subject or an adverb that gives more information about the verb, as indicated in parentheses.

old
EXAMPLE: My uncle snores. (adjective)

Answers will vary.
Sample answers shown.

amazing
1. His snoring is loud. (adjective)

usually
2. His wife wears earplugs. (adverb)

little
3. The earplugs help her sleep. (adjective)

sometimes
4. She calls him "the human bullfrog." (adverb)

ten-year
5. Their marriage has withstood this challenge. (adjective)

H. Phrases

9. Phrase: A group of words that is not a complete sentence because it is missing a subject or a verb or both. It also does not express a complete thought.

A **phrase** is a group of words that is not a complete sentence because it is missing a subject or a verb or both. It also does not express a complete thought.

> under the table
>
> running through the woods
>
> his face a stony mystery

Phrases cannot stand on their own, but within a sentence a phrase can give more information about the subject (or other nouns or pronouns), the verb, or the whole sentence. In other words, phrases often function as adjectives and adverbs.

> The cat ran *under the table*.
>
> *Running through the woods*, I tripped on a tangled vine.

10. Preposition: A word that connects a noun, pronoun, or verb with some other information about it. A prepositional phrase starts with a preposition and ends with a noun or pronoun.

A **prepositional phrase** is a phrase that begins with a preposition and ends with a noun or pronoun. A **preposition** is a word that connects a noun, pronoun, or verb with some other information about it. (See the list of common prepositions on this page.)

preposition

I want to put my new picture on that wall.

prepositional phrase

preposition

He ran through the swamp to avoid capture.

prepositional phrase

TIP: *Preposition* is sometimes abbreviated *prep.*

The subject of a sentence is *never* in a prepositional phrase. (When you are looking for the subject, you can cross out the prepositional phrase.)

ESL
You can also give students a list of common prepositional phrases that they may not be familiar with (*over the hill, up a creek, beat around the bush,* and so on). (SG)

TEAMWORK
To help students work with rather than just look at the list of common prepositions, have them use each preposition in the list to complete a sentence. You can give prompts using students' names or names and places you are all familiar with; they have to write complete sentences that include prepositional phrases. (BO)

Common Prepositions

about	before	except	of	to
above	behind	for	off	toward
across	below	from	on	under
after	beneath	in	out	until
against	beside	inside	outside	up
along	between	into	over	upon
among	by	like	past	with
around	down	near	since	within
at	during	next to	through	without

I. Clauses

11. Clause: A group of words that has a subject and a verb.

A **clause** is a group of words that has a subject and a verb.

There are two kinds of clauses. **Independent clauses** have a subject, a verb, and a complete thought. In other words, independent clauses can stand on their own as sentences.

The car is already sold.

The cat is always hungry.

I will finish this chapter.

Independent clause	=	Sentence

Other clauses have a subject and a verb but do *not* express a complete thought; they cannot stand on their own as sentences. These are called **dependent clauses** or **subordinate clauses.**

that my uncle told me about

who lives next door

before the week is over

Within sentences, these clauses usually give more information about the subject (or other nouns or pronouns), the verb, or the whole sentence. In other words, dependent clauses function as adjectives and adverbs.

The car *that my uncle told me about* is already sold.

The cat *who lives next door* is always hungry.

Before the week is over, I will finish this chapter.

J. Conjunctions

12. Conjunction: A word that joins words, phrases, or clauses. The conjunctions *and, but, for, nor, or, so,* and *yet* are called coordinating conjunctions.

A **conjunction** is a word that joins words, phrases, or clauses.

The conjunctions *and, but, for, nor, or, so,* and *yet* are called **coordinating conjunctions.** They are often used to join two subjects, verbs, or modifiers to make **compound subjects, compound verbs,** and **compound modifiers.**

COMPOUND SUBJECTS   The *man and woman* walked hand-in-hand.

COMPOUND VERBS   Stephanie *walks or runs* every day.

COMPOUND MODIFIERS   The child was *excited and happy.*

Summary: Twelve Basic Sentence Terms

1. **Sentence:** The basic unit of written communication. It must have a subject and a verb, and it must express a complete thought. (See p. 256.)

2. **Subject:** The person, place, or thing that the sentence is about. The subject can be a noun or a pronoun. (See p. 257.)

3. **Noun:** The name of a person, place, or thing. A noun can be a subject. (See p. 257.)

4. **Pronoun:** Replaces a noun in a sentence. A pronoun can be a subject. (See p. 257.)

5. **Verb:** Tells what the subject does or links the subject to a word that describes it. (See p. 258.)

6. **Complete Thought:** An idea that makes sense independent of other sentences around it. (See p. 261.)

7. **Adjective:** A word or group of words that modifies (gives more information about) the subject (or any noun or pronoun). (See p. 262.)

8. **Adverb:** A word or group of words that modifies (gives more information about) a verb (or an adjective or another adverb). Often, but not always, an adverb ends in *-ly*. (See p. 263.)

9. **Phrase:** A group of words that is not a complete sentence because it is missing a subject or a verb or both. It also does not express a complete thought. (See p. 264.)

10. **Preposition:** A word that connects a noun, pronoun, or verb with some other information about it. A prepositional phrase starts with a preposition and ends with a noun or pronoun. (See p. 264.)

11. **Clause:** A group of words that has a subject and a verb. (See p. 265.)

12. **Conjunction:** A word that joins words, phrases, or clauses. The conjunctions *and, but, for, nor, or, so,* and *yet* are called coordinating conjunctions. (See p. 265.)

22

Fragments

Incomplete Sentences

A. Fragments That Start with Prepositions
B. Fragments That Start with Dependent Words
C. Fragments That Start with *-ing* Verb Forms
D. Fragments That Start with Examples or Explanations

Understand What Sentence Fragments Are

A **sentence** is a group of words that has a subject and a verb and expresses a complete thought, independent of other sentences.

A **sentence fragment** is a group of words that looks like a sentence but is missing a subject, a verb, or a complete thought. It is only a piece of a sentence, and it is considered a serious mistake in formal writing.

SENTENCE   I got home late, so I ate some cold pizza and drank a whole liter of Pepsi.

FRAGMENT   I got home late, so I ate some cold pizza. *And drank a whole liter of Pepsi.*

> [*And drank a whole liter of Pepsi* contains a verb (*drank*) but no subject. It is a fragment.]

In the Real World, Why Is It Important to Correct Fragments?

SITUATION: Karen has just graduated from the licensed practical nurse (LPN) program, and she's applying for a job at an excellent hospital. She sends her résumé along with a cover letter. She really wants a job at this hospital. Unfortunately, her cover letter hurts her chances. Here is a portion of her letter:

Students should underline fragments for Practice 1, on this page.

I graduated from the Nurse Practitioner program at Roxbury Community College./In May of this year. Even though I have just graduated, I have held responsible positions that will help me become part of your team quickly,/Including Office Assistant at the Pediatrics Center, Assistant Manager at TLC Day Care, and Shift Manager at Pizza Hut. These positions have given me experience in office procedures, child care, and patient interaction. This experience will help me in the position on the nursing staff at Children's Hospital./Because it is directly relevant to the job.

Students should correct fragments for Practice 7, p. 277. Answers will vary.

RESPONSE: We gave Ann Colangelo, director of Critical Care Nursing at Children's Hospital in Boston, a cover letter containing Karen's paragraph. This is how Colangelo reacted to the letter:

I'm not a stickler for perfect grammar, and our business is health care, not writing. But I noticed the errors in the letter right away. The résumé looks decent, but those kinds of mistakes mark Karen as either sloppy or lacking in basic writing skills. I don't need nursing staff with either of those traits, and we have lots of applicants for every position.

People outside the English classroom notice major grammar errors, and while they may not assign you a course grade, they do judge you by your communication skills.

Practice 1 ▷ **Finding Fragments**

Find and underline the three fragments in Karen's letter.

Practice Finding and Correcting Fragments

Fragments are missing a subject, a verb, or a complete thought. How do you find these problems in your own writing? Look for the four trouble spots that often signal sentence fragments.

TROUBLE SPOTS: SENTENCE FRAGMENTS

1. A word group that starts with a preposition

     Examples of prepositions: *at, with, in*

2. A word group that starts with a dependent word

     Examples of dependent words: *after, because, who, that*

3. A word group that starts with an *-ing* verb form

     Examples of *-ing* verb forms: *running, studying, listening*

4. A word group that starts with an example or explanation of something mentioned in the previous sentence

     Example: *For instance the fire escape*

TWO WAYS TO CORRECT A FRAGMENT:

1. Add what is missing (a subject, a verb, or both)
2. Attach the fragment to the sentence before or after it

Thinking Critically about Fragments

FOCUS	Whenever you see one of the four trouble spots in your writing, stop to check for a possible fragment.
ASK	• Does it have a subject? • Does it have a verb? • Does it express a complete thought independent of other sentences?
EDIT	If your answer to any of these questions is no, you have a fragment that must be corrected.

TIP: Remember, the subject of a sentence is *never* in a prepositional phrase. (See p. 264.)

A. Fragments That Start with Prepositions

Whenever a preposition starts what you think is a sentence, check for a subject, a verb, and a complete thought. If the group of words is missing any of these, it is a fragment.

I pounded as hard as I could. *Against the door.*

[*Against the door* lacks both a subject and a verb. It is a fragment.]

Correct a fragment that starts with a preposition by connecting it to the sentence either before or after it. If you connect such a fragment to the sentence after it, put a comma after the fragment to join it to the next sentence.

I pounded as hard as I could/ ^a^ gainst the door.

In the very bottom of the largest shopping bag, underneath the bags of apples and oranges,/I found my car keys.

Common Prepositions

about	before	except	of	to
above	behind	for	off	toward
across	below	from	on	under
after	beneath	in	out	until
against	beside	inside	outside	up
along	between	into	over	upon
among	by	like	past	with
around	down	near	since	within
at	during	next to	through	without

Practice 2 ▸ **Correcting Fragments That Start with Prepositions**

Circle all prepositions at the beginnings of word groups. Use the Thinking Critically guide on page 269 to identify any fragments. Then correct each fragment by connecting it to the previous or the next sentence.

EXAMPLE: (For) students of agriculture,/ ^t^ The Biosphere II project in the

Arizona desert held special interest.

Answers may vary. Possible edits shown.

1. The eight men and women who spent two years inside the glass-and-

    steel dome had to grow their own food/ ^w^ (With) almost no help from the

    outside world.

2. Biosphere II duplicated natural conditions/ ^i^ In a controlled, inside

    atmosphere.

3. The 3.2-acre greenhouse-like structure included a rain forest, a savan-nah, a desert, and even a small "ocean/" ~~With~~ a machine for generating waves.

4. ~~Under~~ difficult conditions/. The crew members in Biosphere II had to produce enough food to live on.

5. The air they breathed almost became depleted because the compost in the soil produced carbon dioxide/ ~~In~~ place of the oxygen in the air.

B. Fragments That Start with Dependent Words

DISCUSSION
Ask students to jot down what they think the word *dependent* means in real life, with an example. Then get some responses. Ask how *dependent* in *dependent clause* is similar to *dependent* in real life.

A **dependent word** is the first word in a dependent clause.

We got home early *because* we left early.

> [*Because* is a dependent word introducing the dependent clause *because we left early.*]

A dependent clause cannot be a sentence because it doesn't express a complete thought, even if it has a subject and a verb. Whenever a dependent word starts what you think is a sentence, stop to check for a subject, a verb, and a complete thought.

He fiddled with the lock for an hour. *Before* he lost his temper.

> [*Before he lost his temper* has a subject (*he*) and a verb (*lost*), but it doesn't express a complete thought. It is a fragment.]

COMPUTER
Suggest that students become aware of the dependent words they use most and do a computer search for them as they edit their own writing. They can then make sure that dependent clauses are attached to sentences. (EG)

Common Dependent Words

after	since	where
although	so that	whether
as	that	which(ever)
because	though	while
before	unless	who(ever)
even though	until	whose
how	what(ever)	
if	when(ever)	

Correct a fragment that starts with a dependent word by connecting it to the sentence before or after it. You may need to put a comma before or after the fragment to join it to the complete sentence.

He fiddled with the lock for an hour/ ^b^ Before he lost his temper.

Since he lost his job six months ago/, ^m̂^ My tenant has not paid the rent.

Practice 3 ▶ **Correcting Fragments That Start with Dependent Words**

In the following items, circle the dependent words. Use the Thinking Critically guide on page 269 to find any fragments, and correct them by connecting them to the previous or the next sentence.

EXAMPLE: (Since) space travel heated up in the 1960s/, ^m^ Many "firsts" have

been achieved. *Answers may vary. Possible edits shown.*

1. No American had orbited the earth/ (Before) ^b^ John Glenn did so on

   February 20, 1962.

2. July 20, 1969, was another historic moment in space travel/, (When) ^w^ Neil

   Armstrong walked on the moon for the first time.

3. (While) they walked on the surface of the moon/, Armstrong and Buzz

   Aldrin collected samples of moon rock and moon soil to bring back to

   earth.

4. In July 1975, the U.S. *Apollo 18* and the Russian *Soyuz 19* had a

   rendezvous in space/, (Where) ^w^ the two crews communicated 145 miles

   above the earth.

5. Americans had begun to feel that space travel was as safe as flying in

   an airliner/ (Until) ^u^ the *Challenger* exploded soon after takeoff on

   January 28, 1986.

C. Fragments That Start with *-ing* Verb Forms

Sometimes an *-ing* verb form is used at the beginning of a complete sentence.

Walking is good exercise.

[*Walking* is the subject.]

Sometimes an *-ing* verb form introduces a fragment. When an *-ing* verb form starts what you think is a sentence, stop and check it for a subject, a verb, and a complete thought.

I was running as fast as I could. *Hoping to get there on time.*

[*Hoping to get there on time* lacks a subject and a verb. It is a fragment.]

Correct a fragment that starts with an *-ing* verb form either by adding whatever sentence elements are missing (usually a subject and a helping verb) or by connecting it to the previous or the next sentence.

I was running as fast as I could/, ʰHoping to get there on time.

I was still hoping
I was running as fast as I could. ~~Hoping~~ to get there on time.
                              ^

Practice 4 ▶ **Correcting Fragments That Start with *-ing* Verb Forms**

Circle the *-ing* verb forms in the following items. Use the Thinking Critically guide on page 269 to find any fragments, and correct them either by adding the missing sentence elements or by connecting them to the previous or the next sentence.

EXAMPLE: People sometimes travel long distances in unusual ways/,

ᵗ
(Trying) to set new world records.
^
Answers may vary. Possible edits shown.

1. In 1931, Plennie Wingo set out on a journey/ (ᵂWalking) backward
                                              ^
around the world.

2. (Wearing) sunglasses with rearview mirrors/, ʰHe set out on his trip early
                                            ^
one morning.

3. After eight thousand miles, Wingo's journey was interrupted by a war/
ᵗ
(Taking) place in Pakistan.
^

4. For two and a half years during the late 1970s, Hans Mullikin was en

   route to the White House. ~~Crawling~~ *He was crawling* from Texas to Washington, D.C.
   ^

5. Mullikin's trip took so long because he lingered/, ~~Taking~~ *t*aking time out to
   ^

   earn money as a logger and a Baptist minister.

D. Fragments That Start with Examples or Explanations

As you reread what you have written, pay special attention to groups of words that are examples of something you presented in the previous sentence. They may be fragments.

> I thought of other ways to get out of my locked apartment. *For example through the window.*

> I don't like climbing out of windows. *Especially from the third floor.*

>> [*For example through the window* and *Especially from the third floor* lack subjects, verbs, and complete thoughts. They are fragments.]

This last fragment trouble spot is harder to recognize because there is no single word or kind of word to look for. Here are a few starting words that may signal a fragment, but fragments that are examples or explanations do not always start with these words.

especially	for example
like	such as

When a group of words that you think is a sentence gives an example of something in the previous sentence, stop to check it for a subject, a verb, and a complete thought.

> I decided to call someone who could help me get out of my apartment. *Like a locksmith.*

>> [*Like a locksmith* has no verb and doesn't express a complete thought. It is a fragment.]

Correct a fragment that starts with an example or explanation by connecting it to the previous or the next sentence. Sometimes you can add whatever sentence elements are missing (a subject or verb or both) instead.

> I decided to call someone who could help me get out of my

> apartment/, ~~L~~like a locksmith.
   ^

I considered getting out of my apartment by using the fire escape. The

one outside my window,/*was pretty strong.*

| Practice 5 | **Correcting Fragments Starting with an Example or Explanation** |

Circle the example or explanation in the following items. Use the Thinking Critically guide on page 269 to find any fragments, and correct them either by connecting them to the previous or the next sentence or by adding the missing sentence elements.

EXAMPLE: Coca-Cola has been phenomenally successful. ~~One~~ *It is one* of the

most profitable products in the world.

Answers may vary. Possible edits shown.

1. Coca-Cola has been successful partly because of its producers' willing-

   ness to expand into new markets,/Not just in North America and

   Europe but throughout the world.

2. In recent years Coca-Cola has prospered in nations once hostile to

   capitalism,/such as China and Vietnam.

3. You can see Coke's famous red-and-white logo almost anywhere.
   You can see it even
   ~~Even~~ in the former Soviet Union.

4. Coke has also sponsored major television events,/such as the 1996

   Summer Olympics.

5. It has had some big marketing successes,/including the return of Coke

   Classic in the mid-1980s.

Edit Paragraphs and Your Own Writing

| Practice 6 | **Editing Paragraphs for Fragments** |

Find and correct any fragments in the paragraphs beginning on the following page. You may want to refer to the Summary on page 278.

Answers may vary. Possible edits shown.

1.   (1) Wilma Rudolph was born in 1940 in Tennessee. (2) When she was four, she became ill with scarlet fever and pneumonia. (3) ~~So~~ *She was so* sick that everyone thought she would die. (4) She survived but one of her legs was damaged. (5) She was told that she would never walk again. (6) Rudolph did manage to walk again, despite the doctors' predictions. (7) After years of treatment, braces, and determination, (8) ^s^ She started running for exercise. (9) In 1960, Rudolph became the second American woman in history to win three gold medals in a single Olympics.

2.   (1) Louis Braille was born in France in 1809. (2) In a tragic accident, he punctured one of his eyes when he was three. (3) Infection set in, and he lost sight in both eyes. (4) He attended a special school for the blind where students were taught a system of communication. (5) *It was a* A very cumbersome and difficult system. (6) Becoming fascinated with the idea of inventing a writing system the blind could read, (7) Braille worked for two years on his own idea. (8) He developed the raised dot system, called Braille, that is used universally.

3.   (1) Most people think of Thomas Edison as a famous inventor, (2) ~~The man~~ who invented the lightbulb. (3) Most people don't know that Edison was considered learning disabled as a child. (4) An illness had prevented him from entering school until he was eight, and his teachers told his parents that he couldn't learn. (5) His parents took him out of school, (6) ^b^ Because they did not believe the teachers. (7) He was then home-schooled, (8) ^b^ By his very determined mother. (9) By the age of ten, Edison was already experimenting with what would become his great inventions.

| Practice 7 | ▷ | Editing Karen's Letter |

Look back at Karen's letter on page 268. You may have already identified the fragments; if not, do that now. Next, using what you've learned in this chapter about correcting fragments, correct each fragment in the paragraph.

| Practice 8 | ▷ | Editing Your Own Writing for Fragments |

As a final practice, edit fragments in a piece of your own writing—a paper you are working on for this class, a paper you've already finished, a paper for another course, or a recent piece of writing from your work or everyday life.

First, do the following "Focus—and Refocus" activity. Then use the Thinking Critically guide on page 269 or the Summary on page 278 to find and correct any fragments in your own writing.

TEACHING TIP
This activity should help students understand that they must shift their focus to edit successfully. They need to see their writing in a new way to identify errors that have been there all along. This activity works well in small groups; point out that different people see different things and that by working in a group, writers can learn to see things they would overlook if each was working separately. Additional "Focus—and Refocus" activities are in the critical thinking section in *Practical Suggestions*.

FOCUS—AND REFOCUS
Focus on this picture and write what you see.

I see a _____.

Did you see the old woman or the young woman? Check with other people in your class to find out what they saw. Now *refocus* your eyes to look for the other image. Can you see it?

Refocusing is an important part of editing. Before editing your writing, refocus, looking for fragments that you may not have seen before (but that were there). This refocusing will help you find any fragments you didn't see at first.

Summary and Quick Review Chart: Fragments

- A **sentence** is a group of words that has a subject and a verb and expresses a complete thought. (See p. 267.)
- A **sentence fragment** seems to be a complete sentence but is only a piece of one. It lacks a subject, a verb, or a complete thought. (See p. 267.)
- There are four **fragment trouble spots** that often signal sentence fragments:
  - A word group that begins with a preposition: *about, in, of* (see p. 269)
  - A word group that begins with a dependent word: *because, until, when* (see p. 271)
  - A word group that begins with an *-ing* verb form: *eating, driving* (see p. 273)
  - A word group that begins with an example or explanation: *like my apartment, such as flowers* (see p. 274)
- To correct fragments, you can add the missing sentence elements or connect the fragment to the sentence before or after it. (See p. 269.)

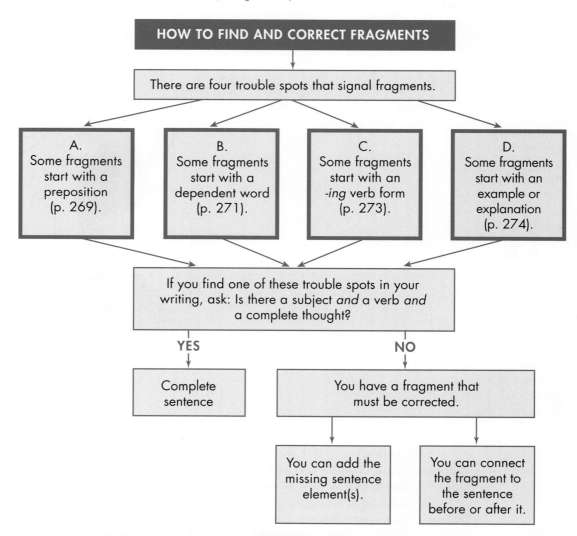

23

Run-Ons

Two Sentences Joined Incorrectly

TIP: To find and correct run-ons, you need to be able to identify a complete sentence. For review, see Chapter 21.

RESOURCES
Additional Resources contains tests and supplemental practice exercises for this chapter as well as a transparency master for the summary chart at the end of the chapter.

A.   Add a Period
B.   Add a Comma and a Conjunction
C.   Add a Semicolon
D.   Add a Dependent Word
E.   A Word That Can Cause Run-Ons: *Then*

Understand What Run-Ons Are

A **sentence** is a group of words that has a subject and a verb and expresses a complete thought. Sometimes two sentences are joined to form one larger sentence. (Each sentence within the larger sentence is called an **independent clause.**)

independent clause   independent clause

The college offers financial aid, and it encourages students to apply.

Run-ons are two complete sentences joined together incorrectly. There are two kinds of run-ons. A **fused sentence** is two complete sentences joined without any punctuation at all.

independent clause   independent clause

FUSED SENTENCE   Smoking is a bad habit it can kill you.

no punctuation

Two sentences must be joined with the proper punctuation. Fusing them together with no punctuation creates a run-on error.

A **comma splice** is two complete sentences joined only by a comma without a conjunction.

independent clause   independent clause

**COMMA
SPLICE**   My mother smoked continuously, she lit one cigarette off another.

└ only a comma

Two sentences must be joined with the proper punctuation and sometimes with a conjunction. Splicing them together with only a comma creates a run-on error.

In the Real World, Why Is It Important to Correct Run-Ons?

SITUATION: Naomi is applying to a special program for returning students at Simmons College. Here is one of the essay questions on the application, followed by a paragraph from Naomi's response.

Statement of Purpose: In two hundred words or less, please describe your intellectual and professional goals and how a Simmons College education will assist you in achieving them.

Students should underline run-ons for Practice 1, p. 281.

For many years I did not take control of my life; I just drifted along without any purpose or goals. I realized one day as I was meeting with my daughter's guidance counselor that I hoped my daughter would not turn out like me. From that moment, I decided I would focus my energy on doing something to help myself and others. I set a goal of becoming a nutritionist. To begin on that path, I took a brush-up course in math at night school, *and* then I took another in chemistry. I passed both courses. *W*ith hard work and persistence I know I can do well in the Simmons program. I am committed to the professional goal I finally found. *I*t has given new purpose to my whole life.

Students should correct run-ons for Practice 7, p. 288. Answers will vary.

RESPONSE: When Jean Heaton, director of admissions for the Dorothea Lynde Dix Scholars Program at Simmons College, read Naomi's essay, she noticed the run-ons and made the following comment:

DISCUSSION
Is the response fair?
What should Jean Heaton
do? What do you think
happened? (Naomi had
a personal interview and
was accepted into the
program.)

We take these essays very seriously. We want students who are thoughtful, hardworking, and mature. Although Naomi's essay indicates that she has some of these qualities, her writing gives another impression. The errors she makes are numerous and significant; I can't help but wonder if she took the time to really think about this essay. If she is careless on a document that represents her admission, will she be careless in other areas as well? It's too bad, because her qualifications are quite good otherwise.

Run-ons, like sentence fragments, are errors that people notice and consider major mistakes.

Practice 1 ▶ Identifying Run-Ons

Find and underline the four run-ons in Naomi's essay.

Practice Finding and Correcting Run-Ons

To find run-ons, focus on each sentence in your writing, one at a time. Until you get used to finding the run-ons (or until you don't make the error anymore), this takes extra time. But if you spend that time on editing the four most serious grammar errors, your writing will improve.

Thinking Critically about Run-Ons

FOCUS   Read each sentence aloud, and listen carefully as you read.

ASK
- Am I pausing in the middle of the sentence?
- If so, are there two subjects and two verbs?
- If so, are there two complete sentences in this sentence? (If I break the sentence into two sentences, does each make sense when I read it aloud? Would each make sense if it weren't next to the other one?)
- If there *are* two complete sentences in this sentence, how are they joined? Is there no punctuation between them? Is there only a comma?

EDIT   If the answer to either of the last questions is yes, the sentence is a run-on and needs to be corrected.

Once you have found a run-on, there are four ways to correct it.

FOUR WAYS TO CORRECT A RUN-ON:

1. Add a period
2. Add a comma and a conjunction
3. Add a semicolon
4. Add a dependent word

TEACHING TIP
To illustrate this diagram and others in the chapter, ask students to give you examples and write them on the board.

A. Add a Period

You can correct a run-on by adding a period to make two separate sentences. Capitalize the letter after the period that begins the new sentence. Reread your two sentences to make sure they make sense.

$$\boxed{\text{S}} \; + \; \boxed{\text{V}} \; . \qquad \boxed{\text{S}} \; + \; \boxed{\text{V}} \; .$$

FUSED SENTENCE   I interviewed a candidate for a job. *S* ƒhe gave me the

"dead fish" handshake.

COMMA SPLICE   The "dead fish" is a limp handshake*.* *T* ƒhe person plops

her hand into yours.

> **Practice 2**   Correcting a Run-On by Adding a Period

For each of the following run-ons, indicate in the space to the left whether it is a fused sentence (F) or a comma splice (CS). Then correct the run-on by adding a period and capitalization as necessary to make two sentences.

EXAMPLE: ___*CS*___ A class at Duke University uses no paper in class*.* *T* ƒhey

use only laptop computers and wireless receivers.

___*F*___ 1. Working together, fifty students and their professor set up the

classroom*.* *I* ɨt took them less than twenty minutes.

___*CS*___ 2. The professor can display any student's computer screen to the

whole class*.* *T* ƚhis allows the class to work together easily.

___*CS*___ 3. Students can continue to interact outside of class*.* *T* ƚhe laptops

and receivers allow them to set up wireless networks.

___*F*___ 4. The wireless networks can be set up anywhere*.* *C* ¢ommon sites are

dorms, the library, and the laundromat.

_____ 5. Duke was a test site,*~~the~~* **T** the students received free software and dis-

counted laptop computers from Apple.

B. Add a Comma and a Conjunction
(*and, but, or, nor, so, for, yet*)

Another way to correct a run-on is to add a comma and one of these conjunctions: *and, but, or, nor, so, for,* or *yet.* If the run-on is a comma splice, it already has a comma, so you need to add only a conjunction. Before adding a conjunction, read the sentences aloud to see which word best expresses the relationship between the two sentences.

ESL
Notice that the comma does not follow the conjunction. The comma follows the word *before* the conjunction. (JS)

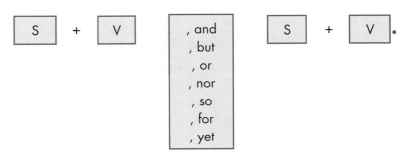

FUSED SENTENCE Naomi was qualified for the job, *but* she hurt her chances

by mumbling.

COMMA SPLICE The candidate mumbled softly, *and* she kept her head down.

Practice 3 ▶ **Correcting a Run-On by Adding a Comma and a Conjunction**

Correct each of the following run-ons by adding a comma if necessary and an appropriate conjunction. ***Answers will vary.***

EXAMPLE: The Internet offers access to huge storehouses of information,

and it delivers the information very quickly.

TEACHING TIP
You may want to have students identify whether each run-on in this practice is a comma splice (CS) or a fused sentence (F): 1-CS, 2-CS, 3-CS, 4-F, 5-F.

1. The Internet used to be very difficult to use, *but* many companies now

offer software that provides easy access.

2. The Internet was not originally designed to be easy, *for* there was no plan

for it to be used by "everyday people."

3. The Internet was created to allow computers to survive a bomb
   but
   attack, its military role eventually became obsolete.

4. Over the years the use of the Internet steadily grew,
   yet
   it did not become
   widely used until the early 1990s.

5. We now have public access to the Internet,
   and
   the number of users continues to increase.

TEACHING TIP
Remind students that a semicolon balances two independent clauses. What is on either side of it must be able to stand alone as a complete sentence. (EG) Use the semicolon only when you have some mastery over it—do not think it is always a safe choice. (JS)

C. Add a Semicolon

A third way to correct a run-on is to use a semicolon (;) to join the two sentences. Use a semicolon when the two sentences express closely related ideas. A semicolon can be used only where a period could also be used; the words on each side of the semicolon must be able to stand alone as a complete sentence.

$$ \boxed{S} \ + \ \boxed{V} \ ; \quad \boxed{S} \ + \ \boxed{V} \ . $$

FUSED SENTENCE Slouching creates a terrible impression ; it makes you seem uninterested, bored, or lacking in self-confidence.

COMMA SPLICE It is important in an interview to hold your head up ; it is just as important to sit up straight.

Practice 4 ▶ **Correcting a Run-On by Adding a Semicolon**

Correct each of the following run-ons by adding a semicolon.

EXAMPLE: The Internet has all kinds of possible uses ; even rock concerts can come across the Net.

1. Fifty thousand people attended the Rolling Stones concert at the Dallas Cotton Bowl ; many thousands more experienced the concert via the Internet.

TEACHING TIP
You may want to have
students identify whether
each run-on in this prac-
tice is a comma splice
(CS) or a fused sentence
(F): 1-F, 2-CS, 3-F, 4-F,
5-F.

2. Stones fans all over the world gathered around computer screens ; rock

    and roll history was being made by one of the Internet's components,

    the MBone.

3. The MBone is short for Multicast Backbone ; the MBone is capable of

    multicasting.

4. Multicasting is the network's ability to make multiple copies of any

    packet of information ; it is then sent to and simulcast in any destina-

    tion that has requested it.

5. The MBone is completely interactive ; it carries audio, video, and a

    "white board" feature that allows viewers to share text, images, and

    sketches.

D. Add a Dependent Word

A fourth way to correct run-ons is to make one of the sentences a dependent clause by adding a dependent word. Choose the dependent word
that best expresses the relationship between the two sentences.

Because a dependent clause is not a complete sentence, it can be joined
to a complete sentence without creating a run-on. You may need to put a
comma before or after the dependent clause to join it to the complete sentence. If you are correcting a comma splice, you may need to delete the
comma.

ESL
Note that only two of
these dependent words
are made up of two
words. Also note that
unless is as useful as *if*,
but it means *if + not*. (I
will go *if* I am invited. I
will *not* go *unless* I am
invited.) (JS)

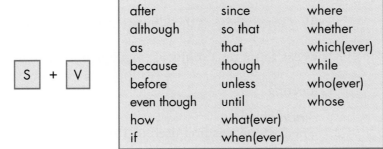

after	since	where
although	so that	whether
as	that	which(ever)
because	though	while
before	unless	who(ever)
even though	until	whose
how	what(ever)	
if	when(ever)	

FUSED SENTENCE   Your final <u>statement</u> <u>should express</u> your interest in the

                     although
   position, <u>you</u> <u>don't want</u> to sound desperate.

COMMA SPLICE   It <u>is</u> important to end an interview on a positive note⟋
be<u>cause</u>
<u>that</u> <u>is</u> what the interviewer will remember.

You can also put the dependent clause first. When the dependent clause comes first, make sure to put a comma after it.

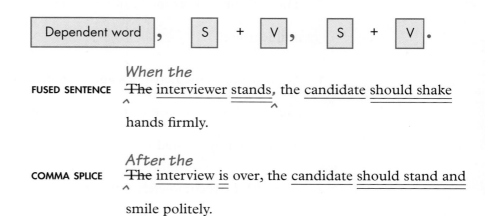

FUSED SENTENCE   *When the*
~~The~~ interviewer <u>stands</u>, the <u>candidate</u> <u>should shake</u>

<u>hands</u> firmly.

COMMA SPLICE   *After the*
~~The~~ interview <u>is</u> over, the <u>candidate</u> <u>should stand and</u>

<u>smile</u> politely.

| Practice 5 | **Correcting a Run-On by Making a Dependent Clause** |

Correct each of the following run-ons by adding a dependent word to make a dependent clause.

TEACHING TIP
You may want to have students identify whether each run-on in this practice is a comma splice (CS) or a fused sentence (F): 1-CS, 2-F, 3-CS, 4-CS, 5-CS.

When a
EXAMPLE: ⱯA researcher was too pregnant to travel to a meeting⟍ she

suggested using an experimental technology that would allow

her to "attend" the meeting without traveling there.

1. Two researchers at the University of Southern California worked for
   so that
   weeks to set up a multicast facility⟋the researcher could attend the

   meeting.

   Since the
2. ~~The~~ MBone was first used in 1992⟍more than one hundred events

   have been sent over it.

   While the
3. ~~The~~ MBone is still not perfect, its inventors consider it successful.

4. Broadcasts that are sent over the MBone can slow down the entire
because
Internet/ they use huge amounts of network capacity.
^

Although the
5. ~~The~~ audio and video quality needs refinement, the MBone has great
^

possibilities not only for rock broadcasts but also for scientific study.

E.   A Word That Can Cause Run-Ons: *Then*

Many run-ons are caused by the word *then. Then* can be used to join
two sentences, but without the correct punctuation, it will result in a run-
on. Often writers use just a comma before *then,* but that makes a comma
splice.

RUN-ON   I picked up my laundry, then I went home.

Correct run-ons caused by *then* using any of the four methods you have just
practiced.

T
I picked up my laundry/. then I went home.
^

and
I picked up my laundry/ then I went home.
^

before
I picked up my laundry/ ~~then~~ I went home.
^

;
I picked up my laundry/ then I went home.
^

Edit Paragraphs and Your Own Writing

| Practice 6 | Editing Paragraphs for Run-Ons |

Find and correct any run-ons in the following paragraphs. Make the
corrections using whichever of the four methods seem best to you. You may
want to refer to the Summary on page 290.
                    Answers will vary. Possible edits shown.

(1) If you read a newspaper anywhere in the world, the ink will

smudge off on your hands. (2) The newspaper industry has been look-

TEACHING TIP
Read the sentences in these paragraphs from the bottom up, one sentence at a time, to focus on finding run-ons. Have students read the paragraphs aloud to listen for errors. (BO)

but
ing for a solution for more than forty years, it has not found one.
(3) Newspapers use oil-based inks that never completely dry; they come off on your hands. (4) Newspaper ink also contains a much higher percentage of carbon black pigment than other printing inks. (5) The carbon black pigment is mixed with an oil that is like car lubricating oil.
T
the result is the big smudge factor.

(6) Smudging has become a bigger problem in recent years than in the past. (7) Newspaper publishers use heavier ink *because* they want the papers to be more readable. (8) The *New York Times* uses very heavy ink; the *Wall Street Journal* uses a light ink. (9) For that reason, the *New York Times* smudges more. (10) It has higher contrast than many papers, *so* it looks easier to read. (11) The price of high contrast is a very high "rub-off" factor.

(12) Rub-resistant inks do exist, *but* they are more expensive.
(13) They neutralize the carbon black by adding resins and waxes.
(14) The regular black ink that newspapers use on their presses costs about 45 cents per pound; rub-resistant inks cost about 55 cents per pound. (15) Even if newspapers were to use the more expensive ink, the smudge factor would only decrease. *I*t would not be eliminated.

Practice 7 ▶ Editing Naomi's Application

Look back at Naomi's application paragraph on page 280. You may have already identified the run-ons; if not, do that now. Next, using what you've learned in this chapter about correcting run-ons, correct each run-on.

| Practice 8 | Editing Your Own Writing for Run-Ons |

As a final practice, edit run-ons in a piece of your own writing—a paper you are working on for this course, a paper you've already finished, a paper for another course, or a recent piece of writing from your work or everyday life.

First, do the following "Focus—and Refocus" activity. Then use the Thinking Critically guide on page 281 or the Summary on page 290 to find and correct any run-ons in your own writing.

FOCUS—AND REFOCUS

Focus on this picture and write what you see.

I see _____ .

Did you see the vase or two faces? Check with other people in your class to find out what they saw. Now *refocus* your eyes to look for the other image. Can you see it?

Refocusing is an important part of editing. Before editing your writing, refocus, looking for run-ons that you may not have seen before (but that were there). This refocusing will help you find any run-ons you didn't see at first.

Summary and Quick Review Chart: Run-Ons

- A **sentence** (or **independent clause**) is a group of words that includes a subject and a verb and expresses a complete thought. (See p. 279.)
- A **run-on** is two complete sentences that are joined incorrectly and written as one sentence. (See p. 279.)
  - A **fused sentence** is two complete sentences joined without any punctuation.
  - A **comma splice** is two complete sentences joined by only a comma.
- There are four ways to correct run-ons:
  - Add a **period** (see p. 282).
  - Add a **comma and a conjunction:** *and, but, or, nor, so, for, yet* (see p. 283).
  - Add a **semicolon** (see p. 284).
  - Add a **dependent word** (see p. 285).
- The word **then** in the middle of a sentence may signal a run-on. (See p. 287.)

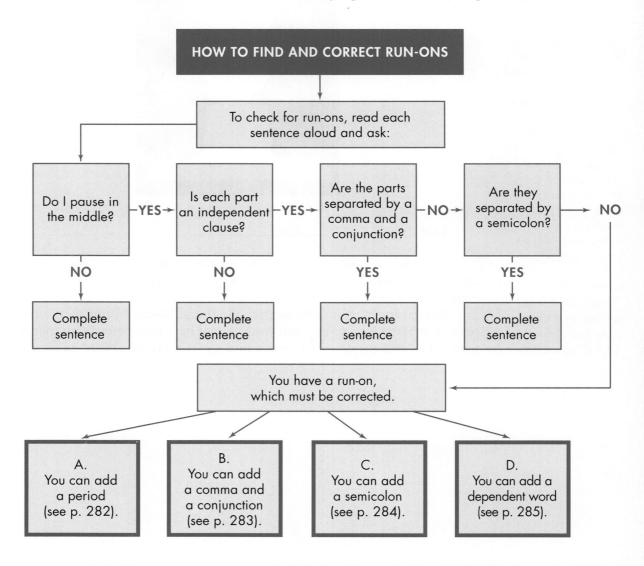

24

Problems with Subject-Verb Agreement

When Subjects and Verbs Don't Match

EVER THOUGHT THIS?
"I know sometimes the verb is supposed to end with -s and sometimes it isn't, but I always get confused."
—Mayerlin Fana, Student

A.   The Verb Is a Form of *Be, Have,* or *Do*
B.   Words Come between the Subject and the Verb
C.   The Subject Is a Compound Subject
D.   The Subject Is an Indefinite Pronoun
E.   The Verb Comes before the Subject

TIP: To find and correct errors in subject-verb agreement, you need to be able to identify a subject, a verb, a prepositional phrase, and a dependent clause. For review, see Chapter 21.

RESOURCES
Additional Resources contains tests and supplemental practice exercises for this chapter as well as a transparency master for the summary chart at the end of the chapter.

Understand What Subject-Verb Agreement Is

In any sentence, the subject and the verb must match—or **agree**—in terms of number. If the subject is singular (one person, place, or thing), then the verb must also be singular. If the subject is plural (more than one), the verb must also be plural.

SINGULAR   The <u>athlete</u> <u>runs</u> around the track.

PLURAL   The <u>athletes</u> <u>run</u> around the track.

Regular verbs have two forms in the present tense: one that ends in *-s* and one that has no ending. The chart on the next page shows which subjects need the form that ends in *-s*. As you can see, the subjects *he, she, it,* and singular nouns always use the form that ends in *-s*.

291

Singular	Plural
I walk.	We walk.
You walk.	You walk.
He (she, it) walks. Joe walks. The student walks.	They walk. Joe and Alice walk. The students walk.

In the Real World, Why Is It Important to Correct Errors in Subject-Verb Agreement?

SITUATION: Ray Owen read an editorial in the local newspaper that made him mad. The editorial (by someone we'll call Mr. X) was about how lazy and untrustworthy students are when they default on college loans. Ray decided to write directly to Mr. X. Here is a portion of his letter:

Students should underline errors for Practice 1, p. 293.

Students should correct errors for Practice 11, p. 304.

I am writing in response to your editorial that accuse*s* students who default on loans of being lazy. You don't know what you're talking about. Many students ~~has~~ *have* to borrow a lot of money to get an education, and most work during college. Getting a college education ~~be~~ *is* a hardship, but most students are willing to work hard to get one. You should find out the facts before you make accusations.

RESPONSE: Mr. X read Ray's letter, circled the errors, and sent it back to Ray with this response:

Dear Mr. Owen:

You claim that you are not lazy. If that's true, why didn't you spend some time making sure your letter was correct and error-free before sending it? Maybe you never bothered to learn how to write in the first place. Either way, you seem to be an example of what I was talking about in the editorial: a student who won't take responsibility for his actions.

Sincerely,

Mr. X

DISCUSSION
Ask students if they think Mr. X is right. What would they say to him about Ray's errors?

Chapter 24 • Problems with Subject-Verb Agreement 293

Problems with subject-verb agreement are serious errors. Most people notice them and consider them major mistakes.

| Practice 1 | Identifying Problems with Subject-Verb Agreement |

Find and underline the three problems with subject-verb agreement in Ray's letter.

Practice Finding and Correcting Errors in Subject-Verb Agreement

TEACHING TIP
Point out to students that correcting each of the four major grammar errors depends on being able to identify the subject and the verb in a sentence.

How can you find problems with subject-verb agreement in your own writing? Learn to look for the five trouble spots that often cause subject-verb agreement errors.

TROUBLE SPOTS: SUBJECT-VERB AGREEMENT

1. The verb is a form of *be, have,* or *do*

   I am in a great mood today.

2. Words or phrases come between the subject and the verb

   The dogs that live in the parking lot bark all night.

3. There is a compound subject (more than one subject for one verb)

   The student and her friend study together.

4. The subject is an indefinite pronoun

   Everyone eats in the cafeteria.

5. The verb comes before the subject

   Where is that turtle?

Thinking Critically about Subject-Verb Agreement

FOCUS Whenever you see one of the five trouble spots in your writing, stop to check for subject-verb agreement problems.

ASK • Where is the subject in this sentence? Where is the verb?
• When I read them aloud together, do they sound right?
• Do they match in terms of number? (Both singular? Both plural?)

EDIT If your answer to either of the last two questions is no, you have a problem with subject-verb agreement that must be corrected.

| Practice 2 | Subject-Verb Agreement |

In each of the following sentences, circle the proper form of the verb in parentheses. Use the Thinking Critically guide on page 293.

EXAMPLE: The common cold (produce /(produces)) many familiar symptoms.

1. Symptoms of the common cold ((include)/ includes) a sore throat, coughing, and congestion or a runny nose.

2. Almost two hundred different viruses ((cause)/ causes) common colds.

3. People ((catch)/ catches) colds by breathing in infected droplets or by hand-to-hand contact.

4. A school-age child sometimes (suffer /(suffers)) up to ten colds in a single year.

5. As an older person (build up /(builds up)) immunity, he or she catches colds less often.

6. No cure (exist /(exists)) for the common cold.

7. One theory (suggest /(suggests)) that large doses of vitamin C can prevent colds, but most doctors dismiss this idea.

8. Cold sufferers often ((rely)/ relies) on over-the-counter medicines that treat the symptoms, not the virus itself.

9. The typical cold (last /(lasts)) for about a week.

10. Although colds are relatively harmless, they sometimes ((create)/ creates) more serious bacterial infections in the ears, lungs, or throat.

A.   The Verb Is a Form of *Be, Have,* or *Do*

The verbs *be, have,* and *do* do not follow the usual rules for forming singular and plural forms; they are **irregular verbs.**

Forms of the Verb *Be*

	SUBJECT	VERB
PRESENT		
Singular	I	am
	you	are
	she, he, it	is
	the student	is
Plural	we	are
	you	are
	they	are
	the students	are
PAST		
Singular	I	was
	you	were
	she, he, it	was
	the student	was
Plural	we	were
	you	were
	they	were
	the students	were

Forms of the Verb *Have*

	SUBJECT	VERB
PRESENT		
Singular	I	have
	you	have
	she, he, it	has
	the student	has
Plural	we	have
	you	have
	they	have
	the students	have

Forms of the Verb *Do*

	SUBJECT	VERB
PRESENT		
Singular	I	do
	you	do
	she, he, it	does
	the student	does
Plural	we	do
	you	do
	they	do
	the students	do

These verbs cause problems for many writers because they are harder to memorize. Another reason is that in casual conversation people sometimes use the same form in all cases: *He do the laundry. They do the laundry.*

In college and at work you need to use the correct forms of these verbs, making sure that they agree with the subject in number. If you confuse the forms, refer to the charts until you feel confident that your use is correct.

     are
They ~~is~~ sick today.
     ^

     does
Mark ~~do~~ the laundry every Wednesday.
     ^

               has
Without a doubt, Andrea ~~have~~ the best taste in shoes.
               ^

Practice 3 ▶ The Verbs *Be, Have,* and *Do*

In each sentence, underline the subject and circle the correct form of the verb. Use the Thinking Critically guide on page 293.

EXAMPLE: Sarah (is/ are) a good friend.

1. Harold (doesn't/ don't) like to get up early in the morning.

2. He (is/ are) a computer animator.

3. His computer programs (has / have) the ability to create logos and landscapes, among other things.

4. His company (is/ are) Rhythm & Hues, and it takes good care of its employees.

5. It (has / have) a complete kitchen with free food and soft drinks.

6. Employees (has / have) to be careful or they might eat all day long.

7. Computer animation (is / are) a growing field.

8. Los Angeles and New York (is / are) the centers, but others (appears / appear) every month.

9. The Disney Studio (has / have) several films that are completely produced by computer animation.

10. Computers (has / have) possibilities far beyond what we can presently imagine.

Practice 4   **The Verbs *Be, Have*, and *Do***

In each sentence, underline the subject and fill in the correct form of the verb indicated in parentheses. Use the Thinking Critically guide on page 293.

EXAMPLE: Fresh herbs _____*are*_____ (*be*) always better in cooking than dried ones.

1. Dried parsley, for example, _____*has*_____ (*have*) almost no flavor.

2. However, fresh parsley _____*is*_____ (*be*) a key ingredient in many summer salads.

3. Mint _____*is*_____ (*be*) an herb that can be grown easily in a backyard garden.

4. Skillful cooks _____*do*_____ (*do*) many things with these herbs.

5. Dried herbs _____*have*_____ (*have*) one obvious advantage: The cook doesn't have to spend time cutting them up.

B. Words Come between the Subject and the Verb

In short sentences, you may have no trouble finding the subject and the verb. In longer sentences, words often come between the subject and the verb, so it is more difficult to find them to make sure they agree. Most often, either a prepositional phrase or a dependent clause comes between the subject and the verb.

TIP: For a list of common prepositions, see p. 264.

Prepositional Phrase between Subject and Verb

A **prepositional phrase** starts with a preposition and ends with a noun or pronoun: I took my bag *of books* and threw it *across the room*.

The subject of a sentence is never in a prepositional phrase. When you are looking for the subject of the sentence, you can cross out any prepositional phrases. This should make it easier for you to find the real subject and decide whether there is a subject-verb agreement problem.

COMPUTER
Have students highlight the prepositional phrase and read only the nonhighlighted parts of the sentence.

The leader ~~of the bikers~~ (wear / wears) ten gold nose rings.

The speaker ~~of the U.S. House of Representatives~~ (give / gives) many interviews.

Practice 5 ▶ **Subject and Verb Separated by Prepositional Phrase**

In each of the following sentences, cross out the prepositional phrase and circle the correct form of the verb. Use the Thinking Critically guide on page 293.

> **EXAMPLE:** The Enneagram system ~~of personality types~~ (**defines** / define) nine basic types of people.

1. The list ~~of personality types~~ (begin / **begins**) with the "perfectionist."

2. The "perfectionist" ~~in any group~~ (want / **wants**) everything to be right.

3. Numbers two and three ~~on the scale~~ (is / **are**) the "giver" and the "achiever."

4. "Givers" ~~by nature~~ (**wish** / wishes) to be helpful and to give.

5. The "achievers," ~~in all areas of their lives,~~ (**want** / wants) to see results.

6. The "tragic romantic" ~~in love situations~~ (get / **gets**) hurt often.

7. The "observer" ~~of life's people and situations~~ (remain / **remains**) cool and objective.

8. My best friend ~~from my high school years~~ (fit / **fits**) the description of the "questioner."

9. The "epicure" ~~across the restaurant in one of the booths~~ (seem / **seems**) relaxed and ready to enjoy herself.

10. The "boss" ~~of the basketball players~~ (make / **makes**) most of the decisions. The "mediator" ~~of the group~~ (want / **wants**) everyone to be happy.

Dependent Clause between Subject and the Verb

A **dependent clause** has a noun and a verb, but it does not express a complete thought. When a dependent clause comes between the subject and the verb, it usually starts with the word *who, whose, whom, that,* or *which.*
The subject of a sentence is never in a dependent clause. When you are looking for the subject of the sentence, you can cross out any dependent clauses. This should make it easier for you to find the real subject and decide whether there is a subject-verb agreement problem.

The coins ~~that I found last week~~ (seem / seems) very valuable.

The obese person ~~whose stomach was stapled~~ (eat / eats) very little now.

Practice 6 ▸ **Subject and Verb Separated by Dependent Clause**

In each of the following sentences, cross out any dependent clauses. Then use the Thinking Critically guide on page 293 to correct any problems with subject-verb agreement. If there is no problem, write "OK" next to the sentence.

EXAMPLE: The company ~~that laid off thousands of workers~~ is not   *OK*

profitable.

1. The person ~~whose orders resulted in layoffs~~ run the company as its
                                                          s
CEO.

2. Almost every year the board ~~that the company asks to review its~~
                            s
~~practices~~ increase the CEO's salary.

3. The same person ~~whom the workers call "the Breadline Boss"~~ makes

millions of dollars a year.   *OK*

4. The annual report ~~that the company publishes~~ praises the CEO for

his leadership and vision.   *OK*

5. The reporter ~~who wrote the article I read~~ think this is unfair.
                                            s

DISCUSSION
Ask students what *compound* means in everyday life (for example, *compound fracture*).

C. The Subject Is a Compound Subject

A **compound subject** consists of two (or more) subjects joined by *and* or *or*. If two subjects are joined by *and*, they combine to become a plural subject, and the verb must be plural too.

plural subject

The teacher *and* her aide grade all of the exams.

TIP: Whenever you see a compound subject joined by *and*, try replacing it in your mind with *they*.

If two subjects are separated by the word *or*, they are not combined. The verb should agree with whichever subject is closer to it.

singular subject

The teacher *or* her aide grades all of the exams.

plural subject

The teacher *or* her aides grade all of the exams.

> **Practice 7**   **Compound Subjects**

In each of the following sentences, underline the word (*and* or *or*) that joins elements in the compound subject. Then circle the correct form of the verb. Use the Thinking Critically guide on page 293.

EXAMPLE: Jean <u>and</u> Joseph (wants /(want)) to find a job.

1. Counselors <u>and</u> friends (gives /(give)) them advice and information.

2. The newspaper <u>and</u> the college employment office (is /(are)) good sources of job listings.

3. A contact <u>or</u> a friend in a particular company ((provides)/ provide) good information on that organization.

4. Annual reports <u>or</u> press releases also (gives /(give)) information on companies.

5. Job fairs <u>and</u> recruiting sessions (is /(are)) good ways to meet people and find out about possible jobs.

6. A letter of inquiry <u>or</u> a telephone call to the personnel department ((is)/ are) another route into an interview.

7. A résumé <u>and</u> a good cover letter (is /(are)) essential.

8. A clean suit <u>or</u> jacket ((gives)/ give) a professional appearance.

9. A follow-up letter <u>and</u> a phone call (makes /(make)) a good impression.

10. Persistence <u>and</u> luck (brings /(bring)) rewards to the job hunter.

D. The Subject Is an Indefinite Pronoun

An **indefinite pronoun** does not stand in for a specific person, place, or thing: It is general. Most indefinite pronouns are either always singular or always plural.

Indefinite Pronouns

ALWAYS SINGULAR			ALWAYS PLURAL
another	everyone	no one	any
anybody	everything	nothing	both
anything	much	one (of)	few
each (of)	neither (of)	somebody	many
either (of)	nobody	someone	several
everybody	none	something	

SINGULAR   <u>Everyone</u> <u>wants</u> the semester to end.

PLURAL   <u>Many</u> <u>want</u> the semester to end.

Often an indefinite pronoun is followed by a prepositional phrase or dependent clause. Remember that the verb of the sentence must agree with the subject of the sentence and *the subject of a sentence is never in a prepositional phrase or dependent clause.* Focus on the indefinite pronoun—you can cross out the prepositional phrase or dependent clause.

<u>Everyone</u> ~~in all of the classes~~ (want / <u>wants</u>) the term to end.

<u>Few</u> ~~of the students~~ (is / <u>are</u>) looking forward to exams.

Practice 8	Subject Is an Indefinite Pronoun

Underline the subject, cross out any prepositional phrases or dependent clauses that come between the subject and the verb, and circle the correct verb. Use the Thinking Critically guide on page 293.

EXAMPLE: <u>One</u> ~~of the strangest human experiences~~ (result / results) from the "small world" phenomenon.

1. <u>Everyone</u> (remembers / remember) an example of the "small world" phenomenon.

2. Someone ~~that you have just met~~ ((tells)/ tell) you a story.

3. During the story, one ~~of you~~ ((realizes)/ realize) that you are connected somehow.

4. One ~~of your friends~~ ((lives)/ live) next door to the person.

5. Someone ~~in your family~~ ((knows)/ know) someone in the person's family.

6. Each ~~of your families~~ ((owns)/ own) a home in the same place.

7. One ~~of your relatives~~ ((plans)/ plan) to marry his cousin.

8. One interesting theory ((holds)/ hold) that if you know one hundred people and talk to someone who knows one hundred people, together you are linked to one million people through friends and acquaintances.

9. Someone ~~in this class~~ probably ((connects)/ connect) to you in one way or another.

10. Each ~~of you~~ probably ((recognizes)/ recognize) a good "small world" story of your own.

E. The Verb Comes before the Subject

In most sentences, the subject comes before the verb. When that order is reversed, you might make errors in subject-verb agreement. Two kinds of sentences reverse the usual subject-verb order: questions and sentences that begin with *here* or *there*.

TEAMWORK
Divide the class down the middle. One side asks questions (students go in turns according to where they are sitting). The other side turns the questions around (anyone can answer by raising his or her hand or calling out the answer). Keep a fairly fast pace.

Questions

In questions, the verb or part of the verb comes before the subject. To help find the subject and verb, you can turn the question around as if you were going to answer it.

Where is the bookstore? / The bookstore is . . .

Are you insane? / You are insane.

When is the bus going to leave? / The bus is going to leave . . .

Sentences That Begin with Here or There

When *here* or *there* begins a sentence, it is never the subject. Turn the sentence around to find the subject and verb.

Here is your key to the apartment. / Your key to the apartment is here.

There are four keys on the table. / Four keys are on the table.

| Practice 9 ▶ | **Verb Comes before the Subject** |

Using the Thinking Critically guide on page 293, correct any problems with subject-verb agreement in the following sentences. If a sentence is already correct, write "OK" next to it.

EXAMPLE: Where ~~is~~ you going?
    are ^

1. What is the best day care center in the area?   *OK*

2. How can I register my son?   *OK*

3. There are twenty-five centers listed in the telephone book.   *OK*

4. There ~~are~~ not a center near my house.
    is ^

5. Is one better than the rest?   *OK*

6. ~~Are~~ there a minimum age?
    Is ^

7. ~~Do~~ it have spaces available?
    Does ^

8. ~~Are~~ the day care center on a bus line?
    Is ^

9. What ~~are~~ the schedule of fees?
    is ^

10. Here ~~are~~ some information on the center.
    is ^

Edit Paragraphs and Your Own Writing

| Practice 10 ▶ | **Editing Paragraphs for Subject-Verb Agreement** |

Find and correct any problems with subject-verb agreement in the following paragraphs. You may want to refer to the Summary on page 306.

TEAMWORK
This practice works well in small groups. One person should read the paragraph aloud. Then the group suggests corrections.

1.   (1) A study I came across while doing research for my sociology
class rate U.S. cities on "most things to do." (2) The categories ~~be~~ sun, sea,
    s ^   *are*
snow, nature, sports, and culture. (3) Each of the cities ~~were~~ assigned
                                                          was ^

a total from 0 to 100 in each category. (4) The number was determined by the level of recreational activities available. (5) Los Angeles and San Diego, which have a warm, coastal climate, have perfect scores. (6) Either of these places ~~are~~ *is* a good place to visit. (7) Miami, New York, and Washington, D.C., are the other cities ranked in the top five.

2. (1) Another study measures the fastest and slowest talkers. (2) Postal workers in different cities talk at different rates when explaining the class of mail. (3) Workers in Columbus, Ohio, speak the fastest. (4) Atlanta and Detroit ~~has~~ *have* the next fastest talkers. (5) There ~~is~~ *are* also fast talkers in Boston and Bakersfield, California. (6) The slowest talkers in the country are in Sacramento, California. (7) Other postal workers who speak very slowly live in Los Angeles; Shreveport, Louisiana; and Chattanooga, Tennessee. (8) How do you think your city ranks?

3. (1) The color of eggs comes from the pigment in the outer layer of the shell. (2) Colors of the shell range from pure white to deep brown. (3) The only determining factor of egg color is the breed of the chicken. (4) Each of the breeds produce*s* a slightly different-colored egg. (5) There is a simple way to tell what color egg a hen will produce. (6) Hens with white earlobes lay white eggs. (7) Any of the hens with red earlobes produce brown eggs.

Practice 11 ▶ Editing Ray's Letter

Look back at Ray's letter on page 292. You may have already identified the subject-verb agreement errors; if not, do that now. Next, using what you've learned in this chapter, correct each error.

| Practice 12 | **Editing Your Own Writing for Subject-Verb Agreement** |

Use your new skill at editing for subject-verb agreement on a piece of your own writing—a paper you are working on for this class, a paper you've already finished, a paper for another course, or a recent piece of writing from your work or everyday life.

First, do the following "Focus—and Refocus" activity. Then use the Thinking Critically guide on page 293 or the Summary on page 306 to find and correct any problems with subject-verb agreement in your own writing.

FOCUS—AND REFOCUS

Focus on this picture and write down whether you are looking at the top of the blocks or the bottom.

I see the _____ *of the blocks.*

Did you see the top or the bottom of the blocks? Check with the people in your class to find out what they saw. Now *refocus* your eyes to look for the other image. Can you see it?

Refocusing is an important part of editing. Before editing your writing, refocus, looking for problems with subjects and verbs that you may not have seen before (but that were there). This refocusing will help you find any errors you didn't see at first.

Summary and Quick Review Chart: Subject-Verb Agreement Problems

- The **subject** and the **verb** in a sentence must **agree** (match) in terms of number. They must both be singular or they must both be plural. (See p. 291.)
- Five trouble spots can cause errors in subject-verb agreement.
  - The verb is a form of *be, have,* or *do* (see p. 294).
  - Words or phrases (**prepositional phrases** or **dependent clauses**) come between the subject and the verb (see p. 297).
  - There is a **compound subject** joined by *and* or *or* (see p. 300).
  - The subject is an **indefinite pronoun** (see p. 301).
  - The **verb comes before the subject** (see p. 302).

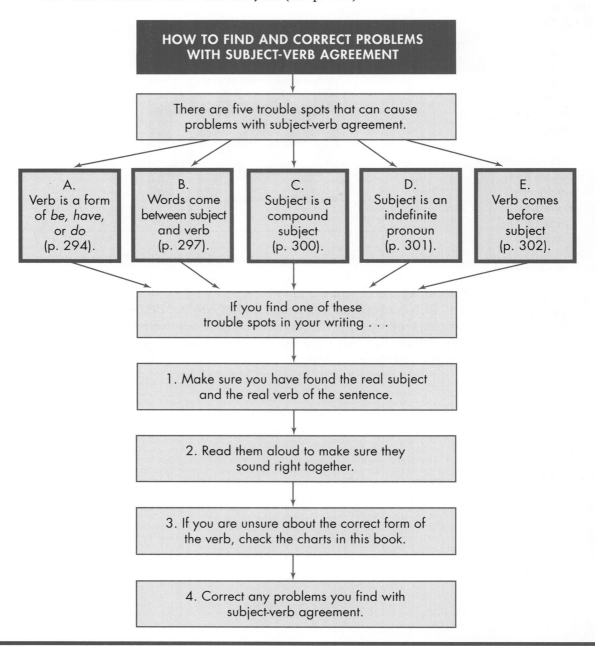

HOW TO FIND AND CORRECT PROBLEMS WITH SUBJECT-VERB AGREEMENT

There are five trouble spots that can cause problems with subject-verb agreement.

| A. Verb is a form of *be, have,* or *do* (p. 294). | B. Words come between subject and verb (p. 297). | C. Subject is a compound subject (p. 300). | D. Subject is an indefinite pronoun (p. 301). | E. Verb comes before subject (p. 302). |

If you find one of these trouble spots in your writing . . .

1. Make sure you have found the real subject and the real verb of the sentence.

2. Read them aloud to make sure they sound right together.

3. If you are unsure about the correct form of the verb, check the charts in this book.

4. Correct any problems you find with subject-verb agreement.

25

Verb Problems

Mistakes in Verb Form and Verb Tense

A. Regular Verbs
B. Irregular Verbs
C. Using Past Participles

TIP: To find and correct problems with verbs, you need to be able to identify the subject and the verb in a sentence. For review, see Chapter 21.

RESOURCES
Additional Resources contains tests and supplemental practice exercises for this chapter as well as a transparency master for the summary chart at the end of the chapter.

Understand What Verb Form and Verb Tense Are

Verb forms are the different ways a verb can be spelled and pronounced. These are different forms of the same verb:

like   likes   liked

The correct form depends on how the verb is used in the sentence: whether it is singular or plural, past or present, and so on.

I <u>like</u> my sister's new apartment.

She <u>likes</u> the low rent.

My sister <u>liked</u> her last apartment, but it was too expensive.

Verb tense tells *when* the action of a sentence occurred: in the past, in the present, or in the future. Verbs change their form and use helping verbs to indicate different tenses.

ESL

Many nonnative speakers will write using the present tense only, avoiding any other verb forms. ESL students may have more extensive problems with verbs in general and need extra practice.

DISCUSSION

Should Martina's boss tell her about this? Would you want to know? What would you say in response?

Students should underline verb errors for Practice 1, on this page.

Students should correct verb errors for Practice 11, p. 323.

PRESENT TENSE	Michael <u>sings</u> quite well.
PAST TENSE	He <u>sang</u> on the ride home.
FUTURE TENSE	He <u>will sing</u> for us again soon.

Using the wrong form of a verb is one of the errors that people notice most.

In the Real World, Why Is It Important to Use Correct Verbs?

SITUATION: Martina is a new intern at an accounting firm. She'd like to get a part-time secretarial position there because she knows that she'll learn a lot about accounting, which she's studying in college. Since Martina is trying to make a good impression, she takes on extra work and tells her supervisor about it in a note:

Last night, I file Mr. Shackler's letters, and I also ~~make~~ *made* copies of those folders you ~~give~~ *gave* me. I enjoy this work and hope I can do more of it.

RESPONSE: Although Martina's boss was impressed by her responsibility and intelligence, she also noticed that Martina made several grammar errors. When a part-time secretarial position did open up at the firm, Martina was not considered for it because her boss was worried that Martina's poor communication skills would make a bad impression on clients.

> **Practice 1** ▷ **Identifying Problems with Verb Form**

Find and underline the three problems with verb form in Martina's note.

Practice Using Correct Verbs

English verbs can be very complicated. There are some general rules that you can learn, but there are also many verb forms that must simply be memorized. The best way to learn the correct forms is to read, write, and speak them as often as possible.

Some people leave off verb endings or use a different pattern for verb forms in their everyday speech. When these people write, they sometimes spell verbs the same way they would say them. This can lead to mistakes in verb form that are very obvious to most readers. If you use verb forms different from the ones shown in this chapter in your everyday speech, be particularly careful to check for standard forms in your writing.

ESL
It is helpful for students to *hear* the verb forms, particularly for irregular verbs. If you have access to a language lab, you might have them listen to prerecorded verb tapes. If students can record, have them record examples for each other, using personalized examples.

Thinking Critically about Verbs

FOCUS	If you think you may have a problem with the verb in a sentence, stop to check.
ASK	• Is this the main verb in the sentence? • Is my sentence about the present? about the past? about something that happened before something else? • Is this a regular verb? an irregular verb? • Do I have the tense I need to express my meaning? Have I written the correct form?
EDIT	Edit to correct any problems with verb form.

TIP: For more about making verbs match subjects, see Chapter 24.

A. Regular Verbs

Most verbs in English are **regular verbs**—their forms follow standard rules. Practice using the right forms so that you do not leave endings off when you use these verbs in your writing.

Two Regular Present-Tense Forms: -s Ending and No Ending

The **present tense** is used for actions that are happening at the same time that they are being written about (the present). It is also used for things that happen all the time. There are two forms for the present tense of regular verbs:

DISCUSSION
A common error is using only the present tense in writing. If your students do this, ask why. A common answer is that they know the present form and are less certain about others. Point out that using the present-tense form of a verb where past tense is correct is as serious an error as using an incorrect past form.

-S ENDING	NO ENDING
jumps	jump
walks	walk
lives	live

Use the *-s* ending when the subject is *he, she, it,* or the name of one person or thing. Use no ending for all other subjects.

TIP: Sometimes the *-s* ending is spelled *-es: he rushes, she tosses.* If a verb ends in *-y,* usually the *-y* changes to *-i* when *-es* is added: *I spy / he spies; you try / she tries.* For more on spelling, see Chapter 35.

PRESENT	SUBJECT	VERB
SINGULAR	I	jump
	you	jump
	she, he, it	jump<u>s</u>
PLURAL	we	jump
	you	jump
	they	jump

| Practice 2 ▶ | **Using the Correct Form for Regular Verbs in the Present Tense** |

In each of the following sentences, first underline the subject and then circle the correct verb form.

EXAMPLE: I (handles /(handle)) many important responsibilities in my position.

1. My job responsibilities (includes /(include)) reviewing all spending requests.

2. My supervisor, in turn, ((reviews)/ review) my work.

3. Our department ((applies)/ apply) for more money than does any other part of the company.

4. Therefore, it is very important that we (uses /(use)) the money we receive wisely.

5. Sometimes when I turn down someone's spending request, the person ((asks)/ ask) for an explanation in writing.

6. I (tries /(try)) my best to explain why the request was turned down.

7. Sometimes the person ((complains)/ complain) to my supervisor.

8. These complaints, of course, (annoys /(annoy)) me.

9. Fortunately, my supervisor usually ((supports)/ support) my decision.

10. Sometimes we (discusses /(discuss)) ways of dealing with my colleagues' concerns.

TIP: If the verb already ends in -e, just add -d: *dance/danced.* If a verb ends in -y, usually the -y changes to -i when -ed is added: *spy/spied; try/tried.* For more on spelling, see Chapter 35.

One Regular Past-Tense Form: -ed Ending

The **past tense** is used for actions that have already happened. An *-ed* ending is needed on all regular verbs in the past tense.

PRESENT TENSE	PAST TENSE
I avoid trouble.	I avoided the freeway this morning.
He walks in the door.	He walked in the same door yesterday.

| Practice 3 ▶ | **Using the Correct Form for Regular Verbs in the Past Tense** |

In each of the following sentences, fill in the correct form of the verb in parentheses.

ESL
Ask ESL students if there is a standard rule for forming the past tense in their first language and, if so, what it is. Have students fill in a chart with the past-tense rule from their first language and the past-tense rules in English.

EXAMPLE: When the airplane _____crashed_____ (*crash*), it _____exploded_____ (*explode*) into a ball of fire.

Several years ago I _____traveled_____ (*travel*) from Boston to Seattle on Christmas Eve. As we _____approached_____ (*approach*) the Seattle area, we _____learned_____ (*learn*) that the airport was fogged in. The captain _____reported_____ (*report*) that he was considering landing in Portland, 180 miles south. While the airliner _____circled_____ (*circle*) the area, passengers _____asked_____ (*ask*) nervous questions about how much fuel _____remained_____ (*remain*). When I _____gazed_____ (*gaze*) out the window I could see the fog down below us. It _____looked_____ (*look*) thick and white. Finally the captain _____decided_____ (*decide*) to attempt a landing. Some passengers _____expressed_____ (*express*) concern, but most of us were glad not to be going to Portland. Soon we _____plunged_____ (*plunge*) deep into the fog and _____waited_____ (*wait*) for something to happen; suddenly the runway's blue landing lights _____rushed_____ (*rush*) up to meet us. A moment later the plane _____touched_____ (*touch*) down, and the entire aircraft _____seemed_____ (*seem*) to shudder with relief.

One Regular Past Participle: -ed Ending

The **past participle** is a verb that can be used with helping verbs, such as *have*. For all regular verbs, the past-participle form is the same as the past-tense form: It uses an *-ed* ending.

PAST-TENSE FORM	PAST-PARTICIPLE FORM
My kids <u>watched</u> cartoons.	They <u>have watched</u> cartoons before.
George <u>visited</u> his cousins.	He <u>has visited</u> them every year.

> **Practice 4** ▶ **Using the Correct Form for the Past Participles of Regular Verbs**

In each of the following sentences, underline the helping verb (a form of *have*) and fill in the correct form of the verb in parentheses.

EXAMPLE: In the past two decades, technology has ___*caused*___ (*cause*) significant changes in education.

1. Since the 1970s, many students have ___*relied*___ (*rely*) on pocket calculators to help them solve math problems.

2. Calculators have ___*decreased*___ (*decrease*) the emphasis on memorizing multiplication tables.

3. Although calculators have ___*changed*___ (*change*) education in important ways, the personal computer has ___*created*___ (*created*) an even greater effect.

4. Computers, which can provide pictures and sounds as well as text, have ___*weakened*___ (*weaken*) the dominance of the printed word.

5. School districts throughout the nation have ___*embraced*___ (*embrace*) the concept of "multimedia education."

6. The case of a kindergarten in Colorado, which has ___*installed*___ (*install*) computers for use by preschoolers, shows how this technology has ___*affected*___ (*affect*) education at all levels.

7. Many parents have ___*discovered*___ (*discover*) that their children know more about computers than they do.

8. At the college level, some schools have ___*established*___ (*establish*) electronic correspondence courses, in which students and instructors communicate entirely by modem.

9. In college libraries, CD-ROM databases and online services have

   ___*replaced*___ (*replace*) many of the printed versions of reference

   works and indexes.

10. The publishers of the *Oxford English Dictionary,* the largest and most

    authoritative English dictionary in the world, have ___*decided*___

    (*decide*) to issue future editions in CD-ROM version only.

DISCUSSION
Ask students what the
word *irregular* means in
real life (for example, *irregular* clothing or *irregular* behavior).

B. Irregular Verbs

Not all verbs in English are regular—some are irregular. **Irregular
verbs** do not follow the regular pattern for the different verb forms. Practice
using these verbs so that you learn to use the correct forms in your writing.

Irregular Present-Tense Forms

Only a few verbs are irregular in the present tense. However, these
verbs are very common, so it is important to learn the correct forms.

Present-Tense Forms for Two Irregular Verbs			
BE		**HAVE**	
I am	we are	I have	we have
you are	you are	you have	you have
he, she, it is	they are	he, she, it has	they have
the editor is	the editors are		
Denise is	Denise and Sarah are		

Practice 5 ▷ **Using the Correct Forms for *Be* and *Have* in the Present Tense**

In each of the following sentences, fill in the correct form of the verb
indicated in parentheses.

EXAMPLE: Because of my university's internship program, I ___*am*___

(*be*) able to receive academic credit for my summer job.

1. I ___*have*___ (*have*) a job lined up with a company that provides

   private security to businesses and residential developments.

2. The company _____*has*_____ (*have*) a good record of keeping its clients safe from crime.

3. The company _____*is*_____ (*be*) part of a fast-growing industry.

4. Many people no longer _____*have*_____ (*have*) faith in the ability of the police to protect them.

5. People with lots of money _____*are*_____ (*be*) willing to pay for their own protection.

6. Concern about crime _____*is*_____ (*be*) especially noticeable in so-called gated communities.

7. In these private residential areas, no one _____*has*_____ (*have*) the right to enter without authorization.

8. If you _____*are*_____ (*be*) a visitor, you must obtain a special pass.

9. Once you _____*have*_____ (*have*) the pass, you show it to the security guard when you reach the gate.

10. In a gated community, the residents _____*are*_____ (*be*) likely to appreciate the security.

Irregular Past-Tense Forms

Irregular verbs do not use the *-ed* ending for the past-tense form. They show the past tense in some other way.

PRESENT-TENSE FORM	PAST-TENSE FORM
I <u>begin</u> today.	I <u>began</u> yesterday.
You <u>sleep</u> very soundly.	You <u>slept</u> late this morning.
I <u>let</u> the dog in today.	I <u>let</u> the dog in yesterday.

The Verb *Be*

The verb *be* is particularly tricky because it has two different forms for the past tense as well as several forms in the present tense. Here are all the forms of *be* together:

PRESENT		PAST	
I am	we are	I was	we were
you are	you are	you were	you were
he, she, it is	they are	he, she, it was	they were
the tax is	the taxes are	the tax was	the taxes were

There is no simple rule for how irregular verbs form the past tense. Until you memorize them, consult the chart on the next two pages.

Practice 6   Using the Correct Form for Irregular Verbs in the Past Tense

In each of the following sentences, fill in the correct past-tense form of the verb in parentheses.

EXAMPLE: John Steinbeck ____*wrote*____ (*write*) *The Grapes of Wrath*, his most famous novel, near the end of the Great Depression.

1. The novel ____*won*____ (*win*) the 1940 Pulitzer Prize and later helped Steinbeck win the Nobel Prize for Literature.

2. Despite his success, Steinbeck always ____*thought*____ (*think*) he was not talented.

3. When writing *The Grapes of Wrath*, he ____*said*____ (*say*) to a friend, "I'm not a writer. I've been fooling myself and other people."

4. In a recent biography, the writer Jay Parini ____*told*____ (*tell*) about Steinbeck's unhappy personal life.

5. Steinbeck ____*drank*____ (*drink*) heavily.

NOTE: Practice 6 continues on page 318.

316

TEACHING TIP
Give students a few minutes in class or as homework to review the list of irregular verbs and underline the fifteen verbs they use most frequently.

COMPUTER
Students can use the find or search function on a computer to find the present-tense form of the fifteen irregular verbs they underlined (or those they missed in the dictation) to see if they have used the correct past-tense and past-participle forms.

Irregular Verb Forms

PRESENT-TENSE FORM	PAST-TENSE FORM	PAST PARTICIPLE
am/are/is	was/were	been
become	became	become
begin	began	begun
bite	bit	bitten
blow	blew	blown
break	broke	broken
bring	brought	brought
build	built	built
buy	bought	bought
catch	caught	caught
choose	chose	chosen
come	came	come
cost	cost	cost
do	did	done
draw	drew	drawn
drink	drank	drunk
drive	drove	driven
eat	ate	eaten
fall	fell	fallen
feed	fed	fed
feel	felt	felt
fight	fought	fought
find	found	found
forget	forgot	forgotten
get	got	got *or* gotten
give	gave	given
go	went	gone
grow	grew	grown
have/has	had	had
hide	hid	hidden
hit	hit	hit
hold	held	held
hurt	hurt	hurt
keep	kept	kept
know	knew	known
lay	laid	laid
leave	left	left

(continued)

PRESENT-TENSE FORM	PAST-TENSE FORM	PAST PARTICIPLE
let	let	let
lie	lay	lain
lose	lost	lost
make	made	made
mean	meant	meant
meet	met	met
pay	paid	paid
put	put	put
quit	quit	quit
read	read	read
ride	rode	ridden
run	ran	run
say	said	said
see	saw	seen
sell	sold	sold
send	sent	sent
shut	shut	shut
sing	sang	sung
sink	sank	sunk
sit	sat	sat
sleep	slept	slept
speak	spoke	spoken
spend	spent	spent
stand	stood	stood
steal	stole	stolen
stick	stuck	stuck
sting	stung	stung
take	took	taken
teach	taught	taught
tear	torn	torn
tell	told	told
think	thought	thought
throw	threw	thrown
understand	understood	understood
wake	woke	woken
wear	worn	worn
win	won	won
write	wrote	written

TEACHING TIP
Students are often surprised to find out they don't know the forms of very common irregular verbs. Dictate some of the present-tense forms on this list and have students supply the past and past-particular forms (do the first one for them). They should check their answers against the list. As a follow-up, have students write sentences using any forms they missed. (BO)

6. He ___*let*___ (*let*) his first two marriages fall apart.

7. His two sons ___*grew*___ (*grow*) up emotionally distant from him.

8. Nonetheless, in Parini's view, Steinbeck ___*brought*___ (*bring*) to his work a deep compassion and respect for the individual.

9. He ___*understood*___ (*understand*) the importance of people's connection to nature.

10. In his works, he ___*fought*___ (*fight*) against the dehumanizing forces of modern technology.

Irregular Past Participles

For regular verbs, the **past-participle form** (used with helping verbs such as *have*) is the same as the past-tense form; they both use the -*ed* ending. For irregular verbs, the past-participle form is often different from the past-tense form.

	PAST-TENSE FORM	PAST-PARTICIPLE FORM
REGULAR VERB	I <u>walked</u> home.	I have <u>walked</u> home before.
IRREGULAR VERB	I <u>drove</u> home.	I have <u>driven</u> home before.

It is difficult to predict how irregular verbs form the past participle. Until you are familiar with them, find them in the chart on pages 316–17.

Practice 7 ▶ **Using Correct Past-Participle Forms for Irregular Verbs**

In each of the following sentences, underline the helping verb (a form of *have*) and fill in the correct past-participle form of the verb in parentheses.

EXAMPLE: Lately, many businesses <u>have</u> ___*begun*___ (*begin*) to hire temporary workers.

1. This <u>has</u> ___*given*___ (*give*) businesses more flexibility.

2. Studies have _____*found*_____ (*find*) that most companies have more

   people on their payrolls than they really need.

3. Companies that have _____*made*_____ (*make*) use of temporary workers

   report that they are more efficient.

4. Some temporary workers have _____*come*_____ (*come*) to appreciate the

   freedom of not being a permanent employee.

5. Others have _____*gone*_____ (*go*) from being temporary workers to

   full-time employees in a relatively short time.

6. However, many "temps" have _____*said*_____ (*say*) they feel unappre-

   ciated by their employers.

7. They also have _____*felt*_____ (*feel*) that they are underpaid.

8. Economists have _____*written*_____ (*write*) reports showing that the use of

   temporary workers results in lower wages for permanent employees.

9. Temporary workers, these economists say, have _____*become*_____

   (*become*) a permanent reserve pool of labor.

10. Economists also have _____*shown*_____ (*show*) that good jobs in

    many fields have declined as companies rely more on temporary

    workers.

C. Using Past Participles

So far in this chapter, you have studied only the *form* of past participles; now you will study what they are used for. The past participle cannot be the main verb of a sentence on its own, but it can be used together with another verb (a **helping verb**) to make the present perfect tense and the past perfect tense.

TIP: You can think of the helping verb as a cane that the other verb needs to get where it's going.

TEACHING TIP
As you introduce this section, remind students that the purpose of this chapter is not to memorize the terms but to use verbs correctly in writing.

Have/Has + *Past Participle* **=** *Present Perfect Tense*

Use a present-tense form of the verb *have* plus the past participle to make the **present perfect tense.**

present tense of *have* (helping verb)   past participle

PRESENT PERFECT TENSE   My car has stalled several times recently.

The present perfect tense is used for an action begun in the past that either continues into the present or was completed at some unspecified time in the past.

PAST TENSE   My car stalled.

> [This sentence says that the car stalled once and that it's over.]

PRESENT PERFECT TENSE   My car has stalled several times.

> [This sentence says the stalling began in the past but may continue into the present.]

Practice 8   **Using the Present Perfect Tense**

In each of the following sentences, circle the correct verb tense.

> **EXAMPLE:** For three months now, the board of overseers (refused / (has refused)) to vote on our proposal.

1. Again and again, they (told /(have told)) us that they need more information.

2. We first ((presented)/ have presented) our plan in February.

3. At that time, board members ((said)/ have said) that they would reach a decision within a month.

4. Since then, we (grew /(have grown)) increasingly impatient.

5. So far this month I (made /(have made)) numerous calls to several of the board members.

6. They (returned /(have returned)) every one of my calls.

7. By now, however, I (began /(have begun)) to doubt their sincerity.

8. On Monday when I ((spoke)/ have spoken) to Ralph Johnson, he ((said)/ have said) he needed to consult the zoning map.

9. For several days now, we (waited /(have waited)) for him to do so.

10. Most of my neighbors and I (lived /(have lived)) on Pleasant Street for a decade or more.

Had + *Past Participle* = *Past Perfect Tense*

Use *had* (the past-tense form of *have*) plus the past participle to make the **past perfect tense**.

past tense of *have* (helping verb)   past participle

PAST PERFECT TENSE   My car <u>had stalled</u> several times before I called the mechanic.

The past perfect tense is used for an action begun in the past that was completed before some other past action.

PAST TENSE   My car <u>stalled</u>.

PRESENT PERFECT TENSE   My car <u>has stalled</u> several times recently.

PAST PERFECT TENSE   My car <u>had stalled</u> three times before I called the mechanic.

[This sentence says that both the *stalling* and *calling the mechanic* happened in the past, but the stalling happened before the calling.]

Practice 9   ### Using the Past Perfect Tense

In each of the following sentences, circle the correct verb tense.

EXAMPLE: By the time firefighters finally arrived, the fire (destroyed / (had destroyed)) most of the building.

1. Tenants who (rushed /(had rushed)) outside when the fire began now watched in shock and disbelief as the firefighters turned their hoses on the blaze.

2. Firefighters were relieved to see that everyone (got /(had gotten)) out of the building safely.

3. Although there were no major injuries, paramedics ((treated)/ had treated) two of the tenants for mild smoke inhalation.

4. A cat that never (went /(had gone)) outside of its apartment before came racing down the stairs at the first sign of flames.

5. Firefighters also ((rescued)/ had rescued) a pet rabbit.

6. By the time the sun set that evening, authorities (declared /(had declared)) the building a total loss.

7. Once the fire finally (burned /(had burned)) itself out, investigators began sifting through the ashy ruins.

8. The next day investigators reported that someone (left /(had left)) a saucepan filled with water on top of a lighted stove burner.

9. Once all the water (boiled /(had boiled)) away, the bottom of the saucepan began to melt.

10. Investigators also ((suggested)/ had suggested) that a roll of paper towels may have been left on top of the stove.

Edit Paragraphs and Your Own Writing

> **Practice 10**   **Editing Paragraphs for Correct Verbs**

Find and correct any problems with verbs in the following paragraphs. You may want to refer to the Summary on page 324.

TEAMWORK
Students can work in small groups to first read paragraphs aloud and then correct errors together.

1.   (1) When Teresa saw her friend Jan drop makeup into her bag, she
frown. (2) She ~~know~~ *knew* that Jan was stealing. (3) She also ~~knowed~~ *knew* that Jan
would be mad if Teresa said anything. (4) What if someone from secu-
rity had seen Jan? (5) As they ~~leave~~ *left* the store, Teresa's heart beat~~ed~~ *d*
hard. (6) When nothing happened, she was relieve *d*. (7) Still, she ~~feel~~ *felt*
bad, so she spoke to Jan. (8) Jan ~~say~~ *said* she was sorry and ~~has~~ returned the makeup.

2.   (1) George Crum, a Native American chef, invent *ed* potato chips in
1853. (2) A customer ~~has~~ *had* returned an order of french fries with a note
that they were too thick. (3) Crum decide *d* to make super-thin fries to
get even. (4) The customer loved the thin fries, and since then they
become *have* a favorite snack. (5) In the 1920s, Herman Lay ~~brang~~ *brought* the
potato chip to grocery stores. (6) The chips sold first in the South, and

their popularity quickly spread. (7) Since then, people ~~has ate~~ *have eaten* millions
of chips.

| Practice 11 | ### Editing Martina's Note |

Look back at Martina's note on page 308. You may have already identi-fied the verb errors; if not, do that now. Next, using what you've learned in this chapter, correct each error.

| Practice 12 | ### Editing Verbs in Your Own Writing |

RESOURCES
Diagnostic tests and addi-tional practice sets are in *Additional Resources.*

Use your new skill at editing verbs on a piece of your own writing—a paper you are working on for this course, a paper you've already finished, or a recent piece of writing from your work or everyday life.

First, do the following "Focus—and Refocus" activity. Then use the Thinking Critically guide on page 309 or the Summary on page 324 to find and correct any problems with verbs in your own writing.

FOCUS—AND REFOCUS
Focus on this picture and write down the color of the arrows you see.

I see _____.

TEACHING TIP
This activity should help students understand that they must shift their focus to edit successfully. They need to see their writing in a new way to identify errors that have been there all along. This activity works well in small groups; point out that dif-ferent people see differ-ent things and that by working in a group, writ-ers can learn to see things they would overlook if each was working separately. Addi-tional "Focus—and Refo-cus" activities are in the critical thinking section in *Practical Suggestions.*

Did you see the black arrows or the white arrows? Check with other people in your class to find out what they saw. Now *refocus* your eyes to look for the other image. Can you see it?

Refocusing is an important part of editing. Before editing your writing, refocus, looking for verb problems that you may not have seen before (but that were there). This refocusing will help you find any errors you didn't see at first.

Summary and Quick Review Chart: Verb Problems

- **Verb forms** are the different ways a verb can be spelled and pronounced. (See p. 307.)
- **Verb tense** indicates when the action in a sentence happens:
  - Happening right now: **present tense** (see pp. 309, 313)
  - Happened in the past: **past tense** (see pp. 310, 314)
  - Started in the past and is still happening: **present perfect tense** (see p. 320)
  - Happened before something else in the past: **past perfect tense** (see p. 321)
- **Regular verbs** follow a standard rule to make the different forms. (See p. 309.)
  - For the present tense, use the form of the verb with the *-s* ending or no ending.
  - For the past tense and past participle, use the form of the verb with the *-ed* ending.
- **Irregular verbs** do not follow a standard rule to make the different forms. Until you memorize the forms, consult the charts in this book. (See pp. 316–17.)

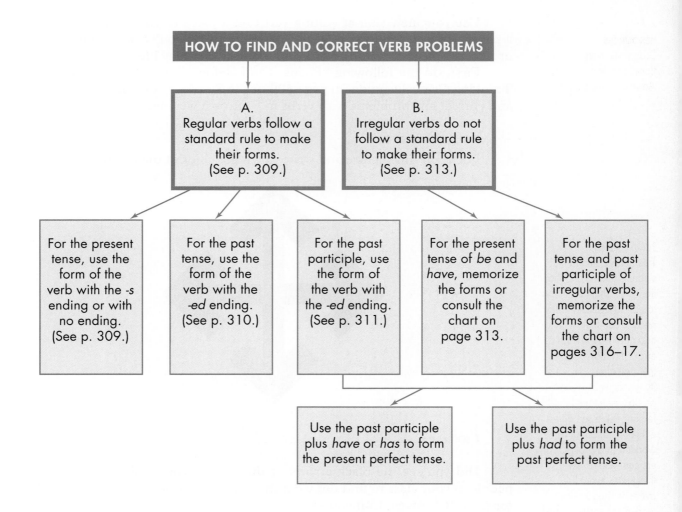

HOW TO FIND AND CORRECT VERB PROBLEMS

A.
Regular verbs follow a standard rule to make their forms. (See p. 309.)

B.
Irregular verbs do not follow a standard rule to make their forms. (See p. 313.)

For the present tense, use the form of the verb with the *-s* ending or with no ending. (See p. 309.)

For the past tense, use the form of the verb with the *-ed* ending. (See p. 310.)

For the past participle, use the form of the verb with the *-ed* ending. (See p. 311.)

For the present tense of *be* and *have*, memorize the forms or consult the chart on page 313.

For the past tense and past participle of irregular verbs, memorize the forms or consult the chart on pages 316–17.

Use the past participle plus *have* or *has* to form the present perfect tense.

Use the past participle plus *had* to form the past perfect tense.

EDITING

Part Six

Other Grammar Concerns

325

26

Pronouns

Using Substitutes for Nouns

TIP: To understand this chapter, you need to know what a *subject,* a *noun,* and a *conjunction* are. For review, see Chapter 21.

RESOURCES
Additional Resources contains tests and supplemental exercises for this chapter as well as a transparency master for the summary chart at the end.

A.   Check for Pronoun Agreement
B.   Make Pronoun Reference Clear
C.   Use the Right Type of Pronoun (Subject, Object, Possessive)

Understand What Pronouns Are

TIP: For a list of common pronouns, see Chapter 21.

Pronouns replace nouns or other pronouns in a sentence so that you will not have to repeat them.

her
Sheryl got into ~~Sheryl's~~ car.

He
I like Mario. ~~Mario~~ is a good dancer.

ESL
ESL students may have particular trouble with pronouns and benefit from extra practice exercises. (JS)

In most cases, a pronoun **refers to** a specific noun or pronoun mentioned nearby. This is how readers know what the pronoun means.

TIP: The noun or pronoun that a pronoun refers to is called the *antecedent* or the *referent.*

My roommate has a new car. His old car was stolen.

327

| Practice 1 | Identifying Pronouns |

In each of the following sentences, circle the pronoun, underline the noun it refers to, and draw an arrow from the pronoun to the noun.

EXAMPLE: Scientists successfully cloned (their) first sheep in 1996.

1. The sheep caused a sensation when (her) existence was announced.

2. Dolly, as (she) was known, could be seen on magazine covers and news programs around the world.

3. Cloning, which means growing an individual genetically identical to (its) parent, sounds like science fiction.

4. Dolly's birth proved that although cloning sounds fantastic, (it) is actually possible.

5. Journalists rushed to give (their) opinions on whether cloning humans is a good idea.

Practice Using Pronouns Correctly

A. Check for Pronoun Agreement

A pronoun must **agree with** (match) the noun or pronoun it refers to in terms of number (singular or plural). If the pronoun is singular, it must also match in terms of gender.

Magda and Bruce sold *their* old television set.

> [*Their* agrees with *Magda and Bruce* because both are plural.]

Magda sold *her* old television set.

> [*Her* agrees with *Magda* because both are singular and feminine.]

Two types of words can cause errors in pronoun agreement: indefinite pronouns and collective nouns.

Indefinite Pronouns

An **indefinite pronoun** does not refer to a specific person, place, or thing: It is general. Most indefinite pronouns are either always singular or always plural.

Indefinite Pronouns

ALWAYS SINGULAR			ALWAYS PLURAL
anybody	everyone	no one	any
anyone	everything	nothing	both
anything	much	one (of)	few
each (of)	neither (of)	somebody	many
either (of)	nobody	someone	several
everybody	none	something	

Whenever a pronoun refers to an indefinite pronoun, check for agreement.

> *her*
> Someone left ~~their~~ purse in the cafeteria.

> *his*
> The monks got up at dawn. Everybody had ~~their~~ chores for the day.

NOTE: Many people object to using only the masculine pronoun *he* when referring to a singular indefinite pronoun such as *everyone*. Although it is grammatically correct, it is considered sexist to use only the masculine form. There are several ways to avoid this problem:

1. Use *his or her.*

    Everybody took *his or her* books home.

2. Alternate between *his* and *her.*

    Everyone took *her* books home.

3. Change the sentence so that the pronoun refers to a plural noun or pronoun.

    The students took *their* books home.

| Practice 2 | Using Indefinite Pronouns |

Circle the correct pronoun or group of words in parentheses.

(1) Anyone who wants to start (their /his or her) own business had better be prepared to work hard. (2) One may find, for example, that (her/ their) work is never done. (3) There is always something waiting, with (its/ their) own peculiar demands. (4) Nothing gets done on (their /its) own. (5) Anybody who expects to have more freedom now that (he no longer works/ they no longer work) for a boss may be disappointed. (6) After all, when you work as an employee for a company, there is always someone above you who must make decisions as (they see /he or she sees) fit. (7) When you are your own boss, there is no one else to place (themselves /himself) in the position of final responsibility.

(8) Somebody starting a business may also be surprised by how much tax (they /she) must pay. (9) Each employee at a company pays only about half as much toward social security as what (they /he) would pay if self-employed. (10) And neither medical nor dental coverage can be obtained as inexpensively as (it/ they) can when a person is an employee at a corporation.

Collective Nouns

A **collective noun** names a group that acts as a single whole.

Common Collective Nouns		
audience	company	group
class	crowd	jury
college	family	society
committee	government	team

Collective nouns are usually singular, so when you use a pronoun to refer to a collective noun, it too must be singular.

The team had ~~their~~ *its* sixth consecutive win of the season.

TEAMWORK
In small groups, have students expand the list of collective nouns. See which group adds the most and have all students write the added words next to the box. (BO)

The jury returned ~~their~~ *its* verdict.

Practice 3 ▶ **Using Collective Nouns and Pronouns**

Circle the correct pronoun in each set of parentheses.

(1) In basketball, a team with less individual ability than (*its*/ their) opponent can often win through greater teamwork and co-operation. (2) A group of basketball players, in other words, is greater than (*its*/ their) individual parts. (3) This was the case in the NBA finals in 1977, when the Philadelphia 76ers' collection of stars, led by Julius Erving, could not demonstrate that (*it was*/ they were) superior to a less glamorous but more cohesive squad from Portland. (4) After losing the first two games in Philadelphia, Portland won three straight games at home, with its own crowd loudly expressing (*its*/ their) approval. (5) Soon, a nationwide jury of sportswriters and fans could declare (*its*/ their) verdict: Portland was the better team.

B. Make Pronoun Reference Clear

If the reader isn't sure what noun or pronoun a pronoun refers to, the meaning of a sentence becomes confusing. You should edit any sentence that has an ambiguous, vague, or repetitious pronoun reference.

In an **ambiguous pronoun reference,** the pronoun could refer to more than one noun.

AMBIGUOUS	Michael told Jim *he* needed a haircut.
	[Did Michael tell Jim that Michael himself needed a haircut? Or did Michael tell Jim that Jim needed a haircut?]
EDITED	Michael thought he needed a haircut, and told Jim he was going to get one.
AMBIGUOUS	I drove my car into a fence, and *it* crumpled.
	[Did the car crumple, or did the fence?]
EDITED	I drove my car into a fence, and the car crumpled.

In a **vague pronoun reference,** the pronoun does not refer clearly to any particular person or thing.

TEACHING TIP
See how many examples students can give of *they* statements. Start off with "They say smoking is bad for you." Ask students to correct the sentence. (BO)

VAGUE   When Michael got to the barbershop, *they* told him it was closed.

> [Who told Michael the barbershop was closed?]

EDITED   When Michael got to the barbershop, the barber told him it was closed.

VAGUE   Before I finished printing my report, it ran out of paper.

> [What was out of paper?]

EDITED   Before I finished printing my report, the printer ran out of paper.

In a **repetitious pronoun reference,** a pronoun is used unnecessarily to *repeat* a reference to a person or thing rather than to *replace* a noun.

The man at the barbershop ~~he~~ told Michael that it was closed.

> **Practice 4**   **Avoiding Ambiguous, Vague, or Repetitious Pronoun References**

ESL
Repetitious pronoun reference is a very common error among ESL students. Read aloud some sentences with this problem (from their own writing, if possible) and ask students to raise hands when they hear a repetitious pronoun reference.

Edit each sentence to eliminate any ambiguous, vague, or repetitious pronoun references. Some sentences may be revised in more than one way. *Answers may vary.*

the car owners
EXAMPLE: When I first looked at the car, ~~they~~ said that the price was far below the real value.

the bank
1. The loan officer at the bank said ~~they~~ would lend me the money for the car if I filled out a full report of my credit history.

the loan officer   *he*
2. But when I sent in the application, ~~they~~ said ~~they~~ wanted a more detailed account of my credit history.

3. The statement that I gave to the loan officer ~~it~~ included two previous automobile loans and one long-term apartment rental.

4. The loan officer ~~he~~ was very polite, but he told me I had to submit a new credit history.

the people at the bank
5. I don't understand why ~~they~~ still demand more information from me.

6. The loan officer told the customer service representative to make sure
    the loan officer
    ~~he~~ had a full report by tomorrow.
    ^

    the owners
7. When I was finding out about the car, ~~they~~ said they expected it to sell
                                          ^
    quickly.

    having the car is
8. I need to drive to work and to visit my mother in the hospital, so ~~it's~~
                                                                        ^
    not just a luxury.

9. The car ~~it~~ has all the features I need and want.

    the loan officer hasn't
10. I would be happy to give the bank more information, but ~~they haven't~~
                                                            ^
    he   *s*
    told me what ~~they~~ want.
    ^   ^

C. Use the Right Type of Pronoun

There are three types of pronouns: subject pronouns, object pronouns, and possessive pronouns.

TIP: Never put an apostrophe in a possessive pronoun.

Pronoun Types

	SUBJECT	OBJECT	POSSESSIVE
SINGULAR			
1st person	I	me	my, mine
2nd person	you	you	your, yours
3rd person	he, she, it, who	him, her, it, whom	his, her, hers, its, whose
PLURAL			
1st person	we	us	our, ours
2nd person	you	you	your, yours
3rd person	they, who	them, whom	their, theirs, whose

Subject pronouns serve as the subject of a verb.

He lives next door to a graveyard.

The phone rang as soon as *I* opened the door.

Object pronouns either are part of a prepositional phrase (the *object* of the preposition) or receive the action of a verb (the *object* of the verb).

OBJECT OF THE PREPOSITION	Jay gave his car to *me*.
OBJECT OF THE VERB	Jay gave *me* his car.

TIP: If you are looking at a pronoun in a sentence and you are sure it is not a subject pronoun or a possessive pronoun, it is probably an object pronoun.

Possessive pronouns show ownership.

Dave is *my* uncle.

That books is *yours*, I think.

There are three trouble spots that make it difficult to know what type of pronoun to use: compound subjects and objects, comparisons, and sentences that need *who* or *whom*.

TIP: In grammar, *compound* means containing two or more equal elements.

Using the Right Pronoun with Compound Subjects and Objects

A **compound subject** is a subject with more than one element joined by a conjunction such as *and* or *or*. A **compound object** is an object with more than one element joined in the same way.

COMPOUND SUBJECT	*Michelle and I* are working on this together.
COMPOUND OBJECT	My boss gave the assignment to *Michelle and me*.

To decide what type of pronoun to use in a compound construction, try leaving out the other elements and saying the sentence aloud to yourself.

~~Joan and~~ (me /(I)) went to the movies last night.

[Think: *I went to the movies last night.*]

The car was headed right for ~~Chuck and~~ (she /(her)).

[Think: *The car was headed right for her.*]

TIP: When you are writing about yourself and someone else, always put yourself *after* everyone else: *My friends and I went to a club,* not *I and my friends went to a club.*

If the pronoun is the object in a prepositional phrase, remember that an object pronoun must be used.

Let's keep that information just between you and (I /(me)).

[*Between you and me* is a prepositional phrase, so an object pronoun, *me*, is required.]

| Practice 5 | Editing Pronouns in Compound Constructions |

Edit each sentence using the proper type of pronoun. If a sentence is already correct, put a "C" next to it.

EXAMPLE: This porcelain bowl was given as a wedding gift to my wife
and ~~I.~~ *me*

1. My friend Kenny and ~~me~~ *I* like to water ski on Lake Chelan.

2. We trade off driving the boat so that ~~him~~ *he* and ~~me~~ *I* both have a chance to ski.

3. Sometimes the wind will force Kenny and me to wait until it calms down.   *C*

4. We often hook up an inner tube to the boat. One time Kenny and I even did this in the dark.   *C*

5. That night in bed, I started thinking: What would have happened if ~~him~~ *he* or ~~me~~ *I* had hit a log?

6. Once in a while Jackie and Sue join us. Then Kenny and ~~them~~ *they* and ~~me~~ *I* all take turns skiing and driving the boat.

7. Last summer Jackie was dating Kenny; I used to see ~~she~~ *her* and Kenny walking along the edge of the lake at night.

8. Kenny wishes that he and she would get back together.   *C*

9. He claims that it would be a good thing for ~~he~~ *him* and ~~she~~ *her* both.

10. Sue told me—just between ~~she~~ *her* and ~~I~~ *me*—that Jackie is dating somebody else.

TIP: To find comparisons, look for the words *than* or *as*.

Using the Right Type of Pronoun in Comparisons

Using the right type of pronoun in comparisons is particularly important because using the wrong type can change the meaning of the sentence. Editing comparisons can be tricky because they often imply words that aren't actually included in the sentence.

TEACHING TIP
Have each student write a sentence that uses implied words in a comparison. Then have the students read the sentences aloud and ask other class members to supply the missing words.

Bob likes Donna more than *I*.

> [This sentence means *Bob likes Donna more than I like her.* The implied words are *like her.*]

Bob likes Donna more than *me*.

> [This sentence means *Bob likes Donna more than he likes me.* The implied words are *he likes.*]

To decide whether to use a subject or object pronoun in a comparison, try adding the implied words and saying the sentence aloud.

The registrar is much more efficient than (us /we).

> [Think: *The registrar is much more efficient than we are.*]

Susan paid more for the computer than (she/her).

> [Think: *Susan paid more for the computer than she did.*]

Practice 6 ▶ **Editing Pronouns in Comparisons**

Edit each sentence using the correct pronoun type. If a sentence is already correct, put a "C" next to it.

I
EXAMPLE: Mark likes science fiction television shows as much as ~~me~~.
                                                                    ^

we
1. Not too many people watch as much *Star Trek* as ~~us~~.
                                                    ^

he
2. I think I remember more than ~~him~~ about the show's characters.
                               ^

3. But Mark remembers the plots much better than I.   *C*

I
4. Mark also has more *Star Trek* toys than ~~me~~.
                                            ^

we
5. The characters on *Star Trek* have explored more of space than ~~us~~.
                                                                 ^

6. Mark likes the episodes where people must live up to a duty that's

they
   bigger than ~~them~~.
               ^

7. I laugh when the characters meet aliens who are smarter than they.   *C*

8. Mark doesn't like *The Twilight Zone* as much as ~~me~~, although he
   ^*I*^

   watches it sometimes.

9. My favorite episode is the one with the woman surrounded by people
   who think she is uglier than ~~them.~~
   ^*they*^

10. The television viewer can see, though, that the other people are far
    more hideous than ~~her.~~
    ^*she*^

TIP: *Whoever* is a subject pronoun; *whomever* is an object pronoun.

Choosing between Who *and* Whom

Who is always a subject; *whom* is always an object. If the pronoun performs an action, use the subject form *who.* If the pronoun does not perform an action, use the object form *whom.*

> **WHO IS SUBJECT**   I would like to know <u>who caused</u> this problem.
>
> **WHOM IS OBJECT**   He told me to whom <u>I should report.</u>

If you have trouble choosing between *who* and *whom,* try restating the sentence or the troublesome part of it using *he* or *him.* (If the sentence is a question, try answering it with *he* or *him.*) If you need to use *he* when you restate the sentence, then you should use *who* in the real sentence. If you need *him,* then you should use *whom.*

> The person ((who)/ whom) sold me the car left town.
>
> > [Think: *He <u>sold me the car.</u>*]
>
> (Who /(Whom)) did you ask?
>
> > [Think: *I asked <u>him.</u>*]

Practice 7 ▶ Choosing between *Who* and *Whom*

In each sentence on the following page, circle the correct word, *who* or *whom.*

> **EXAMPLE:** Andrew Johnson, ((who)/ whom) took office after Abraham Lincoln was assassinated, is the only American president to be impeached.
>
> > [Think: *He took office . . .*]

1. Although Johnson was from the South, he remained loyal to Lincoln, (who̲/ whom) chose him as his running mate in 1864.

2. After the Civil War, Johnson clashed with members of Congress (who̲/ whom) demanded that the southern states be punished more severely.

3. The most powerful person (who /whom̲) Johnson defied was Thaddeus Stevens of Pennsylvania.

4. Johnson was impeached after trying to fire Secretary of War Edwin Stanton, (who /whom̲) he suspected of conspiring with Johnson's congressional opponents.

5. Johnson, (who̲/ whom) remained as president until the end of his term, came within one vote of being removed from office.

Edit Paragraphs and Your Own Writing

Practice 8 ▶ **Editing Paragraphs for Pronoun Use**

Find and correct any problems with pronoun use in the following paragraphs. You may want to refer to the Summary on page 340.

(1) You won't believe what happened to Jim and ~~I~~ *me* over the weekend. (2) We went to a party and were talking to some people we'd never met before. (3) Jim liked them more than ~~me,~~ *I* but I hung around for a while anyway.

(4) A woman ~~whom~~ *who* was very loud told us she'd seen a house she wanted to buy. (5) At the real estate office ~~they~~ *an agent* said the house was for sale, but ~~they~~ *he* didn't have the phone number of the owners. (6) This woman,~~/she~~ tried to reach the owners all weekend, but they weren't home.

(7) You can imagine how surprised Jim and ~~me~~ *I* were when we learned that the house was ours. (8) The woman made us a good offer on the spot, and we accepted it. (9) A few minutes later, every person

his or her

at the party raised ~~their~~ glass in a toast. (10) The real estate agency will
                    ^

its

include an article about us in ~~their~~ next newsletter.
                               ^

Practice 9 ▶	**Editing Your Own Writing for Pronoun Use**

LEARNING JOURNAL
Do you understand the terms *pronoun agreement* and *pronoun reference*? How would you explain them to someone else?

TEACHING TIP
Have students underline every pronoun in their paragraphs and draw an arrow to the word or words it refers to. (EG)

As a final practice, edit a piece of your own writing for pronoun use. It can be a paper you are working on for this course, a paper you've already finished, a paper for another course, or a recent piece of writing from your work or everyday life. Record in your learning journal any problem sentences you find, along with their corrections. You may want to use the Summary on page 340.

Summary and Quick Review Chart: Pronouns

- **Pronouns** replace nouns or other pronouns in a sentence. (See p. 327.)
- In most cases, a pronoun **refers to** a specific noun or pronoun mentioned nearby. (See p. 327.)
- A pronoun must **agree with** (match) the noun or pronoun it refers to in terms of number and gender. (See p. 328.)
- An **indefinite pronoun** does not refer to a specific person or thing. (See p. 329.) A **collective noun** names a group that acts as a single whole. (See p. 330.)
- Pronoun reference should be clear, not ambiguous, vague, or repetitious. (See p. 331.)
- **Subject pronouns** are used as subjects, **object pronouns** are used as objects, and **possessive pronouns** are used to show ownership. (See p. 334.)
- **Who** is used when the sentence needs a subject pronoun, **whom** when it needs an object pronoun. (See p. 337.)

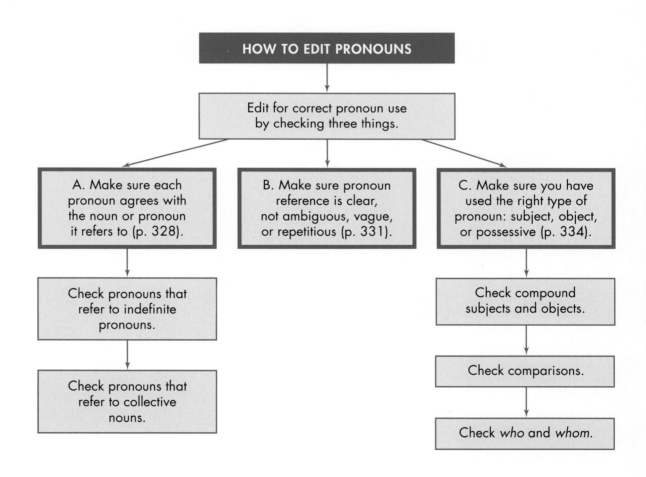

27

Adjectives and Adverbs

Describing *Which One?* or *How?*

A. Choosing between Adjectives and Adverbs
B. Using Comparative and Superlative Forms
C. *Good, Well, Bad,* and *Badly*

TIP: To understand this chapter on adjectives and adverbs, you need to know what *nouns, pronouns,* and *verbs* are. For review, see Chapter 21.

DISCUSSION
To get students focused on adjectives and adverbs, throw out a few sentences containing adjectives with students in the class as the subjects ("Dan is wearing a black leather jacket"). Ask the student in the sentence what the adjectives are. Keep the pace up. Or ask a student to give you a sentence about a desk (or a book or something else in the room) using an adjective.

ESL
Refer students to Chapter 32, where the standard order of adjectives is presented.

LEARNING JOURNAL
Use your learning journal as a place to record sentences with adjective and adverb problems that you find in your writing. You should also record edited versions of the sentences, with the problems corrected.

Understand What Adjectives and Adverbs Are

Adjectives and adverbs describe or **modify** (give more information about) other words. Adjectives and adverbs can come before or after the words they modify. You can use more than one to modify a word.

Adjectives describe or modify nouns (words that name people, places, or things) and pronouns (words that replace nouns). They add information about *what kind, which one,* or *how many.*

The *final* exam was today.

It was *long* and *difficult.*

The *three shiny new* cars are parked outside.

Adverbs describe or modify verbs (words that tell what happens in a sentence), adjectives, or other adverbs. They add information about *how, how much,* or *when.*

RESOURCES
Additional Resources contains tests and supplemental practice exercises for this chapter as well as a transparency master for the summary chart at the end.

MODIFYING VERB	Sharon <u>accepted</u> the job *yesterday*.
MODIFYING ADJECTIVE	The *very* young lawyer handled the case.
MODIFYING ANOTHER ADVERB	The team played *surprisingly* well.

Practice Using Adjectives and Adverbs Correctly

A. Choosing between Adjectives and Adverbs

Some adverbs are formed by adding -*ly* to the end of an adjective.

ADJECTIVE

She received a *quick* answer.
The *new* student introduced himself.
That is an *honest* answer.

ADVERB

Her sister answered *quickly*.
The couple is *newly* married.
Please answer *honestly*.

The similarity between adjectives and adverbs can make it difficult to choose between them. To decide whether to use an adjective or an adverb, find the word it is describing or modifying. If that word is a noun or pronoun, use an adjective. If it is a verb, adjective, or another adverb, use an adverb.

Practice 1   Choosing between Adjectives and Adverbs

In each sentence, circle the correct word in parentheses and underline the word in the sentence that it describes or modifies.

EXAMPLE: When I was asked if I wanted to become the manager of an Outback restaurant, I (quick/quickly)) <u>accepted</u> the offer.

1. The chain started in 1987 and <u>grew</u> (rapid/rapidly)) to more than two hundred stores by 1994.

2. The restaurants are (creative/creatively)) <u>designed</u> to look like the Australian bush.

3. The success of the chain, however, is a result of its (unique)/uniquely) management <u>structure</u>.

4. To become the manager of an Outback restaurant, I (initial/initially)) <u>invested</u> $25,000 of my own money.

5. I felt that I was taking a risk, but I also <u>was</u> (confident)/confidently) that the restaurant would succeed.

6. I knew that I would be getting 10 percent of my restaurant's (annual/ annually) profits on top of my base salary.

7. I also knew that an Outback manager's (total/ totally) income (typical /typically) is at least $120,000.

8. As a (high /highly) compensated manager, I feel more like an owner than an employee.

9. I try to make sure that service in my restaurant is (true /truly) outstanding and that diners are (quick /quickly) seated and served.

10. Customers tell me they appreciate the value and service that we (consistent /consistently) provide.

ESL
Point out that comparative constructions often use the word *than*.

B. Using Comparative and Superlative Forms

To compare two things, use the **comparative** form of adjectives or adverbs.

Carol ran *faster* than I did.

Johan is *more intelligent* than his sister.

Comparative and Superlative Forms		
ADJECTIVE OR ADVERB	**COMPARATIVE**	**SUPERLATIVE**
ADVERBS AND ADJECTIVES OF ONE SYLLABLE		
tall	taller	tallest
fast	faster	fastest
ADJECTIVES ENDING IN -Y		
happy	happier	happiest
silly	sillier	silliest
ADVERBS AND ADJECTIVES OF MORE THAN ONE SYLLABLE		
graceful	more graceful	most graceful
gracefully	more gracefully	most gracefully
intelligent	more intelligent	most intelligent
intelligently	more intelligently	most intelligently

To compare three or more things, use the superlative form of adjectives or adverbs.

Carol ran *fastest* of all the women runners.

Johan is the *most intelligent* of the five children.

Comparative and superlative forms can be made either by adding an ending to an adjective or adverb or by adding a word. If the adjective or adverb is short (one syllable), add the endings *-er* to make the comparative and *-est* to make the superlative. Use this pattern also for adjectives that end in *-y*, (change the *-y* to *-i* before adding *-er* or *-est*). If the adjective or adverb is longer than one syllable, add the words *more* to make the comparative and *most* to make the superlative.

Use either an ending (*-er* or *-est*) or an extra word (*more* or *most*) to form a comparative or superlative—not both at once.

Jackie Joyner-Kersee is the ~~most~~ fastest woman runner.

TIP: For more on changing a final *-y* to *-i* when adding endings, see Chapter 35.

Practice 2 ▶ **Using Comparatives and Superlatives**

In the space provided in each sentence, write the correct form of the adjective or adverb in parentheses.

EXAMPLE: In Greek mythology, heroes were superhuman; only a god was
___*greater*___ (*great*) than a hero.

1. Perhaps the ___*most famous*___ (*famous*) Greek hero is Achilles.

2. Achilles was not only the ___*biggest*___ (*big*) of all the soldiers;
he was also the ___*most stubborn*___ (*stubborn*) of them.

3. Achilles' heel was the ___*weakest*___ (*weak*) point in his body and
the only place in which he could be fatally wounded.

4. When his mother, Thetis, dipped him in the river Styx, she had hoped
that his life would be ___*closer*___ (*close*) to a god's than a man's.

5. Thetis, herself a goddess, was destined to bear Zeus a son who would
become the ___*greatest*___ (*great*) god of all.

6. But Zeus wanted no one to be _____*more powerful*_____ (*powerful*) than he, and he forced Thetis to marry a human.

7. At the wedding, a spiteful god tossed among the guests an apple intended for the _____*most beautiful*_____ (*beautiful*) of all women.

8. This act is said to have led to the Trojan War, a conflict that lasted _____*longer*_____ (*long*) than either side expected.

9. For many readers, the _____*most exciting*_____ (*exciting*) scene in Homer's *Iliad* is Achilles' defeat of the Trojan warrior Hector.

10. Hector tried to run away, but he could not run _____*faster*_____ (*fast*) than Achilles.

C. *Good, Well, Bad,* and *Badly*

TIP: *Irregular* means not following a standard rule.

Four common adjectives and adverbs have irregular forms: *good, well, bad,* and *badly.*

	COMPARATIVE	SUPERLATIVE
ADJECTIVE		
good	better	best
bad	worse	worst
ADVERB		
well	better	best
badly	worse	worst

People often get confused about whether to use *good* or *well. Good* is an adjective, so use it to describe a noun or pronoun. *Well* is an adverb, so use it to describe a verb or an adjective.

ADJECTIVE   She has a *good* job.

ADVERB   He works *well* with his colleagues.

Well can also be an adjective to describe someone's health: *I am not well today.*

| Practice 3 | **Using *Good* and *Well*** |

Complete each sentence by filling in either *good* or *well*.

EXAMPLE: Many Americans have difficulty obtaining _____*good*_____ health care.

1. Part of the problem is that policy makers cannot agree on what a _____*good*_____ health care plan should include.

2. Some politicians, for example, feel that the U.S. system works _____*well*_____ as it is.

3. According to some critics, President Clinton's plans to change the health insurance system failed because Clinton did not do a _____*good*_____ job of presenting his ideas.

4. Supporters say that no matter how _____*well*_____ Clinton had explained his plan, the health insurance industry would have prevented any major changes.

5. Everyone would agree that a person who is sick should see a doctor, but what about a person who is _____*well*_____?

| Practice 4 | **Using Comparative and Superlative Forms of *Good* and *Bad*** |

Complete each sentence on the next page by filling in the correct comparative or superlative form of *good* or *bad*.

EXAMPLE: I am sorry to report that apartment units 2 and 7 are in

_____*worse*_____ shape than they were before.

1. The units are partly below ground and will be in danger of being

   flooded if the rain we've been having gets any ___*worse*___.

2. Unfortunately, this has been one of the ___*worst*___ months of rain

   in several years.

3. Tenants report that despite their heavy use of disinfectant, the buildup

   of mold on the walls has not gotten any ___*better*___.

4. Bill Soeltz, of unit 7, says the ___*worst*___ thing is the smell.

5. I told him that we were determined to do what was ___*best*___,

   regardless of the expense.

Edit Paragraphs and Your Own Writing

| Practice 5 | Editing Paragraphs for Correct Adjectives and Adverbs |

TEAMWORK
Copy an article from the newspaper or some other source and have students find all the adjectives and adverbs, drawing arrows from the modifiers to the words they modify. This can be done in small groups in class or assigned as homework to go over the next day in class.

Find and correct any problems with adjectives and adverbs in the following paragraphs. You may want to refer to the Summary on page 349.

(1) One of the *most important* ~~importantest~~ things I've learned since starting college is to avoid waiting until the last minute to begin my work. (2) I used to think that I could successfully write a paper the night before it was due. (3) This technique worked *well* ~~good~~ for me in high school. (4) But when I tried it in my history class freshman year I received a bad grade, much *worse* ~~badder~~ than I had expected. (5) I promised myself that I would do *better* ~~gooder~~ than that in the future.

persistently

(6) I've also learned to work ~~persistent~~ at a task, even when I feel

frustrated. (7) If a task is ~~more~~ harder than I expected, I will arrange to

ask the professor or a tutor for help. (8) This often turns out to be the

fastest

~~faster~~ way of all to solve the problem. (9) If no outside help is available,

I will usually put the work away for a few hours, or overnight, and

resume my efforts when I feel ~~more~~ better about my ability to con-

centrate.

useful   *stronger*

(10) Patience is also a ~~usefully~~ habit. (11) I tend to do a ~~strong~~ job

slowly

when I work more ~~slow~~ than when I work faster. (12) Sometimes I

quickly,

dive into a project too ~~quick,~~ before I have a full understanding of

what is expected of me. (13) I also get into trouble when I try to tackle

well.

something when I'm overtired or not feeling ~~good.~~ (14) Then I have to

needlessly   *good*

start over, and I end up ~~needless~~ wasting time. (15) It's a ~~well~~ idea to

best.

do my most important work when I'm feeling my ~~bestest.~~

Practice 6 ▶ **Editing Your Own Writing for Correct Adjectives and Adverbs**

LEARNING JOURNAL
What kind of mistake with adjectives or adverbs do you make most often in your writing? What are some ways to avoid or correct this mistake?

   As a final practice, edit a piece of your own writing for correct use of adjectives and adverbs. It can be a paper you are working on for this course, a paper you've already finished, a paper for another course, or a recent piece of writing from your work or everyday life. Record in your learning journal any problem sentences you find, along with their corrections. You may want to use the Summary on page 349.

Summary and Quick Review Chart: Adjectives and Adverbs

- Adjectives and adverbs describe or **modify** (give more information about) other words. (See p. 341.)
- **Adjectives** modify nouns and pronouns. (See p. 341.)
- **Adverbs** modify verbs, adjectives, or other adverbs. Many adverbs are formed by adding *-ly* to an adjective. (See p. 341.)
- The **comparative** form of an adjective or adverb is used to compare two things. It is formed by adding *-er* or the word *more*. (See p. 343.)
- The **superlative** form of an adjective or adverb is used to compare three or more things. It is formed by adding *-est* or the word *most*. (See p. 344.)
- *Good, well, bad,* and *badly* have irregular and similar comparative and superlative forms. Use *good* as an adjective and *well* as an adverb. (See p. 345.)

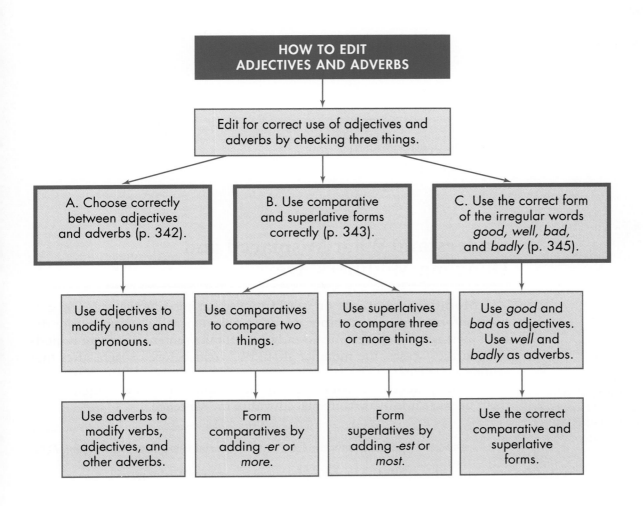

28

Misplaced and Dangling Modifiers

Avoiding Confusing Descriptions

TIP: To understand this chapter, you need to know what *nouns, verbs, adjectives, adverbs, phrases,* and *clauses* are. For review, see Chapter 21.

A. Misplaced Modifiers
B. Dangling Modifiers

RESOURCES
Additional Resources contains tests and supplemental practice exercises for this chapter as well as a transparency master for the summary chart at the end.

Understand What Misplaced and Dangling Modifiers Are

Modifiers are words or word groups that modify (describe or give more information about) other words in a sentence. To communicate the right message, a modifier must clearly point to the sentence element it modifies. In most cases, the modifier should be right before or right after that sentence element.

A **misplaced modifier** ends up describing the wrong sentence element because it is incorrectly placed within the sentence.

LEARNING JOURNAL
Use your learning journal as a place to record sentences you find in your writing with misplaced or dangling modifiers. You should also record edited versions of the sentences, with the problems corrected.

MISPLACED   Margaret saw the Lincoln Memorial *flying over Washington, D.C.*

[Was the Lincoln Memorial flying over Washington?]

CLEAR   *Flying over Washington, D.C.,* Margaret saw the Lincoln Memorial.

350

TEACHING TIPS
• With an introductory modifier, the noun that follows the comma should be the one that is doing the action or being described.
• Remind students that possessive nouns and pronouns can't be modified. (EG)

A **dangling modifier** is said to "dangle" because the sentence element it is supposed to modify is implied but not actually in the sentence; with nothing to attach itself to, the modifier is left dangling. A dangling modifier usually appears at the beginning of the sentence and seems to modify the noun or pronoun that immediately follows it.

DANGLING   *Rushing to class,* the books fell out of my bag.

[Were the books rushing to class?]

CLEAR   *Rushing to class,* I dropped my books.

Misplaced and dangling modifiers can create confusion. Be sure to look for and correct misplaced and dangling modifiers in your writing.

Practice Correcting Misplaced and Dangling Modifiers

TEAMWORK
As homework, have each student write a sentence that is funny because of a misplaced or dangling modifier. Collect the sentences and read some aloud, asking the class for corrections.

A. Misplaced Modifiers

To correct a misplaced modifier, place the modifier as close as possible to the sentence element it modifies. The safest choice is often to put the modifier directly before the sentence element it modifies.

Wearing my bathrobe,
I went outside to empty the trash ~~wearing my bathrobe.~~

Three constructions in particular often lead to misplaced modifiers. Be sure to check for these in your writing.

LIMITING MODIFIERS SUCH AS *ONLY, ALMOST, HARDLY, NEARLY,* **AND** *JUST*

only
I ~~only~~ need fifty dollars.

almost
Joan ~~almost~~ ran ten miles.

PREPOSITIONAL PHRASES

in my car
I was talking to a police officer ~~in my car.~~

that she found
Emma hid the worm under the carpet ~~that she found.~~

PHRASES BEGINNING WITH -*ING* VERB FORMS

Using my credit card,
I bought the puppy using my credit card.
             ^

Wearing a glove,
Kim caught the ball wearing a glove.
         ^   ^

> **Practice 1**   **Correcting Misplaced Modifiers**

Find and correct any misplaced modifiers in the following sentences. If a sentence is correct, write a "C" next to it. It may be necessary to add new words or ideas to sentences that need editing.

                                            Jennifer thought
EXAMPLE: Concerned about riding on city streets, this bike seemed safer
                              she   ^
     than the others ~~Jennifer~~ had looked at. *Answers may vary.*
                          ^   *Possible editing shown.*

1. Jennifer also bought a helmet that was rated highly in *Consumer*

   Reports.   *C*

   Wearing her helmet, she
2. ~~She~~ took a test ride on the bike in her helmet.
   ^   ^

   In the morning, she
3. ~~She~~ took a route to school her friends had recommended ~~in the morning.~~
   ^   ^

        in the tunnel
4. Traffic was so bad that she later wrote a letter to the city council ~~in~~
                        ^   ^

   ~~the tunnel.~~

        along the new road
5. Potholes bent one of her wheels ~~along the new road.~~
                        ^   ^

                   nearly   *only*
6. It had ~~nearly~~ taken her two hours ~~only~~ to go five miles.
                              ^   ^

                       that was much better
7. Jennifer discovered a route on another map ~~that was much better.~~
                                    ^   ^

                only
8. The next day she ~~only~~ needed twenty minutes to reach the campus.
                          ^

   Looking at her watch, she
9. ~~She~~ was pleased with her bike ~~looking at her watch.~~
   ^   ^

                       that saved her time
10. She recommended the route to a friend ~~that saved her time.~~
                               ^   ^

COMPUTER
Have students highlight introductory phrases in their writing. Then direct them to look at the first word after the phrase to make sure that it is the noun or pronoun the phrase describes.

TEACHING TIP
Students sometimes try to correct a dangling modifier by adding a subordinating conjunction (such as *while*) without sufficiently reworking the sentence itself. Point out that adding *while* alone does not correct the problem with this sentence: *While trying to eat a hot dog...*

B. Dangling Modifiers

When an opening modifier is not followed by the word it describes, it is a **dangling modifier.** Writers often fail to include the word being modified because they think the meaning is clear. Be sure to include it.

I drove
Distracted by the bright lights, my car ~~drove~~ off the road.

[The word being modified, *I,* was not included in the original sentence.]

There are two basic ways to correct dangling modifiers. Use the one that makes the most sense. You can add the word being modified right after the opening modifier so that the connection between the two is clear.

I
Trying to eat a hot dog, ~~my bike~~ swerved off the path, *on my bike.*

You can also add the word being modified in the opening modifier itself.

While I was trying
~~Trying~~ to eat a hot dog, my bike swerved off the path.

Practice 2   Correcting Dangling Modifiers

Find and correct any dangling modifiers in the following sentences. It may be necessary to add new words or ideas to some sentences.

EXAMPLE: Titled "The Forces Making for an Economic Collapse,"
the article by
Thomas Palley argues ~~in his article~~ against a completely

balanced budget.   *Answers will vary. Possible editing shown.*

the article discusses
1. Published in the *Atlantic Monthly,* falling wages, corporate layoffs, and

attempts to eliminate inflation ~~are discussed.~~

many workers were able to afford
2. Earning higher wages than ever before, homes ~~became widely~~

~~affordable~~ in the 1950s and 1960s.

With wages
3. F̶alling nearly fifty dollars per week between 1973 and 1991, workers

have recently found it impossible to buy homes.

workers become frustrated.
4. Unable to buy their own homes, ~~frustration results.~~

5.   *corporations usually leave*

Taking advantage of cheaper labor overseas, American workers ~~usually~~ *when they relocate.*

~~are left~~ behind ~~by corporate relocations.~~

6.   Creating huge budget deficits, ~~Palley blames~~ presidential mismanage-

has caused

ment ~~for~~ the problem/, *Palley argues.*

7.   *Palley believes*

Convinced the problem could be fixed with a balanced budget, the

economy could be healthy again.

8.   *other economists think*

Citing different sources of the problem, a balanced budget could

result in ruin ~~according to other economists.~~

9.   *American workers feel*

Unconcerned with the cause of the problem, fear and frustration ~~are~~

~~felt by many American workers.~~

10. *workers think*

Wanting basic things like homes and jobs, the government is not

responsive.

Edit Paragraphs and Your Own Writing

Practice 3   Editing Paragraphs for Misplaced and Dangling Modifiers

Find and correct any misplaced or dangling modifiers in the following paragraphs. You may want to refer to the Summary on page 356.

Answers will vary. Possible editing shown.

Dear Mr. Bolton:

(1) I am responding to your advertisement in the *Courier-Ledger*

I have strong

seeking a summer intern for your law practice. (2) A hard worker, ~~my~~

qualifications ~~are strong.~~ (3) I am currently working on a bachelor's

nearly

degree in political science and ~~nearly~~ have taken fifty credit hours of

courses. (4) These include classes in jurisprudence, law and public pol-

icy, and business law.

(5) Business law is especially of interest to me. (6) Sometimes

while sitting in class

I dream of becoming a corporate attorney ˄ ~~while sitting in class~~.
˄

(7) Someday I'd like to work for one of the major firms in New York.

I am already   *and*

(8) ~~Already~~ planning to go on to law school, my grade point average is
˄   ˄

in the top 10 percent of my class.

(9) I realize that I will not earn much money as an intern.

someday

(10) But ~~someday~~ I am confident that I will be able to find a good-
˄

I find

paying job. (11) Thinking of the experience I could gain, a summer job
˄

at your firm ~~is~~ highly appealing.

| Practice 4 ▶ | **Editing Your Own Writing for Misplaced and Dangling Modifiers** |

LEARNING JOURNAL
Which is more difficult for you, finding misplaced and dangling modifiers or correcting them? What can you do to help yourself improve at it?

As a final practice, edit a piece of your own writing for misplaced and dangling modifiers. It can be a paper you are working on for this course, a paper you've already finished, a paper for another course, or a recent piece of writing from your work or everyday life. Record in your learning journal any problem sentences you find, along with their corrections. You may want to use the Summary on page 356.

Summary and Quick Review Chart: Misplaced and Dangling Modifiers

- **Modifiers** are words or word groups that modify (describe or give more information about) other words in a sentence. (See p. 350.)

- A **misplaced modifier** describes the wrong sentence element because it is incorrectly placed within the sentence. (See p. 350.)

- When an opening modifier is not followed by the word it describes, it is a **dangling modifier.** Often the sentence element it is supposed to modify is implied but not actually in the sentence. (See p. 351.)

- Edit both misplaced and dangling modifiers by making sure that the sentence element to be modified is in the sentence and that it is placed as close as possible to the modifier. (See pp. 351 and 353.)

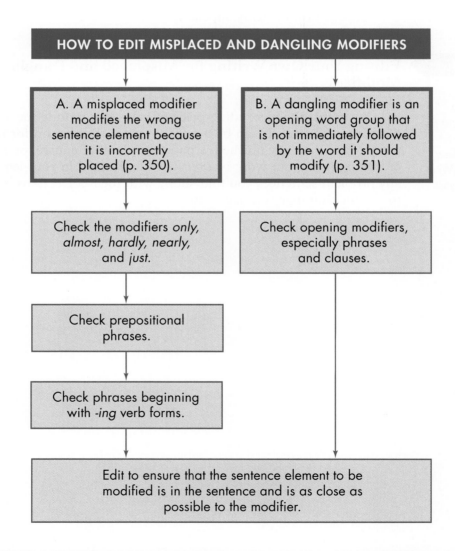

HOW TO EDIT MISPLACED AND DANGLING MODIFIERS

A. A misplaced modifier modifies the wrong sentence element because it is incorrectly placed (p. 350).

B. A dangling modifier is an opening word group that is not immediately followed by the word it should modify (p. 351).

Check the modifiers *only, almost, hardly, nearly,* and *just.*

Check opening modifiers, especially phrases and clauses.

Check prepositional phrases.

Check phrases beginning with *-ing* verb forms.

Edit to ensure that the sentence element to be modified is in the sentence and is as close as possible to the modifier.

29

Coordination and Subordination

Joining Ideas

TIP: To understand this chapter, you need to know what *sentences* and *conjunctions* are. For review, see Chapter 21.

RESOURCES *Additional Resources* contains tests and supplemental practice exercises for this chapter as well as a transparency master for the summary chart at the end.

A.   Coordination Using Coordinating Conjunctions
B.   Coordination Using Semicolons
C.   Subordination Using Subordinating Conjunctions

Understand Coordination and Subordination

Coordination and subordination are ways to join sentences with related ideas. If all of your sentences are short, they will seem choppy and hard to read. To vary the rhythm and flow of your writing and to clarify the relationship of ideas, use coordination or subordination.

Coordination should be used to join two sentences when the ideas in them are equally important.

LEARNING JOURNAL Use your learning journal as a place to record sentences with weak coordination and subordination. You should also record edited versions of the sentences, once you have corrected them.

TWO SENTENCES	The continent of Antarctica is unpopulated. Scientists are studying its habitability.
JOINED THROUGH COORDINATION	The continent of Antarctica is unpopulated, *but* scientists are studying its habitability.

Subordination should be used to join two sentences when one idea is more important than the other.

TWO SENTENCES	Mt. Erebus in Antarctica is a mountain. It erupts like a volcano.
JOINED THROUGH SUBORDINATION	*Although* Mt. Erebus in Antarctica is a mountain, it erupts like a volcano.

[*Although* makes the first part of this sentence subordinate and puts more emphasis on the second part, the idea that Mt. Erebus erupts.]

Practice Using Coordination and Subordination

A. Coordination Using Coordinating Conjunctions

A conjunction is a word that joins words, phrases, or clauses. **Coordinating conjunctions** are the words *and, but, for, nor, or, so,* and *yet.* They join ideas of equal importance. To join two sentences with ideas that are equally important, put a comma and one of these conjunctions between the sentences. Choose the conjunction that makes the most sense for the meaning of the two sentences.

Equal idea	, and , but , for , nor , or , so , yet	Equal idea
Antarctica is huge	, and	it is 98 percent ice.
It is very dry	, for	it receives only as much rain as a desert.
Perhaps people could live there	, or	it could be used for other purposes.

> **Practice 1**   **Coordinating Ideas with Coordinating Conjunctions**

Combine each pair of sentences into a single sentence by using a comma and a coordinating conjunction. Choose a coordinating conjunction by considering how the ideas in the two sentences are related to each other. In some cases, there may be more than one correct answer.

EXAMPLE: Pete hurried to catch the bus/. ~~He~~ *but he* could not board it because he lacked exact change.

Answers will vary. Possible editing shown.

1. He argued with the driver, ~~He~~ *but he* finally gave up and walked to a nearby

    convenience store.

2. He spoke to a cashier, ~~He~~ *and he* asked her if she could make change.

3. She said he could buy something, ~~He~~ *or he* could wait until someone else

    bought something.

4. No one else was in the store, ~~Pete~~ *so* Pete decided to buy an apple turnover.

5. He waited impatiently for the cashier to give him his change, ~~The~~ *for the* next

    bus was already approaching.

6. He wanted to run right out the door, ~~He~~ *but he* knew he had to wait.

7. Pete finally got his change, ~~He~~ *and he* ran as fast as he could.

8. Pete missed this bus, too, ~~He~~ *so he* decided to eat the apple turnover.

9. The turnover was delicious, ~~He~~ *so he* went back to the store for another one.

10. Pete never made it to work that day, ~~He~~ *but he* decided it was a good day

    anyway.

B. Coordination Using Semicolons

Another way to join sentences through coordination is to use a semi-colon between two sentences with related ideas. Make sure when you use a semicolon that the ideas are very closely related.

TEACHING TIP
Remind students that a semicolon balances two independent clauses; what's on either side must be able to stand alone as a complete sentence. (EG)

Equal idea	;	Equal idea

Antarctica is a mystery	;	no one knows too much about it.
Its climate is extreme	;	few people want to endure it.
My cousin went there	;	he loves to explore the unknown.

A semicolon alone does not tell readers much about the relationship between the two ideas. To give more information about the relationship, use a semicolon followed by a word that indicates the relationship; put a comma after the word. Here are some of the most common words used this way.

Equal idea	; also, ; instead, ; still, ; then, ; as a result, ; besides, ; however, ; in addition, ; in fact, ; therefore,	Equal idea

Antarctica is largely unexplored	; as a result,	it is unpopulated.
It receives little rain	; also,	it is incredibly cold.
It is a huge area	; therefore,	scientists are becoming more interested in it.

Practice 2   ▶   **Coordinating Ideas with Semicolons**

Join each pair of sentences by using a semicolon alone.

 EXAMPLE: Tanning booths can cause skin to age. ~~They~~ *they* may also promote

cancer.

1. Exposure to the sun can cause both short-term and long-term side effects. ~~Using~~ *using* tanning booths has similar risks.

2. Using a tanning booth does not mean that you will definitely harm yourself. ~~What~~ *what* it does mean is that you are taking a chance.

3. It's easy to ignore long-term health dangers. ~~The~~ *the* desire to look good is often of more immediate concern.

4. Some people wear no clothes in a tanning booth. ~~This~~ *this* behavior can damage skin that is normally covered by a bathing suit.

5. Ultraviolet light can injure the eyes. *tanning* ~~Tanning~~ salon patrons should always wear protective goggles.

Practice 3   **Joining Ideas with Semicolons and Connecting Words**

Join each pair of sentences by using a semicolon and a connecting word. Choose a connecting word that makes sense for the relationship between the two ideas. In some cases, there may be more than one correct answer.

EXAMPLE: Kirk's business professor turned in her grades late. *therefore, there* ~~There~~ was a blank space on Kirk's grade sheet when it arrived. *Answers will vary. Possible editing shown.*

1. He tried phoning the professor. *also, he* ~~He~~ sent her several e-mail messages.

2. When the professor finally called Kirk back, the news was not good. *in fact, he* ~~He~~ wished that the grade had remained blank.

3. Kirk asked if he could do extra work to raise the grade to at least a C. *however, the* ~~The~~ professor said that there was nothing either of them could do.

4. Kirk felt that he could not afford to let his grade point average go any lower. *therefore, he* ~~He~~ asked the professor once more if she could help.

5. She agreed to meet with him the next day. *as a result,* Kirk hoped to be able to change her mind.

TEACHING TIP
Do the same kind of board exercise with subordinating conjunctions as you did with coordinating conjunctions. Write two sentences on the board and have students suggest how they would have to change to accommodate different subordinating conjunctions.

C. Subordination Using Subordinating Conjunctions

A conjunction is a word that joins words, phrases, or clauses. **Subordinating conjunctions** join two ideas when one idea is more important than the other. The idea that has the subordinating conjunction in front of it becomes a **subordinate clause** or **dependent clause**; because of the subordinating conjunction, it no longer expresses a complete thought and cannot stand by itself as a sentence.

Choose the conjunction that makes the most sense with the two sentences. Some of the most common subordinating conjunctions are on the next page.

after	since
although	so that
as	unless
as if	until
because	when
before	where
even though	while
if	

Main idea   Subordinate idea

MAIN IDEA		SUBORDINATE IDEA
Scientists study the interior of Mt. Erebus	because	it might provide clues about global warming.
It is difficult to study the interior	since	it is composed of boiling lava.

You can also put the subordinating conjunction and subordinate idea at the beginning of the new sentence. When the subordinate idea comes first, use a comma to separate it from the rest of the sentence.

Subordinating conjunction	Subordinate idea	,	Main idea
When	it erupts	,	Mt. Erebus hurls lava bombs.
Because	it is dangerous	,	scientists are hesitant to go inside.

Practice 4 ▶ Joining Ideas through Subordination

Join the following pairs of sentences into a single sentence by using an appropriate subordinating conjunction either at the beginning or between the two sentences. Use a conjunction that makes sense with the two sentences. In some cases, there may be more than one correct answer.

EXAMPLE: Revising your writing on a computer saves time. *because you* ~~You~~ can make changes without having to retype your entire paper.

Answers will vary. Possible editing shown.

1. Almost all college students used typewriters until about ten years ago. *when computers* ~~Computers~~ became more affordable.

2. Typewriters were used less often. *after computers* ~~Computers~~ became more widespread.

3. Computers offer many advantages/ *although there* ~~There~~ are also some drawbacks.

4. *If you* ~~You~~ have not saved what you have written/ *a* ~~A~~ power outage could cause you to lose your work.

5. *When computers* ~~Computers~~ became widely used in the 1980s/ *professors* ~~Professors~~ were surprised to hear students say, "The computer ate my paper."

6. *When you* ~~You~~ have written a rough draft of a paper/ *you* ~~You~~ should print it out.

7. Some people like to print out a document to proofread it/ *because they* ~~They~~ fail to catch all their mistakes on the screen.

8. *Although the* ~~The~~ quality of computer screens is getting better/ *people* ~~People~~ still complain about eyestrain.

9. *Although spell-checking* ~~Spell-checking~~ programs prevent many errors/ *only* ~~Only~~ a person is able to recognize sound-alikes such as *their* and *there*.

10. Using a grammar-check program can also cause problems/ *if writers* ~~Writers~~ assume that understanding the grammar rules is not important.

Edit Paragraphs and Your Own Writing

| Practice 5 | Editing Paragraphs for Coordination and Subordination |

In the following paragraphs, join the underlined sentences using either coordination or subordination. Do not forget to punctuate correctly.

Answers will vary. Possible editing shown.

(1) *Although* Herman Melville is now considered one of the greatest American writers/ (2) *his* ~~His~~ books were mostly forgotten at the time of his death in 1891. (3) His novel *Moby Dick,* perhaps the most admired

work in all of American literature, was viewed as nothing more than a curious adventure story that might hold the interest of teenage boys.
(4) The book's more complex themes remained invisible. (5) *until a* A new generation of literary critics rediscovered them in the 1920s.

(6) The Dutch painter Vincent van Gogh was another nineteenth-century artist unappreciated during his lifetime. (7) Potential buyers were not interested in his work. (8) *and even* Even van Gogh himself considered much of it "ugly." (9) Sadly, the most inspired period in the artist's life ended with his suicide in July 1890. (10) He had moved to Arles, France, in February 1888. (11) *where he* He created some of his most famous works, including the disturbingly powerful *Starry Night*.

(12) Great art is often far ahead of its time. (13) *so it* It is frequently misunderstood. (14) Numerous writers and painters better known in their day than Melville or van Gogh have long since been forgotten. (15) These people gave the public what it wanted. (16) *but they* They failed to create anything of lasting worth.

Practice 6 ▶ **Editing Your Own Writing for Coordination and Subordination**

As a final practice, edit a piece of your own writing for coordination and subordination. It can be a paper you are working on for this course, a paper you've already finished, a paper for another course, or a recent piece of writing from your work or everyday life. Record in your learning journal any problem sentences you find, along with their corrections. You may want to use the Summary on page 365.

Summary and Quick Review Chart: Coordination and Subordination

- Coordination and subordination can be used to join sentences with related ideas. (See p. 357.)
- **Coordination** can be used to join two sentences when the ideas in them are equally important. (See p. 357.)
- **Subordination** can be used to join two sentences when one idea is more important than another. (See p. 357.)
- When using a coordinating conjunction or a subordinating conjunction, choose the one that best fits the meaning of the two sentences.
- The idea that has the subordinating conjunction in front of it becomes a **subordinate clause** or **dependent clause.** Because of the subordinating conjunction, it no longer expresses a complete thought and cannot stand by itself as a sentence. (See p. 361.)

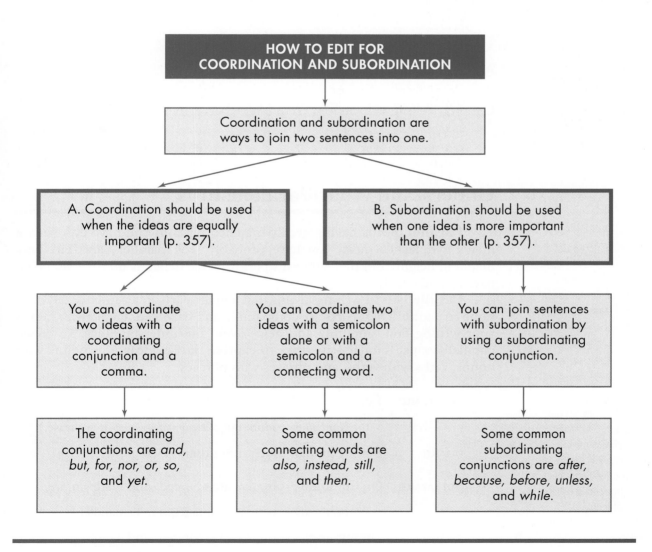

HOW TO EDIT FOR COORDINATION AND SUBORDINATION

Coordination and subordination are ways to join two sentences into one.

A. Coordination should be used when the ideas are equally important (p. 357).

B. Subordination should be used when one idea is more important than the other (p. 357).

You can coordinate two ideas with a coordinating conjunction and a comma.

You can coordinate two ideas with a semicolon alone or with a semicolon and a connecting word.

You can join sentences with subordination by using a subordinating conjunction.

The coordinating conjunctions are *and, but, for, nor, or, so, and yet.*

Some common connecting words are *also, instead, still, and then.*

Some common subordinating conjunctions are *after, because, before, unless, and while.*

30

Parallelism

Balancing Ideas

TIP: To understand this chapter, you need to know what *nouns, verbs,* and *phrases* are. For review, see Chapter 21.

A. Parallelism in Pairs and Lists
B. Parallelism in Comparisons
C. Parallelism with Certain Paired Words

RESOURCES
Additional Resources contains tests and supplemental practice exercises for this chapter.

Understand What Parallelism Is

TEACHING TIP
When explaining parallelism, tell students to visualize an old-fashioned scale; it won't balance unless the contents of both trays are equal. (EG)

Parallel means having evenly matched parts. If you have ever seen a men's gymnastics meet, you have probably seen parallel bars. The bars match in height, and the gymnast's performance depends on the bars being parallel and evenly balanced.

Parallelism in writing means that similar parts in a sentence have the same structure: Their parts are comparable and balanced. Parallelism makes your writing flow smoothly and helps avoid misunderstandings. To create parallelism, use similar structures to express similar ideas. Put nouns with nouns, verbs with verbs, and phrases with phrases.

LEARNING JOURNAL
Use your learning journal as a place to record sentences with problems in parallelism that you find in your writing. You should also record edited versions of these sentences, with the problems corrected.

NOT PARALLEL	I enjoy <u>pinball</u> much more than <u>playing video games</u>.
	[*Pinball* is a noun, but *playing video games* is a phrase.]
PARALLEL	I enjoy <u>pinball</u> much more than <u>video games</u>.
NOT PARALLEL	On our anniversary, we <u>ate</u>, <u>danced</u>, and <u>were singing</u>.
	[Verbs must be in the same tense to be parallel.]
PARALLEL	On our anniversary, we <u>ate</u>, <u>danced</u>, and <u>sang</u>.

ESL
Refer ESL students to Chapter 32. Many of the parallel constructions depend on using infinitives and idioms correctly.

NOT PARALLEL   This weekend we can go <u>to the beach</u> or <u>walking in the mountains</u>.

> [*To the beach* and *walking in the mountains* are both phrases, but they have different forms. *To the beach* should be paired with another prepositional phrase: *to the mountains.*]

PARALLEL   This weekend we can go <u>to the beach</u> or <u>to the mountains</u>.

Practice Writing Parallel Sentences

A. Parallelism in Pairs and Lists

When you present two or more things in a series, use a similar form for each thing.

NOT PARALLEL   The criminal conspiracy involved <u>a lawyer</u> and <u>an assistant</u> from the mayor's office <u>was also part of it</u>.

PARALLEL   The criminal conspiracy involved <u>a lawyer</u> and <u>an assistant</u> from the mayor's office.

NOT PARALLEL   The story was <u>in the newspaper</u>, <u>on the radio</u>, and <u>the television</u>.

PARALLEL   The story was <u>in the newspaper</u>, <u>on the radio</u>, and <u>on the television</u>.

TEACHING TIP
Help students see that the problem with parallelism in this sentence is that the preposition *on* is left out of the last phrase.

Practice 1   Parallelism in Lists

In each sentence, underline the parts of the sentence that should be parallel. Then edit the sentence to make it parallel.

Answers may vary. Possible editing shown.

EXAMPLE: Although I like driving, I don't like <u>searching for a parking</u>

            waiting
<u>spot</u> or <u>~~to wait~~ for someone to leave</u>.
         ∧

1. Finding a space near the campus can be <u>frustrating</u>, <u>time-consuming</u>,

     annoying.
<u>and ~~it annoys me.~~</u>
     ∧

2. Yesterday, just when I finally found an open space, another car

                  took it.
<u>appeared</u>, <u>sped up</u>, and <u>~~was taking it.~~</u>
                 ∧

3.   I yelled at the driver, an older man <u>wearing a tan sportcoat</u> and
   carrying
   <u>~~who carried~~ a leather briefcase.</u>
   ^

4.   I felt a mixture of <u>anger,</u> ~~frustrated,~~ and <u>disappointment.</u>
   frustration
   ^

5.   Then, while I was still <u>circling the parking lot</u> and ~~checked~~ my watch,
   checking
   ^

   I realized that the man I had shouted at was my professor.

B.   Parallelism in Comparisons

In comparisons, items being compared should have parallel structure. Comparisons often use the words *than* or *as*. When you edit for parallelism, check to make sure that the items on either side of those words (the things being compared) are parallel.

NOT PARALLEL	<u>Driving downtown</u> is *as* fast as <u>the bus</u>.
PARALLEL	<u>Driving downtown</u> is *as* fast as <u>taking the bus</u>.
NOT PARALLEL	<u>To admit a mistake</u> is better *than* <u>denying it</u>.
PARALLEL	<u>To admit a mistake</u> is better *than* <u>to deny it</u>.
	<u>Admitting a mistake</u> is better *than* <u>denying it</u>.

Practice 2   Parallelism in Comparisons

In each sentence, underline the parts of the sentence that should be parallel. Then edit the sentence to make it parallel.

Answers may vary. Possible editing shown.

EXAMPLE: Leasing a new car may be <u>less expensive</u> than ~~to buy~~ one.
buying
^

1.   Car dealers often require less money down for <u>leasing a car</u> than
   purchasing
   <u>for ~~the purchase of~~ one.</u>
   ^

2.   <u>The monthly payments for a leased car</u> may be as low as ~~paying for a~~
   loan payments.
   ^
   ~~loan.~~

3.   You should check the terms of <u>leasing</u> to make sure they are as favor-
   the terms of buying.
   able as <u>~~to buy~~.</u>
   ^

4. You may find that ~~to lease~~ is a safer bet than buying.
        leasing
                  ^

5. You will be making less of a financial commitment by leasing a car
        by owning
    than ~~to own~~ it.
         ^

C. Parallelism with Certain Paired Words

When a sentence uses certain paired words, called **correlative conjunctions,** the items joined by them must be parallel. Here are the paired words:

both . . . and   neither . . . nor   rather . . . than

either . . . or   not only . . . but also

When you use the first part of a pair, be sure you always use the second part as well.

NOT PARALLEL	Bruce wants *both* to be rich *and* freedom.
PARALLEL	Bruce wants *both* to be rich *and* to be free.
NOT PARALLEL	He can *neither* fail the course and quitting his job is also impossible.
PARALLEL	He can *neither* fail the course *nor* quit his job.

Practice 3 ▶ **Parallelism with Certain Paired Words**

In each sentence, circle the paired words and underline the parts of the sentence that should be parallel. Then edit the sentence to make it parallel.

EXAMPLE: Choosing a mate can be (both) romantic (and) ~~it can be a~~
                                                              heartbreaking.
                                                                    ^
~~heartbreak.~~ *Answers may vary. Possible editing shown.*

1. People hope to find someone who is (not only) a good lover (but also)

    ~~to find~~ a friendly person.

2. Sometimes a person must (either) make a long-term commitment (or)

    let~~ting~~ go of the relationship.

3. People often feel that they want ⟨neither⟩ to break up ~~and are against~~
   nor to marry.
   ^
   ~~marrying.~~

4. Sometimes people ask, "Would I ⟨rather⟩ risk being lonely ⟨than⟩
   risk being unhappy?"
   ~~unhappiness?"~~
   ^

5. Compromising may be wise; ~~to settle~~ for a bad partner is not.
   settling
   ^

Practice 4 ▶ **Completing Sentences with Paired Words**

Edit each sentence by completing the correlative conjunction and adding more information. Make sure that the structures on both sides of the correlative conjunction are parallel.

Answers will vary. Possible editing shown.

1. I could bring to this job not only youthful enthusiasm *but also*
   relevant experience.

2. I am willing to work either in your Chicago office *or in your*
   San Francisco office.

3. My current job neither encourages creativity *nor allows*
   flexibility.

4. I would rather work in a difficult job *than work in an*
   unchallenging job.

5. In college I learned a lot both from my classes *and from other*
   students.

Edit Paragraphs and Your Own Writing

Practice 5 ▶ Editing Paragraphs for Parallelism

Find and correct any problems with parallelism in the following paragraphs. You may want to refer to the Summary on page 372.

TEAMWORK
Have students form small groups. Each group writes five sentences that are not parallel. Each group exchanges sentences with another group and corrects the other group's sentences.

(1) As a young man, Sigmund Freud, the founder of psychoanalysis, was determined to use the methods of science to unlock the secrets of human behavior. (2) But as biographer Peter Gay explains, the effort was slow, time-consuming, and ~~that it was~~ often discouraging. (3) A medical doctor by training, in the 1890s Freud began studying and *documenting*
~~to document~~ causes of hysteria, and he discovered that many of his female patients had been sexually abused by their fathers. (4) Through this, Freud came to understand how traumatic events from childhood *forgotten*
that are ignored or ~~one forgets them~~ can cause emotional problems later.

(5) To test his theories, Freud analyzed himself. (6) Studying his *disturbing.*
own violent and erotic impulses was frightening and ~~disturbed him.~~
(7) But it was also deeply rewarding, not only to Freud as a scientist *to*
but also Freud as an individual. (8) His own neurotic symptoms gradually disappeared. (9) Soon he published his most famous book, *The Interpretation of Dreams.* (10) Here he describes how even in sleep the *disguises*
subconscious mind often distorts and ~~is disguising~~ forbidden wishes so that they become unrecognizable. (11) A dream takes on meaning only when understood symbolically — "interpreted" through the methods of psychoanalysis.

LEARNING JOURNAL
How would you explain parallelism to someone who had never heard of it before? How would you explain how to edit for it?

Practice 6   Editing Your Own Writing for Parallelism

As a final practice, edit a piece of your own writing for parallelism. It can be a paper you are working on for this course, a paper you've already finished, a paper for another course, or a recent piece of writing from your work or everyday life. Record in your learning journal any problem sentences you find, along with their corrections. You may want to use the Summary on page 372.

Summary and Quick Review Chart: Parallelism

- **Parallelism** is the use of similar grammatical structures for similar ideas. (See p. 366.)
- Problems with parallelism occur most often in **pairs** and **lists,** in **comparisons,** and with **certain paired words.** (See pp. 367, 368, and 369.)

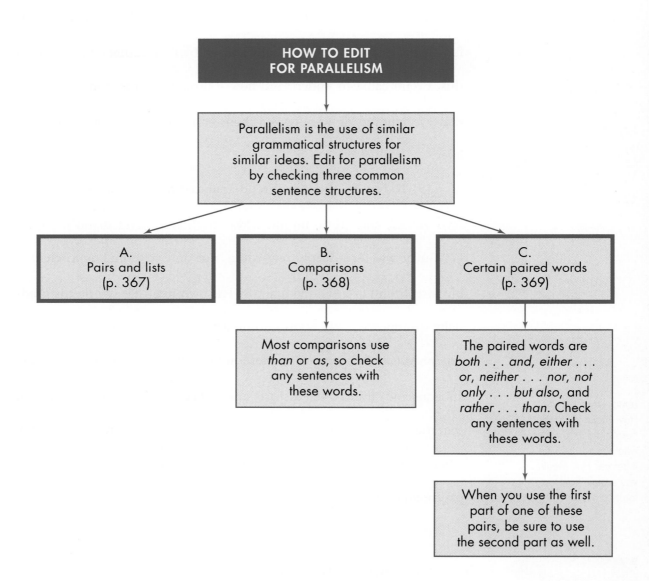

HOW TO EDIT FOR PARALLELISM

Parallelism is the use of similar grammatical structures for similar ideas. Edit for parallelism by checking three common sentence structures.

A. Pairs and lists (p. 367)

B. Comparisons (p. 368)

C. Certain paired words (p. 369)

Most comparisons use *than* or *as,* so check any sentences with these words.

The paired words are *both . . . and, either . . . or, neither . . . nor, not only . . . but also,* and *rather . . . than.* Check any sentences with these words.

When you use the first part of one of these pairs, be sure to use the second part as well.

31

Sentence Variety
Putting Rhythm in Your Writing

TIP: To understand this chapter, you need to know what *adverbs, phrases, modifiers, verbs, subjects,* and *clauses* are. For review, see Chapter 21.

A.   Start Some Sentences with Adverbs
B.   Join Ideas Using an *-ing* Verb Form
C.   Join Ideas Using an *-ed* Verb Form
D.   Join Ideas Using an Appositive
E.   Join Ideas Using an Adjective Clause

RESOURCES
Additional Resources contains tests and supplemental practice exercises for this chapter, as well as a transparency master for the summary chart at the end.

LEARNING JOURNAL
Use your learning journal as a place to record an example of a brief passage with short, similar-sounding sentences. Also record edited versions of these sentences, after you have introduced some sentence variety.

Understand What Sentence Variety Is

Using **sentence variety** in your writing means using assorted sentence patterns, lengths, and rhythms. Most of us like variety: We don't want to have the same dinner every night, or have ten shirts of the same style and color, or listen to the same song ten times in a row.

If your sentences are all the same pattern and length, your readers will quickly tire of them and may not keep reading long enough to understand your point. Many writers use too many short, simple sentences, mistakenly thinking that short is always easier to understand than long. In fact, that is not true, as you can see in these examples.

WITH SHORT, SIMPLE SENTENCES

The tiger shark is sometimes called the garbage can of the sea. It reaches six meters in length. A tiger shark weighs up to a ton. It eats almost anything. It has been known to eat fish, boots, beer bottles, dogs, and humans. Surprising things were found in tiger sharks' stomachs. These include overcoats, raincoats, a cow's hoof, a deer's antlers, and a chicken coop with feathers and bones still inside.

TEAMWORK
After they have completed the chapter, small groups can reexamine this sample paragraph. Have students try to identify which kinds of sentence variety the author has used.

WITH SENTENCE VARIETY

The tiger shark, which reaches six meters in length, is sometimes called the garbage can of the sea. Weighing up to a ton, it eats almost anything, including fish, boots, beer bottles, dogs, and humans. Surprising things, such as overcoats, raincoats, cows' hooves, deer antlers, and a chicken coop with feathers and bones still inside have been found in the stomachs of tiger sharks.

—Adapted from E. O. Wilson, *Diversity of Life*

Good writing is a mix of long and short sentences with a variety of patterns. Sentence variety is what gives your writing good rhythm and flow.

Practice Creating Sentence Variety

COMPUTER
Students can get a visual measure of the length of their sentences by inserting two returns after every period in a paragraph. (They can use the search and replace function to do this.)

To create sentence variety, you need to edit your writing so that it has sentences of different types and lengths. Most writers tend to write short sentences that start with the subject, so this chapter will focus on techniques for starting with something other than the subject and for writing a variety of longer sentences.

Remember that the goal is to use variety to achieve a good rhythm. Do not simply change all your sentences from one pattern to another pattern or you still won't have variety: You'll have just another set of similar-sounding sentences.

A. Start Some Sentences with Adverbs

ESL
Remind students that an adverb answers the question *How? When? Where? Why?* or *How often?* (JS)

Adverbs are words that modify or describe verbs, adjectives, or other adverbs; they often end with -*ly*. As long as the meaning is clear, adverbs can be placed at the beginning of a sentence instead of in the middle.

ADVERB IN MIDDLE	Stories about haunted houses *frequently* surface at Halloween.
STARTS WITH ADVERB	*Frequently*, stories about haunted houses surface at Halloween.
ADVERB IN MIDDLE	They *often* focus on sea captains lost at sea.
STARTS WITH ADVERB	*Often* they focus on sea captains lost at sea.

Practice 1   Starting Sentences with an Adverb

Edit each sentence so it begins with an adverb. Remember that many adverbs end in -*ly*.

         Invariably, the
EXAMPLE: ~~The~~ story of the parked lovers ~~invariably~~ scares everyone, even

though it's been around a long time.

1. *Understandably, the*
   ~~The~~ two teenagers ~~understandably~~ wanted to be alone.
   ^

2. *Intentionally, they*
   ~~They~~ situated themselves ~~intentionally~~ far away from any of the

   other cars.

3. *Gradually, they*
   ~~They gradually~~ began to relax while listening to some soft songs on
   ^

   the car radio.

4. *Suddenly they*
   ~~They~~ heard a loud scratching noise ~~suddenly.~~
   ^   ^

5. *Frantically, one*
   ~~One~~ of them tried ~~frantically~~ to start the engine, but they soon
   ^

   discovered that the car battery was dead.

TIP: For more on joining ideas, see Chapter 29.

B. Join Ideas Using an *-ing* Verb Form

One way to combine sentences is to use an **-*ing* verb form** (the form of a verb that ends in *-ing*) to make one of the sentences into a phrase.

TWO SENTENCES	A pecan roll from our bakery is not dietetic. It contains eight hundred calories.
JOINED WITH *-ING* VERB FORM	*Containing* eight hundred calories, a pecan roll from our bakery is not dietetic.

ESL
Remind students that an *-ing* verb form that modifies the subject cannot be the main verb in the sentence.

To combine sentences this way, add *-ing* to the verb in one of the sentences and delete the subject. You now have a modifier phrase that can be added to the beginning or the end of the other sentence, depending on what makes the most sense.

equaling
The fat content is also high. ~~It equals~~ the fat in a huge country
^

breakfast.

If you put the phrase starting with the *-ing* verb form at the beginning of the sentence, be sure the word that the phrase modifies follows immediately. Otherwise, you will create a dangling modifier.

TIP: For more on finding and correcting dangling modifiers, see Chapter 28.

TWO SENTENCES	I ran through the rain. My raincoat got all wet.
DANGLING MODIFIER	*Running* *my* ~~I ran~~ through the rain. ~~My~~ raincoat got all wet.
EDITED	*I got* Running through the rain, my raincoat ~~got~~ all wet.

| Practice 2 | **Joining Ideas Using an *-ing* Verb Form** |

Combine each pair of sentences into a single sentence by using an *-ing* verb form.

Hoping to get a better price, the

EXAMPLE: ~~The~~ city is seeking new bids for its proposed sewage
           ^

treatment plant. ~~It hopes to get a better price.~~
                Answers may vary. Sample editing shown.
                                          recognizing
1. A majority of voters approved the project last spring, ~~They recognized~~
                                                      ,   ^

   that the old system is inadequate.

   Fearing a sharp increase in taxes, some
2. ~~Some~~ citizens oppose the project. ~~They fear a sharp increase in taxes.~~
   ^

   Seeking reelection, the
3. ~~The~~ mayor is determined to keep everybody happy. ~~She is seeking~~
   ^

   ~~reelection.~~

   Speaking to a group of homeowners, she
4. ~~She~~ said that federal aid may help avoid an increase in property taxes.
   ^

   ~~She was speaking to a group of homeowners.~~

5. The sewage treatment plant would be the largest in Whitefield
                  serving
   County, ~~It would serve~~ twenty thousand homes.
         ,   ^

C.   Join Ideas Using an *-ed* Verb Form

Another way to combine sentences is to use an **-ed verb form** (the form of a verb that ends in *-ed*) to make one of the sentences into a phrase.

| TWO SENTENCES | Leonardo da Vinci was a man of many talents. He was noted for his painting. |
| JOINED WITH *-ED* VERB FORM | *Noted* for his painting, Leonardo da Vinci was a man of many talents. |

TIP: For more on helping verbs, see Chapters 21 and 25.

To combine sentences this way, drop the subject and the helping verb from a sentence that has an *-ed* verb form. You now have a modifier phrase that can be added to the beginning or the end of the other sentence, depending on what makes the most sense.

Interested   *Leonardo*
~~Leonardo was interested~~ in many areas, ~~He~~ investigated problems of
^   ,   ^

geology, botany, mechanics, and hydraulics.

TIP: For more on finding and correcting dangling modifiers, see Chapter 28.

If you put the phrase starting with the *-ed* verb form at the beginning of the sentence, be sure the word that the phrase modifies follows immediately. Otherwise, you will create a dangling modifier.

Practice 3 ▶ **Joining Ideas Using an *-ed* Verb Form**

Combine each pair of sentences into a single sentence by using an *-ed* verb form.

Classified as retarded by mistake,

EXAMPLE: Marie Balter actually was quite intelligent. ~~She was classified~~
             ^

~~as retarded by mistake.~~

Answers may vary. Sample editing shown.

Deserted

1. ~~She was deserted~~ by her mother, Marie was placed in a home for the
      ^

   mentally retarded.

Labeled   *she*

2. ~~She was labeled~~ as unteachable, ~~She~~ was not expected to learn much.
      ^   ^

3. Marie learned very simple tasks, ~~They were~~ created just to keep her

   occupied.

Saved

4. ~~She was saved~~ by a perceptive teacher, Marie went to college and
      ^

   graduate school.

Inspired

5. ~~She was inspired~~ by the teacher who saved her, Marie became a
      ^

   teacher herself.

D. Join Ideas Using an Appositive

TEACHING TIP
Say aloud a sentence that has as its subject something familiar to students in the class (e.g., the president, a celebrity). Ask them to suggest a good appositive. If you wish, have them suggest humorous possibilities.

An **appositive** is a phrase that renames a noun. Appositives can be used to combine two sentences into one.

TWO SENTENCES	Mushroom tea was a fad not long ago. It was a so-called miracle drink.
JOINED WITH AN APPOSITIVE	Mushroom tea, *a so-called miracle drink*, was a fad not long ago.

[The phrase *a so-called miracle drink* renames the noun *tea*.]

To combine sentences this way, drop the subject and verb in a sentence that describes a noun in that or another sentence. You now have an appositive phrase that can be placed right after the noun. Use commas to set off the appositive.

The tea~~,was~~ a dangerous fad~~, It~~ caused a few deaths.

| Practice 4 | **Joining Ideas Using an Appositive** |

Combine each pair of sentences into a single sentence by using an appositive. Be sure to use commas to set off the appositive.

EXAMPLE: Dolphins, ~~are~~ sea-dwelling mammals, ~~They~~ are well adjusted to their lives in the ocean.

1. Marine biologists, *scientists who study ocean life forms,* have long been fascinated by the dolphin. ~~Marine biologists are scientists who study ocean life forms.~~

2. Terrie Williams, ~~is~~ a physiologist, ~~Williams~~ has been doing research on dolphins for years.

3. ~~A blow-hole is a small opening on the top of an aquatic mammal's head.~~ A dolphin needs to surface occasionally to breathe through its blow-hole, *a small opening on the top of an aquatic mammal's head.*

4. Williams learned that when dolphins make a deep-water dive, their *a dive of more than fifty meters,* lungs actually collapse. ~~A deep-water dive is a dive of more than fifty meters.~~

5. This physiological trick, *a clever evolutionary adaptation,* explains how dolphins can spend so little energy to dive so deep. ~~This physiological trick is a clever evolutionary adaptation.~~

E. Join Ideas Using an Adjective Clause

An **adjective clause** is a group of words with a subject and a verb that modifies or describes a noun. It can be used to combine two sentences into one.

TWO SENTENCES	Vashti has won many teaching awards. She teaches at a community college.
JOINED WITH AN ADJECTIVE CLAUSE	Vashti, *who teaches at a community college*, has won many teaching awards.

TIP: Use *who* to refer to a person, *which* to refer to places or things (but not to people), and *that* for people, places, or things. When referring to a person, *who* is preferable to *that.*

TIP: An *adjective clause* is sometimes called a *relative clause.*

To join sentences this way, use *who, which,* or *that* to replace the subject of a sentence that describes a noun in another sentence. You now have an adjective clause that you can move next to the noun it describes.

which

Rocío attributes her success to the Puente Project. It helped her meet

the challenges of college.

NOTE: Punctuating adjective clauses can be tricky. If the adjective clause can be taken out of the sentence without completely changing the meaning of the sentence, put commas around the clause.

Vashti, *who teaches at a community college,* has won many teaching awards.

[The phrase *who teaches at a community college* adds information about Vashti, but it is not essential; the sentence *Vashti has won many teaching awards* means almost the same thing as the sentence in the example.]

If the adjective clause is an essential part of the meaning of the sentence, do not put commas around it.

Vashti is the teacher *who changed Reggie's life.*

[*Who changed Reggie's life* is an essential part of this sentence. The sentence *Vashti is the teacher* is very different in meaning from the whole sentence in the example.]

Practice 5 ▶ Joining Ideas Using an Adjective Clause

Combine each pair of sentences into a single sentence by using an adjective clause beginning with *who, which,* or *that.*

who has been going to college for the past three years,

EXAMPLE: My friend Erin had her first child last June. ~~She has been going to college for the past three years.~~

Answers may vary. Sample editing shown.

1. While Erin goes to classes, her baby boy stays at a day care center*/,*
   which
   ~~The day care center~~ costs Erin about $100 a week.
   ^

2. Twice when her son was ill Erin had to miss her geology lab*/* ~~The lab~~   *which*
   ^

   is an important part of her grade for that course.

3. Occasionally, Erin's parents *who live about seventy miles away,* come up and watch the baby while Erin is
   ^

   studying. ~~They live about 70 miles away.~~

4. Sometimes Erin feels discouraged by the extra costs*/* ~~The costs~~ have   *that*
   ^

   resulted from her having a child.

5. She feels that some of her professors aren't very sympathetic. ~~These~~   *who have never been mothers themselves*
   ^

   ~~are the ones who have never been mothers themselves.~~

Edit Paragraphs and Your Own Writing

> **Practice 6** ▶ **Editing Paragraphs for Sentence Variety**

TEAMWORK
Break students into groups and have each group write a paragraph for the other groups to edit. The sentences should all be between five and ten words long. Have groups exchange and edit the paragraphs, and then invite groups to read their unedited and edited versions.

Create sentence variety in the following paragraphs. Join at least two sentences in each of the paragraphs. Try to use several of the techniques covered in this chapter. There are many possible ways to edit each paragraph.

Answers will vary. Possible editing shown.

(1) In the last few decades of the nineteenth century, more and more of western Europe became prosperous and stable. (2) ~~Instead~~ *Unfortunately, instead* of
^

being a time of lasting peace, this ~~unfortunately~~ turned out to be a

period building toward war. (3) Part of the reason was the attempt by
Germany*,* to match England as a world power. (4) ~~Germany had lagged~~   *which had lagged far behind its rivals,*
^

~~far behind its rivals.~~ (5) ~~The~~ German emperor Wilhelm II launched a   *Hoping to take advantage of new technology, the*
^

massive project to build up Germany's navy. (6) ~~He was hoping to take~~

~~advantage of new technology.~~

(7) By the turn of the century a deadly arms race was under way. *Determined to maintain its superiority at sea,* (8) Britain built more and more warships. (9) ~~It was determined to maintain its superiority at sea.~~ (10) Meanwhile, in Germany, the military was becoming more influential. (11) Civilian leaders lacked the skill of Otto von Bismarck, (12) ~~He was~~ the legendary figure who had managed to create a unified Germany in 1866. (13) The situation in Europe was further complicated by the complex relationships among England, France, Russia, Austria-Hungary, and Turkey.

(14) The disaster erupted in the Balkan state of Bosnia. (15) The old Ottoman Empire, *which had played a major role in southeastern Europe since the fourteenth century,* ~~was disintegrating.~~ (16) ~~The Ottoman Empire had played a major role in southeastern Europe since the fourteenth century.~~ (17) Russia and Austria-Hungary vied to gain influence over small states such as Serbia, Bulgaria, and Greece, (18) ~~These~~ states previously ~~had been~~ controlled by Turkey. (19) On June 28, 1914, Serbian nationalists in Sarajevo assassinated Archduke Francis Ferdinand, (20) *who* ~~He~~ was the heir to the Austro-Hungarian throne. (21) Soon Austria declared war on Serbia. (22) This led, not surprisingly, first to a Russian threat against Austria and then to German mobilization. (23) By the end of the summer, much of Europe was entangled in the war.

LEARNING JOURNAL
Do you tend to write short, similar-sounding sentences? Which type of sentence pattern covered in this chapter do you think you will use most often when you are editing for sentence variety?

Practice 7 ▶ Editing Your Own Writing for Sentence Variety

As a final practice, edit a piece of your own writing for sentence variety. It can be a paper you are working on for this course, a paper you've already finished, a paper for another course, or a recent piece of writing from your work or everyday life. Record in your learning journal any examples of short, choppy sentences you find, along with the edited versions. You may want to use the Summary on page 382.

Summary and Quick Review Chart: Sentence Variety

- Using **sentence variety** means using assorted sentence patterns and lengths in your writing. Sentence variety is important to give your writing good rhythm and flow. (See pp. 373–74.)
- If you tend to write short, similar-sounding sentences, try using some of these techniques: Start some sentences with **adverbs** (p. 374), join ideas using an **-ing verb form** (p. 375), join ideas using an **-ed verb form** (p. 376), join ideas using an **appositive** (p. 377), join ideas using an **adjective clause** (p. 379).
- An **appositive** is a word or phrase that renames a noun. (See p. 377.)
- An **adjective clause** is a clause starting with *who*, *which*, or *that* that modifies or describes a noun or pronoun. (See p. 379.)

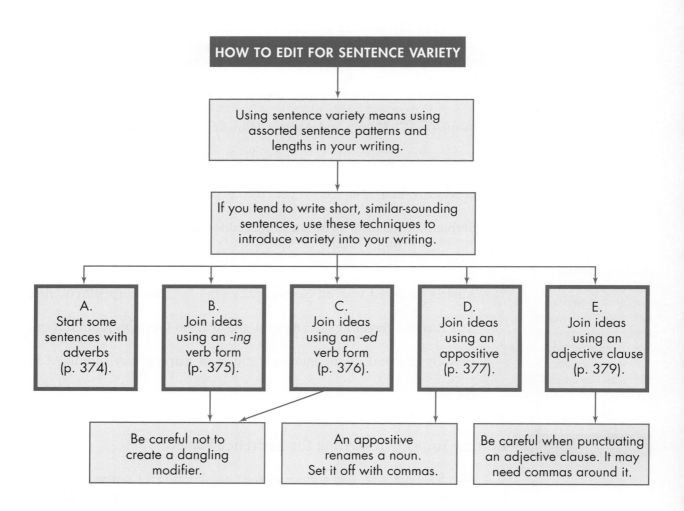

32

ESL Concerns

Areas of Special Interest to Nonnative Speakers

TIP: This chapter focuses on problems that many nonnative speakers of English have when they write papers for college, but native speakers may find it useful as well.

TEACHING TIP
This chapter was written with the needs of ESL students in mind, but you may want to assign it to native speakers of nonstandard dialects or to other students who have any of the problems covered here.

TIP: Reading and listening to standard English are some of the best ways to improve your ability to write and speak it.

RESOURCES
Additional Resources contains tests and supplemental practice exercises for this chapter.

Nouns and Articles
Verbs
Prepositions
Negatives and Questions
Adjectives

Most of the information that you need to write correct English for college papers is the same as what students whose first language is English need. You may need more help, though, with some matters that are very different from your own first language. This chapter will focus on those areas.

Nouns and Articles

A. Subjects

The **subject** of a sentence is the person, place, or thing the sentence is about. It is either a noun or a pronoun (a word that substitutes for a noun). Be sure to include a subject in every sentence and every dependent clause.

It is
~~Is~~ raining here today.
 ^

                                                          he
My boss has taught me a great deal, although is difficult to work for.
                                                          ^

B. Count and Noncount Nouns

A **noun** is a word that names a person, place, or thing. English nouns fall into two categories, depending on whether they name things that can be counted.

COUNT NOUN	I bought two new *chairs*.
NONCOUNT NOUN	I bought some new *furniture*.

The noun *chair* (plural, *chairs*) is a **count noun** because it names a distinct individual thing that can be counted. The noun *furniture* is a **noncount noun** because it represents a general category or group that can't be divided into distinct, countable individuals. It would not make sense to say in English, *I bought two new furnitures.* Here are some more examples:

COUNT	NONCOUNT
apple	fruit
tree	grass
dollar	money
beach	sand
fact	information

Count nouns can be made plural. Noncount nouns cannot be plural; they are always singular.

I got ~~two~~ information~~s~~ to use in my paper.

The coach looked over the team's equipment~~s~~.

C. Articles

The words *a, an,* and *the* are called **articles;** they are used with nouns. The correct article depends on (1) whether the noun is count or noncount, (2) whether the noun is singular or plural, and (3) whether or not the identity of the individual or group is specific and known to the reader.

The identity of a noun is known to the reader if there is only one possibility or if the writer has given (or is about to give) all the information the reader needs to know to identify the noun.

IDENTITY KNOWN   *The dog* who lives next door barks constantly.

> [This sentence narrows the possibilities down to one: the dog who lives next door.]

The identity of a noun is not known if there is more than one possibility or if the writer is referring to a general group or whole category.

Articles with Count and Noncount Nouns

COUNT NOUNS	ARTICLE
SINGULAR	
Identity Known	*the*
	I want to read *the book* on taxes that you recommended.
Identity Not Known	*a* or *an*
	I want to read *a book* on taxes.
PLURAL	
Identity Known	*the*
	I enjoyed *the movies* we saw.
Identity Not Known or a General Category	(nothing or another kind of word)
	I usually enjoy *movies* like that.
	I usually enjoy *those movies*.

NONCOUNT NOUNS	ARTICLE
SINGULAR	
Identity Known	*the*
	I put *the food* in the refrigerator.
Identity Not Known or a General Category	(nothing or another kind of word)
	There is *food* all over the kitchen.
	Give *some food* to the neighbors.

IDENTITY NOT KNOWN   *A dog* in my neighborhood barks constantly.

Dogs who bark constantly are a nuisance.

Here are some guidelines for using articles:

- Use *the* if the identity is known, whether the noun is count, noncount, singular, or plural: *the old dog, the two dogs, the weather.*
- Use *a* or *an* for all singular count nouns if their identity is unknown or nonspecific: *a question, a good question, an orange.*
- Use *a* before words that start with a consonant sound; use *an* before words that start with a vowel sound: *a dog, an elevator.*

- Never use *a* or *an* with noncount nouns.
- Noncount nouns (which are always singular) and any plural count noun whose identity is unknown can use either no article at all or some other kind of word, such as *this, these, that, those, many, some: jewelry, this jewelry; buses, many buses.*

Practice 1 ▶ **Editing Nouns and Articles**

Edit the following paragraph, adding and changing articles and nouns as necessary. Also add a subject to any sentence that is missing one.

Answers may vary. Possible editing shown.

(1) I think I'll have *a* hamburger for lunch. (2) ~~Always~~ *I always* wonder why *the* bottom half of *a* hamburger bun is so thin and always falls apart. (3) You get *the* burger off *the* grill, put onion*s*, ketchup*s*, and mustard*s* on it, and you begin to eat *the* burger, but *the* bottom bun is wet and crumbling. (4) What is ~~an~~ *the* answer? (5) ~~Hamburger~~ *A hamburger* expert uses *the* thicker top bun on the bottom. (6) This way *the* burger stays together, and *the* person having *the* meal is happy. (7) ~~Food~~ *The food* industry shouldn't make such odd buns.

Verbs

Verbs tell what action the subject in the sentence performs or link the subject to a word that describes it.

TIP: For prepositions after verbs, see page 389. For the position of verbs in questions, see page 391. For other problems with verbs, see Chapter 25.

D. Using the *-ing* Form or the *to* Form after Certain Verbs

A **gerund** is a verb form that ends in *-ing*. An **infinitive** is a verb form that has no ending but is preceded by the word *to*. These forms cannot function as the main verbs in sentences; the sentences must have another word that functions as the main verb.

GERUND I enjoy *swimming.*

INFINITIVE I like *to swim.*

Whether to use a gerund or an infinitive often depends on the main verb in the sentence. Some verbs can be followed by either a gerund or an infinitive, some can be followed only by a gerund, and some can be followed only by an infinitive. Knowing which to use can be tricky, since the correct form is based on convention, not logic. Practice using the correct structures for the verbs you use most often.

VERB + INFINITIVE OR GERUND

begin	hate	remember	try
continue	like	start	
forget	love	stop	

These verbs can be followed by either an infinitive or a gerund. Sometimes the meaning is about the same.

He <u>hates</u> *staying* out late. = He <u>hates</u> *to stay* out late.

Sometimes the meaning changes depending on whether you use an infinitive or a gerund.

Mario <u>stopped</u> *smoking.*

> [This means that Mario no longer smokes.]

Mario <u>stopped</u> *to smoke.*

> [This means that Mario stopped what he was doing and smoked a cigarette.]

VERB + INFINITIVE

agree	decide	manage	pretend
ask	expect	need	promise
beg	fail	offer	refuse
choose	hope	plan	want
claim			

Teresa <u>agreed</u> *to help.*

Roberto <u>chose</u> *to ignore* my advice.

VERB + GERUND

admit	discuss	keep	risk
avoid	enjoy	miss	suggest
consider	finish	practice	
deny	imagine	quit	

The man <u>admitted</u> *robbing* the bank.

You can't <u>avoid</u> *paying* bills.

E. Progressive Tense

The **progressive tense** consists of a form of the verb *be* plus an *-ing* form of a verb. It is used to indicate a continuing activity.

Kim *is reading* a novel about Asian American immigrants.

Not all verbs can form the progressive tense. Certain verbs that indicate sensing or a state of being are not usually used this way.

VERBS THAT CANNOT FORM THE PROGRESSIVE TENSE

appear	have	mean	taste
believe	hear	need	understand
belong	know	see	want
cost	like	seem	weigh

I ~~am~~ belong~~ing~~ to several student associations on campus.

The author ~~is meaning~~ *means* that unions have damaged our economy.

Practice 2   **Editing Verbs**

Edit the following paragraph to make sure that verbs are used correctly.

(1) Many students ~~are believing~~ *believe* that the college should provide on-campus day care. (2) These students want ~~improving~~ *to improve* their ability to get a good job. (3) They consider ~~to get~~ *getting* a better job a worthwhile goal. (4) They come to college where they try to take courses that will make them attractive to employers. (5) The courses ~~are~~ cost~~ing~~ a lot, but the expense is worth it to these students. (6) Unfortunately, since they continue to be responsible for their families, they often have difficulty ~~to arrange~~ *arranging* for child care. (7) They stop taking the courses they really need, so they don't achieve their goal. (8) Shouldn't the college agree ~~helping~~ *to help* these students? (9) The college would also be helped because more and better students would want to come to a college that met more of the students' needs.

Prepositions

TIP: For more on prepositions, see Chapter 21.

A **preposition** is a word that connects a noun, pronoun, or verb with some other information about it; some prepositions have two words.

Knowing which preposition to use can be difficult because the correct preposition is often determined by idiom or convention rather than logic. An **idiom** is any combination of words that is always used the same way, even though there is no logical or grammatical explanation for it. The best way to learn idioms is to practice writing and speaking the correct forms.

F. Prepositions with Adjectives

Adjectives are often followed by prepositions. Here are some common examples.

afraid of	full of	scared of
ashamed of	happy about	sorry for
aware of	interested in	tired of
confused by	proud of	
excited about	responsible for	

Marina is excited ~~of~~ *about* getting a good grade in the course.

However, she is tired ~~with~~ *of* all this work.

G. Prepositions with Verbs

Many verbs consist of a verb plus a preposition (or adverb). They must be learned by heart because their meaning usually has nothing to do with the literal meaning of the verb plus the preposition. Often, the meaning of the verb changes completely depending on which preposition is used.

You must *take out* the trash.

You must *take in* the exciting sights of New York City.

Here are a few common examples.

call off	They decided to *call off* the wedding.
call on	The professor never *calls on* me.
fill in	Please *fill in* the blanks.
fill out	You must *fill out* this application form.
fill up	I told him to *fill up* the gas tank.
go over	Let's *go over* what we learned last week.

grow up	All children *grow up.*
hand in	You must *hand in* your homework now.
look up	I decided to *look up* the word in the dictionary.
pick out	Richard *picked out* a dependable car.
pick up	Allison *picked up* her cat at the kennel.
put off	I often *put off* my work until the last minute.

Practice 3 ▸ **Editing Prepositions**

Edit the following paragraph to make sure that prepositions are used correctly.

(1) People were once afraid ~~to~~ *of* comets in the sky. (2) They thought that these giant snowballs were signs of bad luck. (3) There are historical examples of rulers calling ~~down~~ *off* battles and holidays when they saw comets in the sky. (4) Today, most people are excited ~~for~~ *about* the idea of seeing a comet, as long as there is no danger of its colliding with the earth. (5) Scientists are interested ~~to~~ *in* learning more about each comet that passes through our solar system. (6) Since there is no way we can travel to visit comets, we need to wait until they come to us.

Negatives and Questions

H. Negatives

To form a negative statement, you can usually use one of these words.

| never | nobody | no one | nowhere |
| no | none | not | |

The word *not* is often combined with the verb in a shortened form called a **contraction.**

TIP: A clause is a group of words with a subject and verb. It may or may not be able to stand on its own as a sentence. For more on clauses, see Chapter 21.

They *aren't* finished. = They *are not* finished.

In standard English, there can be only one negative word in each clause.

Caryl will ~~not~~ ask no one for help.

Caryl will not ask ~~no one~~ for help.

When writing a negative statement using the word *not,* the *not* must come after the first helping verb in the sentence. If there is no helping verb, you must add a form of *do* as well as *not* to make a negative statement.

POSITIVE   Jane *will run* with us.

NEGATIVE   Jane *will not run* with us.

POSITIVE   I *enjoyed* listening to the music.

NEGATIVE   I *did not enjoy* listening to the music.

> [Notice that the verb *enjoyed* changed to *enjoy* once the verb *did* was added.]

I.   Questions

To turn a statement into a question, move the helping verb in the statement so that it comes before the subject. If the only verb is a form of *be,* it can also be moved before the subject. If there is no helping verb or form of *be* in the statement, you must add a form of *do* and put it before the subject. Be sure to end the question with a question mark.

STATEMENT   Jim *can drive* tonight.

QUESTION   *Can* Jim *drive* tonight?

STATEMENT   He *is* unhappy.

QUESTION   *Is* he unhappy?

STATEMENT   You *passed* the test.

QUESTION   *Did* you *pass* the test?

> [Notice that the verb *passed* changed to *pass* once the verb *did* was added.]

Practice 4   **Editing Negatives and Questions**

For each positive statement, write one negative statement and one question.

EXAMPLE: Our professor gives us interesting assignments.

NEGATIVE: *Our professor does not give us interesting*

assignments.

QUESTION: *Does our professor give us interesting*

assignments?

Answers may vary. Possible answers shown.

1. We were writing about why we want to take this course.

   NEGATIVE: *We were not writing about why we want to take this course.*

   QUESTION: *Were we writing about why we want to take this course?*

2. We are working on papers about our family histories.

   NEGATIVE: *We are not working on papers about our family histories.*

   QUESTION: *Are we working on papers about our family histories?*

3. My family has lived in this country for five years.

   NEGATIVE: *My family has not lived in this country for five years.*

   QUESTION: *Has my family lived in this country for five years?*

4. We enjoy all there is to do and see here.

   NEGATIVE: *We do not enjoy all there is to do and see here.*

   QUESTION: *Do we enjoy all there is to do and see here?*

5. The weather is difficult to get used to.

   NEGATIVE: *The weather is not difficult to get used to.*

   QUESTION: *Is the weather difficult to get used to?*

Adjectives

TIP: For more on adjectives, see Chapter 27.

Adjectives modify or describe nouns and pronouns. Many sentences have several adjectives that modify the same word.

The *big old red* truck rolled by.

J. Order of Adjectives

When you use more than one adjective to modify the same word, you should use the conventional order for adjectives in standard English.

1. Judgment/overall opinion: *awful, friendly, intelligent, strange, terrible*
2. Size: *big, huge, tiny, large, short, tall*
3. Shape: *round, square, fat, thin, circular, square*
4. Age: *old, young, new, youthful*
5. Color: *blue, green, yellow, red*
6. Nationality/location: *Greek, Indian, California, southern*
7. Material: *paper, glass, plastic, wooden*

Practice 5 ▷ **Editing Adjectives**

Write sentences using the nouns and adjectives supplied. Be sure to put the adjectives in the correct order.

EXAMPLE: desk (wooden, huge, old)

The huge old wooden desk was covered with papers.

Answers will vary. Possible answers shown.

1. hair (black, long)

Her long black hair was beautiful.

2. jacket (leather, new, brown)

The new brown leather jacket is too expensive.

3. man (tall, old, scary)

I ran from the scary tall old man.

4. calculator (tiny, complicated, new)

The complicated tiny new calculator is hard to use.

5. chair (green, ugly, plastic)

The ugly green plastic chair sat by the pool all winter.

EDITING

Part Seven

Word Use

33

Word Choice
Avoiding Language Pitfalls

A.   Vague and Abstract Words
B.   Slang
C.   Stuffy Language
D.   Wordy Language
E.   Clichés

Understand the Importance of Choosing Words Carefully

In conversation, a large part of your meaning is conveyed by your facial expression, your tone of voice, gestures, the tilt of your head. In writing, you have only the words on the page to make your point, so you must choose them carefully. If you use vague or inappropriate words, your readers may not understand or care about what you have to say. Carefully chosen, precise words have more "punch" and more life and tell your readers exactly what you mean.

This chapter shows five common pitfalls and how to avoid them. These pitfalls weaken the forcefulness of your writing and make it hard for you to get your point across. Eliminating these whenever you find them and replacing them with specific words that fit your meaning will make your writing clearer and more effective.

Two resources will help you find the best words for your meaning: a dictionary and a thesaurus.

ESL
ESL students can use a dictionary written specifically for nonnative speakers (such as *The Longman Dictionary of American English*) in addition to a standard English dictionary. (JS)

Dictionary

You need a dictionary. For a very small investment, you can have a complete word resource that gives all kinds of useful information about any word: spelling, division of the word into syllables, pronunciation, parts of speech, other forms of the word, definitions, and examples of how the word is used. Here is a sample dictionary entry.

spelling and end-of-line division   pronunciation   parts of speech   other forms

con • crete (kon´kret, kong´-, kon kret´, kong-), *adj., n., v.,* **-cret • ed,** **-cret • ing.** —*adj.* **1.** constituting an actual thing or instance; real; perceptible; substantial: *concrete proof.* **2.** pertaining to or concerned with realities or actual instances rather than abstractions; particular as opposed to general: *concrete proposals.* **3.** referring to an actual substance or thing, as opposed to an abstract quality: *The words "cat," "water," and "teacher" are concrete, whereas the words "truth," "excellence," and "adulthood" are abstract. . . .*

definition ———

example ———

— *Random House Webster's College Dictionary*

COMPUTER
Many word processing programs include a thesaurus (sometimes called a "word finder"). Encourage students to use it if they want to explore other word options. (EG)

TEACHING TIP
Warn students that they can't just plug in every word in a thesaurus as if they were all interchangeable. If they're not confident about how a word should be used, they should look it up in a dictionary.

Thesaurus

A thesaurus gives synonyms (words that have the same meaning) for the word you look up. Like a dictionary, it comes in inexpensive editions. Use a thesaurus when you can't find the right word for what you mean.

Concrete, *adj.* **1.** Particular, specific, single, singular, certain, special, unique, sole, peculiar, individual, individualized; separate, isolated, distinct, discrete; exact, precise, direct, strict, minute; explicit, definite, express; plain, evident, manifest, obvious; pointed, marked, emphasized; restrictive, limiting, limited, bounded; determinate, well-defined, clear-cut, fixed, finite; determinative, determining, conclusive, decided; graphic, vivid, detailed, striking, telling.

—J. I. Rodale, *The Synonym Finder*

Practice Avoiding Five Language Pitfalls

A. Vague and Abstract Words

Your words need to create a clear, strong picture for your readers. Vague and abstract words are so general that your readers will not have a clear idea of what you mean. They are also dull. Here are some common vague and abstract words.

Vague and Abstract Words		
big	a lot	happy
small	very	sad
nice	pretty	house
good	beautiful	car
OK (okay)	dumb	school
bad	young	person
awful	old	job

When you see one of these words or a similarly general word in your writing, try to replace it with a concrete specific word. A **concrete** word names something that can be seen, heard, felt, tasted, or smelled. A **specific** word names a particular individual or quality. Compare these two sentences:

VAGUE AND ABSTRACT   A very old man went across the street.

CONCRETE AND SPECIFIC   An eighty-seven-year-old priest sprinted across Main Street.

The first version is too general to be interesting. The second version creates a clear, strong image.

Practice 1 ▶ Avoiding Vague and Abstract Words

In the following sentences, underline the vague, abstract words. Then edit to replace them with concrete, specific words. You can invent any details you like.

EXAMPLE: The beach where we vacationed was ~~beautiful.~~ *private, with fine white sand and grassy dunes.*

Answers will vary. Sample editing shown.

1. We ~~had a good time and a lot of fun.~~ *enjoyed swimming in the warm water.*

2. However, the place we stayed in was ~~awful.~~ *run-down and filthy.*

3. The food was ~~pretty bad, too.~~ *bland and overcooked.*

4. The people who rented the place next to ours ~~were old.~~ *had been retired for fifteen years.*

5. They ~~were friendly.~~ *invited us to have dinner with them.*

B. Slang

Slang is informal and casual language and should be used only in informal and casual situations. Avoid using slang when you write, and never use it in writing for college or work. Use language that is appropriate for your audience and purpose.

SLANG	EDITED
If I don't get this job, I'll be *bummed*.	If I don't get this job, I will be disappointed.
I would be *psyched* to work for this company.	I would welcome the chance to work for this company.
Getting this job would be really *phat*.	Getting this job would be exciting.

Practice 2 ▶ Avoiding Slang

In the following sentences, underline the slang. Then edit by replacing the slang with language appropriate for a formal audience and purpose. Imagine that you are writing to a supervisor at work.

EXAMPLE: I want to know why you have been ~~on my case so much~~ *so critical of me*

recently. *Answers will vary. Possible editing shown.*

1. I don't see why it is necessary for you to ~~chew me out~~ *reprimand me* so often.

2. During my last evaluation you asked me to ~~get my act together,~~ *improve my performance,* and I

   feel that I have done so.

3. I was really ~~fired up~~ *enthusiastic* about the last project I worked on.

4. I wish that our relationship could be more ~~laid back.~~ *relaxed.*

5. This is ~~an awesome~~ *a wonderful* place to work, and I'd like to ~~hang around~~ *remain* here for

   at least another year.

C. Stuffy Language

Sometimes when people write, they think that big or fancy words and overly formal language make them sound smart and their ideas sound more important. This is wrong. Stuffy language makes your writing more difficult to understand, and it often makes you sound unnatural or pretentious. Use straightforward language instead.

STUFFY

I will *utilize* this pan for cooking.

Reading will *maximize* your vocabulary *development*.

We will have to *abrogate* this contract.

EDITED

I will use this pan for cooking.

Reading will improve your vocabulary.

We will have to cancel this contract.

Practice 3   **Avoiding Stuffy Language**

In the following sentences, underline the words and phrases that are stuffy. Then edit by replacing them with straightforward language.

EXAMPLE: This agency ~~services~~ *helps* many groups through programs that most people are not even ~~cognizant of.~~ *aware of.*   *Answers will vary.*
Possible editing shown.

1. The superintendent announced, "Schools will ~~commence operation~~ *open* on August 28 this year."

2. She continued, "I have appointed a committee to ~~formulate a document~~ *write a report* on enrollment and special programs."

3. The committee will ~~contemplate the fiscal ramifications~~ *study the costs* of a preschool program.

4. The town will ~~enlist the expertise of~~ *hire* a consultant.

5. ~~In a cooperative endeavor,~~ *Working together,* the committee and the consultant will study programs that are not ~~exorbitant in cost.~~ *too expensive.*

D. Wordy Language

People sometimes use too many words for the same reason they use stuffy language: They think it sounds smart and important. But too many words can get in the way of your point and weaken it. Be concise.

COMPUTER
Students can use the computer's search or find function to locate these phrases (or others like them) in their writing.

WORDY

In the opinion of this writer, I think the directions are not clear.

In point of fact, they are impossible to understand.

I'm not interested *at this point in time*.

EDITED

I think the directions are not clear.

They are impossible to understand.

I'm not interested now.

TEACHING TIP
Encourage students to eliminate "I think," "I believe," and "I feel" from their writing. Tell them that readers assume the opinions are the writer's unless the writer credits someone else. (EG)

Common Wordy Expressions

WORDY	EDITED
As a result of	Because
Due to the fact that	Because
In spite of the fact that	Although
It is my opinion that	I think
In the event that	If
The fact of the matter is that	(*Just state the point.*)
A great number of	Many
At that time	Then
In this paper I will show that . . .	(*Just make the point; don't announce it.*)

DISCUSSION
Have students come up with at least five additional common wordy phrases.

▶ **Practice 4**   Avoiding Wordy Language

TEACHING TIP
As homework, have each student write at least two hundred words on an event that influenced them. In class, tell them they must cut at least ten words without losing any meaning. (BO)

In the following sentences, underline the wordy language. Then edit by replacing it with concise language.

EXAMPLE: Inflation occurred in the 1970s ~~due to the fact that~~ the price
  because
of oil rose sharply.

Answers will vary.
Possible editing shown.

1. During ~~this period of~~ time, ~~a great number of~~ countries suffered
     that   *many*

    economic hardship.

2. ~~In spite of the fact that~~ inflation normally accompanies economic
     Although

    growth, many economies ~~at this point in time~~ stagnated.
                                then

3. Economists had never before ~~at any point in the past~~ seen this combination of rising prices and stagnating growth.

4. They named this phenomenon, which ~~in their opinion~~ they believed represented a serious long-term danger, "stagflation."

5. "Stagflation" ~~came to a final end~~ *ended* in the early 1980s, when recession brought down inflation ~~to a significantly lower level.~~

E. Clichés

Certain phrases are used so often that people no longer pay attention to them. These phrases are clichés. To get your point across, you want your readers to pay attention to what you have written, so avoid clichés. Replace them with fresh language that precisely expresses your meaning.

CLICHÉS	EDITED
I can't *make ends meet*.	I don't have enough money to live on.
My uncle *worked his way up the corporate ladder*.	My uncle started as a shipping clerk but ended up managing his region's sales division.

ESL
Point out to students that some clichés are also idioms (phrases that cannot be understood by their literal meaning alone). Another reason to avoid clichés is that nonnative speakers may get the idiom wrong.

COMPUTER
Students can use the computer's search or find function to locate these phrases (or others like them) in their own writing.

Common Clichés

as big as a house	last but not least
the best/worst of all times	light as a feather
better late than never	no way on earth
break the ice	110 percent
the corporate ladder	playing with fire
crystal clear	spoiled brat
a drop in the bucket	spoiled rotten
easier said than done	starting from scratch
hard as a rock	sweating blood
hell on earth	work like a dog
	worked his/her way up

| Practice 5 | Avoiding Clichés |

In the following sentences, underline the clichés. Then edit by replacing them with fresh language that precisely expresses your meaning.

Answers will vary. Possible editing shown.

EXAMPLE: Riding a bicycle one hundred miles in a single day can be ~~hell~~ *excruciating* ~~on earth~~ unless you're willing to ~~give 110 percent.~~ *work extremely hard.*

1. You have to persuade yourself to ~~sweat blood and~~ ~~work like a dog~~ for *devote every bit of your strength to the challenge*

   up to ten hours.

2. ~~There's no way on earth you can~~ do it without extensive training. *It's impossible to*

3. Staying on your bike until ~~the bitter end,~~ of course, is ~~easier said than~~ ~~done.~~ *the very last mile,* *an enormously* *difficult task.*

4. The important thing is that you ~~still have the fire in your belly~~ and *maintain your determination*

   that you're able to keep your goal of finishing the race ~~crystal clear~~ in *always present*

   your mind.

5. No matter how long it takes you to cross the finish line, remind your-

   self that ~~it's better late than never.~~ *finishing at all is a tremendous achievement.*

TEAMWORK
In small groups, have students write five sentences with clichés other than those given here. Each group should exchange paragraphs with another group and edit the sentences to eliminate the clichés.

Edit Paragraphs and Your Own Writing

| Practice 6 | Editing Paragraphs for Word Choice |

Find and edit any examples of vague and abstract language, slang, stuffy language, wordy language, or clichés in the following paragraphs. You may want to refer to the Summary on page 406.

Answers will vary. Possible editing shown.

(1) Throughout recorded history, ~~the human populace has~~ done *people have* ~~bad~~ things to the environment. (2) For example, the need for firewood *devastating* ~~really screwed up~~ the forests of Europe. (3) ~~Due to the fact that~~ char- *destroyed* *Because*

coal has a high carbon-to-hydrogen ratio, the burning of wood is a

dirty and inefficient source of fuel. (4) Coal was ~~utilized~~ *used* as an alterna-

tive, but ~~as we know,~~ coal is ~~not so nice either.~~ *also harmful to the environment.* (5) ~~At this point in time~~

~~when~~ *When* oil furnaces began to replace coal furnaces, the air in many cities

slowly became somewhat cleaner.

(6) ~~Another thing that blows my mind is that~~ *Amazingly,* whales were the

main source of fuel for lamps for much of the nineteenth century.

(7) Each year, thousands of sperm whales were ~~apprehended and ter-~~ *killed,*

~~minated,~~ until ~~the time came when~~ they were almost extinct. (8) When

petroleum oil was discovered in 1859, people thought that their energy

problems were over~~forever after.~~ (9) However, ~~in my opinion I feel that~~

our dependence on oil is a ~~big-time~~ *significant* problem. (10) During the energy

crisis of the 1970s, for example, we really had to ~~bite the bullet.~~ *restrict our fuel consumption.* (11) It

is ~~dumb~~ *foolish* to continue to use fossil fuels when scientists have ~~demon-~~ *shown*

~~strated~~ that they contribute to global warming.

Practice 7 ▶ Editing Your Own Writing for Word Choice

LEARNING JOURNAL
Which language pitfall do you get trapped by most often? Why do you think you have this problem? How can you avoid it in your writing?

    As a final practice, edit a piece of your own writing for word choice. It can be a paper you are working on for this course, a paper you've already finished, a paper for another course, or a recent piece of writing from your work or everyday life. Record in your learning journal any problem sentences you find, along with their corrections. You may want to use the Summary on page 406.

Summary and Quick Review Chart: Word Choice

- In writing, you have only your words to express your meaning, so choose them carefully. (See p. 397.)
- A **dictionary** and a **thesaurus** will help you choose words. (See p. 398.)
- Avoid these five language pitfalls:
    - **Vague and abstract words:** These create a general, uninteresting picture. Use concrete, specific words instead. (See p. 398.)
    - **Slang:** Slang is too casual and informal for college writing. Replace it with language appropriate for your audience and purpose. (See p. 400.)
    - **Stuffy language:** Overly fancy or formal language usually sounds pretentious and confusing, not important or intelligent. Use straightforward language instead. (See p. 400.)
    - **Wordy language:** Too many words can get in the way of your meaning. Be concise. (See p. 401.)
    - **Clichés:** Replace overused phrases with fresh words that precisely express your meaning. (See p. 403.)

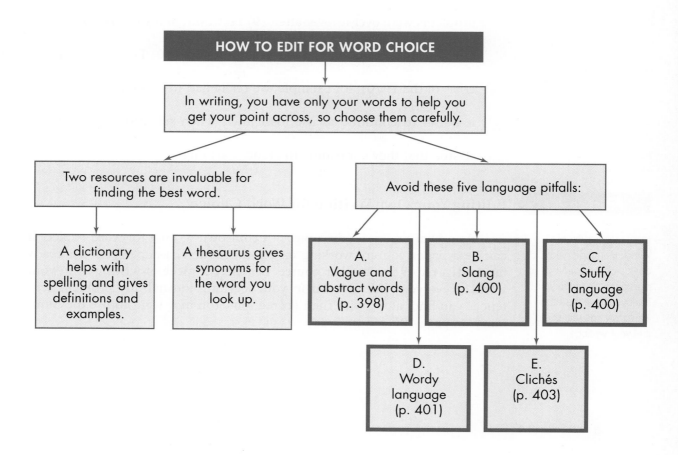

34

Commonly Confused Words

Avoiding Mistakes with Sound-Alikes

TIP: To understand this chapter, you need to know what *nouns, verbs, adjectives,* and *adverbs* are. For review, see Chapter 21.

Understand Why Certain Words Are Commonly Confused

RESOURCES
Additional Resources contains tests and supplemental practice exercises for this chapter.

People confuse certain words in English because they sound alike and often mean similar things. In speech, words that sound alike are not a problem. But in writing, words that sound alike may be spelled differently, and people rely on the spelling to understand what you mean. When you use a word that sounds like the one you want but is spelled differently and has a different meaning, it will confuse your reader. Edit your writing carefully to make sure that you have used the correct word.

1. Proofread carefully, using techniques discussed on page 421.
2. Use a dictionary to look up any words you are unsure about.
3. Focus on finding and correcting mistakes you make with the twenty-two sets of commonly confused words covered in this chapter.
4. Develop a personal list of words you confuse often. In your learning journal or on an index card, record the words that you confuse in your writing, and write their meanings. Before you turn in any piece of writing, consult your personal list to make sure you have used the words on it correctly.

LEARNING JOURNAL
Use your learning journal as a place to start a personal list of words you commonly confuse. When you edit your papers, be sure to check for words on your personal list.

Practice Using Commonly Confused Words Correctly

Study the different meanings and spellings of these twenty-two sets of commonly confused words. Complete the sentences after each set of words using the correct word.

A/An/And

a: used before a word that begins with a consonant sound

A friend of mine just won the lottery.

an: used before a word that begins with a vowel sound

An old friend just won the lottery.

and: used to join two words

My friend *and* I went out to celebrate.

*A friend *and* I ate at *an* Italian restaurant.*

Other lottery winners were ___*an*___ old farmer ___*and*___ ___*a*___ bowling team.

Accept/Except

accept: to agree to receive or admit (verb)

I will *accept* the job offer.

except: but, other than

All the stores are closed *except* the Quik-Stop.

I *accept* all the job conditions *except* the low pay.

Do not ___*accept*___ gifts from clients ___*except*___ those who are also personal friends.

Advice/Advise

advice: opinion (noun)

I would like your *advice* before I make a decision.

advise: to give an opinion (verb)

 Please *advise* me what to do.

Please *advise* me what to do; you always give me good *advice*.

If you don't like my _____*advice*_____, please _____*advise*_____ me how to

proceed.

Affect/Effect

affect: to make an impact on, to change something (verb)

 The whole city was *affected* by the hurricane.

effect: a result (noun)

 What *effect* will the hurricane have on the local economy?

Although the storm will have many bad *effects*, it will not *affect* the
price of food.

The _____*effect*_____ of the disaster will _____*affect*_____ many people.

Are/Our

are: a form of the verb *be*

 The workers *are* about to go on strike.

our: a pronoun showing ownership

 The children played on *our* porch.

My relatives *are* staying at *our* house.

_____*Our*_____ new neighbors _____*are*_____ moving in today.

Conscience/Conscious

conscience: a personal sense of right and wrong (noun)

 Jake's *conscience* wouldn't allow him to cheat.

conscious: awake, aware (adjective)

 The coma patient is now *conscious*.

I am *conscious* that it's getting late.

The judge was *conscious* that the accused had acted according to his *conscience* even though he broke the law.

The man said he was not _____conscious_____ that what he had done was illegal

or his _____conscience_____ would not have let him do it.

Its / It's

its: pronoun showing ownership

The dog chased *its* tail.

it's: a contraction of the words *it is*

***It's* about time you got here.**

It's very hard for a dog to keep *its* teeth clean.

_____It's_____ surprising that the college lowered _____its_____ tuition.

Knew / New / Know / No

knew: understood; recognized (past tense of the verb *know*)

I *knew* the answer, but I couldn't think of it.

new: unused, recent (adjective)

The building has a *new* security code.

know: to understand, to have knowledge of (verb)

I *know* the answer, but I can't think of it.

no: used to form a negative

I have *no* idea what the answer is.

I never *knew* how much a *new* car costs.

The _____new_____ teacher _____knew_____ many of her students already.

There is *no* way Tom could *know* where Celia is hiding.

I _____know_____ that there is _____no_____ cake left.

Loose/Lose

loose: baggy, not fixed in place (adjective)

In hot weather, people tend to wear *loose* clothing.

lose: to misplace, to forfeit possession of (verb)

Every summer I *lose* about three pairs of sunglasses.

If the ring is too *loose* on your finger, you might *lose* it.

I _____*lose*_____ my patience with _____*loose*_____ rules in schools.

Of/Have

of: coming from; caused by; part of a group; away from; made from (preposition)

The leader *of* the band played bass guitar.

have: to possess (verb). Also used as a helping verb.

I *have* one more course to take before I graduate.

I should *have* started studying earlier.

Note: Do not use *of* after *would, should, could,* and *might.* Use *have* after those words.

If I'd known we were out *of* coffee, I would *have* bought some.

Sidney could _____*have*_____ been one _____*of*_____ the winners.

Passed/Past

passed: went by or went ahead (past tense of the verb *pass*)

We *passed* the hospital on the way to the airport.

past: time that has gone by (noun); gone by, over, in front of

In the *past,* I was able to stay up all night and not be tired.

The snow fell *past* my window.

This *past* school year, I *passed* all of my exams.

Trish _____*passed*_____ me as we ran _____*past*_____ the one-mile marker.

Peace/Piece

peace: no disagreement; calm

> **Could you all quiet down and give me a little *peace?***

piece: a part of something larger

> **May I have a *piece* of that pie?**

The feuding families found *peace* after they sold the *piece* of land.

To keep the _____*peace*_____, give your sister a _____*piece*_____ of candy.

Principal/Principle

principal: chief, head of a school (noun); main (adjective)

> **Corinne is a *principal* in the management consulting firm.**
>
> **Ms. Edwards is the *principal* of Bolton Elementary School.**

principle: a standard of beliefs or behaviors (noun)

> **Although tempted, she held on to her moral *principles*.**

The *principal* questioned the delinquent student's *principles*.

The_____*principal*_____problem is that you want me to act against

my_____*principles*_____.

Quiet/Quite/Quit

quiet: soft in sound; not noisy (adjective)

> **The library was very *quiet*.**

quite: completely, very (adverb)

> **After the marathon, the eighty-year-old runner was *quite* tired.**

quit: to stop (verb)

> **She *quit* her job.**

After the band *quit* playing, the hall was *quite quiet*.

If you would_____*quit*_____shouting and be_____*quiet*_____, you would

find that the scenery is_____*quite*_____pleasant.

Right/Write/Rite

right: correct; in a direction opposite from left (adjective)

> **You definitely made the *right* choice.**

> **When you get to the stoplight, make a *right* turn.**

write: to put words on paper (verb)

> **Will you *write* your phone number for me?**

rite: a ritual (noun)

> **Getting a driver's license at age sixteen is a common *rite* of passage.**

Please *write* the *right* answer in the space provided.

You were _____*right*_____ to _____*write*_____ a letter of complaint about the

practice of hazing; it is a barbaric _____*rite*_____ .

Than/Then

than: word used to compare two or more things or persons

> **It's colder inside *than* outside.**

then: at a certain time

> **I got out of the car and *then* realized the keys were still in it.**

Clara ran more miles *than* she ever had before, and *then* she collapsed.

Back_____*then*_____ I smoked more _____*than*_____ three packs a day.

Their/There/They're

their: a pronoun showing ownership

> **I borrowed *their* jumper cables to start the car.**

there: a word indicating placement or existence

> **Just put the package *there* on the desk.**

> ***There* are too many lawyers.**

they're: a contraction of the words *they are*

> ***They're* about to leave.**

Their home entertainment center placed *there* in the middle of the room indicates that *they're* interested in media.

_____*Their*_____ beach house is empty except for the one week that

_____*they're*_____ vacationing _____*there*_____ .

Though / Through / Threw

though: however; nevertheless; in spite of

> ***Though* he's short, he plays great basketball.**

through: finished with (adjective); from one side to the other (preposition)

> **I'm *through* arguing with you.**

> **The baseball went right *through* the window.**

threw: hurled, tossed (past tense of the verb *throw*)

> **She *threw* the basketball.**

Even *though* it was illegal, she *threw* the empty cup *through* the window onto the road.

_____*Though*_____ she didn't really believe it would bring good luck, Jan

_____*threw*_____ a penny _____*through*_____ the air into the fountain.

To / Too / Two

to: a word indicating a direction or movement (preposition); part of the infinitive form of a verb

> **Please give the message *to* Sharon.**

> **It is easier *to* ask for forgiveness than *to* get permission.**

too: also; more than enough (adverb)

> **I'm tired *too*.**

> **Dan ate *too* much and felt sick.**

two: the number between one and three

> **There were only *two* computers in the lab.**

They went out *to* a restaurant and ordered *too* much food for *two* people.

When Marty went _____*to*_____ pay for his meal, the cashier charged him

_____*two*_____ dollars _____*too*_____ much.

Use/Used

use: to employ or utilize (verb)

> **How do you plan to *use* that blueprint?**

used: past tense of the verb *use*. *Used to* can indicate a past fact or state, or it can mean "familiar with."

> **He *used* his lunch hour to do errands.**

> **He *used* to go for a jog during his lunch hour.**

She *used to* be a chef so she knows how to *use* all kinds of kitchen gadgets. She is also *used to* improvising in the kitchen.

Tom _____*used*_____ the prize money to buy a fancy car; his family hoped

he would _____*use*_____ it for his education.

Who's/Whose

who's: a contraction of the words *who is*

> ***Who's* at the door?**

whose: a pronoun showing ownership

> ***Whose* shoes are these?**

Who's the person *whose* car sank in the river?

The student _____*whose*_____ name is first on the list is the one

_____*who's*_____ in charge.

Your/You're

your: a pronoun showing ownership

> **Did you bring *your* wallet?**

you're: a contraction of the words *you are*

You're not telling me the whole story.

***You're* going to have *your* third exam tomorrow.**

_____*Your*_____ teacher says _____*you're*_____ very good with numbers.

> **Practice 1**   Using the Right Word

In each of the following items, circle the correct word in parentheses.

1. I just can't (accept/except) your decision.
2. She (use/used) to live right next door.
3. (Their/There/They're) on (their/there/they're) way to the mountains.
4. The baby has more toys (than/then) he knows what to do with.
5. You should always act in accordance with your (principals/principles).
6. After cheating on the test, she had a very guilty (conscience/conscious).
7. His greed (knows/nos) (know/no) bounds.
8. Are you going to (your/you're) class today?
9. I should (of/have) left (are/our) car at the garage.
10. I think it's going to be (a/an) horrible day.

Edit Paragraphs and Your Own Writing

> **Practice 2**   Editing Paragraphs for Commonly Confused Words

Edit the following paragraphs to ensure that commonly confused words are used correctly.

(1) More and more women are purchasing handguns, against the
advice
~~advise~~ of law enforcement officers. (2) Few of these women are crimi-
                                                        know
nals or plan to commit crimes. (3) They ~~no~~ the risks of guns, and they

accept those risks. (4) They buy weapons primarily because ~~their~~ *they're* tired

of feeling like victims. (5) They don't want to contribute ~~too~~ *to* the vio-

lence in ~~are~~ *our* society, but they also realize that women are the victims of

violent attacks far ~~to~~ *too* often. (6) Many women ~~loose they're~~ *lose their* lives because

they can't fight off their attackers. (7) Some have made a ~~conscience~~ *conscious*

decision to arm themselves for protection. (8) The National Rifle Asso-

ciation (NRA) has even produced a series of advertisements with this

aim as ~~it's~~ *its* main message.

(9) But critics question if women buying guns has made things

worse rather ~~then~~ *than* better. (10) Having a gun in your house makes it

three times as likely that someone will be killed there—and that some-

one is just as likely to be the woman herself or her children as ~~a~~ *an* as-

sailant. (11) Most young children can't tell the difference between a

real gun and a play one. (12) Every year, ~~their~~ *there* are tragic examples of

children who accidentally shoot and even kill other youngsters while

they are "playing" with guns. (13) A mother ~~who's~~ *whose* children are injured

while "playing" with her gun will never again think that a gun provides

~~piece~~ *peace* of mind. (14) Reducing the violence in our society—not redis-

tributing it—may be a better solution.

Practice 3 ➤ Editing Your Own Writing for Commonly Confused Words

As a final practice, edit a piece of your own writing for commonly confused words. It can be a paper you are working on for this course, a paper
you've already finished, a paper for another course, or a recent piece of writing from your work or everyday life. Add any misused words you find to
your personal list of words you confuse most often. You may want to use the
Summary on page 418.

Summary: Commonly Confused Words

- Certain words are commonly confused because they sound alike but are spelled differently. It is important to use the right word; otherwise, your readers may be confused.

- Editing for the most commonly confused words and learning to use them correctly will greatly improve your writing.

TEACHING TIP
Ask students for a few more commonly confused words. Start them off by putting one pair on the board and then list others that they suggest.

- Here are the twenty-two sets of the most commonly confused words.

a / an / and	peace / piece
accept / except	principal / principle
advice / advise	quiet / quite / quit
affect / effect	right / write / rite
are / our	than / then
conscience / conscious	their / there / they're
its / it's	though / through / threw
knew / new / know / no	to / too / two
loose / lose	use / used
of / have	who's / whose
passed / past	your / you're

35

Spelling
Using the Right Letters

Two Important Tools: Dictionary and Spelling List
Three Steps for Finding and Correcting Mistakes
Four Strategies for Becoming a Better Speller

Some very smart people are very poor spellers. Unfortunately, spelling errors are generally easy for readers to spot—and they make a bad impression. In fact, spelling errors can be considered the fifth most serious error that writers can make. Successful, smart writers who are also poor spellers learn to find and correct their spelling errors before they submit any formal writing. If you are not a good speller, you need to do this too.

Two Important Tools: Dictionary and Spelling List

If you are serious about improving your spelling, you need to have a dictionary and a spelling list and use them.

Dictionary

A dictionary contains the correct spellings of words, along with information on how they are pronounced, what they mean, and where they came from. Buy a dictionary; everyone needs one. When editing your papers, use a dictionary whenever you are unsure about the spelling of a word. **Learning to check the dictionary is the single most important thing you can do to improve your spelling.**

TIP: For a sample dictionary entry, see page 398.

Buy a current dictionary rather than an old one because current editions have current definitions and words that are new to the language (such as *Internet, downsizing, byte,* and *Web page,* for example). If you have trouble finding words in a regular dictionary, get a spelling dictionary, which is designed to help you find a word even if you have no idea how to spell it.

Spelling List

Most people misspell the same words over and over. A spelling list will show you what your problem areas are and will help you improve them.

Set aside a section of your course notebook for your spelling list. Every time you edit a paper, write down all the words that you misspelled. Put the correct spelling first, and then in parentheses put the way you actually wrote it. After you have recorded the spelling errors for three pieces of writing, spend ten minutes analyzing your spelling list. Ask yourself:

TEACHING TIP
Ask students to write on a scrap of paper a word they often misspell. Collect the pieces of paper and make up a list of class spelling demons.

- What words have I misspelled more than once?
- What do I get wrong about them? Do I always misspell them the same way?
- What are my personal spelling "demons"? ("Demons" are the five to ten words that you tend to spell wrong over and over.)
- Are there any other mistakes that I tend to make over and over (leaving the final -*s* off words, for example)?

TEACHING TIP
Telling students they will have to turn in their spelling lists reinforces the importance of their making one. If you have time, you can make up individualized spelling quizzes.

Write your demon words (five to ten words), spelled correctly, on an index card and keep it somewhere handy so that you can consult the card whenever you write.

Every couple of weeks, go back to your spelling list to see if your problem areas have changed. Are you misspelling fewer words in each paper? What are your current spelling demons? Keeping and using a spelling list may sound like a lot of extra work, but if you do it constantly, your spelling will certainly improve.

TEACHING TIP
Tell students to take a moment to make a mental picture of their spelling demons; they should visualize the words spelled correctly. (SG)

Three Steps for Finding and Correcting Mistakes

Every time you write a paper, you need to edit it for spelling. To edit for spelling, you need to focus on spelling. Don't try to correct your grammar or improve your message at the same time. Remember to check the dictionary whenever you are unsure about the spelling of a word and to add all the spelling mistakes you find to your personal spelling list.

COMPUTER
Tell students to use the spell checker before they proofread.

Step 1. Use a Spell Checker

If you use a word processor, it probably has a spell checker. A spell checker finds and highlights a word that may be misspelled, suggests other spellings, and gives you the opportunity to change the spelling of the word. Use this feature after you have completed a piece of writing but before you print it out.

ESL
Tell students that many words in English aren't spelled as they sound. Also warn students that some English words may be similar in sound and meaning to words in their first language, but they may be spelled slightly differently.

Never rely on the spell checker to do your editing for you. A spell checker ignores anything it recognizes as a word, so it will not help you find words that are misused or misspellings that are also words. For example, a spell checker would not highlight any problems in these phrases:

Just *to* it.   (Correct: *Just do it.*)

pain in the *nick*   (Correct: *pain in the neck*)

my writing *coarse* (Correct: *my writing course*)

Step 2. Use Proofreading Techniques

Proofreading is reading to find and correct errors. Use some of the following proofreading techniques to focus on the spelling of one word at a time. Different techniques work for different people, so try them all and then decide which ones work for you.

PROOFREADING TECHNIQUES

- Put a piece of paper under the line that you are reading.
- Cut a "window" in an index card that is about the size of a long word (such as *misunderstanding*) and place it over your writing to focus on one word at a time.
- Proofread your paper backwards, one word at a time.
- If you are using a word processor, print out a version of your paper that looks noticeably different: Make the words larger, make the margins larger, triple-space the lines, or do all of these.
- Read your paper aloud. This will help if you tend to leave words out.
- Exchange papers with a partner and proofread your partner's paper. You should only identify possible misspellings. The writer of the paper should be responsible for checking the spelling and correcting any mistakes.

Step 3. Check Your Personal Spelling List

After you have proofread each word in your paper, look at your personal spelling list and your list of demon words one more time. Have you used any of these words in your paper? If so, go back and check their spelling again. You may be surprised to find that you missed seeing the same old spelling mistakes.

Practice 1 Using the Three Steps for Finding and Correcting Mistakes

Take the last paper you wrote—or one that you are working on now—and use the three steps for finding and correcting spelling mistakes. How many spelling mistakes did you find? Were you surprised? How was the experience different from what you normally do to edit for spelling? How confident are you that your paper now contains no spelling mistakes?

Four Strategies for Becoming a Better Speller

Learning to find and correct spelling mistakes that you have already made is only half the battle. You also need to become a better speller so that you do not make so many mistakes in the first place. Here are four strategies.

Strategy 1. Master Ten Troublemakers

The ten words in the following list were identified by writing teachers around the United States as the words most commonly misspelled by students of all ages and backgrounds. Master these, and you will be ahead of the crowd. Because there are only ten, you should be able to learn them.

Phrases related to the spelling of the word can help people remember the correct spellings. Silly as these memory aids may seem, they can work, so try them.

TROUBLEMAKERS	COMMON MISSPELLINGS	MEMORY AIDS
1. **a lot**	alot	means more than one and is more than one word
2. **develop**	develope	*lop* off the *e*
3. **receive**	recieve	*i* before *e* except after *c*, or when sounded like *a*, as in *neighbor* or *weigh*
4. **separate**	seperate	there's *a rat* in there
5. **until**	untill	sounds like *one l*
6. **light**	lite	
7. **necessary**	necesary, nesesary	
8. **argument**	arguement	
9. **definite**	definate, defenite	
10. **surprise**	surprize	

Practice 2 ▶ **Creating Memory Aids for the Troublemakers**

Create memory aids for the other five troublemakers in the list.

light

Answers will vary.

necessary

argument
_____

definite
_____

surprise
_____

Strategy 2. Master Your Personal Spelling Demons

Once you know what your spelling demons are, you can start to conquer them. If your list of spelling demons is long, you may want to start by focusing on the top five or the top three. When you have mastered these, you can go on to the next few. Different techniques work for different people. Try them all and then stick with the ones that work for you.

- Create a memory aid, as you did for the ten troublemakers.
- Break the word into parts and try to master each part. You can break it into syllables (*Feb ru ar y*) or separate the prefixes and endings (*dis ap point ment*).
- Write the word (*correctly*) ten times.
- Say the letters of the word out loud. See if there's a rhythm or a rhyme you can memorize.
- Write a paragraph in which you use the word at least three times.
- Say the word out loud, emphasizing each letter and syllable — even if that's not the way you normally say it. For example, say *pro bab ly* instead of *prob ly.* Try to pronounce the word this way in your head each time you spell it.
- Ask a partner to give you a spelling test.

Strategy 3. Master Commonly Confused Words

Chapter 34 covers twenty-two sets of words that are commonly confused because they sound similar, such as *write* and *right* or *its* and *it's.* If you can master these commonly confused words, you will avoid many spelling mistakes.

Strategy 4. Learn Six Spelling Rules

The questions and rules in this chapter cover spelling situations in which people often hesitate and think, What do I do here? If you can remember the rules, you can correct many of the spelling errors in your writing.

Before the six rules, here is a quick review of vowels and consonants:

Vowels: *a, e, i, o, u*

Consonants are all the letters that are *not* vowels: *b, c, d, f, g, h, j, k, l, m, n, p, q, r, s, t, v, w, x, z*

The letter *y* can be either a vowel or a consonant. It is a vowel when it sounds like the *y* in *fly* or *hungry*. It is a consonant when it sounds like the *y* in *yellow*.

IE *or* EI?

RULE **1** *I* before *e*
Except after *c*,
Or when sounded like *a*
As in *neighbor* or *weigh*.

Many people repeat this rhyme to themselves as they decide whether a word is spelled with an *ie* or an *ei*.

piece (*i* before *e*)

rec**ei**ve (except after *c*)

eight (it sounds like *a*)

EXCEPTIONS: *either, neither, foreign, height, seize, society, their, weird*

▶ Practice 3 ▶ **Using Rule 1**

In the spaces provided, write more examples of words that follow the rule. Do not use the words that have already been covered.

Answers will vary. Possible answers shown.

1. *niece*

2. *siege*

3. *believe*

4. *deceive*

5. *freight*

6. *sieve*

Drop the Final E *or Keep It?*

RULE **2** **Drop the final *e*** when adding an ending that begins with a vowel.

hop**e** + **i**ng = hoping

imagin**e** + **a**tion = imagination

Keep the final *e* when adding an ending that begins with a consonant.

> achiev**e** + **m**ent = achievement
>
> definit**e** + **l**y = definitely

EXCEPTIONS: *argument, truly, awful, simply,* and others

Practice 4 ▸ **Using Rule 2**

For each item, circle the first letter in the ending, and decide whether it is a consonant or a vowel. Then add the ending to the word and write the new word in the space.

1. peace + (f)ul = *peaceful*

2. separate + (l)y = *separately*

3. believe + (i)ng = *believing*

4. schedule + (e)d = *scheduled*

5. value + (a)ble = *valuable*

6. write + (i)ng = *writing*

7. pure + (e)r = *purer*

8. create + (i)ve = *creative*

9. shame + (f)ul = *shameful*

10. converse + (a)tion = *conversation*

Change the **Y** *to* **I,** *or Not?*

RULE 3   When adding an ending, **change the *y* to *i*** when a consonant comes before the *y.*

> lone**l**y + est = loneli̇est
>
> hap**p**y + er = happi̇er
>
> apolo**g**y + ize = apologi̇ze
>
> like**l**y + hood = likeli̇hood

Do not change the *y* when a vowel comes before the *y.*

> b**o**y + ish = boyish
>
> p**a**y + ment = payment
>
> surv**e**y + or = surveyor
>
> b**u**y + er = buyer

EXCEPTIONS: 1. When adding *-ing* to a word ending in *y*, always keep the *y.*

2. *daily, dryer, said, paid,* and others

| Practice 5 | Using Rule 3 |

For each item, circle the letter before the *y*, and decide whether it is a vowel or a consonant. Then add the ending to the word and write the new word in the spaces provided.

1. pl(a)y + ful = *playful*

2. pl(i)y + ers = *pliers*

3. comed(i)y + an = *comedian*

4. carr(i)y + er = *carrier*

5. def(i)y + ant = *defiant*

6. pl(a)y + ed = *played*

7. bur(i)y + al = *burial*

8. merr(i)y + ment = *merriment*

9. puff(i)y + ness = *puffiness*

10. pr(a)y + ers = *prayers*

Should the Final Consonant Be Doubled?

RULE **4** When adding an ending that starts with a vowel to a one-syllable word, follow these rules.

Double the final consonant only if the word ends with a consonant-vowel-consonant.

> tr**ap** + ed = tra**pp**ed
> oc**cur** + ence = occu**rr**ence
> pre**fer** + ed = prefe**rr**ed
> com**mit** + ed = commi**tt**ed

Do not double the final consonant if the word ends with some other combination.

VOWEL-VOWEL-CONSONANT	VOWEL-CONSONANT-CONSONANT
cl**ean** + est = clean**e**st	sl**ick** + er = slicker
p**oor** + er = poorer	te**ach** + er = teacher
cl**ear** + ed = cleared	l**ast** + ed = lasted

RULE **5** When adding an ending that starts with a vowel to a word with two or more syllables, follow these rules.

TIP: The syllable you "stress" is the one you say with most emphasis.

Double the final consonant only if the word ends with a consonant-vowel-consonant *and* the stress is on the last syllable.

> sub**mit** + ing = submi**tt**ing
> con**trol** + er = contro**ll**er
> ad**mit** + ed = admi**tt**ed

Do not double the final consonant in other cases.

problem + atic = proble**m**atic

understand + ing = understan**d**ing

offer + ed = offe**r**ed

Using Rules 4 and 5

For each item, circle the last three letters in the word, and decide whether they fit the consonant-vowel-consonant pattern. In words with more than one syllable, underline the stressed syllable. Then add the ending to the words and write the new word in the space provided.

1. lift + ed = _lifted_

2. happen + ed = _happened_

3. command + er = _commander_

4. omit + ed = _omitted_

5. cheap + er = _cheaper_

6. disgust + ing = _disgusting_

7. spot + ed = _spotted_

8. slip + ery = _slippery_

9. scrap + ed = _scrapped_

10. return + able = _returnable_

Add -S or -ES?

The endings *-s* and *-es* are used to make the plural form of most nouns (*two books*) and the *he/she/it* form of most verbs (*he runs*).

RULE **6**   **Add -*s*** to most words and words that end in *o* preceded by a vowel.

MOST WORDS	WORDS THAT END IN VOWEL PLUS *O*
book + **s** = books	vid**eo** + **s** = videos
college + **s** = colleges	ster**eo** + **s** = stereos
jump + **s** = jumps	rad**io** + **s** = radios

Add -*es* to words that end in *o* preceded by a consonant and words that end in *s, sh, ch,* or *x.*

WORDS THAT END IN CONSONANT PLUS *O*	WORDS THAT END IN *S, SH, CH,* OR *X*
pota**to** + **es** = potatoes	class + **es** = classes
he**ro** + **es** = heroes	push + **es** = pushes
go + **es** = goes	ben**ch** + **es** = benches
	fax + **es** = faxes

EXCEPTIONS: *pianos, solos,* and others

| Practice 7 | **Using Rule 6** |

For each word, circle the last two letters and decide which of the patterns this word fits (most words, vowel plus *o*, consonant plus *o* or *s* / *sh* / *ch* / *x*). Add *-s* or *-es* and write the new word in the space provided.

1. address — *addresses*

2. bicycle — *bicycles*

3. tomato — *tomatoes*

4. church — *churches*

5. stretch — *stretches*

6. studio — *studios*

7. dash — *dashes*

8. construct — *constructs*

9. discover — *discovers*

10. box — *boxes*

Seventy-Five Commonly Misspelled Words

Use this list as an easy reference to check your spelling.

absence	definite	humorous	rhythm
achieve	describe	illegal	roommate
across	different	immediately	schedule
a lot	disappoint	interest	secretary
already	dollar	jewelry	separate
analyze	embarrass	judgment	sincerely
answer	environment	knowledge	sophomore
argument	especially	license	succeed
athlete	exaggerate	loneliness	successful
awful	excellent	meant	surprise
basically	exercise	necessary	truly
beginning	fascinate	noticeable	until
business	February	occasion	usually
calendar	finally	occurrence	vegetable
career	foreign	perform	weight
coming	friend	prejudice	weird
commitment	government	probably	writing
conscious	harass	receive	written
convenient	height	recognize	

Edit Paragraphs and Your Own Writing

Practice 8   Editing Paragraphs for Spelling

Find and correct any spelling mistakes in the following paragraphs.

(1) In today's schools, there is a ~~rageing~~ *raging* argument about whether to ~~seperate~~ *separate* children of different ~~abilitys~~ *abilities* into classes with others of similar ~~achievment~~ *achievement* levels. (2) Some experts claim that children ~~develope~~ *develop* and learn best when they are in mixed-ability classes. (3) These same experts state that ~~divideing~~ *dividing* students will ~~prejudise~~ *prejudice* teachers against the slower students. (4) When students of lesser ability are grouped together, they don't learn as fast, their self-esteem drops, their ~~absenses~~ *absences* increase, and they may drop out. (5) ~~Basicaly,~~ *Basically,* the experts claim, students lose all motivation to ~~acheive.~~ *achieve.*

(6) Other experts present another side of the ~~arguement.~~ *argument.* (7) They say that grouping by ability allows students to learn at a more natural rate. (8) Teachers ~~usally~~ *usually* have ~~alot~~ *a lot* more time to spend with students because they aren't trying to teach students of all abilities. (9) For example, if students with similar writing skills are together in a class, the teacher either can spend a lot of time with grammar if the class needs it or can skip over it if the students have mastered the basic rules. (10) These experts claim that grouping by ability provides a more efficient learning environment, gets a good class ~~rythym~~ *rhythm* going, and results in the ~~happyest,~~ *happiest,* most enthusiastic learners.

interesting,
(11) Both sides have ~~intresting,~~ persuasive arguments that they
                     ^
                                        government
present to local, state, and federal ~~goverment~~ officials. (12) So far,
                                          ^
neither side has persuaded the other, and the heated debate continues.

| Practice 9 ▶ | Editing Your Own Writing for Spelling |

As a final practice, edit a piece of your own writing for spelling, using the techniques described in this chapter. It can be a paper you are working on for this course, a paper you've already finished, a paper for another course, or a recent piece of writing from your work or everyday life. Record in your learning journal any mistakes you find, along with their corrections.

Summary: Spelling

- Correct spelling is important and easy to master.
- **Two important tools** for good spelling are a dictionary and a personal spelling list. (See p. 419.)
- **Three steps for finding and correcting spelling mistakes** are using a spell checker, using proofreading techniques, and checking your personal spelling list every time you edit for spelling. (See pp. 420–21.)
- **Four strategies for becoming a better speller** are mastering ten troublemakers, mastering your personal spelling demons, mastering commonly confused words, and learning six spelling rules. (See pp. 422–24.)

EDITING

Part Eight

Punctuation and Capitalization

36

Commas

TIP: To understand this chapter, you need to know what *nouns, sentences, phrases,* and *clauses* are. If you need to review, see Chapter 21.

LEARNING JOURNAL
Use your learning journal as a place to record sentences with comma problems. Also record edited versions of these sentences, with the problems corrected.

TEACHING TIP
To make sure that students understand the differences among the sentences, have a student read each aloud and ask what the meaning is.

Understand What Commas Do

Commas (,) are punctuation marks that help readers understand a sentence. Read aloud the following three sentences. How does the use of commas change the meaning of the words?

NO COMMA	When you call Sarah I'll start cooking.
ONE COMMA	When you call Sarah, I'll start cooking.
TWO COMMAS	When you call, Sarah, I'll start cooking.

RESOURCES
Additional Resources contains tests and supplemental exercises for this chapter.

Using commas correctly helps your readers understand what you mean. When you use a comma in a sentence, it signals a particular meaning to your readers, so it is important that you understand when and how to use it.

Practice Using Commas Correctly

TIP: How does a comma change the way you read the sentence aloud? Most readers pause when they come to a comma.

A. Commas between Items in a Series

Use commas to separate the items in a series (three or more items). This includes the last item in the series, which usually has *and* before it.

ESL
Because different languages have different intonation patterns, students should not rely on intonation alone to decide where to put commas.

I *work, go to school,* and *take care of my family.*

To get from South Dakota to Texas, we will drive through *Nebraska, Kansas,* and *Oklahoma.*

We can *sleep in the car, stay in a motel,* or *camp outside.*

Practice 1 ▶ **Using Commas in Series**

Edit the following sentences by adding commas where they are needed in the series. If a sentence is already correct, put a "C" next to it.

EXAMPLE: Sales of our fruit juices have expanded in the Northeast,the
                                                                    ^
South,and the Midwest.
       ^

1. Continued expansion relies on our ability to promote novelty
    beverages such as papaya,mango,and boysenberry juices in grocery
                            ^   ^
    stores and restaurants.

2. We also present juice as an alternative to beverages such as soda,beer,
                                                                     ^   ^
    and water.

3. In Washington and northern California we are already doing well
    against our major competitors.   *C*

4. In these areas our increase in market share over the past three years

    has been 7 percent, 10 percent, and 7 percent.

5. In areas where our juice is relatively new, we'd like to see increases of

    10 percent, 20 percent, or 25 percent.

6. In each section of the country, the regional sales director, his or her as-

    sistant, and local salespeople will develop a plan for that area.

7. We want to target New England states such as Connecticut,

    Massachusetts, and New Hampshire, where attitudes about fruit juice

    are similar to those in Seattle, Portland, and other Northwest cities.

8. Our advertising should emphasize our small-scale production

    methods, our commitment to quality, and our juices' delicious flavor.

9. We also should provide free samples of our juices at outdoor concerts,

    county fairs, and arts festivals.

10. Careful planning, hard work, and individual initiative will ensure the

    growth of our company this year, next year, and the years that follow.

B. Commas in Compound Sentences

A **compound sentence** contains two complete sentences joined by
one of these words: *and, but, for, or, nor, so, yet.* Use a comma before the joining word to separate the two complete thoughts.

| Sentence | **,** | and, but, for, or, nor, so, yet | Sentence |

I called my best friend, and *she agreed to drive me to work.*

I asked my best friend to drive me to work, but *she was busy.*

I can take the bus to work, or *I can call another friend.*

| Practice 2 | Using Commas in Compound Sentences |

Edit the following compound sentences by adding commas where they are needed. If a sentence is already correct, put a "C" next to it.

EXAMPLE: Yesterday I went to bed early, but my brother called and woke me up.

1. He told me that our father was in the hospital, but I didn't believe him.

2. My brother slowly repeated the news, and I realized that he was serious.

3. I quickly got dressed, and then I called for a taxi.   *C*

4. I asked the taxi driver to drive fast, but he said he had to obey the speed limit.

5. Traffic was unusually light, so we reached the hospital sooner than I expected.

6. My brother was waiting for me in the lobby, and I asked him if he had learned anything more.

7. Our father had suffered a minor heart attack, but he was now resting comfortably.

8. He looked pale and weak, but he said he felt fine.

9. The doctor told us that there was no real danger, so my brother and I took his advice and went home.

10. When I got home I felt extremely tired, but I did not feel like sleeping.

C. Commas after Introductory Word Groups

Use a comma after an introductory word or word group. The comma lets your readers know that the main part of the sentence is starting.

| Introductory word group | , | Rest of sentence |

However, the president is coming to visit our city.

By the way, I don't have a babysitter for tomorrow night.

While I waited outside, Susan went backstage to meet the band.

Practice 3   **Using Commas after Introductory Word Groups**

Edit the following sentences by adding commas after introductory word groups where they are needed.

EXAMPLE: According to most medical researchers, the chance of

the AIDS virus being spread through athletic contact is

very low.

1. As we all know, AIDS is spread mainly through sexual contact and

   through drug use that involves the sharing of needles.

2. Nonetheless, some people feel that all college athletes should be tested

   for the HIV virus before competing.

3. Since basketball star Magic Johnson revealed in 1991 that he is HIV-

   positive, an NBA player must be removed from a game if he is

   bleeding.

4. Once the wound is properly bandaged, the player is allowed to return

   to the game.

5. Not surprisingly, many college sports follow similar rules.

6. However, requiring athletes to leave a contest when bleeding is quite different from forcing them to be tested for HIV.

7. According to some student-athletes, mandatory HIV testing would violate their civil liberties.

8. Using the same argument, many student-athletes object to being tested for the use of drugs.

9. In their view, student-athletes should be treated no differently from other students.

10. In this case, some would say that public health is more important than civil liberties.

D.   Commas around Appositives and Interrupters

TIP: For more on appositives, see Chapter 31.

An **appositive** comes directly after a noun or pronoun and renames it.

Lily, *my cousin*, will take her nursing exam this summer.

The prices are reasonable at Chapters, *the campus bookstore*.

An **interrupter** is an aside or transition that interrupts the flow of a sentence and does not affect its meaning.

TIP: Most of the transitions (time, space, and importance) covered in earlier chapters are interrupters that should be set off with commas.

My sister, *actually*, has very good reasons for being late.

Her car broke down, *for example*.

Putting commas around appositives and interrupters tells readers that these elements give extra information but are not essential to the meaning of the sentence. If the appositive or interrupter is in the middle of the sentence, set it off with a comma before and a comma after. If it comes at the beginning or end of the sentence, separate it from the rest of the sentence with one comma.

TIP: An interrupter that appears at the beginning of a sentence is the same as an introductory word group.

By the way, your proposal has been accepted.

Your proposal, *by the way*, has been accepted.

Your proposal has been accepted, *by the way*.

Practice 4   **Using Commas to Set Off Appositives and Interrupters**

Edit the following sentences by using commas to set off appositives and interrupters.

EXAMPLE: Vancouver, a large Canadian city west of Toronto, is located near the mouth of the Fraser River.

1. Grouse Mountain, a ski area, overlooks the city and the Strait of Georgia.

2. The Strait of Georgia, a long body of water connected to Puget Sound, provides excellent fishing opportunities.

3. There are, in addition, numerous places for hiking.

4. Stanley Park, a peninsula near downtown, is popular with visitors and local residents.

5. The Vancouver area, however, has much to offer beyond recreation.

6. Vancouver, unlike many other large urban areas, is surprisingly relaxed.

7. The city, in addition, is known as a bustling commercial center.

8. It is an important part of the Pacific Rim, a vast region that includes China, Japan, Korea, Australia, Peru, and the west coast of North America.

9. Vancouver, like San Francisco and Seattle, has a large Asian population.

10. Many residents of Hong Kong, for example, moved to Vancouver in the 1980s and 1990s.

E. Commas around Adjective Clauses

An **adjective clause** is a group of words with a subject and a verb that begins with *who, which,* or *that* and describes a noun right before it in the sentence. Whether or not an adjective clause should be set off from the rest of the sentence by commas depends on its meaning in the sentence.

If the adjective clause can be taken out of the sentence without completely changing the meaning of the sentence, put commas around the clause.

Lily, *who is my cousin,* will take her nursing exam this summer.

Chapters, *which is the campus bookstore,* charges outrageous prices.

I complained to Mr. Kranz, *who is the bookstore manager.*

If the adjective clause is essential to the meaning of the sentence, do not put commas around it. You can tell whether the clause is essential by taking it out and seeing if the meaning of the sentence changes significantly, as it would if you took the clause out of the following examples.

The only grocery store *that sold good bread* went out of business.

Students *who cheat on exams* often get caught.

Salesclerks *who sell liquor to minors* are breaking the law.

Noun	Adjective clause essential to meaning	Rest of sentence

Noun	,	Adjective clause not essential to meaning	,	Rest of sentence

> **Practice 5** ▶ Using Commas to Set Off Adjective Clauses

Edit the following sentences by putting commas around adjective clauses where they are needed. Remember that if the adjective clause is essential to the meaning of the sentence, you should not use commas. If a sentence is already correct, put a "C" next to it.

EXAMPLE: The Grandview Movie House, which opened in 1923, will

shut down soon.

1. Robert Kramer, who bought the theater two years ago, said that he is

losing money.

2. Kramer,who owns a car wash,was new to the movie theater business.

3. The Grandview,which is known for its comfortable seats and wide screen,has been in financial trouble for at least a decade.

4. Theaters that have only one screen are struggling to survive.   *C*

5. Multiplex theaters,which are often located in shopping malls,now dominate the industry.

6. Patrons who regularly attend movies at the Grandview were disappointed by the news.   *C*

7. Brad Warren,who works as an accountant in a nearby office,has been watching films at the Grandview since the 1960s.

8. Warren's father,who died in 1989,attended a movie at the Grandview the year it opened.

9. A group that views the theater as a historic landmark hopes to save it.   *C*

10. Gerald Jordan,who wants to buy the property,said he would tear down the theater and replace it with an athletic club.

F.   Other Uses for Commas

Commas with Quotation Marks

TIP: For more on quotation marks, see Chapter 38.

Quotation marks are used to show that you are exactly repeating what someone said. Use commas to set off the words inside quotation marks from the rest of the sentence.

"Let me see your license," demanded the police officer.

"Did you realize," she asked, "that you were going eighty miles per hour?"

I exclaimed, "I didn't!"

Notice that a comma never comes directly after a quotation mark.

Commas in Addresses

Use commas to seperate the elements of an address included in a sentence. However, do not use one before the ZIP code.

My address is 2512 Windermere Street, Jackson, Mississippi 40720.

If the sentence continues after the address, put a comma after the address.

I moved here from Detroit, Michigan, when I was eighteen.

Commas in Dates

Separate the day from the year with a comma. If you give the month and year, do not separate them with a comma.

My daughter was born on November 8, 1992.

The next conference is in August 1998.

If the sentence continues after the date, put a comma after the date.

In April 1988, residents of our town made a banana split that was four miles long.

Commas with Names

Put commas around the name of someone you are addressing by name.

Don, I want you to come look at this.

Unfortunately, Marie, you need to finish the report by next week.

Commas with Yes or No

Put commas around the word *yes* or *no* in response to a question.

Yes, I believe you are right.

Practice 6   Using Other Commas

Edit the following sentences by adding commas where they are needed. If a sentence is already correct, put a "C" next to it.

EXAMPLE: On December 12, 1994, beachfront property was badly damaged by a fast-moving storm.

1. Some homeowners were still waiting to settle their claims with their insurance companies in January 1996.   *C*

2. Rob McGregor of 31 Hudson Street,Wesleyville,is one of those home-owners.

3. Asked if he was losing patience, McGregor replied,"Yes,I sure am."

4. "I've really had it up to here," McGregor said.

5. His wife said,"Rob,don't go mouthing off to any reporters."

6. "Betty, I'll say what I want to say," Rob replied.

7. An official of Value-Safe Insurance of Wrightsville,Ohio,said the company will process claims within the next few months.

8. "No,there is no way we can do it any sooner," the official said.

9. Customers unhappy with their service may write to Value-Safe Insurance,P.O. Box 225,Wrightsville,Ohio 62812.

10. The company's regional office in Worcester,Massachusetts,can be reached by a toll-free number.

Edit Paragraphs and Your Own Writing

| Practice 7 | ▶ | Editing Paragraphs for Commas |

TEAMWORK
Put students in small groups to edit paragraphs. Then have a member of each group read the edited paragraph aloud.

Edit the following paragraphs by adding commas where they are needed.

(1) In April 1990, the book *You Just Don't Understand* was published by William Morrow in New York, New York. (2) The subject of

the book is the differences in the way men and women use language, including how they listen, how they speak, how they interact, and generally how they communicate. (3) It gives examples of how men and women misunderstand each other, and it describes the causes and possible solutions to their language expectations. (4) Deborah Tannen, the author, starts with childhood experiences that shape the way girls and boys use language.

(5) Tannen writes, "Even if they grow up in the same house, girls and boys grow up in different worlds of words. (6) Although they often play together, boys and girls spend most of their time playing in same-sex groups. (7) And although some of their play activities are similar, their favorite games are different, and their ways of using language in their games are also different." (8) Tannen continues, "Boys tend to play outside, for example, in large groups that have a hierarchy. (9) Girls, on the other hand, play in small groups or pairs. (10) Many of their activities (such as playing house) don't have winners or losers."

(11) Later in life, these differences can cause disagreements between men and women. (12) Tannen says, for example, "For everyone, home is a place to be offstage. (13) The comfort of home, however, can have opposite meanings for men and women. (14) For many men, the comfort of home means freedom from having to talk. (15) They are free to remain silent. (16) For women, on the other hand, home is a place where they feel the greatest need to talk, and they want to talk to those closest to them." (17) Needless to say, conflict results from these different expectations.

Practice 8 ➤ Editing Your Own Writing for Commas

As a final practice, edit a piece of your own writing for commas. It can be a paper you are working on for this course, a paper you've already finished, a paper for another course, or a recent piece of writing from your work or everyday life. In your learning journal, record any examples of sentences with comma problems that you find, along with the edited versions. You may want to use the Summary on this page.

Summary: Commas

LEARNING JOURNAL
What mistake with commas do you make most often? Why do you think you make this mistake?

- A **comma** (**,**) is a punctuation mark that helps readers understand your sentence. A comma often indicates a pause.

- Use commas to separate these elements from one another:
  - **Items in a series** of three or more (see p. 434)
  - Two sentences within a **compound sentence** (see p. 435)
  - **Parts of an address** (see p. 442)
  - **Parts of a date** (see p.442)

- Use commas to set off any of these elements from the rest of the sentence:
  - **Introductory word groups** (see p. 437)
  - An **appositive** (see p. 438)
  - An **interrupter** (see p. 438)
  - An **adjective clause** (see p. 440)
  - A **quotation** (see p. 441)
  - The name of the **person being addressed** (see p. 442)
  - The word *yes* or *no* in response to a question (see p. 442)

37

Apostrophes

A. Apostrophes to Show Ownership
B. Apostrophes in Contractions
C. Apostrophes with Letters, Numbers, and Time

Understand What Apostrophes Do

An **apostrophe** (') is a punctuation mark that either shows ownership (*Susan's*) or indicates that a letter has been intentionally left out to form a **contraction** (*I'm, that's, they're*). Although an apostrophe looks like a comma (,), it is not used for the same purpose, and it is written higher on the line than commas are.

apostrophe ʼ   comma ,

Practice Using Apostrophes Correctly

A. Apostrophes to Show Ownership

Add -*'s* to a singular noun to show ownership even if the noun already ends in -*s*.

Karen's apartment is on the South Side.

They all followed the *college's* rules.

James's roommate is looking for him.

If the noun is plural and ends in -*s*, just add an apostrophe. If it is plural but does not end in -*s*, add -*'s*.

My *books'* covers are all falling off.

[More than one book]

The *kids'* father was building them a playhouse.

[More than one kid]

The *children's* toys were all broken.

The placement of an apostrophe makes a difference in meaning.

My *sister's* six children are at my house for the weekend.

[One sister who has six children]

My *sisters'* six children are at my house for the weekend.

[More than one sister who together have six children]

Do not use an apostrophe to form the plural of a noun.

Gina went camping with her sister's and their children.

All of the highway's to the airport are under construction until the end of the summer.

Do not use an apostrophe with a possessive pronoun—these already show ownership (possession).

Is that bag your's?

No, it is our's.

Possessive Pronouns

my	his	its	their
mine	her	our	theirs
your	hers	ours	whose
yours			

Its or *It's*?

The single most common error with apostrophes and pronouns is confusing *its* (a possessive pronoun) with *it's* (a contraction meaning "it is"). Remember, when you mean that something belonged to *it,* always use *its*; never use *it's*. Whenever you write *it's,* test to see if it's correct by replacing it with *it is* and reading the sentence aloud.

Practice 1 ▸ Using Apostrophes to Show Ownership

Edit the following sentences by adding -*'s* or an apostrophe alone to show ownership and by crossing out any incorrect use of an apostrophe or *s'*.

EXAMPLE: People must respect other peoples need/s for personal space.

1. A person's feelings about personal space depend on his or her's culture.

2. Personal space is especially important in cultures/ that are formal and reserved.

3. Standing too close to another person's face when you speak is considered rude.

4. Fistfights often are preceded by someone's aggressive violation of someone else's space.

5. The expression "Get out of my face!" is a warning meant to prevent the confrontation's violent conclusion.

6. A dog's interaction with a member of it/s own species can follow a similar pattern; dogs are determined to defend what is their/s.

7. The hair on dogs' neck/s may stand on end.

8. A researcher's recent work examines various species' personal space.

9. For example, seagulls' positions on a log follow a pattern similar to that of people lined up waiting for a bus.

10. Studies show that an animal's overcrowded environment can lead to violent behavior.

B. Apostrophes in Contractions

ESL
Because contractions are often new to ESL students, you may want to advise them to avoid all contractions in college work that they are submitting for a grade. They should use apostrophes only to show ownership.

A **contraction** is formed by joining two words and leaving out one or more of the letters. Use an apostrophe to show where the letter or letters have been left out. Be sure to put the apostrophe in the right place.

She's on her way. = *She is* on her way.

I'll see you there. = *I will* see you there.

TIP: Do not use contractions in formal papers or reports for college or work. If you are unsure whether using contractions is acceptable for a college assignment, ask your professor.

Common Contractions

aren't = are not	she'll = she will
can't = cannot	she's = she is, she has
couldn't = could not	there's = there is
didn't = did not	they'd = they would, they had
don't = do not	they'll = they will
he'd = he would, he had	they're = they are
he'll = he will	they've = they have
he's = he is, he has	who'd = who would, who had
I'd = I would, I had	who'll = who will
I'll = I will	who's = who is, who has
I'm = I am	won't = will not
I've = I have	wouldn't = would not
isn't = is not	you'd = you would, you had
it's = it is, it has	you'll = you will
let's = let us	you're = you are
she'd = she would, she had	you've = you have

| Practice 2 | Using Apostrophes in Contractions |

Edit the following sentences by adding apostrophes where needed and crossing out incorrectly used apostrophes.

EXAMPLE: Although we observe personal space boundaries in our daily lives, they're not something we spend much time thinking about.

1. You'll notice right away if a stranger leans over and talks to you so his face is practically touching yours.

2. Perhaps you'd accept this kind of behavior from a family member.

3. There isn't one single acceptable boundary we'd use in all situations.

4. An elevator has its own rules: You wouldn't stand right next to a person if there were space in one of the corners.

5. With co-workers, we're likely to keep a personal space of four to twelve feet.

6. We'll accept a personal space of four feet down to eighteen inches with friends.

7. The last sixteen inches is reserved for people we're most intimate with.

8. When people hug or kiss, they show that they're willing to surrender their personal space to each other, at least temporarily.

9. A supervisor who's not aware of the personal space boundaries of his or her employees risks committing a serious transgression.

10. Even if the supervisor doesn't intend anything by the gestures, it's his or her responsibility to act appropriately.

C. Apostrophes with Letters, Numbers, and Time

Use -'s to make letters and numbers plural.

In Scrabble games, there are more *e*'s than any other letter.

In women's shoes, size *8*'s are more common than size *10*'s.

Use -'s in certain expressions about time.

This year's graduating class is huge.

Last week's exams were awful.

She took *four weeks'* maternity leave after the baby was born.

Practice 3 ▸ **Using Apostrophes with Letters, Numbers, and Time**

Edit the following sentences by adding apostrophes where needed and crossing out incorrectly used apostrophes.

EXAMPLE: When I returned to work after two weeks' vacation, I had what

looked like a decade's worth of work in my box.

1. I sorted letters alphabetically, starting with *A*'s.

2. There were more letters by names starting with *M*'s than any other.

3. When I checked my e-mail, the screen flashed 48's to show that I had

    forty-eight messages.

4. My voice mail wasn't much better, telling me that in two weeks' time I

    had received twenty-five messages.

5. I needed another week's time just to return all the phone calls.

6. During each day's work, I returned five of the calls.

7. One phone number was composed entirely of 6's and 7's:

    767-7766.

8. Another number included five 2's: 722-2242.

9. I wondered whether by taking a month's vacation, I would end up with ninety-six e-mail messages.

10. I devoted a few minutes' thought to whether I'd be better off with a different job.

Edit Paragraphs and Your Own Writing

Practice 4　Editing Paragraphs for Apostrophes

Edit the following paragraphs by adding apostrophes where needed and crossing out incorrectly used apostrophes.

(1) People's names often have strange stories attached to them. (2) Oprah Winfrey's first name, for example, is very unusual. (3) It's actually misspelled. It was supposed to be "Orpah," a biblical name, but a clerk's error on the birth certificate resulted in "Oprah." (4) Somehow, *The Orpah Winfrey Show* doesn't sound like a popular television program. (5) "Oprah," on the other hand, with it's resemblance to "opera," makes us think of a performer on a stage. (6) Winfrey herself is certainly not upset that she didn't end up with her parents' choice of names; her production company's name is "Harpo," which is "Oprah" spelled backward. (7) While Winfrey is not the only entertainer with an unusual first name, hers is especially memorable.

(8) As Winfrey's example suggests, names on birth certificates are often mixed up. (9) If a clerk's *a*'s look like *o*'s, for example, "Dana" becomes "Dona" and "Jarvis" becomes "Jorvis." (10) But unusual names don't all result from mistakes. (11) You've probably heard of names

such as "Candy Cane" or "Spring Raines" or "Stormy Winters." (12)
Some people's names sound like job titles. (13) Think, for example, of
a surgeon who's named "Carver," or a dentist called "Dr. Drill."
(14) Early in his career, the baseball pitcher Eric Plunk was known for
hitting batters' with his wild pitches. (15) There's no way to explain any
of these names except by attributing them to pure chance. (16) Each
name has its own meaning and origin; we're all affected by our names,
whether we like them or not.

> **Practice 5**   Editing Your Own Writing for Apostrophes

As a final practice, edit a piece of your own writing for apostrophes. It
can be a paper you are working on for this course, a paper you've already
finished, a paper for another course, or a recent piece of writing from your
work or everyday life. In your learning journal, record examples of sentences
with apostrophe problems that you find, along with the edited versions. You
may want to use the Summary on this page.

Summary: Apostrophes

LEARNING JOURNAL
What type of mistake
with apostrophes do
you make most often?
How can you avoid this
mistake or be sure to edit
for it?

- An **apostrophe** (') is a punctuation mark that usually either shows
  ownership or indicates where a letter or letters have been left out in
  contractions. (See p. 446.)
- To show **ownership,** add -'s to a singular noun, even if the noun
  already ends in -s. For a plural noun, add an apostrophe alone if the
  noun ends in -s; add -'s if the noun does not end in -s. (See p. 446.)
- Do not use an apostrophe with a possessive pronoun. (See p. 447.)
- Do not confuse *its* and *it's*. *Its* shows ownership; *it's* is a contraction
  meaning "it is." (See p. 448.)
- A **contraction** is formed by joining two words and leaving out one or
  more of the letters. Use an apostrophe to show where the letter or letters have been left out. (See p. 449.)
- Use -'s to make **letters and numbers plural.** (See p. 451.)
- Use -'s in certain **expressions about time.** (See p. 451.)

38

Quotation Marks

" "

TIP: To understand this chapter, you need to know what a *sentence* is. For review, see Chapter 21.

RESOURCES
Additional Resources contains tests and supplemental practice exercises for this chapter.

TEACHING TIP
Remind students that they will probably need to use quotation marks when writing narration (Chapters 8 and 18) and argument (Chapters 14 and 19) and when using quotations in opening paragraphs of essays (Chapter 16).

LEARNING JOURNAL
Use your learning journal as a place to record sentences with mistakes in the use of quotation marks. Also record edited versions of these sentences, with the problems corrected.

A. Quotation Marks for Direct Quotations
B. No Quotation Marks for Indirect Quotations
C. Quotation Marks for Certain Titles

Understand What Quotation Marks Do

Quotation marks (" ") always appear in pairs. Quotation marks have two common uses in college writing: They are used with some quotations, and they are used to set off titles.

A **quotation** is the report of another person's words. There are two types of quotations: **direct quotations** (the exact repetition, word for word, of what someone said) and **indirect quotations** (a restatement of what someone said, not word for word). Quotation marks are used only for direct quotations.

DIRECT QUOTATION   He said, "You should get the downtown bus."

INDIRECT QUOTATION   He said I should get the downtown bus.

454

Practice Using Quotation Marks Correctly

A. Quotation Marks for Direct Quotations

When you write a direct quotation, you need to use quotation marks around the quoted words. These tell readers that the words used are exactly what was said.

1. "I don't know what she means," I said to my friend Lina.
2. Lina said, "Do you think we should ask a question?"
3. "Excuse me, Professor Soames," I ventured, "but could you explain that again?"
4. "Certainly," said Professor Soames. "Please ask questions whenever you don't understand something."
5. "Thanks." Then I smiled and said, "Sometimes it seems like teachers just want to tell you what they know. I'm glad you're not like that."

Quoted words are usually combined with words that identify who is speaking, such as *I said to my friend Lina* in the first example. The identifying words can come after the quoted words (example 1), before them (example 2), or in the middle (example 3). Here are some guidelines for capitalization and punctuation:

TEACHING TIP
As you read each of these rules regarding capitalization, put a sentence on the board without any quotation marks and ask students where the quotation marks should go and which letters should be capitalized.

TEACHING TIP
Tell students that if they put identifying words in a sentence on their own, this will probably be a fragment. Identifying words need to be attached to their quotations.

TIP: For more on commas with quotation marks, see Chapter 36.

- Capitalize the first letter in a complete sentence that's being quoted, even if it comes after some identifying words (example 2).

- Do not capitalize the first letter in a quotation if it's not the first word in a complete sentence (*but* in example 3).

- If it is a complete sentence, a quotation can stand on its own, without any identifying words (example 4).

- Identifying words must be attached to a quotation; they cannot be a sentence on their own.

- Use commas to separate identifying words from quoted words in the same sentence.

- Always put quotation marks after commas, periods, question marks, and exclamation points.

quotation mark   question mark   quotation mark

Lina said, "Do you think we should ask a question?"

comma

Setting Off a Quotation within Another Quotation

Sometimes when you directly quote someone, part of what that person said quotes something or someone else. Put single quotation marks (‘ ’) around the quotation within a quotation so that readers understand who says what.

The college handbook said, "Students must be given the opportunity to make up work missed for legitimate reasons."

Terry told his instructor, "I'm sorry I missed the exam, but that isn't reason to fail me for the term. Our handbook says, 'Students must be given the opportunity to make up work missed for legitimate reasons,' and I have a good reason."

Practice 1 ▶ **Punctuating Direct Quotations**

Edit the following sentences by adding quotation marks and commas where needed.

EXAMPLE: A radio journalist asked a nurse at a critical-care facility, "Do you feel that the medical community needlessly prolongs the life of the terminally ill?"

TEAMWORK
Have students write two of their own direct quotations without correct punctuation or capitalization. Each student should exchange sentences with a partner and edit the other person's sentences.

1. "If I could quickly answer that question," the nurse replied, "I'd deserve an honorary degree in ethics."

2. She added, "But I see it as the greatest dilemma we face today."

3. "How would you describe that dilemma?" the reporter asked the nurse.

4. The nurse said, "It's a choice of when to use our amazing medical technology and when not to."

5. The reporter asked, "So there are times when you'd favor letting patients die on their own?"

6. "Yes," the nurse replied, "I would."

7. The reporter asked, "Under what circumstances should a patient be

allowed to die?"

8. "I can't really answer that question because there are so many variables

involved," the nurse replied.

9. "Is this a matter of deciding how to allocate scarce resources?" the

reporter asked.

10. "In a sense, it is," the nurse replied. "We shouldn't try to keep everyone

alive for as long as possible just because we have the technical know-

how to do so."

B. No Quotation Marks for Indirect Quotations

When you report what someone said but do not use the person's exact words, you are writing an indirect quotation. Do not use quotation marks for indirect quotations. Indirect quotations often begin with the word *that*.

INDIRECT QUOTATION	DIRECT QUOTATION
Sam said that there was a fire downtown.	Sam said, "There was a fire downtown."
The police told us to move along.	"Move along," directed the police.
Tara told me that she is graduating.	Tara said, "I am graduating."

Practice 2 ▶ **Punctuating Direct and Indirect Quotations**

Edit the following sentences by adding quotation marks where needed and crossing out quotation marks that are incorrectly used. If a sentence is already correct, put a "C" next to it.

EXAMPLE: Three days before her apartment was robbed, Jocelyn told a

friend, "I have concerns about the safety of this building."

1. "Have you complained to the landlord yet?" her friend asked.

2. "Not yet," Jocelyn replied, "although I know I should."

3. The next day Jocelyn phoned the landlord and asked him if he could install a more secure lock on the front door.   *C*

4. The landlord said that she felt the lock was fine the way it was.

5. When Jocelyn phoned the landlord after the burglary, she said, "I know this wouldn't have happened if that lock had been installed."

6. "I'm sorry about your stereo being stolen," the landlord replied, "but there's nothing I can do about it now."

7. The next day Jocelyn asked a tenants' rights group whether she had grounds for a lawsuit.   *C*

8. The person she spoke to said that she probably did.

9. "If I were you," the person said, "I'd let your landlord know right away about your plans."

10. When Jocelyn told her landlord of the possible lawsuit, he said that he would reimburse her for the loss of her stereo.   *C*

C. Quotation Marks for Certain Titles

When you refer to a short work such as a magazine or newspaper article, a chapter in a book, a short story, an essay, a song, or a poem, put quotation marks around the title of the work.

NEWSPAPER ARTICLE   "President Promises No New Taxes"

SHORT STORY   "The Lady or the Tiger?"

ESSAY   "A Brother's Murder"

Usually titles of longer works such as novels, books, magazines, and newspapers are underlined or italicized.

BOOK   <u>Gone with the Wind</u> or *Gone with the Wind*

NEWSPAPER   <u>Washington Post</u> or *Washington Post*

If you are writing a paper with many outside sources, your instructor will probably refer you to a particular system of citing sources. Follow that system's guidelines when deciding how to show titles in your paper.

Practice 3 ▶ **Using Quotation Marks for Titles**

Edit the following sentences by adding quotation marks around titles as needed. None of these titles needs underlining or italics.

> **EXAMPLE:** One of Flannery O'Connor's best-known short stories is "A Good Man Is Hard to Find."

1. As in her story "Good Country People," the title of "A Good Man Is Hard to Find" is ironic: The man who appears late in the story is actually a deranged killer.

2. In "Good Country People," a simple young Bible salesman is revealed to be a cynical schemer with no belief in God.

3. As O'Connor made clear in her essay "Novelist and Believer," her own faith as a Catholic deeply influenced her fiction.

4. Some of her stories have strongly Christian titles, such as "A Temple of the Holy Ghost."

5. But as she explained in the essay "The Nature and Aim of Fiction," O'Connor was less interested in grand themes than in concrete human experiences.

Edit Paragraphs and Your Own Writing

Practice 4 ▶ **Editing Paragraphs for Quotation Marks**

Edit the following paragraphs by adding quotation marks where needed and crossing out any incorrectly used quotation marks.

(1) When Ruiz first came into my office, he told me that he was a poor student. (2) I asked, "What makes you think that?"

(3) Ruiz answered, "I've always gotten bad grades, and I don't know how to get any better." (4) He shook his head. (5) "I've just about given up."

(6) I told him that ⁄there were some resources on campus he could use and that we could work together to help him."

(7) "What kind of things are you talking about?" asked Ruiz. (8) "What exactly will I learn?"

(9) I said, "There are plenty of programs to help you. (10) You really have no excuse to fail."

(11) "Can you be a little more specific?" he asked.

(12) "Certainly," I said. (13) I told him about the survival skills program. (14) I also pulled out folders on study skills such as time management, memory, note taking, and positive attitude. (15) "Take a look at these," I said.

(16) Ruiz said, "No, I'm not interested in that. (17) And I don't have time."

(18) I replied, "That's your decision, Ruiz, but remember that education is one of the few things that people are willing to pay for and

not get." (19) I paused and then added, "Sounds to me like you're wasting the money you spent on tuition. (20) Why not try to get what you paid for?"

(21) Ruiz thought for a moment, looking out the window, and finally told me that he'd try.

(22) "Good," I said. (23) "I'm glad to hear it."

Practice 5 ▶ **Editing Your Own Writing for Quotation Marks**

As a final practice, edit a piece of your own writing for quotation marks. It can be a paper you are working on for this course, a paper you've already finished, a paper for another course, or a recent piece of writing from your work or everyday life. In your learning journal, record any examples of sentences with mistakes in the use of quotation marks that you find, along with the edited versions. You may want to use the Summary on this page.

Summary: Quotation Marks

LEARNING JOURNAL
In your own words, explain the difference between direct quotations and indirect quotations. Write one example of each.

- **Quotation marks** look like this: " ". They always appear in pairs. (See p. 454.)
- A **quotation** is the report of another person's words. (See p. 454.)
- A **direct quotation** is the exact, word-for-word repetition of what someone said. Use quotation marks around direct quotations. (See p. 455.)
- An **indirect quotation** is a restatement of what someone said, not word for word. Do not use quotation marks with indirect quotations. (See p. 457.)
- To set off a **quotation within a quotation,** use single quotation marks: ' '. (See p. 456.)
- Put quotation marks around **titles** of short works such as magazine or newspaper articles, short stories, songs, and poems. For longer works (magazines, novels, books, newspapers, and so on) either underline or italicize the title. (See p. 458.)

39

Other Punctuation

TIP: To understand this chapter, you need to know what *sentences* and *independent clauses* are. For review, see Chapter 21.

A. Colon   **:**
B. Semicolon   **;**
C. Parentheses   **( )**
D. Dash   **--**
E. Hyphen   **-**

RESOURCES
Additional Resources contains tests and supplemental practice exercises for this chapter.

Understand What Punctuation Does

Punctuation helps readers understand writing. If punctuation is not used correctly, it sends readers a confusing—or, even worse, a wrong—message. This chapter covers marks of punctuation that people sometimes use incorrectly because they aren't quite sure what they are supposed to do.

LEARNING JOURNAL
Use your learning journal as a place to record sentences you find in your writing that should use these punctuation marks. Try to find one sample sentence each for colons, semicolons, parentheses, dashes, and hyphens. Show the sentence both before and after you edit it.

COLON	**:**	introduces a list announces an explanation
SEMICOLON	**;**	joins two independent clauses into one sentence separates items in a complicated list
PARENTHESES	**( )**	set off extra information that is not essential
DASH	**--**	sets off words for emphasis indicates a pause

HYPHEN	-	joins two words that together form a single description
		shows a word break at the end of a line

Practice Using Punctuation Correctly

TIP: See Commas (Chapter 36), Apostrophes (Chapter 37), and Quotation Marks (Chapter 38) for coverage of these punctuation marks.

A. Colon :

Colons before Lists

Use a colon after an independent clause to introduce a list.

Many companies had booths at the computer fair: Apple, Microsoft, IBM, and Digital, to name just a few.

There was a vast array of software: financial management, games, educational, college applications, and so on.

Colons before Explanations

TIP: An independent clause contains a subject, a verb, and a complete thought. It can stand on its own as a sentence. (See p. 265.)

Use a colon after an independent clause to let readers know that you are about to provide an explanation or example of what you just wrote.

The fair was overwhelming: too much hype about too many things.

I picked up something I've been looking for: a new printer.

NOTE: A colon in a sentence must follow an independent clause. One of the most common misuses of colons is to use them after a phrase instead of an independent clause.

TEACHING TIP
After each of the explanations and examples in this chapter, ask students to write an example of their own. Call on a few students to put their examples on the board.

INCORRECT	Tonya has six cousins. *Named*: Joe, Stella, Monique, Sid, Ian, and Tomas.
CORRECT	Tonya has six cousins: Joe, Stella, Monique, Sid, Ian, and Tomas.
INCORRECT	Jeff has many interests. *For example*: bicycle racing, sculpture, and building musical instruments.
CORRECT	Jeff has many interests: bicycle racing, sculpture, and building musical instruments.

Colons in Business Correspondence

Use a colon after a greeting (called a *salutation*) in a business letter and after the standard heading lines at the beginning of the memorandum.

Dear Mr. Hernandez:

To: Pat Toney
From: Susan Anker

B. Semicolon   `;`

Semicolons to Join Independent Clauses

Use a semicolon to join two very closely related sentences into one sentence.

> In an interview, hold your head up and don't slouch; it is important to look alert.

> Slouching creates a terrible impression; it makes you seem uninterested.

> Make good eye contact; looking down is not appropriate in an interview.

Semicolons in Lists Containing Commas

When one or more items in a list contain commas, use semicolons to separate the items. Otherwise, it is difficult for readers to tell where one item ends and another begins.

> For dinner, Bob ate an order of onion rings, extra large; a sixteen-ounce steak, medium rare; a baked potato with sour cream, bacon bits, and chives; a green salad; and a huge bowl of ice cream topped with fudge sauce, nuts, whipped cream, and a maraschino cherry.

C. Parentheses   `( )`

Use parentheses to set off information that is not essential to the meaning of the sentence. Parentheses are always used in pairs.

> My grandfather (a truly wonderful person) was always inventing things.

> His most successful invention (and also his first) was the electric blanket.

> When he died (at the age of ninety-six) he had more than 150 patents registered.

D. Dash   `--`

Dashes can be used like parentheses to set off additional information, particularly information that you want to emphasize.

> The final exam -- worth 25 percent of your total grade -- will be next Thursday.

> There will be no makeup exam -- no exceptions -- for this course.

COMPUTER
Show students how to create true dashes on the computer rather than typing two hyphens.

A dash can also indicate a pause, much like a comma does.

My uncle went on long fishing trips —— without my aunt and cousins.

E. Hyphen –

Hyphens to Join Words That Form a Single Description

We often join two or more words that together form a single description of a person, place, or thing. To join the words, use a hyphen.

Being a stockbroker is a high-risk position.

Michelle is the ultimate decision-maker in our department.

Jill was a lovely three-year-old girl.

Hyphens to Divide a Word at the End of a Line

Use a hyphen to divide a word when part of the word must continue on the next line.

Critics accuse the tobacco industry of increasing the amounts of nicotine in cigarettes to encourage addiction and boost sales.

If you are not sure where to break a word, look it up in a dictionary. The main entry word will show you where you can break the word: **dic • tio • nary**. If you still aren't confident that you are putting the hyphen in the right place, don't break the word; write it all on the next line.

COMPUTER
Most word processing programs automatically put a whole word on the next line without hyphenating it ("word wrap"). Most have a hyphenation feature, however, that can be turned on. Be sure to tell your students if you have a strong preference.

Edit Paragraphs and Your Own Writing

Practice 1   **Editing Paragraphs for Other Punctuation Marks**

Edit the following paragraphs by adding colons, semicolons, parentheses, dashes, and hyphens where needed. Circle the marks of punctuation that you add. Keep in mind that in some places more than one type of punctuation may be acceptable.   *Answers may vary. Possible edits shown.*

(1) More than fifty thousand domestic adoptions take place in this country each year; despite minor difficulties most of them go smoothly. (2) But a few years ago, the case of four-year-old Baby Richard highlighted an important issue: the rights of adoptive parents versus the rights of birth parents. (3) Richard was in a good situa-

tion; healthy, happy, loved by the couple who had adopted him at birth. (4) Then Richard's other parents—the natural, biological ones—appeared on the scene. (5) They were prepared to spend years battling the case in court; they desperately wanted their son back.

(6) The birth mother had given up her baby for several reasons—she was alone, frightened, and angry; her boyfriend had left her two weeks before Richard was born; she had heard stories that he was seeing an old girlfriend. (7) A few days after the baby's birth, the baby was put up for adoption—his mother didn't want him. (8) When the boyfriend (the father of the baby) returned later, he was told that the baby had died. (9) Eventually, however, the father discovered that his former girlfriend had lied; his son was still alive. (10) After several years of searching, the biological parents found their long-lost child, who was living happily with his adoptive parents. (11) After years of legal arguments, the Illinois Supreme Court reached its verdict: Baby Richard belonged to the parents whose genes he shared. (12) The adoptive parents—the people who had loved and cared for Baby Richard for his first four years—were bitterly disappointed.

| **Practice 2** | ### Editing Your Own Writing for Other Marks of Punctuation |

As a final practice, edit a piece of your own writing for colons, semicolons, parentheses, dashes, and hyphens. It can be a paper you are working on for this course, a paper you've already finished, a paper for another course, or a piece of writing from your work or everyday life. You may want to try more than one way to use these marks of punctuation in your writing. In your learning journal, record any examples of sentences you edited, showing the sentences both before and after you edited them. You may want to use the Summary on page 467.

Summary: Colons, Semicolons, Parentheses, Dashes, and Hyphens

LEARNING JOURNAL
What is one useful thing
you learned in this
chapter?

- **Colons** : can be used
  - After an independent clause to introduce a list (see p. 463)
  - After an independent clause to announce an explanation or example (see p. 463)
  - After the greeting in a business letter or the standard lines in a memorandum (see p. 463)

- **Semicolons** ; can be used
  - To join two independent clauses into one sentence (see p. 464)
  - To separate items in a list when the items contain commas (see p. 464)

- **Parentheses** ( ) set off information that is not essential to the sentence. (see p. 464)

- **Dashes** -- also set off information in the sentence, usually information that you want to emphasize. (See p. 464.)

- **Hyphens** - can be used
  - To join two or more words that together form a single description (see p. 465)
  - To divide a word at the end of a line when there isn't room for the whole word (see p. 465)

40

Capitalization
Using Capital Letters

TIP: To understand this chapter, you need to know what a *sentence* is. For review, see Chapter 21.

RESOURCES
Additional Resources contains tests and supplemental practice exercises for this chapter.

A.   Capitalization of Sentences
B.   Capitalization of Names of Specific People, Places, Dates, and Things
C.   Capitalization of Titles

Understand Three Rules of Capitalization

TEACHING TIP
Remind students that they should not write or type in all capital letters; they will have more trouble in the editing stage with recognizing their capitalization problems.

There are three basic rules of capitalization. Capitalize the first letter

1.   Of every new sentence
2.   In names of specific people, places, dates, and things
3.   Of important words in titles

If you can remember these three rules, you will avoid the most common errors in capitalization.

Practice Capitalization

A. Capitalization of Sentences

Capitalize the first letter in each new sentence, including the first word in a direct quotation.

TIP: For more on punctuating direct quotations, see Chapter 38.

The superintendent was angry.

He asked, "What's going on here?"

| **Practice 1** | Capitalizing the First Word in a Sentence |

Edit the following paragraph by adding capitalization as needed.

(1) Occasionally a phrase or sentence uttered by a president is so memorable that it becomes part of American history. (2) *O*ne example occurred before the start of the Civil War, when Abraham Lincoln stated, "*A* house divided against itself cannot stand." (3) *A*lmost seventy years later, in the midst of the Great Depression, Franklin Roosevelt declared "*W*e have nothing to fear but fear itself."

B. Capitalization of Names of Specific People, Places, Dates, and Things

TEACHING TIP
Have students come up with their own "specific" and "not specific" examples.

The general rule is to capitalize the first letter in names of specific people, places, dates, and things. Do not capitalize names of general categories. Look at the examples for each group.

People

Capitalize the first letter in names of specific people and in titles used with names of specific people.

SPECIFIC	NOT SPECIFIC
Jean Heaton	my neighbor
Professor Fitzgerald	your math professor
Dr. Cornog	the doctor

Places

Capitalize the first letter in names of specific buildings, streets, cities, states, regions, and countries.

ESL
Ask ESL students to identify any English capitalization rules that differ from the rules in their first language. (BO)

SPECIFIC	NOT SPECIFIC
Bolton Town Hall	the town hall
Arlington Street	our street
Dearborn Heights	my hometown
Arizona	this state
the South	the southern region
Spain	that country

Dates

Capitalize the first letter in the names of days, months, and holidays. Do not capitalize the names of the seasons (winter, spring, summer, fall).

SPECIFIC	NOT SPECIFIC
Wednesday	tomorrow
June 15	summer
Thanksgiving	my birthday

Organizations, Companies, and Groups

SPECIFIC	NOT SPECIFIC
Bunker Hill Community College	my college
Microsoft	that software company
Alcoholics Anonymous	the self-help group

Languages, Nationalities, and Religions

SPECIFIC	NOT SPECIFIC
English, Greek, Spanish	my first language
Christianity, Buddhism	your religion

Courses

SPECIFIC	NOT SPECIFIC
Composition 101	writing course
Introduction to Psychology	my psychology course

Commercial Products

SPECIFIC	NOT SPECIFIC
Diet Pepsi	a diet cola
Skippy	peanut butter

Practice 2 Capitalizing Names

Edit the sentences on the following page by capitalizing as needed.

EXAMPLE: One of the most interesting courses I've taken was called

      I   *W*   *R*

introduction to world religions.

1. The course was taught last fall at the *S*springfield *A*adult *E*education *C*center.

2. The instructor, *G*gerald *R*ryan, originally had wanted to become a *C*catholic priest, but he dropped out of the seminary before he was ordained.

3. In those days, he told us, many *C*catholic rites were still conducted in *L*latin.

4. Gerald later spent two years working and traveling in *A*asia, where he became interested in the study of *B*buddhism and other eastern religions.

5. He also studied for a time with *H*harvey *C*cox, a well-known scholar, at the *H*harvard *D*divinity *S*school.

6. During our class, *G*gerald explained how *T*tibetan *B*buddhism is different from *Z*zen *B*buddhism, which places more emphasis on solitary meditation.

7. Gerald devoted one session near the end of *O*october to discussing the ideas of *M*martin *L*luther and *J*john *C*calvin.

8. Calvin was born in *F*france in 1509.

9. In 1536, he began work in *G*geneva, in the *F*french-speaking section of *S*switzerland.

10. I learned from *G*gerald's course that some of *C*calvin's ideas contributed to the rise of capitalism in northern *E*europe.

C. Capitalization of Titles

When you write the title of a book, movie, television program, magazine, newspaper, article, story, song, paper, poem, and so on, capitalize the first word and all important words. The only words that do not need to be capitalized (unless they are the first word) are *the, a, an,* and prepositions.

TIP: For more on punctuating titles, see Chapter 38. For a list of common prepositions, see Chapter 21.

I Love Lucy was a long-running television program.

Both *USA Today* and the *New York Times* are popular newspapers.

"Once More to the Lake" is one of Chuck's favorite essays.

Practice 3   **Capitalizing Titles**

Edit the following sentences by capitalizing titles as needed.

EXAMPLE: In her book *Who S̲tole F̲eminism?* Christina Hoff Sommers criticizes arguments that some feminists have made.

1. Sommers claims that feminists such as Susan Faludi, in her book *Backlash: The U̲ndeclared W̲ar against American W̲omen,* have exaggerated the inequality between men and women that still exists in the workplace.

2. Sommers cites an in-depth article in the *New York T̲imes* that shows how much women have gained in the 1980s and 1990s.

3. "Younger women," says this article in the *T̲imes,* "now earn 80 cents for every dollar earned by men of the same age, up from 69 cents in 1980."

4. On the other side is an article entitled "D̲oes the M̲arket for W̲omen's L̲abor N̲eed F̲ixing?" by Barbara Bergmann, a leading economist.

5. This article, published in the *Journal of E̲conomic Perspectives,* claims that widespread and severe discrimination against women still exists.

Edit Paragraphs and Your Own Writing

Practice 4 ▶ **Editing Paragraphs for Capitalization**

TEAMWORK
This exercise works well in pairs.

Edit the following paragraphs by capitalizing as needed.

(1) In 1992 the *L* *B* la bahia *R* road became the first highway in *T* texas to be designated as scenic and historic by the *T* texas *H* historical *C* commission. (2) Among those who traveled it were *S* sam *H* houston, *D* davy *C* crockett, and *S* stephen *A* austin. (3) It housed a fort built by *S* spanish explorers in the early eighteenth century and was a major overland route, according to *S* sam *H* houston *R* regional *L* library *D* director *R* robert *S* schaadt. (4) Sam *H* houston rode it after signing the *T* texas *D* declaration of *I* independence at *W* washington-on-the-*B* brazos. (5) Along it lies the town of *I* independence, which, according to the *T* texas *B* baptist *H* historical *C* center *M* museum *N* news, features fifty-five sites of historical interest. (6) For *B* baylor *U* university and *T* texas *B* baptists, *I* independence holds special meaning. (7) There, in 1845, *B* baylor received its charter and opened its doors. (8) Soon thereafter, *I* independence became known as the *A* athens of *T* texas. (9) In 1885, *B* baylor relocated to *W* waco. (10) In 1830, *T* texas *B* baptists built a church there that still holds services on *S* sundays and *W* wednesdays. (11) It may be the oldest active *B* baptist church in *T* texas. (12) Thousands of visitors travel the *L* *B* la bahia *R* road to *I* independence, particularly in the spring when the wildflowers blaze along the road as far as the eye can see.

| Practice 5 | Editing Your Own Writing for Capitalization |

As a final practice, edit a piece of your own writing for capitalization. It can be a paper you are working on for this course, a paper you've already finished, a paper for another course, or a recent piece of writing from your work or everyday life. In your learning journal, record any examples of sentences with capitalization problems that you find, along with the edited versions. You may want to use the Summary on this page.

Summary: Capitalization

LEARNING JOURNAL
What problem do you have most often with capitalization? What can you do to edit more effectively for it in the future?

- Capitalize the first letter of every **new sentence.** (See p. 468.)
- Capitalize the first letter in **names of specific people, places, dates,** and **things.** (See p. 469.)
- Capitalize the first letter of important words in **titles.** (See p. 472.)

READINGS FOR WRITERS

41

Introduction to the Reading Process

EVER THOUGHT THIS?
- I failed the test because I didn't read the directions right.
- I had to redo the application because I put information in the wrong place.
- The insurance agent told me I'm not covered for the damage. I thought I was, but I didn't read the policy carefully.
- My boss yelled at me because I made a mistake. She said I would have known what to do if I'd read the memo carefully.

In "Readings for Writers," you will find twenty essays that demonstrate the types of writing you have studied in this book: illustration, narration, description, process analysis, classification, definition, comparison and contrast, cause and effect, and argument. However, these readings provide more than just good models of writing. They also tell gripping tales of adventure, argue passionately about controversial issues, and describe some surprising practices from diverse cultures. Some of the essays may even help you work more efficiently, with tips on the best time of day to study and strategies for successful job interviews. These essays can also provide you with ideas for your own writing, both in and out of school. Most important, they offer you a chance to practice your reading skills — skills that will help you to become a better writer.

Why Is Reading Important?

Often our lives follow a **READ-DO** pattern: We have to *read* before we can *do,* and how well we *do* depends on how well we understand what we *read.* Make no mistake about it: Reading is important — in college, at work, and in everyday life.

Look at these typical read-do situations:

SITUATION ONE: COLLEGE

English assignment: Read the essay and answer the question.

Math assignment: Read pages 109–14 and do Exercise Set 2.1.

SITUATION TWO: WORK

Read the memo and respond by five o'clock.

Read the manual before operating.

Read the procedures carefully before filling the order.

Read the complaint letter and suggest a response.

SITUATION THREE: EVERYDAY LIFE

Read the lease agreement before signing.

Read the insurance policy before signing.

Read the assembly directions before putting together.

Read the safety directions before using.

In each of these situations, if you *read* carefully, you will understand what you need to *do* next.

How Can These Readings Help You?

As you can see, reading plays an important role in many areas of your life. The more you read, the better you become at it. This part of the book presents some strategies for reading and then lets you practice those strategies on essays by professional writers. In fact, you can apply the strategies to any material that requires careful reading.

Reading the essays in this part of the book will help you in the following situations:

In Your Writing

The essays presented in this section are good models of the types of essays you are probably writing in your writing course. Carefully reading a good model can help improve your own writing. By looking at how someone else states main ideas, provides supporting details, organizes ideas, and introduces and concludes an essay, you gain a better sense of how you might write a similar essay. The readings can also give you ideas to write about: As you react to an author's ideas in a selection, you may discover ideas of your own to explore.

In Your Ability to Read Closely and Critically

To get the most out of what you read, you need to read closely and critically. Close reading means that you understand every word the author has written and every point he or she makes. Critical reading means that you ask yourself why the author has made these points in this way and then ask whether you agree. The more you practice close and critical reading, the better you will do it. To help you read closely and critically, the essays in this section contain many notes and questions. Soon you will find that questioning, checking, and probing will come naturally to you. (For more on these notes and questions, see Becoming an Active, Critical Reader, p. 479.)

In Your Ability to Understand Other Experiences and Points of View

The authors of these selections vary in age, gender, race, culture, and experience, and their writing reflects their many differences. In a rapidly changing world, your ability to understand, appreciate, and interact with people whose outlooks and experiences are very different from your own is essential.

Increasingly, employers value social skills, communication skills, and the ability to work as part of a team. Being able to understand new and different viewpoints can help you work well in a group. Another benefit may be more personal: As you read more and learn to see things through other people's eyes, you may discover new perspectives on your own life or learn about lives that differ from yours.

In Your Ability to Help Yourself

Much practical information about living in the modern world is contained in writing. As a strong reader, you will be able to read about whatever you need to know. You can read expert tips on making money, investing, starting your own business, finding a job, moving, raising a family, protecting yourself from unfair treatment, buying a car at the best price, buying a house, negotiating what you want, and so on: The list is endless. When you read well, you can find help to get what you need.

Becoming an Active, Critical Reader

TIP: Keeping a separate reading journal can be a useful strategy for active, critical reading. If you keep a reading journal, you can use it to record your responses to the questions and suggestions in this reader.

Close, critical reading requires an active reader. An active reader takes part in the experience of reading and doesn't passively sit and look at words. Before beginning to read, prepare to actively engage in reading. Find a place where you can be comfortable and where you won't be distracted or interrupted. You need to be mentally alert and ready to concentrate when you read. Be physically alert too: For most people, reading while lying down or slouching results in sleepiness (and even a tendency to nod off). Instead, try sitting at a table or a desk with a good light source nearby.

When you are ready to begin reading, try some of these strategies:

Before Reading

Get an Overview.

Before you begin reading, get an overview. Skim the reading for a general sense of what it contains. This will help you decide what to look for as you read and help keep you on track.

TEACHING TIP
For more information on reading journals, see *Practical Suggestions.*

Most written works have one or more aids to understanding. It is a good idea to look over these aids before you read the work: They were put there to help you. Some of these aids are listed on the next page.

- *Title.* The title usually indicates the topic and main idea of a piece of writing.
- *Author line.* The author's name is usually given at either the beginning or end of a work. Ask yourself whether you have ever heard of this person and, if so, whether he or she is an expert on the topic of the work.
- *Headnote.* A headnote is a paragraph (or more) found at the beginning of a written work that gives information about the author, the writing itself, or both. The background information in a headnote can be useful in understanding what an author is trying to say.
- *Headings and words in boldface.* Headings usually appear on a line by themselves within the work. Boldface words look darker than the surrounding text—**like this**. Both are used to indicate important points. Headings also show the major sections within a piece of writing.
- *Definitions and other notes.* Sometimes books define important or difficult words in notes placed in the margins or at the bottom of the page. Other notes about key points may be found there as well. Read the definitions and notes when you skim for a sense of what the writing is about. Read them again later to make sure you understand what the writing says.

The readings in this section of *Real Writing* contain titles, author lines, headnotes, headings, and definitions. Before you read any essay here, use these aids to get an overview.

Ask a Guiding Question.

After you get an overview, you will have some sense of what the reading is about. Now ask yourself a question that you expect the reading will be able to answer. Usually, you can make the title into a question. For example, for an essay by humorist Russell Baker entitled "The Plot against People," you could ask, "What kind of plot will Baker describe, and who or what will be involved?" For an article by news reporter Joe Klein entitled "The Education of Berenice Belizaire," you could ask, "What is important or unusual about Berenice Belizaire's education?"

If the reading has been assigned to you, consider what your instructor wants you to learn from it: This may help you form a guiding question. For example, if you were told to read Chapter 4, "Respiratory Illnesses," in your nursing textbook, and then write a list of the illnesses and their treatments, you might ask, "What are the different respiratory illnesses, and how are they treated?"

As you read, try to answer your question. A guiding question gives you a purpose when you are reading and helps keep you focused. This book supplies a guiding question for each essay in the Readings section. Be sure to read it before you read the essay and keep it in mind while you read.

TIP: If you keep a reading journal, you can record your guiding question there.

While Reading

Keep Asking Questions.

Active readers keep asking questions and trying to answer them. You already have a guiding question. As you read, ask yourself, "Have I answered my guiding question yet? If not, why not?" Ask yourself other questions, too: "What does this mean? Do I understand everything so far? Do I agree with it? Is this useful?"

Sometimes it helps to pause in the middle of a reading. Otherwise, you may find yourself at the last sentence without understanding what you've read. Try to pause about midway through each reading and predict what's going to come next. Will the author provide another example? Will the plot of a story take a new twist? Will a completely new topic be introduced?

TIP: If you keep a reading journal, you can write your notes there.

Take Notes.

Another way to stay active while reading is to take notes. Taking notes can help you understand a reading, and the act of writing notes keeps you alert. Your notes can be written in the margin of a book, in a separate reading journal, or on note cards. You also can underline, use check marks and other symbols, or highlight phrases in a different color. Find a method that works for you. Here are some ideas for how to take notes:

- Note the main idea (double-underline it).
- Note the supporting points (underline them).
- Note things you agree with (put a check mark in the margin).
- Note things you don't agree with (put an exclamation point in the margin).
- Note points or words you don't understand (put a question mark in the margin).
- Note information that answers your guiding question.
- Note thoughts or reactions you have while reading (write them in the margin).

After Reading

TIP: If you keep a reading journal, you can write your answers there.

Answer Questions.

After you've read the selection, you will be able to answer questions about it. Sometimes you may need to read all or parts of it again to fully answer questions.

First, look at your guiding question and try to answer it.

Second, if you are reading a college textbook, you will probably find study questions at the end of each reading or chapter. Try to answer all of them, even if they aren't assigned.

Third, you should always try to answer the following basic questions about what you've read, even if you don't have study questions:

CLOSE READING QUESTIONS

What is the author's main point?

What are the supporting points?

Do I understand everything I've just read?

CRITICAL READING QUESTIONS

Why is the author making this main point?

How strong are the supporting points?

>   Does the author use opinions or facts as supporting points?

>   Do I agree with the opinions?

>   Do the facts seem sound and relevant?

How has the author tried to convince me of his or her point of view?

Is there another way to look at this topic?

What do I think about the author's message? Why do I think this?

Each essay in this section is followed by two kinds of questions: Check Your Comprehension questions help you read closely, and Read Critically questions help you read critically. Be sure to answer them when you finish a reading.

Write.

The best way to make ideas and information your own is to use them. So the best way to be an active reader is to write something about what you have read. If you take notes while you read, you already have started to do this. But now you can try three other kinds of writing:

TIP: For more information on summarizing, see Chapter 20.

SUMMARIZE: A summary is a short account, in your own words, of the main point and supporting points in a reading. Writing an informal summary helps you understand the author's key points. A summary also reminds you of these key points during class discussion, while preparing for a writing assignment, and when studying for a test.

TIP: If you keep a reading journal, you can summarize and respond to the reading there.

RESPOND: A response is your personal reaction to the reading. We learn new things by connecting them to what we already know. What connections can you make between what you've read and your own life? Have you ever experienced anything similar? How did the reading make you feel? What was your first thought when you finished reading?

WRITE A PARAGRAPH OR ESSAY: Try writing your own paragraph or essay on the same topic. Do you agree or disagree with what the author said? Set out your own reasons clearly and persuasively. You also can use the reading as a model: Can you write something similar?

Each essay in "Readings for Writers" is followed by a Summarize and Respond suggestion and by topics for paragraphs and essays. Writing after reading is the best way to make what you've read work for you.

An Active Reader at Work

Here is a sample reading. Its notes show how one student, Angela, read the essay. The things that Angela did *before* reading are in black; the things she did *while* reading are in color. You may want to use this as a model as you work through the readings in the following chapters.

read author,
title,
headnote

Arthur Levine
Student Expectations of College

Dedicated to the pursuit of improving educational experiences for students of every kind, Arthur Levine is president of Teachers College at Columbia University and chair of the Institute for Educational Management at Harvard University. Before writing this article, Levine interviewed students on thirty campuses as part of a study of undergraduate values and beliefs. Based on those interviews, he presents some of his interpretations of what students want—and do not want—from colleges. His findings indicate that colleges need to change in order to provide today's students with what they want and need.

read
Guiding
Question

GUIDING QUESTION
What are student expectations of college, and do you agree with what the author says?

relates to
Guiding
Question

Perhaps the most profound change in higher education today is in the expectations students have of their schools. Higher education is not the central feature of their lives, but just one of a multiplicity[1] of activities in which they are engaged every day. For many, college is not even the most important of these activities. Work and family overshadow it.   ✓ *my night job!*   1

The relationship students want with their college is like the one they already have with their banks, supermarkets, and the other organizations they patronize.[2] They want education to be nearby and to operate during convenient hours. They want easy, accessible parking, short lines, and polite and efficient personnel and services. They also want high-quality products but are eager for low costs. They are very willing to comparison shop—placing a premium[3] on time and money.   ✓   2

! I don't
totally
agree

Guiding
Question

What they don't want are the extras colleges traditionally offer. Just as they do not expect their banks to arrange softball games for them or family picnics or religious services or mental health clinics, increasingly they do not expect these things of their colleges. They prefer to tend to their own entertainment, health care, and spiritual needs and do not want to pay a college for these services. All they want of higher education is simple procedures, good service, quality courses, and low costs—with course quality ranked as the highest priority and price, procedures, and service ranking lower. Students are bringing to higher education exactly the same consumer expectations they have for every other commercial enterprise with which they deal.   ?   3

[1] **multiplicity:** great number
[2] **patronize:** be a regular customer of
[3] **premium:** high value

noticed vocabulary glosses

42

Illustration

TIP: For information on writing illustration, see Chapter 7.

Each essay in this chapter uses illustration to get its main point across to the reader. Illustration uses one or more examples to show, explain, or prove a main point. Good illustration contains detailed and specific examples and gives enough examples to make the point. Sometimes one extended example is all that's needed, but often writers use a series of briefer examples. As you read these essays, pay attention to how these writers use convincing, interesting examples.

Maya Angelou
Our Boys

Maya Angelou was born Marguerite Johnson in St. Louis in 1928. She lived much of her young life in Stamps, Arkansas, with her paternal grandmother, Annie Henderson, and her brother Bailey. Though burdened with the sadness of a broken family, rape, racism, and teenage pregnancy, Angelou was uplifted by her grandmother's faith and her brother's love. She went on to perform with a dance company, act in a number of plays and films, and write six books of poetry, various scores and songs, and a six-volume autobiography. Angelou is perhaps best known for the first of these personal accounts: *I Know Why the Caged Bird Sings* (1970). For the January 1993 presidential inauguration ceremony, President William Jefferson Clinton asked her to compose and deliver an original poem ("On the Pulse of Morning").

Maya Angelou continues to chronicle her life experience in collections of autobiographical essays. The following selection is from *Wouldn't Take Nothing for My Journey Now* (1993). As an African American woman, she writes not to point out differences or dwell on past injustices but to illustrate the need for connection, tolerance, and self-exploration. Maya Angelou is Reynolds Professor of American Studies at Wake Forest University.

GUIDING QUESTION

Why is this essay an example of illustration, and what point does Angelou illustrate?

"I like the use of the word *tapestry* to illustrate that no matter what color we are, we are all equal."
—Jimmy Munoz, Student

The plague[1] of racism is insidious,[2] entering into our minds as smoothly and quietly and invisibly as floating airborne microbes enter into our bodies to find lifelong purchase[3] in our bloodstreams.

Here is a dark little tale which exposes the general pain of racism. I wrote ten one-hour television programs called *Blacks, Blues, Blacks,* which highlighted Africanisms[4] still current in American life. The work was produced in San Francisco at KQED.

The program "African Art's Impact in Western Art" was fourth in a series. In it I planned to show the impact African sculpture had on the art of Picasso,[5] Modigliani,[6] Paul Klee,[7] and Rouault.[8] I learned that a Berkeley collector owned many pieces of East African Makonde[9] sculpture. I contacted the collector, who allowed me to select thirty pieces of art. When they were arranged on lighted plinths,[10] the shadows fell from the sculptures on to the floor, and we photographed them in dramatic sequence. The collector and his wife were so pleased with the outcome that at my farewell dinner they presented me with a piece of sculpture as a memento.[11] They were white, older, amused and amusing. I knew that if I lived in their area, we would become social friends.

I returned to New York, but three years later I moved back to Berkeley to live. I telephoned the collector and informed him of my move. He said, "So glad you called. I read of your return in the newspaper. Of course we must get together." He went on, "You know I am the local president of the National Council of Christians and Jews. But you don't know what I've been doing since we last spoke. I've been in Germany trying to ameliorate[12]

[1] **plague:** widespread, destructive problem or situation
[2] **insidious:** having a gradually harmful effect
[3] **purchase:** influence
[4] **Africanisms:** words, ideals, and behaviors adopted from African culture and tradition
[5] **Picasso:** Pablo Picasso (1881–1973); Spanish painter and sculptor
[6] **Modigliani:** Amedeo Modigliani (1884–1920); Italian painter and sculptor
[7] **Paul Klee:** (1879–1940); Swiss painter and etcher
[8] **Rouault:** Georges Rouault (1871–1958); French painter
[9] **Makonde:** East African people known for their wood carving
[10] **plinths:** square blocks that serve as bases
[11] **memento:** keepsake or souvenir
[12] **ameliorate:** improve

TEACHING TIP

This essay is an extended example: One detailed example supports the main idea. Have students find the main point (thesis statement) and underline details that make the one example come to life.

Read the poem at the end of the essay aloud. Which lines state the author's main point? ("We are more alike, my friends, than we are un-alike.") What examples does the poem give?

the conditions for American soldiers." His voice was weighted with emotion. He said, "You know, the black soldiers are having a horrific time over there, and our boys are having a hard time, too."

I asked, "What did you say?"

He said, "Well, I'm saying that the black soldiers are having it particularly rough, but our guys are having a bad time, too."

I asked, "Would you repeat that?"

He said, "Well, I'm saying . . ." Then his mind played back his statement, or he reheard the echo of his blunder hanging in the air.

He said, "Oh, my God, I've made such a stupid mistake, and I'm speaking with Maya Angelou." He said, "I'm so embarrassed, I'm going to hang up." I said, "Please don't. Please don't. This incident merely shows how insidious racism is. Please, let's talk about it." I could hear embarrassment in his voice, and hesitations and chagrin.[13] Finally, after about three or four minutes, he managed to hang up. I telephoned him three times, but he never returned my telephone calls.

The incident saddened and burdened me. The man, his family and friends were lessened by not getting to know me and my family and friends. And it also meant that I, my family, and my friends were lessened by not getting to know him. Because we never had a chance to talk, to teach each other and learn from each other, racism had diminished all the lives it had touched.

It is time for the preachers, the rabbis, the priests and pundits,[14] and the professors to believe in the awesome wonder of diversity so that they can teach those who follow them. It is time for parents to teach young people early on that in diversity there is beauty and there is strength. We all should know that diversity makes for a rich tapestry,[15] and we must understand that all the threads of the tapestry are equal in value no matter their color; equal in importance no matter their texture.

Our young must be taught that racial peculiarities do exist, but that beneath the skin, beyond the differing features and into the true heart of being, fundamentally,[16] we are more alike, my friend, than we are unalike.

> . . . Mirror twins are different
> although their features jibe,
> and lovers think quite different
>   thoughts
> while lying side by side.
>
> We love and lose in China,
> we weep on England's moors,
> and laugh and moan in Guinea,
> and thrive on Spanish shores.

[13] **chagrin:** disappointment

[14] **pundits:** authorities

[15] **tapestry:** hand-woven cloth with designs or pictures

[16] **fundamentally:** basically

IDEA JOURNAL
Give your own examples
to support the author's
main point.

We seek success in Finland,
are born and die in Maine.
In minor ways we differ,
in major we're the same.

I note the obvious differences
between each sort and type,
but we are more alike, my friends,
than we are unalike.

We are more alike, my friends,
than we are unalike.
We are more alike, my friends,
than we are unalike.

Summarize and Respond

In your reading journal or elsewhere, write a brief summary (three to five sentences) of "Our Boys." Next, jot down a quick response to the reading. What did the essay make you think or feel? Is racism something you see or experience in your own life? Where and when?

Check Your Comprehension

1. An alternative title for this essay could be
   a. "Racism on the Rise in American Cities."
   b. "African Art, American Artists."
   c. "The Experiences of Black American Soldiers."
   d. "Why We Still Need to Teach about Racism."

2. The main idea of this essay is that
   a. black soldiers suffer more than white soldiers.
   b. sometimes we aren't aware of our racist words and behaviors.
   c. many Americans still have a racist view of African American folk art.
   d. interracial friendships are not possible.

3. Why does the collector hang up on Angelou?
   a. He is embarrassed about what he has said.
   b. He is angry about the living conditions of American soldiers in Germany.
   c. He mistakes her for someone else.
   d. He no longer collects African art.

4. If you are still unfamiliar with the following words, use a dictionary to check their meanings: impact (para. 3); horrific (4); blunder (8); burdened (10); diversity (11).

Read Critically

1. Successful writers think about their purpose when they write. What do you think Angelou's purpose in writing this essay is?
2. Take another look at paragraph 1 of the essay. Why do you think Angelou chose to begin with this image? Is it effective?
3. What was the collector's "stupid mistake"?
4. How does Angelou propose to ease racial tensions? Do you agree with her ideas? Why, or why not?
5. Angelou begins the poem that ends the essay with "Mirror twins." What is a mirror twin? How do you think the idea of mirror twins helps to illustrate her point?

WRITING TIP
Remember that good illustration
1. Makes a point
2. Contains detailed, specific examples that show, explain, or prove the point
3. Gives enough examples to get the point across

Write

WRITE A PARAGRAPH: Write a paragraph showing that racism is an unjust and shameful act. Provide examples that illustrate this point.

WRITE AN ESSAY: Angelou makes a compelling point about racism by presenting a common example of racist behavior. Write an essay in which you illustrate the harmful effects of racism through examples. Think about your own experiences as an eyewitness to or victim of racism.

Susan Perry and *Jim Dawson*
What's Your Best Time of Day?

Susan Perry, born in Cleveland, Ohio, in 1950, has worked as a freelance writer and editor for various publications, including those from the Center for Science in the Public Interest and Time-Life Books. Jim Dawson, born in 1949 in Tampa, Florida, has worked as a reporter specializing in science for the *Minneapolis Star* and *Tribune*. Their first book, *Nightmare: Women and the Dalkon Shield* (1985), presents the individual cases, court transcripts, and legal findings that led to the recall of the deadly birth control device, the Dalkon Shield.

In "What's Your Best Time of Day?" excerpted from their second book, *The Secrets Our Body Clocks Reveal* (1988), Perry and Dawson explore the field of chronobiology—the study of how the season and time of day can affect our moods and productivity. Notice how the authors use detailed examples to illustrate what the science of chronobiology has revealed about our daily lives.

GUIDING QUESTION
What does the question "What's Your Best Time of Day?" have to do with the authors' main idea?

Every fall, Jane, a young mother and part-time librarian, begins to eat more and often feels sleepy. Her mood is also darker, especially when she awakens in the morning; it takes all her energy just to drag herself out of bed. These symptoms persist until April, when warmer weather and longer days seem to lighten her mood and alleviate[1] her cravings for food and sleep.

Joseph, a forty-eight-year-old engineer for a Midwestern computer company, feels cranky early in the morning. But as the day progresses, he becomes friendlier and more accommodating.[2]

All living organisms, from mollusks[3] to men and women, exhibit biological rhythms. Some are short and can be measured in minutes or hours. Others last days or months. The peaking of body temperature, which occurs in most people every evening, is a daily rhythm. The menstrual cycle is a monthly rhythm. The increase in sexual drive in the autumn—not in the spring, as poets would have us believe—is a seasonal, or yearly, rhythm.

The idea that our bodies are in constant flux is fairly new—and goes against traditional medical training. In the past, many doctors were taught to believe the body has a relatively stable, or homeostatic,[4] internal environment. Any fluctuations were considered random and not meaningful enough to be studied.

As early as the 1940s, however, some scientists questioned the homeostatic view of the body. Franz Halberg, a young European scientist working in the United States, noticed that the number of white blood cells in laboratory mice was dramatically higher and lower at different times of day. Gradually, such research spread to the study of other rhythms in other life forms, and the findings were sometimes startling. For example, the time of day when a person receives X-ray or drug treatment for cancer can affect treatment benefits and ultimately mean the difference between life and death.

This new science is called chronobiology,[5] and the evidence supporting it has become increasingly persuasive. Along the way, the scientific and medical communities are beginning to rethink their ideas about how the human body works, and gradually what had been considered a minor science just a few years ago is being studied in major universities and medical centers around the world. There are even chronobiologists working for the National Aeronautics and Space Administration, as well as for the National Institute of Health and other government laboratories.

With their new findings, they are teaching us things that can literally change our lives—by helping us organize ourselves so we can work *with* our natural rhythms rather than *against* them. This can enhance our outlook on life as well as our performance at work and play.

Because they are easy to detect and measure, more is known of daily— or circadian[6] (Latin for "about a day")—rhythms than other types. The most obvious daily rhythm is the sleep/wake cycle. But there are other daily cycles as well: temperature, blood pressure, hormone levels. Amid these and

[1] **alleviate:** lessen
[2] **accommodating:** agreeable
[3] **mollusks:** shellfish
[4] **homeostatic:** unchanging
[5] **chronobiology:** study of rhythms in living organisms
[6] **circadian:** daily

IDEA JOURNAL
Give some personal
examples of your best
time of day for certain
activities.

the body's other changing rhythms, you are simply a different person at 9 A.M. than you are at 3 P.M. How you feel, how well you work, your level of alertness, your sensitivity to taste and smell, the degree with which you enjoy food or take pleasure in music—all are changing throughout the day.

Most of us seem to reach our peak of alertness around noon. Soon after that, alertness declines, and sleepiness may set in by midafternoon.

Your short-term memory is best during the morning—in fact, about 15 percent more efficient than at any other time of day. So, students, take heed: When faced with a morning exam, it really does pay to review your notes right before the test is given.

Long-term memory is different. Afternoon is the best time for learning material that you want to recall days, weeks or months later. Politicians, business executives or others who must learn speeches would be smart to do their memorizing during that time of day. If you are a student, you would be wise to schedule your more difficult classes in the afternoon, rather than in the morning. You should also try to do most of your studying in the afternoon, rather than late at night. Many students believe they memorize better while burning the midnight oil because their short-term recall is better during the wee hours of the morning than in the afternoon. But short-term memory won't help them much several days later, when they face the exam.

By contrast, we tend to do best on cognitive[7] tasks—things that require the juggling of words and figures in one's head—during the morning hours. This might be a good time, say, to balance a checkbook.

Your manual dexterity—the speed and coordination with which you perform complicated tasks with your hands—peaks during the afternoon hours. Such work as carpentry, typing or sewing will be a little easier at this time of day.

What about sports? During afternoon and early evening, your coordination is at its peak, and you're able to react the quickest to an outside stimulus—like a baseball speeding toward you at home plate. Studies have also shown that late in the day, when your body temperature is peaking, you will *perceive* a physical workout to be easier and less fatiguing—whether it actually is or not. That means you are more likely to work harder during a late-afternoon or early-evening workout, and therefore benefit more from it. Studies involving swimmers, runners, shot-putters and rowing crews have shown consistently that performance is better in the evening than in the morning.

In fact, all of your senses—taste, sight, hearing, touch, and smell— may be at their keenest during late afternoon and early evening. That could be why dinner usually tastes better to us than breakfast and why bright lights irritate us at night.

Even our perception of time changes from hour to hour. Not only does time seem to fly when you're having fun, but it also seems to fly even faster if you are having that fun in the late afternoon or early evening, when your body temperature is also peaking.

---

[7] **cognitive:** involving the mind

While all of us follow the same general pattern of ups and downs, the   17
exact timing varies from person to person. It all depends on how your "biological" day is structured—how much of a morning or night person you are.
The earlier your biological day gets going, the earlier you are likely to
enter—and exit—the peak times for performing various tasks. An extreme
morning person and an extreme night person may have circadian cycles that
are a few hours apart.

Each of us can increase our knowledge about our individual rhythms.   18
Learn how to listen to the inner beats of your body; let them set the pace of
your day. You will live a healthier—and happier—life. As no less an authority than the Bible tells us, "To every thing there is a season, and a time to
every purpose under heaven."

Summarize and Respond

In your reading journal or elsewhere, write a brief summary (three to
five sentences) of "What's Your Best Time of Day?" Next, jot down a quick
response to the reading. How do the authors' observations relate to *your*
body rhythms? What is *your* best time of day?

Check Your Comprehension

1. An alternate title for this essay could be
   a. "Circadian Rhythms."
   b. "Morning People."
   c. "A Good Excuse for Failing Afternoon Exams."
   d. "Winter: The Time to Fall in Love."

2. The main idea of this essay is that
   a. understanding the rhythm of our bodies is a new science.
   b. reviewing materials in the morning may be a good test-taking
      tactic.
   c. understanding the rhythm of our bodies can improve the quality
      of our lives.
   d. women may have different daily rhythms than men.

3. When is the best time for a politician to learn a speech?
   a. late at night
   b. afternoon
   c. early morning
   d. between 9 A.M. and 3 P.M.

4. If you are still unfamiliar with the following words, use a dictionary to
   check their meanings: persist (para. 1); flux (4); dexterity (13); coordination (14).

Read Critically

1. Do the authors believe in the ideas of chronobiology? Can you think of any questions to ask them?

2. The authors claim that "how you feel, how well you work, your level of alertness, your sensitivity to taste and smell . . . all are changing throughout the day." What two examples do they use to support this claim?

3. Explain why you liked or didn't like how the authors open the essay with the example of "Jane."

4. Throughout the essay, the authors provide many examples to support their main point. What other qualities of good illustration can you find in their essay?

5. What traditional advice about studying do the authors claim to be incorrect?

Write

WRITING TIP
Remember that good illustration
1. Makes a point
2. Contains detailed, specific examples that show, explain, or prove the point
3. Gives enough examples to get the point across

WRITE A PARAGRAPH: Write a paragraph that applies the authors' findings to your body rhythms. Find examples in the essay that might explain your behaviors—for example, like feeling more energetic in the late afternoon. Be sure to use a detailed example from your own life to support your idea.

WRITE AN ESSAY: Write an essay that supports the ideas on body rhythms you read about. Use your experiences as examples. You may want to draw on the ideas you developed for Summarize and Respond. In what ways do your observations support the authors' findings? In what ways do they disagree?

43

Narration

TIP: For information on writing narration, see Chapters 8 and 18.

Each essay in this chapter uses narration to get its main point across to the reader. Narration tells a story that reveals something meaningful. Good narration includes all the important events in a story, brings each event to life with details, and presents events in a clear order. As you read these essays, note how the writers use meaningful and vivid stories to convey a message.

Roger Hoffmann
The Dare

When we look back on our childhoods, we sometimes see for the first time the risks we took to gain the approval of our peers. Roger Hoffmann's narrative takes us to his own childhood, when he was "struggling to make the cut in a tough Atlanta grammar school." At the time, the desire to belong to a group was stronger than his own sense of personal safety. Though we may not have responded in the same way to "The Dare," Hoffmann's essay reminds us that taking risks and seeking approval are life experiences that follow us into adulthood.

First printed in the *New York Times Magazine* (1986), this essay illustrates how a narration essay can tell a suspenseful and vivid story. As you read, notice the details Hoffmann provides to make his essay grab your attention.

GUIDING QUESTION
What was the dare, and why was it important to the author?

TEACHING TIP
Have students read the essay, list the major incidents, and circle the transitions the author uses. Which paragraphs are most lifelike? What details bring the story to life? What is the purpose of the essay? Why is it important to the author?

The secret to diving under a moving freight train and rolling out of the other side with all your parts attached lies in picking the right spot between the tracks to hit with your back. Ideally, you want soft dirt or pea gravel, clear of glass shards[1] and railroad spikes that could cause you instinctively, and fatally, to sit up. Today, at thirty-eight, I couldn't be threatened or baited enough to attempt that dive. But as a seventh grader struggling to make the cut in a tough Atlanta grammar school, all it took was a dare.

I coasted through my first years of school as a fussed-over smart kid, the teacher's pet who finished his work first and then strutted around the room tutoring other students. By the seventh grade, I had more A's than friends. Even my old cronies,[2] Dwayne and O. T., made it clear I'd never be one of the guys in junior high if I didn't dirty up my act. They challenged me to break the rules, and I did. The I-dare-you's escalated:[3] shoplifting, sugaring teachers' gas tanks, dropping lighted matches into public mailboxes. Each guerrilla act won me the approval I never got for just being smart.

Walking home by the railroad tracks after school, we started playing chicken with oncoming trains. O. T., who was failing that year, always won. One afternoon he charged a boxcar from the side, stopping just short of throwing himself between the wheels. I was stunned. After the train disappeared, we debated whether someone could dive under a moving car, stay put for a 10-count, then scramble out the other side. I thought it could be done and said so. O. T. immediately stepped in front of me and smiled. Not by me, I added quickly, I certainly didn't mean that I could do it. "A smart guy like you," he said, his smile evaporating, "you could figure it out easy." And then, squeezing each word for effect, "I . . . DARE . . . you." I'd just turned twelve. The monkey clawing my back was Teacher's Pet. And I'd been dared.

As an adult, I've been on both ends of life's implicit[4] business and social I-dare-you's, although adults don't use those words. We provoke[5] with body language, tone of voice, ambiguous[6] phrases. I dare you to: argue with the boss, tell Fred what you think of him, send the wine back. Only rarely are the risks physical. How we respond to dares when we are young may have something to do with which of the truly hazardous male inner dares—attacking mountains, tempting bulls at Pamplona[7]—we embrace or ignore as men.

For two weeks, I scouted trains and tracks. I studied moving boxcars close up, memorizing how they squatted on their axles, never getting used to the squeal or the way the air felt hot from the sides. I created an imaginary, friendly train and ran next to it. I mastered a shallow, head-first dive with a simple half-twist. I'd land on my back, count to ten, imagine wheels and, locking both hands on the rail to my left, heave myself over and out. Even

[1] **shards:** sharp fragments
[2] **cronies:** close friends
[3] **escalated:** rose, increased
[4] **implicit:** understood but not directly stated
[5] **provoke:** cause anger
[6] **ambiguous:** having more than one meaning
[7] **Pamplona:** city in the north of Spain

under pure sky, though, I had to fight to keep my eyes open and my shoulders between the rails.

The next Saturday, O. T., Dwayne and three eighth graders met me below the hill that backed up to the lumberyard. The track followed a slow bend there and opened to a straight, slightly uphill climb for a solid third of a mile. My run started two hundred yards after the bend. The train would have its tongue hanging out.   6

The other boys huddled off to one side, a circle on another planet, and watched quietly as I double-knotted my shoelaces. My hands trembled. O. T. broke the circle and came over to me. He kept his hands hidden in the pockets of his jacket. We looked at each other. BB's[8] of sweat appeared beneath his nose. I stuffed my wallet in one of his pockets, rubbing it against his knuckles on the way in, and slid my house key, wired to a red-and-white fishing bobber, into the other. We backed away from each other, and he turned and ran to join the four already climbing up the hill.   7

I watched them all the way to the top. They clustered together as if I were taking their picture. Their silhouette resembled a round shouldered tombstone. They waved down to me, and I dropped them from my mind and sat down on the rail. Immediately, I jumped back. The steel was vibrating.   8

The train sounded like a cow going short of breath. I pulled my shirttail out and looked down at my spot, then up the incline of track ahead of me. Suddenly the air went hot, and the engine was by me. I hadn't pictured it moving that fast. A man's bare head leaned out and stared at me. I waved to him with my left hand and turned into the train, burying my face into the incredible noise. When I looked up, the head was gone.   9

I started running alongside the boxcars. Quickly, I found their pace, held it, and then eased off, concentrating on each thick wheel that cut past me. I slowed another notch. Over my shoulder, I picked my car as it came off the bend, locking in the image of the white mountain goat painted on its side. I waited, leaned forward like the anchor in a 440-relay, wishing the baton up the track behind me. Then the big goat fired by me, and I was flying and then tucking my shoulder as I dipped under the train.   10

A heavy blanket of red dust settled over me. I felt bolted to the earth. Sheet-metal bellies thundered and shook above my face. Count to ten, a voice said, watch the axles and look to your left for daylight. But I couldn't count, and I couldn't find left if my life depended on it, which it did. The colors overhead went from brown to red to black to red again. Finally, I ripped my hands free, forced them to the rail, and, in one convulsive jerk, threw myself into the blue light.   11

I lay there face down until there was no more noise, and I could feel the sun against the back of my neck. I sat up. The last ribbon of train was slipping away in the distance. Across the tracks, O. T. was leading a cavalry charge down the hill, five very small, galloping boys, their fists whirling above them. I pulled my knees to my chest. My corduroy pants puckered wet across my thighs. I didn't care.   12

[8] **BB's:** pellets used in air guns

IDEA JOURNAL
Tell a scary story from your past. Organize the incidents chronologically, and use lifelike details to convey what frightened you.

Summarize and Respond

In your reading journal or elsewhere, write a brief summary (three to five sentences) of "The Dare." Next, jot down a quick response to the reading. How did it make you feel? Describe any childhood experiences you were reminded of by reading it.

Check Your Comprehension

1. An alternate title for this essay could be
   a. "How to Survive Being Teacher's Pet."
   b. "Hazardous Male Dares."
   c. "Being Invincible."
   (d.) "Peer Pressure."

2. The main idea of this essay is that
   a. the secret to surviving a dive beneath a moving freight train involves hitting the right spot.
   b. you must avoid acting smart in school if you want to be accepted.
   c. how adults respond to dares depends on how they responded as children.
   (d.) the pressure to be accepted by a group can make us do things we never would do when alone.

3. According to the essay, what kind of dares do adults face?
   a. walking past strangers on the street
   (b.) threatening body language and vague phrases
   c. orders from the boss
   d. gambling

4. If you are still unfamiliar with the following words, use a dictionary to check their meanings: debated, evaporating (para. 3); hazardous (4); silhouette (8).

Read Critically

1. Find the two points in the narrative where Hoffmann comments from the perspective of an adult. Explain why you think the author does this.
2. Hoffmann tells us that he performed the dare to be accepted by his peers, yet he ends his essay without telling how his friends responded. Why do you think the author leaves out the friends' responses? What is the effect of ending the essay with the line "I didn't care"?
3. In paragraph 3, Hoffmann writes that "the monkey clawing my back was Teacher's Pet." What do you think he means? Why do you think he says it this way?

4. In paragraph 6 Hoffmann writes that "the train would have its tongue hanging out." What does this image make you think of? Explain why you think (or don't think) this image works.

5. Does Hoffmann's relationship with his friends seem realistic to you? Does it change over the course of the story?

Write

WRITE A PARAGRAPH: Write a paragraph about something you did to be accepted by a particular group.

WRITE AN ESSAY: Write an essay about a dare that you faced. This dare does not have to be from your childhood, but if it is, you can begin with your entry for Summarize and Respond. Include all the important events in the story, such as who dared you, what the dare involved, and why you felt you had to accept the dare. Use details to help your readers understand what happened.

Brent Staples
A Brother's Murder

Brent Staples (b.1951) was raised in Chester, Pennsylvania, an industrial city that was plagued by poverty and violence. Staples escaped the life of the streets by earning his B.A. at Widener University (in Chester, where he later returned to teach) and then by leaving the East Coast to complete a Ph.D. in psychology at the University of Chicago. While living in Chicago he wrote extensively about jazz for a number of magazines, worked as a staff reporter for the *Chicago Sun Times,* and in 1981 received a fine arts grant for creative writing. In 1985, Staples joined the staff of the *New York Times,* working first as an editor for the *Book Review* and then joining the editorial board in 1990.

Staples frequently writes about issues of race, examining what it means to be a black male in contemporary American culture. In "A Brother's Murder" (from the *New York Times,* 1986), Staples questions the circumstances that drove him to leave home to obtain an education but led his brother Blake to stay behind and embrace the street life.

GUIDING QUESTION
What does Staples want us to learn from his brother's life and death?

It has been more than two years since my telephone rang with the news that my younger brother Blake—just twenty-two years old—had been murdered. The young man who killed him was only twenty-four. Wearing a ski mask, he emerged from a car, fired six times at close range with a massive

1

.44 Magnum, then fled. The two had once been inseparable friends. A senseless rivalry—beginning, I think, with an argument over a girlfriend—escalated from posturing,[1] to threats, to violence, to murder. The way the two were living, death could have come to either of them from anywhere. In fact, the assailant[2] had already survived multiple gunshot wounds from an incident much like the one in which my brother lost his life.

As I wept for Blake I felt wrenched backward into events and circumstances that had seemed light-years gone. Though a decade apart, we both were raised in Chester, Pennsylvania, an angry, heavily black, heavily poor, industrial city southwest of Philadelphia. There, in the 1960s, I was introduced to mortality,[3] not by the old and failing, but by beautiful young men who lay wrecked after sudden explosions of violence. The first, I remember from my fourteenth year — Johnny, brash lover of fast cars, stabbed to death two doors from my house in a fight over a pool game. The next year, my teenage cousin, Wesley, whom I loved very much, was shot dead. The summers blur. Milton, an angry young neighbor, shot a crosstown rival, wounding him badly. William, another teen-age neighbor, took a shotgun blast to the shoulder in some urban drama and displayed his bandages proudly. His brother, Leonard, severely beaten, lost an eye and donned a black patch. It went on.

I recall not long before I left for college, two local Vietnam veterans—one from the Marines, one from the Army—arguing fiercely, nearly at blows about which outfit had done the most in the war. The most killing, they meant. Not much later, I read a magazine article that set that dispute in context. In the story, a noncommissioned officer—a sergeant, I believe—said he would pass up any number of affluent, suburban-born recruits to get hard-core soldiers from the inner city. They jumped into the rice paddies with "their manhood on their sleeves," I believe he said. These two items—the veterans arguing and the sergeant's words—still characterize for me the circumstances under which black men in their teens and twenties kill one another with such frequency. With a touchy paranoia[4] born of living battered lives, they are desperate to be *real* men. Killing is only machismo[5] taken to the extreme. Incursions[6] to be punished by death were many and minor, and they remain so: They include stepping on the wrong toe, literally; cheating in a drug deal; simply saying "I dare you" to someone holding a gun; crossing territorial lines in a gang dispute. My brother grew up to wear his manhood on his sleeve. And when he died, he was in that group—black, male and in its teens and early twenties—that is far and away the most likely to murder or be murdered.

I left the East Coast after college, spent the mid- and late-1970s in Chicago as a graduate student, taught for a time, then became a journalist.

[1] **posturing:** acting tough

[2] **assailant:** attacker

[3] **mortality:** condition of eventually having to die

[4] **paranoia:** belief that people are out to get you

[5] **machismo:** aggressive male behavior (see the essay on p. 538)

[6] **incursions:** attacks

Within ten years of leaving my hometown, I was overeducated and "upwardly mobile," ensconced[7] on a quiet, tree-lined street where voices raised in anger were scarcely ever heard. The telephone, like some grim umbilical, kept me connected to the old world with news of deaths, imprisonings and misfortune. I felt emotionally beaten up. Perhaps to protect myself, I added a psychological dimension to the physical distance I had already achieved. I rarely visited my hometown. I shut it out.

As I fled the past, so Blake embraced it. On Christmas of 1983, I traveled from Chicago to a black section of Roanoke, Virginia, where he then lived. The desolate public housing projects, the hopeless, idle young men crashing against one another—these reminded me of the embittered town we'd grown up in. It was a place where once I would have been comfortable, or at least sure of myself. Now, hearing of my brother's forays[8] into crime, his scrapes with police and street thugs, I was scared, unsteady on foreign terrain.[9]

I saw that Blake's romance with the street life and the hustler image had flowered dangerously. One evening that late December, standing in some Roanoke dive among drug dealers and grim, hair-trigger losers, I told him I feared for his life. He had affected the image of the tough he wanted to be. But behind the dark glasses and the swagger, I glimpsed the baby-faced toddler I'd once watched over. I nearly wept. I wanted desperately for him to live. The young think themselves immortal, and a dangerous light shone in his eyes as he spoke laughingly of making fools of the policemen who had raided his apartment looking for drugs. He cried out as I took his right hand. A line of stitches lay between the thumb and index finger. Kickback from a shotgun, he explained, nothing serious. Gunplay had become part of his life.

I lacked the language simply to say: Thousands have lived this for you and died. I fought the urge to lift him bodily and shake him. This place and the way you are living smells of death to me, I said. Take some time away, I said. Let's go downtown tomorrow and buy a plane ticket anywhere, take a bus trip, anything to get away and cool things off. He took my alarm casually. We arranged to meet the following night—an appointment he would not keep. We embraced as though through glass. I drove away.

As I stood in my apartment in Chicago holding the receiver that evening in February 1984, I felt as though part of my soul had been cut away. I questioned myself then, and I still do. Did I not reach back soon or earnestly[10] enough for him? For weeks I awoke crying from a recurrent dream in which I chased him, urgently trying to get him to read a document I had, as though reading it would protect him from what had happened in waking life. His eyes shining like black diamonds, he smiled and danced just beyond my grasp. When I reached for him, I caught only the space where he had been.

5

6

7

8

[7] **ensconced:** settled comfortably
[8] **forays:** trips
[9] **terrain:** ground
[10] **earnestly:** sincerely

Summarize and Respond

In your reading journal or elsewhere, write a brief summary (three to five sentences) of "A Brother's Murder." Next, jot down a quick response to the reading. What did it make you feel? How did Staples feel about his brother?

Check Your Comprehension

1. An alternate title for this essay could be
    a. "Their Manhood on Their Sleeves."
    b. "Pennsylvania's Inner Cities."
    c. "Why I Left the City."
    d. "Drug Dealers and Hair-Trigger Losers."

2. The main idea of this essay is that
    a. in order to survive, you must leave your past behind.
    b. many black males in the inner city are likely to kill or be killed trying to prove their toughness.
    c. killing is a glorified form of manhood.
    d. acting macho is a good way to protect yourself.

3. What group did Blake belong to?
    a. a violent street gang
    b. a group of drug dealers
    c. Vietnam veterans
    d. a group most likely to murder or be murdered

4. If you are still unfamiliar with any of the following words, use a dictionary to check their meanings: escalated (para. 1); wrenched (2); umbilical (4).

Read Critically

1. Why do you think Staples begins his narrative by telling about Blake's death? How did you feel when you read the opening of the essay? Why didn't the author mention his brother's death at the end of the essay?

2. Staples fills his narrative with details to help him tell his story. For example, in paragraph 6 he tells of "a line of stitches" in Blake's hand. Find another example of a vivid detail. What effect did it have on you as you read the story?

3. In this essay Staples also writes about his own life and how it differed from his brother's. What effect does this comparison between the lives of the two brothers have on the essay?

4. In quoting the veterans, Staples writes that "they jumped into the rice paddies with 'their manhood on their sleeves.' " What do you think he means by this phrase? How does it pertain to Blake?

WRITING TIP
Remember that good
narration
1. Tells a story that
   reveals something
   meaningful
2. Includes all the important events in a story
3. Brings each event to
   life with details
4. Presents events in a
   clear order, usually
   chronological

5. In paragraph 3, Staples writes that young black men are "desperate to be *real* men." How do you think Staples would describe what it means to be "real men"?

Write

WRITE A PARAGRAPH: Write a paragraph that tells how you relate to a brother or sister (or another family member or close friend). Present details in a clear order about an event (like a party or shopping trip) that describes the nature of your relationship (such as whether you get along or fight).

WRITE AN ESSAY: Write an essay that tells a story about a dramatic experience you have had. Be sure to tell what the incident is, why it's important, when it occurred, and who or what was involved. Include vivid details to help your reader experience the event as you did.

44

Description

TIP: For information on writing description, see Chapters 9 and 18.

Description creates a picture with words. Good descriptions use vivid details to create a picture so realistic that readers can see it for themselves. These details can appeal to any of the five senses—sight, sound, smell, touch, or taste.

The essays in this chapter use description to get their main points across to the reader. The essay may simply describe an object or an experience or may make a larger point. Each essay succeeds when the author uses sensory details to bring an experience to life.

Maxine Hong Kingston
"Eat! Eat!"

Maxine Hong Kingston, born in 1940 to Chinese immigrants, was raised in Stockton, California, among the Chinese American community. Her parents, who were well educated in China (her mother, in fact, was a doctor), worked as laundry operators in the United States. Kingston earned a degree from the University of California at Berkeley in 1962 and taught English and creative writing for a number of years. Eventually, she turned to a career in writing and has published poetry, fiction, and memoirs. This essay is excerpted from her autobiography, *The Woman Warrior: Memoirs of a Girlhood among Ghosts* (1976).

In "'Eat! Eat!'" Kingston skillfully describes her mother's techniques for cooking unconventional foods and her stories about traditional feasts in China.

GUIDING QUESTION
What effects do Kingston's images have on you, and how does she achieve these effects?

"This is very descriptive writing with a realistic point of view. Some parts of the essay made me believe I was in Kingston's kitchen looking at the strange foods her mother made."

—*Laura Sterck, Student*

TEACHING TIP
This essay uses vivid sensory details—especially sight, sound, and taste. Have students read the essay, underline images that appeal to the senses, and write in the margin the sense each image appeals to. Which paragraph is most vivid? Why?

My mother has cooked for us: raccoons, skunks, hawks, city pigeons, wild ducks, wild geese, black-skinned bantams,[1] snakes, garden snails, turtles that crawled about the pantry floor and sometimes escaped under the refrigerator or stove, catfish that swam in the bathtub. "The emperors used to eat the peaked hump of purple dromedaries,"[2] she would say. "They used chopsticks made from rhinoceros horn, and they ate ducks' tongues and monkeys' lips." She boiled the weeds we pulled up in the yard. There was a tender plant with flowers like white stars hiding under the leaves, which were like the flower petals but green. I've not been able to find it since growing up. It had no taste. When I was as tall as the washing machine, I stepped out on the back porch one night, and some heavy, ruffling, windy, clawed thing dived at me. Even after getting chanted back to sensibility, I shook when I recalled that perched everywhere there were owls with great hunched shoulders and yellow scowls. They were a surprise for my mother from my father. We children used to hide under the beds with our fingers in our ears to shut out the bird screams and the thud, thud of the turtles swimming in the boiling water, their shells hitting the sides of the pot. Once the third aunt who worked at the laundry ran out and bought us bags of candy to hold over our noses; my mother was dismembering[3] skunk on the chopping block. I could smell the rubbery odor through the candy.   1

In a glass jar on a shelf my mother kept a big brown hand with pointed claws stewing in alcohol and herbs. She must have brought it from China because I do not remember a time when I did not have the hand to look at. She said it was a bear's claw, and for many years I thought bears were hairless. My mother used the tobacco, leeks, and grasses swimming about the hand to rub our sprains and bruises.   2

Just as I would climb up to the shelf to take one look after another at the hand, I would hear my mother's monkey story. I'd take my fingers out of my ears and let her monkey words enter my brain. I did not always listen voluntarily, though. She would begin telling the story, perhaps repeating it to a homesick villager, and I'd overhear before I had a chance to protect myself. Then the monkey words would unsettle me; a curtain flapped loose inside my brain. I have wanted to say, "Stop it. Stop it," but not once did I say, "Stop it."   3

"Do you know what people in China eat when they have the money?" my mother began. "They buy into a monkey feast. The eaters sit around a thick wood table with a hole in the middle. Boys bring in the monkey at the end of a pole. Its neck is in a collar at the end of the pole, and it is screaming. Its hands are tied behind it. They clamp the monkey into the table; the   4

---

[1] **bantams:** breed of chicken
[2] **dromedaries:** one-humped camels
[3] **dismembering:** chopping off body parts

whole table fits like another collar around its neck. Using a surgeon's saw, the cooks cut a clean line in a circle at the top of its head. To loosen the bone, they tap with a tiny hammer and wedge here and there with a silver pick. Then an old woman reaches out her hand to the monkey's face and up to its scalp, where she tufts some hairs and lifts off the lid of the skull. The eaters spoon out the brains."

Did she say, "You should have seen the faces the monkey made"? Did she say, "The people laughed at the monkey screaming"? It was alive? The curtain flaps closed like merciful[4] black wings.

"Eat! Eat!" my mother would shout at our heads bent over bowls, the blood pudding awobble[5] in the middle of the table.

She had one rule to keep us safe from toadstools[6] and such: "If it tastes good, it's bad for you," she said. "If it tastes bad, it's good for you."

We'd have to face four- and five-day-old leftovers until we ate it all. The squid eye would keep appearing at breakfast and dinner until eaten. Sometimes brown masses sat on every dish. I have seen revulsion on the faces of visitors who've caught us at meals.

"Have you eaten yet?" the Chinese greet one another.

"Yes, I have," they answer whether they have or not. "And you?"

I would live on plastic.

IDEA JOURNAL
Describe one of your eating rituals that might seem strange to someone from another culture.

Summarize and Respond

In your reading journal or elsewhere, write a brief summary (three to five sentences) of " 'Eat! Eat!' " Next, jot down a quick response to the reading. What did it make you think or feel? Can you recall an experience from your childhood that centers around a particular food?

Check Your Comprehension

1. An alternate title for this essay could be
   a. "The Monkey Story: Remembering Tastes and Trials of Childhood."
   b. "What the Emperors Used to Eat."
   c. "Attack of the Owls."
   d. "The White Star Plant."

2. The main idea of the essay is that
   a. as a child the author found her mother's cooking strange and unappetizing.
   b. the customs of one culture can be inappropriate for another.

[4] **merciful:** sympathetic
[5] **awobble:** unsteady
[6] **toadstools:** mushrooms

    c.   plastic tastes better than some foods.

    d.   if it tastes good, it's bad for you; if it tastes bad, it's good for you.

3. Why does Kingston's third aunt bring the children bags of candy?

    a.   She believes candy is the only healthy food.

    (b.)   She wants to calm them and block the odor of the skunk.

    c.   She brings them candy every day.

    d.   She wants to reward the children for surviving the owl attack.

4. If you are still unfamiliar with the following words, use a dictionary to check their meanings: sensibility (para. 1); leeks (2); tufts (4); revulsion (8).

Read Critically

1. Kingston uses images throughout her story. Pick one image, and explain how you think that image works as description.

2. In paragraph 1, Kingston writes, "We children used to hide under the beds with our fingers in our ears to shut out the bird screams and the thud, thud of the turtles swimming in the boiling water, their shells hitting the sides of the pot." Why does Kingston repeat the word "thud" here? What senses is she appealing to in this sentence? What effect does this have?

3. In the opening sentence, the author lists the exotic foods her mother has cooked. What effect did this sentence have on you? What did it lead you to expect the author would discuss in her essay?

4. In your opinion, what does Kingston think of the foods her mother cooked for her? What in the essay supports your answer?

5. Kingston concludes her essay by stating, "I would live on plastic." What do you think she means?

Write

WRITE A PARAGRAPH: Write a paragraph that describes your most recent meal. Include the meal's smell, its taste, how it looked, what it reminded you of, and why you chose that particular food. Avoid telling what the food is; let your description speak for itself.

WRITE AN ESSAY: Write an essay that describes an experience with a particular food you had as a child. This food may be something you fully enjoyed or, like Kingston's descriptions, something you would rather not have eaten. Consider how the food—the smell, the taste, the touch—made you feel. What emotions does the food stir up? Draw on the ideas you developed for Summarize and Respond, if you like.

WRITING TIP
Remember that good description
1. Creates a single main impression
2. Uses specific and concrete details that appeal to the senses (sight, sound, touch, taste, and smell)

Deems Taylor

The Monster

When Deems Taylor died in 1966, he was eighty years old and hailed as the composer of the first successful American operas. Taylor wrote his first piece of music at the age of ten and eventually wrote more than fifty works over the course of his life. In addition to composing, he worked as a newspaper editor, war correspondent, translator of prose and poetry, radio narrator, landscape painter, and public speaker. When asked about his many interests, Taylor replied, "I have tried teaching and found it an intolerable bore. No one would dream of hiring me as a conductor, and I am a dreadful pianist. So, long ago, I hit on a fourth choice: I would be subsidized. . . . I, the composer, have been supported by me, doing other things."

In this essay, an excerpt from *Of Men and Music* (1937), Taylor offers a mysterious description of a famous figure.

GUIDING QUESTION
Why doesn't Taylor include the composer's name in the title of the essay?

"The detailed description of the main character helped me get a feel for the overall idea of the essay."
—Lori Hassan, Student

He was an undersized little man, with a head too big for his body—a sickly little man. His nerves were bad. He had skin trouble. It was agony for him to wear anything next to his skin coarser than silk. And he had delusions[1] of grandeur.[2]

He was a monster of conceit.[3] Never for one minute did he look at the world or at the people, except in relation to himself. He was not only the most important person in the world, to himself; in his own eyes he was the only person who existed. He believed himself to be one of the greatest dramatists in the world, one of the greatest thinkers, and one of the greatest composers. To hear him talk, he was Shakespeare, and Beethoven, and Plato,[4] rolled into one. And you would have had no difficulty in hearing him talk. He was one of the most exhausting conversationalists that ever lived. An evening with him was an evening spent in listening to a monologue.[5] Sometimes he was brilliant; sometimes he was maddeningly tiresome. But whether he was being brilliant or dull, he had one sole topic of conversation: himself. What *he* thought and what *he* did.

[1] **delusions:** false beliefs
[2] **grandeur:** magnificence
[3] **conceit:** exaggerated opinion of oneself
[4] **Plato:** philosopher in ancient Greece (c. 428–348 B.C.)
[5] **monologue:** long speech by one person

He had a mania[6] for being in the right. The slightest hint of disagreement, from anyone, on the most trivial point, was enough to set him off on a harangue[7] that might last for hours, in which he proved himself right in so many ways, and with such exhausting volubility,[8] that in the end his hearer, stunned and deafened, would agree with him, for the sake of peace.

It never occurred to him that he and his doings were not of the most intense and fascinating interest to anyone with whom he came in contact. He had theories about almost any subject under the sun, including vegetarianism, the drama, politics, and music; and in support of these theories he wrote pamphlets, letters, books . . . thousands upon thousands of words, hundreds and hundreds of pages. He not only wrote these things, and published them—usually at somebody else's expense—but he would sit and read them aloud, for hours, to his friends and his family.

He wrote operas; and no sooner did he have the synopsis[9] of a story, but he would invite—or rather summon—a crowd of his friends to his house and read it aloud to them. Not for criticism. For applause. When the complete poem was written, the friends had to come again, and hear *that* read aloud. Then he would publish the poem, sometimes years before the music that went with it was written. He played the piano like a composer, in the worst sense of what that implies, and he would sit down at the piano before parties that included some of the finest pianists of his time, and play for them, by the hour, his own music, needless to say. He had a composer's voice. And he would invite eminent[10] vocalists to his house and sing them his operas, taking all the parts.

He had the emotional stability of a six-year-old child. When he felt out of sorts, he would rave and stamp, or sink into suicidal gloom and talk darkly of going to the East to end his days as a Buddhist monk. Ten minutes later, when something pleased him, he would rush out of doors and run around the garden, or jump up and down on the sofa, or stand on his head. He could be grief-stricken over the death of a pet dog, and he could be callous and heartless to a degree that would have made a Roman emperor shudder.

He was almost innocent of any sense of responsibility. Not only did he seem incapable of supporting himself, but it never occurred to him that he was under any obligation to do so. He was convinced that the world owed him a living. In support of this belief, he borrowed money from everybody who was good for a loan—men, women, friends, or strangers. He wrote begging letters by the score, sometimes groveling[11] without shame, at others loftily offering his intended benefactor[12] the privilege of contributing to his support, and being mortally offended if the recipient declined[13] the honor. I

6 **mania:** intense enthusiasm
7 **harangue:** long, pompous speech
8 **volubility:** talking too much
9 **synopsis:** outline of a story
10 **eminent:** well-known
11 **groveling:** begging
12 **benefactor:** patron, someone who supports another
13 **declined:** turned down, rejected

have found no record of his ever paying or repaying money to anyone who did not have a legal claim upon it.

What money he could lay his hands on he spent like an Indian rajah.[14] The mere prospect of a performance of one of his operas was enough to set him to running up bills amounting to ten times the amount of his prospective[15] royalties. On an income that would reduce a more scrupulous[16] man to doing his own laundry, he would keep two servants. Without enough money in his pocket to pay his rent, he would have the walls and ceiling of his study lined with pink silk. No one will ever know—certainly he never knew—how much money he owed. We do know that his greatest benefactor gave him $6,000 to pay the most pressing of his debts in one city, and a year later had to give him $16,000 to enable him to live in another city without being thrown into jail for debt.

He was equally unscrupulous in other ways. An endless procession[17] of women marched through his life. His first wife spent twenty years enduring and forgiving his infidelities.[18] His second wife had been the wife of his most devoted friend and admirer, from whom he stole her. And even while he was trying to persuade her to leave her first husband he was writing to a friend to inquire whether he could suggest some wealthy woman—*any* wealthy woman—whom he could marry for her money.

He was completely selfish in his other personal relationships. His liking for his friends was measured solely by the completeness of their devotion to him, or by their usefulness to him, whether financial or artistic. The minute they failed him—even by so much as refusing a dinner invitation—or began to lessen in usefulness, he cast them off without a second thought. At the end of his life he had exactly one friend left whom he had known even in middle age.

He had a genius for making enemies. He would insult a man who disagreed with him about the weather. He would pull endless wires in order to meet some man who admired his work and was able and anxious to be of use to him—and would proceed to make a mortal[19] enemy of him with some idiotic and wholly uncalled-for exhibition of arrogance[20] and bad manners. A character in one of his operas was a caricature[21] of one of the most powerful music critics of his day. Not content with burlesquing[22] him, he invited the critic to his house and read him the libretto[23] aloud in front of his friends.

The name of this monster was Richard Wagner. Everything that I have said about him you can find on record—in newspapers, in police reports, in the testimony of people who knew him, in his own letters, between the

[14] **rajah:** prince in India
[15] **prospective:** upcoming
[16] **scrupulous:** conscientious
[17] **procession:** parade
[18] **infidelities:** unfaithful acts
[19] **mortal:** deadly
[20] **arrogance:** overbearing pride
[21] **caricature:** exaggerated portrait that pokes fun at the subject
[22] **burlesquing:** mocking
[23] **libretto:** text of an opera

lines of his autobiography. And the curious thing about this record is that it doesn't matter in the least.

Because this undersized, sickly, disagreeable, fascinating little man was right all the time. The joke was on us. He *was* one of the world's great dramatists; he *was* a great thinker; he *was* one of the most stupendous musical geniuses that, up to now, the world has never seen. The world did owe him a living. People couldn't know those things at the time, I suppose; and yet to us, who know his music, it does seem as though they should have known. What if he did talk about himself all the time? If he had talked about himself for twenty-four hours every day for the span of his life he would not have uttered half the number of words that other men have spoken and written about him since his death.

When you consider what he wrote—thirteen operas and music dramas, eleven of them still holding the stage, eight of them unquestionably worth ranking among the world's great musico-dramatic masterpieces—when you listen to what he wrote, the debts and heartaches that people had to endure from him don't seem much of a price. Eduard Hanslick, the critic whom he caricatured in *Die Meistersinger* and who hated him ever after, now lives only because he was caricatured in *Die Meistersinger*. The women whose hearts he broke are long since dead; and the man who could never love anyone but himself has made them deathless atonement, I think, with *Tristan und Isolde.* Think of the luxury with which for a time, at least, fate rewarded Napoleon,[24] the man who ruined France and looted Europe; and then perhaps you will agree that a few thousand dollars' worth of debts were not too heavy a price to pay for the *Ring* trilogy.

What if he was faithless to his friends and to his wives? He had one mistress to whom he was faithful to the day of his death: Music. Not for a single moment did he ever compromise with what he believed, with what he dreamed. There is not a line of his music that could have been conceived by a little mind. Even when he is dull, or downright bad, he is dull in the grand manner. There is greatness about his worst mistakes. Listening to his music, one does not forgive him for what he may or may not have been. It is not a matter of forgiveness. It is a matter of being dumb with wonder that his poor brain and body didn't burst under the torment of the demon of creative energy that lived inside him, struggling, clawing, scratching to be released; tearing, shrieking at him to write the music that was in him. The miracle is that what he did in the little space of seventy years could have been done at all, even by a great genius. Is it any wonder that he had no time to be a man?

Summarize and Respond

In your reading journal or elsewhere, write a brief summary (three to five sentences) of "The Monster." Next, jot down your response to the reading. What did it make you think or feel? Were you surprised to learn that a famous and highly respected composer was such a "monster" in his personal life?

---

[24] **Napoleon:** Napoleon Bonaparte, French dictator who changed the course of Western history with his military genius (1769–1821)

Check Your Comprehension

1. Who is "the monster" in this essay?
    a. Shakespeare
    b. Beethoven
    c. Richard Wagner
    d. Napoleon

2. An alternate title for this essay could be
    a. "The Hardships of a Great Composer."
    b. "Roll over Beethoven: Richard Wagner's Here."
    c. "Society's Tolerance for Genius."
    d. "Casanova: The Man behind the Ring."

3. The main idea of this essay is that
    a. gifted people are usually not very nice.
    b. dictators and composers have much in common.
    c. you can't judge a genius by the same standards used for an ordinary person.
    d. it's okay to be dull if you're dull in a grand manner.

4. If you are still unfamiliar with the following words, use a dictionary to check their meanings: agony (para. 1); dramatists, maddeningly (2); theories (4); summon, criticism (5); rave, shudder (6); debts, atonement (14).

Read Critically

1. Why does Taylor keep Wagner's identity a secret until halfway through the essay?
2. Taylor provides many images in his description. Choose one that you particularly like, and explain how it helps the author make his point.
3. Taylor concludes his essay with "Is it any wonder he had no time to be a man?" Why do you think he ends with this? Answer his question.
4. Does Taylor really consider Wagner a monster? Where in the essay do you find support for your answer?
5. Taylor writes that "the joke was on us." Explain what you think he means.

WRITING TIP
Remember that good description
1. Creates a single main impression
2. Uses specific and concrete details that appeal to the senses (sight, sound, touch, taste, and smell)

Write

WRITE A PARAGRAPH: Write a paragraph that describes a person you know, but doesn't name that person.

WRITE AN ESSAY: Think of a famous person and write an essay that describes this person's character. Use images that appeal to your readers' senses. For example, instead of telling us that somebody is miserly, show us how he reuses the same piece of aluminum foil day after day to wrap his jelly sandwich. Feel free to invent details: You do not have to rely on the truth.

45

Process Analysis

TIP: For information on writing process analysis, see Chapters 10 and 18.

Each essay in this chapter uses process analysis to get its main point across to the reader. Process analysis explains how something works or how to do something. Good process analysis lists the essential steps in the process, explains each step in detail, and presents the steps in a logical order. Instructions are process analyses that give readers enough information to complete the steps themselves. Other process analyses are intended simply to educate the reader. As you read these essays, note how their writers present a series of clear, simple steps.

Kirby W. Stanat
The Job Interview

Kirby Stanat claims to have hired more than eight thousand people in his work as a personnel specialist and recruiter. He spent seven years as the Director of Career Planning and Placement at the University of Wisconsin before becoming the University's director of Auxiliary Enterprises. As a placement director, Stanat's function was "teaching students how the hiring process works . . . how the system works and how you can work it."

In "The Job Interview," an excerpt from his book *Job Hunting Secrets and Tactics* (1977), Stanat outlines the process of applying for—and getting—a job. Although the essay focuses on interviews conducted on campus by recruiters from big companies, his advice applies equally well to all job seekers.

GUIDING QUESTION
What advice does Stanat give about taking job interviews, and does it sound like good advice?

To succeed in campus job interviews, you have to know where that recruiter is coming from. The simple answer is that he is coming from corporate headquarters.

That may sound obvious, but it is a significant point that too many students do not consider. The recruiter is not a free spirit as he flies from Berkeley to New Haven, from Chapel Hill to Boulder. He's on an invisible leash to the office, and if he is worth his salary, he is mentally in corporate headquarters all the time he's on the road. If you can fix that in your mind—that when you walk into that bare-walled eight-by-ten cubicle in the placement center you are walking into a branch office of Sears, Bendix, or General Motors—you can avoid a lot of little mistakes and maybe some big ones. If, for example, you assume that because the interview is on campus the recruiter expects you to look and act like a student, you're in for a shock. A student is somebody who drinks beer, wears blue jeans, and throws a Frisbee. No recruiter has jobs for student Frisbee whizzes.

A cool spring day in late March. Sam Davis, a good recruiter who has been on the college circuit for years, is on my campus talking to candidates. He comes out to the waiting area to meet the student who signed up for an 11 o'clock interview. I'm standing in the doorway of my office, taking in the scene.

Sam calls the candidate: "Sidney Student." There sits Sidney. He's at a 45-degree angle, his feet are in the aisle, and he's almost lying down. He's wearing well-polished brown shoes, a tasteful pair of brown pants, a light brown shirt, and a good-looking tie. Unfortunately, he tops off this well-coordinated outfit with his Joe's Tavern Class A Softball Championship jacket, which has a big woven emblem over the heart. If that isn't bad enough, in his left hand is a cigarette and in his right hand is a half-eaten apple.

When Sam calls his name, the kid is caught off guard. He ditches the cigarette in an ashtray, struggles to his feet, and transfers the apple from the right to the left hand. Apple juice is everywhere, so Sid wipes his hand on the seat of his pants and shakes hands with Sam. Sam, who by now is close to having a stroke, gives me that what-the-hell-do-I-have-here look and has the young man follow him into the interview room.

The situation deteriorates even further—into pure Laurel and Hardy.[1] The kid is stuck with the half-eaten apple, doesn't know what to do with it, and obviously is suffering some discomfort. He carries the apple into the interviewing room with him and places it in the ashtray on the desk—right on top of Sam's freshly lit cigarette. The interview lasts five minutes.

I have told that story to scores of students and have asked them, "Did that kid get the job?" Invariably, they answer, "No, he didn't," and, of course, they're right. The students readily accept the idea that the kid lost the job in the waiting room. No student has ever asked me, "Did Sam Davis

---

[1] **Laurel and Hardy:** Hollywood actor-comedians who made films from 1915 to the 1950s

investigate to find out if the kid had any talent?" or "Did Sam Davis ask around to see if the kid might be smarter than that?" Of course, Sam did not.

After Sam gave Sidney the lightning brush-off, I asked Sidney to come into my office. I slammed the door and started to chew him out, because a stunt like that reflects badly on the university and on the placement center and, most important, it certainly doesn't do Sidney any good. I told him, "You handled yourself like some dumb student," and he said, "Well, Mr. Stanat, that's what I am. I am a student." I had to do a lot of talking to convince him that he had blown the interview, that Sam Davis wanted a professional, not a student.

That was an extreme case, but similar things happen, in varying degrees, over and over again in campus placement offices all over the country.

Recruiters want to meet professionals—with professional attitudes, professional objectives, and professional clothes. Behave and dress for the campus interview as if you were going to talk to the president of Ford Motor Company in his office.

Let us move in for a closer look at how the campus recruiter operates.

Let's say you have a 10 o'clock appointment with the recruiter from XYZ Corporation. The recruiter gets rid of the candidate in front of you at about 5 minutes to 10, jots down a few notes about what he is going to do with him or her, then picks up your résumé or data sheet. (Students usually fill out standard data sheets provided by the placement center. Sometimes they give the placement center copies of their résumés. These are given to the recruiter before the interview. [Some employment counselors] will strongly advise you, in certain situations, not to submit your résumé before meeting the recruiter. That does not apply when you go through the college placement center. The reason for not submitting your résumé in advance in some other situations is that submitting it could prevent you from getting an interview. But at the placement center, once you sign up for the interview, your interview is guaranteed.)

The importance of your data sheet or résumé comes into play here. Although the recruiter is still in the interview room and you are still in the lobby, your interview is under way. You're on. The recruiter will look over your sheet pretty carefully before he goes out to call you. He develops a mental picture of you. He thinks, "I'm going to enjoy talking with this kid," or, "This one's going to be a turkey." The recruiter has already begun to make a screening decision about you.

His first impression of you, from reading your sheet, could come from your grade point. It could come from misspelled words. It could come from poor erasures or from the fact that necessary information is missing. By the time the recruiter has finished reading your sheet, you've already hit the plus or minus column. You might not be very far into either column, but you probably didn't land squarely on the neutral line dividing the two columns. I defy anybody to read ten data sheets or résumés without forming an opinion about all ten candidates.

Let's assume the recruiter got a fairly good impression from your sheet.

Now the recruiter goes out to the lobby to meet you. He almost shuffles along, and his mind is somewhere else. Then he calls your name, and at that instant he visibly clicks into gear. He just went to work. As he calls your

4

5

6

7

8

9

10

11

12

TEACHING TIP
Have students read the
essay and underline the
essential steps in the
process. Are the author's
examples of each step
detailed enough? Ask
groups to give another
detail for each step and
then rewrite the process
analysis in a simplified
how-to format.

name, he looks quickly around the room, waiting for somebody to move. If you are sitting on the middle of your back, with a book open and a cigarette going, and if you have to rebuild yourself to stand up, the interest will run right out of the recruiter's face. You, not the recruiter, made the appointment for 10 o'clock, and the recruiter expects to see a young professional come popping out of that chair like today is a good day and you're anxious to meet him.

At this point, the recruiter does something rude. He doesn't walk across the room to meet you halfway. He waits for you to come to him. Something very important is happening. He wants to see you move. He wants to get an impression about your posture, your stride, and your briskness. If you slouch over to him, sidewinderlike,[2] he is not going to be impressed. He'll figure you would probably slouch your way through workdays. He wants you to come at him with lots of good things going for you. If you watch the recruiter's eyes, you can see the inspection. He glances quickly at shoes, pants, coat, shirt; dress, blouse, hose—the whole works.

He'll stick out his hand and say, "Good morning, Bill, my name is Joe Recruiter." Your handshake is extremely important.

> **Tip:** I would rather have a [person] bring me to my knees with a powerful handshake than give me a weak one. . . .

Next the recruiter will probably say, "Okay, Bill, please follow me," and he'll lead you into his interviewing room.

When you get to the room, you may find that the recruiter will open the door and gesture you in—with him blocking part of the doorway. There's enough room for you to get past him, but it's a near thing.

As you scrape past, he gives you a closeup inspection. He looks at your hair; if it's greasy, that will bother him. He looks at your collar; if it's dirty, that will bother him. He looks at your shoulders; if they're covered with dandruff, that will bother him. If you're a man, he looks at your chin. If you didn't get a close shave, that will irritate him. If you're a woman, he checks your makeup. If it's too heavy, he won't like it.

Then he smells you. An amazing number of people smell bad. Occasionally a recruiter meets a student who smells like a canal horse. That student can expect an interview of about four to five minutes (the average interview is twenty-five to thirty minutes). Students who stretch their budgets don't have their clothes dry-cleaned often enough. And every recruiting season a recruiter will run into somebody who stopped at a student union before the interview to wolf down a hamburger with onions and then tried to cover up the smell with breath mints. That doesn't work. The kid ends up smelling like onions and breath mints, and the interview has been severely damaged.

Next the recruiter inspects the back side of you. He checks your hair (is it combed in front but not in back?), your heels (are they run down?), your pants (are they baggy?), your slip (is it showing?), your stockings (do they have runs in them?).

[2] **sidewinderlike:** in an indirect manner

IDEA JOURNAL

How would you present
yourself as a "profes-
sional" in a job inter-
view?

Then he invites you to sit down.   20

At this point, I submit, *the recruiter's decision on you is 75 to 80 percent*   21
made.

Think about it. The recruiter has read your résumé. He knows who you   22
are and where you are from. He knows your marital status, your major, and
your grade point. And he knows what you've done with your summers. He
has inspected you, exchanged greetings with you, and smelled you. There is
very little additional hard information that he must gather on you. From
now on, it's mostly body chemistry.

Many recruiters have argued strenuously[3] that they don't make such   23
hasty decisions. So I tried an experiment. I told several recruiters that I
would hang around in the hall outside the interview room when they took
candidates in.

I told them that as soon as they had definitely decided not to recom-   24
mend the candidate they were interviewing, they should snap their fingers
loud enough for me to hear. It went like this:

First candidate: thirty-eight seconds after the candidate sat down: 25
Snap! Second candidate: one minute, forty-two seconds: Snap! Third candidate: forty-five seconds: Snap!

One recruiter was particularly adamant.[4] "Hell, no," he said; he didn't   26
rush to judgment on candidates. I asked him to participate in the snapping
experiment. He went out in the lobby, picked up his first candidate of the
day, and headed for an interview room. As he passed me in the hall, he
glared at me. And his fingers went "Snap!"

Summarize and Respond

In your reading journal or elsewhere, write a brief summary (three to five
sentences) of "The Job Interview." Next, jot down a quick response to the
reading. As a student, is there anything you would like to say to Kirby Stanat?

Check Your Comprehension

1. An alternate title for this essay could be
    a.   "When Students Were Studious."
    b.   "Losing the Job."
    c.   "Making the Grade: How to Pass a Job Interview."
    d.   "No Chemistry Finals Here."

2. The main idea of this essay is that
    a.   students should act like students at job interviews.
    b.   recruiters are not judgmental.

---

[3] **strenuously:** trying hard
[4] **adamant:** unyielding

c. how you present yourself to the world involves more than what you say.

d. a good student is not necessarily a good worker.

3. What is the first impression a student makes on the recruiter?

   a. his or her appearance

   b. his or her talent

   c. the information on his or her résumé and how it is presented

   d. whether he or she is a smoker or a nonsmoker

4. If you are still unfamiliar with the following words, use a dictionary to check their meanings: emblem, deteriorates (para. 2).

Read Critically

1. What process is Stanat analyzing? Why is he analyzing it? Use examples from the text to support your answer.

2. Does Stanat present the steps of the process in chronological order?

3. In paragraph 24, Stanat says he told the recruiters to "snap their fingers loud enough for me to hear." What is the purpose of the snapping? What function does it serve in his essay?

4. In paragraph 9 Stanat writes, "Although the recruiter is still in the interview room and you are still in the lobby, your interview is under way." What does he mean by this statement?

5. Describe the tone the author uses in the essay and how you responded to it.

Write

WRITING TIP
Remember that good process analysis
1. Tells what process is being analyzed and why
2. Lists all the essential steps in the process
3. Explains each step in detail
4. Presents the steps in a logical order, usually chronological

WRITE A PARAGRAPH: List your ideas about what a student should do for a successful job interview. Then write a paragraph that presents your list in chronological order.

WRITE AN ESSAY: Write an essay that explains how to balance the various "lives" that today's students have (college, work, family, and so on). You might want to expand on the ideas you addressed in your reading journal for Summarize and Respond. Your essay should be a guide to how to be a student at the end of the twentieth century. Based on your experiences and the challenges you have faced, what advice could you give a younger student?

Joey Green

Beauty and the Beef

A humorist and observer of American culture, Joey Green is the author of several books: *Hi, Bob! The Unofficial Guide to the Bob Newhart Show, Polish Your Furniture with Panty Hose, The Partridge Family Album, The Get Smart Handbook, The Unofficial Gilligan's Island Handbook,* and *Hellbent on Insanity — College Humor of the 70s and 80s.* Green graduated from Cornell University, despite near-expulsion for selling fake football programs at the 1979 Cornell-Yale homecoming game. After college, he served as a contributing editor for *National Lampoon* and *Spy* magazine. Green has spent part of his professional life at the J. Walter Thompson agency, writing television commercials for Burger King, Hyatt Hotels, Eastman Kodak (he won a Clio award for a print ad he created for Kodak), and Walt Disney World. A native of Miami, Florida, he currently lives in West Hills, California.

In "Beauty and the Beef," originally published in *Spy* magazine (1987), Green provides many colorful details as he shows, step-by-step, how a hamburger is made into a television star.

GUIDING QUESTION
How does the title of the essay relate to the process being analyzed?

"I like the way Green analyzes the process used to get consumers to buy their products."
—*Deborah Baker, Student*

When was the last time you opened a carton in a fast-food restaurant to find a hamburger as appetizing as the ones in the TV commercials? Did you ever look past the counter help to catch a glimpse of a juicy hamburger patty, handsomely branded by the grill, sizzling and crackling as it glides over roaring flames, with tender juices sputtering into the fire? On television the burger is a magnificent slab of flame-broiled beef — majestically topped with crisp iceberg lettuce, succulent red tomatoes, tangy onions, and plump pickles, all between two halves of a towering sesame-seed bun. But, of course, the real-life Whoppers don't quite measure up.

The ingredients of a TV Whopper are, unbelievably, the same as those used in real Whoppers sold to average consumers. But like other screen personalities, the Whopper needs a little help from makeup.

When making a Burger King commercial, J. Walter Thompson, the company's advertising agency, usually devotes at least one full day to filming "beauty shots" of the food. Burger King supplies the agency with several large boxes of frozen beef patties. But before a patty is sent over the flame broiler, a professionally trained food stylist earning between $500 and $750 a day prepares it for the camera.

The crew typically arrives at 7:00 A.M. and spends two hours setting up lights that will flatter the burger. Then the stylist, aided by two assistants,

TEACHING TIP
Have students underline the steps in the process and circle at least five details. Ask them if they found the essay interesting, and why. Discuss with them whether they think advertising distorts the truth and ask them to bring in examples of ads they think are good examples of distortion. Have them analyze this distortion in a paragraph or essay.

begins by burning "flame-broiling stripes" into the thawed hamburger patties with a special Madison Avenue[1] branding iron. Because the tool doesn't always leave a rich, charcoal-black impression on the patty, the stylist uses a fine paintbrush to darken the singed crevices[2] with a sauce the color of used motor oil. The stylist also sprinkles salt on the patty so when it passes over the flames, natural juices will be encouraged to rise to the meat's surface.

Thus branded, retouched, and juiced, the patties are run back and forth over a conveyor-belt broiler while the director films the little spectacle from a variety of angles. Two dozen people watch from the wings: lighting assistants, prop people, camera assistants, gas specialists, the client, and agency people — producers, writers, art directors. Of course, as the meat is broiled blood rises to the surface in small pools. Since, for the purpose of advertising, bubbling blood is not a desirable special effect, the stylist, like a prissy[3] microsurgical nurse, continually dabs at the burger with a Q-Tip.

Before the patty passes over the flame a second time, the food stylist maneuvers a small electric heater an inch or so above the burger to heat up the natural fatty juices until they begin to steam and sizzle. Otherwise puddles of grease will cover the meat. Sometimes patties are dried out on a bed of paper towels. Before they're sent over the flame broiler again, the stylist relubricates them with a drop of corn oil to guarantee picturesque crackling and sizzling.

If you examine any real Whopper at any Burger King closely, you'll discover flame-broiling stripes only on the top side of the beef patty. Hamburgers are sent through the flame broiler once; they're never flipped over. The commercials imply otherwise. On television a beef patty, fetchingly covered with flame-broiling stripes, travels over the broiler, indicating that the burger has been flipped to sear stripes into the other side.

In any case, the camera crew has just five or ten seconds in the life cycle of a TV Whopper to capture good, sizzling, brown beef on film. After that the hamburger starts to shrink rapidly as the water and grease are cooked from it. Filming lasts anywhere from three to eight hours, depending upon the occurrence of a variety of technical problems — heavy smoke, grease accumulating on the camera equipment, the gas specialist's failure to achieve a perfect, preternaturally[4] orange glowing flame. Out of one day's work, and anywhere between fifty and seventy-five hamburgers, the agency hopes to get five seconds of usable footage. Most of the time the patties are either too raw, bloody, greasy, or small.

Of course, the cooked hamburger patty depicted sitting on a sesame-seed bun in the commercial is a different hamburger from those towel-dried, steak-sauce-dabbed, corn-oiled specimens that were filmed sliding over the flames. This presentation patty hasn't been flame-broiled at all. It's been branded with the phony flame-broiling marks, retouched with the steak sauce — and then microwaved.

Truth in advertising, however, is maintained, sort of: When you're shown the final product — a completely built hamburger topped with sliced

---

[1] **Madison Avenue:** street in New York where many big advertising companies are located

[2] **crevices:** narrow openings

[3] **prissy:** extremely proper

[4] **preternaturally:** extraordinary; beyond what is natural

vegetables and condiments—you are seeing the actual quantities of ingredients found on the average real Whopper. On television, though, you're only seeing half of the hamburger—the front half. The lettuce, tomatoes, onions and pickles have all been shoved to the front of the burger. The stylist has carefully nudged and manicured the ingredients so that they sit just right. The red, ripe tomatoes are flown in fresh from California the morning of the shoot. You might find such tomatoes on your hamburger—if you ordered several hundred Whoppers early in the morning, in Fresno. The lettuce and tomatoes are cut, trimmed, and then piled on top of a cold cooked hamburger patty, and the whole construction is sprayed with a fine mist of glycerine[5] to glisten and shimmer seductively. Finally the hamburger is capped with a painstakingly handcrafted sesame-seed bun. For at least an hour the stylist has been kneeling over the bun like a lens grinder, positioning each sesame seed. He dips a toothpick in Elmer's glue and, using a pair of tweezers, places as many as 300 seeds, one by one, onto a formerly bald bun.

When it's all over, the crew packs up the equipment, and seventy-five gorgeous-looking hamburgers are dumped in the garbage.   11

IDEA JOURNAL
Think of a common process (e.g., ATM withdrawals, college course registrations), and write a how-to process analysis of it.

Summarize and Respond

In your reading journal or elsewhere, write a brief summary (three to five sentences) of "Beauty and the Beef." Next, jot down a quick response to the reading. Were you surprised by how much is done to a hamburger to make it look appetizing? What other products have you seen advertised that probably go through a similar process?

Check Your Comprehension

1. An alternate title for this essay could be
   a. " 'Truth' in Advertising."
   b. "Fast Food in America."
   c. "Why Hamburgers Are Good to Eat."
   d. "J. Walter Thompson: King of Madison Avenue."

2. The main idea of this essay is that
   a. food stylists make a lot of money.
   b. advertising agencies are totally unethical.
   c. advertisements create better-than-real-life products.
   d. Burger King spends a lot of money on advertising.

3. What does the author say about truth in advertising?
   a. It doesn't exist.
   b. It is stretched.
   c. It is always the primary concern of advertisers.
   d. It is easy to find.

[5] **glycerine:** colorless liquid

4. If you are still unfamiliar with the following words, use a dictionary to check their meanings: succulent (para. 1); flatter, singed (4); maneuvers, relubricates (6); sear (7); depicted (9).

Read Critically

1. What do you think is the author's purpose in writing this essay?

2. The essay opens with a question. Why is this question more effective than a simple statement such as "Hamburgers never look as good as they do in TV commercials"?

3. What, to you, was the most interesting step in the process of "beautifying" a burger? Why? What details made it stand out?

4. How does the author organize his ideas? Would another order of organization work well? Why, or why not?

5. How would you describe the author's attitude about the "beautifying" of beef? Find three examples in the essay that reveal this attitude.

Write

WRITING TIP
Remember that good process analysis
1. Tells what process is being analyzed and why
2. Lists all the essential steps in the process
3. Explains each step in detail
4. Presents the steps in a logical order, usually chronological

WRITE A PARAGRAPH: Write a paragraph that explains how to "beautify" something or someone (for example, how to put on makeup or how to make something look good in order to sell it). Feel free to exaggerate and use humor.

WRITE AN ESSAY: Look through some magazines or watch a few TV commercials to find an advertisement that you think makes something look better than it really is. You may want to look at the ideas you wrote in your reading journal for Summarize and Respond. Then write an essay that explains what steps the advertiser might have taken to create the better-than-real image.

46

Classification

TIP: For information on writing classification, see Chapters 11 and 18.

The essays in this chapter use classification to get their main point across to the reader. Classification organizes things into useful categories, follows a single organizational principle, and gives examples of what belongs in each category. As you read these essays, note how these writers simplify a complex topic by sorting items into clearly defined categories.

Russell Baker
The Plot against People

Russell Baker, born in Virginia in 1925 to a working-class family, began his career as a journalist for the *Baltimore Sun* at the age of twenty-two. Over Baker's fifty-year career as a journalist, he has written autobiographies, fiction, magazine articles, and collected writings. A noted humorist and political writer, Baker has been published regularly in the *Washington Post* and the *New York Times.* He is best known for his *New York Times* "Observer" column, where since 1962 he has aimed his wit at politicians, government, and the frustrations of contemporary life. The "Observer" earned Baker a Pulitzer Prize for Distinguished Commentary in 1979.

In "The Plot against People," which appeared in his prize-winning column in 1978, Baker humorously classifies the difficulties created by everyday objects.

GUIDING QUESTION
How does Baker classify the three types of inanimate objects, and what examples does he provide?

TEACHING TIP
Have students read this essay and diagram it using an organizing principle, three categories, and examples. A blank classification form can be found in *Additional Resources*. Ask students to think up new categories of everyday objects following Baker's model.

Washington, June 17 — Inanimate[1] objects are classified scientifically into three major categories — those that don't work, those that break down, and those that get lost.

The goal of all inanimate objects is to resist man and ultimately to defeat him, and the three major classifications are based on the method each object uses to achieve its purpose. As a general rule, any object capable of breaking down at the moment when it is most needed will do so. The automobile is typical of the category.

With the cunning[2] typical of its breed, the automobile never breaks down while entering a filling station with a large staff of idle mechanics. It waits until it reaches a downtown intersection in the middle of the rush hour, or until it is fully loaded with family and luggage on the Ohio turnpike.

Thus it creates maximum misery, inconvenience, frustration, and irritability among its human cargo, thereby reducing its owner's life span.

Washing machines, garbage disposals, lawn mowers, light bulbs, automatic laundry dryers, water pipes, furnaces, electrical fuses, television tubes, hose nozzles, tape recorders, slide projectors — all are in league with the automobile to take their turn at breaking down whenever life threatens to flow smoothly for their human enemies.

Many inanimate objects, of course, find it extremely difficult to break down. Pliers, for example, and gloves and keys are almost totally incapable of breaking down. Therefore, they have had to evolve a different technique for resisting man.

They get lost. Science has still not solved the mystery of how they do it, and no man has ever caught one of them in the act of getting lost. The most plausible theory is that they have developed a secret method of locomotion[3] which they are able to conceal the instant a human eye falls upon them.

It is not uncommon for a pair of pliers to climb all the way from the cellar to the attic in its single-minded determination to raise its owner's blood pressure. Keys have been known to burrow three feet under mattresses. Women's purses, despite their great weight, frequently travel through six or seven rooms to find hiding space under a couch.

Scientists have been struck by the fact that things that break down virtually never get lost, while things that get lost hardly ever break down.

A furnace, for example, will invariably break down at the depth of the first winter cold wave, but it will never get lost. A woman's purse, which after all does have some inherent capacity for breaking down, hardly ever does; it almost invariably chooses to get lost.

Some persons believe this constitutes[4] evidence that inanimate objects are not entirely hostile to man, and that a negotiated peace is possible. After all, they point out, a furnace could infuriate a man even more thoroughly by getting lost than by breaking down, just as a glove could upset him far more by breaking down than by getting lost.

---

[1] **inanimate:** not living
[2] **cunning:** shrewd
[3] **locomotion:** movement
[4] **constitutes:** makes up or builds

Not everyone agrees, however, that this indicates a conciliatory[5] atti-   12
tude among inanimate objects. Many say it merely proves that furnaces,
gloves, and pliers are incredibly stupid.

The third class of objects—those that don't work—is the most curious   13
of all. These include such objects as barometers, car clocks, cigarette
lighters, flashlights, and toy-train locomotives. It is inaccurate, of course, to
say that they never work. They work once, usually for the first few hours
after being brought home, and then quit. Thereafter, they never work again.

In fact, it is widely assumed that they are built for the purpose of not   14
working. Some people have reached advanced ages without ever seeing
some of these objects—barometers, for example—in working order.

Science is utterly baffled[6] by the entire category. There are many theo-   15
ries about it. The most interesting holds that the things that don't work have
attained the highest state possible for an inanimate object, the state to which
things that break down and things that get lost can still only aspire.[7]

They have truly defeated man by conditioning him never to expect   16
anything of them, and in return they have given man the only peace he receives from inanimate society. He does not expect his barometer to work, his
electric locomotive to run, his cigarette lighter to light, or his flashlight to illuminate, and when they don't, it does not raise his blood pressure.

He cannot attain that peace with furnaces and keys, and cars and   17
women's purses as long as he demands that they work for their keep.

IDEA JOURNAL
Write about your experi-
ences with one of the
three types of everyday
objects that Baker
presents.

Summarize and Respond

In your reading journal or elsewhere, write a brief summary (three to
five sentences) of "The Plot against People." Next, jot down a brief response
to the reading. What did the essay make you think or feel? Explain why you
could or could not relate to what the author described.

Check Your Comprehension

1. An alternative title for this essay could be
   a.   "How to Fix a Furnace."
   b.   "The Really Big Frustrations."
   c.   "The Creative Side of Things."
   (d.) "The Objects of Modern Life: More Hassle Than Help."

2. The main idea of this essay is that
   (a.) the objects meant to simplify everyday life can actually cause the
         greatest stress.
   b.   when you most rely on something, it will fail you.

[5] **conciliatory:** making peace
[6] **baffled:** confused
[7] **aspire:** strive for

    c.   things that don't work are worse than things that get lost.

    d.   things that break down never get lost.

3. Which objects have truly defeated man?

    a.   washers, dryers, and refrigerators

    b.   keys, women's purses, and pliers

    (c.) flashlights, cigarette lighters, and barometers

    d.   hose nozzles, tape recorders, and slide projectors

4. If you are still unfamiliar with the following words, use a dictionary to check their meanings: barometers (para. 13); conditioning, illuminate (16).

Read Critically

1. Describe the tone of this essay.

2. Baker uses classification to organize objects into categories. Make a chart with his categories at the top of each column. Then list the objects Baker mentions in the correct column.

3. Baker refers to scientists and the scientific community throughout this essay. For example, in paragraph 7 he writes that "science has still not solved the mystery." Do scientists really study the problems he describes? If not, why do you suppose he includes these references?

4. In paragraph 12 Baker writes, "Many say it merely proves that furnaces, gloves, and pliers are incredibly stupid." What kind of characteristics is he attributing to inanimate objects, and what is the effect?

5. Baker tells us that the third class of objects "have truly defeated man." Why does he say this is so?

Write

WRITING TIP
Remember, good classification
1. Organizes things into useful categories
2. Follows a single organizing principle
3. Gives examples of what belongs in each category

WRITE A PARAGRAPH: Create another category that inanimate objects might be placed in. Write a paragraph about this category, and provide examples.

WRITE AN ESSAY: Write an essay that follows Baker's classification model but has a different topic. For a topic, consider classifying types of drivers (perhaps based on the types of cars they drive) or types of shoppers (perhaps the kind that end up in front of you in the check-out lane). You may want to use humor to describe your categories.

Stephanie Ericsson

The Ways We Lie

Stephanie Ericsson is a freelance writer for television, film, and magazines. She was born in Dallas, Texas, in 1953 and has lived in a variety of places, including San Francisco, New York, Los Angeles, London, Spain, and Minnesota. Ericsson had a major turning point in her life when her husband died suddenly when she was two months pregnant with their daughter. She began a journal to help cope with her grief and loss and later used her writing to help others cope with similar struggles. An excerpt from her journal was published in the *Utne Reader,* and her writings were published in a book entitled *Companion through the Darkness: Inner Dialogues on Grief* (1993). About her book, Ericsson writes, "It belongs to those who have had the blinders ripped from their eyes, who suddenly see the lies of our lives and the truths of existence for what they are."

In the following essay, taken from her follow-up work *Companion into the Dawn: Inner Dialogues on Loving* (1994), Ericsson continues her search for truth by examining and classifying our daily lies.

GUIDING QUESTION
As you read this essay, pay attention to the examples Ericsson provides. What examples of lying can you think of from your own experience?

"Ericsson uses specific personal experiences to relate something familiar. Her message is clear."
—*David Frey, Student*

The bank called today and I told them my deposit was in the mail, even though I hadn't written a check yet. It'd been a rough day. The baby I'm pregnant with decided to do aerobics on my lungs for two hours, our three-year-old daughter painted the living-room couch with lipstick, the IRS put me on hold for an hour, and I was late to a business meeting because I was tired. 1

I told my client that the traffic had been bad. When my partner came home, his haggard face told me his day hadn't gone any better than mine, so when he asked, "How was your day?" I said, "Oh, fine," knowing that one more straw might break his back. A friend called and wanted to take me to lunch. I said I was busy. Four lies in the course of a day, none of which I felt the least bit guilty about. 2

We lie. We all do. We exaggerate, we minimize, we avoid confrontation, we spare people's feelings, we conveniently forget, we keep secrets, we justify lying to the big-guy institutions. Like most people, I indulge in small falsehoods and still think of myself as an honest person. Sure I lie, but it doesn't hurt anything. Or does it? 3

I once tried going a whole week without telling a lie, and it was paralyzing. I discovered that telling the truth all the time is nearly impossible. It 4 means living with some serious consequences: The bank charges me $60 in overdraft fees, my partner keels over when I tell him about my travails, my client fires me for telling her I didn't feel like being on time, and my friend takes it personally when I say I'm not hungry. There must be some merit to lying.

But if I justify lying, what makes me any different from slick politicians or the corporate robbers who raided the S&L industry? Saying it's okay to lie one way and not another is hedging.[1] I cannot seem to escape the voice deep inside me that tells me: When someone lies, someone loses.

What far-reaching consequences will I, or others, pay as a result of my lie? Will someone's trust be destroyed? Will someone else pay *my* penance because I ducked out? We must consider the *meaning of our actions*. Deception, lies, capital crimes, and misdemeanors[2] all carry meanings. *Webster's* definition of *lie* is specific:

> 1: a false statement or action especially made with the intent to deceive; 2: anything that gives or is meant to give a false impression.

A definition like this implies that there are many, many ways to tell a lie. Here are just a few.

The White Lie

The white lie assumes that the truth will cause more damage than a simple, harmless untruth. Telling a friend he looks great when he looks like hell can be based on a decision that the friend needs a compliment more than a frank opinion. But, in effect, it is the liar deciding what is best for the lied to. Ultimately, it is a vote of no confidence. It is an act of subtle arrogance[3] for anyone to decide what is best for someone else.

Yet not all circumstances are quite so cut and dried. Take, for instance, the sergeant in Vietnam who knew one of his men was killed in action but listed him as missing so that the man's family would receive indefinite compensation instead of the lump-sum pittance[4] the military gives widows and children. His intent was honorable. Yet for twenty years this family kept their hopes alive, unable to move on to a new life.

Facades

We all put up facades[5] to one degree or another. When I put on a suit to go to see a client, I feel as though I am putting on another face, obeying the expectation that serious businesspeople wear suits rather than sweatpants. But I'm a writer. Normally, I get up, get the kid off to school, and sit at my computer in my pajamas until four in the afternoon. When I answer the phone, the caller thinks I'm wearing a suit (though the UPS man knows better).

---

[1] **hedging:** avoiding the question
[2] **misdemeanors:** minor violations of rules
[3] **arrogance:** belief in one's superiority
[4] **pittance:** small amount
[5] **facades:** masks

But facades can be destructive because they are used to seduce others 11
into an illusion. For instance, I recently realized that a former friend was a liar.
He presented himself with all the right looks and the right words and offered
lots of new consciousness theories, fabulous books to read, and fascinating insights. Then I did some business with him, and the time came for him to pay
me. He turned out to be all talk and no walk. I heard a plethora⁶ of reasonable
excuses, including in-depth descriptions of the big break around the corner. In
six months of work, I saw less than a hundred bucks. When I confronted him,
he raised both eyebrows and tried to convince me that I'd heard him wrong,
that he'd made no commitment to me. A simple investigation into his past revealed a crowded graveyard of disenchanted former friends.

Ignoring the Plain Facts

In the sixties, the Catholic Church in Massachusetts began hearing 12
complaints that Father James Porter was sexually molesting children. Rather
than relieving him of his duties, the ecclesiastical authorities simply moved
him from one parish to another between 1960 and 1967, actually providing
him with a fresh supply of unsuspecting families and innocent children to
abuse. After treatment in 1967 for pedophilia,⁷ he went back to work, this
time in Minnesota. The new diocese⁸ was aware of Father Porter's obsession
with children, but they needed priests and recklessly believed treatment had
cured him. More children were abused until he was relieved of his duties a
year later. By his own admission, Porter may have abused as many as a hundred children.

Ignoring the facts may not in and of itself be a form of lying, but con- 13
sider the context of this situation. If a lie is *a false action done with the intent to
deceive,* then the Catholic Church's conscious covering for Porter created irreparable consequences. The church became a co-perpetrator with Porter.

Stereotypes and Clichés

Stereotype and cliché serve a purpose as a form of shorthand. Our 14
need for vast amounts of information in nanoseconds⁹ has made the stereotype vital to modern communication. Unfortunately, it often shuts down
original thinking, giving those hungry for truth a candy bar of misinforma-
tion instead of a balanced meal. The stereotype explains a situation with just
enough truth to seem unquestionable.

All the *isms*—racism, sexism, ageism, et al.—are founded on and 15
fueled by the stereotype and the cliché, which are lies of exaggeration, omis-
sion, and ignorance. They are always dangerous. They take a single tree and
make it a landscape. They destroy curiosity. They close minds and separate
people. The single mother on welfare is assumed to be cheating. Any black
male could tell you how much of his identity is obliterated¹⁰ daily by stereo-

IDEA JOURNAL
Think of another common
human behavior. Break
it into categories, and
give examples for each
category.

---

⁶ **plethora:** excess
⁷ **pedophilia:** sexual abuse of children
⁸ **diocese:** district or churches under the guidance of a bishop
⁹ **nanoseconds:** billionths of a second
¹⁰ **obliterated:** wiped out

types. Fat people, ugly people, beautiful people, old people, large-breasted women, short men, the mentally ill, and the homeless all could tell you how much more they are like us than we want to think. I once admitted to a group of people that I had a mouth like a truck driver. Much to my surprise, a man stood up and said, "I'm a truck driver, and I never cuss." Needless to say, I was humbled.

Out-and-Out Lies

Of all the ways to lie, I like this one the best, probably because I get tired of trying to figure out the real meanings behind things. At least I can trust the bald-faced lie. I once asked my five-year-old nephew, "Who broke the fence?" (I had seen him do it.) He answered, "The murderers." Who could argue?

At least when this sort of lie is told it can be easily confronted. As the person who is lied to, I know where I stand. The bald-faced lie doesn't toy with my perceptions — it argues with them. It doesn't try to refashion reality, it tries to refute[11] it. *Read my lips* . . . No sleight[12] of hand. No guessing. If this were the only form of lying, there would be no such thing as floating anxiety or the adult-children of alcoholics movement.

These are only a few of the ways we lie. Or are lied to. As I said earlier, it's not easy to entirely eliminate lies from our lives. No matter how pious[13] we may try to be, we will still embellish, hedge, and omit to lubricate[14] the daily machinery of living. But there is a world of difference between telling functional lies and living a lie. Martin Buber once said, "The lie is the spirit committing treason against itself." Our acceptance of lies becomes a cultural cancer that eventually shrouds[15] and reorders reality until moral garbage becomes as invisible to us as water is to a fish.

How much do we tolerate before we become sick and tired of being sick and tired? When will we stand up and declare our *right* to trust? When do we stop accepting that the real truth is in the fine print? Whose lips do we read this year when we vote for president? When will we stop being so reticent about making judgments? When do we stop turning over our personal power and responsibility to liars?

Maybe if I don't tell the bank the check's in the mail I'll be less tolerant of the lies told to me every day. A country song I once heard said it all for me: "You've got to stand for something or you'll fall for anything."

Summarize and Respond

In your reading journal or elsewhere, write a brief summary (three to five sentences) of "The Ways We Lie." Next, jot down a response to the read-

[11] **refute:** deny
[12] **sleight:** skillful trick
[13] **pious:** religious
[14] **lubricate:** oil
[15] **shrouds:** covers

ing. What did it make you think about or feel? Do you agree with Ericsson's claim that we all tell lies every day? Provide examples from your own experience that support this idea.

Check Your Comprehension

1. An alternate title for this essay could be
    a.   "Lying Never Hurt Anyone."
    b.   "The Check's in the Mail: The Greatest Lie of All."
    c.   "Justification for Lying."
    d.   "Lies in our Lives."

2. The main idea of this essay is that
    a.   small lies are okay because everyone lies.
    b.   we should reevaluate the role that lies play in our lives.
    c.   lies are worst when told by someone you trust.
    d.   to trust and be trusted, we must refuse to lie.

3. What distinction does Ericsson make between telling a functional lie and living a lie?
    a.   Telling a functional lie makes someone feel bad, and living a lie cheats big institutions.
    b.   Telling a functional lie is relatively harmless, but living a lie can put you in jail.
    c.   Telling a functional lie has no merit, and living a lie is a good idea.
    d.   Telling a functional lie is honest, and living a lie is dishonest.

4. If you are still unfamiliar with the following words, use a dictionary to look up their meanings: confrontation (para. 3); merit (4); penance (6); irreparable (13); cliché, vital (14); refashion (17); tolerant (20).

Read Critically

1. Describe Ericsson's tone in this essay. For example, what is her tone in paragraph 1 when she tells us that "the baby I'm pregnant with decided to do aerobics on my lungs for two hours"?
2. How does Ericsson organize her essay? How does she classify the way we tell lies?
3. What images does Ericsson associate with telling lies? Select one that you like and explain why.
4. What is Ericsson's attitude toward lying? What examples in the essay support your answer?
5. In paragraph 16 Ericsson writes, "At least I can trust the bald-faced lie." What do you think she means by trusting a lie?

Write

WRITE A PARAGRAPH: Write a paragraph that describes another category of lies. Be sure to provide examples for your readers.

WRITE AN ESSAY: Write an essay that continues Ericsson's classification of the ways we lie. Provide detailed examples from your experiences—or the experiences of people you know—for at least two of the categories she provides. Develop two new categories of your own. Feel free to include the ideas you wrote about in your reading journal for Summarize and Respond.

47

Definition

TIP: For information on writing definition, see Chapter 12.

The essays in this chapter use definition to get their main point across to the reader. Definition explains what a term means. Good definitions give a clear and precise meaning, include examples of the term, and use words and information that the reader will understand. An essay may present and explore a definition of a term, or a definition may be one piece in a larger discussion. As you read these essays, note the ways that these writers use easy-to-understand examples and information to explain their terms.

Janice Castro
Spanglish

Raised on a northern California cattle ranch, Janice Castro went on to study English literature and city planning at the University of California at Berkeley. She began what would become a more than twenty-year career with *Time* magazine in 1973, working as a reporter-researcher and then as a writer. Castro manages to play softball and do mountain biking in addition to writing major stories on the defense industry, economic devastation, and other business-related interests.

Castro spends much of her time in cyberspace, working as an online journalist for Time, Inc., an electronic publishing house. As editor of *Time Daily*, the electronic version of *Time* magazine, she presents the news in an interactive format that promotes communication between readers and journalists. In "Spanglish," first published in *Time* (1988), the author provides a definition essay that also encourages communication—specifically among English- and Spanish-speaking Americans.

GUIDING QUESTION
How does the author define Spanglish, and how do her examples support different aspects of the definition?

"The author's details re-late to real people and real experiences. "Span-glish isn't something I ever thought about—it is just another language that I speak."
—Marie Vazquez, Student

TEACHING TIP
As students read, have them underline the defini-tion of *Spanglish* and identify the sentence structure (term + *means/is* + basic definition). Castro extends the defini-tion by explaining how the word came about and by showing it in context. Have students explain the word's origin in their own words. Ask students to underline sev-eral examples of Span-glish in the reading and share them with the class.

The word *Spanglish* came into existence be-cause of a changing population mix. Ask groups to list other new words (and their defini-tions) (e.g., Internet, e-mail, download).

In Manhattan a first grader greets her visiting grandparents, happily exclaiming, "Come here, *siéntate!*" Her bemused[1] grandfather, who does not speak Spanish, nevertheless knows she is asking him to sit down. A Miami personnel officer understands what a job applicant means when he says, "*Quiero un* part time." Nor do drivers miss a beat reading a billboard alongside a Los Angeles street advertising CERVEZA—SIX-PACK!

This free-form blend of Spanish and English, known as Spanglish, is common linguistic[2] currency wherever concentrations of Hispanic Ameri-cans are found in the United States. In Los Angeles, where 55 percent of the city's 3 million inhabitants speak Spanish, Spanglish is as much a part of daily life as sunglasses. Unlike the broken-English efforts of earlier immi-grants from Europe, Asia, and other regions, Spanglish has become a widely accepted conversational mode used casually—even playfully—by Spanish-speaking immigrants and native-born Americans alike.

Consisting of one part Hispanicized English, one part Americanized Spanish and more than a little fractured syntax,[3] Spanglish is a bit like a Robin Williams comedy routine: a crackling line of cross-cultural patter[4] straight from the melting pot. Often it enters Anglo homes and families through the children, who pick it up at school or at play with their young Hispanic contemporaries. In other cases, it comes from watching TV; many an Anglo child watching *Sesame Street* has learned *uno dos tres* almost as quickly as one two three.

Spanglish takes a variety of forms, from the Southern California An-glos who bid farewell with the utterly silly "*hasta la* bye-bye" to the Cuban American drivers in Miami who *parquean* their *carros*. Some Spanglish sen-tences are mostly Spanish, with a quick detour for an English word or two. A Latino friend may cut short a conversation by glancing at his watch and excusing himself with the explanation that he must "*ir al* supermarket."

Many of the English words transplanted in this way are simply handier than their Spanish counterparts. No matter how distasteful the subject, for example, it is still easier to say "income tax" than *impuesto sobre la renta*. At the same time, many Spanish-speaking immigrants have adopted such terms as *VCR, microwave,* and *dishwasher* for what they view as largely American phenomena. Still other English words convey a cultural context that is not implicit[5] in the Spanish. A friend who invites you to *lonche* most likely has in mind the brisk American custom of "doing lunch" rather than the lan-guorous afternoon break traditionally implied by *almuerzo*.

[1] **bemused:** slightly confused
[2] **linguistic:** relating to the study of languages
[3] **syntax:** arrangement of words in sentences
[4] **patter:** rapid speech
[5] **implicit:** understood without being directly stated

Mainstream Americans exposed to similar hybrids of German, Chinese, or Hindi might be mystified. But even Anglos who speak little or no Spanish are somewhat familiar with Spanglish. Living among them, for one thing, are 19 million Hispanics. In addition, more American high school and university students sign up for Spanish than for any other foreign language.

6

Only in the past ten years, though, has Spanglish begun to turn into a national slang. Its popularity has grown with the explosive increases in U.S. immigration from Latin American countries. English has increasingly collided with Spanish in retail stores, offices, and classrooms, in pop music, and on street corners. Anglos whose ancestors picked up such Spanish words as *rancho, bronco, tornado,* and *incommunicado,* for instance, now freely use such Spanish words as *gracias, bueno, amigo,* and *por favor.*

7

Among Latinos, Spanglish conversations often flow easily from Spanish into several sentences of English and back.

8

Spanglish is a sort of code for Latinos: The speakers know Spanish, but their hybrid language reflects the American culture in which they live. Many lean to shorter, clipped phrases in place of the longer, more graceful expressions their parents used. Says Leonel de la Cuesta, an assistant professor of modern languages at Florida International University in Miami: "In the United States, time is money, and that is showing up in Spanglish as an economy of language." Conversational examples: *taipiar* (type) and *winshiwiper* (windshield wiper) replace *escribir a máquina* and *limpia-parabrisas.*

9

Major advertisers, eager to tap the estimated $134 billion in spending power wielded by Spanish-speaking Americans, have ventured into Spanglish to promote their products. In some cases, attempts to sprinkle Spanish through commercials have produced embarrassing gaffes. A Braniff airlines ad that sought to tell Spanish-speaking audiences they could settle back *en* (in) luxuriant *cuero* (leather) seats, for example, inadvertently said they could fly without clothes (*encuero*). A fractured translation of the Miller Lite slogan told readers the beer was "Filling, and less delicious." Similar blunders are often made by Anglos trying to impress Spanish-speaking pals. But if Latinos are amused by mangled Spanglish, they also recognize these goofs as a sort of friendly acceptance. As they might put it, *no problema.*

10

IDEA JOURNAL
Take a new word from your group's list and write a basic definition, a context for the word, and several examples.

Summarize and Respond

In your reading journal or elsewhere, write a brief summary (three to five sentences) of "Spanglish." Next, jot down a brief response to the reading. Note any instances of Spanglish that you have used or heard. Have you heard or used any other hybrid or mixed languages?

Check Your Comprehension

1. An alternate title for this essay could be
   a. "Language in the 1990s."
   b. "The Butchering of Languages."

   c.   "Easier Than English."

   d.   "Coded Linguistics."

2. The main idea of this essay is that

   a.   advertisers will shape their ads to appeal to any group with
        spending power.

   (b.) a hybrid language provides a common speaking ground.

   c.   language changes as a form of rebellion.

   d.   language reflects the economy.

3. According to the essay, what is the main reason Spanglish has become
    a national slang in the past ten years?

   a.   More children are learning Spanish from *Sesame Street.*

   (b.) Increased immigration from Latin American countries has intro-
        duced Spanish into more neighborhoods.

   c.   It's easier than using one language.

   d.   It's easier than saying *impuestro sobre la renta.*

4. If you are unfamiliar with these words, use a dictionary to check their
    meanings: currency, inhabitants, mode (para. 2); cross-cultural (3).

Read Critically

1. Does the author directly state why Spanglish is being defined? Why do
    you think the author wrote about this subject?

2. The author provides numerous examples of Spanglish, many of which
    are not translated. Do you think she forgot to provide translations? Is
    there another reason she does not explain what the words mean?

3. In paragraph 9, the author quotes from a language teacher who said
    that "in the United States, time is money, and that is showing up in
    Spanglish as an economy of language." What does this statement mean?
    How do the examples that immediately follow demonstrate this point?

4. According to the author, who speaks Spanglish?

5. How would you describe the tone of this essay?

Write

WRITING TIP
Remember that a good
definition
1. Explains what a term
   means
2. Gives a clear and
   precise meaning
3. Includes examples of
   the term
4. Uses words and infor-
   mation that the reader
   will understand

WRITE A PARAGRAPH: Write a paragraph defining a term or phrase that is
used by members of a particular group. For example, consider terms such as
dude, yo, or *whatever.* Be sure to provide at least one example for your readers.

WRITE AN ESSAY: Write an essay that defines a term or concept that is used
by members of a particular group you belong to (for example, a church
group, an ethnic group, or a group of friends). You might use slang or jargon
or select a term unfamiliar to an outsider. Develop what you prepared for
Write a Paragraph, if you like. Be sure to explain the term, tell why you're
defining it, and provide detailed examples.

Isaac Asimov

What Is Intelligence, Anyway?

The son of Russian Jews, Isaac Asimov (1920–1992) emigrated with his family to New York at the age of three. He began writing stories when he was eleven, entered Columbia University at fifteen, and eventually earned a Ph.D. in chemistry. He went on to become one of the greatest and most productive science fiction writers of the twentieth century. He once called writing "my idea of a vacation." Dr. Asimov's career spanned more than fifty years and led to numerous awards and honors. In addition to fiction, he has written histories, scientific essays, children's stories, and pamphlets for the United States Atomic Energy Commission.

In "What Is Intelligence, Anyway?" Asimov combines a sense of humor with an interest in scientific inquiry. His essay asks us to think about our own definitions of intelligence.

GUIDING QUESTION
Does Asimov answer his question, "What Is Intelligence, Anyway?"?

"I like how the writer doesn't put himself up on a pedestal. He related his message clearly and with a touch of humor."
—Beverly Rehfeldt, Student

What is intelligence, anyway? When I was in the Army, I received a kind of aptitude[1] test that all soldiers took and, against a normal of 100, scored 160. No one at the base had ever seen a figure like that, and for two hours they made a big fuss over me. (It didn't mean anything. The next day I was still a buck private with KP[2] as my highest duty.)   1

All of my life I've been registering scores like that, so that I have the complacent[3] feeling that I'm highly intelligent, and I expect other people to think so, too. Actually, though, don't such scores simply mean that I am very good at answering the type of academic questions that are considered worthy of answers by the people who make up the intelligence tests—people with intellectual bents[4] similar to mine?   2

For instance, I had an auto repairman once, who, on these intelligence tests, could not possibly have scored more than 80, by my estimate. I always took it for granted that I was far more intelligent than he was. Yet, when anything went wrong with my car, I hastened to him with it, watched him anxiously as he explored its vitals,[5] and listened to his pronouncements as though they were divine oracles[6]—and he always fixed my car.   3

[1] **aptitude:** ability, talent
[2] **KP:** kitchen patrol
[3] **complacent:** pleased with oneself, often without being aware of some defect
[4] **bents:** talents
[5] **vitals:** main parts of something
[6] **oracles:** wise answers

TEACHING TIP
Ask students to underline the sentence that defines *intelligence* and identify the topic sentence structure (term + *is not* + expected definition). Does Asimov's essay give a clear and precise meaning of the term *intelligence*? (No, he explains that the meaning of *intelligence* is relative.) How does context help define *intelligence*?

IDEA JOURNAL
Define *intelligence* using one of your strengths as the measure of intelligence (e.g., the ability to work well with your hands, to figure out how engines work, to diagnose and fix problems, to explain ideas to other people).

Well then, suppose my auto repairman devised questions for an intelligence test. Or suppose a carpenter did, or a farmer, or, indeed, almost anyone but an academician.[7] By every one of those tests, I'd prove myself a moron. And I'd *be* a moron, too. In a world where I could not use my academic training and my verbal talents but had to do something intricate or hard, working with my hands, I would do poorly. My intelligence, then, is not absolute but is a function of the society I live in and of the fact that a small subsection of that society has managed to foist[8] itself on the rest as an arbiter[9] of such matters.

Consider my auto repairman, again. He had a habit of telling me jokes whenever he saw me. One time he raised his head from under the automobile hood to say, "Doc, a deaf-and-dumb guy went into a hardware store to ask for some nails. He put two fingers together on the counter and made hammering motions with the other hand. The clerk brought him a hammer. He shook his head and pointed to the two fingers he was hammering. The clerk brought him nails. He picked out the sizes he wanted, and left. Well, doc, the next guy who came in was a blind man. He wanted scissors. How do you suppose he asked for them?"

Indulgently, I lifted my right hand and made scissoring motions with my first two fingers. Whereupon my auto repairman laughed raucously[10] and said, "Why, you dumb jerk, he used his *voice* and asked for them." Then he said, smugly, "I've been trying that on all my customers today." "Did you catch many?" I asked. "Quite a few," he said, "but I knew for sure I'd catch *you*." "Why is that?" I asked. "Because you're so goddamned educated, doc, I *knew* you couldn't be very smart."

And I have an uneasy feeling he had something there.

Summarize and Respond

In your reading journal or elsewhere, write a brief summary (three to five sentences) of "What Is Intelligence, Anyway?" Next, jot down a quick response to the reading. What did it make you think or feel? Give an example of being "smart" that requires more than being educated.

Check Your Comprehension

1. An alternate title for this essay could be
   a. "Why I Hate My Auto Repair Man."
   (b.) "More Than One Kind of Intelligence."
   c. "How to Increase Your Score on an Intelligence Test."
   d. "Test Makers: Always Right."

---

[7] **academician:** someone who teaches at a college
[8] **foist:** pass off as valuable
[9] **arbiter:** person who decides an issue
[10] **raucously:** rowdily

2. The main idea of this essay is that
    a. academicians are not very smart.
    b. people who "get" jokes are more intelligent than people who don't.
    c. all standardized tests should have questions about farming.
    (d.) there are many different types of intelligence, not just the one measured by standardized tests.

3. What is the author not skilled in?
    a. understanding jokes
    b. taking intelligence tests
    (c.) working with tools and machines
    d. verbal talents

4. If you are still unfamiliar with the following words, use a dictionary to check their meanings: private (para. 1); estimate, granted, hastened (3); devised, intricate (4).

Read Critically

1. In paragraph 2, Asimov writes, "I have the complacent feeling that I'm highly intelligent, and I expect other people to think so, too." Do you think he feels the same way by the end of the essay? Why, or why not?

2. What do you think intelligence is? How do you think Asimov would answer this question?

3. How do you think the auto repair man would define *intelligence*?

4. Why do you think Asimov tells readers about the joke? How does the story contribute to the point of his essay?

5. Think of another example that shows how different situations call for different types of intelligence. Where would you put your examples in Asimov's essay?

Write

WRITING TIP
Remember that a good definition
1. Explains what a term means
2. Gives a clear and precise meaning
3. Includes examples of the term
4. Uses words and information that the reader will understand

WRITE A PARAGRAPH: Write a paragraph that discusses a time when you used a different type of intelligence than the kind you are tested on in school. For example, you could write about how you fixed a leaky faucet, cheered up a friend who was feeling down, or played a game of tennis.

WRITE AN ESSAY: Write an essay that answers the question, "What is intelligence, anyway?" Use examples from your personal experience to help define the concept of intelligence. If you wrote about this topic for Summarize and Respond, you may want to develop your ideas here. Explain why you think Asimov would agree or disagree with your definition.

48

Comparison and Contrast

TIP: For information on writing comparison and contrast, see Chapters 13 and 18.

The essays in this chapter use comparison and contrast to get their main point across to the reader. Comparison looks at the similarities of two subjects, and contrast looks at the differences of two subjects. Good comparison and contrast uses subjects that have enough in common to be compared or contrasted, presents several points of comparison or contrast, and arranges the points in a useful manner—either point-by-point or whole-to-whole. Sometimes writers use comparison and contrast to identify what makes each subject unique; sometimes they use it to choose the better of two possibilities. As you read these essays, note how the similarities and differences of the subjects are presented.

Rose Del Castillo Guilbault
Americanization Is Tough on Macho

Rose Del Castillo Guilbault earned a B.A. in broadcast journalism from San Jose State University and an M.B.A. from Pepperdine University. In her career in journalism she has written stories for print, radio, and television. Since 1975, Guilbault has worked for the San Francisco–based KGO-TV, a public television station that, under her leadership, has sustained a commitment to special community projects. The recipient of numerous awards in journalism, Guilbault was the only journalist appointed in 1991 to President George Bush's Advisory Commission on Educational Excellence for Hispanic Students.

Guilbault's former monthly column on the Hispanic experience in the *San Francisco Chronicle,* in which this essay first appeared (1989), won a Eugene Block Journalism Award for advancing social justice and human rights. In "Americanization Is Tough on Macho," Guilbault compares and contrasts how American and Hispanic cultures define the concept of macho.

GUIDING QUESTION
How does the author define *macho*?

What is *macho?* That depends which side of the border you come from.   1

Although it's not unusual for words and expressions to lose their subtlety in translation, the negative connotations[1] of *macho* in this country are troublesome to Hispanics.   2

Take the newspaper descriptions of alleged[2] mass murderer Ramon Salcido. That an insensitive, insanely jealous, hard-drinking, violent Latin male is referred to as *macho* makes Hispanics cringe.   3

"*Es muy macho,*" the women in my family nod approvingly, describing a man they respect. But in the United States, when women say, "He's so macho," it's with disdain.   4

The Hispanic *macho* is manly, responsible, hardworking, a man in charge, a patriarch. A man who expresses strength through silence. What the Yiddish language would call a *mensch.*   5

The American *macho* is a chauvinist, a brute, uncouth, selfish, loud, abrasive, capable of inflicting pain, and sexually promiscuous.[3]   6

Quintessential *macho* models in this country are Sylvester Stallone, Arnold Schwarzenegger, and Charles Bronson. In their movies, they exude toughness, independence, masculinity. But a closer look reveals their machismo is really violence masquerading as courage, sullenness[4] disguised as silence, and irresponsibility camouflaged as independence.   7

If the Hispanic ideal of *macho* were translated to American screen roles, they might be Jimmy Stewart, Sean Connery, and Laurence Olivier.   8

In Spanish, *macho* ennobles[5] Latin males. In English, it devalues them. This pattern seems consistent with the conflicts ethnic minority males experience in this country. Typically the cultural traits other societies value don't translate as desirable characteristics in America.   9

I watched my own father struggle with these cultural ambiguities.[6] He worked on a farm for twenty years. He laid down miles of irrigation pipe, carefully plowed long, neat rows in fields, hacked away at recalcitrant[7] weeds and drove tractors through whirlpools of dust. He stoically[8] worked twenty-hour days during harvest season, accepting the long hours as part of agricultural work. When the boss complained or upbraided[9] him for minor mistakes, he kept quiet, even when it was obvious the boss had erred.   10

[1] **connotations:** ideas associated with words
[2] **alleged:** presumed
[3] **promiscuous:** engaging in sexual intercourse with many partners
[4] **sullenness:** bad temper
[5] **ennobles:** glorifies
[6] **ambiguities:** unclear meanings
[7] **recalcitrant:** defiant
[8] **stoically:** without complaining
[9] **upbraided:** scolded

He handled the most menial tasks with pride. At home he was a good provider, helped out my mother's family in Mexico without complaint, and was indulgent with me. Arguments between my mother and him generally had to do with money, or with his stubborn reluctance to share his troubles. He tried to work them out in his own silence. He didn't want to trouble my mother—a course that backfired, because the imagined is always worse than the reality.

Americans regarded my father as decidedly un-*macho*. His character was interpreted as nonassertive,[10] his loyalty nonambition, and his quietness ignorance. I once overheard the boss's son blame him for plowing crooked rows in a field. My father merely smiled at the lie, knowing the boy had done it, but didn't refute[11] it, confident his good work was well known. But the boss instead ridiculed him for being "stupid" and letting a kid get away with a lie. Seeing my embarrassment, my father dismissed the incident, saying, "They're the dumb ones. Imagine, me fighting with a kid."

I tried not to look at him with American eyes because sometimes the reflection hurt.

Listening to my aunts' clucks of approval, my vision focused on the qualities America overlooked. "He's such a hard worker. So serious, so responsible." My aunts would secretly compliment my mother. The unspoken comparison was that he was not like some of their husbands, who drank and womanized. My uncles represented the darker side of *macho*.

In a patriarchal society, few challenge their roles. If men drink, it's because it's the manly thing to do. If they gamble, it's because it's how men relax. And if they fool around, well, it's because a man simply can't hold back so much man! My aunts didn't exactly meekly sit back, but they put up with these transgressions[12] because Mexican society dictated this was their lot in life.

In the United States, I believe it was the feminist movement of the early seventies that changed *macho*'s meaning. Perhaps my generation of Latin women was in part responsible. I recall Chicanos complaining about the chauvinistic nature of Latin men and the notion they wanted their women barefoot, pregnant and in the kitchen. The generalization that Latin men embodied chauvinistic traits led to this interesting twist of semantics.[13] Suddenly a word that represented something positive in one culture became a negative prototype in another.

The problem with the use of *macho* today is that it's become an accepted stereotype of the Latin male. And like all stereotypes, it distorts truth.

The impact of language in our society is undeniable. And the misuse of *macho* hints at a deeper cultural misunderstanding that extends beyond mere word definitions.

IDEA JOURNAL
Contrast two meanings of the same word (e.g., *feminism, conservative, liberal*) from different perspectives.

[10] **nonassertive:** passive
[11] **refute:** challenge
[12] **transgressions:** violations of a law or commandment
[13] **semantics:** the meaning of words

Summarize and Respond

In your reading journal or elsewhere, write a brief summary (three to five sentences) of "Americanization Is Tough on Macho." Next, jot down your response to the reading. When you think of the term *macho,* what comes to mind? What do you think of Guilbault's definitions?

Check Your Comprehension

1. An alternate title for this essay could be
    a.   "The Darker Side of Macho."
    b.   "Wanting to Be Macho."
    c.   "More Than One Kind of Macho."
    d.   "Macho: Violence Masquerading as Courage?"

2. The main idea of this essay is that
    a.   American women do not understand the meaning of *macho.*
    b.   traits that are valued in other societies can be misunderstood or not valued in America.
    c.   the notion of macho has become an unaccepted stereotype of the Latin male.
    d.   American men need to be less macho.

3. According to the essay, what changed the meaning of *macho* in the United States?
    a.   movies with Arnold Schwarzenegger and Charles Bronson
    b.   men who worked menial tasks at home
    c.   the feminist movement of the early 1970s
    d.   men who are loud, abrasive, capable of inflicting pain, and sexually promiscuous

4. If you are still unfamiliar with the following words, use a dictionary to check their meanings: chauvinist, uncouth (para. 6); indulgent (11); prototype (16).

Read Critically

1. Think about Guilbault's methods. Does she arrange her ideas point-by-point or whole-to-whole?
2. Consider the author's perspective. Which definition of *macho* does she favor? What in the essay supports your answer?
3. What do you think is Guilbault's purpose in writing this essay? Is she simply comparing and contrasting meanings of *macho,* or is she writing about other themes as well? Explain your response.

4. In paragraph 13, Guilbault writes, "I tried not to look at him with American eyes because . . . the reflection hurt." What does she mean?

5. How would you describe the two types of macho that Guilbault presents? What in the essay supports your answer?

Write

WRITING TIP
Remember, good comparison and contrast
1. Uses subjects that have enough in common to be compared and contrasted
2. Presents several points of comparison or contrast
3. Arranges the points in a useful manner—either point-by-point or whole-to-whole

WRITE A PARAGRAPH: Write a paragraph that continues Guilbault's comparison and contrast of the meanings of *macho*. Use your own examples to support her ideas, including examples from another culture's perception of macho.

WRITE AN ESSAY: Guilbault writes that "typically the cultural traits other societies value don't translate as desirable characteristics in America." Write an essay about a behavior that is valued in one culture and not in another. For example, you might consider how members of a particular group dress or act, and then decide whether their appearance or behavior is accepted by others outside of that group. For this assignment, you can use a broad definition of *culture* that includes a peer group, a work group, or an ethnic group. In other words, *culture* might mean any group that shares the same goals and values.

Mike Royko

Two Extremes Miss Target over Guns

Mike Royko (1932–1997) got his first job as a reporter by lying about previous journalist experience. From then on, he worked for virtually every Chicago newspaper in virtually every capacity. For more than twenty years, Royko reigned in his home town, holding the title of Chicago's most prominent journalist. In his daily column Royko often tackled controversial subjects.

In "Two Extremes Miss Target over Guns," Royko, who was a gun owner himself and a member of the LaSalle Street Rod and Gun Club, criticizes both gun lovers and gun haters about their attitudes toward gun control. He examines the lack of communication that plagues the debate on gun control by comparing and contrasting the attitudes of opponents and supporters. The article originally appeared in the *Chicago Tribune* (1995).

GUIDING QUESTION
Based on Royko's title, what do you expect the essay to focus on?

When the subject is guns, we definitely have a failure to communicate.   1

Those who hate guns seem to believe that those who don't are a lot of lowbrow, beady-eyed, beer-guzzling neofascists who are constantly leaving pistols around the house so children can find them and shoot their siblings.[1]   2

Those who defend gun ownership seem to think that gun-control advocates[2] are a bunch of left-wing, government-loving, wine-sipping sissies who believe that the best way to handle a criminal is to kneel at his feet and blubber: "Don't hurt me. Take my money. I know you had a disadvantaged childhood, and I share your pain."   3

That's why I seldom write about the endless struggle between gun owners and gun haters, even though I think I understand them better than they understand each other.   4

For example, many gun lovers seem to believe that any gun-control law that imposes any restriction on gun ownership is a bad law.   5

If you carry that to its illogical[3] conclusion, we would have no gun laws and no restrictions. It would be legal for anyone—responsible citizen or nut—to buy a gun as easily as a bottle of root beer. And for anyone to carry it everywhere and anywhere, openly or concealed.   6

We might even have a situation that I once jokingly proposed[4]—and the Archie Bunker show shamelessly stole—in which all passengers on airplanes would be issued loaner pistols so they could blow away skyjackers.   7

We need gun laws. How restrictive they should be, I don't know. But reasonable people should be able to agree on terms that would help keep guns away from dangerous hands while letting decent people protect themselves.   8

"Protect themselves?" someone is scornfully[5] saying. "They don't protect themselves or anyone else. They just let their guns fall into the hands of children or criminals."   9

That's the response of many of those who dislike guns and want a European approach: Nobody has them but the cops or rigidly[6] controlled sportsmen.   10

And I think they truly believe that hardly anyone ever uses a gun to shoot or fend[7] off a criminal.   11

Maybe that's the fault of the media. We seldom overlook a story about a child using his dad's gun to shoot his older sister.   12

But we aren't as alert to stories about people who ping a crook.   13

There are sources for both kinds of stories.   14

The gun-control advocates keep large files on every case of careless gun use they can find.   15

But they don't have any records of people successfully defending themselves against criminals.   16

[1] **siblings:** brothers and sisters
[2] **advocates:** people in favor of something
[3] **illogical:** without reason
[4] **proposed:** offered or volunteered
[5] **scornfully:** with disdain or strong dislike
[6] **rigidly:** tightly
[7] **fend:** hold off

At the same time, the National Rifle Association has thick files of honest citizens using guns to kill, wound, or capture criminals.

But under *F* in its file cabinets, there is nothing about family gun tragedies.

Chances are you didn't read about the great jewelry store shootout in Richmond, Va., a couple of months ago. I know about it only because a friend in Virginia called me.

This is what happened:

Two gunmen barged into the Beverly Jewelry Store. Both were career criminals with long records for stickups, burglaries, drug running, and other crimes across the South and Southeast. One was being sought[8] on a murder rap. He was later described by an acquaintance[9] this way: "He won't kill you unless he has to. But if he has to, he will."

They had picked the wrong jewelry store. The owner is a gutsy guy and an expert marksman. His employees had all been trained in using guns and had so many guns hidden in the store that he and his salespeople were never more than an outstretched arm away from one.

So when one of the gunmen jumped on a display case and let loose with a warning blast from his shotgun, the owner and his five employees all reached down and came up shooting. Six guns going at the same time.

The robbers got off a few shots that didn't hit anyone, but within seconds, both were dead.

The owner of the store said he doesn't believe in being passive when someone threatens his life with a sawed-off shotgun.

There are those who would disagree. Don't fight back and you won't get hurt is their approach. But that's no longer a safe bet, if it ever was. Today, punks with guns take the money, then kill their victims just to see how it feels.

So if the police can't protect people from murderers—and they admit that is beyond them—who will? That jewelry store owner knew. He and his employees were on their own, as most of us are.

It's not a simple subject.

IDEA JOURNAL
Compare and/or contrast the different sides of a controversial issue (e.g., abortion, capital punishment, English only). Decide whether to show the similarities, the differences, or both.

Summarize and Respond

In your reading journal or elsewhere, write a brief summary (three to five sentences) of "Two Extremes Miss Target over Guns." Next, jot down a quick response to the reading. What did it make you think or feel? Do you think Royko presents both sides of the issue fairly? Why, or why not?

Check Your Comprehension

1. An alternate title for this essay could be
   a. "Guns: More Protective Than Destructive When in the Right Hands."

[8] **sought:** looked for
[9] **acquaintance:** someone not known very well

b.   "Gun Lovers and Archie Bunker."

c.   "Family Gun Tragedies Fill the Media."

d.   "The Wrong Gutsy Guy."

2.   The main idea of this essay is that

a.   any gun-control law that restricts gun ownership is a bad law.

b.   gun control is a simple subject.

c.   reasonable people should be able to keep guns out of the hands of criminals and in the hands of decent people.

d.   under *F*, there's nothing about family gun tragedies.

3.   What is the European approach to gun control?

a.   Anyone can carry a concealed weapon, anywhere, anytime.

b.   Only hunters have guns.

c.   Only the police and hunters have guns.

d.   Reach down and come up shooting.

4.   If you are still unfamiliar with the following words, use a dictionary to check their meanings: neofascists (para. 2); imposes (5); restrictive (8); ping (13); marksman (22).

Read Critically

1.   Does Royko say more about how "gun lovers" and "gun-control advocates" are alike or different? What examples can you find?

2.   Consider Royko's example of the "gutsy" jewelry store owner. Which side of the issue does this example support? Does he offer an example for the other side? What does this suggest about his perspective?

3.   Royko concludes with the statement that "it's not a simple subject." What do you think he means by this? What examples for and against gun control can you add to the essay?

4.   What is the "target" that Royko refers to in his title?

5.   Royko tells us that "the robbers got off a few shots that didn't hit anyone, but within seconds, both were dead." How do you think supporters of gun control might feel about this incident?

WRITING TIP
Remember, good comparison and contrast
1. Uses subjects that have enough in common to be compared or contrasted
2. Presents several points of comparison or contrast
3. Arranges the points in a useful manner — either point-by-point or whole-to-whole

Write

WRITE A PARAGRAPH: Write a paragraph that compares two people's attitudes towards an issue. Be sure to use good examples to support your point.

WRITE AN ESSAY: Write an essay that compares and contrasts the two sides of the gun-control issue. You should address some of the complexities that Royko does not focus on. Remember that regardless of *your* response to the issue, both sides of the issue must be treated fairly. If you wrote about gun control in Write a Paragraph, you may write your essay on this, too.

49

Cause and Effect

TIP: For information on writing cause and effect, see Chapter 18.

The essays in this chapter explain causes and effects to get their main points across to the reader. A cause is why something happened. An effect is what happens after an event takes place. Often, writers explain both causes and effects in a single essay.

Good cause-and-effect explanations provide clear, logical links between causes and effects. They offer examples and other evidence to support their points. Finally, they arrange their points in a logical order (usually according to time or importance). Sometimes writers use cause and effect to introduce a topic, but sometimes they want to persuade the reader that their ideas about cause and effect are correct. As you read these essays note why and how cause-and-effect explanations are used.

Anne Roiphe
Why Marriages Fail

Anne Roiphe (b. 1935) grew up in New York City, where she currently lives. A novelist and nonfiction writer, Roiphe often explores the topics of divorce, aging, and religious tradition. She is best known for her second novel, *Up the Sandbox,* in which she explores the issues of feminism, marriage, and Jewish identity.

Roiphe's first marriage ended in divorce after five years, and she now is married to psychoanalyst Herman Roiphe. Together they wrote *Your Child's Mind: The Complete Book of Infant and Child Emotional Well-Being* (1986). In "Why Marriages Fail," originally published in *Family Weekly* (1983), Roiphe offers a serious investigation of the reasons for divorce, exploring the issues of cause and effect. She also suggests ways to strengthen relationships.

GUIDING QUESTION
What explanation does Roiphe provide for why marriages fail?

"This essay provides some insight into the importance of good communication in a marriage. Poor communication causes problems."
—Elizabeth Velasco, Student

TEACHING TIP
Have students fill in the ring diagram in Chapter 18 using this essay. A reproducible blank form for the rings is in *Additional Resources.* Is Roiphe presenting causes, effects, or both?

These days so many marriages end in divorce that our most sacred vows no longer ring with truth. "Happily ever after" and "Till death do us part" are expressions that seem on the way to becoming obsolete.[1] Why has it become so hard for couples to stay together? What goes wrong? What has happened to us that close to one-half of all marriages are destined for the divorce courts? How could we have created a society in which 42 percent of our children will grow up in single-parent homes? If statistics could only measure loneliness, regret, pain, loss of self-confidence, and fear of the future, the numbers would be beyond quantifying.   1

Even though each broken marriage is unique, we can still find the common perils,[2] the common causes for marital despair. Each marriage has crisis points, and each marriage tests endurance,[3] the capacity for both intimacy and change. Outside pressures such as job loss, illness, infertility, trouble with a child, care of aging parents, and all the other plagues of life hit marriage the way hurricanes blast our shores. Some marriages survive these storms, and others don't. Marriages fail, however, not simply because of the outside weather but because the inner climate becomes too hot or too cold, too turbulent or too stupefying.[4]   2

When we look at how we choose our partners and what expectations exist at the tender beginnings of romance, some of the reasons for disaster become quite clear. We all select with unconscious accuracy a mate who will recreate with us the emotional patterns of our first homes. Dr. Carl A. Whitaker, a marital therapist and emeritus professor of psychiatry at the University of Wisconsin, explains, "From early childhood on, each of us carried models for marriage, femininity, masculinity, motherhood, fatherhood and all the other family roles." Each of us falls in love with a mate who has qualities of our parents, who will help us rediscover both the psychological happiness and miseries of our past lives. We may think we have found a man unlike Dad, but then he turns to drink or drugs, or loses his job over and over again, or sits silently in front of the TV just the way Dad did. A man may choose a woman who doesn't like kids just like his mother or who gambles away the family savings just like his mother. Or he may choose a slender wife who seems unlike his obese mother but then turns out to have other addictions that destroy their mutual happiness.   3

A man and a woman bring to their marriage bed a blended concoction[5] of conscious and unconscious memories of their parents' lives together. The human way is to compulsively repeat and recreate the patterns of the past. Sigmund Freud so well described the unhappy design that many of us get   4

[1] **obsolete:** outdated
[2] **perils:** dangers
[3] **endurance:** power to tolerate hardship
[4] **stupefying:** dulling the senses
[5] **concoction:** mixture

trapped in: the unmet needs of childhood, the angry feelings left over from frustrations of long ago, the limits of trust, and the reoccurrence of old fears. Once an individual senses this entrapment,[6] there may follow a yearning to escape, and the result could be a broken, splintered marriage.

Of course people can overcome the habits and attitudes that developed in childhood. We all have hidden strengths and amazing capacities for growth and creative change. Change, however, requires work—observing your part in a rotten pattern, bringing difficulties out into the open—and work runs counter to the basic myth of marriage: "When I wed this person all my problems will be over. I will have achieved success and I will become the center of life for this other person and this person will be my center, and we will mean everything to each other forever." This myth, which every marriage relies on, is soon exposed. The coming of children, the pulls and tugs of their demands on affection and time, place a considerable strain on that basic myth of meaning everything to each other, of merging together and solving all of life's problems.

Concern and tension about money take each partner away from the other. Obligations to demanding parents or still-depended-upon parents create further strain. Couples today must also deal with all the cultural changes brought on in recent years by the women's movement and the sexual revolution. The altering of roles and the shifting of responsibilities have been extremely trying for many marriages.

These and other realities of life erode the visions of marital bliss the way sandstorms eat at rock and the ocean nibbles away at the dunes. Those euphoric,[7] grand feelings that accompany romantic love are really self-delusions, self-hypnotic dreams that enable us to forge a relationship. Real life, failure at work, disappointments, exhaustion, bad smells, bad colds, and hard times all puncture the dream and leave us stranded with our mate, with our childhood patterns pushing us this way and that, with our unfulfilled expectations.

The struggle to survive in marriage requires adaptability, flexibility, genuine love and kindness, and an imagination strong enough to feel what the other is feeling. Many marriages fall apart because either partner cannot imagine what the other wants or cannot communicate what he or she needs or feels. Anger builds until it erupts into a volcanic burst that buries the marriage in ash.

It is not hard to see, therefore, how essential[8] communication is for a good marriage. A man and a woman must be able to tell each other how they feel and why they feel the way they do; otherwise they will impose on each other roles and actions that lead to further unhappiness. In some cases, the communication patterns of childhood—of not talking, of talking too much, of not listening, of distrust and anger, of withdrawal—spill into the marriage and prevent a healthy exchange of thoughts and feelings. The answer is to set up new patterns of communication and intimacy.

---

[6] **entrapment:** process of luring into a trap

[7] **euphoric:** elated, extremely joyful

[8] **essential:** necessary

At the same time, however, we must see each other as individuals. "To achieve a balance between separateness and closeness is one of the major psychological tasks of all human beings at every stage of life," says Dr. Stuart Bartle, a psychiatrist at the New York University Medical Center.   10

If we sense from our mate a need for too much intimacy, we tend to push him or her away, fearing that we may lose our identities in the merging of marriage. One partner may suffocate the other partner in a childlike dependency.   11

A good marriage means growing as a couple but also growing as individuals. This isn't easy. Richard gives up his interest in carpentry because his wife, Helen, is jealous of the time he spends away from her. Karen quits the choir group because her husband dislikes the friends she makes there. Each pair clings to each other and is angry with each other as life closes in on them. This kind of marital balance is easily thrown as one or the other pulls away and divorce follows.   12

IDEA JOURNAL
List the possible causes and effects of student success that an article on "Why Students Succeed" would present.

Sometimes people pretend that a new partner will solve the old problems. Most often extramarital sex destroys a marriage because it allows an artificial split between the good and the bad—the good is projected on the new partner, and the bad is dumped on the head of the old. Dishonesty, hiding, and cheating create walls between men and women. Infidelity[9] is just a symptom of trouble. It is a symbolic complaint, a weapon of revenge, as well as an unraveler of closeness. Infidelity is often that proverbial[10] last straw that sinks the camel to the ground.   13

All right—marriage has always been difficult. Why then are we seeing so many divorces at this time? Yes, our modern social fabric is thin, and yes the permissiveness of society has created unrealistic expectations and thrown the family into chaos. But divorce is so common because people today are unwilling to exercise the self-discipline that marriage requires. They expect easy joy, like the entertainment on TV, the thrill of a good party.   14

Marriage takes some kind of sacrifice, not dreadful self-sacrifice of the soul, but some level of compromise. Some of one's fantasies, some of one's legitimate desires have to be given up for the value of the marriage itself. "While all marital partners feel shackled at times, it is they who really choose to make the marital ties into confining chains or supporting bonds," says Dr. Whitaker. Marriage requires sexual, financial, and emotional discipline. A man and a woman cannot follow every impulse, cannot allow themselves to stop growing or changing.   15

Divorce is not an evil act. Sometimes it provides salvation for people who have grown hopelessly apart or were frozen in patterns of pain or mutual unhappiness. Divorce can be, despite its initial devastation, like the first cut of the surgeon's knife, a step toward new health and a good life. On the other hand, if the partners can stay past the breaking up of the romantic myths into the development of real love and intimacy, they have achieved a work as amazing as the greatest cathedrals of the world. Marriages that do   16

[9] **infidelity:** act of being unfaithful
[10] **proverbial:** commonly referred to

not fail but improve, that persist despite imperfections, are not only rare these days but offer a wondrous shelter in which the face of our mutual humanity can safely show itself.

Summarize and Respond

In your reading journal or elsewhere, write a brief summary (three to five sentences) of "Why Marriages Fail." Next, jot down a quick response to the reading. What did it make you think or feel? Why did you agree or disagree with Roiphe's conclusions? Can you think of any examples of good or bad marriages that fit Roiphe's explanations?

Check Your Comprehension

1. An alternate title for this essay could be
   a. "Why Some Marriages Endure."
   b. "A Marriage Made in Heaven."
   c. "How Children Affect a Marriage."
   d. "Why People Should Not Marry."

2. The main idea of this essay is that
   a. divorce is an evil act.
   b. a successful marriage requires work and compromise.
   c. failed marriages cause loneliness.
   d. we all marry our parents in our partners.

3. According to the author, what is the basic myth of marriage?
   a. that the partners will mean everything to one another
   b. that communication is essential to a good marriage
   c. that infidelity is a symptom of trouble
   d. that a good marriage means growing as a couple and as individuals

4. If you are still unfamiliar with the following words, use a dictionary to check their meanings: turbulent (para. 2); compulsively (4); forge (7); permissiveness (14); compromise, impulse (15); salvation (16).

Read Critically

1. Choose one of the images that Roiphe uses to describe marriage and discuss why you think it works.
2. How does Roiphe arrange her points? Does she provide clear links between cause and effect? What in the essay supports your answer?
3. According to marital therapist Dr. Carl A. Whitaker, how do most people choose their marriage partners?

4. What is Roiphe's attitude toward divorce? What examples from the essay support your answer?

5. According to Roiphe, what is necessary for a marriage to endure? Explain why you agree or disagree.

WRITING TIP
Remember, good cause-and-effect explanations
1. Provide clear, logical links between causes and effects
2. Offer examples and other evidence to support their points
3. Arrange their points in a logical order (usually according to time or importance)

Write

WRITE A PARAGRAPH: Write a cause-and-effect paragraph about the causes of a good marriage. Try to use an example from your own experience or the experience of parents or friends.

WRITE AN ESSAY: Roiphe uses a few personal examples to support her ideas about marriage. In an essay that discusses the cause and effect of failed marriages, use examples from relationships of real people to support your ideas. If you addressed this issue in your reading journal for Summarize and Respond, feel free to use those ideas.

Joe Klein
The Education of Berenice Belizaire

Joe Klein was born in New York in 1946. He earned a degree from the University of Pennsylvania in 1968 and began a career as a reporter a year later. Says Klein about his work, "I've generally specialized in reporting on 'unfamous' people—a worker dying of cancer caused by his job, a union official, a grocer in Florida, the marketing executive who decided to sell granola in boxes." Not all of his writing is about the "unfamous," however. *Primary Colors* (1996), an anonymous book satirizing the Clinton administration, was in fact written by Klein.

In "The Education of Berenice Belizaire," Klein profiles Haitian immigrant Berenice Belizaire, examining how her experiences led her to become valedictorian of her high school class and to be admitted as a student at the Massachusetts Institute of Technology. The article originally appeared in *Newsweek* (1993).

GUIDING QUESTION
Why did Klein choose to write about Berenice Belizaire, and what examples does he use to describe her education?

"'The Education of Berenice Belizaire' is an inspiring story showing that immigrants can make it in the United States of America."
—*Ricky Alyassi, Student*

W hen Berenice Belizaire arrived in New York from Haiti with her mother and sister in 1987, she was not very happy. She spoke no English. The family had to live in a cramped Brooklyn apartment, a far cry from the   1

TEACHING TIP
Ask students what
caused Berenice's move
to the United States from
Haiti. Have them under-
line the *effects* (out-
comes) of Berenice's
move to a U.S. high
school. Have students un-
derline how immigrants
positively affect New
York City. Why does the
author start with the
story of Berenice and
then move to all
immigrants?

comfortable house they'd had in Haiti. Her mother, a nurse, worked long hours. School was torture. Berenice had always been a good student, but now she was learning a new language while enduring constant taunts from the Americans (both black and white). They cursed her in the cafeteria and threw food at her. Someone hit her sister in the head with a book. "Why can't we go home?" Berenice asked her mother.

Because home was too dangerous. The schools weren't always open anymore, and education—her mother insisted—was the most important thing. Her mother had always pushed her: Memorize everything, she ordered. "I have a pretty good memory," Berenice admitted last week. Indeed, the other kids at school began to notice that Berenice always, somehow, knew the answers. "They started coming to me for help," she says. "They never called me a nerd."

Within two years Berenice was speaking English, though not well enough to get into one of New York's elite[1] public high schools. She had to settle for the neighborhood school, James Madison—which is one of the magical American places, the alma mater of Ruth Bader Ginsburg[2] among others, a school with a history of unlikely success stories. "I didn't realize what we had in Berenice at first," says math teacher Judith Khan. "She was good at math, but she was quiet. And the things she didn't know! She applied for a summer program in Buffalo and asked me how to get there on the subway. But she always seemed to ask the right questions. She understood the big ideas. She could think on her feet. She could explain difficult problems so the other kids could understand them. Eventually, I realized: she wasn't just pushing for grades, she was hungry for *knowledge.* . . . And you know, it never occurred to me that she also was doing it in English and history, all these other subjects that had to be much tougher for her than math."

She moved from third in her class to first during senior year. She was selected as valedictorian,[3] an honor she almost refused (still shy, she wouldn't allow her picture in the school's yearbook). She gave the speech, after some prodding[4]—a modest[5] address about the importance of hard work and how it's never too late to try hard: an immigrant's valedictory. Last week I caught up with Berenice at the Massachusetts Institute of Technology where she was jumpstarting her college career. I asked her what she wanted to be doing in ten years: "I want to build a famous computer, like IBM," she said. "I want my name to be part of it."

Berenice Belizaire's story is remarkable but not unusual. The New York City schools are bulging with overachieving immigrants. The burdens they place on a creaky, corroded system are often cited as an argument against liberal immigration policies, but teachers like Judith Khan don't seem to mind. "They're why I love teaching in Brooklyn," she says. "They have a

---

[1] **elite:** having superior status
[2] **Ruth Bader Ginsburg:** an Associate Justice of the United States Supreme Court
[3] **valedictorian:** student with highest grade average who delivers the valedictory address at graduation
[4] **prodding:** urging
[5] **modest:** humble

IDEA JOURNAL
Write about an event in your life that you did not look forward to (e.g., moving to a new home, going to a new school, getting a new boss, learning how to use a computer). What caused it, and what came about as a result of it?

drive in them we no longer seem to have. You see these kids, who aren't prepared academically and can barely speak the language, struggling so hard. They just sop it up. They're like little sponges. You see Berenice, who had none of the usual, preconceived[6] racial barriers in her mind—you see her becoming friendly with the Russian kids, and learning chess from Po Ching [from Taiwan]. It is *so* exciting."

Indeed, it is possible that immigrant energy reinvigorated[7] not just 6 some schools (and more than a few teachers)—but *the city itself* in the 1980s. "Without them, New York would have been a smaller place, a poorer place, a lot less vital[8] and exciting," says Prof. Emanuel Tobier of New York University. They restored the retail life of the city, starting a raft of small businesses—and doing the sorts of entry-level, bedpan-emptying jobs that nonimmigrants spurn.[9] They added far more to the local economy than they removed; more important, they reminded enlightened New Yorkers that the city had always worked best as a vast, noisy, dreamy hothouse for the cultivation[10] of new Americans.

The Haitians have followed the classic pattern. They have a signifi- 7 cantly higher workforce participation rate than the average in New York. They have a lower rate of poverty. They have a higher rate of new-business formation and a lower rate of welfare dependency. Their median household income, at $28,853, is about $1,000 less than the citywide median (but about $1,000 higher than Chinese immigrants, often seen as a "model" minority). They've also developed a traditional network of fraternal societies, newspapers, and neighborhoods with solid—extended, rather than nuclear—families. "A big issue now is whether women who graduate from school should be allowed to live by themselves before they marry," says Lola Poisson, who counsels Haitian immigrants. "There's a lot of tension over that."

Such perverse propriety[11] cannot last long. Immigrants become Amer- 8 icans very quickly. Some lose hope after years of menial[12] labor; others lose discipline, inebriated[13] by freedom. "There's an interesting phenomenon," says Philip Kasinitz of Williams College. "When immigrant kids criticize each other for getting lazy or loose, they say, 'You're becoming American.'" (Belizaire said she and the Russians would tease each other that way at Madison.) It's ironic, Kasinitz adds, "Those who work hardest to keep American culture at bay have the best chance of becoming American success stories." If so, we may be fixed on the wrong issue. The question shouldn't be whether immigrants are ruining America, but whether America is ruining the immigrants.

---

[6] **preconceived:** determined in advance
[7] **reinvigorated:** brought back to life
[8] **vital:** essential
[9] **spurn:** reject
[10] **cultivation:** careful growing
[11] **propriety:** correct behavior
[12] **menial:** relating to a job felt to be suitable for a servant
[13] **inebriated:** drunk

Summarize and Respond

In your reading journal or elsewhere, write a brief summary (three to five sentences) of "The Education of Berenice Belizaire." Next, jot down a quick response to the reading. What did the essay make you think or feel? What did it remind you of? Do you think Berenice Belizaire's is a typical example of an immigrant success story? Why, or why not?

Check Your Comprehension

1. An alternate title for this essay could be
   a. "Hungry for Knowledge."
   b. "Are Immigrants Ruining America?"
   c. "Hothouse for New Americans."
   d. "Shy Girl No More."

2. The main idea of this essay is that
   a. hard work is important.
   b. immigrants become Americanized very quickly.
   c. immigrants have much to teach America about hard work and success.
   d. Americans are lazy.

3. According to Belizaire, why did the kids at school finally stop taunting her?
   a. She was part of an extended family and large community.
   b. She was accepted to a summer program in Buffalo.
   c. She always knew the answers and began providing help.
   d. She spoke no English.

4. If you are still unfamiliar with the following words, use a dictionary to check their meanings: enduring (para. 1); formation, fraternal, nuclear (7); perverse, phenomenon (8).

Read Critically

1. What causes does Klein give for Belizaire's success?
2. Why do you think Klein quotes people other than Berenice Belizaire? What does this add to his essay?
3. What effect does the author's use of statistics as examples have on the essay? Do you find his statistics surprising? Why, or why not?
4. Judging from the essay, what do you think is Klein's attitude toward immigration?

5. In paragraph 8, Klein includes the quote, "Those who work hardest to keep American culture at bay have the best chance of becoming American success stories." What do you think this quote means?

Write

WRITE A PARAGRAPH: Write a paragraph that discusses why Berenice Belizaire has become so successful. Discuss at least two of Klein's causes or reasons.

WRITE AN ESSAY: Write an essay about *your* education and the causes and effects that influenced your schooling. As Klein does with Belizaire, include childhood experiences that may have contributed to your pursuit of education.

50

Argument

TIP: For information on writing argument, see Chapters 14 and 19.

The essays in this chapter use argument to get their main points across to the reader. Argument takes a strong and definite position on an issue. Good arguments consider the opposing view, give solid evidence to defend and support the position, and have energy from start to finish. As you read these essays, note how these writers use evidence to make their point.

In this section, we have provided a pro and con essay on each topic so that you can compare and contrast the argumentative strategies used. As you read the essays in each pair, decide which essay you find stronger and why.

Andrew Sullivan

Let Gays Marry

When he was about ten years old, Andrew Sullivan began thinking of himself as homosexual. For a young boy growing up Catholic in England, being gay did not promise the kind of freedoms that Sullivan argues for in his essay. In fact, being gay meant feeling, in Sullivan's words, "that love was about being accepted on the condition that you suppressed what you really felt." The loneliness that Sullivan felt finally faded when he acknowledged he was gay. This acknowledgment led to an acceptance of self.

Sullivan earned his B.A. from Oxford University and a Ph.D. in political science from Harvard University. He currently lives in Washington, D.C., where he was formerly the senior editor for the *New Republic*. Sullivan is also the author of *Virtually Normal: An Argument about Homosexuality* (1995), a book that explores how society deals with its gay and lesbian citizens. The following essay, "Let Gays Marry," originally appeared in *Newsweek* (1996).

GUIDING QUESTION

What parts of Sullivan's arguments are convincing to you, and what parts are not particularly effective?

"Part of the author's strategy is to define the term marriage. Based on this definition, he makes a very reasonable, powerful argument."

—Li Pan, Student

TEACHING TIP

Sullivan favors allowing gays to marry and responds to the next selection, which opposes gay marriages. His essay is an excellent example of considering and responding to opposing views. Have students identify the four opposing views Sullivan cites and his answers to the opposition. What evidence does Sullivan give to refute Bennett's claims? Discuss Sullivan's statement that gay marriage is "a deeply conservative cause." What points in his argument are conservative? Is Sullivan's argument convincing? Is his evidence strong? Have students counter Sullivan's points.

"A state cannot deem[1] a class of persons a stranger to its laws," declared the Supreme Court last week. It was a monumental statement. Gay men and lesbians, the conservative court said, are no longer strangers in America. They are citizens, entitled, like everyone else, to equal protection — no special rights, but simple equality.   1

For the first time in Supreme Court history, gay men and women were seen not as some powerful lobby trying to subvert[2] America, but as the people we truly are — the sons and daughters of countless mothers and fathers, with all the weaknesses and strengths and hopes of everybody else. And what we seek is not some special place in America but merely to be a full and equal part of America, to give back to our society without being forced to lie or hide or live as second-class citizens.   2

That is why marriage is so central to our hopes. People ask us why we want the right to marry, but the answer is obvious. It's the same reason anyone wants the right to marry. At some point in our lives, some of us are lucky enough to meet the person we truly love. And we want to commit to that person in front of our family and country for the rest of our lives. It's the most simple, the most natural, the most human instinct in the world. How could anyone seek to oppose that?   3

Yes, at first blush, it seems like a radical proposal, but, when you think about it some more, it's actually the opposite. Throughout American history, to be sure, marriage has been between a man and a woman, and in many ways our society is built upon that institution. But none of that need change in the slightest. After all, no one is seeking to take away anybody's right to marry, and no one is seeking to force any church to change any doctrine[3] in any way. Particular religious arguments against same-sex marriage are rightly debated within the churches and faiths themselves. That is not the issue here: There is a separation between church and state in this country. We are only asking that when the government gives out *civil* marriage licenses, those of us who are gay should be treated like anybody else.   4

Of course, some argue that marriage is *by definition* between a man and a woman. But for centuries, marriage was *by definition* a contract in which the wife was her husband's legal property. And we changed that. For centuries, marriage was *by definition* between two people of the same race. And we changed that. We changed these things because we recognized that human dignity is the same whether you are a man or a woman, black or white. And no one has any more of a choice to be gay than to be black or white or male or female.   5

Some say that marriage is only about raising children, but we let childless heterosexual couples be married (Bob and Elizabeth Dole, Pat and   6

---

[1] **deem:** consider

[2] **subvert:** ruin

[3] **doctrine:** guiding principles

IDEA JOURNAL
How would you gather evidence for an argument you want to make? What kind of evidence is most convincing?

Shelley Buchanan, for instance). Why should gay couples be treated differently? Others fear that there is no logical difference between allowing same-sex marriage and sanctioning[4] polygamy and other horrors. But the issue whether to sanction multiple spouses (gay or straight) is completely separate from whether, in the existing institution between two unrelated adults, the government should discriminate between its citizens.

This is, in fact, if only Bill Bennett[5] could see it, a deeply conservative[6] cause. It seeks to change no one else's rights or marriages in any way. It seeks merely to promote monogamy,[7] fidelity,[8] and the disciplines of family life among people who have long been cast to the margins of society. And what could be a more conservative project than that? Why indeed would any conservative seek to oppose those very family values for gay people that he or she supports for everybody else? Except, of course, to make gay men and lesbians strangers in their own country, to forbid them ever to come home.

Summarize and Respond

In your reading journal or elsewhere, write a brief summary (three to five sentences) of "Let Gays Marry." Next, jot down a quick response to the essay. What did it make you think or feel? Do you agree with Sullivan's argument? Why, or why not?

Check Your Comprehension

1. An alternative title for this essay could be
    a.   "Family Values for Everyone."
    b.   "The Conservative Point of View."
    c.   "Subverting America."
    d.   "Life on the Margins."

2. The main idea of this essay is that
    a.   polygamy should be sanctioned by the courts.
    b.   gays deserve special rights.
    c.   everyone deserves the right to marry.
    d.   gay marriage has the same concerns as interracial marriage.

3. According to Sullivan, why is gay marriage a deeply conservative cause?
    a.   because fighting for it follows the tradition of freedom of speech
    b.   because it promotes a stable family life

---

[4] **sanctioning:** granting permission
[5] **Bill Bennett:** See p. 559.
[6] **conservative:** keeping traditional values and tending to be against change
[7] **monogamy:** the practice of having only one mate
[8] **fidelity:** sexual loyalty

    c.   because it recognizes the value of all people

    d.   because it promises equality

4.   If you are still unfamiliar with the following words, use a dictionary to check their meanings: lobby (para. 2); radical, debated (4); heterosexual, polygamy, discriminate (6).

Read Critically

1.   Identify the opposing views that Sullivan considers.

2.   Which of Sullivan's points in favor of gay marriage do you find the most convincing? Why?

3.   Who do you think Sullivan's audience is? Who is he writing for?

4.   What emotions do you think Sullivan is appealing to? Give two examples of how he appeals to emotions.

5.   In paragraph 5, Sullivan notes that marriage used to make women the legal property of their husbands and that only people of the same race could marry. Why do you think he raises these issues here?

WRITING TIP
Remember, good arguments
1. Consider the opposing view
2. Give solid evidence to defend and support your position
3. Have energy from start to finish

Write

WRITE A PARAGRAPH: Write a paragraph that argues either in favor of or against Sullivan's position. Use strong examples to support your point.

WRITE AN ESSAY: Write an essay that responds to Sullivan, either by adding more points to his argument or by challenging it. If you wish, include any ideas you developed for Summarize and Respond or Write a Paragraph.

William J. Bennett
Leave Marriage Alone

Republican conservative William J. Bennett (b. 1943) served as director of the Office of National Drug Control Policy under President George Bush and as secretary of education and chair of the National Endowment for Humanities under President Ronald Reagan. Bennett holds a B.A. from Williams College, a Ph.D. from the University of Texas, and a law degree from Harvard University. He is currently codirector of Empower America and a senior editor of *National Review* magazine.

Bennett is also editor of *The Book of Virtues: A Treasury of Great Moral Stories* (1993), which explores self-discipline, compassion, courage, perseverance, and other virtues. In "Leave Marriage Alone," from *Newsweek* (1996), he argues against giving official approval to same-sex unions.

GUIDING QUESTION
What evidence does Bennett present to make his case?

There are at least two key issues that divide proponents[1] and opponents[2] of same-sex marriage. The first is whether legally recognizing same-sex unions would strengthen or weaken the institution.[3] The second has to do with the basic understanding of marriage itself.

The advocates of same-sex marriage say that they seek to strengthen and celebrate marriage. That may be what some intend. But I am certain that it will not be the reality. Consider: The legal union of same-sex couples would shatter the conventional definition of marriage, change the rules which govern[4] behavior, endorse[5] practices which are completely antithetical[6] to the tenets[7] of all of the world's major religions, send conflicting signals about marriage and sexuality, particularly to the young, and obscure marriage's enormously consequential[8] function—procreation and child-rearing.

Broadening the definition of marriage to include same-sex unions would stretch it almost beyond recognition—and new attempts to expand the definition still further would surely follow. On what *principled* ground can Andrew Sullivan exclude others who most desperately want what he wants, legal recognition and social acceptance? Why on earth would Sullivan exclude from marriage a bisexual who wants to marry two other people? After all, exclusion would be a denial of that person's sexuality. The same holds true of a father and a daughter who want to marry. Or two sisters. Or men who want (consensual)[9] polygamous arrangements. Sullivan may think some of these arrangements are unwise. But having employed sexual relativism[10] in his own defense, he has effectively lost the capacity to draw any lines and make moral distinctions.

Forsaking all others is an essential component of marriage. Obviously it is not always honored in practice. But it is the ideal to which we rightly aspire, and in most marriages the ideal is in fact the norm. Many advocates of same-sex marriage simply do not share this ideal; promiscuity[11] among homosexual males is well known. Sullivan himself has written that gay male relationships are served by the "openness of the contract" and that homosexuals should resist allowing their "varied and complicated lives" to be flat-

[1] **proponents:** people in favor of something

[2] **opponents:** people against something

[3] **institution:** custom—here, the custom of marriage

[4] **govern:** rule

[5] **endorse:** sponsor

[6] **antithetical:** opposite

[7] **tenets:** principles

[8] **consequential:** significant

[9] **consensual:** by mutual agreement

[10] **relativism:** the theory that truth or goodness is determined by the beliefs of an individual or group

[11] **promiscuity:** engaging in sexual relations with multiple partners

tened into a "single, moralistic model." But that "single, moralistic model" has served society exceedingly well. The burden of proof ought to be on those who propose untested arrangements for our most important institution.

A second key difference I have with Sullivan goes to the very heart of marriage itself. I believe that marriage is not an arbitrary construct[12] which can be redefined simply by those who lay claim to it. It is an honorable estate, instituted of God and built on moral, religious, sexual, and human realities. Marriage is based on a natural teleology,[13] on the different, complementary nature of men and women—and how they refine,[14] support, encourage, and complete one another. It is the institution through which we propagate, nurture, educate, and sustain our species.

That we have to engage in this debate at all is an indication of how steep our moral slide has been. Worse, those who defend the traditional understanding of marriage are routinely referred to (though not to my knowledge by Sullivan) as "homophobes," "gay-bashers," "intolerant," and "bigoted." Can one defend an honorable, 4,000-year-old tradition and not be called these names?

This is a large, tolerant, diverse country. In America people are free to do as they wish, within broad parameters.[15] It is also a country in sore need of shoring up some of its most crucial institutions: marriage and the family, schools, neighborhoods, communities. But marriage and family are the greatest of these. That is why they are elevated and revered. We should keep them so.

IDEA JOURNAL
Which essay do you agree with? Why?

Summarize and Respond

In your reading journal or elsewhere, write a brief summary (three to five sentences) of "Leave Marriage Alone." Next, jot down a quick response to Bennett's essay. What did it make you think or feel? Do you agree or disagree with Bennett's argument? Why?

Check Your Comprehension

1. An alternative title for this essay could be
    a.   "Marriage under Lock and Key."
    b.   "A Celebration of Marriage."
    c.   "Keeping to Conventions."
    d.   "Debating Marriage."

2. The main idea of this essay is that
    a.   gays are immoral and should not be allowed to marry.
    b.   bigotry and tradition sometimes go hand in hand.

[12] **construct:** concept
[13] **teleology:** study of the purpose of natural acts
[14] **refine:** improve
[15] **parameters:** boundaries

      (c.) the institution of marriage should remain unchanged.

      d. same-sex unions would strengthen marriage.

3. According to Bennett, what is the primary purpose of marriage?

      (a.) to produce and raise children

      b. to honor men and women

      c. to destroy moral standards

      d. to exclude outsiders

4. If you are still unfamiliar with the following words, use a dictionary to check their meanings: conventional (para. 2); forsaking, essential (4); arbitrary, propagate, sustain (5); bigoted (6); revered (7).

Read Critically

1. What is Bennett's argument? What evidence does he present to support his argument?

2. Bennett addresses Sullivan's arguments in favor of same-sex marriage. What other arguments does he address?

3. Which do you think is Bennett's strongest point? Why?

4. What does Bennett say will happen if gay marriage is legalized?

5. What is the "complementary nature of men and women" to which Bennett refers?

Write

WRITING TIP
Remember, good arguments
1. Consider the opposing view
2. Give solid evidence to defend and support your position
3. Have energy from start to finish

WRITE A PARAGRAPH: Write a paragraph that argues in favor of abolishing marriage altogether. Remember to consider your opponents' views and provide evidence that supports your position.

WRITE AN ESSAY: Write an essay that responds to Bennett's discussion, either by adding more points to his argument or by challenging it. You may include the ideas you developed in your reading journal when you addressed the issue under Summarize and Respond.

Terry Crawford

Affirmative Action Causes Imbalance

Terry Crawford was born in 1973 in Atlanta, Georgia. He was deeply influenced by a high school English teacher who continued to mentor him during his college years. Although Crawford lacked confidence as a first-year student at the University of Virginia, during his senior year he wrote a weekly column for *The Cavalier Daily,* the newspaper in which this essay appeared. Crawford currently teaches English at the junior high level in Japan.

In 1995, Crawford wrote "Affirmative Action Causes Imbalance" about the consequences of affirmative action, a policy that gives preferred treatment to groups that have been discriminated against in the past. Although he says that he continues to rethink his position on the issue, in this article Crawford argues passionately against such policies.

GUIDING QUESTION
What is Crawford's main point, and how does he support his argument?

"It was interesting to hear another point of view about affirmative action. I felt the writer clearly argued his position on this controversial issue."
—*Farrah Burgos, Student*

Affirmative action should be abolished. Not because past injustices against minorities—like the original numbers in an equation—can be disputed, but because the equation's two parameters[1]—fairness and the government's role—are entered into the equation incorrectly.   1

On the surface, affirmative action seems fair. It is an attempt to correct past injustices against women and minorities. But affirmative action penalizes[2] people for past injustices they did not commit. Like holding a son accountable[3] for his father's crimes, society is punishing innocent people for the racism of prior generations. Furthermore, affirmative action helps advance people who may not be disadvantaged. If affirmative action would punish only those who discriminate and assist only those who need assistance, it would be a viable[4] option.   2

TEACHING TIP
This essay begins with a strong statement of position as the thesis statement. Have students label it and identify two places where the author cites and answers the opposing view. What other points does the author make? Which evidence is the most convincing and why? Discuss how the concluding sentence relates back to the thesis statement. Is it a good conclusion?

Supporters of affirmative action may argue that unfairness is the unfortunate side effect of achieving a greater good in America. However, why are the proponents[5] of affirmative action in academia[6] and the business world unwilling to step down and fill their position with people more disadvantaged than themselves? These programs are easy to endorse[7] when one gains or is protected by them. In reality, the pastors of race-preferential hiring practices rarely practice what they preach.   3

The government cannot ensure everyone is equal, but it can at least treat everyone equally. Affirmative action does not serve individual justice. Race and gender are the only considerations in laws governing hiring practices, but they are not the only qualifications to consider when determining whether someone is disadvantaged. By reducing the inputs of the equation to only two parts, race and gender, the government can ensure positive statistical results while ignoring the negative outcome: individual injustice to people who have not committed any wrong.   4

---

[1] **parameters:** boundaries
[2] **penalizes:** punishes
[3] **accountable:** responsible
[4] **viable:** possible, likely
[5] **proponents:** supporters
[6] **academia:** institutions for the study of arts and sciences
[7] **endorse:** support

IDEA JOURNAL
Choose an issue you feel strongly about. List the opposing views—arguments that can be made against your position.

We do not have a perfect meritocracy.[8] The best person is not always hired. Connections often get one's foot in the door. But the government must not place another obstacle in the way of society's attempts to reward the best with the most, particularly without giving the most racially tolerant generation in the United States's history a chance.

Affirmative action takes a complex social problem and reduces it to a simple equation of two plus two equals four. Like with any mathematical equation, however, if you distort the necessary considerations, you will get the wrong answer.

Summarize and Respond

In your reading journal or elsewhere, write a brief summary (three to five sentences) of "Affirmative Action Causes Imbalance." Next, jot down a quick response to the reading. Were you convinced by Crawford's argument? Why, or why not? Which do you think is Crawford's strongest point? Why?

Check Your Comprehension

1. An alternate title for this essay could be
   a. "Leave the Past to the Past and Look Forward."
   b. "Affirmative Action Solves the Equation."
   c. "Guilty for Our Father's Acts."
   d. "Why Affirmative Action Should Not Be Abolished."

2. The main idea of this essay is that
   a. a son is accountable for his father's crimes.
   b. affirmative action punishes people who are not guilty and helps people who may not be disadvantaged.
   c. affirmative action considers only gender and not ability.
   d. affirmative action prevents people from getting their foot in the door.

3. According to the author, who does affirmative action punish?
   a. people who are not disadvantaged
   b. people who are not personally guilty of discrimination
   c. fathers who are guilty of crimes
   d. people related to the presidents of companies

4. If you are still unfamiliar with the following words, use a dictionary to look up their meanings: equation (para. 1); option (2).

---

[8] **meritocracy:** system in which talent is recognized and rewarded

Read Critically

1. Identify Crawford's argument. How does he address opposing viewpoints?

2. How would you describe the tone of this essay? Give two specific examples.

3. What evidence does Crawford provide to support his argument? Choose one point that you find most convincing.

4. How do you think Crawford feels about people who get jobs because they *know* someone? What in the essay supports your answer?

5. According to Crawford, what is the main problem with affirmative action? Explain why you agree or disagree.

Write

WRITING TIP
Remember, good arguments
1. Consider the opposing view
2. Give solid evidence to defend and support your position
3. Have energy from start to finish

WRITE A PARAGRAPH: Write a paragraph that supports affirmative action. You may address the arguments Crawford makes, if you like.

WRITE AN ESSAY: Write an essay that argues in favor of affirmative action and addresses some of the points Crawford does not discuss. If the paragraph you developed begins to explore this topic, include it in your discussion. If you wrote in your journal about parts of Crawford's discussion that you agreed with, include those points in your essay as opposing viewpoints.

Raphael Allen
A Need for Affirmative Action

Raphael Allen (b. 1975) grew up in Chicago and studied world politics at Hamilton College in Clinton, New York. At Hamilton, he was a member of Pentagon, a leadership honor society for seniors. He also served as secretary for black cultural affairs within the Black and Latin Student Union.

Allen says he still struggles with writing. However, his passions—community activism, social change, and political debate—motivate him to write. According to Allen, an African American, "it would be a scary America" if companies were to abandon their affirmative action programs. In the following selection, Allen presents his argument for maintaining such programs. The essay originally appeared in the "Pros and Cons" section of *The Spectator* (1996), the author's college newspaper.

GUIDING QUESTION
What is Allen's attitude toward affirmative action, and what opposing viewpoints does he address?

There is a need for affirmative action in America. The Constitution commits us to the ideals of education and equal economic opportunities to all, regardless of race or gender. However, institutionalized racism[1] and other forms of discrimination present in America make these ideals unobtainable for a large number of citizens. The current attack on affirmative action is based on the illusion of a short supply of jobs and the progressive loss of white male elitist[2] control over the national economy. This attack is based on two myths: (1) People of color and white women dominate the workforce, and (2) programs are set aside for unqualified minorities and white women.

Myth: People of color and white women dominate the workforce. Although white women and minorities are making progress through affirmative action programs, their relative success encompasses[3] a small percentage of the total workforce. According to the 1990 census, the average on-the-job earnings for all American adults totaled $15,105. Blacks' average on-the-job annual earnings came to $10,912; Hispanics', $11,219; and Native Americans', $11,949. Also, women held 40 percent of the nation's jobs while white men constituted[4] 47 percent of the American workforce. Ninety-five percent of upper-managerial positions were held by white men. These statistics do not show the domination of minorities and white women in the workforce.

Myth: Programs are set aside for unqualified minorities and white women. Many people believe that the government can make America a color-blind and sexually equal society by abandoning race and gender-based preferences (affirmative action) in favor of preferences based solely on merit. This argument assumes that the people who benefit from affirmative action programs would be considered unqualified in a system based on merit. However, the entire purpose of affirmative action is to make sure that *qualified* candidates who had been historically overlooked by employers are now given a fair chance to get good jobs. Up until now, the people who control the American economy—white males—have been unwilling to share the control with qualified white women and people of color. The criticisms of affirmative action work to reinforce white male privilege and make the real victims of discrimination in this country appear to be racists.

In order to survive into the twenty-first century, affirmative action must continue to dismantle[5] institutionalized racism and sexism. America cannot be an egalitarian society as long as racism and other forms of discrimination continue. Affirmative action policies allow the many qualified minorities and white women access to those areas in the workforce that have historically been denied to them by racist and sexist hiring practices.

[1] **institutionalized racism:** discrimination that is based on race and is part of a culture's structure
[2] **elitist:** believing that a certain group deserves favored treatment
[3] **encompasses:** covers
[4] **constituted:** made up
[5] **dismantle:** take apart

Summarize and Respond

In your reading journal or elsewhere, write a brief summary (three to five sentences) of Allen's essay. Next, jot down a quick response to the reading. What did you think about Allen's ideas? Explain why you think his argument is or isn't convincing. How do you think he feels about his opponents' views? Would you say he is fair? Why, or why not?

Check Your Comprehension

1. An alternate title for this essay could be
   a. "No Need for Affirmative Action."
   b. "Dismantling the Myths."
   c. "Native Americans' Earnings."
   d. "The Illusion of White Male Privilege."

2. The main idea of this essay is that
   a. the conservative aim of affirmative action must be challenged.
   b. women make up only 47 percent of the workforce.
   c. programs should not be set aside for unqualified people.
   d. a large need still remains for affirmative action programs.

3. What is the second myth on which the attack on affirmative action is based?
   a. White men believe their jobs are threatened by women and people of color.
   b. Affirmative action works against the goal of achieving a society where all are equal regardless of race or gender.
   c. The average income for blacks was $10,912 in 1990.
   d. Affirmative action gives jobs to unqualified women and minorities.

4. If you are still unfamiliar with the following words, use a dictionary to check their meanings: ideals, discrimination, unobtainable, myths, dominate (para. 1); relative (2); abandoning, merit, privilege (3).

Read Critically

1. Identify the two myths Allen attacks. Have you heard people expressing these views before? When?

2. What evidence does Allen use to support his argument? Which pieces of evidence did you find most powerful?

3. In what paragraph does Allen first address his opponents' views? How does he bring them into the essay?

4. Why do you think Allen does not use any personal examples to persuade his readers? How would this change the essay?

5. Allen begins paragraphs 2 and 3 with the word "Myth." How does using this word help his argument?

WRITING TIP
Remember, good arguments
1. Consider the opposing view
2. Give solid evidence to defend and support your position
3. Have energy from start to finish

Write

WRITE A PARAGRAPH: Write a paragraph arguing against affirmative action. You should address some of the issues that Allen mentions.

WRITE AN ESSAY: Write an essay that argues against affirmative action and addresses some of the points that Allen does not discuss. If the paragraph you developed begins to explore this topic, include it in your discussion. If you wrote in your reading journal about parts of Allen's discussion that you agreed with, include those points in your essay as opposing viewpoints.

USEFUL APPENDICES

Appendix A

How to Make an Oral Presentation

Five Surefire Strategies

In college, at work—sometimes even in your everyday life—you will need to make oral presentations. While most people rate public speaking as one of life's most stressful experiences, there are a number of practical strategies for giving an oral presentation that will help you cope with the anxiety caused by this task. Knowing how to prepare for a presentation will help you feel confident and in control of the situation.

You have probably witnessed an embarrassing oral presentation where the speaker fell apart and the audience felt as uncomfortable as the speaker. The following is an example of such a situation.

SITUATION: Jean is in the middle of reviewing her presentation notes when she hears herself being introduced. Startled, she gathers her materials into a messy stack of notes and papers, apologizes for not being ready, and walks quickly to the front of the room.

Obviously flustered, she tries to reorganize her notes, shuffling papers, frowning, and sighing loudly. She begins reading her presentation with her head down, speaking quickly and softly. Several people call out, "I can't hear you" or "Speak up."

Jean clears her throat and starts from the beginning. She's so rattled that her voice quivers and then breaks. She looks up, red in the face, and says, "Sorry. I'm really nervous."

She continues but moves too quickly from one point to the next because she doesn't want to bore people. She forgets to introduce or summarize any of her points, so the audience finds it difficult to follow her speech. People start to tune out.

Aware that she's not doing very well, Jean nervously fiddles with her hair while speaking. She reads quickly and with no emphasis, thinking that the sooner she gets through this, the sooner she can sit down. The words that looked so good in writing sound stupid and awkward when said aloud.

As Jean turns to the second page, she realizes that her papers are out of order. There is an awkward silence as she searches desperately for the right page. She finally finds it and begins again. Soon she comes to a word that she can't read, and she has to stop again to figure it out. Still fiddling with her hair, she now looks as if she's about to pull it out.

Jean skips the word and continues. Her only goal now is to finish. But she's run out of time because of her fumbling and because her presentation was too long to begin with. The warning signal goes off, indicating that one minute remains.

This is the last straw for Jean. She looks up, bright red and nearly in tears, and says, "I guess I've run out of time. I only got through one of my points. I don't have time for what I really wanted to say." She grabs her papers and returns to her seat.

Jean sits in utter misery, sure that everyone is looking at her. She can't listen to anyone else's presentation. All she can do is stare at the floor and wait impatiently for the moment she can escape the room.

ANALYSIS: Jean's presentation was not successful because of some common pitfalls she could easily have avoided. She wasn't adequately prepared, she was obviously very nervous, she hadn't structured her presentation to make her points clear to her audience, she hadn't practiced reading her presentation, and she fled at the end. If she had practiced five simple strategies for making an oral presentation, her experience would have been much less painful, and her presentation would have been much better.

Strategy 1. Be Prepared

Jean's first mistake was not being well prepared. She wasn't psychologically prepared to speak, and she hadn't organized the materials for her presentation properly. Because she was busy reviewing her notes at the last minute, she was caught off guard. Her papers got messed up, she was startled, and she was off to a bad start.

Organize Your Notes

Before you go into the room where you are giving your presentation, make sure all of your notes are in order. Number all pages or note cards so you can quickly reorganize them if they get mixed up, and carry all of your materials in a folder.

Keep Your Notes in Order

If you want to review your main points while waiting to make your presentation, try to run through them in your head. Leave the folder closed. If you need to refresh your memory on a particular point, open the folder and carefully go through your notes until you find the answer.

Use Your Energy

Be aware of when your turn is coming, and focus on being calm. Tell yourself that you're prepared and you know what you're doing. Breathe deeply. Don't worry if your heart is beating hard and fast; that's normal. Nervous energy before a performance of any sort is natural and can make you a more engaging speaker. You just need to learn to channel that energy and make it work *for* you. Use that adrenaline to fuel your enthusiasm for your topic.

Build Yourself Up

Keep breathing normally. However silly it may seem, remind yourself of your strengths and repeat them in your head as your turn to speak approaches: "I know what I'm talking about." "I look good today." "I have a good voice." Remember that your audience isn't waiting for you to fail. Most people understand the stress of oral presentations and are sympathetic. Your audience wants you to do well.

Carry Yourself like Royalty

When it's your turn, take a deep breath, calmly pick up your folder, and walk to the front of the room. Walk slowly, stand straight, and focus on projecting a confident image. Remember that you're in control.

Strategy 2. Act with Confidence

Jean's second mistake was not acting with confidence and authority. She was visibly upset as she tried to get her notes in order, and when she did start, she spoke too softly to be heard. When her voice broke, she apologized to the audience and announced her nervousness. Practicing several techniques would have made her appear confident and in control.

Take Your Time

After you've walked to the front of the room, take a few moments to calmly arrange your notes and papers before you begin. Relax. The timing of your presentation won't start until you begin speaking, so make sure you've got things where you need them before beginning. Remember that even professional speakers need a few moments to lay out their materials.

Take Command

When you're ready to begin, stand up straight and look up and out at the audience. Remember that you are in command of the room. Pause for a few seconds to let people know you're about to begin, and wait for them to give you their attention. When you have the attention of the audience, take a deep breath and begin.

Greet Your Audience

Smile and greet the audience, surveying the room as you do so. Your greeting should be something simple, like "Good morning and thank you all for coming." If there are people in the audience who don't know you, be sure to introduce yourself. Even though you may be nervous, don't forget to smile: It will relax you as well as your audience.

Slow Down and Speak Up

Make sure that you speak slowly, clearly, and loudly. If you're nervous, your tendency will be to speak too quickly, so focus on slowing your speech a bit. Look at the last row of the audience and try to project your voice so that people that far back can hear you. It may feel as if you're shouting, but you won't be. Don't be embarrassed to ask if everyone can hear you. Experienced speakers often break the ice by encouraging an audience to tell them if they need to speak up.

Strategy 3. Structure Your Presentation

Jean's third mistake was not giving her presentation a clear structure that would make it easy for her audience to follow her main points. Your presentation should include lots of verbal cues that let people know when you're making a point, what it is, and when you're moving to another point. The structure of an oral presentation must be much more obvious than the structure of a written paper, so that people can understand as they are listening.

Limit Your Focus

Choose a manageable topic for the time allotted and limit the number of points you plan to make. Listening is hard work, and most people can absorb only a few key points from a speech. Try to limit yourself to three main points in your presentation, and be sure to support each of them with concrete examples. As you give more complex presentations, you will need to use visual aids such as transparencies or slides that will allow you to illustrate and reinforce your points.

State Your Thesis and Preview Your Main Points

Let your audience know what your topic is and what main point you are going to make. State your thesis (your main point) slowly so that people understand the purpose of your presentation. Tell them: "My topic today is _____," and "I will be arguing [or showing, or explaining] _____."

Let your audience in on the structure of your presentation by giving them a preview of your key points. You might tell them: "There are three major points I'd like to make about _____. First I'll present _____. Second I'll discuss _____. And my third point will be _____. This presentation should take approximately three minutes, and there will be time for questions at the end."

Use Transitions to Move from Point to Point

Use transitions to let your audience know when you're finished with one point and about to make another. In your preview, you told the audience what your major points would be. As you speak, you should give clear verbal cues when introducing and summarizing each point. For example:

- My first point is _____.
- Examples/explanation
- Repeat or summarize the first point (to remind the audience of what it is and to let them know you're about to move to another point).

- My second point is _____.
- Examples/explanation
- Repeat or summarize second point.

- My third and final point is _____.
- Examples/explanation
- Repeat or summarize third point.

Conclude by Reviewing Your Main Points

Let people know when you're coming to the end of your presentation by using a verbal cue such as

In conclusion,
To summarize,
To review,

Then review your major points. Conclude with a simple, strong sentence that restates the overall purpose of your presentation—the main point you want to make.

Strategy 4. Practice Your Presentation

Like many people, Jean made the mistake of not adequately practicing her presentation. The right kind of practice would have helped her avoid the following problems: fidgeting with her hair, writing a presentation that sounded awkward when presented orally, losing her place in the middle of her talk, being unable to decipher her handwriting, and running out of time.

Even professional speakers practice their speeches. You should allow plenty of time to practice giving your oral presentation.

Practice Aloud

Things that sound good in writing often sound stilted or awkward when spoken. You need to read your presentation aloud—several times—to make sure that it sounds right. You'll feel silly, but do it anyway. Stop and make changes when things sound awkward. Be aware of any distracting habits you may have, such as interrupting the flow of your speech with repeated expressions like "uh," "you know," or "see."

Practicing aloud will help you remember your points. Practice your speech again and again until you feel comfortable with it. Be sure to practice aloud a final time on the day of your presentation.

Practice in Front of a Mirror

You need to see what you look like as you give your presentation, so try practicing in front of a mirror. This will make you feel even sillier than just saying it aloud, but it will also make you feel much more confident when it comes time to give the presentation.

- Stand straight and look up at the mirror frequently. Pretend you are looking out at an audience.
- Be aware of any distracting habits you have while speaking, such as fidgeting with your hair, as Jean did. Some people shift their weight from one leg to another, or sway back and forth, or stand with their legs far apart in a military stance.
- Practice keeping your hands still, except when you want to gesture or point to something for emphasis. You can hold your notes at your side or in front of you, or you can place them on a table or podium.
- Practice keeping your feet slightly apart and your weight evenly distributed. Don't shift back and forth or rock.
- If you know you will be seated when giving your presentation, you should sit in a chair while practicing. Don't jiggle your feet or swing your legs. Keep your feet flat on the floor.

Practice Working with Your Material

Figure out in advance how you will handle your notes and papers. After you've said your presentation aloud a couple of times to get the wording right, decide whether you will work with the whole presentation written out, an outline, or note cards.

THE WHOLE PRESENTATION: Many people feel insecure unless they have their whole presentation, written out word for word, to read from. If you feel that you need the whole presentation in writing, that's fine, but don't think you don't have to practice. You have to be comfortable enough with the written version to be able to deliver it naturally, not as if you're reading, and to look up at your audience without fear of losing your place. If your eyes are glued to the page, you'll lose your audience's attention.

In addition to practicing, you should format your presentation so it will be easy for you to find your place:

- Highlight your main points in color or by obvious underlining so you'll be able to find your place quickly if you get lost.

- Double-space between the lines of your presentation so you won't have trouble reading it.

- Use a large size type. If you must handwrite your presentation, make sure that you can read your handwriting.

- Write the numbers of your main points in the margin, next to the paragraphs where you introduce those points, write "conc." next to your conclusion, and so on.

- Make sure your pages are clearly numbered so they can easily be put in order if you mix them up.

OUTLINE: Instead of writing out your entire presentation, word for word, you may want to write out your main points in outline form. An outline should include all of the main points you want to make, with examples or explanations. It should also include the points to be made in the introduction and conclusion.

NOTE CARDS: Some people prefer to work from 3″ x 5″ note cards rather than pieces of paper. They prepare a note card for each major point that lists the point and an example. If you use note cards, be sure to number them in the top right corner so that you can easily reassemble them if they get out of order.

Time Yourself

As you practice aloud, time yourself. You need to be sure that you can finish your presentation within the time limit you've been given.

If you find that you don't have enough time to make your major points, don't just speak more quickly. Go back and revise your presentation. Keep the points simple and the examples clear. If necessary, cut back on the number of points you are making, keeping only the strongest ones.

Be sure to time yourself at least twice after you have your presentation in final form.

Strategy 5. Create a Good Final Impression

Jean's last mistake was that when she ran short on time, she panicked and ended on a bad note. Practicing aloud and timing yourself will help you avoid this situation, but if you do run short on time, don't panic.

Usually speakers are given a warning signal of some sort to let them know that they need to finish. If you get your warning signal before you've said all you wanted to, remember that it's a warning. You have a bit of time left to conclude your presentation.

You may have enough time to go on as planned and finish, but if you know you can't fit everything in the time remaining, you will need to condense. You may need to move to your final point and give it without an example. Then say, "Again, here are the major points," repeat them briefly, and conclude.

The main thing to remember if you run out of time is not to panic. Stay calm and confident and use the remaining time well. Reduce the details about your points and move to a very brief conclusion.

When the time is over, look up, smile at your audience, thank them for their attention, and ask if they have any questions. Give the audience time to respond. It may take them a while to get started on questions. Wait calmly, and look around the room. If there are no questions, thank the audience again and return to your seat.

Assignment

Choose one of the following topics and prepare a three-minute oral presentation.

COLLEGE

A good instructor

What you learned in your last class

The last exam you took

The kind of exam you like

Grades

A model student

WORK

The kind of job you want

The skills you can offer an employer

A nightmare boss

Interviews

How to ask for a raise

EVERYDAY LIFE

Saving a public park

Recycling

Police corruption

Any local issue you feel strongly about

The best deal in your hometown

Appendix B

How to Write a Résumé

A résumé presents your experience and skills in brief written form. When you apply for a job, you should have an up-to-date résumé that you can send to a prospective employer and carry with you to an interview. Because the quality of your résumé will often determine whether you are called for an interview, it is worth your time to put together a good one.

The following descriptive guide was written by Jill Lee, coordinator of career services at the University of Toledo Community and Technical College. Jill is profiled in Chapter 10.

The appearance of your résumé is very important. Use a good-quality paper and print copies of your résumé on a laser printer. Spelling and grammar are also important. A spelling error or an obvious grammar error may rule you out of consideration for a job, so proofread your résumé carefully. Emphasize your positive qualities in your résumé, highlighting your skills and accomplishments. Within each section, list the most recent information first and then work back in time. For example, under "Experience or Employment" you should list your current or most recent position first, then the one before that, and so on.

A competitive résumé must be concise and well organized. Prospective employers spend an average of six to eight seconds deciding whether to give a résumé serious consideration, so you should be brief and highlight your skills and experience. Try to keep your résumé to one page.

A résumé should include the following categories of information (see the sample résumé on p. 580).

1. Identifying Information

At the top of the page, put your identifying information: your full name, address, and telephone number, including your area code. Include your work number if it's all right for someone to contact you there. It's important to include a number where a caller can leave a message. Each piece of information should be on its own line and centered.

2. Objective

If you have a specific career objective, you can list it under this category. It should be a clearly defined, short-term goal such as the following:

OBJECTIVE: To obtain a position as an engineering technician

OBJECTIVE: To obtain an accounting position

You should be sure that your objective matches the career opportunities available at the company you are sending your résumé to.

3. Education

Under education, be sure to correctly identify your degree(s). Under most conditions, you should not include your high school. Note: Associate degrees do not have an *s* at the end of the word *associate*.

Associate of Applied Business/Science degree in Medical Technology

B.A. in Communication

M.A. in Counseling Psychology

Include the date you received each degree, or your "anticipated" or "expected" graduation date:

B.A. in Communication, May 1999

Associate degree in Medical Technology, May 1999 (anticipated)

Include the complete name of each school you attended, along with the city and state where it is located.

The University of Toledo Community and Technical College, Toledo, Ohio

List any relevant additional information, such as grade point average (GPA) if it was 3.0 or higher, dean's list, honorary society, or other academic honors or awards.

4. Experience

List both paid employment and any volunteer work or internships, focusing on the experience that is most relevant to your career objective. If you like, you can create both an "Employment" category listing paid positions and a separate "Related Experience" section listing unpaid positions such as computer lab tutor, campus guide, or senior mentor.

Each entry in the experience section should include the following:

Title of position

Company name and location (city, state)

Dates of employment/experience

Summarize the positions you've held and highlight your accomplishments. Include all concrete skills and abilities you developed, particularly those skills relevant to your current career goals. Remember that a résumé is not the place for undue modesty about your achievements. You need to emphasize your skills to prospective employers. Tell an employer what you can do for him or her. Imagine a reader who is asking the question "Why should I hire you?" and provide reasons. Use action verbs to describe your achievements:

Developed a proposal for marketing career services.

Assisted with legal research.

Analyzed reports and data and *compiled* results.

5. Skills

List any special abilities and skills in this category, such as computer skills, language skills, budgeting skills, math skills, telephone abilities, and equipment skills. Don't skimp on this section. Brainstorm a list of everything you can do and then pare your list down to skills that may be relevant to an employer.

6. References

References are people who will vouch for you. They should be people who have worked closely with you, such as former employers or instructors, who you think will say positive things about you. Be sure to check with the people you plan to list to make sure it's okay to use them as references.

On your résumé you may list the names, positions, companies, and telephone numbers of your references or you may simply write "References available upon request." If you state that references are available, make sure you have people and contact numbers lined up.

7. Other Possible Headings

You may have qualifications or abilities you want to include on your résumé that don't fit neatly into any of the categories. Don't omit them; consider adding categories to fit them, such as "Special Training" or "Certifications." You want your résumé to include any information that will build you up as a good potential employee.

SAMPLE RÉSUMÉ

Megan Ormsby

2005 Garden Park Drive
Toledo, OH 43612
(419) 555-0622

CAREER OBJECTIVE	To obtain a position as a legal secretary
EDUCATION	Associate degree in Legal Secretarial Technology, June 1999 The University of Toledo Community and Technical College, Toledo, Ohio
	GPA: 3.5 (A=4.0) • Dean's list • Golden Key National Honor Society
EXPERIENCE	**March 1996 – present:** Legal secretary Johnson's Legal Services, Perrysburg, Ohio
	• Combined and entered expert testimony into database • Drafted distribution and settlement letters • Entered and updated claims in Lawtrac • Filled out and filed probate forms • Attended administrative hearings • Helped organize information for spreadsheets
	January 1994 – March 1996: Secretary The University of Toledo, Toledo, Ohio
	• Developed an office procedures manual • Typed documents • Organized the office • Provided courteous personal service
SKILLS	• Proficient in WordPerfect, Excel, Windows, Lotus Notes, Microsoft Word, PageMaker, QuarkXpress • Excellent written and oral communication skills • Excellent editing and proofreading skills • Certified legal secretary
REFERENCES	Available upon request

Appendix C

How to Set Goals

Ten Steps to Taking Control of Your Life

Setting goals is one way to take some control of your life. Rather than just taking what comes your way, you can decide for yourself what you want and what you can do to get it. You may not always get what you want, but you'll have a better chance of achieving your goals once you've decided what they are.

Ideally, you should think about both your short-term goals (for today, this week, this month, or this year) and your middle-range goals (two to five years) and long-term goals (five to ten years and longer).

Like everything else, goal setting takes an initial investment of time and then a routine that makes the activities that will help you achieve your goal a part of your daily life. Read the ten steps in this section and fill in your responses where indicated. For now, focus on a short-term goal, something you want to accomplish in the next year. Try out the strategies discussed in this section for just one month to see what progress you make.

The following guide to goal setting is based on a seminar entitled "Thinking Positively: Working Positively" presented by Dr. Rita Losee. When she was in her forties, Dr. Losee transformed her own life in several ways, including starting her own business, successfully training for and completing a triathlon, and writing a book.

1. Decide on the Goal

Make your goal specific and concrete, not vague or abstract.

EXAMPLE (*too vague*): I want to lead a healthier lifestyle.

EXAMPLE (*specific, concrete*): I want to be more physically fit.

Think about a serious short-term goal you would like to achieve and record it here. Make sure it is specific and concrete.

GOAL: _____

2. Post the Goal Where You Will See It

Post your goal somewhere where you will be reminded of it every day. That might be on a mirror, a refrigerator door, a car dashboard, or your computer screen saver; you just need a daily visual reminder.

WHERE WILL I POST MY GOAL? _____

3. List the Reasons You Want to Achieve the Goal

If, for example, your goal is to be more physically fit, some of your reasons might be to reduce stress, to participate in athletic activities with friends, and to decrease your risk of heart disease and other illnesses.

Push yourself to make your list of reasons as long as possible. When you think you've thought of everything, force yourself to think up one more reason, and then another.

REASONS FOR ACHIEVING MY GOAL: _____

_____

_____

_____

_____

_____

_____

_____

4. List the Barriers to Achieving the Goal

If there wasn't some difficulty involved in reaching your goal, you would have done it already. There are barriers that stand in the way of achieving most goals.

If your goal is getting fit, one barrier might be that your busy schedule at work or at school makes it hard to find time to exercise.

Push yourself to become aware of as many barriers to achieving your goal as possible. The more you are aware of these barriers, the more likely you are to overcome them.

BARRIERS TO ACHIEVING MY GOAL: _____

_____

_____

_____

_____

_____

5. Establish a Routine for Focusing on Your Goal

Once every day, at the same time of day or during the same activity, remind yourself of your goal. Set aside just one minute every day—first thing in the morning, as you're showering, or as you're going to work or school—to focus on your goal.

WHEN I'LL FOCUS ON MY GOAL: _____

6. Break the Goal into Subgoals

According to an old Chinese proverb, "A journey of a thousand miles begins with a single step." So does the achievement of your goal. Ask yourself what steps you need to take to reach your goal. Keep these steps reasonable and realistic.

If your goal is to get fit, you might decide to set aside some time each week to go for a walk or to do sit-ups. Or you might decide to join a health club and set up an exercise program with the help of a fitness trainer. The important thing is to make sure that you are being realistic—that it won't be too difficult for you to follow the steps you come up with for achieving your goal.

List as many steps as you can think of and cross them off each week as you complete them. Keep your crossed-off lists in a notebook or file that you can refer to so that you can see you're making progress.

STEPS / SUBGOALS: _____

_____

_____

_____

_____

_____

_____

7. Review Your Progress and Don't Get Discouraged by Occasional Slip-Ups

You should review your progress at least once a week. Schedule a time to do so in your calendar or notebook and be sure to keep the appointment.

What did you do well? Where were there problems or slip-ups? No one is perfect, so expect that you'll slip up sometimes. When that happens, don't despair, and don't give up your goal.

If, for example, you go for two weeks without exercising because of the pressure from finals or a deadline on a project at work, accept it as a normal misstep. Don't say to yourself, "Well, now I might as well give up my health club membership; I'm never going to use it." Accept your behavior and remind yourself that tomorrow represents a chance for a new start. Don't beat yourself up; it doesn't do any good.

Try to learn from your slip-ups. Ask yourself what triggered them and how you might handle a similar situation in the future. Once you become aware of the kinds of situations that trigger slip-ups, you can plan strategies for coping with them.

8. Visualize Your Achievement of the Goal

Imagine yourself as you will be when you achieve your goal. You can do this either by taking a few seconds to close your eyes and visualize yourself or by coming up with statements about how things will be when you've achieved your goal.

Make the statements in the present. For example, "I am walking three miles with friends every evening." "I feel great." "I am proud of myself and am confident." "I'm not falling behind and holding the group up."

GOAL ACHIEVEMENT STATEMENTS: _____

_____

_____

_____

_____

_____

9. Do Not Make Negative Self-Evaluations

Become aware of the things you say to yourself about yourself. Most of us occasionally send ourselves negative messages about what failures we are, how we don't deserve to have what we want, or how we'll always be some way we don't want to be.

When you find yourself saying something like "I'll always be out of shape" or "I'm a loser," or anything else that is negative about yourself, immediately correct the thought with a positive counterstatement like "I'm on my way to being fit" or "I know how to be a winner and I will be one."

You may have years of negative thoughts about yourself floating around in your head. Those negative thoughts are poison, and you must try to counter them with positive thoughts.

10. Celebrate Your Successes

Write down all of your successes. For example, "I did twenty push-ups today." Think of small rewards you will give yourself for each success (obviously they can't be the things you're trying to avoid; you should think of appropriate rewards in advance).

POSSIBLE REWARDS FOR MY SUCCESSES: _____

_____

_____

_____

_____

Once You Have Achieved Your Goal, Set Another One

If you commit yourself to following these ten strategies for just a month, you will be surprised at the progress you'll make. Setting goals will become a way of life for you. Once you achieve your initial goal, set another one. Having achieved one goal, you're ready to set and achieve others. You can take control.

A GRAMMAR REFERENCE

Use this section of *Real Writing* as a tool to find a definition, an example, or an editing strategy quickly. Once you find what you're looking for, this reference will point you to a more complete discussion of the topic in one of *Real Writing*'s grammar chapters (see Chapters 21–40).

In each of the examples throughout this section, the subject of the sentence is underlined once, and the verb is underlined twice. This system of indicating subject and verb is the same one used throughout the rest of the book.

A. A Dozen Sentence Terms

Real Writing tries to avoid terms that are not tools you need right now. The twelve terms that follow are the same terms presented in Chapter 21. These are the tools you need to start editing your writing.

1. A **sentence** is the basic unit of written communication. A complete sentence in standard written English must have a subject and a verb, and it must express a complete thought.

I work at the dry cleaner.

For more information about **sentences**, see Chapters 21, 22, and 23.

2. The **subject** of the sentence is the person, place, or thing that the sentence is about. The subject can be a noun or a pronoun. To find the subject, ask: Who or what is the sentence about?

Maureen studies all week long. [Who is the sentence about? *Maureen.*]

For more information about **subjects**, see Chapters 21 and 32.

3. A **noun** is the name of a person, place, or thing. A noun can name a specific person, place, or thing.

Jack is overweight.

A noun can also name a nonspecific person, place, or thing.

Computer technicians can make a good salary.

For more information about **nouns**, see Chapters 21 and 32.

4. A **pronoun** stands in for a noun. People use pronouns to avoid repeating nouns.

The students finished the test. ~~The students~~ They passed in their exams.

For more information about **pronouns**, see Chapters 21, 26, and 32.

5.   A **verb** tells what the subject does or links the subject to another word that describes it.

- An **action verb** tells what action the subject performs. To find the main action verb in a sentence, ask: What action does the subject perform?

  Kevin snores all night.

    [What is the subject? *Kevin.* What action does the subject perform? *Snores.*]

- A **linking verb** connects (links) the subject to another word or words that describe the subject. Linking verbs show no action.

  The professor is late.

    [The verb *is* links the subject *professor* to a word that describes the professor: *late.*]

- A **helping verb** joins with another verb. The helping verb is often a form of *be, have,* or *do.* Together, the helping verb and the other verb (called the main verb) are called a complete verb.

  I was studying for the test.

    [The helping verb is *was;* the complete verb is *was studying.*]

For more information about **verbs,** see Chapters 21, 24, 25, and 32.

6.   A **complete thought** is an idea that makes sense by itself, without other sentences. An incomplete thought leaves readers wondering what's going on.

INCOMPLETE THOUGHT	because my alarm didn't go off
COMPLETE THOUGHT	I was late because my alarm didn't go off.

For more information about **complete thoughts,** see Chapter 21.

7.   An **adjective** is a word or group of words that modifies (gives more information about) the subject.

The old man laughed.

    [The adjective *old* gives more information about the subject *man.*]

For more information about **adjectives,** see Chapters 21, 27, and 32.

8.   An **adverb** is a word or group of words that modifies (gives more information about) a verb. Often, but not always, an adverb ends in *-ly.*

The skinny man laughed loudly.

[The adverb *loudly* gives more information about the verb *laughed*.]

For more information about **adverbs**, see Chapter 21.

9.   A **phrase** is a group of words that is not a complete sentence because it is missing a subject or a verb or both. It also does not express a complete thought. A **prepositional phrase** is a phrase that begins with a preposition and ends with a noun or pronoun.

under the table

For more information about **phrases** and **prepositional phrases**, see Chapter 21.

10.   A **preposition** is a word that connects a noun, pronoun, or verb with some other information about it. See the list on page 264.

preposition

The cat ran under the table.

prepositional phrase

For more information about **prepositions**, see Chapters 21 and 32.

11.   A **clause** is a group of words that has a subject and a verb.

- An **independent clause** has a subject, a verb, and a complete thought. Independent clauses can stand on their own as sentences.

    The cat is always hungry.

- A **dependent clause** (or **subordinate clause**) has a subject and a verb but does not express a complete thought; it cannot stand on its own as a sentence.

    who lives next door

Within sentences, these clauses usually give more information about the subject, the verb, or the whole sentence.

    The cat *who lives next door* is always hungry.

For more information about **clauses**, see Chapters 21 and 29.

12.   A **conjunction** is a word that joins words, phrases, or clauses. The words *and, but, for, nor, or, so,* and *yet* are called **coordinating conjunctions**.

The <u>man</u> *and* <u>woman</u> walked hand-in-hand.

For more information about **conjunctions**, see Chapters 21 and 29.

B. Finding and Correcting the Four Most Serious Errors

This book puts special emphasis on four grammar errors, the four that people most often notice. If you can edit your writing to correct the four most serious errors, your writing will be clearer, and your grades will improve.

1. Fragments

A **sentence fragment** is a group of words that looks like a sentence but is missing a subject, a verb, or a complete thought. Correct fragments either by adding the missing sentence elements or by connecting the fragment to the sentence before or after it. To find fragments, look for these trouble spots:

- Some fragments start with a preposition.

  FRAGMENT   I pounded as hard as I could. *Against the door.*

  > [*Against the door* lacks both a subject and a verb.]

  EDITED   I pounded as hard as I could/ ᵃAgainst the door.

- Some fragments start with a dependent word.

  FRAGMENT   He fiddled with the lock for an hour. *Before he lost his temper.*

  > [*Before he lost his temper* has a subject (*he*) and a verb (*lost*), but it doesn't express a complete thought.]

  EDITED   He fiddled with the lock for an hour/ ᵇBefore he lost his temper.

- Some fragments start with *-ing* verb forms.

  FRAGMENT   I was running as fast as I could. *Hoping to get there on time.*

  > [*Hoping to get there on time* lacks a subject and a verb.]

  EDITED   I was running as fast as I could. ~~Hoping~~ *I was still hoping* to get there on time.

- Some fragments start with examples or explanations.

FRAGMENT   I considered getting out of my apartment by using the fire escape. *The one outside my window.*

[*The one outside my window* lacks a verb and a complete thought.]

EDITED   I considered getting out of my apartment by using the fire escape. The one outside my window/ *was pretty strong.*
                                                                 ^

For more information about **fragments,** see Chapter 22.

2. Run-Ons

Run-ons are two complete sentences joined together incorrectly and written as one sentence. There are two kinds of run-ons. A *fused sentence* is two complete sentences joined without any punctuation at all.

Smoking is a bad habit it can kill you.
                    ↑no punctuation

A *comma splice* is two complete sentences joined only by a comma without a conjunction.

My mother smoked continuously, she lit one cigarette off another.
                             ↑only a comma

There are four ways to correct run-on sentences.

- You can correct a run-on by adding a period.

    RUN-ON   I interviewed a candidate for a job she gave me the "dead fish" handshake.

    EDITED   I interviewed a candidate for a job. *She* she gave me the "dead fish" handshake.
                                              ^

- You can correct a run-on by adding a comma and one of these conjunctions: *and, but, or, so, for, nor,* or *yet.*

    RUN-ON   Naomi was qualified for the job, she hurt her chances by mumbling.

    EDITED   Naomi was qualified for the job, *but* she hurt her chances by mumbling.
                                              ^

- You can correct a run-on by using a semicolon (;) to join the two sentences.

    RUN-ON   Slouching creates a terrible impression it makes you seem uninterested, bored, or lacking in self-confidence.

EDITED   Slouching <u>creates</u> a terrible impression[;] it <u>makes</u> you seem uninterested, bored, or lacking in self-confidence.

- You can correct a run-on by adding a dependent word and making one of the sentences a dependent clause. (You may need to put a comma before or after the dependent clause to join it to the complete sentence. If you are correcting a comma splice, you may need to delete the comma.)

RUN-ON   It <u>is</u> important to end an interview on a positive note, <u>that</u> <u>is</u> what the interviewer will remember.

EDITED   It <u>is</u> important to end an interview on a positive note, *because* <u>that</u> <u>is</u> what the interviewer will remember.

Many run-ons are caused by the word *then. Then* can be used to join two sentences, but without the correct punctuation, it will result in a run-on. You can correct run-ons caused by *then* using any of the four methods just discussed.

RUN-ON   I <u>picked</u> up my laundry, then I <u>went</u> home.

    comma splice

EDITED   I <u>picked</u> up my laundry. Then I <u>went</u> home.

EDITED   I <u>picked</u> up my laundry, and then I <u>went</u> home.

EDITED   I <u>picked</u> up my laundry; then I <u>went</u> home.

EDITED   After I <u>picked</u> up my laundry, ~~then~~ I <u>went</u> home.

For more information about **run-ons**, see Chapter 23.

3. *Problems with Subject-Verb Agreement*

In any sentence, the subject and the verb must match in terms of number. When they do, this is called **subject-verb agreement.** If the subject is singular (one person, place, or thing), then the verb must also be singular. If the subject is plural (more than one), the verb must also be plural.

SINGULAR   The <u>athlete</u> <u>runs</u> around the track.

PLURAL   The <u>athletes</u> <u>run</u> around the track.

SUBJECT-VERB DISAGREEMENT   Most <u>students</u> here <u>takes</u> four courses.

To correct problems with subject-verb agreement, find the real subject and the real verb of the sentence, and read them aloud to make sure they sound right together. If you are unsure about the correct form of the verb, check the charts in Chapter 24. To find problems with subject-verb agreement, be aware of the five potential trouble spots.

- You may have a problem with subject-verb agreement if **the verb is a form of *be*, *have*, or *do*.** The verbs *be*, *have*, and *do* do not follow the usual rules for forming singular and plural forms; they are **irregular verbs.**

  are
  They ~~is~~ sick today.

  does
  Mark ~~do~~ the laundry every Wednesday.

  has
  Without a doubt, Andrea ~~have~~ the best taste in shoes.

- You may have a problem with subject-verb agreement if **words come between the subject and the verb.** In longer sentences, it may be more difficult to find the subject and the verb and make them agree. Most often, either a prepositional phrase or a dependent clause comes between the subject and the verb. The subject of the sentence is *never* in a prepositional phrase or a dependent clause. To locate the subject of the sentence, cross out prepositional phrases and dependent clauses.

  The speaker ~~of the U.S. House of Representatives~~ gives many interviews.

  The coins ~~that I found last week~~ seem very valuable.

- You may have a problem with subject-verb agreement if **the subject is a compound subject.** A compound subject consists of two (or more) subjects joined by *and* or *or*. If two subjects are joined by *and*, they combine to become a plural subject, and the verb must be plural too.

  The teacher *and* her aide grade all of the exams.

  If the two subjects are separated by the word *or*, they are not combined. The verb should agree with whichever subject is closer to it.

  The teacher *or* her aide grades all of the exams.

- You may have a problem with subject-verb agreement if **the subject is an indefinite pronoun.** An indefinite pronoun does not stand in for a specific person, place, or thing. It is general. Most indefinite pronouns are either always singular or always plural. Check the chart in Chapter 24 if you are unsure of which are singular and which are plural.

  SINGULAR   *Everybody* wants the semester to end.

PLURAL   *Many* <u>want</u> the semester to end.

- You may have a problem with subject-verb agreement if **the verb comes before the subject.** Two kinds of sentences reverse the usual subject-verb order: questions and sentences that begin with *here* or *there*. To find the subject and verb, turn the question or sentence around.

     Where <u>is</u> the <u>bookstore</u>? / The <u>bookstore</u> <u>is</u> . . .

     Here <u>is</u> the <u>key</u> to your apartment. / The <u>key</u> to your apartment <u>is</u> here.

For more information about **subject-verb agreement,** see Chapter 24.

4. *Problems with Verb Forms*

Verb forms are the different ways a verb can be spelled and pronounced. The correct form depends on how the verb is used in the sentence: whether it is singular or plural, past or present, and so on.

     I <u>like</u> my sister's new apartment.

     She <u>likes</u> the low rent.

     My sister <u>liked</u> her last apartment, but it was too expensive.

Verb tense tells *when* the action of the sentence occurred: in the past, in the present, or in the future. Verbs change their form and use helping verbs to indicate different tenses.

PRESENT TENSE   Michael <u>sings</u> quite well.

PAST TENSE   He <u>sang</u> on the ride home.

FUTURE TENSE   He <u>will sing</u> for us again soon.

Most verbs in English are **regular verbs** — their forms follow standard rules.

- The **present tense** is used for actions that are happening at the same time they are being written about (the present). It is also used for things that happen all the time. Use an *-s* ending when the subject is *he, she, it,* or the name of one person or thing. Use no ending for all other subjects.

     I jump.

     She jump<u>s</u>.

     We jump.

- The **past tense** is used for actions that have already happened. An *-ed* ending is needed on all regular verbs in the past tense.

    I avoid<u>ed</u> the freeway this morning.

    He walk<u>ed</u> in the same door yesterday.

- The **past participle** is a verb that can be used with helping verbs, such as *have*. For all regular verbs, the past-participle form is the same as the past-tense form: It uses an *-ed* ending.

    PAST-TENSE FORM   My kids <u>watched</u> cartoons.

    PAST-PARTICIPLE FORM   They <u>have watched</u> cartoons before.

Irregular verbs do not follow the regular pattern for the different verb forms.

- Only a few verbs are irregular in the **present tense**. Since the irregular verbs *be* and *have* are very common, it is important to learn the correct forms. See the chart on page 313 for the correct present-tense forms of these two verbs.

- Irregular verbs do not use the *-ed* ending for the **past-tense** form. They change in some other way. Also, the **past-participle** form of irregular verbs is often different from the past-tense form.

    PRESENT-TENSE FORM   I <u>take</u> the commuter train to work.

    PAST-TENSE FORM   I <u>took</u> the early train yesterday.

    PAST-PARTICIPLE FORM   I <u>have taken</u> the commuter train to work for the

    past two years.

There is no simple rule for how irregular verbs form the past tense and the past participle. Until you memorize them, check the chart on pages 316–17.

For more information about **verb problems,** see Chapter 25.

C. Some Basic Punctuation

Using correct punctuation in a sentence makes your meaning clearer to your reader. Here are some practical tips for using two of the most common punctuation marks, the comma and the apostrophe. See Chapters 38 and 39 for information about using other punctuation.

1. Commas

Commas are punctuation marks that help readers understand a sentence. A comma often indicates a pause.

- Use commas to separate the items in a **series** (three or more items).

  I *work, go to school,* and *take care of my family.*

- Use a comma before the word *(and, but, for, or, so, yet, nor)* joining two complete thoughts in a **compound sentence.**

  I called my best friend, and *she agreed to drive me to work.*

- Use a comma after an **introductory word group.** The comma lets your readers know that the main part of the sentence is starting.

  By the way, I don't have a babysitter for tonight.

- Use commas to set off **appositives** and **interrupters.**

  An **appositive** comes directly after a noun or pronoun and renames it.

  Lily, *my cousin,* will take her nursing exam this summer.

  An **interrupter** is an aside or transition that interrupts the flow of a sentence and does not affect its meaning.

  My sister, *actually,* has very good reasons for being late.

- Use commas to set off an **adjective clause** *if the clause can be taken out of the sentence without completely changing the meaning of the sentence.* An adjective clause is a group of words with a subject and a verb that begins with *who, which,* or *that* and describes a noun right before it in the sentence.

  Chapters, *which is the campus bookstore,* charges outrageous prices.

For other uses of **commas,** see Chapter 36.

2. Apostrophes

An **apostrophe** is a punctuation mark that either shows ownership (*Susan's*) or indicates that a letter has been intentionally left out to form a contraction (*I'm, that's, they're*).

- Add -*'s* to a singular noun to show ownership (even if the noun already ends in -*s*).

  Karen's apartment is on the South Side.

- If the noun is plural and ends in -*s,* just add an apostrophe. If it is plural but does not end in -*s,* add -*'s.*

The *kids'* father was building them a playhouse. [More than one kid]

The *children's* toys were all broken.

- *Its* or *it's?* Remember that *its* shows possession (something belongs to *it*); *it's* is a contraction meaning "it is". When you use *it's,* test to see if it's correct by replacing it with *it is* and reading the sentence aloud.

   The dog runs in circles after *its* tail.

   It's funny to watch the dog do that over and over.

- A **contraction** is formed by joining two words and leaving out one or more of the letters. Use an apostrophe to show where the letter or letters have been left out.

   I'll see you there. = *I will* see you there.

See page 449 for a list of common contractions.

For more information about **apostrophes,** see Chapter 37.

Answers to Odd-Numbered Exercises

CHAPTER 21

Practice 21–1, page 258
Answers: **1.** he   **3.** people   **5.** They   **7.** Students   **9.** courses

Practice 21–2, page 258
Answers: **1.** Subject: Oak Grove International; action verb: sells   **3.** Subject: Oak Grove; action verb: creates   **5.** Subject: coffin; action verb: costs   **7.** Subject: coffins; action verb: carry   **9.** Subject: owners; action verb: started

Practice 21–3, page 260
Answers: **1.** Subject: They; linking verb: taste; the word that describes the subject: good   **3.** Subject: colors; linking verb: taste; the word that describes the subject: different   **5.** Subject: Forrest Mars and Bruce Murries; linking verb: were; the word that describes the subject: inventors

Practice 21–4, page 261
Answers: **1.** Subject: Students; complete verb: can learn   **3.** Subject: officials; complete verb: have claimed   **5.** Subject: students; complete verb: must compete

Practice 21–5, page 261
Answers and possible edits: **1.** I (incomplete thought); I will wait until the store closes at midnight.   **3.** C (complete thought)   **5.** C (complete thought)

Practice 21–6, page 263
Answers and possible edits: **1.** Subject: snoring; verb: is; with addition of adjective: amazing snoring   **3.** Subject: earplugs; verb: help; with addition of adjective: little earplugs   **5.** Subject: marriage; verb: has withstood; with addition of adjective: ten-year marriage

CHAPTER 22

Practice 22–2, page 270
Possible edits: **1.** The eight men and women who spent two years inside the glass-and-steel dome had to grow their own food with almost no help from the outside world.   **3.** The 3.2-acre greenhouse-like structure included a rain forest, a savannah, a desert, and even a small "ocean" with a machine for generating waves.   **5.** The air they breathed almost became depleted because the compost in the soil produced carbon dioxide in place of the oxygen in the air.

Practice 22–3, page 272
Answers and possible edits: **1.** Dependent word: before. No American had orbited the earth before John Glenn did so on February 20, 1962.   **3.** Dependent word: while. While they walked on the surface of the moon, Armstrong and Buzz Aldrin collected samples of moon rock and moon soil to bring back to earth.   **5.** Dependent word: until. Americans had begun to feel that space travel was as safe as flying in an airliner until the *Challenger* exploded soon after takeoff on January 28, 1986.

Practice 22–4, page 273
Answers and possible edits: **1.** *-ing* verb: walking. In 1931, Plennie Wingo set out on a journey walking backward around the world.   **3.** *-ing* verb: taking. After eight thousand miles, Wingo's journey was interrupted by a war taking place in Pakistan.   **5.** *-ing* verb: taking. Mullikin's trip took so long because he lingered, taking time out to earn money as a logger and a Baptist minister.

Practice 22–5, page 275
Answers and possible edits: **1.** Example or explanation: Not just in North America and Europe but throughout the world; edited sentence: Coca-Cola has been successful partly because of its producers' willingness to expand into new markets, not just in North America and Europe but throughout the world.   **3.** Example or explanation: Even in the former Soviet Union; edited sentences: You can see Coke's famous red–and–white logo almost anywhere. You can see it even in the former Soviet Union.   **5.** Example or explanation: Including the return of Coke Classic in the mid-1980s; edited sentence: It has had some big marketing successes, including the return of Coke Classic in the mid-1980s.

Practice 22–6, page 275
Answers and possible edits:
1. (1) Correct (3) She was so sick that everyone thought she would die. (5) Correct (7) After years of treatment, braces, special shoes, and determination, she started run-

ning for exercise. (9) Correct **3.** (1) Most people think of Thomas Edison as a famous inventor who invented the lightbulb. (3) Correct (5) His parents took him out of school because they did not believe the teachers. (7) He was then home-schooled by his very determined mother. (9) Correct

CHAPTER 23

Practice 23–2, page 282
Answers: **1.** F (fused sentence); Working together, fifty students and their professor set up the classroom. It took them less than twenty minutes. **3.** CS (comma splice); Students can continue to interact outside of class. The laptops and receivers allow them to set up wireless networks. **5.** F (fused sentence); Duke was a test site. The students received free software and discounted laptop computers from Apple.

Practice 23–3, page 283
Possible edits: **1.** The Internet used to be very difficult to use, but many companies now offer software that provides easy access. **3.** The Internet was created more than twenty years ago to allow computers to survive a bomb attack, but its military role eventually became obsolete. **5.** We now have public access to the Internet, and the number of users continues to increase.

Practice 23–4, page 284
Answers: **1.** Fifty thousand people attended the Rolling Stones concert at the Dallas Cotton Bowl; many thousands more experienced the concert via the Internet. **3.** The MBone is short for Multicast Backbone; the MBone is capable of multicasting. **5.** The MBone is completely interactive; it carries audio, video, and a "white board" feature that allows people watching to share text, images, and sketches.

Practice 23–5, page 286
Possible edits: **1.** Two researchers at the University of Southern California worked for weeks to set up a multicast facility so that the researcher could attend the meeting. **3.** While the MBone is still not perfect, its inventors consider it successful. **5.** Although the audio and video quality needs refinement, the MBone has great possibilities not only for rock broadcasts but also for scientific study.

Practice 23–6, page 287
Answers and possible edits: **1.** Correct **3.** Newspapers use oil-based inks that never completely dry; they come off on your hands. **5.** The carbon black pigment is mixed with an oil that is like car lubricating oil. The result is the big smudge factor. **7.** Newspaper publishers use heavier ink because they want the papers to be more readable. **9.** Correct **11.** Correct **13.** Correct

15. Even if newpapers were to use the more expensive ink, the smudge factor would only decrease. It would not be eliminated.

CHAPTER 24

Practice 24–2, page 294
Answers: **1.** include **3.** catch **5.** builds up **7.** suggests **9.** lasts

Practice 24–3, page 296
Answers: **1.** Subject: Harold; verb: doesn't **3.** Subject: programs; verb: have **5.** Subject: It; verb: has **7.** Subject: animation; verb: is **9.** Subject: Disney Studio; verb: has

Practice 24–4, page 297
Answers: **1.** Subject: parsley; verb: has **3.** Subject: Mint; verb: is **5.** Subject: herbs; verb: have

Practice 24–5, page 298
Answers: **1.** Prepositional phrase: of personality types; verb: begins **3.** Prepositional phrase: on the scale; verb: are **5.** Prepositional phrases: in all areas of their lives; verb: want **7.** Prepositional phrase: of life's people and situations; verb: remains **9.** Prepositional phrases: across the restaurant in one of the booths; verb: seems

Practice 24–6, page 299
Answers: **1.** Dependent clause: whose orders resulted in layoffs; verb: runs **3.** Dependent clause: whom the workers call "the Breadline Boss"; verb is OK. **5.** Dependent clause: who wrote the article I read; verb: thinks

Practice 24–7, page 300
Answers: **1.** Subject joined by: and; verb: give **3.** Subject joined by: or; verb: provides **5.** Subject joined by: and; verb: are **7.** Subject joined by: and; verb: are **9.** Subject joined by: and; verb: make

Practice 24–8, page 301
Answers: **1.** Subject: Everyone; verb: remembers **3.** Subject: one; verb: realizes **5.** Subject: Someone; verb: knows **7.** Subject: One; verb: plans **9.** Subject: Someone; verb: connects

Practice 24–9, page 303
Answers: **1.** OK **3.** OK **5.** OK **7.** Does it have spaces available? **9.** What is the schedule of fees?

Practice 24–10, page 303
Answers:
1. (1) A study I came across while doing research for my sociology class rates U.S. cities on "most things to do." (3) Each of the cities was assigned a total from 0 to 100 in each category. (5) Correct (7) Correct **3.** (1) Correct

(3) Correct (5) Correct (7) Any of the hens with red earlobes produce brown eggs.

CHAPTER 25

Practice 25–2, page 310
Answers: **1.** Subject: responsibilities; verb: include **3.** Subject: department; verb: applies **5.** Subject: person; verb: asks **7.** Subject: person; verb: complains **9.** Subject: supervisor; verb: supports

Practice 25–4, page 312
Answers: **1.** Helping verb: have; verb: relied **3.** Helping verb: have; verb: changed; helping verb: has; verb: created **5.** Helping verb: have; verb: embraced **7.** Helping verb: have; verb: discovered **9.** Helping verb: have; verb: replaced

Practice 25–5, page 313
Answers: **1.** have **3.** is **5.** are **7.** has **9.** have

Practice 25–6, page 315
Answers: **1.** won **3.** said **5.** drank **7.** grew **9.** understood

Practice 25–7, page 318
Answers: **1.** Helping verb: has; past participle: given **3.** Helping verb: have; past participle: made **5.** Helping verb: have; past participle: gone **7.** Helping verb: have; past participle: felt **9.** Helping verb: have; past participle: become

Practice 25–8, page 320
Answers: **1.** have told **3.** said **5.** have made **7.** have begun **9.** have waited

Practice 25–9, page 321
Answers: **1.** had rushed **3.** treated **5.** rescued **7.** had burned **9.** had boiled

Practice 25–10, page 322
Answers:
1. (1) When Teresa saw her friend Jan drop makeup into her bag, she frowned. (3) She also knew that Jan would be mad if Teresa said anything. (5) As they left the store, Teresa's heart beat hard. (7) Still, she felt bad, so she spoke to Teresa.

CHAPTER 26

Practice 26–1, page 328
Answers: **1.** Pronoun: her; noun: sheep **3.** Pronoun: its; noun: individual **5.** Pronoun: their; noun: Journalists

Practice 26–2, page 330
Answers: **1.** his or her **3.** its **5.** he no longer works **7.** himself **9.** he

Practice 26–3, page 331
Answers: **1.** its **3.** it was **5.** its

Practice 26–4, page 332
Possible edits: **1.** The loan officer at the bank said the bank would lend me the money for the car if I filled out a full report of my credit history. **3.** The statement that I gave to the loan officer included two previous automobile loans and one long-term apartment rental. **5.** I don't understand why the people at the bank still demand more information from me. **7.** When I was finding out about the car, the owners said they expected it to sell quickly. **9.** The car has all the features I need and want.

Practice 26–5, page 335
Answers: **1.** My friend Kenny and I like to water ski on Lake Chelan. **3.** C (correct) **5.** That night in bed, I started thinking: What would have happened if he or I had hit a log? **7.** Last summer Jackie was dating Kenny; I used to see her and Kenny walking along the edge of the lake at night. **9.** He claims that it would be a good thing for him and her both.

Practice 26–6, page 336
Answers: **1.** Not too many people watch as much *Star Trek* as we. **3.** C (correct) **5.** The characters on *Star Trek* have explored more of space than we. **7.** C (correct) **9.** My favorite episode is the one with the woman surrounded by people who think she is uglier than they.

Practice 26–7, page 337
Answers: **1.** who **3.** whom **5.** who

Practice 26–8, page 338
Answers: **(1)** You won't believe what happened to Jim and me over the weekend. **(3)** Jim liked them more than I, but I hung around for a while anyway. **(5)** At the real estate office an agent said the house was for sale, but he didn't have the phone number of the owners. **(7)** You can imagine how surprised Jim and I were when we learned that the house was ours. **(9)** A few minutes later, every person at the party raised his or her glass in a toast.

CHAPTER 27

Practice 27–1, page 342
Answers: **1.** *Rapidly* describes *grew*. **3.** *Unique* describes *structure*. **5.** *Confident* describes *I*. **7.** *Total* describes *income*; *typically* describes *is*. **9.** *Truly* describes *outstanding*; *quickly* describes *seated*.

Practice 27–2, page 344
Answers: **1.** most famous **3.** weakest **5.** greatest
7. most beautiful **9.** most exciting

Practice 27–3, page 346
Answers: **1.** good **3.** good **5.** well

Practice 27–4, page 346
Answers: **1.** worse **3.** better **5.** best

Practice 27–5, page 347
Answers: **(1)** One of the most important things I've learned since starting college is to avoid waiting until the last minute to begin my work. **(3)** This technique worked well for me in high school. **(5)** I promised myself that I would do better than that in the future, and I have improved. **(7)** If a task is harder than I expected, I will arrange to ask the professor or a tutor for help. **(9)** If no outside help is available, I will usually put the work away for a few hours, or overnight, and resume my efforts when I feel better about my ability to concentrate. **(11)** I tend to do a stronger job when I work more slowly than when I work faster. **(13)** I also get into trouble when I try to tackle something when I'm overtired or not feeling well. **(15)** It's a good idea to do my most important work when I'm feeling my best.

CHAPTER 28

Practice 28–1, page 352
Answers and possible edits: **1.** C (correct) **3.** In the morning, she took a route to school her friends had recommended. **5.** Potholes along the new road bent one of her wheels. **7.** Jennifer discovered a route that was much better on another map. **9.** Looking at her watch, she was pleased with her bike.

Practice 28–2, page 353
Possible edits: **1.** Published in the *Atlantic Monthly*, the article discusses falling wages, corporate layoffs, and attempts to eliminate inflation. **3.** With wages falling nearly fifty dollars per week between 1973 and 1991, workers have recently found it impossible to buy homes. **5.** Taking advantage of cheaper labor overseas, corporations usually leave American workers behind when they relocate. **7.** Convinced the problem could be fixed with a balanced budget, Palley believes the economy could be healthy again. **9.** Unconcerned with the cause of the problem, American workers feel fear and frustration.

Practice 28–3, page 354
Possible edits: **(1)** Correct **(3)** I am currently working on a bachelor's degree in political science and have taken nearly fifty credit hours of courses. **(5)** Correct **(7)** Correct **(9)** Correct **(11)** Thinking of the experience I could gain, I find a summer job at your firm highly appealing.

CHAPTER 29

Practice 29–1, page 358
Possible edits: **1.** He argued with the driver, but he finally gave up and walked to a nearby convenience store. **3.** She said he could buy something, or he could wait until someone else bought something. **5.** He waited impatiently for the cashier to give him his change, for the next bus was already approaching. **7.** Pete finally got his change, and he ran as fast as he could. **9.** The turnover was delicious, so he went back to the store for another one.

Practice 29–2, page 360
Answers: **1.** Exposure to the sun can cause both short-term and long-term side effects; using tanning booths has similar risks. **3.** It's easy to ignore long-term health dangers; the desire to look good is often of more immediate concern. **5.** Ultraviolet light can injure the eyes; tanning salon patrons should always wear protective goggles.

Practice 29–3, page 361
Possible edits: **1.** He tried phoning the professor; also, he sent her several e-mail messages. **3.** Kirk asked if he could do extra work to raise the grade to at least a C; however, the professor said that there was nothing either of them could do. **5.** She agreed to meet with him the next day; as a result, Kirk hoped to be able to change her mind.

Practice 29–4, page 362
Possible edits: **1.** Almost all college students used typewriters until about ten years ago when computers became more affordable. **3.** Computers offer many advantages although there are also some drawbacks. **5.** When computers became widely used in the 1980s, professors were surprised to hear students say, "The computer ate my paper." **7.** Some people like to print out a document to proofread it because they fail to catch all their mistakes on the screen. **9.** Although spell-checking programs prevent many errors, only a person is able to recognize homophones such as *their* and *there*.

Practice 29–5, page 363
Possible edits: **(1)** Although Herman Melville is now considered one of the greatest American writers, his books were mostly forgotten at the time of his death in 1891. **(3)** Correct **(5)** The book's more complex themes remained invisible, until a new generation of literary critics rediscovered them in the 1920s. **(7)** Potential buyers were not interested in his work, and even van Gogh himself considered much of it "ugly." **(9)** Correct **(11)** He had moved to Arles, France, in February 1888, where he created some of his most famous works, including the disturbingly powerful *Starry Night*. **(13)** Great art is often far ahead of its time, so it is frequently misunderstood. **(15)** These people gave

the public what it wanted, but they failed to create anything of lasting worth.

CHAPTER 30

Practice 30–1, page 367
Possible edits: **1.** Parts that should be parallel: frustrating, time-consuming, it annoys me. Finding a space near the campus can be frustrating, time-consuming, and annoying. **3.** Parts that should be parallel: wearing a tan sportcoat, who carried a leather briefcase. I yelled at the driver, an older man wearing a tan sportcoat and carrying a leather briefcase. **5.** Parts that should be parallel: circling the parking lot, checked my watch. Then, while I was still circling the parking lot and checking my watch, I realized that the man I had shouted at was my professor.

Practice 30–2, page 368
Possible edits: **1.** Parts that should be parallel: for leasing a car, for the purchase of one. Car dealers often require less money down for leasing a car than for purchasing one. **3.** Parts that should be parallel: the terms of leasing, to buy. You should check the terms of leasing to make sure they are as favorable as the terms of buying. **5.** Parts that should be parallel: leasing, to own. You will be making less of a financial commitment by leasing a car than by owning it.

Practice 30–3, page 369
Possible edits: **1.** Paired words: not only, but also; parts that should be parallel: a good lover, to find a friendly person. People hope to find someone who is not only a good lover but also a friendly person. **3.** Paired word: neither; parts that should be parallel: to break up, are against marrying. People often feel that they want neither to break up nor to marry. **5.** Parts that should be parallel: Compromising, to settle. Compromising may be wise; settling for a bad partner is not.

Practice 30–4, page 370
Possible edits: **1.** I could bring to this job not only youthful enthusiasm but also relevant experience. **3.** My current job neither encourages creativity nor allows flexibility. **5.** In college I learned a lot both from my classes and from other students.

Practice 30–5, page 370
Possible edits: **(1)** Correct **(3)** A medical doctor by training, in the 1890s Freud began studying and documenting causes of hysteria, and he discovered that many of his female patients had been sexually abused by their fathers. **(5)** Correct **(7)** But it was also deeply rewarding, not only to Freud as a scientist but also to Freud as an individual. **(9)** Correct **(11)** Correct

CHAPTER 31

Practice 31–1, page 374
Answers: **1.** Understandably, the two teenagers wanted to be alone. **3.** Gradually, they began to relax while listening to some soft songs on the car radio. **5.** Frantically, one of them tried to start the engine, but they soon discovered that the car battery was dead.

Practice 31–2, page 376
Possible edits: **1.** A majority of voters approved the project last spring, recognizing that the old system is inadequate. **3.** Seeking reelection, the mayor is determined to keep everyone happy. **5.** The sewage treatment plant would be the largest in Whitefield County, serving twenty thousand homes.

Practice 31–3, page 377
Possible edits: **1.** Deserted by her mother, Marie was placed in a home for the mentally retarded. **3.** Marie learned very simple tasks, created just to keep her occupied. **5.** Inspired by the teacher who saved her, Marie became a teacher herself.

Practice 31–4, page 378
Answers: **1.** Marine biologists, scientists who study ocean life forms, have long been fascinated by the dolphin. **3.** A dolphin needs to surface occasionally to breathe through its blow-hole, a small opening on top of an aquatic mammal's head. **5.** This physiological trick, a clever evolutionary adaptation, explains how dolphins can spend so little energy to dive so deep.

Practice 31–5, page 379
Possible edits: **1.** While Erin goes to classes, her baby boy stays at a day care center, which costs Erin about $100 a week. **3.** Occasionally, Erin's parents, who live about seventy miles away, come up and watch the baby while Erin is studying. **5.** She feels that some of her professors who have never been mothers themselves aren't very sympathetic.

Practice 31–6, page 380
Possible edits: **(1)** Correct **(3)** Part of the reason was the attempt by Germany, which had lagged far behind its rivals, to match England as a world power. **(5)** Hoping to take advantage of the new technology, the German emperor Wilhelm II launched a massive project to build up Germany's navy. **(7)** Correct **(9)** Determined to maintain its superiority at sea, Britain built more and more warships. **(11)** Civilian leaders lacked the skill of Otto von Bismarck, the legendary figure who had managed to create a unified Germany in 1866. **(13)** Correct **(15)** The old Ottoman Empire, which had played a major role in southeastern Europe since the fourteenth century, was disintegrating. **(17)** Russia and Austria-Hungary vied to gain influence over small states such as Serbia,

Bulgaria, and Greece, states previously controlled by Turkey. **(19)** On June 28, 1914, Serbian nationalists in Sarajevo assassinated Archduke Francis Ferdinand, who was the heir to the Austro-Hungarian throne. **(21)** Correct **(23)** Correct

CHAPTER 32

Practice 32–1, page 386
Possible edits: **(1)** I think I'll have a hamburger for lunch. **(3)** You get the burger off the grill, put onions, ketchup, and mustard on it, and you begin to eat the burger, but the bottom bun is wet and crumbling. **(5)** A hamburger expert uses the thicker top bun on the bottom. **(7)** The food industry shouldn't make such odd buns.

Practice 32–2, page 388
Answers: **(1)** Many students believe that the college should provide on-campus day care. **(3)** They consider getting a better job a worthwhile goal. **(5)** The courses cost a lot, but the expense is worth it to these students. **(7)** Correct **(9)** Correct

Practice 32–3, page 390
Answers: **(1)** People were once afraid of comets in the sky. **(3)** There are historical examples of rulers calling off battles and holidays when they saw comets in the sky. **(5)** Scientists are interested in learning more about each comet that passes through our solar system.

Practice 32–4, page 391
Answers:
1. Negative: We were not writing about why we want to take this course.   Question: Were we writing about why we want to take this course?
3. Negative: My family has not lived in this country for five years.   Question: Has my family lived in this country for five years?
5. Negative: The weather is not difficult to get used to. Question: Is the weather difficult to get used to?

Practice 32–5, page 393
Answers: **1.** Her long black hair was beautiful.   **3.** I ran from the scary tall old man.   **5.** The ugly green plastic chair sat by the pool all winter.

CHAPTER 33

Practice 33–1, page 399
Answers and possible edits: **1.** Abstract words: good, a lot. We enjoyed swimming in the warm water. **3.** Abstract words: pretty bad. The food was bland and overcooked. **5.** Abstract word: friendly. They invited us to have dinner with them.

Practice 33–2, page 400
Answers and possible edits: **1.** Slang: chew me out. I don't see why it is necessary for you to reprimand me so often. **3.** Slang: fired up. I was really enthusiastic about the last project I worked on.   **5.** Slang: awesome, hang around. This is a wonderful place to work, and I'd like to remain here for at least another year.

Practice 33–3, page 401
Answers and possible edits: **1.** Stuffy language: commence operation. The superintendent announced, "Schools will open on August 28 this year." **3.** Stuffy language: contemplate the fiscal ramifications. The committee will study the costs of a preschool program. **5.** Stuffy language: In a cooperative endeavor; exorbitant in cost. Working together, the committee and the consultant will study programs that are not too expensive.

Practice 33–4, page 402
Answers and possible edits: **1.** Wordy phrases: this period of; a great number of. During that time, many countries suffered economic hardship. **3.** Wordy phrase: at any point in the past. Economists had never before seen this combination of rising prices and stagnating growth. **5.** Wordy phrases: came to a final end; to a significantly lower level. "Stagflation" ended in the early 1980s, when recession brought down inflation.

Practice 33–5, page 404
Answers and possible edits: **1.** Clichés: sweat blood; work like a dog. You have to persuade yourself to devote every bit of your strength to the challenge for up to ten hours. **3.** Clichés: the bitter end; easier said than done. Staying on your bike until the very last mile, of course, is an enormously difficult task.   **5.** Cliché: better late than never. No matter how long it takes you to cross the finish line, remind yourself that finishing at all is a tremendous achievement.

Practice 33–6, page 404
Possible edits: **(1)** Throughout recorded history, people have done devastating things to the environment. **(3)** Because charcoal has a high carbon-to-hydrogen ratio, the burning of wood is a dirty and inefficient source of fuel. **(5)** When oil furnaces began to replace coal furnaces, the air in many cities slowly became somewhat cleaner. **(7)** Each year, thousands of sperm whales were killed, until they were almost extinct. **(9)** However, our dependence on oil is a significant problem. **(11)** It is foolish to continue to use fossil fuels when scientists have shown that they contribute to global warming.

CHAPTER 34

Practice 34–1, page 416
Answers: **1.** accept **3.** They're **5.** principles
7. knows **9.** have; our

Practice 34–2, page 416
Answers: **(1)** More and more women are purchasing handguns, against the advice of law enforcement officers. **(3)** They know the risks of guns, and they accept those risks. **(5)** They don't want to contribute to the violence in our society, but they also realize that women are the victims of violent attacks far too often. **(7)** Some have made a conscious decision to arm themselves for protection. **(9)** But critics question if women buying guns has made things worse rather than better. **(11)** Most young children can't tell the difference between a real gun and a play one. **(13)** A mother whose children are injured while "playing" with her gun will never again think that a gun provides peace of mind.

CHAPTER 35

Practice 35–3, page 424
Answers will vary.

Practice 35–4, page 425
Answers: **1.** peaceful **3.** believing **5.** valuable
7. purer **9.** shameful

Practice 35–5, page 426
Answers: **1.** playful **3.** comedian **5.** defiant **7.** burial **9.** puffiness

Practice 35–6, page 427
Answers: **1.** lifted **3.** commander **5.** cheaper
7. spotted **9.** scrapped

Practice 35–7, page 428
Answers: **1.** addresses **3.** tomatoes **5.** stretches
7. dashes **9.** discovers

Practice 35–8, page 429
Answers: **(1)** In today's schools, there is a raging argument about whether to separate children of different abilities into classes with others of similar achievement levels. **(3)** These same experts state that dividing students will prejudice teachers against the slower students. **(5)** Basically, the experts claim, students lose all motivation to achieve. **(7)** They say that grouping by ability allows students to learn at a more natural rate. **(9)** Correct **(11)** Both sides have interesting, persuasive arguments that they present to local, state, and federal government officials.

CHAPTER 36

Practice 36–1, page 434
Answers: **1.** Continued expansion relies on our ability to promote novelty beverages such as papaya, mango, and boysenberry juices. **3.** C (correct) **5.** In areas where our juice is relatively new, we'd like to see increases of 10 percent, 20 percent, or 25 percent. **7.** We want to target New England states such as Connecticut, Massachusetts, and New Hampshire, where attitudes about fruit juice are similar to those in Seattle, Portland, and other Northwest cities. **9.** We also should provide free samples of our juices at outdoor concerts, county fairs, and arts festivals.

Practice 36–2, page 436
Answers: **1.** He told me that our father was in the hospital, but I didn't believe him. **3.** C (correct) **5.** Traffic was unusually light, so we reached the hospital sooner than I expected. **7.** Our father had suffered a minor heart attack, but he was now resting comfortably. **9.** The doctor told us that there was no real danger, so my brother and I took his advice and went home.

Practice 36–3, page 437
Answers: **1.** As we all know, AIDS is spread mainly through sexual contact and through drug use that involves the sharing of needles. **3.** Since basketball star Magic Johnson revealed in 1991 that he is HIV-positive, an NBA player must be removed from a game if he is bleeding. **5.** Not surprisingly, many college sports follow similar rules to prevent blood contact between players. **7.** According to some student-athletes, mandatory HIV testing would violate their civil liberties. **9.** In their view, student-athletes should be treated no differently from other students.

Practice 36–4, page 439
Answers: **1.** Grouse Mountain, a ski area, overlooks the city and the Strait of Georgia. **3.** There are, in addition, numerous places for hiking. **5.** The Vancouver area, however, has much to offer beyond recreation. **7.** The city, in addition, is known as a bustling commercial center. **9.** Vancouver, like San Francisco and Seattle, has a large Asian population.

Practice 36–5, page 440
Answers: **1.** Robert Kramer, who bought the theater two years ago, said that he is losing money. **3.** The Grandview, which is known for its comfortable seats and wide screen, has been in financial trouble for at least a decade. **5.** Multiplex theaters, which are often located in shopping malls, now dominate the industry. **7.** Brad Warren, who works as an accountant in a nearby office, has been watching films at the Grandview since the 1960s. **9.** C (correct)

Practice 36–6, page 442

Answers: **1.** C (correct) **3.** Asked if he was running out of patience, McGregor replied, "Yes, I sure am." **5.** His wife said, "Rob, don't go mouthing off to any reporters." **7.** An official of Value-Safe Insurance of Wrightsville, Ohio, said the company will process claims within the next few months. **9.** Customers unhappy with their service may write to Value-Safe Insurance, P.O. Box 225, Wrightsville, Ohio 62812.

Practice 36–7, page 443

Answers: **(1)** In April 1990, the book *You Just Don't Understand* was published by William Morrow in New York, New York. **(3)** It gives examples of how men and women misunderstand each other, and it describes the causes and possible solutions to their language expectations. **(5)** Tannen writes, "Even if they grow up in the same house, girls and boys grow up in different worlds of words. **(7)** And although some of their play activities are similar, their favorite games are different, and their ways of using language in their games are also different." **(9)** Girls, on the other hand, play in small groups or pairs. **(11)** Later in life, these difficulties can cause disagreements between men and women. **(13)** The comfort of home, however, can have opposite meanings for men and women. **(15)** Correct **(17)** Needless to say, conflict results from these different expectations.

CHAPTER 37

Practice 37–1, page 448

Answers: **1.** A person's feelings about personal space depend on his or her culture. **3.** Standing too close to another person's face when you speak is considered rude. **5.** The expression "Get out of my face!" is a warning meant to prevent the confrontation's violent conclusion. **7.** The hair on dogs' necks may stand on end. **9.** For example, seagulls' positions on a log follow a pattern similar to that of people lined up waiting for a bus.

Practice 37–2, page 450

Answers: **1.** You'll notice right away if a stranger leans over and talks to you so his face is practically touching yours. **3.** There isn't one single acceptable boundary we'd use in all situations. **5.** With co-workers, we're likely to keep a personal space of four to twelve feet. **7.** The last sixteen inches is reserved for people we're most intimate with. **9.** A supervisor who's not aware of the personal space boundaries of his or her employees risks committing a serious transgression.

Practice 37–3, page 451

Answers: **1.** I sorted letters alphabetically, starting with *A*'s. **3.** When I checked my e-mail, the screen flashed 48's to show that I had forty-eight messages. **5.** I needed another week's time just to return all the phone calls. **7.** One phone number was composed almost entirely of 6's and 7's: 767-7766. **9.** I wondered whether by taking a month's vacation, I would end up with ninety-six e-mail messages.

Practice 37–4, page 452

Answers: **(1)** People's names often have strange stories attached to them. **(3)** It's actually misspelled. It was supposed to be "Orpah," a biblical name, but a clerk's error on the birth certificate resulted in "Oprah." **(5)** "Oprah," on the other hand, with its resemblance to "opera," makes us think of a performer on a stage. **(7)** While Winfrey is not the only entertainer with an unusual first name, hers is especially memorable. **(9)** If a clerk's *a*'s look like *o*'s, for example, "Dana" becomes "Dona" and "Jarvis" becomes "Jorvis." **(11)** You've probably heard of names such as "Candy Cane" or "Spring Raines" or "Stormy Winters." **(13)** Think, for example, of a surgeon who's named "Carver," or a dentist called "Dr. Drill." **(15)** There's no way to explain any of these names except by attributing them to pure chance.

CHAPTER 38

Practice 38–1, page 456

Answers: **1.** "If I could quickly answer that question," the nurse replied, "I'd deserve an honorary degree in ethics." **3.** "How would you describe that dilemma?" the reporter asked the nurse. **5.** The reporter asked, "So there are times when you'd favor letting patients die on their own?" **7.** The reporter asked, "Under what circumstances should a patient be allowed to die?" **9.** "Is this a matter of deciding how to allocate scarce resources?" the reporter asked.

Practice 38–2, page 457

Answers: **1.** "Have you complained to the landlord yet?" her friend asked. **3.** C (correct) **5.** When Jocelyn phoned the landlord after the burglary, she said, "I know this wouldn't have happened if that lock had been installed." **7.** C (correct) **9.** "If I were you," the person said, "I'd let your landlord know right away about your plans."

Practice 38–3, page 459

Answers: **1.** As in her story "Good Country People," the title of "A Good Man Is Hard to Find" is ironic: The man who appears late in the story is actually a deranged killer. **3.** As O'Connor made clear in her essay "Novelist and Believer," her own faith as a Catholic deeply influenced her fiction. **5.** But as she explained in the essay "The Nature and Aim of Fiction," O'Connor was less interested in grand themes than in concrete human experiences.

Practice 38–4, page 460

Answers: **(1)** Correct **(3)** Ruiz answered, "I've always gotten bad grades, and I don't know how to get any better." **(5)** "I've just about given up." **(7)** Correct **(9)** I said, "There are plenty of programs to help you. **(11)** "Can you be a little more specific?" he asked. **(13)** Correct **(15)** "Take a look at these," I said. **(17)** And I don't have time." **(19)** I paused and then added, "Sounds to me like you're wasting the money you spent on tuition. **(21)** Ruiz thought for a moment, looking out the window, and finally told me that he'd try.

CHAPTER 39

Practice 39–1, page 465

Answers and possible edits: **(1)** More than fifty thousand domestic adoptions take place in this country each year; despite minor difficulties most of them go smoothly. **(3)** Richard was in a good situation: healthy, happy, loved by the couple who had adopted him at birth. **(5)** They were prepared to spend years battling the case in court; they desperately wanted their son back. **(7)** A few days after the baby's birth, the baby was put up for adoption—his mother didn't want him. **(9)** Eventually, however, the father discovered that his former girlfriend had lied; his son was still alive. **(11)** After years of legal arguments, the Illinois Supreme Court reached its verdict: Baby Richard belonged to the parents whose genes he shared.

CHAPTER 40

Practice 40–1, page 469

Answers: **(1)** Correct **(3)** Almost seventy years later, in the midst of the Great Depression, Franklin Roosevelt declared, "We have nothing to fear but fear itself."

Practice 40–2, page 470

Answers: **1.** The course was taught last fall at the Springfield Adult Education Center. **3.** In those days, he told us, many Catholic rites were still conducted in Latin. **5.** He also studied for a time with Harvey Cox, a well-known scholar, at the Harvard Divinity School. **7.** Gerald devoted one session near the end of October to discussing the ideas of Martin Luther and John Calvin. **9.** In 1536, he began work in Geneva, in the French-speaking section of Switzerland.

Practice 40–3, page 472

Answers: **1.** Sommers claims that feminists such as Susan Faludi, in her book *Backlash: The Undeclared War against American Women*, have exaggerated the inequality between men and women that still exists in the workplace. **3.** "Younger women," says this article in the *Times*, "now earn 80 cents for every dollar earned by men of the same age, up from 69 cents in 1980." **5.** This article, published in the *Journal of Economic Perspectives*, claims that widespread and severe discrimination against women still exists.

Practice 40–4, page 473

Answers: **(1)** In 1992, the La Bahia Road became the first highway in Texas to be designated as scenic and historic by the Texas Historical Commission. **(3)** It housed a fort built by Spanish explorers in the early eighteenth century and was a major overland route, according to Sam Houston Regional Library Director Robert Schaadt. **(5)** Along it lies the town of Independence, which, according to the *Texas Baptist Historical Center Museum News*, features fifty-five sites of historical interest. **(7)** There, in 1845, Baylor received its charter and opened its doors. **(9)** In 1885, Baylor relocated to Waco. **(11)** It may be the oldest active Baptist church in Texas.

Index

(Continued from page iv)

Joe Klein, "The Education of Berenice Belizaire." From *Newsweek*, August 9, 1993. Copyright © 1993 by Newsweek, Inc. Reprinted by permission.

Arthur Levine, "Student Expectations of College" (excerpt). From *Change*, September/October 1993, page 4. Published by Heldref Publications, 1319 18th St. N.W., Washington, D.C. 20036-1802. Copyright © 1993. Reprinted by permission of the Helen Dwight Reid Educational Foundation.

Rita Losee, from "Thinking Positively: Working Positively." Reprinted by permission of the author. For further information or to book Dr. Losee as a speaker, please write her at PO Box 163, Boxford, MA 01921.

Bruce McCabe, "Mental Illness: Escape From Hell" (excerpt). From the *Boston Globe*, April 8, 1995. Reprinted courtesy of the *Boston Globe*.

Susan Perry and Jim Dawson, "What's Your Best Time of Day?" From a Reader's Digest (1988) condensed version of *The Secrets Our Body Clocks Reveal*. Copyright © 1988. Reprinted by permission of Sanford Greenburger Associates, 55 Fifth Avenue, New York, NY 10003.

"Portable CD Players." Copyright © 1995 by Consumers Union of U.S., Inc., Yonkers, N.Y. 10703-1057. Reprinted by permission of *Consumer Reports*, December 1995. Although this material originally appeared in *Consumer Reports*, the selective adaptation and resulting conclusions presented are those of the author(s) and are not sanctioned or endorsed in any way by Consumers Union, the publisher of *Consumer Reports*.

Anne Roiphe, "Why Marriages Fail." Copyright © 1993 by Anne Roiphe. Reprinted by permission of International Creative Management, Inc.

Mike Royko, "Two Extremes Miss Target over Guns." From the *Chicago Tribune*. Copyright © 1995. Reprinted by permission of Tribune Media Services.

Kirby W. Stanat, with Patrick Reardon, "How to Take a Job Interview." From *Job Hunting Secrets and Tactics*. Copyright © 1977 by Westwind Press. Reprinted by permission of the author.

Brent Staples, "A Brother's Murder." From the *New York Times*. Copyright © 1986 by the New York Times Co. Reprinted by permission.

Andrew Sullivan, "Let Gays Marry." From *Newsweek*, June 3, 1996. Copyright © 1993 by Newsweek, Inc. Reprinted by permission.

Deems Taylor, "The Monster." Copyright © 1937 by Deems Taylor. Reprinted by permission of Curtis Brown, Ltd.

Wallace Terry, "When His Sound Was Silenced" (excerpt). Published by *Parade*. Copyright © 1994 by Wallace Terry. Reprinted by permission of the author and the author's agents, Scovil Chichak Galen Literary Agency, Inc., 381 Park Avenue South, New York, New York 10016.

Photograph Credits

Page   1: Joseph Schuyler/Stock, Boston
Page 59: Joel Gordon
Page 177: Joel Gordon
Page 211: Charles Gupton/Stock, Boston/PNI
Page 253: Frank Siteman/The Picture Cube
Page 325: Joel Gordon
Page 395: Joel Gordon
Page 431: Bob Daemmrich/Stock, Boston/PNI
Page 475: Hakim Raquib